Initiating Dionysus

Initiating Dionysus

Ritual and Theatre in Aristophanes' *Frogs*

ISMENE LADA-RICHARDS

CLARENDON PRESS · OXFORD

1999

Oxford University Press, Great Clarendon Street, Oxford OX2 6DP
Oxford New York
Athens Auckland Bangkok Bogota Bombay Buenos Aires
Calcutta Cape Town Dar es Salaam Delhi Florence Hong Kong Istanbul
Karachi Kuala Lumpur Madras Madrid Melbourne Mexico City
Nairobi Paris Singapore Taipei Tokyo Toronto Warsaw
and associated companies in
Berlin Ibadan

Oxford is a registered trade mark of Oxford University Press

Published in the United States
by Oxford University Press Inc., New York

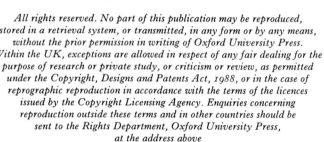

British Library Cataloguing in Publication Data
Data available

Library of Congress Cataloging in Publication Data
Initiating Dionysus : ritual and theatre in
Aristophanes' Frogs / Ismene Lada-Richards.
Includes bibliographical references and index.
1. Aristophanes. Frogs. 2. Greek drama (Comedy)—History and
criticism. 3. Dionysus (Greek deity) in literature. 4. Literature
and anthropology—Greece. 5. Rites and ceremonies in literature.
6. Theater—Religious aspects. 7. Initiations in literature.
8. Ritual in literature. 9. Greece—Religion. I. Title.
PA3875.R3L33 1998 882'.01—dc21 98-25549
ISBN 0-19-814981-6

PA
3895
,R3
L33
1999

1 3 5 7 9 10 8 6 4 2

Typeset by Regent Typesetting, London
Printed in Great Britain on acid-free paper by
Biddles Ltd., Guildford and King's Lynn

For my parents
and
for David
animae dimidium meae

Preface

THIS book originated in my Ph.D. dissertation, written at Trinity College, Cambridge, between 1988 and 1992. It was thoroughly revised and greatly expanded during the last year of my Research Fellowship at St John's College, Cambridge and during a semester's leave very kindly awarded to me by the Classics Department of Nottingham University in the academic year 1996–7. As the final typescript was with the Press in March 1997 I have not been able to take into account: T. H. Carpenter, *Dionysian Imagery in Fifth-Century Athens* (Oxford, 1997); P. E. Easterling (ed.), *The Cambridge Companion to Greek Tragedy* (Cambridge, 1997); A. Laks, and G. W. Most (eds.), *Studies on the Derveni Papyrus* (Oxford, 1997); C. Pelling (ed.), *Greek Tragedy and the Historian* (Oxford, 1997); and the 8th volume of *LIMC*, especially the article 'Mainades' by I. Krauskopf, E. Simon, and B. Simon.

On the practical side, the project would never have got off the ground as a Ph.D. without the financial help generously granted by several institutions. The Alexander S. Onassis Public Benefit Foundation, the British Academy, and the Jebb Fund in Cambridge all supported various stages of my work, while a Fellowship from St John's College provided me not only with the leisure (and the luxury!) in which to pursue research but also with a second home and family, the memory of which I shall forever treasure.

Academically, my greatest debt by far is to my Ph.D. supervisor, Dr R. L. Hunter, who guided my research with a patience and painstaking attention to detail far beyond the call of duty. Having read and reread innumerable successive drafts, from my clumsy English sentences of January 1989 to the book's final typescript, he has been the sharpest critic of my work, from subtle points of textual criticism to broader issues of culture and society, and from things Homeric to late Roman and beyond. Whenever I faltered by way of argument or otherwise he has always been there to reassure me, push me in new directions, and, above all, keep me going. I only hope this book will not make him feel his efforts have been entirely wasted. Dr M. Beard also supervised a term of my research, generously giving up her time and putting at my disposal the wealth of her knowledge of religion, iconography, and anthropology.

My work owes very much to her criticism and penetrating questions.

Prof. E. W. Handley and Prof. P. E. Easterling, Dr S. Goldhill, Dr P. Cartledge, and Prof. D. Konstan have read all or part of the typescript at various stages of its construction and made invaluable contributions. I have profited enormously from Dr A. M. Bowie's and Prof. R. Seaford's (the readers for the Press) stimulating criticism and their numerous suggestions for improvement; besides, their enthusiasm for the project and unfailing encouragement along the way have been very much appreciated. Finally, Prof. A. H. Sommerstein has kindly read several chapters in their final form and subjected them to a thorough scrutiny which saved me from embarrassing blunders, but as I have been stubborn enough not to take on board all of his suggestions I am the only one responsible for any errors that remain.

How much I owe to Eric Handley and Pat Easterling is impossible to express in words. From my very first moments in England some nine years ago and through all kinds of disappointments and troubles they have generously supported me in every possible way. At St John's College, day in and day out Malcolm Schofield, Geoff Horrocks, and John Crook have extended to me a warm and stimulating friendship, much needed encouragement, and enormous human understanding, while Christianne Sourvinou-Inwood has always been at the other end of the phone in Oxford listening, advising, and pushing me on. It is also my greatest pleasure to be able to thank in this place Prof. Eleni Contiades and Prof. John-Theophanes Papademetriou of the University of Athens. Prof. Contiades' brilliant lectures on the *Bacchae* sparked my first interest in Dionysus, while Prof. Papademetriou recruited me in 1985 into his heavenly group of a select few and was the first to lay down for me exacting standards for research and scholarship. If only they could find in this volume a small return for their kindness, their faith in me, and their genuine interest in my career I should be truly delighted, for without them I would never have been able to start. And finally, a special word of thanks to my most inspiring teachers who instilled in me a love of Classics and a spirit of independent critical inquiry: Mrs Stella Marangoudaki and Dr Foula Pispyringou.

Many friends (some of whom are now colleagues at various British and American Universities) have helped me along what has many times been an arduous path; they are too numerous to mention by name, but I hope they will accept my gratitude not only for their support but for endless hours of happiness, leisure, and laughter. Last but not least, my thanks go to Mannucha Lisboa for a very special bond of *philia* and for giving me an adorable god-daughter, and, of course, to the dedicatees of this book, my parents and my husband. Byron and Ida Lada have patiently endured a long separation and have constantly provided unfailing love and moral support; they were the first to believe that I could do it, and so I dedicate this book to them with gratitude and love. My husband, David Richards, has stoically put up with the difficult final stages of my writing and has helped in the collection of the book's illustrations; his loving care and his touching interest in my Dionysiac ramblings has made the completion of this work an infinitely more pleasant experience. But far beyond this book, I am grateful to him for giving me the love that makes my life worth living.

I.L.-R.

Cambridge
March 1997

Acknowledgements

1. 1   Courtesy, Trustees of the British Museum.
1. 2   Courtesy, Antikensammlung, Staatliche Museen zu Berlin Preussischer Kulturbesitz: Archivfoto.
1. 3   William E. Nickerson Fund≠2; Courtesy, Museum of Fine Arts, Boston.
1. 4   Courtesy, Staatliche Antikensammlungen und Glyptothek München (Foto Museum).
1. 5   American School of Classical Studies at Athens, Corinth Excavations. Photo: I. Ioannidou—L. Bartzioou. By courtesy of Nancy Bookidis.
1. 6   Courtesy, National Archaeological Museum, Athens.
1. 7   By courtesy of Dr A. M. Moretti of the Soprintendenza Archeologica per l'Etruria Meridionale, P. le di Villa Giulia; Foto della Soprintendenza Archeologica per l' Etruria Meridionale.
1. 8   Courtesy, Trustees of the British Museum.
1. 9   Courtesy, Biblioth que Nationale de France, Paris.
1. 10   Courtesy, Antikensammlung, Staatliche Museen zu Berlin Preussischer Kulturbesitz. Photo: Johannes Laurentius.
2. 1   Courtesy, Ashmolean Museum, Oxford.
2. 2   By courtesy of Cristiana Morigi Govi, Museo Civico Archeologico, Bologna.
2. 3a   Courtesy, Trustees of the British Museum.
2. 3b   Courtesy, Trustees of the British Museum.
2. 4   Courtesy, The Metropolitan Museum of Art, Fletcher Fund, 1928. (28. 57. 23)
2. 5   By courtesy of Cristiana Morigi Govi, Museo Civico Archeologico, Bologna.
2. 6   Courtesy, Ashmolean Museum, Oxford.
3. 1   By courtesy of Dr. G. Andreassi, Soprintendenza Archeologica della Puglia-Taranto.
3. 2   Catharine Page Perkins Fund; Courtesy, Museum of Fine Arts, Boston.
3. 3   Courtesy, Staatliche Antikensammlungen und Glyptothek München (Foto Museum).

3. 4	Courtesy, Musée du Louvre. Photo: M. Chuzeville.
3. 5	Courtesy, Trustees of the British Museum.
3. 6	Courtesy, Musée du Louvre. Photo: M. Chuzeville.
3. 7	By courtesy of Cristiana Morigi Govi, Museo Civico Archeologico, Bologna.
3. 8	Courtesy, Staatliche Antikensammlungen und Glyptothek München (Foto Museum).
3. 9	Courtesy, Musée du Louvre. Photo: M. Chuzeville.
3. 10	Courtesy, Musée du Louvre. Photo: M. Chuzeville.
4. 1	Courtesy, Trustees of the British Museum.
4. 2	Courtesy, Trustees of the British Museum.
4. 3	By courtesy of Eric Blanchegorge, Musée Antoine Vivenel, Compi gne, France.
4. 4	Courtesy, Trustees of the British Museum.
4. 5	Courtesy, Trustees of the British Museum.
4. 6	Courtesy, Direzione Generale Musei Vaticani, Vatican City.
4. 7	Courtesy, Trustees of the British Museum.
7. 1	Courtesy, Biblioth que Nationale de France, Paris.
7. 2	By courtesy of Cristiana Morigi Govi, Museo Civico Archeologico, Bologna.
A1 (*a–c*)	Courtesy, Ashmolean Museum, Oxford.
A2 (*a–d*)	Courtesy, Musée du Louvre. Photo: M. Chuzeville.

Contents

List of Illustrations

Abbreviations

AA	*Archäologischer Anzeiger*
ABSA	*Annual of the British School at Athens*
ABV	J. D. Beazley, *Attic Black-Figure Vase-Painters* (Oxford, 1956)
AC	*L'Antiquité Classique*
AD	*Archaeologikon Deltion*
AE	*Archaeologike Ephemeris*
AION (*ArchStAnt*)	*Annali dell'Istituto universitario orientale di Napoli, Dipartimento di Studi del mondo classico e del Mediterraneo antico, Sezione di archeologia e storia antica*
AJA	*American Journal of Archaeology*
AJP	*American Journal of Philology*
AK	*Antike Kunst*
Anecd. Graec.	I. Bekker, *Anecdota Graeca*, 3 vols. (Berlin, 1814–21)
Annales, ESC	*Annales (Économie, Sociétés, Civilisations)*
ARV²	J. D. Beazley, *Attic Red-Figure Vase-Painters* (Oxford, 1963)
ASAE	*Annales du Service des Antiquités d'Égypte*
ASNP	*Annali della Scuola Normale Superiore di Pisa, Cl. di Lettere e Filosofia*
AW	*Antike Welt*
BAGB	*Bulletin de l'Association Guillaume Budé*
BCH	*Bulletin de Correspondance Hellénique*
Beazley, *Para.*	J. D. Beazley, *Paralipomena* (Oxford, 1971)
BICS	*Bulletin of the Institute of Classical Studies of the University of London*
BIFG	*Bollettino dell'Istituto di Filologia Greca dell'Univ. di Padova*
CGFP	*Comicorum Graecorum Fragmenta in Papyris Reperta*, ed. C. Austin (Berlin and New York, 1973)
CIL	*Corpus Inscriptionum Latinarum*
CJ	*The Classical Journal*
ClAnt	*Classical Antiquity*
Coll. Alex.	J. U. Powell, *Collectanea Alexandrina* (Oxford, 1925)
CPG	E. L. von Leutsch and F. G. Schneidewin, *Corpus Paroemiographorum Graecorum*, 2 vols. (Hildesheim, 1958)
CPh	*Classical Philology*

CQ	*Classical Quarterly*
CR	*Classical Review*
CVA	*Corpus Vasorum Antiquorum*
CW	*The Classical World*
DA	C. Daremberg and E. Saglio (eds.), *Dictionnaire des antiquités grecques et romaines* (Paris, 1877–1919)
DArch	*Dialoghi di Archeologia*
D–K	H. Diels and W. Kranz (eds.), *Die Fragmente der Vorsokratiker* (6th edn.) (Berlin, 1951–2)
Erbse, *Att. Lex.*	Erbse, H., *Untersuchungen zu den attizistischen Lexika* (Berlin, 1950)
FGrHist	F. Jacoby (ed.), *Die Fragmente der griechischen Historiker* (Berlin and Leiden, 1923–58).
FHG	C. Müller (ed.), *Fragmenta Historicorum Graecorum* (Paris, 1841–70)
G–P	B. Gentili and C. Prato (eds.), *Poetarum Elegiacorum Testimonia et Fragmenta*, 2 vols. (Leipzig, 1979–85)
G&R	*Greece and Rome*
GRBS	*Greek, Roman, and Byzantine Studies*
HSCP	*Harvard Studies in Classical Philology*
HThR	*Harvard Theological Review*
IC	M. Guarducci (ed.), *Inscriptiones Creticae*, i: *Tituli Cretae Mediae Praeter Gortynios* (Rome, 1935)
ICS	*Illinois Classical Studies*
IG	*Inscriptiones Graecae* (Berlin, 1873–)
IMagn.	O. Kern (ed.), *Die Inschriften von Magnesia am Maeander* (Berlin, 1900)
JDAI	*Jahrbuch des Deutschen Archäologischen Instituts*
JHS	*Journal of Hellenic Studies*
JRS	*Journal of Roman Studies*
K–A	R. Kassel and C. Austin (eds.), *Poetae Comici Graeci* (=*PCG*) (Berlin and New York, 1983–)
LCM	*Liverpool Classical Monthly*
LGRM	W. H. Roscher, *Ausführliches Lexicon der griechischen und römischen Mythologie* (Leipzig and Berlin, 1884–1937)
LIMC	*Lexicon Iconographicum Mythologiae Classicae* (Zurich and Munich, 1981–)
MDAI (A)	*Mitteilungen des Deutschen Archäologischen Instituts (Athen. Abt.)*
MEFRA	*Mélanges d'Archéologie et d'Histoire de l'École Française de Rome*
MH	*Museum Helveticum*
MOMC[3]	T. B. L. Webster, *Monuments Illustrating Old and Middle Comedy* (3rd edn., revised and enlarged by J. R. Green) (*BICS*, suppl. 39; London, 1978)

MonAL	*Monumenti antichi pubblicati dall'Accademia dei Lincei, Roma*
MTSP	T. B. L. Webster, *Monuments Illustrating Tragedy and Satyr Play* (2nd edn. with appendix) (*BICS*, suppl. 20; London, 1967)
M–W	R. Merkelbach and M. L. West (eds.), *Hesiodi: Fragmenta Selecta* (3rd edn.) (Oxford, 1990)
NLH	*New Literary History*
PCA	*Proceedings of the Classical Association*
PCPS	*Proceedings of the Cambridge Philological Society*
PEG	A. Bernabé (ed.), *Poetae Epici Graeci: Testimonia et Fragmenta* (pars i) (Leipzig, 1987)
PGM	K. Preisendanz and A. Henrichs (eds.), *Papyri Graecae Magicae: Die griechischen Zauberpapyri* (2nd edn.), 2 vols. (Stuttgart, 1973–4)
PhV²	A. D. Trendall, *Phlyax Vases* (2nd edn.) (*BICS*, suppl. 19; London, 1967)
PMG	D. Page (ed.), *Poetae Melici Graeci* (Oxford, 1962)
PMGF	M. Davies (ed.), *Poetarum Melicorum Graecorum Fragmenta*, vol. 1: *Alcman, Stesichorus, Ibycus* (Oxford, 1991)
QUCC	*Quaderni Urbinati di Cultura Classica*
RA	*Revue Archéologique*
RAC	*Reallexikon für Antike und Christentum* (Stuttgart, 1973–4)
RBPh	*Revue Belge de Philologie et d'Histoire*
RE	A. Pauly, G. Wissowa, and W. Kroll (eds.), *Real-Encyclopädie der classischen Altertumswissenschaft* (Stuttgart, 1894–1980)
REA	*Revue des Études Anciennes*
REG	*Revue des Études Grecques*
RFIC	*Rivista di Filologia e di Istruzione Classica*
RhM	*Rheinisches Museum*
RHR	*Revue de l'Histoire des Religions*
RPh	*Revue de Philologie*
RSC	*Rivista di Studi Classici*
RVAp.	A. D. Trendall and A. Cambitoglou, *The Red-Figured Vases of Apulia*, i (Oxford, 1978); ii (Oxford, 1982)
RVAp. Suppl.	A. D. Trendall and A. Cambitoglou, *The Red-Figured Vases of Apulia, Supplement i* (*BICS*, suppl. 42; London, 1983); *Supplement ii* (*BICS*, suppl. 60; London, 1991)
SMSR	*Studi e materiali di storia delle religioni*
TAPA	*Transactions and Proceedings of the American Philological Association*
TR	*Le Temps de la réflexion*

Walz, *Rhet. Graec.*	C. Walz (ed.), *Rhetores Graeci*, 9 vols. (Stuttgart and London, 1832–6)
West	M. L. West (ed.), *Iambi et elegi Graeci*, 2 vols. (Oxford, 1971–2)
WJA	*Würzburger Jahrbücher für die Altertumswissenschaft*
YClS	*Yale Classical Studies*
ZPE	*Zeitschrift für Papyrologie und Epigraphik*

Fragments of tragic poets are listed as follows:

Aeschylus	S. Radt (= Radt), *Tragicorum Graecorum Fragmenta* (= *TrGF*), iii: Aeschylus (Göttingen, 1985)
Sophocles	S. Radt (= Radt), *Tragicorum Graecorum Fragmenta* (= *TrGF*), iv: Sophocles (Göttingen, 1977)
Euripides	A. Nauck (= N²), *Tragicorum Graecorum Fragmenta* (2nd edn.) (Leipzig, 1889)
Minor Tragedians	B. Snell, *Tragicorum Graecorum Fragmenta*, i: *Didascaliae Tragicae: Catalogi Tragicorum et Tragoediarum: Testimonia et Fragmenta Tragicorum minorum* (edn. corrected and augmented by R. Kannicht) (Göttingen, 1986) (= *TrGF* i)
Adespota	B. Snell and R. Kannicht, *Tragicorum Graecorum Fragmenta*, ii: *Fragmenta Adespota; Testimonia Volumini 1 Addenda; Indices ad volumina 1 et 2* (Göttingen, 1981) (= *TrGF* ii)

Note to the Reader

1. Quotations from *Frogs* follow Dover's text (Oxford, 1993); passages from other Aristophanic plays are cited from the Oxford Classical Text of F. W. Hall and W. M. Geldart (vol. i, 2nd edn., 1906; vol. ii, 2nd edn., 1907); unless otherwise stated, scholia on Aristophanic plays follow the edition of Fr. Dübner, *Scholia Graeca in Aristophanem* (Paris, 1842). Unless otherwise ascribed, translations of passages from *Frogs* and other Aristophanic plays are mine. The same applies to translations from Tragedy, except that displayed quotations of longer tragic passages are all taken from *The Complete Greek Tragedies* series, edited by David Grene and Richmond Lattimore (vols. 1–4, Chicago and London, 1959). However, I have given my own translation for all passages quoted from Euripides' *Bacchae*. Homeric passages are always cited in Richmond Lattimore's translation (1965, *Odyssey*; 1951, *Iliad*). Unless otherwise stated, all other Greek and Latin passages are cited in the Loeb translation (often with some modification). In the case of foreign-language secondary literature translations are mine (unless otherwise ascribed).

2. *LIMC* (*Lexicon Iconographicum Mythologiae Classicae*) references are to the catalogue numbers within each individual entry, so '*LIMC*, s.v. Dionysos, 528', means no. 528 within the 'Dionysos' entry; whenever I refer to pages of a volume of *LIMC* I explicitly say so. I do not list the authors of the various *LIMC* articles in the bibliography, but, given the frequency of my citations, I should mention here that the entry on 'Dionysos' (*LIMC* iii. 1 (1986), pp. 414–514) is authored by C. Gasparri, the entries on 'Herakles' (*LIMC* iv. 1 (1988), pp. 728–838 and *LIMC* v. 1 (1990), pp. 1–192) by J. Boardman *et al.*, and the entry on Demeter (*LIMC* iv. 1 (1988), pp. 844–92) by L. Beschi.

3. I use the Latinized form of names of authors, historical and mythical characters (but NB that Dionysus and Heracles appear as Dionysos and Herakles in refs. from *LIMC*), place names (e.g. Cithaeron), festivals (e.g. Apaturia, Lenaea), and titles of ancient works (e.g. *Choephori*, *Lycurgeia*). However, I have sometimes sacrificed consistency for the sake of not jarring the reader unneces-

sarily, hence *Epitaphios*, Lemnos, Lindos, etc. Greek words integrated in the text (e.g. *ekplexis, euphrosyne*) are used in transliterated form; please note that in my transcriptions I use ch for the Greek letter *chi* and k for the Greek letter *kappa* (so, e.g. *bakchos*) and also that I do not distinguish between long and short 'e' and 'o'. In abbreviating names of authors and titles of ancient works I have opted for the forms which would be most easily recognized not only by the professional classicist but also by the general reader (so, e.g. 'Soph.' rather than 'S', 'Aesch.' rather than 'A', etc.).

4. Please note that I write 'Chorus' with capital 'C' when referring to the Chorus of a play, acting or speaking in the name of its Chorus Leader, but 'chorus' when I refer to the chorus as a social/civic institution. Similarly, I write Mystai when referring to the Chorus of mystic initiates in the *Frogs* but mystai when referring to Eleusinian or Dionysiac initiates in a more general way. And, although I have italicized transliterated Greek words, I have not done so for mystes/mystai, for 'technical' terms referring to parts of the play (e.g. parodos, parabasis), and for terms denoting containers, such as krater, stamnos, etc., which are part of the current archaeological vocabulary.

Introduction

THE first word belongs to Dionysus, the formidable, multifaceted god, who fired the imagination of poets and artists throughout antiquity and beyond, the ambiguous god, who, despite having sparked 'a wider spectrum of different and often contradictory interpretations' (Henrichs 1984a: 240) than any other Greek divinity, still remains as 'elusive' and defying definition (cf. Henrichs 1984a: 209), as mysterious and surprising as ever. What is, then, to be gained by offering the scholarly world yet another study revolving around this indisputable star of the ancient pantheon? And, in particular, how rewarding can it be to focus yet again on Dionysus' most well-ploughed province, fifth-century Athenian drama? It may be true that not much can be new and exciting about Dionysus in the *Bacchae*, especially after the splendid insights afforded by Seaford's work on initiation ritual[1] or Foley's, Segal's, Goldhill's, and Bierl's work on aspects of 'metatheatricality'.[2] The Dionysus of the *Frogs*, however, is a case apart.

Despite being the protagonist of one of the most studied Aristophanic plays (with its two most recent commentaries, by Dover (1993) and Sommerstein (1996), published within four years of each other),[3] the comic Dionysus has not yet fared any better than he did in the remote days of Pascal (1911) and Lapalus (1934): Aristophanes' derision of Dionysus was the key idea of those scholars' work; the allegedly 'burlesque presentation' of Dionysus is still a prominent element in the excellent commentaries of Dover (1993) and Sommerstein (1996), and, even beyond commentaries, in Paul Cartledge's (1990) otherwise highly stimulating book on Aristophanes.[4] The problem arises from the fact that, to date, interpreters of Aristophanes have confined themselves to a *purely theatrical* appreciation of this god as a stock dramatic character, a mere generic type. In essence, not much has changed since Cornford's (1914: 238) schematic categorization of Dionysus in the *Frogs* as a 'Buffoon'; although few scholars now venture one-

---

[1] See esp. Seaford (1981, 1987a, 1996).
[2] Foley (1980); Segal (1982, 1985); Goldhill (1986a, 1988a); Bierl (1991).
[3] Commentaries on *Frogs* are listed in Dover (1993: xii).
[4] See esp. (1990: 4–6).

sided characterizations of Dionysus,[5] Dover's (1993: 40–1) conclusion

> So in *Frogs* the comic Dionysos is treated in isolation from the multifarious legends, cults, and functions of which a divine person, called in all cases 'Dionysos', was the nucleus

is the result of a similar overall restriction of viewpoint and perspective. My book, instead, starts primarily from the assumption that spectators going to the theatre *cannot* and *do not* leave at home the whole framework of more general cultural, ideological, ethical principles which they apply to their extra-theatrical activities (Elam 1980: 52), and that, for this very reason, a 'stage-Dionysus' cannot be separated from the range of aspects, levels of meaning, and functions which were attached to his mythic, ritual, and cultic counterpart. This is particularly true not only for fifth-century Athens, where a dramatic festival, whether the City Dionysia or the Lenaea, is an inherent, organic part of the city's religious, social, cultural, and political life, but also for any classical Greek community, as an ancient god's divine 'personality'[6] is not a fixed and static concept, but flexible, raw, mouldable material, with great capacities of adaptation, transformation, and assimilation. For example, a stage-Dionysus, whether tragic or comic, borrows from the rich conglomerate of his mythical and cultic images; but this new amalgam which, through the medium of the actor, lives, breathes, and moves on stage, cross-fertilizes in its turn the Dionysus of the *polis*' cultural tradition, a tradition which will express itself in iconography, in sculpture, as well as in forms and patterns of ritual and cult. In other words, as there is a constant interaction between cultural context and stage drama, we cannot hope to understand the dramatic hero of the *Frogs* without first attempting to understand what his real-life counterpart, the Dionysus of the *polis*' religious tradition, meant for his original spectators, the Aristophanic audience of late fifth-century Athens. And, as our view of the play in its entirety is bound to be conditioned by our interpretation of its protagonist, this book aims to

---

[5] See e.g. Henderson (1975: 91) (*bomolochos*); Higgins (1977: 64) (*eiron*).

[6] My use of this term with respect to a divine figure follows Sourvinou-Inwood's (1978: 101 n. 3) definition of 'personality' as incorporating the spheres of (i) myth, (ii) cult, i.e. human worship rendered to a deity, (iii) theology 'in the sense of sets of beliefs about the functions and areas of activity of the deity', and (iv) ideology, 'primarily through the agency of literature, involving the deity as an embodiment of certain ideas and concepts'. For further discussion of the problems of the 'self', person/'personality' see primarily Easterling (1990) and the rest of the articles in Pelling's (1990) collection. A masterful treatment of such issues can now be found in Christopher Gill's monograph (1996), which appeared too late for me to take into account in this book.

fill a gap in the scholarship of Old Athenian Comedy by offering a reading of *Frogs* while primarily focusing on the central role and function of Dionysus in it.

1. *Handling Dionysiac Evidence*

An account of Dionysus' cult in the classical Athenian city obviously falls outside the scope of this study. Let it suffice to highlight at this point the main Dionysiac areas that we shall deal with in the chapters to follow, that is, wine, maenadism, theatre, and the afterlife.

Being men's 'companion in festivity' at *symposia* and drunken revelries alike; poured out to the rest of the Olympians at libations in every feast and festival of a *polis*' sacred calendar; being the prototype of a stage-actor's dramatic transformations and the divine model for his experience of 'getting out' of himself; driving women to 'ritual madness' and binding them together in a feeling of 'communion' with his *thiasos*; finally, 'liberating', as Dionysus Lysios, the initiate in his mysteries from the fear of death, and promising to him or her a blissful afterlife, Dionysus is everywhere, an essential part of the everyday life, experience, and activities of the Athenian classical spectator. Furthermore, being the god who has left the most overwhelming and most wide-ranging record of evidence in the ancient world, Dionysus is firmly fixed in the cultural 'encyclopaedia'[7] of every Greek spectator. And it cannot be emphasized too strongly that it is precisely *through this 'encyclopaedia'* which accompanied, as it were, the audience into the theatre, that Dionysiac plays were viewed and mentally processed. In other words, the audience made sense of a stage-Dionysus not independently of but *through* and *because of* its 'kept' Dionysiac knowledge. Most important, however, are the implications of this proposition for the way we approach the *Frogs*. What it actually entails is that we have no hope of decoding a Dionysiac play, while doing justice to the sense-making activities of its original viewers, unless we first attempt to restore this very 'kept' knowledge, this very cultural 'Dionysiac' baggage which they all possessed. But, even so, some clarifications are required at this point.

In the first place, the reader will notice that my documentation often jumps to periods and places other than fifth-century Athens. A Dionysiac rite in Corinth, for example, or a late Hellenistic inscription from Asia Minor are many a time brought into the discussion to support arguments about *Frogs*. Now, any historian of

[7] See Sperber (1975: 91ff.).

religion will promptly emphasize the need for sufficient alertness to the danger of uncritical transpositions of Dionysiac features from one historical or geographical context to others. Nevertheless, necessary though it may be for a project which would aim to describe with exactitude the cultic realities of Dionysiac ritual in a *particular* area and epoch, a rigid synchronic and diachronic segmentation of Dionysus' religious personality ultimately creates more problems than it actually resolves, for it obfuscates the important fact that Dionysus also exhibited a wealth of universal features, cutting across compartments and confinements of time and of space. For this reason, I believe that, once due account is taken of limitations and dangers, a later development in the Dionysiac record *can* be considered to throw some light on earlier, half-hidden characteristics or features still not clearly delineated, while evidence from other spatial settings *can* offer useful suggestions regarding the meanings or the structure of patterns for which local explanation (*exegesis*) is inadequate. In general, then, I have preferred to offer a fuller picture of Dionysiac aspects—even if some of its elements cannot be verified with absolute security for fifth-century Athens— to the alternative of confining myself to those few points which can be safely documented without the slightest doubt.

Secondly, a related difficult issue attaches to the sphere of Dionysiac Mysteries. Not only does the bulk of our information come from the Hellenistic and Roman periods, making it particularly hazardous to rely upon it uncritically for fifth-century ritual practice, but also 'no local center for Bacchic Mysteries' exists, as they appeared 'everywhere from the Black Sea to Egypt and from Asia Minor to southern Italy' (Burkert 1987a: 5). Consequently, as initiations into Dionysiac *thiasoi*, being individual and sporadic and non-compliant with universal schemes, display considerable regional variety, information about initiation rituals into a *thiasos* of, let us say, Asia Minor may have very little to contribute to our knowledge of initiation in Mainland Greece or Southern Italy or Crete. However, even here, a relatively safe fuller picture can still be drawn—provided, of course, that the researcher does not pretend to be reconstructing a totally *accurate*, indisputable account of historical Dionysiac cultic facts. So, for example, speculation on an early phase of a later rite *is* possible because of the well-known conservatism and continuity characterizing all mystery religions (cf. Seaford 1996: 40). This feature is often verbally emphasized in Dionysiac records, such as the well-known Delphic oracle (see *IMagn.* 215a, 24–30) instructing the Magnesians of Asia Minor to import from Thebes maenads who would be 'of the stock of the Cadmeian Ino' (γενεῆς Εἰνοῦς ἄπο Καδμηείης) (26–7)[8] or, to a lesser extent, the edict of Ptolemy IV Philopator, requiring the itinerant practitioners of initiations to be conscious of the provenance and ancestry of their *sacra/hieros logos* for three entire generations.[9] Similarly, the broad geographical range covered by the famous Orphic/Bacchic gold leaves (2.1) testifies to the possibility and ease of the diffusion of eschatological ideas. In this respect, then, although Robert Parker (1983: 287) is right in pointing out that 'the southern Italian initiate's hopes and fears for the afterlife were not necessarily shared by the Athenian farmer, drunk and happy at the Anthesteria', consideration of the rich funerary imagery of the South Italian vases *does* create a wider perspective and a helpful referential frame in which to place the Athenian Dionysus of the *polis*' 'official' eschatology, the god who, in Sophocles' imagination, 'rules over the glens, common to all, of Eleusinian Deo (i.e. Demeter)' (*Ant.* 1119–21);[10] what is even more significant is that the Sophoclean text itself mentions 'Eleusis' in immediate connection to 'Italia' (1119):[11] an Athenian author and, presumably, his audience are able to perceive two regionally distinct faces of Dionysus as ultimately interwoven.

Thirdly, a particular methodological issue arises from the problematic relation of Dionysiac myth to ritual. Much research has been done and much has been written on the difference between those two Dionysiac spheres. Henrichs, in particular, has frequently—and rightly—emphasized the need for a clear-cut distinction between myth and ritual for a historical delineation of the cultic aspects of Dionysiac rites.[12] Nevertheless, myth *does* become an area of cardinal importance for a project which aims at reconstructing the 'perceptual filters' (Sourvinou-Inwood 1990a: 396) through which the members of an ancient community would have been able to understand this god. Dionysiac myth had always had a

---

[8] See Henrichs (1978: 123 ff.).

[9] See Zuntz (1963); cf. also a variety of other mystic cults constructed around an *hieros logos* (see e.g. Hdt. 2. 51. 4, on the Samothracian mysteries; cf. West 1983a on Orphic *hieroi logoi*), to be communicated to the *mystai* in the form of oral presentation as well as to be handed down without interruption through the generations of those who perform the rites. Finally, the continuity of *teletai* through direct and uninterrupted transmission of knowledge is clearly implied in expressions such as μυστηρίων παράδοσιν or τῆς τελετῆς παράδοσις (Theo Smyrn. *Mathem.*, p. 14 Hiller).

[10] See Henrichs (1990: 264 ff.).

[11] See Henrichs' (1990: 268) castigation of Roger Dawe's 'thoroughly un-Dionysiac' Οἰχαλίαν, an 'incongruous' conjecture (and an excellent example of the dangers of reading ancient texts outside their context, restricting one's mind to purely philological issues) (cf. below).

[12] Henrichs (1978, 1982, 1984a). See also Rapp (1872); Dodds (1951: 270–82); Bremmer (1984); Versnel (1990b: 134 ff.).

greater impact on people's minds than any ritual performances, and
it was precisely the close and unfailing interaction between myth
and cult which shaped the distinctive identity of Dionysus through
all epochs.

Take, for example, the case of maenadism, perhaps the most
impressive and well-known ritual in the sphere of this god. We
can be fairly sure that real-life, that is cultic, maenadism was never
practised within the borders of the Attic land—at least not in
historical times (Henrichs 1978, 1982). However, despite the fact
that the rites were enacted far away from the Athenian *polis*, on the
slopes of Mt. Parnassus; that they were restricted to the small
number of female participants who joined in Delphi the Dionysiac
bands of the so-called Thyiads (Θυιάδες) (see Villanueva Puig 1986);
and that by Euripides' time they were probably much more 'tame'
and restrained than the *Bacchae* might suggest, the Athenians'
understanding of the Dionysiac experience was shaped to a very
large extent by the notion of uncontrollable frenzy, ritual madness.
Featuring on inummerable vases of all shapes and uses and on
sculptural reliefs; moulded as miniature statuettes buried with the
dead in tombs; flanking the idol of Dionysus on the famous series of
the 'Lenaean' vases (cf. 2.12(b)), or merely serving as literary
metaphors and models for dramatists and poets, raving maenads in
bodily postures characteristic of ritual ecstasy are an inextricable
part of the Athenian citizen's experience of Dionysus and his world.
Similar is the case with the notorious issue of *omophagia* (eating of
raw meat) (4.8): whether it was actually practised on Greek land in
historical times or not (a fascinating problem for the historian of
religion) is of very little interest or consequence to the thesis of
this book. What *does* matter is that maenads were *imagined* to be
practising it at the heat of their ecstatic rites, and it is this imaginary
picture which comes to contribute to the shaping of the contemporary Athenian's perception of the god. As Obbink (1993: 69) has put
it with respect to maenadic *sparagmos* (dismemberment), what is of
greater significance is not 'what was *actually done*, but rather what
was *believed* to be done, or . . . what was believed to have *once* been
done . . .'. In other words, then, this book holds in view both perspectives simultaneously, and frequently has recourse to the notion
of the Dionysiac 'myth and ritual complex'. I believe that such a
unified view of Dionysiac myth and ritual paves the way for the cir-
cumvention of the highly misleading question of whether Dionysus
should be conceived as 'in' or 'out' of the civic borders. For the
Dionysus of myth, who operates in defiance of the city's norms, and
whose primary function is to demolish and to blur, is inseparable

from the Dionysus of civic cults who may even function as an impulse towards civic cohesiveness and order (cf. Ch. 5). Thus, fundamental for my reading is the appreciation that the classical Athenian city was conscious of Dionysus as a benign, civic, thoroughly 'integrated' figure, while at the same time viewing him as 'another way of thought': elusive and defying definition, this god could also stand as the irruption of alterity into a community's pedantic life, a strange force which had to be purged of its potential subversiveness so as to perform a beneficial function. This ambivalence is obvious in most Dionysiac spheres.

In the conceptual frame of the classical Athenian citizens, the wild maenads of Euripides' *Bacchae* tearing live animals apart could easily be coupled not only with the solemn priestesses of many an Attic deme, duly performing the Dionysiac sacrifice on the altar (4.10), but also with the band of chaste Dionysiac women, the so-called Γεραιραί who, supervised by the Basilinna, the wife of the Archon Basileus, performed 'the secret rituals on behalf of the *polis*' (τὰ ἄρρητα ἱερὰ ὑπὲρ τῆς πόλεως) ([Dem.] 59. 73). The bacchant who raves on the open mountainside is the 'other visage' of the civilized 'maenad' who, despite her name, is many a time portrayed by vase-painters in a posture and a mood indistinguishable from those of the women enclosed in the house's female quarters.[13] On the so-called 'Lenaean' vases especially, one single civic ritual space incorporates the female worshipper of Dionysus both in her exalted and ecstatic madness and in her dignified solemn service to the god.[14] Moreover, in the Hellenistic period—for which, as we have noted just above, evidence is ampler—a city can incorporate maenadic sacrifice both as a disruption and negation of its normal sacrificial code and as a cohesive act performed on behalf of the entire *polis*.[15] The Dionysiac priestesses, correspondingly, act both as a centrifugal force leading the female population 'to the mountain' (εἰς ὄρος) and as Bacchae 'of the city' (πολιήτιδες . . . Βάκχαι),[16] displaying the Dionysiac *sacra* to the vision of the whole city.[17] However, Dionysiac ambiguity

[13] See Frontisi-Ducroux (1986: esp. 171 and 173 ff.); Bérard and Bron (1986: 23–7). Cf. Bérard and Bron (1989: 134) on 'tamed, calmed, dressed, civilized' satyrs.

[14] Many a time the two images are juxtaposed on the sides of one single vase; see Frontisi-Ducroux (1986: 171).

[15] See the famous Milesian inscription (Sokolowski 1955: no. 48), where it is forbidden ὠμοφάγιον ἐμβαλεῖν (not suggesting omophagy (Henrichs 1969c, 1978) but even so, still an aberration (cf. Bremmer 1984: 275–6)) μηθενὶ πρότερον ἢ ἡ ἱέρεια ὑπὲρ τῆς πόλεως (i.e. on behalf of the city) ἐμβάλῃ. For a discussion of Dionysiac sacrifice see Ch. 4.

[16] Line 1 of a Maenadic epigram on a tombstone from Miletus; text in Henrichs (1969c: 225) and Henrichs (1978: 148).

[17] See the emphatic juxtaposition of discordant actions in the same epigram (n. 16), lines 3–4: ὑμᾶς κεἰς ὄρος ἦγε καὶ ὄργια πάντα καὶ ἱρὰ | ἤνεικεμ πάσης ἐρχομένη πρὸ πόλεως.

becomes more impressive when one focuses on the Dionysiac dramatic world.

Leading the god from the *eschara* to the city in an annual re-enactment of his original advent/incorporation into the pantheon of the *polis* (Ch. 3), the 'Great' or 'City' Dionysia festival (see Pickard-Cambridge 1988: 57–101) proclaims publicly his civic, Athenian dimension. Many a time, however, the plays sponsored and staged by this same city, dwelling, as they do, on Dionysus' potentially subversive side, foster a counter-image of Dionysianism as the wild natural impulse which threatens to negate the structure of well-ordered communities. In a series of pre-play sacrifices (Pickard-Cambridge 1988: 61) the Great Dionysia ensures the ritual separation of bestial, human, and divine.[18] Yet, the fictional reality of the Dionysiac spectacle itself exploits the fickleness of forms, enacts the dissolution of polarities, explores the whole spectrum of distorted fusions between those same categories that civic ritual discourse is anxious to keep rigidly apart. Finally, in so far as it is possible that the Dionysiac procession carried and displayed phalluses, a part of which were probably sent to Athens by colonial cities[19] specifically for that particular occasion, the Great Dionysia festival could be considered as a Panhellenic tribute to the male dimension of Dionysus' personality. At the same time, however, the Dionysiac theatre of Athens is the civic space *par excellence* where the rigidly defined male personality is allowed to plunge in every form of 'otherness'. Escaping its own boundaries the male body verges on the feminine either through direct impersonation of women or through *mimesis* of female *pathos* (Zeitlin 1990*a*; cf. Lada-Richards 1997*b*), while physical and ideological confines and constructions of the male world are questioned or renegotiated. And, most significantly, it is Dionysus himself who, embracing femininity into his own being (1.3), becomes the high principle for this annihilation of generic differentiation and allows his own theatre to dramatize his mythical *persona* as a sensual, soft, and feminine youth.

To conclude. Instead of relegating the 'self-questioning portrayal of Dionysus' to the sphere of myth and 'to the realm of the imagination, both ancient and modern' (Henrichs 1990: 269), this book identifies the Athenians' conception of this god as an awareness of his ambiguity. Such a consciousness would have been nourished and consolidated by the daily juxtaposition of their Dionysiac mythical 'encyclopaedia' with their 'civic' experience of Dionysiac rites and cults. In this respect then, rather than forming 'a Dionysus

---

[18] For this function of the sacrificial act see 4.6.
[19] See testimonia and discussion in Pickard-Cambridge (1988: 62 with nn. 3 and 4).

for special occasions', 'the ambivalent Dionysus of tragedy' (Henrichs 1990: 269) should be viewed as an integral part of the Athenian 'kept knowledge' encoded in the multiform articulations of the *polis*' discourse. More significantly still, the *polis*' awareness of Dionysus' duality is nowhere more conspicuously expressed than in the programme and the ideology of the City Dionysia. Evoking, as it does, through the constant interaction of the plays with their wider ceremonial frame a rich range of Dionysiac polarities and undissolved tensions, this civic festival may testify to an Athenian audience's perception of Dionysus as structurally unclassifiable, as the mediator *par excellence* between 'nature' and 'culture'.

My first chapter discusses the complexities of the relationship between Dionysus and Heracles in the comedy's prologue, placing special emphasis on the visual and semantic elements which communicate to the audience the paradox that 'Dionysiac' and 'Heraclean' polarities are not only sharply differentiated but also inextricably interwoven. Chapter 2 argues that the play's structure is arranged in accordance with the tripartite structure of a 'rite of passage': Dionysus, the 'ritual passenger' is 'alienated' in the prologue of the *Frogs* from the intellectual environment of late fifth-century BC Athens to undertake a journey into the Underworld, which qualifies as a 'liminal' transition towards his final 'reaggregation' into the idealized image of the *polis*' community, as this is gradually evoked in the play's agon, through the highly symbolical contest of Euripides and Aeschylus in Hades. Dionysus' initiation into Athens is effected in the three major ways through which the god is accessible to his worshippers, namely, wine, theatrical role-playing, and *myesis* into the Eleusinian/Bacchic mysteries. It is with the vicissitudes of mystic initiation that Chapter 2 is primarily concerned, while the third chapter centres on the wine motif, as reflected in the various stages of Dionysus' itinerary, which can be seen as the dramatic re-enactment of the god's original advent and mythical incorporation into the Athenian *polis*. Chapter 4 discusses the 'metatheatrical' dimension of the god's dramatic identity: Dionysus' 'Heraclean' role-playing functions in such a way as to invite the spectator to conceive the god in the position and the role of an actor. Dionysus interweaves in his *persona* the two antithetical viewpoints from which the phenomenon of 'playing the other' is conceivable, the ritual and the theatrical, both of which are markedly 'Dionysiac' and ultimately based on the experience of *ekstasis*. The same chapter argues that Dionysus' *mimesis* of Heracles results in the channelling of his dramatic personality in one particular direction, that is, the civilized, civic community of the Athenian *polis*. Chapters 5–9 form the second part of the book, dealing exclusively with the play's agon, which both illustrates and complements Dionysus' reintegration into Athens. Dionysus completes his initiation into civic space by being required to reflect upon, and ultimately to choose among, the multicoloured body of positive and negative imagery attached to the contending poets Aeschylus and Euripides. It will be argued that, far from representing an absurd decision, Dionysus' final choice, inspired by his gradual realization of dramatic poetry's communal function, is in intrinsic and internal correspondence with the play's pivotal concerns. Dionysus is fully drawn into the civic orbit, and, placed 'metatheatrically' in the position of the entire city as a spectator, he chooses the *polis*-oriented Aeschylus, whose poetry is inextricably interwoven with a healthy civic image, over the *oikos*-centred Euripides, the catalyst who challenges and questions the building blocks of *polis*, of society, and culture.

2. *Literary Matters*

So far so good about Dionysus, then, and the Dionysiac argument of this book. As regards interpretation now, my aim has not been to uncover and present an 'authentic' meaning, a 'message', so to speak, that the author of the *Frogs* would supposedly have striven to convey to his assembled fellow-citizens. Although I *do* believe that an author in the Graeco-Roman world must be treated as a historically definable *persona*,[20] instead of an abstraction,[21] that is, as the 'genial creator of a work',[22] writing with a specific communicative aim within the realm of a smaller- or larger-scale society, I do not accept that there is or that there should be one single 'correct' way of deciphering a text. Authorial intention can never be fully grasped or accurately reconstructed and, even if it were explicitly avowed, by no means should it become for us restrictive or more valid than other readings, for the voice of the artist is only *one* among the multiplicity of threads whose interweaving circumscribes the aesthetic object.

Rather than being author-centred, then, my interpretation starts from the side of the audience, in so far as I believe that the viewer's or the reader's response can be considered at least as important as the creative role of the author in the determination of the range of

---

[20] See *contra* Culler's (1981: 38) position.

[21] And for this reason I have not banned the more or less 'intentionalist' terms 'Aristophanes' or 'the dramatist' from my discussion.

[22] Proposition rejected by Foucault (1979: 159).

meanings that a work may have.[23] More specifically, my method-
ology belongs to the structuralist/semiotic branch of 'audience-
oriented' criticism, in so far as I treat the text as 'a network of
different messages depending on different codes and working at
different levels of signification' (Eco 1979: 5), and I accept that
every literary work comes to life through the variety of responses
that it generates in its addressees.[24] However, there is still a further
issue to be considered here.

My approach aims neither at describing with exactitude the
mental processes by which an individual fifth-century spectator
would have advanced as a recipient of this text nor at recovering *the*
response of *the* play's original audience in its totality. First, any conception of *the* audience as an homogeneous, indissoluble entity is
very likely to be misleading: even in a relatively small community,
where people can be reasonably expected to share the same cultural
conventions as well as to mobilize the same set of 'interpretive
strategies' (Fish 1976: 476), the range of possible responses may still
be extremely broad.[25] In classical Athens, for example, the sense-
making activity of the man in the street or villager spectator would
by no means have been identical with the perceptual faculties of the
town-bred intellectual or, generally speaking, of the 'informed'[26]
fifth-century recipient. Setting out to reconstruct a collective, a
unanimous response is, therefore, a futile task. Secondly, my
arrangement and interpretation of the play's structural and semantic
units is very likely to be different from that of any fifth-century
spectator, as it is based on my interaction with the text through
reading: affording both privileged knowledge of the future sequence
and the leisure for shifting vantage-points at free will, a reading
experience allows the interweaving of anticipation/retrospection,[27]
and is consequently sustained by the interplay of the sum of the perspectives inherent in the text.[28] In this respect, then, many of the

---

[23] As is the fundamental precept of 'reader-response' criticism; for a general introduction
see Suleiman (1980).

[24] In the language of 'reader-response' criticism, the text is 'realized' by its addressees; see
e.g. Iser (1974: 280).

[25] Cf. Bal and Bryson (1991: 186) on the parallel issue of 'reception' in the viewing of a
work of art: 'even when attention to the conditions of reception discloses a particular group,
which operates codes of viewing in a unique way, analysis of reception must still distinguish
between degrees of *access* to those codes', for 'members of the group have different levels of
access to the group's codes and varying degrees of competence and expertise'.

[26] For the notion of the 'informed reader' see Fish (1970: 145).

[27] The point is stressed by Iser (1974: 281–2).

[28] On the other hand, however, the reader's experience is infinitely poorer than that of the
spectator, since the latter appreciates the text as this is gradually constructed through the
entire complex network of the codes and the signs which 'participate' in the performance and
which are largely irrecoverable once the play is 'flat' on paper. Cf. M. Pfister (1988: 13).

possible connections between patterns of the text are bound to escape the notice of a spectating recipient, whose attention is primarily absorbed into the linear development of the dramatic plot.[29]

Leaving aside the vexed issue of authorial intention, the fundamental principle which guides my approach is that no text can or should be seen as a 'self-sufficient' artefact, existing outside sociocultural conventions. Each theatrical performance makes 'continual appeal to our general understanding of the world' (Elam 1980: 52). For this reason, cutting the text off from its cultural milieu, that is, dissociating theatrical signification from non-theatrical experience, is a task dangerously misleading in all cases, and, as I have emphasized from the start, particularly so with respect to fifth-century Athenian drama, a form of entertainment sponsored and produced by the City for display to the City and nourished by a constant interaction with the *polis* and its values (see esp. Chs. 5–9). Moreover, for all of us who approach Greek drama some twenty-five centuries after its first production, further traps are strewn on our path. For, as Gombrich (1977) has shown, the 'innocent' eye is a myth, and thus the addressee who comes from a different background will inevitably project upon the text his or her own expectations (see Gombrich 1977: 271),[30] which in their turn will inevitably distort the unique identity this work had at the time and the place of its first creation.

The novelty of my general argument, then, resides in its deployment of an entire series of cultural—and more precisely religious—considerations which have never previously been taken into account for the illumination of *Frogs*. In particular, the main question that this book proposes to address is how one's membership in Greek fifth-century society would have determined and shaped one's understanding of the *Frogs*. In other words, I have set out to recover, independently of individual responses, the 'con-textual' frame in which that piece of work originated; to make explicit the implicit knowledge, the underlying conventions which were shared, even if subconsciously, by participants in a fifth-century community, and which would have invested the textual elements with sense and functions. Rather than seeking to pin down *the* authorial purpose or to refashion *the* audience's response, I have sought to reconstitute the original circuit of communication between the play and its recipients, that is, to identify the codes

[29] Nevertheless, a reading public did exist, especially at the end of the 5th-cent. BC and, therefore, taking a reading 'point of view' as well into account means getting a better insight into the potential forms of 'dialogue' between the text and its contemporary addressees.

[30] Cf. Barthes (1975a: 10): 'This "I" which approaches the text is already itself a plurality of other texts, of codes which are infinite or, more precisely, lost (whose origin is lost).'

which would have made possible the emission and decipherment of messages within the original communicative channel between the sender/author of the *Frogs* and his fifth-century addressees, whether spectators or readers. Rather than seeking one single meaning, this book attempts to reconstruct the wider spectrum of *potential* meanings that various segments of the text *could* have in their own sociocultural milieu.

In this respect, questions such as whether the spectators would have been able to recall to mind an obscure Dionysiac myth; to detect a covert allusion to a tragedy performed in the distant past; to think of connections not immediately obvious between mythical *personae*, and so on, are virtually irrelevant. What matters more, I believe, is not the accurate recording of real-life, individual responses (in any case, an impossible task), but rather the sum of interpretative possibilities conditioned by a given culture. To put it in another way, any interpretation which 'makes sense', that is, is both recognizable and intelligible *within its own cultural frame* adds something to the global 'meaning' of the text.[31] And, in the case of the *Frogs*, by sociocultural milieu I do not simply mean the historical realities of its original production—the grim and dangerous political situation, which has been analysed by scholars at great length in relation to the play. I mean first and foremost the entire wider network of cultural presuppositions and assumptions which can enable an addressee's decipherment of textual and theatrical signs. Yet, we are totally unlikely to recover such assumptions either through purely philological means or through the channel of theatrical conventions only; the very nature of the interpretative problems calling for our attention is such that it compels us to 'open up' our limited perspective and be ready to consider material spreading over the widest possible range of media.

So, for example, a strictly textual interpretation of Dionysus' disguise in the prologue of the *Frogs* as an awkward assortment of incongruous paraphernalia ignores the sense-making activities of contemporary Aristophanic viewers, for whom the 'Heraclean' lion-skin that Dionysus has donned as part of his theatrical attire is in fact a manifestation of a vital aspect of his own mythical and cultic personality (1.1). And this is a 'con-textual' reading that we can only arrive at if we broaden the scope of our inquiry so as to take into account, alongside textual evidence, sources as diverse as iconography and sculpture, myth and ritual/cultic practices or, in a word, sources which afford a valuable insight into the range of material available to classical audiences. In a similar way, a strictly

---

[31] Mossman (1995: 8–10) is particularly good on this issue.

'closed', exclusively textual interpretation of Agathon's disguise in Aristophanes' *Thesmophoriazusae* (134 ff.) will lead us to the false conclusion that the majority of Agathon's peculiar accessories have 'nothing to do with Dionysus'. Even such scholars as Kassel (1966), Rau (1967), and Sommerstein (1994) have fallen into the trap of disregarding the plethora of visual images available to Aristophanic audiences and have thus failed to see that *barbitos* (a kind of stringed instrument like the lyre), mirror, and sword are frequent elements in the iconography of Dionysiac *thiasoi* or played a specific cultic function in Dionysiac mystic rites. And I return to *Frogs* for one last example. Stanford (1963), Dover (1993), Sommerstein (1996) have all something to say about Dionysus, 'son of the Wine-Jar' (υἱὸς Σταμνίου) in *Frogs* 22; Dionysus' association with the wine is commented on, and the notes usefully stress the point that the nominative may be either Σταμνίας (a name much like Καπνίας in *Wasps* 151) or σταμνίον. However, the real impact of Dionysus' self-presentation as 'son of the Decanter' is not illuminated, because strictly philological inquiry has been blind to the fact that not only was Dionysus' face painted on stamnoi and all kinds of wine vessels but the wine-god himself was also frequently moulded in the shape of a vase (3.1)! An important contemporary way of gaining access to the meaning of the text for its original spectators has been lost.

Comparable is the case of dramatic scenes which can be easily situated within the frame of generic precedents/conventions. Let us take, for example, Dionysus' rowing in Charon's boat on the waters of the Styx. As we are fortunate to have some fragments of Eupolis' *Taxiarchs*, there is no doubt that the Aristophanic scene guides the spectator's understanding along this 'theatrical' path. However, this is only half the story. For Dionysus' voyaging to Hades through the Styx is also equivalent to an 'arrival' from the water, and as such it would have created meaning for its Athenian spectators through its association with important moments of their cultic/ritual experience, that is, Dionysus' annual advent to Athens from the sea, taking place either at the Great Dionysia festival or the Anthesteria (2.4(b)). Similarly, Dionysus' disguise in the *Frogs* calls, of course, to mind the typical disguises of the comic trickster hero. However, this is not as far as we could—or rather should—be going. For the art of transformation is intrinsically Dionysiac, as lack of stable identity and fluidity of shape lie at the very core of the experience that Dionysus creates for his votaries (4.1). To sum up, then, with all its inherent value to the student of literary conventions and dramatic tropes, a strictly theatrical way of deciphering dramatic scenes as conforming to or deviating from generic traditions represents only *one* among a multiplicity of other possible readings. To insist on treating this particular communicative path as superior to all others would mean 'abusively closing off the plurality of codes' (Barthes 1975*a*: 206). To quote Barthes (1975*a*: 5) again, access to a text can be gained 'by several entrances, none of which can be authoritatively declared to be the main one'. My reading of the play, then, challenges the narrow-minded position that theatrical conventions and generic expectations are the *exclusive* factors in the shaping of what Jauss has named the 'Erwartungshorizont'[32] of a given public and consequently constitute the sole dimension which accounts for a performance's 'intelligibility'.

I believe that the implications of such an approach for the treatment of Dionysus are significant, for my reading understands Dionysus' 'dramatic character'[33] not only as indebted to the dramatic tradition of fifth-century Dionysiac stage-representations and as moulded by the play's action, but also, and most importantly, as a function of his mythic/ritual/cultic 'personality',[34] and of a fifth-

---

[32] See Jauss (1970: 14), where the reader's 'horizon of expectations' is conceived as being determined not only by 'the familiar standards or the inherent poetry of the genre' but also by the work's 'implicit relationships' to other works of the 'literary-historical context'; more significantly, Jauss acknowledges as an important factor 'the possibility that the reader of a new work has to perceive it not only within the narrow horizon of his literary expectations but also within the wider horizon of his experience of life' (1970: 14).

[33] The notion of 'dramatic character'—the focus of so much debate and contestation in recent decades—requires some kind of explanation, not to say justification, for its use. To state my position very briefly, I am inclined to take it for granted that 'the dramatic image of character within space and time is irreducible' (C. R. Lyons 1987: 28) or that, as Barthes (1975*b*: 257) has put it, 'there is not a single narrative in the world without "characters"' (cf. Goldhill 1990*b*: 111). Furthermore, Barthes's specification of the two critical extremes which have to be avoided, i.e. suppressing character on the one hand, while on the other taking 'him' off the page in order to treat him/her 'as a real person, a full, psychologically endowed individual' (Goldhill 1990*b*: 112), is the most helpful contribution to the furtherance of the debate (brought to the attention of classicists mainly through Goldhill's quotations (1986*b*: 164; 1990*b*: 112)). In other words, I believe that a notion of dramatic character should be retained as long as one is willing to acknowledge its 'ineradicable *difference*' (Goldhill 1990*b*: 106) from 'real-life' persons, i.e. admit the fact that 'the same criteria that we use to evaluate or discuss real human behaviour and real human beings' cannot be 'used without question for analysing "character" in a text critically' (Goldhill 1990*b*: 106; cf. Garton 1972: 14–15). 'Character' would, therefore, mean a 'human image' (C. R. Lyons 1987: 30), created by the interrelation of factors operating at all levels within the realms of the text itself. It would denote the 'feeling of a human presence' which can have its own inner world, even if this is not consistently or thoroughly delineated, and even if it is delimited by the play's fictitious existence.

[34] This should not be taken as implying a belief in the independent, extra–theatrical (in the Bradleyan sense) existence of a dramatic hero. A dramatic character is 'a fiction, and whether seen in a technical or an interpretative light has only an existence limited by its play' (Styan 1975: 159); to put it in Garton's (1957: 251) way, 'the figure cannot . . . be set loose, or he would forfeit his power, the power which he has by being in and of the action' (cf. Gould 1978: 44). Now, Barthes (1975*a*: 68) has argued that the figure in a narrative is 'an illegal, impersonal, anachronistic configuration of symbolic relationships . . . As a symbolic ideality, the character has no chronological or biographical standing; he has no Name . . .'. Never-

century Greek audience's 'perceptual filters'. A large part, there-fore, in the shaping of Dionysus' *dramatis persona* is played by 'intertextuality', in so far, of course, as the meaning of this term is not restricted to the issue of a work's dependence on earlier speci-mens belonging to the same genre. For this book exploits 'inter-textuality' in the way this has been elucidated by Julia Kristeva (1974), that is, as the relation of a text to the multiplicity of cultural discourses which provide for it 'un cadre de dialogue voire même un univers sémantique à discuter' (338; cf. 339); in this respect, the entire corpus of fifth-century theatrical production becomes for the *Frogs* and for Dionysus 'un acte de présupposition' (Kristeva 1974: 339).

theless, however much this may be applicable to modern texts, one has to acknowledge that there is a difference between the status of a 'modern' and a 'classical' dramatic hero: the former of course is 'inconceivable' in any 'space' outside the boundaries of his dramatic role. But the latter *does* exist as a legendary or sometimes even as a cultic figure in the mythical traditions and the rituals on which the poets draw for the raw material of their plays. Each poet is *re*shaping and *re*moulding in his own way an already existing mythic/cultic/ritual 'per-sonality'. And the *dramatis persona* of a hero in a given text is, in this respect, the playwright's interpretation/dramatization of an 'episode' out of the hero's mythical life.

I

'Dionysiac' and 'Heraclean' in the Prologue of the *Frogs*

1.1. *Dionysus and Heracles, 'Self' and 'Other'*

If fifth-century Athenian theatre can be defined as an '"other scene" where the city puts itself and its values into question' (Zeitlin 1990*b*: 144), the figure who, at the Lenaea of 405 BC, steps on to the stage at the beginning of the *Frogs* constitutes for his Athenian spectators the quintessence of 'otherness'. A lion-skin upon his shoulders, he verges on bestiality; clad in a female saffron robe (*krokotos*) and wearing buskins (*kothornoi*), he has a share in femininity;[1] when he finally ascribes a name to his hybrid *dramatis persona*, the audience understands that this stage-figure is a god (22 ὅτ' ἐγὼ μὲν ὢν Διόνυσος),[2] participating in the action as a male human being, 'son of the Wine-Jar' (υἱὸς Σταμνίου) (22). Thus, in a society which 'sharply polarizes definitions and distinctions of masculine and feminine roles' (Zeitlin 1990*a*: 65 n. 6), while at the same time emphasizing both man's distance from the gods and the severance of his condition from a state of primitive bestiality, Dionysus, 'the son of Stamnias', presents a challenge to man's claims in a rigidly defined masculine identity. In a theatre where 'the self that is really at stake is to be identified with the male' (Zeitlin 1990*a*: 68), Dionysus in the prologue of the *Frogs* embodies what the Athenian male spectator has learnt that he is not: a woman, a beast, a god.

[1] The *krokotos* is a female dress *par excellence* (Ar. *Lys.* 44–51, 219–20, 645; *Eccles.* 332, 879) and the hallmark of effeminate men (Ar. *Thesm.* 138, 253, 941, 945). For the *kothornos* as expressing femininity see e.g. Ar. *Lys.* 658; *Eccles.* 344–6; Hdt. 1. 155. 4; cf. Smith (1905: 124–9); Pickard-Cambridge (1988: 207). *Contra*, see Kurtz and Boardman (1986: 61 with n. 123).

[2] We lack secure knowledge on (*a*) the extent to which Dionysus' mask was a specifically 'Dionysiac' one (cf. 4.1 n. 2); (*b*) the degree of the Aristophanic Dionysus' visual conformity to other theatrical, whether tragic or comic, dramatizations of this god; (*c*) the degree of his stage-figure's similarity to his representations in art, and (*d*) the extent to which the *krokotos* and the *kothornoi* were perceived as distinctively Dionysiac insignia (see n. 3 below). Nevertheless, the audience's realization of Dionysus' presence on the stage should have been immediate or, at least, should have preceded the utterance of the name 'Dionysus' in line 22 (cf. also the first scene's visual evocation of the Dionysiac story of 'Hephaestus' Return', on which see 3.1).

However, if Dionysus can be envisaged as the epitome of 'other-ness' with respect to the spectators, he also embodies the 'other' in his own self as well. Because, although the *krokotos* and the *kothornoi* qualify as Dionysiac attributes,[3] lion-skin and club are the almost unmistakable insignia of Heracles.[4] In fact, as Dionysus him-self admits, his dressing up is meant to 'imitate' Heracles (109 ἦλθον κατὰ σὴν μίμησιν), the focus of the comedy's prologue thus narrow-ing down to his face-to-face encounter with his model (38 ff.). Interpreters to date have almost always conceived this confrontation as a powerful display of the god's ridiculousness and incongruity,[5] thrust sharply and emphatically into relief through Heracles' unquenchable stream of laughter. Nevertheless, Nicole Loraux (1990: 38)[6] ingeniously enlarged the scope of the discussion by taking into account for the first time the *internal* dimension of the scene, that is, the comic tensions which arise from the interrelation of the stage-characters themselves.

The value of this different approach lies mainly in its considera-tion of a contemporary Athenian audience's perception of the play's *dramatis personae*, that is, of its implicit knowledge and, therefore, understanding, that each of the protagonists appearing on the stage has in reality a greater share in the other's attributes than he would seem to realize or admit (Loraux 1990: 38). In accordance with this line of inquiry, then, femininity could be considered as reflecting the 'other' side of Heracles, the Greek hero of virility. For Greek Tragedy is rich in 'those convulsive moments when . . . the virility

---

[3] *Krokotos*: the extant evidence from the classical period suggests that the *krokotos* was a frequent garment of the god in his theatrical—both tragic and comic—appearances (e.g. Aesch. *Edoni*, fr. 61 Radt; Cratinus' *Dionysalexandrus*, fr. 40 K–A), while the scholiast on *Frogs* 46 as well as Pollux (4. 117), having probably in mind more examples than we do, corroborate this impression. Later material from literature, ritual, and sculpture is abundant, ranging from representations of the god and his followers in fiction (Luc. 4. 2. 20) to Dionysus' cult statues (Athen. 198c) and actual ritual practice (Philostr. *Vit. Apoll.* 4. 21). Artemidorus (*Onirocr.* 2. 3 (p. 103, 8–10 Pack)) ascribes a *poikile* dress to the 'artists of Dionysus', and, although irrefutable documentation is lacking, the wealth of 5th-cent. vase-paintings depicting Dionysus in a long, flowery dress suggests that later Dionysiac literary pictures simply follow an old and well-established pattern.

Kothornoi: Dionysus is almost always wearing some kind of soft loose boot in art: Pickard-Cambridge (1988: 206–8); Bieber, *RE*, s.v. Kothurn; *LIMC*, s.v. Dionysos, *passim*. Iconography establishes the continuity in the connection of Dionysus with the *kothornos* up to late antiquity, for which literary evidence is paramount (cf. e.g. Nonn. *Dion.* 14. 237, 18. 200; Paus. 8. 31. 4, etc.), while, according to Aelian (*NA* 12. 34), it is the buskin which con-secrates the calf as a sacrificial victim for Dionysus on the Greek island of Tenedos (cf. Appendix). In any case, the *kothornos* belongs to the Dionysiac realm already in the classical period, as the shoe of tragic actors (see below, n. 43).

[4] See *LIMC* iv. 1, s.v. Herakles, p. 729; note, however, Bérard's warnings (1983: 115) and, even more strongly (1987b: esp. 165).

[5] e.g. Lapalus (1934: 2–3); Harriott (1986: 110); Cartledge (1990: 4).

[6] First published in 1982.

of the hero quakes' (Loraux 1990: 28ff.),[7] while feminine dress attributed to him both in legend (during his enslavement to the Lydian queen Omphale)[8] and in cult (Plut. *Mor.* 304c–e) becomes the tangible expression of his deep affinity with the female. Furthermore, although classical literature does not anticipate later sources (e.g. Plut. *Mor.* 785e; Luc. 59. 10. 17) in attributing to Heracles the saffron gown, iconography testifies to the existence of the transvestism detail in the Heracles/Omphale myths as early as the fifth century BC (see Figs. 1.1 and 1.2).[9]

Conversely, if the lion-skin is the foremost token of Heraclean prowess, the lion's ferocity is strongly associated with Dionysus' heroic[10] side too. Thus, in representations of the Gigantomachy, while the lion-skin is for Heracles his identifying feature, Dionysus is primarily distinguished by the lions and other wild creatures which, far from being mere weapons, assist him in his fight[11] and, as Lissarrague (1987a: 111) has put it, 'prolongent son énergie guerrière en l'animalisant.' Furthermore, as Carpenter (1986: 66) observes, the implications of the lion as a common element in the Dionysiac and Heraclean iconography should not be overlooked, because 'Dionysos in the Gigantomachy and Herakles and the Nemean Lion are the only mythological scenes that regularly appear in Attic black-figure vase paintings in which gods and lions appear together.' To sum up, then, just as Heracles partakes of Dionysus' femininity, whose emblem is the *krokotos*, the god has a conspicuous share in Heracles' heroism, the lion being the unifying link between the two. The lion-skin, consequently, should not merely be seen as

---

[7] Cf. Zeitlin (1990a: 75 with n. 24).

[8] e.g. Luc. 79. 15. 2, 59. 10; Ov. *Her.* 9. 55ff.; Sen. *HF* 465–71. The literary sources are admittedly late, but iconography can very probably ascribe to the myth an earlier date; see next note.

[9] In his study of Heraclean iconography Vollkommer (1988: 32) considers an Attic rf. pelike of about 430 BC (Fig. 1.1) as its 'oldest and only sure representation in Attic art'; on a Boeotian rf. skyphos too (Fig. 1.2), dating from the same period, Heracles is depicted as giving to a woman (Omphale? Boardman (*LIMC* iv, s.v. Herakles, 1537) does not identify the figure) his bow, while being prepared to offer her his other attributes as well. Vollkommer (1988: 32) interprets the two vases as testifying to 'the beginning of such representations in art, with no general iconography established.'

[10] Dionysus was summoned as 'hero' in the archaic cultic hymn sung by the women of Elis: ἐλθεῖν ἥρω Διόνυσε (fr. 871, 1 *PMG*). Cf. the Bacchic inscription in the Metropolitan Museum of Art, attributing the cult-title Ἥρως to the head of a bacchic *thiasos* in Roman times; see Cumont (1933: 237–9).

[11] See e.g. *LIMC*, s.v. Dionysos, 615, 618, 620, 628, and, most importantly, the Gigantomachy on a well-known dinos of the Lydos Painter, where Dionysus and lions are companions in the fight (M. B. Moore's (1979) reconstruction). On Dionysus' role in the Gigantomachy in 6th-cent. Attic vases see Carpenter (1986: 55ff.) The iconographic theme of Dionysus as an heroic warrior is also prominent in the Athenian *polis'* monumental art, as the second East metope of the Parthenon suggests; see Brommer (1967: i. 23–4, and ii. pls. 42–4).

1.1. Heracles exchanging attributes with Omphale
rf. Attic pelike: British Museum, E 370 (*ARV²* 1134, 7)

1.2. Heracles and Omphale?
rf. Boeotian skyphos: Staatliche Museen zu Berlin, inv. 3414

the famous, distinctive attribute of Heracles but also, and more importantly for our reading of this play, as a telling indicator of an aspect of Dionysus' own multifariousness. It will be argued in this chapter that its striking juxtaposition to the rest of the paraphernalia which construct Dionysus' theatrical disguise in the comedy's prologue is highly evocative: in a classical Greek audience's perspective it can easily build up a wide range of polarities that both stage-figures span. For if Dionysus' mythical and cultic personality is a compound of ambiguities,[12] Heracles is a contradictory hero 'far more markedly . . . than any other', contradictions having always been felt to constitute such 'an essential part of his mythical *persona*, that little attempt was made to reduce or suppress them' (Kirk 1977: 286).

1.2. *Human, Bestial, and Divine*

As a result of Heracles' fight with the Nemean lion, a labour performed through the violence of his hands,[13] the lion-skin reflects his 'power to wrestle on equal terms with monsters' (Kirk 1977: 287)—superhuman prowess, which ultimately assimilates him to them.[14] Within the boundaries of the Heraclean figure, the polar opposites of man and beast dissolve and fuse: his head emerging out of the lion's open mouth, he fights beasts as though he had himself a share in their animality.[15] Yet, it is precisely those bestial fights which secured for him the blessing of Olympian immortality. Thus, an almost standard feature in the pictures of his deification in art (Fig. 1.3)[16] the lion-skin is the reminder that the hero's physical power is, as Kirk (1977: 289) has put it, 'both animal and almost divine', and points to the collocation of beast, man, and god in his mythical *persona*.[17]

The complementarity, therefore, of the two figures becomes

---

[12] See primarily Otto (1965); Henrichs (1982); Segal (1982); Seaford (1994a).

[13] See e.g. Hes. *Theog.* 332; Soph. *Trach.* 1089–94; Eur. *Her.* 153–4. For representations in art see *LIMC* v, s.v. Herakles,'labour I' *passim*.

[14] See Soph. *Trach.* 517–22 (with Easterling 1982: ad loc.); cf. Segal (1977: 119); Silk (1985: 8).

[15] In the literary tradition see e.g. Eur. *Her.* 362–3. The bestiality inherent in this kind of outfit can be gauged *ex silentio* from the fact that Theseus, the utterly civilized hero of the classical Athenian *polis*, although frequently associated with a lion-skin, never wears it *Heracleo modo*, i.e. with the lion's mouth covering his head (Bérard 1983: 115).

[16] See e.g. *LIMC* v, s.v. Herakles, 2850, 2866, 2869, 2873–4, 2877–8 (Fig. 1.3), 2889, 2892, etc.; in a different scheme (lion-skin hanging in the field) see pl. 31 in Carpenter (1986); cf. Verbanck-Piérard (1987: 194 with p. 75).

[17] In cult as well Heracles wavers between man/hero and god, as the double sacrifices offered to him suggest: Farnell (1921: 95 ff.); Woodford (1971: 212–13); Shapiro (1983: esp. 10–14); (sceptical) Verbanck-Piérard (1989).

1.3. Heracles wearing his lion-skin in the chariot procession of his deification

bf. hydria: Museum of Fine Arts, Boston, 67. 1006

apparent. Because, if Heracles 'lies on the margins between human and divine', occupying 'the no-man's-land that is also no-god's-land' (Silk 1985: 6), it is precisely the constant alternation between human shape and manifestation of divine power which best expresses the essence of Dionysus' mythical and cultic personality.[18] Moreover, affinity with the beast is by no means an exclusively Heraclean characteristic either, since it is Dionysus *par excellence* who annihilates the frontiers between beast and god, the lion being perhaps 'the oldest of his bestial shapes' (Dodds 1960: xviii).[19] In this respect, then, as an accessory and complement to his human dimension on the stage, the Heraclean lion-skin evokes the Dionysiac spanning of the 'man and beast' polarity. Furthermore, to the extent to which *kothornoi* and *krokotos* could be suggestive

[18] A good example of the coexistence of the human/god polarity in Dionysus is his puzzling *dramatis persona* in the *Bacchae*; as Henrichs (1993: 21) has put it, 'The dramatic blurring of ritual identities is such that Dionysus' own followers, the Asian maenads who form the chorus, mistake the "stranger god" for the human leader of their ritual thiasos.' In general, it is Dionysus who, more than any other god, 'plays divine visitor' in human shape; see Burnett (1970: 27) and *passim*. For a recent survey of the entire question of 'divinity' and 'humanity' in Dionysus see Henrichs (1993).

[19] See e.g. in art, *LIMC*, s.v. Dionysos, 423, where Dionysus stands face-to-face with his bestial incarnation, a lion; in literature see e.g. Hom. *h.* 7. 44; Eur. *Bacch.* 1017–19 (with Dodds 1960: xviii); Anton. Liber. 10; Nonn. *Dion.* 40. 44, etc. For other bestial shapes of Dionysus see Roux (1972: on *Bacch.* 99–100) and Bérard (1976: 68ff.); cf. *LIMC*, s.v. Dionysos, 154–9.

of Dionysus' divinity to the play's original spectators, 'the son of Stamnias' of the *Frogs* offers a glimpse of the complexity of his divine counterpart in myth, the figure who 'can leap the boundaries between the three major categories of sentient life' (Segal 1982: 11).

1.3. *Male and Female*

Commenting on line 47, the scholiast explains Heracles' laughter at the 'oddity' of Dionysus' attire (τὴν ἄτοπον . . . σκευήν) as astonishment at his half-brother's mixture of discordant (ὅτι τὰ ἄμικτα ἔμιξεν) features, namely male and female: 'because the saffron robe and the buskin befit women (γυναικεῖά ἐστιν), while the lion-skin and club belong to men (ἀνδρῷα).'

However, if Heracles' personality can sometimes verge on femininity, the spanning of the 'male–female' polarity is a permanent, essential feature of Dionysianism. To draw on conceptual pictures which could easily have been evoked by Dionysus' appearance in the *Frogs*, the god was frequently conceived and represented as clad in feminine dress. Thus, *krokotos*, *bassara* (a long, brightly coloured Thracian robe),[20] and *poikilon* (a dress wrought in many colours),[21] are his usual garments both on stage and in art, where the mass of his representations in a long and fine-pleated robe justifies and elucidates his invocation by the chorus of the Theban Elders in Sophocles' *Oedipus Tyrannus* as Μαινάδων ὁμόστολον, that is, 'wearing the same attire as the maenads' (212) (see Fig. 1.4).[22] More importantly still, it is on the fifth-century Athenian stage that Dionysus is mercilessly taunted for his effeminate appearance. In Aeschylus' *Edoni* (fr. 61 Radt) he is scornfully referred to as 'the woman-man' (*gynnis*; cf. below, 1.6(a)), while in the same dramatist's satyric *Theori* or *Isthmiastae* (fr. 78a 67–8 Radt) he fends off the satyrs' slander that he is a feeble, unwarlike, womanish man (*gynnis*),

---

[20] See Aesch. *Edoni*, fr. 59 Radt ὅστις χιτῶνας βασσάρας τε Λυδίας | ἔχει ποδήρεις with the gloss in Phot. *Lex.* β 85 βασσάραι· χιτῶνες οὓς ἐφόρουν αἱ Θρᾷκιαι βάκχαι, καλούμεναι οὕτως ἀπὸ τοῦ Βασσαρέως Διονύσου. ἦσαν δὲ ποικίλοι καὶ ποδήρεις.

[21] See Eupolis' *Taxiarchi*, fr. 280 K–A, suggesting that ποικίλον is a usual Bacchic dress, and cf. Cratinus' *Dionysalexandrus*, fr. 40 K–A, with Pollux 7. 47 (τὸ δὲ ποικίλον, Διονύσου χιτὼν βακχικός). The state of the evidence seems to be confused, but if, as both Hesychius' gloss (ποικίλον ἱμάτιον· ζωγραφητόν) and the name itself suggest, this garment was a flowery one, when worn by the god on stage it would certainly have been appropriate for conveying and emphasizing his links with femininity: cf. Artem. *Onirocr.* 2. 3 (p. 105, 12 Pack) γυναικὶ δὲ ποικίλη καὶ ἀνθηρὰ ἐσθὴς συμφέρει.

[22] See Kenner (1970: 116–20) for a good defence (based primarily on iconographic evidence) of *homostolos* here as 'mit den Mänaden gleichgekleidet' rather than 'mit den Mänaden mitziehend'.

1.4. Dionysus and maenads in similar attires

rf. amphora by Cleophrades: Munich, Staatliche Antikensammlungen, Glyptothek 8732

not to be counted as a male.[23] Besides, Euripides' *Bacchae* brings Dionysus on the stage as a 'stranger of female appearance' (τὸν θηλύμορφον ξένον) (353),[24] with pale complexion (457; cf. 7.4), long locks 'full of desire' (πόθου πλέως) (456), and 'Aphrodite's graces in his eyes' (ὄσσοις χάριτας Ἀφροδίτης ἔχων) (236); correspondingly, the accomplishment of Pentheus' initiation into the Dionysiac mystic rites (Seaford 1981; cf. 2.12) involves his gradual embracing of the feminine dimension,[25] which culminates in his donning 'the equipment of a woman, a maenad, a bacchant' (σκευὴν γυναικὸς μαινάδος βάκχης ἔχων) (915), and his being identical to Cadmus' raving daughters (917 πρέπεις δὲ Κάδμου θυγατέρων μορφὴν μιᾷ).[26]

---

[23] ὡς οὐδέν εἰμι τὴν σιδηρῖτι[ν τέχνην, | γύννις δ' ἄναλκις οὐδ' ἔνειμ' ἐ[ν ἄρσεσιν (incorporating Lobel's and Lloyd-Jones's suggestions).

[24] Cf. Philochorus' reference to Dionysus as θηλύμορφος (*FGrHist* 328 F7a); Luc. 79. 22. 1 ὁ θηλυμίτρης, ὁ ἀβρότερος τῶν γυναικῶν.

[25] See the slow progress from his initial horror (e.g. 822, 828, 836) to his utter willingness to surrender himself to the Stranger's care in the famous 'robing scene' (912ff.).

[26] Cf. the tradition whereby Hermes entrusted the infant Dionysus to Ino and Athamas, whom he persuaded to rear the boy as a girl (τρέφειν ὡς κόρην) (Apollod. 3. 4. 3). The story clearly belongs to that corpus of myths where transvestism reflects a rite of passage, usually

Yet, it is Dionysus who, more than any other god in the Greek pantheon, is strongly associated with the phallus, the symbol of virility *par excellence*.[27] Our own, culturally determined notions of 'effeminacy' and 'transvestism', consequently, can hardly do justice to the nature and the power of Dionysus' sexual ambiguity. In a Greek classical perspective, Dionysus does not merely 'verge upon' or occasionally 'embrace' femininity, but is, instead, a figure who essentially and fundamentally *shares in both sexes simultaneously*, and, therefore, *mediates* between male and female gender.[28] And, although the written sources which explicitly attribute to the god an androgynous *persona* are either late or of dubious chronology,[29] iconography exemplifies Dionysus' transcendence of the 'male–female' polarity as early as the fifth century BC. For in a sharp contrast both to sixth-century vase-painters, who depict a 'dignified bearded god', and to later artists (last decades of fifth and early fourth century), who portray 'a graceful beardless youth' (Dodds 1960: 133),[30] in the bulk of early and mid-fifth-century artistic portraits of Dionysus, his sexual identity is blurred. To put it in another way, in antithesis to the Aristophanic Agathon, who shaves (*Thesm.* 191) from fear of betraying the disguise of his delicate female dress, Dionysus, clad in the feminine *bassara* and in the company of his ecstatic retinue, retains his long, virile beard (cf. Fig. 1.4).[31] Like the representations of 'Anacreontic'/Dionysiac komasts, where the antithetical juxtaposition of male and female signs (e.g. heavy and long black beard[32] versus elegant feminine dress, sash, parasol, and, occasionally, earrings) turns them into bisexual beings,

to adulthood (cf. 2.2). And actually, the procession at the Dionysiac Oschophoria (with clear initiatory traits), setting out from a Dionysiac sanctuary somewhere in the town, is led by δύο νεανίαι κατὰ γυναῖκας ἐστολισμένοι (Procl. *ap.* Phot. *Bibl.* cod. 239, 322a (Henry), 14–15; Bekker, *Anecd. Graec.* s.v. ὠσχοί). For transvestism in Dionysiac ritual see Seaford (1994a: 273). Cf. Bremmer (1992).

[27] For Dionysus and phalluses in the Attic branch of the Dionysiac tradition cf. schol. Ar. *Acharn.* 243; for *phallophoriai* in Attica see Pickard-Cambridge (1988: 62 with nn. 3–4); see, in general, Herter, *RE*, s.v. Phallophorie, and cf. *LIMC*, s.v. Dionysos, 153.

[28] See Jameson (1993: 44): '. . . one might also speak of his bisexuality, the coexistence of elements of *both* genders that may, in effect, cancel each other out, or even of his transcendence of sexuality.'

[29] See e.g. Orph. *h.* 30. 2, 42. 4 (ἄρσενα καὶ θῆλυν, διφυῆ, λύσειον Ἴακχον); Ael. Arist. 4. 52 (pp. 48–9 Dindorf), and the allegorical passages from Porphyry and the Stoics assembled by Jacoby (*FGrHist* 3b (suppl. text), p. 274, on Philochorus 328 F7).

[30] This duality in Dionysiac iconography is rationalistically explained by Diodorus (4. 5. 2) with the existence of two Dionysi, τὸν μὲν παλαιὸν καταπώγωνα . . . τὸν δὲ νεώτερον ὡραῖον καὶ τρυφερὸν καὶ νέον. For the type of the virile, bearded Dionysus see e.g. *LIMC*, s.v. Dionysos, 286–97, 300–7, 326–8, 804–17, and cf. Pausanias' description of the 7th-cent. chest of Cypselus in Olympia (5. 19. 6). For the type of Dionysos *kalos* see e.g. *LIMC*, 356–7, 375–81, 742–50.

[31] See e.g. *LIMC*, s.v. Dionysos, 469 (*c.*480 BC), 472 (480–470 BC), 478 (490–480 BC).

[32] Most probably false (Price 1990: 141–2).

transcending boundaries of gender,[33] the raving god is frequently conceived by the painters as both male and female at once.[34]

1.4. War and Peace

As attributes of Heracles, lion-skin and club function primarily as weapons (cf. Eur. *Her.* 465–6). Because, although a supreme pacifier of the earth, it is only by waging constant war against both bestial and human lawlessness that he succeeds in establishing 'a lifetime of tranquillity for the sake of mankind' (Eur. *Her.* 698–700).[35] Nevertheless, the juxtaposition of beast-hide with saffron robe and buskins creates an analogous antithesis within the stage-figure of Dionysus himself, as, according to Diodorus, Dionysus' martial and pacific sides are reflected in the outfit he dons for each particular occasion. Thus,

in the battles which took place during his wars he arrayed himself in arms suitable for war and in the skins of panthers (καὶ δοραῖς παρδάλεων),[36] but in assemblages and at festive gatherings in time of peace he wore garments which were bright-coloured and luxurious in their effeminacy (ἐσθῆσιν ἀνθειναῖς καὶ κατὰ τὴν μαλακότητα τρυφεραῖς). (Diod. 4. 4. 4)

Now, Diodorus' general account of Dionysus' warlike nature is largely indebted to the Hellenistic conception of Bacchus as a leader

[33] See Frontisi-Ducroux and Lissarrague (1990) and esp. 228–9: 'By appropriating certain signs of the feminine, they show themselves off to be ambisexed beings, striving to transcend gender categories.' On this much discussed corpus of Attic vases (between about 520 and 450 BC) see Caskey and Beazley (1954); Frontisi-Ducroux and Lissarrague (1990 (1983)); Kurtz and Boardman (1986); W. J. Slater (1978); Price (1990); Delavaud-Roux (1995).

[34] In the wider experience of Dionysiac myth and cult, other exemplifications of this cross-sexual game resulting in hybrid, bisexual combinations, would be: women in both satyric loincloth/phallus and female breasts (e.g. late 5th-cent. Attic rf. kylix: *ARV²* 1519, 13 (*LIMC*, s.v. Dionysos, 842) (Fig. 1.5); fragment of a vase found in Miletus (Caruso 1987: fig. 6)); satyrs with either feminine breasts (e.g. Caruso 1987: fig. 17) or female mask (e.g. T. B. L. Webster 1967: CT2 (terracotta statuette)) or with both a phallus and a fine, long, and pleated feminine dress (e.g. Trumpf-Lyritzaki 1969: FV 97). Pride of place among this evidence is held by a chous in the National Museum of Athens (Fig. 1.6) which depicts a man in satyr-mask, dressed up in a maenadic costume: the scene may be inspired by the cultic/ritual transvestisms taking part on the Choes day of the Anthesteria festival (see 4.11; cf. Appendix, n. 19). Cf. Ael. Arist. 4. 54 (p. 50 Dindorf) καὶ οὐ τοὺς ἄνδρας θηλύνειν μᾶλλον ἢ τὰς γυναῖκας εἰς ἀνδρῶν τάξιν καθιστάναι Διονυσιακόν, and see in general Caruso (1987).

[35] Perhaps the clearest illustration of the Heraclean fusion of a warlike and pacific side is offered by the Olympic games, signalling the start of a 'solemn truce' (*spondai*) and armistice in times of war, and yet having been first established from the very spoils of the hero's battles as an ἀκρόθινα πολέμου (Pind. *Ol.* 2. 4).

[36] In the Gigantomachy, where Dionysus is almost always clad in a *dora* (hide), the distinction between a panther/leopard and lion-skin is not always clear-cut; however, on the basis of M. B. Moore's (1979: 85 n. 60) principle that 'the coats of the lions are indicated by dots', while 'that of the panther by widely-spaced circles', in *LIMC*, s.v. Dionysos, 615 and 628 Dionysus fights with a lion-skin spread over his arm (Fig. 1.7).

1.5. (*Left*) Transvestite
games: Dionysus and woman
in a satyr's loincloth and phallus

rf. Attic kylix: Corinth Museum, CP 885 (*ARV*² 1519, 13)

1.6. (*Below*) Transvestite games: man in maenadic costume and satyr mask

rf. Attic chous: Athens, National Museum, no. 1220

1.7. Dionysus fighting in the Gigantomachy
rf. Attic kylix: Rome, Villa Giulia, 50388 (*ARV*² 65, 114)

of armies, a triumphant *stratelates*.[37] Yet, the paradoxic constellation of a pacific and a martial side in Dionysus' *persona* is by no means a late construct, without any bearing on the cultural experience of a classical Greek audience. To start from the perspective of Orphic/Dionysiac initiates (see Ch. 2), the words 'war-peace' (εἰρήνη-πόλεμος) are scratched above the abbreviation *ΔΙΟΝ* (standing for Dionysus) on a bone tablet found in Olbia (of Pontus) and dating from the late fifth century BC (West 1982a: 22). But, more importantly, a wider audience as well could easily envisage Dionysus in terms of a polarity of 'war' and 'peace'.

'Lover of Peace, who is giver of prosperity' (φιλεῖ δ' ὀλβοδότειραν Εἰ | ρήναν) (Eur. *Bacch.* 419–20),[38] Dionysus and his female entourage, the maenads, can also wage war against their mythical opponents.[39] Accessories of *komoi* and festivities, *kothornoi*[40] and

---

[37] See, however, Eur. *Bacch.* 52, where Dionysus warns ξυνάψω μαινάσι στρατηλατῶν. In early Dionysiac myths, cf. also Dionysus' military expedition against Perseus and the Argives: Paus. 2. 20. 4, 2. 22. 1 (tomb of women Διονύσῳ συνεστρατευμέναι).

[38] For Eirene as a member of the Bacchic *thiasos* see *LIMC*, s.v. Eirene, 11–12.

[39] For perceptive remarks on the military terms/imagery associated with the maenads' attack on Pentheus in Euripides' *Bacchae* see March (1989: 43); for a more detailed discussion of the un-hoplitic nature of Dionysiac 'war' see below, 7.4.

[40] The *kothornos* is frequently worn by men in iconographic depictions of *symposia*; see Bieber (1907: 46–7; with refs. to vases); Karouzou (1945: 39); Kurtz and Boardman (1986: 61); extremely relevant to my discussion is an Attic krater in Palermo (Karouzou 1945), where the *kothornoi* are thrown off just under the couch of a reclining Dionysus (*CVA* (Palermo, i), pl. 47).

krokotos can be connotatively associated with the joyful and exuber-
ant Dionysiac side. And yet, although the god of war, 'bringer of
much suffering' (πολύμοχθος), is 'out of tune with Bromios' celebrations' (Βρομίου παράμουσος ἑορταῖς) (Eur. *Phoen.* 784–5), Dionysus
has himself a share in Ares,[41] causing 'the moral and physical
collapse of those who attempt to resist by normal means the fury of
the possessed worshippers'.[42] Finally, as a footwear of tragic actors,
the Dionysiac buskin[43] engraves a pacific element on the acting god's
skeue, since Tragedy is strongly interwoven with a life of peace.[44]
However, fifth-century playgoers could have been well aware that
it is primarily the language and imagery of tragic drama which
depicts the madness of the warrior in terms of bacchic frenzy and
possession.[45] Perhaps the clearest dramatic illustration of Dionysus'
paradoxical relation to 'war' and 'peace' is the parodos of the
Sophoclean *Antigone*. Envisaging the warrior's 'mad impulse' as a
state of *bakcheia* (135–6 μαινομένᾳ ξὺν ὁρμᾷ | βακχεύων ἐπέπνει),[46] the
Theban Elders still invoke Dionysus himself to lead the festive
pannychis (152–4), the choral performance which will celebrate the
polis' relief from civil strife. In other words, within the borders of his
own native land, Dionysus, 'the shaker of Thebes' (ὁ Θήβας ... ἐλελί-
| χθων)(153–4), functions as a force both sinister and buoyant, an
ever-powerful divine presence which rouses up and rocks the city in
the rage of war no less than in the joyful excitement of peace.

[41] Eur. *Bacch.* 302–4 Ἄρεώς τε μοῖραν μεταλαβὼν ἔχει τινά· | στρατὸν γὰρ ἐν ὅπλοις ὄντα κἀπὶ
τάξεσιν | φόβος διεπτόησε πρὶν λόγχης θιγεῖν.

[42] Dodds (1960: ad 302–4); for historical examples see below (7.4, n. 77) and Seaford (1996:
ad 302–5). The ambiguous relation of this god to war and peace remains a fundamental constituent of his mythical *persona* both in late antiquity and in Roman times; see e.g. Plut.
Demetr. 2. 3; Ael. Arist. 4. 53–4 (pp. 49–50 Dindorf); Hor. *Od.* 2. 19. 25–8.

[43] The *kothornos* of the classical period did not have the raised sole of the Hellenistic era
and could certainly not be taken as a symbol of the tragic genre (as e.g. in Roman times).
However, as a low and soft boot with a beak-shaped tip, it *does* appear in classical dramatic
imagery as the footwear of tragic actors. Good examples can be sought in some theatrical
'rehearsal scenes' on vases, such as a bell-krater in Ferrara (*c*.460 BC), where an actor impersonating a maenad wears soft and pointed boots, or a pelike in Boston (*c*.430 BC), where two
chorus men, preparing to take part in a chorus of women, wear (or are depicted in the act of
putting on) soft pointed boots. See figs. 33 and 34 respectively in Pickard-Cambridge (1988).
Another splendid example is a rf. chous in the National Museum of Athens (fig. 37 in Kenner
1970), (Fig. 1.6), where *kothornoi* are worn by two masked figures/actors, impersonating
maenads (I am grateful to Prof. Handley for having drawn my attention to this vase).

[44] For Tragedy and peace see e.g. Ar. *Peace* 530–2 and 695.

[45] The affinities and correspondences between Dionysus and Ares in their ways of possessing, inspiring, and driving out of the mind are interestingly traced by Lonnoy (1985).

[46] Cf. most importantly Aesch. *Sept.* 497–8 ἔνθεος δ' Ἄρει | βακχᾷ πρὸς ἀλκήν, θυιὰς ὥς, φόβον
βλέπων.

1.5. Primitiveness and Civilization

Finally, animal skins place their wearers at the opposite side of the values of the *polis*. So, for example, dressing in a goatskin can be regarded as the hallmark of uncivilized existence (Theognis, 54–6), while asking for *dike*, arbitration, can be presented as incompatible with the wearing of leather garments (*diphtherai*) (Men. *Epitr.* 228–30). In other words, even merely the hide of a domestic animal functions as a means of differentiation, by emphasizing the polarity between the man inside the *asty* and the countryman outsider (e.g. Ar. *Clouds* 70–2) or between the citizen and slave (e.g. Ar. *Eccles.* 723–4; cf. Athen. 657d on the Spartan helots).[47]

Infinitely more suggestive is of course the hide of a wild animal. Whether as an attribute of the social outcast, such as Euripides' Philoctetes,[48] or as an accessory of the warrior[49] and a garment of the hunter,[50] who oscillates perpetually between Civilization and the wilderness of Nature, the skin of a beast—often a lion-skin in the vase-painter's imagination[51]—may function as a sign of brutishness and primitiveness, which should be relegated to the realm outside civic walls. A prime example at this point is the monstrous Polyphemus in the Euripidean *Cyclops*, who wraps up in hides of wild beasts (δοραῖσι θηρῶν) as a protection against wintry weather (Eur. *Cycl.* 329–31). A 'war' with branches, correspondingly, belongs to those downward deviations of civilized fighting tactics which one encounters among Herodotus' barbarian 'others',[52] while in the anti-society of the Homeric savage Cyclopes, Polyphemus is distinguished by his huge club, 'a great bludgeon of olive wood, still green' (*Od.* 9. 319–20).[53] More significantly still, in the Periclean

---

[47] See further Frontisi-Ducroux (1983: 72–3).

[48] According to Dio Chrysostom (*Or.* 59. 5), he entered the stage clothed in the skin of wild beasts (δοραὶ θηρίων καλύπτουσιν αὐτόν).

[49] See Pausanias (4. 11. 3) on Arcadian mountaineers who, instead of wearing breastplates, were protected in their fight against the Lacedaemonians with the hides of wild beasts, wolves, and bears.

[50] An animal-skin is a common attribute of the great mythical hunters and huntresses, e.g. Atalanta (*LIMC*, s.v. Atalanta, 5), Artemis (e.g. *ABV* 107, 1), Argos (e.g. fig. 175 in Schefold 1981: 135), etc. For the club as an attribute of mythical hunters see e.g. Orion (Schefold 1981: 153, fig. 201; cf. Hom. *Od.* 11. 575); Argos (Schefold 1981: 135, fig. 175); Actaeon (Schefold 1981: 143, fig. 188); cf. Bérard (1983: 114–15 and 1987b).

[51] With the individualization of hunting scenes from the end of the 6th cent. onwards, lion-skin becomes a means of iconographical assimilation of the anonymous ephebic hunter to the great mythical models; see Schmitt and Schnapp (1982: 67 with fig. 9).

[52] See e.g. Hdt. 4. 180 (with Rosellini and Saïd 1978: 981, and nn. 179–80) where, in a ritual feast in honour of Athena, young girls among the Auseans of Libya μάχονται πρὸς ἀλλήλας λίθοισί τε καὶ ξύλοισι; for branches as belonging to the pre-civilized phase of mankind see also Lucr. *De Rer. Nat.* 5. 1284; cf. ibid. 5. 975 for the use of clubs (*magno pondere clavae*).

[53] The Euripidean Polyphemus still carries a club (*Cycl.* 210 (cf. 203 with Seaford 1984: ad loc.)).

period hides of beasts and tree-branches became an artist's favourite means for underlining the crudity of monstrous creatures, envisaged as leading an existence which either contradicts or threatens to subvert the order of the city.[54]

Within the cultural complex of Greek perceptions and assumptions, therefore, lion-skin and club as the insignia of Heracles could mobilize associations with conceptual frameworks such as primitiveness and savagery.[55] Simultaneously, however, they could also indicate the essential ambiguity around which this hero's personality revolves: although his toils pave the way for the acculturation of mankind,[56] Heracles himself partakes of 'nature' working, as he does, through sheer brute strength and operating outside the boundaries of civilized space. As Turato (1979: 46) has expressed it, 'Heracles' civilizing work stops at the doorstep of the city. Those same weapons he uses for offensive action, the armour with which he shields himself, exclude him from the city.' Heracles' figure is remarkable for spanning both *nomos*/culture and *bia*, the violence of brute force. Thus, in the notoriously obscure lines of a much discussed Pindaric fragment (169a [A'], 1–5 Maehler), it is Heracles' achievements (ἔργοισιν Ἡρακλέος) which are chosen to exemplify the poet's gnome that 'the most supreme violence' (τὸ βιαιότατον) finds its justification through *nomos*.

Yet, if Heracles occupies a precarious borderline between 'nature' and 'culture', this very same polarity expresses the fundamental paradox on which Dionysus' mythical and ritual *persona* rests.

A visual link to the appearance of the ecstatic god of myth, the Heraclean lion-skin appropriated by the Aristophanic 'son of Stamnias' evokes the picture of the wild Dionysus of nature who, 'equipped with *thyrsoi* and fawn-skins' (*Frogs* 1211–12, from Eur. *Hypsipyle*, fr. 752 N²), 'leaps in the dance' (πηδᾷ χορεύων) (*Frogs*

---

[54] See Vian (1952: 145–6); cf. Schefold (1981: 148, fig. 196) (Apollo versus Tityos in *pardalis*). Literary descriptions follow the trend, e.g. Ar. *Birds* 1249–50; Pl. *Soph.* 246a. Centaurs as well are frequently shown fighting with tree-branches. It is also interesting to note at this point that Herodotus ascribes wooden staffs to Peisistratus' bodyguards, who enabled him to seize the Acropolis: 'yet these men did not become spear-bearers of Pisistratus, but club-bearers, for they attended on him carrying wooden maces' (Hdt. 1. 59; tr. D. Grene 1987) (I owe this reference to Alan Sommerstein).

[55] Note e.g. Aegle's contempt for the beastlike Heracles, clad in 'the skin of a huge lion, untreated and untanned' and carrying 'a sturdy olive branch' (Ap. Rh. *Argon.* 4. 1436ff.). According to Diodorus' chronological segmentation of the Heraclean figure (e.g. at 3. 74. 4), *ropalon* and *leonte* are appropriate τῷ παλαιῷ . . . Ἡρακλεῖ διὰ τὸ κατ' ἐκείνους τοὺς χρόνους μήπω τῶν ὅπλων εὑρημένων τοὺς ἀνθρώπους τοῖς μὲν ξύλοις ἀμύνεσθαι τοὺς ἀντιταττομένους, ταῖς δὲ δοραῖς τῶν θηρίων σκεπαστηρίοις ὅπλοις χρῆσθαι (1. 24. 3); cf. also the post-Homeric poetical conception of Heracles as a figure ἐν λῃστοῦ σχήματι, wandering about on his own ξύλον ἔχοντα καὶ λεοντῆν, a tradition which, according to Athenaeus, originates in Stesichorus (Athen. 512e–13a=Stesichorus, fr. 229 *PMGF*).

[56] For Heracles as a 'culture-hero' see Lacroix (1974).

1213), in opposition to the world of the *polis*' community (Fig. 1.8).[57] Saffron gown and buskin, on the other hand, as accessories of banquets and festive celebrations, which are intrinsically linked to the *polis*' socio-religious identity, transpose Dionysus' dramatic figure to the very core of civic life. In other words, juxtaposed to *kothornoi* and *krokotos*, the hide of a wild beast confronts the audience of the *Frogs* with a visual illustration of Dionysus' duality, since this god could be perceived both as 'Bestower of favours' and 'Kind' (Διόνυσον . . . Χαριδότην καὶ Μειλίχιον) as well as 'Eater of raw flesh' and 'Savage' (Ὠμηστὴς καὶ Ἀγριώνιος) (Plut. *Ant.* 24. 4–5) or, to put it in fifth-century dramatic language, as 'a god in initiation ritual most terrible, but to humankind most gentle' (ἐν τέλει θεός | δεινότατος, ἀνθρώποισι δ᾽ ἠπιώτατος) (Eur. *Bacch.* 860–1).[58]

1.6. *Dionysiac Ambiguities and the Dionysus of the* Frogs

(a) *Visual signs*

The appropriation of the Heraclean 'other', therefore, reveals ultimately provinces which belong to Dionysus' own 'self'. Thus, Dionysus' appearance in the prologue of the *Frogs* evokes both the 'universal' god, inextricably bound up with the wildness of nature (implications of the *leonte*), and the god under whose aegis lie the dramatic festivals, the most specifically and unmistakably Athenian expression of the *polis*' cultural vitality (implications of the *kothornos*). Or, if viewed from a different angle, the stage-figure Aristophanes created stands both for the impulse to 'primitiveness' operating inside human nature[59] and as the god who, through his invention of wine (connotations of 'son of the Wine-Jar'), has elevated human life to the status of civilization (cf. Ch. 3). To translate this duality in visual terms, in the eyes of fifth-century spectators, the Heraclean masquerade would have been able to evoke a figure

---

[57] See e.g. *ARV*² 298, 1643 where Dionysus, clad in his *pardalis*, dismembers a wild beast held over his shoulders (Fig. 1.8).

[58] Tr. Seaford (1996); see also his note ad 860–1. Cf. also Bierl (1991: 35): 'Das Bild des komischen Helden, das auf der Bühne die gegensätzlichen Teile des körperlich starken Haudegens Herakles und des verweichlichten, weibischen Literaten vereinigt, ist in bester Weise Dionysos selbst, der sich selbst in den *Bakchen* als δεινότατος, ἀνθρώποισι δ᾽ ἠπιώτατος (861) charakterisiert.'

[59] In 5th-cent. Greek terms, it is primarily Dionysus' disorderly appearance which conveys the intimation of primitiveness. Amalgamating, as it does, both the human and the bestial, it evokes that pre-civilized phase in mankind's evolution, when boundaries between the species had not yet been fixed, and human life was 'confused' (*pephyrmenos*) and 'beastlike' (*theriodes*) (Eur. *Suppl.* 201–2); see O'Brien (1985); on the notion of the *pephyrmenon* see Lämmli (1962: 63 ff., with sources) and on the *diakrisis*-motif as indicating the progress to civilization see Lämmli (1962: 68–9).

1.8. Dionysus *mainomenos*

rf. Attic stamnos: British Museum, E 439 (*ARV²* 298, 1643)

fundamentally Dionysiac. For, wearing a feminine dress and a *dora*, a hide, this comically shaped version of Dionysus' mythical *persona* is not substantially different from its counterpart on vases, the god with the leopard-skin or the fawn-skin knotted on his shoulders over his long and womanish Thracian dress (*bassara*) (cf. Fig. 1.8).[60]

Besides, it seems that an Athenian spectator may have been used to a constellation of discordant elements not only in the mythical but in the stage-appearances of Dionysus as well. Interestingly, it is another play of Aristophanes himself which points in this direction. When Euripides and his Kinsman visit the effeminate tragic poet Agathon in the *Thesmophoriazusae*, the Kinsman asks:

καί σ᾽, ὦ νεανίσχ᾽, ἥτις εἶ, κατ᾽ Αἰσχύλον
ἐκ τῆς Λυκουργείας ἐρέσθαι βούλομαι.
ποδαπὸς ὁ γύννις; τίς πάτρα; τίς ἡ στολή;
τίς ἡ τάραξις τοῦ βίου; τί βάρβιτος
λαλεῖ κροκωτῷ; τί δὲ λύρα κεκρυφάλῳ;
τί λήκυθος καὶ στρόφιον; ὡς οὐ ξύμφορα.
τίς δαὶ κατόπτρου καὶ ξίφους κοινωνία;

---

[60] According to Philostratus (*Imag.* 1. 15. 2), σκευή . . . ἠνθισμένη (cf. the saffron gown) καὶ θύρσοι καὶ νεβρίδες (cf. the lion-skin) constitute usual elements of Dionysiac images in art.

And now, young sir, I want to ask you in the style of Aeschylus, in words from the Lycurgus plays, what manner of woman you are. 'Whence comes this epicene? What is its country, what its garb?' What confusion of life-styles is this? What has a bass to say to a saffron gown? or a lyre to a hair-net? What's an oil-flask doing with a breast-band? How incongruous! And what partnership can there be between a mirror and a sword? (*Thesm.* 134–40; tr. Sommerstein 1994)

The scholiast on line 135 ascribes only ποδαπὸς ὁ γύννις; to Aeschylus' Dionysiac play *Edoni*. Scholars, however, have considered the possibility that lines 137–40 as well were extracted from the same tragedy[61] and, should this assumption be correct, we can reasonably surmise that Agathon's 'confusion of life-styles' (τίς ἡ τάραξις τοῦ βίου) (137) offers also a glimpse of the Aeschylean conception of Dionysus' 'confused' appearance too. For, although the oil-flask (*lekythos*) and the breast-band (*strophion*) are clearly Agathon's own attributes, that is, not linked with Dionysus in our tradition, saffron gown (*krokotos*), mirror (*katoptron*), sword (*xiphos*), *barbitos* (a stringed instrument similar to the lyre), and maybe also the hair-net (*kekryphalos*) could actually, to a greater or lesser extent, have been perceived by the play's original spectators as appropriate to the mythical and cultic *persona* of Dionysus.[62]

The Dionysiac associations of the saffron robe have already been discussed (1.1). An important instrument of the *thiasos* (Seaford 1984: 106), the *barbitos* is inherently associated with Dionysiac scenes (Maas and Snyder 1989: 113–14), for vase-painters depict not only satyrs, silens, maenads (less frequently), and human komasts, but even Dionysus himself in the act of *barbitizein* (Fig. 1.9).[63] The mirror seems to have been closely associated with the Orphic cluster

---

[61] Rau (1967: 109–11) detects a tragic/Aeschylean ring in the entire passage (136ff.); cf. Sommerstein (1994: ad 136): 'many words and phrases in 137–45 may also be quoted or adapted from Lycurgus' interrogation of Dionysus'. The scholiast on *Thesm.* 137 (τίς ἡ τάραξις τοῦ βίου) cites the line as the beginning of Eubulus' Διονύσιος (fr. 24 K–A=25a Hunter), but see Kassel (1966: 11) and Hunter (1983: 117) for the greater probability of Eubulus' using a 'familiar tag' from Aeschylus rather than 'a pastiche of Aristophanes'.

[62] In iconography, both Dionysus and his female followers often wear some kind of head-dress, although not the particular one-piece cap which archaeologists identify as the *kekryphalos*; for Dionysus and the sash (*mitra*) see e.g. Soph. *OT* 209; Diod. 4. 4. 4, and, in general, Brandenburg (1966); for representations of maenads wearing the *sakkos* (a one-piece cap resembling the *kekryphalos*) see refs. in Kurtz and Boardman (1986: 53 n. 99). I am inclined to believe that the stage-figure of an effeminate-looking male wearing a feminine headdress could easily have triggered off Dionysiac connotations, whether his particular cap looked exactly like the usual Dionysiac accessory or not.

[63] For satyrs/silens/komasts and the *barbitos* see Paquette (1984: B10, B11, B22), etc.; for a maenad with *barbitos* see Maas and Snyder (1989: 137, fig. 19); for Dionysus himself playing the *barbitos* see an Attic rf. kylix (*ARV²* 371, 14) of the Brygos Painter, now in Paris (*LIMC*, s.v. Dionysos, 465) (Fig. 1.9); in general, for representations of the *barbitos* in komastic iconography of the 'Anacreontic' tradition see Kurtz and Boardman (1986: 62–4).

1.9. Dionysus playing the *barbitos*

rf. Attic kylix: Paris, Cabinet des Médailles, 576 (*ARV*² 371, 14)

of Dionysiac myths, as it was one among the playthings with which the Titans enticed the child Dionysus and led him to his (initiatory) death.[64] Clement of Alexandria (*Protr.* 2. 15) refers to all these objects as 'the worthless tokens of this sacrament' (τῆς τελετῆς τὰ ἀχρεῖα σύμβολα) and, on the basis of archaeological and other evidence,[65] West (1983*a*: 156–7) and Seaford (1987*a*) have convincingly argued that mirrors had a specific cultic function in Dionysiac initiation rites—they may have been used 'to stimulate and confuse the initiand' (Seaford 1987*a*: 77). More importantly still, a mirror may have been a stage-property in Euripides' *Bacchae*, thus explaining Pentheus' much discussed 'double vision' in 918–19: 'Pentheus looks in a mirror (held by himself or by Dionysos), which intrigues

---

[64] See e.g. Orph. frs. 34, 209, 214 Kern.

[65] See e.g. the inscription 'Demonassa, daughter of Lenaios, *euai*! and Lenaios son of Demoklos, *eiau*!' on a late 6th-cent. mirror from Olbia of Pontus (West 1983*a*: 156; cf. n. 51). See also Seaford (1987*a*: 77 n. 11).

him, disorientates him, and, as a female instrument, completes his humiliation' (Seaford 1987a: 78),[66] while maenads handling a mirror seem to be familiar figures in Dionysiac iconography (e.g. Balensiefen 1990: nos. K9 and K19; *LIMC*, s.v. Dionysos, 341).[67] As for the sword, maenads armed with *xiphoi* feature in theatrical illustrations of Pentheus' death[68] (probably reflecting a pre-Euripidean version of the myth, such as dramatized e.g. in Xenocles' *Bacchae* of 415 BC) (March 1989: 36–7), while the picture of a maenad who, *xiphos* and the leg of a kid in her hands, dances in the presence of a formally costumed flute-player on both sides of a Berlin pelike (*ARV*² 47), (Fig. 1.10) may be an illustration of a tragic scene (Beazley 1955: 312), perhaps even from Aeschylus' lost *Bassarae* (T. B. L. Webster 1967: 138). Furthermore, in a wider Dionysiac circle too, the sword seems to be 'extraordinarily fixed' (T. B. L. Webster 1967: 138) in representations of Orpheus' death by the Dionysiac Bassarids.[69] In this respect, then, placed within the broader framework of Greek mythical and cultic images and structures, the spectrum of paradoxes created by the juxtaposition of incongruous elements in the 'Dionysiac' stage-figure of Agathon in the *Thesmophoriazusae*[70] is analogous to that constructed through Dionysus' imitation of Heracles in the *Frogs*. Finally, Aesch. fr. 61a Radt 'what can have been agreed between a shield and a drinking cup?' (τί δ' ἀσπίδι ξύνθημα καὶ καρχησίῳ;)[71] calling attention, as it does, to the unharmonious collocation of a martial and pacific side in the tragic *dramatis persona* of the god, enriches the range of contradictions which could have been envisaged as dissolved within the figure of Dionysus on the comic stage (cf. Kassel 1966: 11) and, therefore, broadens the repertory of 'images' on which fifth-century spectators could have drawn in the course of their perceptual assimilation of the *Frogs*.

[66] Cf. Seaford (1987a: 78): 'Just as Dionysos, as an initiand, was enticed and led to his death by a mirror, so the initiand Pentheus sees before him, in the mirror, an obscure but significant image of his companion, before being led off to his death' and his further suggestion (78 n. 16) that 'if Dionysos carried a mirror in Aeschylus' *Lykourgeia*, this would give point to the parody at Ar. *Thesm.* 140.' See now also Seaford (1996: ad 918–19).

[67] Cf. an isolated fragment of a Dionysiac comic play (Alexander, Διόνυσος) which reads: ἰδοὺ κάτοπτρον· εἰπέ μοι, τούτῳ τί χρῇ; (fr. 1 K–A; ref. in Seaford 1996: ad 918–19).

[68] As, for example, on an Italian cup in Naples (pl. 2a in March 1989) or a vase from the Jatta collection in Ruvo (pl. 2c in March 1989).

[69] See e.g. an hydria from Foiano (Caskey and Beazley 1954: 72–6), an Attic lekythos from Palermo (ibid.: n. 9), etc. However, ignoring the wider cultural perspective afforded by Dionysiac iconography, Sommerstein (1994: ad 140) submits that 'a sword would be equally inappropriate for Dionysus.'

[70] With heavy concentration on the male/female polarity (as focused, more explicitly, in *Thesm.* 141–5).

[71] Kassel (1966: 12) connects it with the same speech of Lycurgus in Aeschylus' *Edoni*; note the similarity in the construction between fr. 61 Radt and *Frogs* 47.

1.10. Maenad with *xiphos*

Staatliche Museen zu Berlin Preussischer Kulturbesitz,
Antikensammlung, inv. V. 1. 3223

(b) *Signs of* logos *and action*

If the scope of inquiry is now extended to the level of the comic *logos* and the comic action, it becomes immediately apparent that the sum of incongruities communicated visually through the physical appearance of Dionysus as a signifier on the *polis*' dramatic stage is complemented by a corresponding verbal cluster of thematic ambiguities, created through his words and deeds in the prologue.

Brother of Heracles (see 58, 60, 164), that is, a divine figure, since his relation to the hero is through their common father Zeus, he happily proclaims himself to be a mortal's offspring, son of the Wine-Jar (22).[72] Detectable in his complaint about the lack of intel-

---

[72] A wealth of evidence suggests that Greeks considered a vase to be a living object. With eyes or even with a whole visage carved on its surface (see e.g. Athen. 501d, using the word πρόσωπον for the cup's interior; cf. Ar. *Plut.* 545), with ears, στόμα, χείλη, τράχηλος, γαστήρ or ὀμφαλός (for the use of anatomic language in the Greeks' description of wine-vessels see

lectual 'fertility' in the Athenian city are both the communal voice of the god of drama ('I am in need of a talented poet') (71) and the personal, emotional lament of a spectator and admirer, or even a deceased poet's close friend.[73] 'Dionysus' though he is, he confesses that he ages after each theatrical performance he dislikes (18), a notion incompatible not only with the Greek conception of an ageless divinity, but also with the distinctively Dionysiac miracle of rejuvenation,[74] prominently featuring in the Initiates' mystic song to Iacchus[75] in the parodos of our play:

> old men's knees bound in the dance;
> off they shake their grief
> and the lingering years of old age,
> through honouring you in holy worship.   (345–9)

Furthermore, by emphasizing that he walks and toils (23 αὐτὸς βαδίζω καὶ πονῶ), he deviates from the norm of the Olympians, perceived as 'ignorant of troubles' (Pindar, fr. 143 Maehler), and relegates himself to the rank of human beings, for whom *ponos*, that is, suffering and labour, best describes their everyday lot.[76] Finally, his knocking on the door 'like a Centaur' (κενταυρικῶς) (38–9) ascribes to him a share in bestiality,[77] since the Centaurs, 'on the

primarily Frœhner 1876) or even with a foot in the shape of a phallus (Boardman 1976), the vase becomes an imitation of the human body, not to say 'human' itself since, from early times onwards and in a variety of places (most prominently Corinth and Rhodes), vases have been frequently manipulated in the shape of human (or even a variety of animal) figures; see primarily Amyx (1988: 512 ff.); Ducat (1966: 61 ff., with plates); Trumpf-Lyritzaki (1969).

[73] See *Frogs* 83–4 (about Agathon) ἀπολιπών μ' ἀποίχεται, | ἀγαθὸς ποιητὴς καὶ ποθεινὸς τοῖς φίλοις.

[74] See primarily Eur. *Bacch*. 188–90 (Cadmus and Teiresias): 'We have pleasantly forgotten that we are old.—You are sharing my experience, then! Because I too feel youthful and ready to join in the dances.' Cf. Pl. *Leg*. 666b; Ael. Arist. 4. 53 (p. 50 Dindorf) καὶ ὁ γέρων ἀναβήσει.

[75] For the identification of Dionysus/Iacchus see 2.3, n. 60.

[76] See e.g. Eur. *Hipp*. 189–90; Soph. *Aj*. 866; *Ant*. 1276; Xen. *Mem*. 2. 1. 28; Pl. *Leg*. 653d. See further Loraux (1982a: 181–2).

[77] There is no secure indication about the way Aristophanes envisaged the staging of Dionysus' knocking. Did he have in mind a Dionysus banging on the door wildly, in an 'Heraclean' display of force, or did he mean Dionysus to knock delicately, i.e. in visible contrast to the fiercer elements in his *skeue*? Should the latter be the case, Dionysus' behaviour would be consistent with the way he imagines that his lion-skin has terrified Heracles (40–1; see 4.2), with the delicacy of his saffron gown (cf. below, n. 82), and, in general, with his subsequent cowardice and sham bravado; Heracles' comment, correspondingly, could easily have been perceived by the original spectators as double-edged, i.e. as a joke both on Dionysus' timidity as well as on the mighty lion-slayer's impressionability (thanks to Richard Hunter who focused my attention on this issue). However, significant help can be sought at this point in iconography: as part of a larger thesis on vase-paintings and Athenian drama, Oliver Taplin (1993: 45–7) has convincingly argued that a bell-krater depicting 'a Herakles-figure' who knocks at a door with his club while accompanied by a baggage-laden servant on a donkey, must have been inspired by the opening scene of *Frogs* (see Taplin, fig. 13.7). To the extent, then, that the illustration is an accurate representation of the Aristophanic scene (and, of course, it must be borne in mind that the painted Dionysus/Heracles wears neither *krokotos*

threshold between human and equine nature', 'marked the limit between animal and human being, between *anthropos* and *therion*' (Du Bois 1982: 27).

Laying claim to the domain of *ponos*, inherently interwoven with male physical effort (Loraux 1982*a*: 174–5 with n. 17), he sharply dissociates himself from feminine delicacy (*tryphe*),[78] a blemish that he pointedly ascribes to his slave:

> now, isn't this a perfect example of insolence and utter softness,
> (εἶτ' οὐχ ὕβρις ταῦτ' ἐστὶ καὶ πολλὴ τρυφή)
> when I, Dionysus, son of Stamnias,
> am *myself* walking and toiling, while allowing *him* to ride . . .   (21–3)

And yet, within the mental framework of fifth-century spectators, delicacy is actually associated with Dionysus, the god imagined by his devotees as 'tossing his tender locks (τρυφερόν . . . πλόκαμον) into the air' (Eur. *Bacch.* 150),[79] the Bacchic Lord, who tantalizes his victim with the misleading promise of extravagant *tryphe*.[80] Besides, Dionysus partakes of feminine softness and fastidiousness within the Aristophanic comedy itself, not only through his quest for the less tiring way of descent to Hades,[81] but also through the saffron robe that he wears, for the *krokotos* appears to be closely linked with feminine luxuriousness.[82] A good example of this connection can be sought in a passage with Dionysiac connotations (Seaford 1993: 119–21) from Euripides' *Phoenician Women*, where Antigone, a

nor *kothornoi*), Dionysus *did* bang on the door violently. Yet, whatever the truth may be, Heracles' remark 'how much like a Centaur . . .' is actually enunciated and, consequently, invites the audience to participate in his own 'point of view', thrust emphatically into relief.

[78] For *tryphe* as one of the many opposites of *ponos* see e.g. Pl. *Rep.* 556b; Arist. *Pol.* 1265a33–4; *EN* 1150b; for the feminine connotations of *tryphe* see e.g. Ar. *Clouds* 48; *Lys.* 387, 405; *Eccles.* 973.

[79] Feminine softness seems to have been an essential dimension of Dionysus' 5th-cent. *persona* on the comic stage too, as plays like Eupolis' *Taxiarchi* suggest, where, despite his manly martial aspirations (cf. 2.5), Dionysus attracts comparison to a 'female soldier, a child-bearing woman from Ionia' (λεχὼ στρατιῶτις ἐξ' Ἰωνίας) (fr. 272 K–A). For Dionysus *trypheros* in later sources see Diod. 4. 4. 2 τρυφερὸν καὶ παντελῶς ἁπαλόν and cf. above, n. 30.

[80] See *Bacch.* 968–70, Dionysus' final luring of Pentheus, the initiand into his mystic *teletai* (Seaford 1981; cf. below, 2.12): 'DI. You will come carried . . . PE. What you describe is luxury for me. | DI. In your mother's arms. PE. You will compel me to be pampered even (καὶ τρυφᾶν μ' ἀναγκάσεις). | DI. Pampering in my fashion (τρυφάς γε τοιάσδ') (tr. Seaford 1996). I owe this reference to Richard Seaford.

[81] See *Frogs* 117ff., and esp. Dionysus' statement in 128: 'Yes, indeed, for I'm not a great walker!', which can be compared with Dem. 42. 24, where a rich man's purchase of a chariot so 'that he may not have to travel on foot' is castigated as an indication of utter luxuriousness: τοσαύτης οὗτος τρυφῆς ἐστι μεστός.

[82] See e.g. Ar. *Lys.* 43–4; Philostr. *Vit. Apoll.* 4. 21, where the Athenians' wearing of κροκωτοί makes them look ἁβρότεροι τῶν Ξέρξου γυναικῶν. As a ποικίλη ἐσθής, the *krokotos* can also connote *tryphe* (Artem. *Onirocr.* 2. 3 (p. 105, 12–14 Pack)) and sympotic luxuriousness (Dio Chrys. *Or.* 8. 31. 14–15); for Dionysus' bright-coloured robes as being *trypherai* see Diod. 4. 4. 4 (above, 1.4).

'maenad of the dead' (βάκχα νεκύ|ων), laments her fate of being 'carried on' (φέρομαι), 'relinquishing the saffron luxury of the garment' (στολίδος κροκόεσσαν ἀνεῖσα τρυφάν) (1489–91). Moreover, witnessing Dionysus' experience of an actor's *ponos* on the stage, a fifth-century Greek audience would have been well aware that, within the frame of the democratic city's ideology, it is this god's dramatic festivals[83] *par excellence* which offer a most welcome—and regular—respite from everyday labour.[84]

Bragging of his participation in the naval battle of Arginusae, Dionysus claims for himself a warrior's identity: 'I was aboard, a mariner in Cleisthenes' ship' (ἐπεβάτευον Κλεισθένει) (48),[85] a declaration forcefully conveyed to the spectator, despite the fact that the extravagance of his bravado is mocked by Xanthias[86] ('And then I woke up!', 51)[87] and that his ambiguous *epebateuon Kleisthenei* gives rise to Heracles' suspicion of homosexual intercourse (57). Naming himself a 'son of Stamnias', conversely, and hence alluding to his connection/identification with wine (3.1), he introduces his theatrical *persona* as an embodiment of peace, for Eirene (Peace) is 'grape-giver' (βοτρυόδωρε) (Ar. *Peace* 520) and 'most vine-loving of all goddesses' (θεῶν πασῶν . . . φιλαμπελωτάτην) (*Peace* 308).[88]

Finally, his choice of Heraclean *bia*, an utterly corporeal pattern, as a means of granting him success in the Underworld, is totally discordant with the purely intellectual nature of the quest which motivated his journey down to Hades. The unrefined way in which he hopes to bring his expedition to a happy ending is illustrated not only in the coarser part of his *skeue* but also in his experiments with brusque behaviour. For Heracles' exclamation 'how like a centaur

---

[83] Suggestively evoked by his *kothornoi* (cf. n. 43) and *krokotos* (one among the garments of kings in tragic drama, according to the scholiast on Ar. *Clouds* 70).

[84] Cf. Thuc. 2. 38 Καὶ μὴν καὶ τῶν πόνων πλείστας ἀναπαύλας τῇ γνώμῃ ἐπορισάμεθα, ἀγῶσι μέν γε . . .

[85] See Sommerstein's note (1996: ad loc.)

[86] Or perhaps Heracles, according to a different attribution of line 51. See, however, Dover (1993: ad loc.).

[87] In the light of Eur. *Cycl.* 5–9, where Silenus comically inflates his role in the Gigantomachy, on Dionysus' side, it would rather seem part of a traditional Dionysiac joke to involve Dionysus or members of his entourage in a warlike event, while at the same time undercutting the heroism of their participation by casting upon it the suspicion of unreality. Thus, in the *Cyclops*, the role of Xanthias is fulfilled by the proud narrator Silenus himself, who disbelieves his own boasts (8 φέρ' ἴδω, τοῦτ' ἰδὼν ὄναρ λέγω;). Seaford (1984: ad loc.) compares *Frogs* 51, but without any comments on the parallel. Further evidence is lacking but, should my postulation be correct, such a motif could be explained as the theatrical reflection of the paradox which underlies the conception of the joyful Dionysiac band or, indeed, the god himself, placed in the midst of war.

[88] In the *Acharnians* peace is virtually synonymous with wine, since it is 'materialized' throughout the play in the image of 'wine libations' (*spondai*); see, most explicitly, *Acharn.* 199 and 1033–4 (cf. 1020–1).

(ὡς κενταυρικῶς) he jumped at my door, whoever that was!' (38–9) associating, as it does, the manners of his brother in disguise with that 'galloping army of double-bodied, hostile beasts, violent, lawless, supremely strong' (Soph. *Trach.* 1095–6) he has himself combated in the past, directs the audience's perception of Dionysus towards the conceptual frames of brutishness and savagery.[89] More precisely, it is the Parthenon metopes, where the *polis'* official art has relegated the 'mountain-ranging, savage breed of Centaurs' (Eur. *Her.* 364–5) to the side of the wild, which best allow us to gauge the impact that Heracles' comparison was likely to have had upon the play's original spectators.

1.7. 'Dionysiac' and 'Heraclean'

However, it is not merely Dionysus' *skeue* which exemplifies a tangible *mélange* of 'Dionysiac' and 'Heraclean' elements in the prologue of the *Frogs*. Dionysus' conduct as well is conspicuously 'Heraclean', without having lost the traits of its 'Dionysianism'.

Delicate and soft and 'not much of a walker' (128), Xanthias' master and companion reacts, comments, criticizes, and yearns in a distinctively 'Dionysiac' way. As he confesses to his brother, his admiration for Euripides is stronger than madness (103 μᾶλλά πλεῖν ἢ μαίνομαι)—an appropriate expression in the mouth of the god who instils *mania* in his votaries and who, from Homer onwards (*Il.* 6. 132), is described and portrayed as *mainomenos* in literature and art (cf. Fig. 1.8). The object of his quest is a fertile poet (96)—an aspiration which thoroughly befits a god whose cult is deeply interwoven with the fertility of nature and who, throughout the Greek world and from the earliest times, is worshiped as Endendros or Dendrites (the power in the tree), Anthios (the blossom-bringer), Karpios (the fruit-bringer) and Phleus (teeming with abundance).[90] As for the volume of his *pothos*, this is calculated on a distinctively 'Dionysiac' measure, that is, the size of a stage-actor, the famous (cf. Dem. 19. 246) Molon:

> ῾ΗΡ. πόθος; πόσος τις;
>
> ΔΙΟΝ.　　　　μικρός, ἡλίκος Μόλων.
>
> HER. Desire? how big?
>
> DION.　　　　small—as big as Molon.[91]　(55)

---

[89] Cf. Hesychius' gloss κενταυρικῶς· ἀγροίκως, ἀγρίως.

[90] See Farnell (1909: 118–20, 123–4) and Otto (1965: 152–9).

[91] See Ghiron-Bistagne (1976: 343), index, s.v. Μόλων. In all probability, Dionysus' reply is a παρὰ προσδοκίαν joke for, according to the scholiast ad loc., Molon was a big man: Παίζει. ἔστι γὰρ μεγαλόσωμος ὁ Μόλων. Sommerstein (1996: ad 55) concludes his very informative note: 'In any case it is evident that Dionysus means that his "longing" was very powerful.'

The worthless host of poets, correspondingly, whom *he*, the vine-god, despises, are fittingly reviled in the language of vintage: they are ἐπιφυλλίδες (92), that is, useless grapes left over for the gleaners in the vineyards.[92] His complaint about his 'toiling' (*ponos*), on the other hand, deflects his *dramatis persona* as much as possible from the 'Dionysiac' and draws him closer to the range of the 'Heraclean'. Because in the Dionysiac experience toil becomes 'sweet' and weariness 'unwearying',[93] as the god communicates supernatural power to his worshippers (e.g. *Bacch.* 194). It is, therefore, the feeling of effortlessness, instead of *ponos*, which constitutes Dionysus' distinctive hallmark (see 9.1). Heracles, on the contrary, is envisaged as the hero of *ponos par excellence*.[94] Not only are his Labours explicitly designated as *ponoi* or *kamatoi*, that is, toils, throughout Greek (including Byzantine) literary tradition,[95] but he also figures (Xen. *Mem.* 2. 1. 21–34) as the hero who, on the threshold of adulthood, chose consciously a life of *ponos* over a life of enjoyment, in which he could relish all pleasures 'most effortlessly' (*Mem.* 2. 1. 24 καὶ πῶς ἂν ἀπονώτατα τούτων πάντων τυγχάνοις). However, the fusion of 'Dionysiac' and 'Heraclean' which preoccupies us in this section can be best appreciated in the literary discussion between the two half-brothers in the comedy's prologue.

Trying to explain to Heracles the nature of his undertaking, Dionysus uses the language of desire: while he was reading the *Andromeda* on Cleisthenes' warship, longing (*pothos*) struck his heart—'you couldn't imagine how strongly!' (53–4). In his attempt to make himself more clearly understood (64 ἆρ' ἐκδιδάσκω τὸ σαφές, ἢ 'τέρᾳ φράσω;), he continues to draw on the semantic field of *pothos*: 'so great is the passion (ἵμερος) which lays me waste' (59) or, a little while later, 'similar, then, is the kind of yearning (πόθος) which devours me—a yearning for Euripides' (66–7).[96] Now, a fifth-century spectator would certainly have been familiar with representations of Pothos as a companion of Dionysiac bands.[97] Simultaneously, however, within the larger frame of his mythical

---

[92] See schol. ad loc. οὕτω λέγεται τὰ βοτρύδια τὰ μετὰ τὸ πατεῖσθαι τῶν στεμφύλων ἐξερχόμενα. ταῦτα δὲ οὐ χρήσιμα.

[93] See Eur. *Bacch.* 65–7 θοάζω | Βρομίῳ πόνον ἡδὺν | κάματόν τ' εὐκάματον.

[94] See Hes. frs. 248 and 249 M–W πονηρότατον καὶ ἄριστον, and Loraux (1982a: 185ff.).

[95] Cf. e.g. Eur. *Her.* 22, 357, 388, 427, 575, 1275, 1353; *Alc.* 481, 1149–50; Diod. 1. 2. 4. See Kritzas (1973).

[96] It should be also noted at this point that *pothein* with respect to a deceased approximates in some respect to the language of the city. Cf. e.g. the epitaph for those fallen at Poteidaea (432 BC): 'the city regrets (*pothei*) these men, as do the people of Erechtheus' (*IG* i² 945); cf. [Dem.] 60. 33 (ποθοῦσι δ' οὐ μόνον συγγενεῖς καὶ πολῖται); see Loraux (1986: 47).

[97] See Eur. *Bacch.* 414 with Dodds (1960: ad loc.) on the personified Pothos in Dionysiac iconography.

and literary 'encyclopaedia', this 'language of desire' would have struck him as distinctively 'Heraclean'. For, more than any other hero, it is the Heracles of myth who constantly falls victim to the elemental drive of sexual lust. Just as in the *Frogs* sexual passion and appetite for food (56–7, 62–5) are the only channels through which the 'ethereal nature' of Dionysus' longing (Segal 1961: 210) can penetrate the realm of Heracles' mental terminology—concrete and confined to tangible, corporeal sensations—*pothos* and *deinos himeros* in the erotic sense (for Iole; Soph. *Trach.* 431–2, 476–7) are the very impulses which had thrust the Sophoclean version of his mythical *persona* into the sack of Oechalia. In other words, Dionysus becomes 'Heraclean' in a totally 'un-Heraclean' and distinctively 'Dionysiac' way: speaking the language of his brother, he is none the less dabbed with an intellectual,[98] Dionysiac tinge. Paradoxical though it may seem, low and sublime, subtle and coarse, mind and body, comic and serious, palpable and abstract as well as 'Dionysiac' and 'Heraclean' are inextricably interwoven *as well as* sharply differentiated in this scene.

To conclude, then, the primary impression communicated to the audience in the prologue of the *Frogs* is the simultaneous intermingling and separation of the 'Dionysiac' and 'Heraclean' poles. The broad range of 'Dionysiac' and 'Heraclean' connotations conveyed by Dionysus' theatrical *skeue* constructs upon the visual level the common mythical and ritual ground to which the real counterparts of the Aristophanic stage-characters belong. The same feeling of interrelation is communicated to the spectator at the level of dramatic *logos* and of action, as Dionysus' stage-presence oscillates between a 'Dionysiac' and 'Heraclean' mode of behaviour. Nevertheless, despite the fact that the performance throws sharply into relief the intertwinement of the two sides, 'Dionysiac' and 'Heraclean' are kept clearly apart in the limited perspectives of the two stage-actors: unwilling to admit that his brother's *krokotos* corresponds to an aspect of his own 'personality', the Aristophanic

---

[98] The dramatic exploitation of the 'Dionysus vs. Heracles' polarity follows a well-known comic path, that is, the motif of differentiation through the clash of incompatible intellectual levels; cf. e.g. Ar. *Clouds* (Socrates vs. Strepsiades) and *Thesmophoriazusae* (Euripides vs. the Kinsman). Nevertheless, the prologue of the *Frogs* is also indebted to a tradition specifically 'Heraclean'. Vase-painters draw heavily on stories about Heracles as a disciple of Linus (Boardman in *LIMC* iv, s.v. Herakles, p. 833), the wise master whom the hero, unable διὰ τὴν τῆς ψυχῆς βραδυτῆτα . . . δέξασθαι τὴν μάθησιν (Diod. 3. 67. 2), killed with a *kithara* or a stool (*LIMC* iv, s.v. Herakles 1667–73); a fragment of Alexis' *Linus* gives some insight into the tradition Aristophanes was likely to be familiar with: Linus asks Heracles to choose a book from a collection of epic and tragic poets, a choice which will reveal his *physis*, ἐπὶ τί μάλισθ' ὥρμηκε (fr. 140, 8 K–A), but Heracles, indifferent to intellectual matters, remains attached to food, and picks up a book on cookery (fr. 140, 9–10 K–A).

Heracles bursts into uncontrollable laughter, a clear indication that he perceives Dionysus as 'other' in relation to himself. But for Dionysus too, conversely, 'Heracles' and the 'Heraclean mode' are obviously conceived as an 'alterity', which can be only appropriated through a change of outward appearance, and with the aid of Heracles' distinguishing traits, lion-skin and club. Moreover, confident though he may be in the depth and the completeness of his transformation (4.2), Dionysus holds firmly on to the proud aware-ness of his own intellectual superiority, and persistently alienates himself from the tastes of his model, as lines 105 ('"Let my mind be master in its house"; you've got a house of your own.')[99] and 107 ('you make sure that you only teach me about food!') suggest. Finally, as the prologue intimates that the measure of Dionysus' success is his compliance with the standards implicated in his proto-type's lion-skin and club, the journey to Hades he is prepared to enact physically on the stage may be translated in abstract terms into a journey of the Dionysiac 'self' towards the Heraclean 'other'. In this Dionysiac transition, the dynamics of 'approach' and 'alien-ation' evidenced in the comedy's opening scene will prove of para-mount importance. For once the whole sequence of the links between the impersonator and his model has been displayed to the audience from the start, every further instance of artistic identification of Dionysus with Heracles implies—and, therefore, can be viewed as—his approximation to an area of his own self; his deviations, conversely, from the ways of his prototype entail an analogous 'estrangement' from the corresponding aspects of his own multifaceted *persona*. Read along these lines, then, the comedy ends with a 'ring-composition' effect: while the function of the prologue is to merge 'Dionysiac' and 'Heraclean' *without* eliminating the sense of incongruity arising from their juxtaposition, we shall see in Chapters 5–9 that in the play's literary contest Dionysus' *persona* broadens so as to incorporate harmoniously, without contradictions, the 'Dionysiac' and 'Heraclean' dimensions simultaneously. The 'Heraclean' characteristics intimated by the 'Heraclean' part of Dionysus' *skeue* resurface in the 'civic' frame of the comedy's agon, amalgamated now and remoulded into the dramatic figure of Aeschylus, who acts as an 'Heraclean' force within society (Ch. 7). Yet, as on the level of poetic *techne*, Aeschylus, the chosen artist, proves himself to be a strikingly 'Dionysiac' poet (6.1–2), the final judgement of the god constitutes as much of a 'Dionysiac' move as an approach, or better say, a 'return' to the 'Heraclean' mode and function (7.5).

[99] Tr. Sommerstein (1996).

'Separation', 'Limen', 'Aggregation': The *Frogs* as a 'Rite of Passage'

2.1. *Introduction*

In a highly influential article published in 1961, C. P. Segal (1961: 213) argued that the *Frogs* is to be seen as the representation of 'a carefully worked out development' within the dramatic figure of Dionysus: the journey into the Unknown becomes on a symbolic level the expression of the god's advancement towards a unified conception of himself and the reintegration of his own personality. Segal, however, was not primarily concerned with exploring the wider pattern into which Dionysus' transition falls. It was only in 1986[1] that David Konstan (1986: 291) suggested—in an important development of Segal's position—that there are three levels in this play which follow 'a logical arrangement imitating a ritual of initiation'. But, once again, like Segal, Konstan did not pursue the implications of his own proposition to the very end: although he refers (299–300) to van Gennep's conclusions on the tripartite structure of a 'rite of passage', he restricts his analogy between the anthropologist's classification and the movement of the *Frogs* to the scene 'at the threshold' of the Underworld, that is, the whipping scene, which, he argues, corresponds to the 'liminal' stage in a ritual process.[2] Moreover, although he seems to be venturing an initiatory reading of the play, it is only in passing that he refers (300) to its last section as conforming to the initiatory phase of 'reaggregation'. In 1993 Angus Bowie's innovative treatment of the *Frogs* (as a chapter of his highly stimulating book on Aristophanes) explores at length the idea of initiation as the primary cultural model upon which this comedy is built.[3] Nevertheless, even Bowie is much more concerned

---

[1] Now revised version as Konstan (1995: 61–74).

[2] See Konstan (1986: 299): 'la confusion radicale d'identité entre Dionysos et Xanthias correspond . . . à ce que Victor Turner, poursuivant la pensée de Arnold van Gennep, rapporte comme l'étape liminaire du processus rituel'.

[3] In the years between 1986 and 1993, Moorton (1989) professes to apply van Gennep's structure to the *Frogs*. However, what he really does is to fragment the play—sometimes quite implausibly—into a series of 'brief or extended rites of passage' (308) which contribute

with exploring the specific ways in which the Mysteries are reflected in and interwoven with the play's imagery than with probing the nature of Dionysus' underworld experience itself. In other words, Bowie's extremely valuable reading of the play still does not discuss the importance of Dionysus as *the* unifying element of the play's structure, nor does it raise the question of how one's membership in Greek fifth-century society would have determined and shaped one's understanding of Dionysus' quest within the *Frogs*. By way of contrast, the present chapter proposes to address precisely such issues and, therefore, push the scholarly discussion a step further, by suggesting that it would be helpful to conceive of the play *in its entirety* along the lines of a tripartite transition, as the fictive remoulding of a 'rite of passage'. It is this conception, I shall argue, which illuminates the play's structure both as an organic and a self-consistent unity as well.

To set the scene before proceeding any further, it is important to define from the start a primary anthropological concept that we shall constantly encounter from this point onwards, both in the present as well as in the following chapters of this book, namely, the already mentioned notion of a 'rite of passage'.

In traditional societies, important changes in the life of individuals, such as the passage from adolescence to adulthood, from maidenhood to married life, or from life to death, are not viewed as simple, physiological events, but are marked out by fairly complicated and standardized ritual sequences, which are meant to consummate the transition from one stage of life to the next. The classic study of such ritual structures, which have been classed by anthropologists as 'rites of passage', is that of the Dutch scholar Arnold van Gennep (1960 (1909)), who was the first to detect and to describe the common pattern underlying all rites of transition. van Gennep saw that ritual passages consist of three phases: 'separation', 'limen' (from the latin word which means threshold), and 'aggregation', or 'reintegration'.

Separation signifies the novice's symbolic abandonment of his previous condition as well as his spatial detachment from his original environment and his seclusion in the space where his initiation will take place. Limen or liminality or marginality is the middle period in an initiation ritual: it is a space and a time apart, during

nothing to our understanding of the play's structural cohesion. Thus, the initiatory phase of 'separation' is understood as Dionysus' 'leave-taking with Heracles' (310), 'the invitation of the Mystae has the characteristics of a rite of incorporation' (318), Pluto's off-stage acceptance of Dionysus (after the whipping scene) has the value of an 'incorporation into Hades' (319), etc. Furthermore, ritual liminality is conceived and treated only spatially in his analysis, i.e. as the *limne* of the frogs.

which the initiand hovers 'in between' two other fixed states and conditions, his/her old self, which he/she has, so to speak, left behind, and his/her new identity, which he or she has not acquired yet. Finally, the third phase of aggregation refers to the initiand's reincorporation into the society to which he/she belongs, under a new *persona*. He/she is now, let us say, an Eleusinian initiate, a *bakchos* or a *bakche* in the circle of Dionysus, a warrior in the city's battle ranks, and so on.

Rites of passage are ubiquitous in ancient Greek societies. Not only do they dramatize a variety of individual transitions (e.g. from childhood to adolescence and adulthood, from virginity to matron status),[4] but they also have protracted liminal periods, which exemplify most of the characteristics of ritual marginality that anthropologists have singled out in a broad range of cultures. Nevertheless, of special interest to us with respect to Aristophanes' *Frogs* is the frame of initiation which pertains to mystery religions. Now, throughout the Graeco-Roman world a multiplicity of mystic cults existed (see esp. Burkert 1987a), characterized by a variable degree of acceptance into and dependence on civic official religion. Yet, our sources prove unanimous in recognizing that the supreme, the quintessential, mystic insight throughout Greek antiquity was to be gained at Eleusis, where initiation into the solemn, awful *teletai* of Demeter and Core is described as 'the most horrible and the most joyful' among all humanly experienced events (Ael. Arist. 22. 2 ἀνθρώποις ταυτὸν φρικωδέστατόν τε καὶ φαιδρότατον). Besides, Dionysiac mysteries as well were quickly spreading over vast Greek territories during the second half of the fifth century BC.[5] But to gain the title of a mystes in Eleusis or to be initiated into a Dionysiac *thiasos* was not merely equivalent to realizing a rite of passage, a transition which bestows a new identity, a 'sacred' ritual *persona*, on the individual concerned. It meant primarily to undergo a unique and ἄρρητος, that is, 'unspeakable', experience, intended to imprint a long and lasting memory upon the soul of the *memyemenoi*. And, precisely because mystic initiation was such a deep, 'transformative'[6] ritual process, it comes as no surprise that a variety of texts, whether literary or philosophical, are informed by the emotional and physical vicissitudes of Eleusinian and/or Bacchic mystai, remoulding thus, to some extent, the language and imagery of

---

[4] See e.g. Jeanmaire (1939); Brelich (1969); Calame (1977); S. G. Cole (1984b); Sourvinou-Inwood (1988); Garland (1985); Vidal-Naquet (1986); Bruit-Zaidman (1991).

[5] For a comprehensive account of the evidence available see now Seaford (1996 : 39–44).

[6] For this conception of ritual as 'transformative' see Schechner (1985: 127); Houseman (1993: 207).

initiation.[7] Nevertheless, no text inspired by mystic cults can be taken to constitute an accurate reflection of the rites, a piece of documentary, so to speak, evidence on ancient mysticism. Any dramatized ritual sequence is distinguished by its inventive reuse of cultic elements; it obeys its own rules and has its own logic, which follows the demands of the *fictive*, that is, the literary, rather than the cultic, plot.[8] To put it in another way, the remoulded mystic images are drawn from a variety of ritual moments and, moreover, they are woven in dramatic constellations which are often by no means identical to those belonging to the real-life rituals themselves.

Yet mystic initiation is not the only type of ritual transition reflected in Greek texts. Greek drama, in particular, frequently incorporates in its structure those ritual passages which have a bearing not only on selected groups but, more importantly, on the life of every individual member of a classical Greek *polis'* community. I have obviously in mind here rites of passage to maturity which, while aiming at the male's integration into the community of adult warriors, signify for the maiden her marital transition. Dramatically recast initiation frames, therefore, should by no means be viewed as inflexible but, on the contrary, as freely intermingling and interacting with each other. For example, although Aeschylus' *Oresteia* dramatizes an archetypal scenario of ephebic initiation, Orestes' transition to manhood, it is also a storehouse of Eleusinian language and imagery, as has been demonstrated in detail by Tierney and Thomson, as early as the first decades of our century.[9] Similarly, as I have shown elsewhere (Lada-Richards 1997a),[10] Sophocles' *Philoctetes* is informed by the patterning of both ephebic rites of passage and Eleusinian imagery as well. And, of course, an analogous literary fusion is to be expected between Eleusinian and Dionysiac initiation. Euripides' *Ion*, for example, is richly informed by elements of both Dionysiac and Eleusinian mystic myth and ritual (Zeitlin 1989),[11] while Plato's *Phaedrus* 249c–54b fuses in an

---

[7] See e.g. (literature): Thomson (1935); Tierney (1937); Headlam and Thomson (1938); A. M. Bowie (1993b: esp. 23–6) on Aeschylus' *Oresteia*; Seaford (1981) on Eur. *Bacchae*; Seaford (1994b) on Sophocles' *Ajax* and *Electra*; Zeitlin (1989) on Eur. *Ion*; Byl (1980) and (1988) and A. M. Bowie (1993a) on Aristophanes' *Clouds*, *Knights*, and *Wasps*; (philosophy): Riedweg (1987) on Plato's *Phaedrus* and *Symposion*.

[8] For example, with respect to *Frogs*, Dover (1993: 61) draws attention to the comic elements blended with the features of the Eleusinian cult, and also, very rightly, reminds us of the grave sin attached to anything which could be taken as divulgation of the Eleusinian Mysteries.

[9] See n. 7 above.

[10] Cf. Lada-Richards (1998).

[11] See more specifically Zeitlin (1989: 190 n. 89): 'It is entirely possible that the ensemble of actions in the tent alludes simultaneously to different moments in different mystic rituals without having to make a definite choice among them.'

inextricable complex beliefs and terminology of both Dionysiac and Eleusinian mystic *teletai*.[12] It is this latter case, in particular, which is of special interest to any reading of the *Frogs*, because the literary conflation of Eleusinian and Bacchic cultic features not only represents a theatrical construction but, much more importantly, illustrates an actual ritual merging in the real-life sequence of the Eleusinian mystic cult.

Apart from the evidence (which most scholars now treat as conclusive) for the identification of Dionysus with the Eleusinian Iacchus (see below, 2.3, n. 60), the deity whose statue was carried in procession from Athens to Eleusis,[13] eloquent testimonies of the deep blending of Dionysiac with Eleusinian mystic structures can be sought in the Orphic/Bacchic gold leaves,[14] where Demeter and Persephone play a prominent role. On the recently discovered tablets from Pelinna, for example, the initiand is instructed to 'tell Persephone that Bacchus himself has released you'.[15] But, more importantly still, Dionysus seems to be perceived as linked, in one way or another, with Eleusis in non-mystic literature as well. The fifth ode of Sophocles' *Antigone*, for example, invokes Dionysus 'who rules over the glens, common to all, of Eleusinian Deo (i.e. Demeter)',[16] while the pseudo-Platonic *Axiochus* (371e) preserves a legend whereby the god was himself initiated into the Great Mysteries. And literary sources tally very well with artistic representations, portraying Dionysus in the company of the main Eleusinian deities.[17]

The *Frogs*, then, must be seen as the literary remoulding of a

[12] See Riedweg (1987: 44–5). I owe this reference to Richard Seaford.

[13] See e.g. *IG* ii² 1006, 9 προέπεμψαν (sc. the ephebes) αὐτὰ (sc. τὰ ἱερά) καὶ τὸν Ἴακχον ὡσαύτως. An allusion to the *pompe* may be detected in the refrain of the mystic Chorus in *Frogs* (403, 408, 413) Ἴακχε φιλοχορευτά, συμπρόπεμπέ με. See Graf (1974: 44).

[14] See below, 2.14; the Bacchic character of the leaves has been proved beyond doubt with the discovery of the tablet from Hipponion (2.11, n. 173), where (line 16) μύσται καὶ βάκχοι are envisaged as treading on a sacred road.

[15] εἰπεῖν Φερσεφόνᾳ σ' ὅτι Βάκχιος αὐτὸς ἔλυσε (line 2; text in Tsantsanoglou and Parássoglou 1987: 10).

[16] πολυώνυμε, . . . κλυτὰν ὃς ἀμφέπεις | Ἰταλίαν, μέδεις δὲ | παγκοίνοις Ἐλευσινίας | Δηοῦς ἐν κόλποις, ὦ Βακχεῦ (Soph. *Ant.* 1115–21).

[17] See e.g. *LIMC*, s.v. Demeter, 396 (with Demeter and Core), 400 (with Demeter and Core), 402 (with Demeter, Core, and Pluto), 405 (with Demeter, Core, Triptolemus, Heracles, Athena), 408, 409, etc. See also *LIMC*, s.v. Dionysos, 523–30. Some of these representations are very early (e.g. *LIMC*, s.v. Dionysos, 523 from *c*.480 BC), some date from the first half of the 4th cent., and the majority date from around 330 BC. Of particular interest with respect to the blending of cults is an Attic rf. krater in Oxford, where the artist presumably follows the Orphic genealogy of Dionysus as son of Zeus and Demeter or Persephone, and has therefore depicted an infant Dionysus, clad in a fawn-skin, on the lap of Demeter (see *LIMC*, s.v. Dionysos, 531; first half of the 4th cent. BC) (Fig. 2.1). For sculptural representations of Dionysus with Demeter and Persephone in Athens and elsewhere see *LIMC*, s.v. Demeter, 452–4a, and s.v. Dionysos, 532–4.

2.1. Infant Dionysus on Demeter's lap
fragment of rf. Attic krater: Oxford, Ashmolean Museum, 1956. 355

ritual fusion. Graf (1974) and A. M. Bowie (1993a) have argued conclusively for the unmistakable reflection of Eleusinian cultic moments and eschatological motifs in the play's imagery and plot.[18] But, most importantly, both Segal (1961) and, to a much greater extent, Bowie (1993a: esp. 230–1), have duly alerted scholars to the need to broaden the scope of their inquiry *beyond* Eleusis, towards the frame of Orphic doctrines and, especially, Dionysiac mysteries, given the protagonistic role of the god in the Aristophanic play. My own reasons for exploring the Dionysiac cultural complex in depth, so as to gain a better insight into a classical Greek audience's appreciation of Dionysus' *dramatis persona* in the *Frogs*, have already been expounded in the Introduction to this book. However, the present chapter will seek to illuminate the ritual structure of the *Frogs* by drawing its material *not only* from Eleusis and the Bacchic circle, but also from other initiatory contexts, such as ephebic rites of passage. Now, it is true that this Aristophanic comedy has no ephebic figure in its cast of characters. Nevertheless, I think it *is* important to identify any elements from rites of maturation which may have found their way into the main sequence of the play's mystic plot. For, as the images belonging to this ritual complex would have been easily detectable by classical male audiences, their

---

[18] e.g. the *pannychis* and dance (see below, 2.13), the Iacchus procession, the torches (2.13 and 2.14), the *gephyrismoi* (2.12), the flowery meadows, the eternal sunlight, etc. See Graf (1974: esp. 40–50); A. M. Bowie (1993a: 229ff.). The parallels with the Eleusinian Great Mysteries are too convincing to allow for the consideration of any alternative theories, such as e.g. that the cultic frame of reference is that of the Lesser Mysteries at Agrai or the Lenaean festival at which the comedy was staged (see refs. in Dover 1993: 62 n. 13).

interweaving with the play's mystical imagery, which centres on Dionysus, would have significantly enhanced a classical Greek viewer's understanding of this god as an initiand, a ritual subject who bears striking signs of liminality and undergoes an initiatory transition.

Dionysus' Rite of Passage and Ritual Liminality

2.2. *'Separation', 'Limen', 'Aggregation'*

In the previous chapter an attempt has been made to reconstruct the 'perceptual filters' through which fifth-century spectators would have been able to visualize and understand Dionysus in the prologue of the *Frogs*. The next step is to appreciate that from a Greek point of view Dionysus, the stage-actor, eludes classification.

If envisaged as a member of a citizen community, the incongruous combination of his garments underlines his oscillation between male and female sex. More importantly, however, it is the very nature of his links with a *polis'* community which seems confused and indeterminate: club in hand and lion-skin upon his shoulders, he looks much more like a dweller of the borders (*eschatia*) or the countryside (*agroi*) surrounding the town.[19] And yet, the *logos* he articulates on the stage is definitely a voice from within the space of the city: many a time, as he reveals, he has been a *theates* at the Athenian theatrical performances (16–18); having first-hand knowledge of Athenian drama and its poets (72–107), he is so familiar with the language of the theatre that he can be aware of stock jokes, scenic conventions, and 'what always makes the spectators laugh' (2; cf. 3–20). Furthermore, he takes pride in his participation in the city's victorious enterprise, the sea battle of Arginusae, under Cleisthenes' command (48 ff.).

In anthropological terms, such a defiance of structural classification carries a wide range of implications. In a variety of cultural contexts and social situations, for example, human beings may be treated as placeless, left out in the rigid patterning of the society to which they belong, lying 'betwixt and between', as Turner (1967: 93) would put it, two other fixed states and conditions.[20] Animals as

---

[19] See 1.5 and cf. Pollux 7. 68, where woollen garments are explicitly said to have functioned in the Athens of the Peisistratids as a separation mark between *agros* and city, since those wearing them were meant to 'be ashamed (ὅπως αἰσχύνοιντο) to come down into the city (εἰς ἄστυ κατιέναι)'. See also Nagy (1990: 389–90).

[20] See e.g. Douglas (1966: 95) on the pregnant mother/unborn child; for applications of the notions of interstitiality and ritual ambiguity in the context of Greek and Roman cult see

well may be perceived as structural misfits, classificatory anomalies,[21] when they do not tidily conform to the established criteria determining their category within a given culture's taxonomic system (Douglas 1975*b*: esp. 282–3). Nevertheless, in the specific frame of a cultic/ritual sequence, structural indeterminacy, the condition of being 'neither-nor' and yet 'both', is quite often the distinctive feature of a rite of passage.[22] My purpose in this chapter is, therefore, to explore the ways in which the notion of ritual marginality can be both illuminating for the role of Dionysus in the *Frogs* and informative for the thematic pattern of the play in its entirety as well.

If the tools of anthropology are applied to the Greek world and to the *Frogs*, it would appear that both sexual ambivalence and ambiguous relation to civic space are well-known signs by which Greek social experience encodes marginality.

Thus, in a variety of civic festivals and isolated rites participation in both male and female qualities at once,[23] symbolizing, as it does, the last moment in the ritual subject's sexual ambiguity,[24] becomes a privileged means of dramatizing the passage towards full female or male status and maturity. Besides, viewed from a different perspective, civic dress combined with an animal's *dora*, a garment often emphasizing the ephebe's ties, still unsevered, with the feral realm of nature, is one among the many visual codes in which myth transcribes liminality, as the case of Jason, an archetypal adolescent suggests.[25] When placed within the wider referential frame of Greek cultural experience, Jason's ambiguous relation to the *polis*, both

Beard (1980) on the Vestal Virgins; Versnel (1993: 228–88) on the Roman festival of Bona Dea and the Greek Thesmophoria.

[21] e.g. the animals which are treated as abominable in the Mosaic code (Douglas 1966: 41–57); the pangolin among the Lele in the Congo (Douglas 1975*a*: esp. 33 ff.); the cassowary among the Karam in N. Guinea (Bulmer 1977). See more generally Tambiah (1977: esp. 158 ff.).

[22] See primarily Turner (1967: 93–111, esp. 95–7).

[23] Festivals: see e.g. the Athenian procession at the Oschophoria (1.3, n. 26) or the Argive Hybristica (Plut. *Mor.* 245e–f; see Halliday 1909–10). Rites: see especially wedding rituals from all over the Greek world, e.g. Sparta (Plut. *Lyc.* 15. 3); Cos (Plut. *Mor.* 304e). For discussions of transvestism in rites of passage see e.g. Delcourt (1961: 1–16); Gallini (1963*b*: 215 ff.); Leitao (1995).

[24] I am focusing on transvestism from a Turnerian/Eliadean perspective, i.e. as the symbolical achievement or recovering of 'a primordial situation of totality and perfection' (Eliade 1958: 26); cf. Ivanov (1984: 14). In other words, instead of using the notion of a 'law of symmetrical inversion', as Vidal-Naquet (1986: 114) does, I understand transvestism as a kind of bisexuality, i.e. the symbolic dramatization of the time of puberty during which each sex 'still shared in the nature of the other' (Vernant 1980: 23; cf. Calame 1977: 259). Cf. also n. 28 below.

[25] See Jason's 'twofold' dress (ἐσθάς . . . ἀμφοτέρα) in Pind. *Pyth.* 4. 79, i.e. a panther-skin worn over his local Magnesian robe (80–1). Cf. A. M. Bowie (1993*a*: 238 n. 55), who also considers Paris in the *Iliad*.

a 'stranger' (*xeinos*) and a 'citizen' (*astos*; Pind. *Pyth.* 4. 78),[26] as well as his transition from the height of his dwellings (*Pyth.* 4. 76 αἰπεινῶν ἀπὸ σταθμῶν) to the city and the *agora* of Iolcos (*Pyth.* 4. 85), is a good semantic analogue for Dionysus' fluctuation between wilderness and city, for his dramatized migration from an unspecified point in the periphery, an Attic elsewhere, to the civic centre.[27] Related as they are, then, to a variety of ritualized transitions, the features which build up Dionysus' paradoxical appearance, as he steps onto the Athenian stage, could well have been perceived by the fifth-century spectators of the *Frogs* as indices of in-betweenness, of social or cultic marginality. To put it in another way: within the underlying system of Greek cultural conventions, the multiplicity of statuses and roles that Dionysus combines with the aid of his disguise in the prologue of the *Frogs* invests his *dramatis persona* with the semantic properties of an initiand who, at the edge of liminality, stands for a kind of 'human prima materia', 'undifferentiated raw material' (Turner 1967: 98).[28]

The first movement of Dionysus dramatized in the play is his arrival in the space of the *polis*, the Lenaean theatre of Athens. Yet, no sooner does he appear in the sight of the spectators than he declares his wish to move away from the theatrical milieu he has attained. For, as is stated explicitly in *Frogs* 69–70, his visit to Heracles marks the starting-point for his dramatic journey '*down* to Hades' (εἰς Ἅιδου κάτω), and 'by Zeus, even further down, if any further down there is' (καὶ νὴ Δί' εἴ τι γ' ἐστὶν ἔτι κατωτέρω). But the very scheme of a *descensus ad inferos* is a widely attested initiatory ordeal (e.g. Eliade 1958: 62), which also belongs to the ritual experience of the Greek and Roman world. In the Athenian cultic sequence of the Arrhephoria, for example,[29] two virgin girls (*parthenoi*), carrying each a secret burden, descend (κατίασιν) at

---

[26] See further Segal (1986a: 57–8) and Vidal-Naquet (1986: 108).

[27] Should there be unambiguous evidence for the existence of ephebic *peripoloi* in 5th-cent. Athens (see A. M. Bowie 1993a: 51 n. 24), Dionysus' stage-movement would also correspond to the passage every adolescent effects from a life of 'circling round' (περιπολεῖν) towards the attainment of full membership in his community and phratry.

[28] I should clarify at this point that I draw upon Turner's view of liminality as the period of time when the initiand does not just *verge* on an opposite side of existence, but symbolically recovers a state of 'totality', that is, as Myerhoff (1982: 117) has put it (restating Turner's own conclusions), he/she 'comes to stand for the sentiment of undifferentiated humankind: all that is universal, innate, whole, and unified'. In Turner's perspective, then, totality is opposed to the partiality and differentiation determining the 'status system' (1969: 106) and is conveyed through the neutralization of semiotically significant polarities (see in this line Ivanov 1984: esp. 11–14), i.e. through the collocation of categories which in a well-ordered society would have been viewed as mutually exclusive (e.g. male/female, human/bestial, etc.).

[29] Recognized as initiatory by Jeanmaire (1939: 264–8); Burkert (1966a, 1983: 150ff.); Brelich (1969: esp. 232ff.), *et al.*

night through a natural entrance leading underground (κάθοδος
ὑπόγαιος αὐτομάτη) into the sacred precinct of 'Aphrodite in the
Gardens' (τῆς καλουμένης ἐν Κήποις Ἀφροδίτης); after having left
under the earth the unknown *sacra* that they had been carrying,
they ascend again bringing up to light something 'covered up'
(ἐγκεκαλυμμένον) (Paus. 1. 27. 3).[30] Furthermore, outside the classical
Athenian frame, the existence of physical grottoes and artificially
built underground chambers/pits (*megara*,[31] *pastoi, thalamai/thala-
moi, mychoi*),[32] specifically designated for the performance of secret
teletai[33] in the cult of chthonic deities and deities worshipped
through mystic rites,[34] suggests that some at least of the ceremonies
of initiation were dramatized through the physical enactment of the
initiand's *katabasis*. Besides, the evidence from archaeology is
adequately corroborated by explicit allusions to ritual descents in a
variety of initiatory contexts such as, for example, the rites of
Trophonius at Lebadeia,[35] the cult of Persephone in Magna
Graecia,[36] the Phrygian ritual of Cybele,[37] or even Persian mystic
rites.[38] I would therefore like to suggest that, within the frame of a
play which, through its Chorus of Initiates, remoulds to a large
extent the experience and the feelings of the mystai in Eleusis, the

---

[30] See Burkert (1983: 150–4).

[31] See Hesychius s.v., and in general Festugière (1972: 52–3); Henrichs (1969a: 34–5).

[32] On these terms see e.g. Clem. Alex. *Protr.* 2. 15 (Klotz); schol. Nic. *Alexiph.* 7; Dio
Chrys. *Or.* 12. 33 (probably referring to Eleusis), and Festugière (1972: 48–9). More
significantly, if the writings of Pherecydes of Syros on μυχοὺς καὶ βόθρους καὶ ἄντρα καὶ θύρας
καὶ πύλας (Porph. *De antr. Nymph.* 31 = B 6 D–K) draw actually upon an experience of
mystic rituals (Seaford 1986a: 13), our evidence extends as far back as the 6th cent. BC.

[33] See e.g. Paus. 8. 37. 8 (*telete* enacted inside Despoina's *megaron* at Lycosura); Aelius
Dionysius, s.v. μάγαρον (fr. 254 [μ.2] in Erbse, *Att. Lex.*), etc.

[34] See e.g. Paus. 8. 37. 8 (*megaron* of Despoina, the Arcadian 'Great Goddess'); Paus. 4. 31.
9 (*megaron* of the Couretes in Messene); Paus. 2. 22. 3 (*bothros* for Persephone in Argos); for
a *bothros*, i.e. 'a round structure surrounding a circular pit' within the Anactoron at the
Sanctuary of the Great Gods in Samothrace (although its function in the initiation rites is
uncertain) see S. G. Cole (1984c: 27; cf. 8). For *megara* in the cult of Demeter see below,
2.8(c), n. 158; for Dionysus and caves see below, 2.8(a) with n. 132.

[35] See below, 2.14.

[36] Festugière (1972: 48–62) has rightly argued that the formula δεσποίνας δ' ὑπὸ κόλπον ἔδυν
χθονίας βασιλείας, pronounced by a mystes in one of the Thurian gold leaves (tablet A1, line 7
in Zuntz 1971: 301), signifies a descent into Persephone's other-worldly realm and functions
as a 'mot de passe' by which the deceased can declare himself as an initiate, therefore laying
claim to eternal bliss (1972: 50: 'le fait de dire: "Je suis descendu . . ." révèle immédiatement
l'initié').

[37] Part of the rites was called *katabasis* (Macr. *Sat.* 1. 21. 10); see Halliday (1925: 243).

[38] See Porph. *De antr. Nymph.* 6 οὕτω καὶ Πέρσαι τὴν ἐκ κάτω κάθοδον τῶν ψυχῶν καὶ πάλιν
ἔξοδον μυσταγωγοῦντες τελοῦσι τὸν μύστην. It is also worth noting—although the evidence is
quite late—the 'password' τετέ[λ]εσμαι καὶ εἰς μέγαρον κατέ[βη]ν Δακτύλων on a magical
papyrus (*PGM*, no. LXX, lines 14–15) of the 3rd or 4th cent. AD; see Betz (1980: 292). Cf.
also Pythagoras' variedly attested initiatory *katabaseis* (Porph. *Vit. Pyth.* 17; Diog. Laert. 8.
3), on which see Eliade (1972: 24–7).

dramatic movement of a *katabasis* assumes special significance: undertaken, as it is, by a character who bears striking signs of liminality, it could adequately impart to the spectator the impression that the descender is himself a *mystes*.

According to van Gennep's scheme, the first phase in a ritual passage is the ritual subject's 'separation', signifying the novice's spatial detachment from his environment and his seclusion in the space where his or her ritual transition is going to be effected.[39] In the Greek world, such initiatory separation is evidenced in a variety of ritual contexts. In the Athenian Arrhephoria (see above), for example, the two little Arrhephoroi live for some time 'with the goddess' (παρὰ τῇ θεῷ) (Paus. 1. 27. 3) in a house on the Acropolis, weaving the *peplos* for Athena;[40] similarly, before undertaking his descent into the cave of Trophonius at Lebadeia (2.14), the initiand is required to spend 'an appointed number of days' in a sacred building (Paus. 9. 39. 5).[41] Nevertheless, more pertinent is the symbolical dimension in the notion of the initiand's 'separation', that is, his 'detachment . . . either from an earlier fixed point in the social structure or a set of cultural conditions (a "state")' (Turner 1967: 94). In his first appearance on the stage Dionysus consistently alludes to the feeling of his alienation[42] from his cultural context. So, for example, he makes it clear that he cannot share in the audience's amusement with certain kinds of stock jokes. His reaction as a *theates* (16–18) sets him apart from the bulk of the spectators, the *theomenoi* whom Xanthias mentions in the play's opening lines (1–2). In other words, his quest for a fertile poet stems from his inability to identify with the current cultural conditions. Verses 1–105 of the *Frogs* may therefore correspond to the initiatory phase of 'separation', as they dramatize, or rather re-enact for the sake of the audience, Dionysus' *detachment* from the intellectual back-

---

[39] In tribal societies neophytes are taken away from their home and families and led to the initiatory hut, built for this specific purpose somewhere in the 'wild'.

[40] See Burkert (1983: 150 with n. 62, and 1966a).

[41] For more cases of initiatory seclusion, think of e.g. the separation of boys from their families at the age of 7 in the context of the Spartan *agoge*; the sojourn of the captive youth/initiand in the *andreion* (men's house) in Crete (Ephorus, *FGrHist* 70 F149); the ritual seclusion of little girls, the *arktoi* (see below, 2.7) at the sanctuary of Artemis at Brauron, where they spend their time dancing and running races; a puberty initiation ritual in Corinth, where seven boys and seven girls are secluded for a year in the temple of Hera Akraia (Burkert 1966b: 118–19 with n. 71), etc. See also Burkert (1985: 98, with nn. 35–41). A comic reflection of initiatory 'separation' may be detected in the Socratic οἰκίδιον (*Clouds* 92), where Strepsiades' initiation (A. M. Bowie 1993a) is performed in Aristophanes' *Clouds*: it is a space of seclusion for Socrates' students, who are not allowed to stay out in the open air for long (198–9).

[42] On van Gennep's pattern as comprising changes in an individual's or a group's *psychological* state as well see Turner (1974: 273).

ground of 405 BC Athens, dominated by 'useless grapes and chatter-boxes, music-halls of swallows, degraders of their art' (92–3).

Yet, if Athens is the starting-point of Dionysus' itinerary at the beginning of the *Frogs*, it is Athens again which signifies the expedition's final goal. Because not only is the Dionysiac *pompe* ready to ascend to the extra-dramatic space of Athens in the play's closing scene, but the journey's destination *within* the dramatic fiction of the comedy as well is 'Athens', since it is primarily the Underworld which can be viewed as a dramatic other-worldly *polis*.

A primary characteristic of the play's mood is that life and death, rather than being rigidly distinguished from one another, inter-penetrate and converge; the phrases 'among the dead of the upper world' (ἐν τοῖς ἄνω νεκροῖσιν) (420), 'saying that life is not life' (φασκούσας οὐ ζῆν τὸ ζῆν) (1082), or 'who knows whether life be death' (εἰ τὸ ζῆν μέν ἐστι κατθανεῖν) (1477) are not mere literary parodies, but hint at the overlap or even the inversion of these realms underlying the *Frogs*' thematical context. In the world of 405 BC, as reflected in the comedy, Athens is an intellectual waste land. Deprived of its fertile poets, as Dionysus himself observes, the *polis* suffocates in an atmosphere of sterility (89–97). The corruption of the leading politicians as well as the disintegration in the sphere of morality and ethics causes the city to be held 'in the cradle of the waves' (704). The spark of life has to be sought in the Domain of the Dead. The healthy communal spirit, the values and ideals (such as evoked by Aeschylus) which inspired the citizens of older genera-tions to be 'brave and six-feet tall, and not evading their duties as citizens' (1014) are not to be encountered in real life any more. The Underworld, on the other hand, preserves the memory of the city's glorious past untouched by decay: in an idealizing and nostalgic mood, quite typical of Old Athenian Comedy, the Chorus of deceased Initiates advocate in the parabasis a return to a lost albeit healthy civic spirit, while Aeschylus conjures the picture of a dignified, gleaming Athens (1013–17, 1026–7, 1039–42), such as was reflected in and moulded by his stage dramas.[43] Consequently, Dionysus' admission and mediative function within the Domain of the Dead can be considered as corresponding to the final stage of his initiation, his reaggregation into the real civic core of the Athenian *polis*.

The ways in which the play will effect this Dionysiac reincorpora-tion are significantly the three main avenues through which human votaries can gain access to this god: wine, theatrical role-playing, and initiation into Mysteries. Their reflection in the *Frogs* will be

---

[43] Cf. Whitman (1964: 256–7); Reckford (1987: 419, 431–2).

discussed in Chapters 2–4. For the moment, my object is to focus closely on those specific aspects of Dionysus' itinerary which, in a fifth-century audience's perspective, would have qualified his experience as the limen of an initiation.[44]

2.3. Symbolic Death of the Initiand

One of the universally attested features of a rite of passage is that the initiand's former personality must die symbolically, so that he/she may be reborn into a new identity (for the entire symbolism see 2.14). So, for example, in wedding ritual, which initiates girls into the life of *gynaikes*, the virgin 'dies' before assuming her new, fertile, and productive role in society,[45] while a mock sacrifice, qualifying for the initiand's symbolic death, is a regular feature of a rite of passage (Seaford 1994*a*: ch. 8). Understandably, then, ritual liminality is a period deeply impregnated with the imagery of death, so that in many societies liminal symbols are 'drawn from the biology of death, decomposition, catabolism, and other physical processes that have a negative tinge'.[46]

One of the most impressive reflections of initiatory simulative death in Greek drama can be sought in the Sophoclean *Electra* (Seaford 1994*b*), where Orestes, an archetypal ephebe in the course of his transition to adulthood, is required to undergo a simulative death, 'a death in word' (λόγῳ θανών), as he himself refers to it (59), twice. In the first place he is reported as dead in the deceptive tale of the Old Servant, who announces his fatal accident in a chariot race at Delphi (680–763).[47] Secondly, and most spectacularly, he appears on the stage carrying the urn which allegedly contains his own ashes. As he says to Electra, 'We have the small remains of dead

---

[44] Drawing upon van Gennep, Moorton (1989: 310–11) has rightly emphasized the topographical, i.e. visual, index of liminality in Dionysus' journey through Hades, namely Charon's lake/marsh, which functions as a neutral zone between the living and the dead. The presence of the frogs as well would have enhanced the liminal significance of Dionysus' transition, not simply because in this play they live in the *limne* (Moorton 1989: 312–14), a circular argument which does not lead anywhere, but because frogs are *per se* 'interstitial' creatures *par excellence*: as amphibians, they partake of the mode of being of both aquatic and land creatures, straddling two taxonomic classes and hovering perpetually between two spheres.

[45] A rich corpus of literature has been assembled on the underlying correlation of marriage and death in Greek thought, ritual, literature, vase-painting, etc. See most importantly: Alexiou and Dronke (1971); Sourvinou-Inwood (1973); Foley (1982*a*); Jenkins (1983); Seaford (1987*b*, 1990*a*); Rehm (1994).

[46] Turner (1967: 96): 'In so far as a neophyte is structurally "dead" he or she may be treated, for a long or short period, as a corpse is customarily treated in his or her society.' For initiation as death in Graeco-Roman mystic cults (including Dionysiac) see below, 2.14.

[47] As he puts it later on, people in the palace think of him as 'dead and gone': εἰς τῶν ἐν Ἀιδου μάνθαν' ἐνθάδ' ὢν ἀνήρ (1342).

Orestes in this urn, this little urn you see us carrying' (1113–14; cf. 1118). Electra, in her turn, laments her brother as 'non-existent' (οὐδὲν ὄντα) (1129), reduced to 'dust and idle shade' (σποδόν τε καὶ σκιὰν ἀνωφελῆ) (1159). In Comedy too, when a crown, that is, a well-known initiatory and sacrificial attribute,[48] is presented to Strepsiades before his final induction into the Socratic Phrontisterion, Socrates himself allays his fear of being put to death, 'sacrificed like Athamas' (256–7), by hinting at the symbolical dimension of initiatory ritual actions: 'no, but we do these things to all those who are being initiated' (258–9).[49] Furthermore, the students secluded in the marginal space of the 'Thinking School' are pale (103; cf. 1112),[50] while Chaerephon, apparently the most distinguished among them, gives the impression of being 'half-dead' (ἡμιθνής) (504). Similarly, in the *Frogs* Dionysus enacts a spatial movement symbolic of death, that is, a descent into the Nether regions,[51] which has already been discussed in 2.2.[52] In addition, some of the ordeals he is threatened with or actually undergoes, such as the prospect of being torn to pieces by monstrous creatures (2.6(b)),[53] his nudity (2.7), and flagellation (2.6(c)) at the threshold of Persephone's dwellings, carry the symbolism of a mock death.[54]

However, the symbolic range of initiatory death is even broader, as 'death' may also mean the annihilation of one's social personality or, to put it in another way, signify the initiand's social anonymity.

The neophytes are ground down so that nothing demarcates them from their fellow ritual passengers. As Turner (1967: 96) writes, 'often their very names are taken from them and each is called solely by the generic term for "neophyte" or "initiand"' (cf. Turner 1969: 106). Among the many literary reflections of this feature, a very

---

[48] See Seaford (1994a: 380): 'the crown (στέφανος) was a mark of having achieved the mystic transition' (with refs. in n. 55).

[49] On this scene see Burkert (1983: 268); Byl (1980: 11, 1988: 69). Cf. A. M. Bowie (1993a: 117 n. 62).

[50] Pallor indicates, among other things, deathlike condition; cf. also *Clouds* 94, where Strepsiades refers to Socrates' place as ψυχῶν σοφῶν . . . φροντιστήριον, emphasizing thus its insubstantial nature (Dover 1968: ad loc.).

[51] The jokes about the quickest way to the Underworld (117–34) as well involve some kind of death: hanging, hemlock, throwing oneself from the top of a tower.

[52] For the symbolism of death inherently interwoven with initiatory *katabaseis* see below, 2.14.

[53] See Brelich (1969: 79 n. 82): 'In certi rituali iniziatici l'uccisione del novizio è soltanto "minacciata" (ma la minaccia sul piano rituale, equivale all' esecuzione stessa).'

[54] Mock dismemberment in initiation ritual as death: Eliade (1958: 90–2, 105–6); nudity as death: see 2.7 and Eliade (1958: 32). Flagellation as death: Brelich (1969: 80 n. 85); on Lycurgus' substitution of the human sacrifice practised at the altar of Artemis Orthia with a rite of flagellation of ephebes see Paus. 3. 16. 10. As Seaford (1994a: 294) writes, 'The logic of this story implies that the flagellation, in the rite of passage to adulthood, is envisaged as a kind of death.'

prominent case is that of the Sophoclean Philoctetes who, having lost the *kleos* which lies at the core of an Homeric hero's identity ('You never heard my name then? Never a rumour of all the wrongs I have suffered . . .?', 251–2; cf. 254–5), describes himself in terms of non-existence, and understands his condition as one of structural invisibility, of social death.[55] In Comedy, a reflection of this same ritual aspect can be sought in the initiatory frame of the *Wasps* (A. M. Bowie 1993*a*: ch. 4): by equating himself with smoke (144 καπνὸς ἔγωγ' ἐξέρχομαι), Philocleon effectively effaces his identity, as smoke is 'a common metaphor for nothingness' (A. M. Bowie 1993*a*: 84);[56] and he goes on to appropriate an archetypal example of self-inflicted anonymity by calling himself, in an Odyssean way, Οὖτις (184) (A. M. Bowie). Similarly, Dionysus, while wavering between Dionysiac and Heraclean identities, arrives at a complete rejection of his own *propria persona*, as he cries out to Xanthias: 'this (i.e. his own name, Dionysus) is worse than the other' (300).[57]

To sum up, then, during the limen of a rite of passage the ritual subject 'passes through a realm that has few or none of the attributes of the past or coming state' (Turner 1967: 94). Being conceived as a 'blank state', a 'tabula rasa' (Turner 1969: 103),[58] the initiand is structurally 'invisible' or 'dead' (Turner 1967: 95 and 96). 'Stripped of all that he/she knows and understands' (Myerhoff 1982: 117), debarred from status, property, insignia, rank, he/she possesses nothing and is demarcated by nothing (Turner 1967: 98–9; cf. Turner 1974: 241). As Turner (1967: 99) has expressed it, his condition 'is indeed the very prototype of sacred poverty'. Having this background in mind, then, one can duly appreciate how significant it is that Dionysus is unable to recognize 'himself' either in the frogs' 'sweet-sounding song' (213) to 'Dionysus of mountain Nysa, son of Zeus' (215–16)[59] or in the Mystai's hymnic invocation to Dionysus/Iacchus (316–17, 323–36, 340–53)[60] and furthermore that he remains indifferent to the multiple allusions to sanctuaries and

---

[55] See 946–7 (of Odysseus) κοὐκ οἶδ' ἐναίρων νεκρόν, ἢ καπνοῦ σκιάν, | εἴδωλον ἄλλως; 1030 ὃς οὐδέν εἰμι καὶ τέθνηχ' ὑμῖν πάλαι; 1018 ἄφιλον ἔρημον ἄπολιν ἐν ζῶσιν νεκρόν. Cf. 861, 884–5. I propose to discuss Philoctetes as an initiand in separate work.

[56] Moreover, as Alan Sommerstein points out to me, Philocleon says he is smoke from figwood (145), proverbially the least useful kind of wood.

[57] Nevertheless, for the rich background of superstitions looming large behind this scene see Riess (1897); Borthwick (1968: 204); Radermacher (1921: 176–9) and Stanford (1963: ad loc.); C. S. Brown (1966: 195–6).

[58] Cf. Myerhoff (1982: 117) on the initiand as 'pure undetermined possibility'.

[59] For Nysa as the mountain of Dionysus see Seaford (1984: on Eur. *Cycl.* 68).

[60] Cf. Dionysus' response (321–2) to Xanthias' suggestion: ᾄδουσι γοῦν τὸν Ἴακχον (320). For the identity of Dionysus and Iacchus from at least the mid-5th cent. onwards see Graf (1974: 51 ff.), a conclusive discussion of this long-debated issue. Cf. A. M. Bowie (1993*a*: 232–3); Richardson (1974: 320).

rites of his cult.[61] Similarly, in the *Wasps*, again, Bdelycleon proves to the initiand Philocleon that the tokens of his power, the attributes and qualities which equalled him to Zeus (620–30; cf. 571), were totally illusory: stripped of all the insignia of his greatness, Philocleon feels himself reduced to 'nothing' (997 οὐδέν εἰμ' ἄρα), just before the process of his reintegration into the city's social life begins (A. M. Bowie 1993*a*: 93).

2.4. Initiatory 'Role Reversals'

(a) Role-playing

Absence of property and structural neutrality go hand in hand with confusion of identity as well as with various exemplifications of 'role reversal'. The first expression of role reversal that we shall concentrate on is role-playing, that is, the adoption of a different identity. In the 'encyclopaedic knowledge' of fifth-century spectators this is a feature inherently interwoven with rites of passage, as shown by the multiple examples of disguise (mostly transvestite) of initiands in myth and cult[62] as well as the disguise of mythical adolescents, whose rite of passage is reflected in Greek drama.[63] A well-known illustration of the latter case, for example, is Orestes, who in all the extant dramatizations of his story resorts to some way of shielding his identity, a stratagem inherently interwoven with his attempt to re-establish his position in the *oikos* of his father. Thus, concealed behind the *persona* of a mere servant in Sophocles' *Electra*, disguised as a Thessalian stranger in Euripides' *Electra* (781), he announces that he has got ready the full gear (560) of a Phocian man in Aeschylus' *Choephori*.[64] Likewise, the comic Dionysus of the *Frogs* steps onto the stage dressed up as Heracles; moreover, as the play's plot advances, one level of disguise proves inadequate for warding off the dangers of the Underworld, and thus, the god takes shelter in the costume of his slave Xanthias

---

[61] See e.g. 215–19b, alluding to the old sanctuary ⟨τοῦ⟩ ἐν Λίμναις Διονύσου (Thuc. 2. 15. 4). For the allusions of the parodos to the Anthesteria see below, Ch. 3.

[62] See above, n. 23. In the sphere of Eleusinian initiation, Demeter, the prototype initiand in the myth as reflected in the Homeric *Hymn*, disguises herself during the liminality of her wanderings as an old woman (Hom. *h. Dem.* 101 ff.), while in the Bacchic sphere, the initiand Pentheus has to be disguised as a maenad. For Bacchic initiatory disguise see below, Appendix.

[63] Also, to the extent that one is willing to recognize initiatory motifs remoulded and reflected in the *Odyssey* (see e.g. Segal 1967; *contra*, Versnel 1990*a*: 56–9), Odysseus, on his return to Ithaca in order to reclaim his throne, disguises himself as the lowest of mortals, a mere beggar.

[64] His role-playing has to be so convincing that he and Pylades must even imitate the accent and the dialect of the region of Parnassus (*Choeph.* 563–4).

(494–7, 579–88). In fact, it turns out that Dionysus is utterly unable to abide by either of these borrowed identities. And yet, it is precisely this plunging into 'otherness' through the assumption of two different *personae* which brings Dionysus close to an important act of role reversal in the course of liminality, that is, the initiand's experiments with various modes of alterity with the aid of masks and costumes (Myerhoff 1982: 113; cf. V. and E. Turner 1982: 202). The 'law of dissociation' (Myerhoff 1982: 121) is fundamental in this 'play with forms' (113), whose main purpose is to arouse the neophyte to a state of self-consciousness, bringing him/her 'to the edge of profound self-questioning' (113). Imitation or even mere observation of alterity provides the initiand both with positive examples, that is, illustrations of the social norm, and—most significantly—with specimens of modes of being from which his future status will require him to keep himself estranged. As far as Greek experience is concerned, the multitude of masks excavated in the Spartan sanctuary of Artemis Orthia[65] does not seem to have revealed the secret of its use. However, if one accepts Vernant's hypothesis as at least a possibility,[66] these strange objects would provide an excellent example of liminal alterity: masks of warriors or sometimes realistic studies of the human face (Dickins 1929: 176, types C and D) would have impressed upon the neophytes the visage of their future integration into the society of adults; faces of old women, of bestiality, and of deformity (Dickins 1929: 176, types A, E (satyrs), F (Gorgons), and G (caricatures)) on the other hand, would have offered to them the opportunity to explore successively 'every aspect of marginality and strangeness, assuming every possible form of otherness, learning how to break rules so as the better to internalize rules that they would thereafter have to keep.'[67] In a similar way, as Chapter 4 discusses, it is precisely through playing at being Heracles, that is, through approaching and deviating from the modes his prototype sets forth, that Dionysus gradually discovers the ways of his reincorporation into the community of Athens.

---

[65] See Dickins (1929); Bosanquet (1905–6: 338–43); Dawkins (1905–6: 324–6).

[66] See now Vernant (1991: ch. 13); cf. Vernant and Frontisi-Ducroux (1988: 199–200).

[67] Vernant and Frontisi-Ducroux (1988: 200). I should like to believe that the argument can have full anthropological support: e.g. for an analogous interplay of negative/positive models in African rites of passage see Gluckman (1966: 121), while, as Crumrine (1969: 18) observes on ritual masked impersonations in Mexico, 'participants come to understand the structure of social relations through observing them in new and atypical combination': the grotesque representations enhance the learning and understanding of social/cultural structure. For an entirely different interpretation of the Orthia masks see Carter (1987).

(b) Inversional behaviour

In an anthropological perspective, 'rituals of reversal' are identified as 'periods or sequences of behaviour in which people are expected to behave in a manner which is diametrically opposite to that in which they are otherwise expected to behave' (Weidkuhn 1977: 167). In other words, role reversal in the course of liminality means also the initiand's reacting in ways which contradict his/her everyday life. A memorable reversal of this type is dramatized in the initiatory frame of Sophocles' *Philoctetes*.[68] In this play Neoptolemus, the initiand/ephebe, is required by his cadet commander Odysseus to depart as much as possible from his identity as 'son of Achilles', and to adopt a totally un-Achillean model of behaviour, primarily characterized by an *ethos* of *logos* rather than of deed, by the ruses of sophistic manipulation, rather than straightforward, honest, steadfast action. Odysseus' words exemplify best this idea of temporary reversal upon which the success of the initiand's liminal experience depends.[69]

> I know, young man, it is not your natural bent
> to say such things nor to contrive such mischief.
>
> .   .   .   .
>
> For one brief shameless portion of a day
> give me yourself, and then for all the rest
> you may be called most scrupulous of men.   (79–85)

Returning now to the *Frogs*, the most conspicuous illustration of this type of reversal is Dionysus' incompetence as an impersonator: as it becomes apparent in a large part of the play, the god of theatre himself does not know how to act (4.3). Furthermore, a wealth of evidence could testify to the 'inversional' quality of Dionysus' protest to Charon: 'Why, how shall I manage to pull the oar, me, inexperienced, ignorant of sea (ἀθαλάττωτος), not having been at Salamis?' (203–5).[70] For, many a time, the Athenians and the Greeks of Ionian coastal cities would have witnessed the festive procession celebrating Dionysus' return from the high seas, his cultic image (or perhaps his priest) installed in a ship carried or wheeled along the streets.[71] Vase-paintings, such as the famous kylix of Exekias (Fig.

---

[68] See primarily Vidal-Naquet (1988*b*).

[69] See further Lada-Richards (1998).

[70] Analogous Dionysiac inversions seem to have been staged in Aristophanes' Διόνυσος ναυαγός (fr. 277 K–A (p. 157)) and in Eupolis' *Taxiarchi* (fr. 268, 49–50 K–A), where Dionysus declares: νεῖν | γὰρ οὐκ ἐπίσταμαι (Austin's addition by comparison with *Frogs* 204).

[71] Although the literary sources are quite late, the wagon-ship is depicted in 3 Attic skyphoi dating from around 500 BC (all three in *LIMC*, s.v. Dionysos, 827–9) (Fig. 2.2). For the (still unresolved) controversy about whether the ship procession belonged to the Anthesteria or the Great Dionysia see Burkert (1983: 201 n. 26).

2.2. Return from the high seas: Dionysus' ship-wagon
bf. Attic skyphos: Bologna, Museo Civico Archeologico, 130

3.8) or the Attic black-figure amphora in Tarquinia, which represent the wine-god as navigator; the variety of his cult-titles as 'Aktaios' ('of the coast'), 'Pelagios' ('of the open sea'), or 'Alieus' ('seaman'); drinking-cups bearing the names of ships or boats labelled 'Dionysus', 'Bakche', 'Euia', 'Komos'; and, above all, Dionysus' own gift, the wine, described throughout antiquity as 'mixed with sea-water' (τεθαλαττωμένος), 'drinking brine' (ἁλμοπότις), 'sunk in the sea' (θαλασσίτης),[72] offer a glimpse of the variety of associations that the Athenian *theatai* would have been able to discern between the rower on the Styx and their god who 'is a ship-master on the wine dark sea (ναυκληρεῖ . . . ἐπ' οἴνοπα πόντον)', as the comic poet Hermippus (*Phormophori*, fr. 63, 2 K–A) has vividly expressed it. Furthermore, if the Hermionians' annual dedication of swimming/ diving and boat-races to 'Dionysus of the Black Goatskin'[73] was

---

[72] Dionysus navigator (art): see *LIMC*, s.v. Dionysos, 788 and 790 respectively (see also 3.1) and cf. an Attic kylix (Nilsson 1951) which depicts Dionysus voyaging on a boat whose head is an ass. Cult titles: (Aktaios, Pelagios): Maass (1888); (Alieus): Tümpel (1889), mainly on Philochorus, *FGrHist* 328 F191, where an oracle institutes a cult of Dionysus *Alieus*. Should the Attic deme of Ἀλαὶ Αἰξωνίδες be established beyond doubt as the recipient of the oracle (on the uncertainty see Jacoby, *FGrHist* III b (suppl.) i. 555–6), this fragment would constitute a valuable testimony on the marine dimension of Dionysus in Attica. Drinking-cups: see W. J. Slater (1976: 167 n. 22); boats: see Davies (1978: 86 n. 31). Wine: see Athen. 32d, 32e; Plin. *HN* 14. 78: *tethalassomenon . . . thalassiten*. On the question of the staging of the Aristophanic scene see Dearden (1976: 67–9); Dover (1972: 179–80, 1993: 212–13); Sommerstein (1996: ad 205–6).

[73] Paus. 2. 35. 1 κατὰ ἔτος ἕκαστον . . . ἁμίλλης κολύμβου καὶ πλοίων τιθέασιν ἆθλα. On the ambiguity of the word κόλυμβος (meaning both diving and swimming) see Ginouvès (1962: 124 n. 1 and 110 with n. 3).

actually more widespread,[74] there is good reason to suppose that in a Greek perspective Dionysus' realm could have been felt as quite closely connected with the 'much-diving songs' (πολυκολύμβοισι μέλεσιν) (245) of the croaking Stygian frogs.[75]

(c) *Anti-social behaviour*

However, 'inversional' behaviour during liminality may also be behaviour which structured society regards as deviant and intolerable. As Edmund Leach (1966: 135) has put it, in the liminal space and time apart, one can see 'all manner of sins such as incest, adultery, transvestism, sacrilege and *lèse-majesté* treated as the natural order of the day'; in other words, behaving antisocially is for liminaries 'the proper expression of their marginal condition' (Douglas 1966: 97).[76] Now, legitimization of inversion is particularly applicable in the context of Greek ephebic initiations: our sources, illuminated by researchers such as Brelich (1969), Jeanmaire (1939), Vidal-Naquet (1986), emphasize the trickery and unlawfulness of the ephebe, and press the point that inversional behaviour during liminality is not merely encouraged but 'even enjoined' on the citizens-to-be. According to Plutarch (*Lyc.* 17. 4), the Spartan neophytes are driven by need and hunger into 'boldness and cunning' (ἀναγκάζωνται τολμᾶν καὶ πανουργεῖν), while the *polis'* respect is earned precisely by those liminaries who manage to excel in the enactment of reversal; as Isocrates (12. 212) has put it with reference to the Spartan world, 'those who have accomplished the greatest number of thefts and have been able to escape detection enjoy a higher esteem among their fellow-youths than others'.[77] In other words, it would appear that a Greek community regards transitional initiatory reversal as the indispensable prerequisite for the ultimate achievement of civic virtue, political *arete*.[78] Dramatic reflections of this liminal characteristic abound in plays whose structure and imagery are informed by the civic institution of the *ephebeia*. In Aristophanic Comedy, for example, the old men of

---

[74] See Ginouvès (1962: 420, on divings). The name of Dionysus together with an ivy-crowned amphora appear on Corcyrean coins which celebrate victories of the island in boat-races. See Gardner (1881: esp. 95).

[75] On the role of immersions (*katapontismoi*) in the Dionysiac 'myth-and-ritual' complex and within the frame of initiatory myths and cults (including the Dionysiac/Eleusinian spheres) see Gallini (1963a).

[76] Cf. Turner (1967: 100): 'a normal man acts abnormally because he is obedient to tribal tradition, not out of disobedience to it. He does not evade but fulfills his duties as a citizen.'

[77] Cf. 12. 214, where Isocrates repeats that the Lacedaemonians 'regard those who stand first in such crimes (i.e. wrongdoing (*kakourgein*) and stealing (*kleptein*)) as the best among their youths and honour them the most'.

[78] Cf. again Isocr. 12. 214, where he stresses that the ephebe is only 'seeking through such practices to school himself in virtue'; see further Vernant (1991: 240).

the Chorus of the *Wasps* remember their ephebic garrison duty in the peripheral Byzantium, when they tricked a bread-lady and stole her mortar (235–8), while Philocleon in the same play nostalgically recalls the time of his prime, when he was able to steal (357 ἥβων γὰρ κἀδυνάμην κλέπτειν; cf. 354–5).[79] Moreover, Philocleon resorts to ephebic *dolos* once again, as soon as he starts rolling backwards into youth after the play's parabasis (A. M. Bowie 1993a: 93–6). Likewise, the Sausage-Seller in the *Knights*, whose role conforms to patterns of ephebic transitions (Bowie 1993a: 52–8), operates by deceit. His cunning is so masterful that it outshines the wittiness even of the celebrated arch-trickster Themistocles (*Knights* 884; see A. M. Bowie 1993a: 54), a comparison which could be coupled with the Chorus's conception of Dionysus in the *Frogs* as a 'truly born Theramenes' (καὶ φύσει Θηραμένους) (541), the notorious archetype of inconstancy and flexibility in the last decade of the Peloponnesian war. But in Tragedy as well *dolos* is the only means which can ensure Orestes' successful reclamation of his patrimony and social status, while the ephebic task enjoined upon Neoptolemus in Sophocles' *Philoctetes* is entirely dependent on *apate* and *klope*,[80] as well as on the art of versatility.[81]

Dionysus' initiatory transition in the *Frogs* has a conspicuous share in this marginal characteristic, for an important dimension of his dramatic character, such as portrayed in the journey to the Underworld, is his proneness to cunning and deception. Whenever his disguise proves to be the cause of trouble, his immediate reaction is to cast away the Heraclean insignia and to have recourse to the *dramatis persona* of his slave (494ff., 579ff.). But when Heraclean identity appears to be leading to *tryphe* and special honours (503ff.), he is quick once more to trick Xanthias into reassuming his subordinate position, so that he can play at being the hero once again (522–33). It is at this very moment that the Chorus comments on his adaptability, or rather his resourceful inconsistency:

> this is the trait of a man
> of wisdom and intelligence,
> one who has sailed round a lot:
> always to roll over
> towards the comfortable side (of the ship)
> rather than stand, like a painted
> image, in one fixed

---

[79] Cf. Philocleon's trickery in the comedy's opening scenes (e.g. 175–96), which draw heavily on images belonging to ephebic liminality (A. M. Bowie 1993a: 81–6).

[80] See e.g. *Phil.* 55, 77–8, 101, 108, 928–9, 949, 1228, 1282, etc.

[81] *Phil.* 130–1 οὐ δῆτα, τέκνον, ποικίλως αὐδωμένου | δέχου τὰ συμφέροντα τῶν ἀεὶ λόγων.

> pose. Nay, turning round
> to a more comfortable position
> is the hallmark of a clever man,
> a truly born Theramenes.[82]   (534a–41)

The chief allusion here is, of course, to the Homeric Odysseus, the man *par excellence* who has 'sailed much' (Dover 1993: ad 535). However, this passage is also informed by a negative picture, and this is the reversal of the values of permanence and constancy that every hoplite is expected to display, once having taken his place in the battle ranks. Whereas the hoplite has sworn never to abandon his comrade-in-arms and to remain fixed in his post wherever he be stationed,[83] Dionysus is praised here for his readiness to pick and choose the softer (*malthakoteron*) and less arduous side, that is, his skill in being flexible and versatile.

Now, by no means do I wish to insinuate that Dionysus' transition in the *Frogs* has any qualitative affinities with ephebic liminality (cf. above, 2.1). Yet, I *do* believe it is important that many a time Dionysus verges on a code of behaviour which is so strikingly—even if not exclusively—characteristic of what is perhaps the most widespread type of ritual passage in ancient Greek society, namely, a youth's transition to maturity. For such a similarity in ways of behaving lends further support to the thesis that the journey undertaken by the god could be envisaged as the re-enactment of an initiatory experience. Besides, Dionysus seems to be inherently interwoven with one of the city's most important festivals, the Ionian Apaturia,[84] which initiates young boys at the age of 16 in the phratry of their father, while commemorating the exemplary *apate* whereby parts of the Attic territory came under Athenian control in the mythical remote past. To put it in another way, Dionysus is linked with the very festival which *re*creates and *re*states annually the *archetypal model* for the inversional values marking for the Athenian future citizens the threshold to adolescence. More importantly still, some of our sources ascribe to Dionysus himself (as Dionysus 'Melanaigis', i.e. Dionysus 'with the black goatskin') the trick by which the defender of Athens Melanthus defeated his Boeotian opponent Xanthus[85] and, if Kolb (1977) is right in arguing that this version of the legend goes as far back as the fifth

---

[82] See Dover (1993: 261–2); Stanford (1963: 119).

[83] οὐδὲ λείψω τὸν παραστάτην ὅπου ἂν στ⟨οι⟩χήσω; see Chap. 7, n. 87.

[84] At least two of the extant sources (Bekker, *Anecd. Graec.* i. 416, s.v. Ἀπατούρια; schol. Ar. *Peace* 800) explicitly designate the ἑορτή as ἀγομένη Διονύσῳ. For a list of the most important sources on the Apaturia see Vidal-Naquet (1986: 123 n. 15).

[85] See Conon, *FGrHist* 26 F1. 39; schol. Ar. *Acharn.* 146; schol. *Peace* 800; Bekker, *Anecd. Graec.* i. 416–17; Apostolius in *CPG* (2), iii. 31.

century,[86] in the 'encyclopaedic' knowledge of Greek classical spectators Dionysiac guilefulness would have been closely connected with a ritual passage and a feast which played a decisive role in the life of every Athenian citizen alike.

(d) The 'world upside-down'

Finally, as Turner (1978: 281) has expressed it, 'in the betwixt-and-between states, social-structure categories are forced to relax their grip on thought and behavior'. When everyday rules have been suspended and 'ordinary social time has stopped' (Leach 1966: 134), the world is turned upside-down: 'the low play at being lords' (Turner 1978: 278) or, as Versnel (1993: 115) has put it, 'the fool is king and rules at will'.[87] A good literary example of the 'world upside-down' motif as part of initiatory reversals can be sought in Aristophanes' *Wasps*: when, according to A. M. Bowie's (1993a: 95) reading, Philocleon returns to the status of ephebic marginality in the play's closing scenes, the father–son relation binding him to Bdelycleon is 'turned completely upon its head'. As he reassures the flute-girl he has stolen from a banquet,

If you're not a bad girl now, when my son dies I'll set you free . . . As it is, I don't have control over my own money, because I'm very young and kept under close watch. It's my little son who keeps his eyes on me . . .

(Wasps 1351–5; tr. A. M. Bowie 1993a: 95)

In the *Frogs* status reversal is evident throughout Dionysus' liminary experience, as the spectator is given the strong impression that it is the slave rather than the god who is often in command. Not only is the hierarchical relation between them reversed visibly through the multiple exchanges of their garments, but Xanthias goes as far as to pronounce verbal insults as well against his master (480, 486) who, in his turn, is self-humiliated to the extent of binding himself with oaths and curses (584–8; cf. his implorations at 579ff.) that Xanthias is free to accept or to reject (see his concessive reply at 589, and cf. 532–3). The peak of this inversion is certainly the whipping scene, where Xanthias/Heracles feels so secure in his new position as a master that he openly declares his former lord to be his slave (616 τὸν παῖδα τουτονὶ λαβών)[88] over whom he seems to have

---

[86] See especially Kolb (1977: 127), where he considers the Dionysiac version as 'zweifellos die richtige und ursprüngliche'.

[87] For social inversions in Greek festivals especially see Halliday (1909–10: 218–19) and Versnel (1993: ch. 2).

[88] What has not been remarked with respect to the whipping scene is that it is not solely the role exchange with Xanthias which reduces Dionysus to the status of a slave, but primarily, and most importantly, the mere fact that he is being touched, let alone flagellated. For a

a power of life and death (625; cf. 618ff. and especially 623–4).[89] And according to the 'law' of liminality, where equality among initiands (Turner 1974: 232)[90] as well as the feeling of 'communitas' (ibid.: 274)[91] and 'undifferentiated humanness' (Myerhoff 1982: 117) are paramount, Dionysus, despite his emphatic proclamation of identity (628–32), is totally unable in the whipping scene to re-establish his superior status.[92] However, if the scene is focused from a specifically Dionysiac angle, it would appear that it carries distinctively Dionysiac overtones. For in the Greek religious frame lack of hierarchical distinctions is inherently interwoven with the range of experiences Dionysus creates, as it is in the Dionysiac realm *par excellence* where, to speak the language of the *Bacchae*, wealthy and poor alike (421–2) mingle, while barriers of sex, age, and social status are prone to collapse (see further 7.2).

citizen's 'physical person may in no case be touched' (Winkler 1990a: 179). As Halperin (1990: 96) has put it, 'At the boundaries of a citizen's body the operation of almost all social and economic power halted', and, consequently, the strongest marker separating citizens from slaves was the principle of the 'inviolability' of the former's body. In other words, even without Xanthias' presence, Dionysus is immediately designated as socially inferior through the workings of classical Athenian democratic ideology *per se* (cf. P. J. Wilson 1991).

[89] Cf. Ivanov's (1984: 11) summary (drawing on Turner 1969: 167ff.) of rituals of status reversal as periods when groups of people, 'usually occupying an inferior position, exercise ritual authority over their superiors' who must accept their 'ritual degradation with good will'; furthermore, 'the inferiors accompany such rituals with vulgar verbal and nonverbal behavior and treat their superiors scornfully, mocking them and addressing them in obscenities . . . the inferiors often establish a hierarchy that resembles a parody of the normal hierarchical order of the superiors'.

[90] In the world of Greek ritual, degradation aiming at the establishment of liminary 'equality' is a well-known feature of rites of passage. We hear, for example, that in Crete, the liminaries secluded in the 'men's house', the *andreion* (cf. n. 41) διακονοῦσί τε καὶ ἑαυτοῖς καὶ τοῖς ἀνδράσι (Ephorus, FGrHist 70 F149) or that in the island of Ceos the girls of marriageable age spend their evenings waiting upon (διηκονοῦντο) one another's parents and brothers even to the point of washing their feet (Plut. *Mor.* 249d).

[91] i.e. the feeling of homogeneity, the all-pervasive psychic unity and the 'generic bond' (Turner 1969: 128) which can arise among participants in ritual ceremonies, such as e.g. a sacred journey, a pilgrimage, etc. For a reflection of the bond between initiands in ancient mystic ritual see the neophyte's oath at his induction in a mystery cult (according to Merkelbach (1967), the cult of Isis), where the fellow-initiands are referred to as brothers: καὶ τοὺς συνμύστας τε καὶ φιλτάτους ἀδελφούς (Cumont's restoration of *PSI* 1162, lines 9–10; see Merkelbach 1967: 73). Cf. also Sopatrus, in Walz, *Rhet. Graec.* viii. 123. 27.

[92] The initiand's utter degradation is a feature often reflected in literary remouldings of transition rites. Philoctetes in Sophocles' play, for example, deprived not only of human company and social commodities but also of his *toxon* as a means both of social recognition and of bare survival, reaches the ultimate degree of humiliation before he is persuaded by Heracles to end his *ponoi* through the conquest of everlasting glory (see esp. *Phil.* 1418–22; cf. below, n. 160).

2.5. *Initiatory* mathos

One of the basic aims of initiation is to impart new knowledge to the novice,[93] covering a wide variety of topics and sometimes even including the initiand's instruction 'in the various manly arts' (H. Webster 1932: 55). Dionysus, 'inexperienced' (ἄπειρος) in the art of rowing, as he declares himself to be (204), is forced by Charon to take his place 'on the oar' (ἐπὶ κώπην) (197)[94] and, in view of the close intertwinement of citizenship and military status in ancient Greek society, Dionysus' apprenticeship could have been conceived as a means towards his incorporation into the citizen body of the *polis*.[95] In the linear perspective of the play's narrative discourse the active participation of Dionysus in rowing is to be set in contrast to his own recollection of his intellectual idleness as a sailor in Arginusae (52–4), and in anticipation of his support of the martial values of Aeschylus in the agon (cf. Chs. 5–8). Furthermore, it should be noted that perhaps a decade before the production of the *Frogs* Eupolis' *Taxiarchi* had staged an analogous Dionysiac apprenticeship, as can be gauged from the scholiast on Aristophanes' *Peace*, who notes that Dionysus was presented as 'learning under Phormion the rules of generals and wars' (schol. *Peace* 348e (Holwerda); see Eupolis, *Taxiarchi*, fr. 274 K–A).[96] True, the play is lost to us; however, I would still surmise that the fifth-century spectators' laughter should not be conceived, as A. M. Wilson (1974: 250) thought, as mockery at Dionysus' inability to perform a quite familiar task, but rather as amusement with the soft and sluggish way in which the god was learning to become 'like them'. In other words, in his depiction of Dionysus as 'an unaccomplished rower battling against the difficulties and discomforts of the task', Aristophanes is not 'exploiting an easy source of humour' (A. M. Wilson) but rather following an already exploited possibility for the

---

[93] Eliade (1958: 37–40); Seaford (1981: 253).

[94] Apart from Eupolis' *Taxiarchi* (with a possible illustration on an Athenian oenochoe) (see below, n. 96) and Dionysius Chalcus, fr. 5 G–P referring to the 'oarage of Dionysus' (3.1), I am not aware of any other image, either textual or iconic, depicting Dionysus in the act of rowing. Some tenuous further evidence can be gleaned from an epic fragment (Theolytus Methymnaeus, fr. 1. 3, p. 9 in Powell, *Coll. Alex.*), where Dionysus is said to have released the vine fetters of the sea-god Glaucus when the latter revealed his *genos*: πατὴρ δέ με γείνατο Κωπεύς; quoted by Maass (1888: 76).

[95] On the experience of rowing a trireme as being an 'important part of the political education of the Athenian thete', imparting and consolidating the democratic ideals of the *polis* see now Strauss (1996: 317 and *passim*).

[96] For the *Taxiarchi* as probably staged *c*.415 BC see Handley (1982). A fragment of an oenochoe from the Athenian Agora (see fig. 86 in Pickard-Cambridge 1988) portrays two fat, comic figures inscribed as [ΔΙ] ΟΝΥΣΟΣ and ΦΟΡ, and is therefore very probably an illustration of Eupolis' play; see Crosby (1955).

incorporation of Dionysus into the community of the Athenian *polis*.

Nevertheless, a classical Greek audience could also have 'received' the rowing scene as a powerful and clever comic blending of initiatory apprenticeship with initiatory gender reversal, as Dionysus experiments with the manly martial art of rowing while being clad in the delicate female *krokotos*. As war had always been in Greek society an exclusively male enterprise, the rowing scene could have created a burlesque effect comparable to the impact of early modern European exploitations of the 'world upside-down' motif: on prints and brochures of all size and kind, the paradox of 'woman goes to war' took a variety of forms for the amusement (or sometimes even the challenging) of male viewers.[97]

2.6. Initiatory Ordeals (Initiatory pathos)

One of the commonest characteristics of an initiation's limen is the neophyte's subjection to a variety of initiatory ordeals, ranging from threats and terrifying sights to actual tortures of the greatest cruelty.[98] For example, a good comic version of the initiand's need to tolerate hardship can be found in *Clouds* 414–16, where the goddesses of the Socratic Phrontisterion promise to Strepsiades great glory if only

> your soul craves
> to endure hardship, and you don't get exhausted whatever you are
> doing,
> and you don't get too frustrated at feeling cold, nor do you feel like
> having supper,

a chart of endurance (*karteria*) to which the initiand, whole-heartedly committed, replies:

> But, as far as a hard soul and a restless care (ψυχῆς στερρᾶς
> δυσκολοκοίτου τε μερίμνης) are concerned,
> and a thrifty belly, wearing out and supping on bitter herbs,
> don't you worry and fear not: I could give you myself to use me as an
> anvil. (420–2)

Turning now to the *Frogs*, the initiand Dionysus' ordeal is linked with terrifying apparitions, threat of dismemberment, and flagellation.

---

[97] See Garrard (1989: 144 ff., 165 ff. on the motif of the 'femme forte'); Maclean (1977 and 1980); Dekker (1989) for pictures.

[98] See e.g. H. Webster (1932: 34 ff.). Twentieth-cent. evidence: La Fontaine (1986: 114).

(a) *Apparitions*

All kinds of apparitions and monsters, either imagined or 'real',[99] are frequent 'habitants of liminality' (Turner 1974: 239) and, therefore, Xanthias' pretence of seeing Empusa in the *Frogs* (288ff.)[100] fits well into the initiatory framework of the play, corroborating the liminal significance of Dionysus' journey in the Underworld.

In the context of Greek rituals especially, Hecate's *katharsia* and *teletai* seem to have been renowned for ghostly apparitions (φάσματα πολλὰ καὶ ποικίλα), as Dio Chrysostom (*Or.* 4. 90) attests.[101] But, more importantly still, being a shape-changing monster, which blurs the taxonomical categories of ordered society by fusing human and animal, male and female modes of existence, the Empusa of the *Frogs* fits nicely into the patterns of ritual marginality from another point of view as well: being 'now a bull, now a mule, now some very pretty woman' (290–1), now 'already a dog' (292), she resembles those boundary-crossing, ambiguous liminary creatures, in which the components of a culture are disassembled and recombined 'in any and every possible pattern however deviant, grotesque, unconventional, or outrageous' (V. and E. Turner 1982: 204). Victor Turner refers to examples such as animal-headed gods or animal gods with human heads, or monstrous combinations, such as a man's head on a lion's body, and so forth. Dissociating and isolating the elements of divinity, humanity, and animality from their familiar context, such grotesque configurations throw them better into relief, and help liminaries become 'vividly and rapidly aware of what may be called the "factors" of their culture' (Turner 1967: 105).

In the range of Greek ambiguous liminal symbolism lending itself

---

[99] That is, in the form of masked men personifying ancestral spirits, mythical creatures, etc.; see Brelich (1969: 36–7). On ritual monsters in the Greek world see Lada-Richards (forthcoming).

[100] Dover (1993: ad 286f.) rightly comments: 'Whether Xanthias is genuinely afraid or playing a practical joke on Dionysos, we cannot tell for sure from the text.' However, I am inclined to suggest that Xanthias actually plays a trick: in the perspective of 5th-cent. spectators a trick of false vision played upon Dionysus himself would have seemed doubly funny, as it could have easily evoked the deceptive *phasma* through which Dionysus helped Melanthus to kill his opponent at the mythical contest over the borders of the Attic land which lies at the origin of the Athenian Apaturia (cf. above, 2.4(c)). Moreover, as will become apparent in my discussion below (2.12(b)), Xanthias' control over Dionysus' emotions would place him in a position analogous to that of the Stranger/Dionysus towards the initiand Pentheus in Euripides' *Bacchae*. But, in any case, I cannot see, along with Dover (1993: ad 286f.), why Xanthias' 'ποῖ δ' ἐγώ at 296 suggests that he is actually frightened'; it could well be a pretended reaction of sham terror.

[101] It is impossible to gauge how far back the specific phase of the ritual described in Dio Chrysostom goes, but it can certainly be emphasized that from classical times onwards Hecate was the 'mistress of phantoms (φαντάσματα) and similar creatures'; see Johnston (1990: 34 with n. 15); cf. Kannicht (1969) on Eur. *Hel.* 569–70, and C. G. Brown (1991: 47 n. 29).

to this kind of interpretation, one could mention, for example, the grotesque masks at the Spartan sanctuary of Artemis Orthia (cf. 2.4(a)), some of which fuse the categories of bestial and human,[102] the animal-headed figures along the selvage of the marble drapery of Despoina's cult statue at Lycosura, or the multitude of animal-headed votive terracotta statuettes excavated at this same town of Arcadia (see Appendix). But in so far as literary remouldings of ritual apparitions are concerned, I would like to suggest that it is first and foremost the goddesses of the Socratic Phrontisterion in the *Clouds*, the Νεφέλαι, who fit perfectly into this pedagogic model of initiatory visions we have just discussed. For, in addition to their multiple and obvious Eleusinian connotations,[103] these creatures of remarkable fluidity of form enjoy a shapelessness which causes them to constantly straddle manifestations of human, bestial, and divine nature.[104] And, as they pride themselves on their ability to mould their appearance in accordance with character traits of individuals prominent in the public life of the community (348–55), they provide an intellectual stimulus to members of the audience to adopt a probing attitude, to view from different perspectives things they had been previously overlooking or simply taking for granted (see 353–4).

(b) *Dismemberment*

An extremely widespread initiatory ordeal is the novice's dismemberment, either imagined in a state of trance, as is the case in Shamanic initiations (Eliade 1958: 90–3; cf. 105–6, on Indian initiations), or carried out through a variety of symbolic actions, as happens usually in initiations into secret societies (Eliade 1958: 74). Similarly, in *Frogs* 473–8 the initiand Dionysus is confronted with the terrifying prospect of this kind of death. Explicit evidence from Greek ritual practice is almost non-existent, except for some faint reflections of the rite in later prose fiction[105] which, nevertheless,

---

[102] Categories E and G in Dickins's (1929: 176) classification.

[103] See primarily Byl (1980 and 1988). Although he admits the Eleusinian connotations of Νεφέλαι, A. M. Bowie (1993a: 123 n. 102) never makes the connection between the apparition of the *Clouds* and Eleusinian visions.

[104] They may look like 'mortal women' (341); centaurs, leopards, bulls, wolves (346–7); deer (354); and yet they are divine, the only divinities in the universe, according to Socrates (365 αὗται γάρ τοι μόναι εἰσὶ θεαί; cf. 265, 297, 316, 329).

[105] See primarily Lollianus' (2nd-cent. AD) *Phoinikika*, fr. Bi recto, 10–17, p. 92 Henrichs, with Henrichs's discussion (Henrichs 1972: 56ff.; 1969b). Note, however, Winkler's (1980) cautious remarks, both concerning the initiatory quality of the rite (171–5) and the 'ultimately unanswerable' (173) question of whether the scene describes an actual murder or a 'scheintod' (173–5). Furthermore, to the extent that one is willing to accept the reflection of initiatory motifs in the Greek Novel, a fake dismemberment scene is elaborately described in Achil. Tat. 3. 15. 4–6; see Merkelbach (1962: 126–7).

describe the initiand's *sparagmos* in language whose realistic vividness resembles the impact of the menaces uttered by the enraged Doorkeeper in the *Frogs*. More importantly still, the Greek mythical corpus is rich in tales of dismemberment (followed by boiling/recomposition),[106] some of which may be supposed to reflect to a certain extent initiatory ritual practice (see e.g. Thomson 1946: 118).

(c) *Flagellation*

The ordeal destined to leave the most memorable impact on the initiand's 'personality' is the various bodily torments (see e.g. Brelich 1969: 31 ff.; Eliade 1958: 21 ff.). In our play, Xanthias suggests that Dionysus be subjected to maltreatment (616 βασάνιζε γάρ . . .), and gives the Underworld Doorkeeper full liberty to torture him 'in any mode (πάντα τρόπον)' (618) he pleases:

> Tie him on a ladder,
> hang him, flog him with a whip of prickly bristles, flay him,
> wrench him, even pour vinegar into his nostrils,
> pile bricks upon him, do anything else except this:
> don't beat him with leek or with a soft-leaved onion.

(618–22)

This series of tortures brings to mind Strepsiades' expectation of suffering when he offers his consent to be initiated into the Socratic School:

> I give and afford
> My body to these, to treat as they please,
> To have and to hold, in squalor, in cold,
> In hunger and thirst, yea by Zeus, at the worst,
> To be flayed out of shape from my heels to my nape.

(*Clouds* 439–42; tr. B. B. Rogers)

Similarly, in the Platonic *Euthydemus*, when Socrates and Ctesippus surrender themselves[107] to Euthydemus and Dionysodorus, the

---

[106] In the Peloponnesian legends, for example, see, most importantly, the myths of Pelops, whose flesh was served up to the gods, and of Atreus, who cut up Thyestes' sons limb from limb (Apollod. *Ep.* 2. 13 μελίσας); see further Burkert (1983: 93–116 with sources). Cf. also the myths around Medea and Pelias (see e.g. Diod. 4. 52); Procne's and Philomela's cutting up of Itys (see e.g. Ov. *Met.* 6. 644–5 *membra | dilaniant*), etc. For the dismemberment/recomposition of Dionysus see below, 2.12(b). For the dismemberment of animal sacrificial victims in the circle of Dionysus see 4.7; see also Paus. 8. 37. 8 for dismemberment (instead of normal sacrificial cutting) of the victim during the mystic *telete* of the Arcadian Great Goddess Despoina: τῶν ἱερείων δὲ οὐ τὰς φάρυγγας ἀποτέμνει ὥσπερ ἐπὶ ταῖς ἄλλαις θυσίαις, κῶλον δὲ ὅ τι ἂν τύχῃ, τοῦτο ἕκαστος ἀπέκοψε τοῦ θύματος.

[107] *Euthd.* 285c παραδίδωμι ἐμαυτὸν Διονυσοδώρῳ τούτῳ . . . ἕτοιμός εἰμι παρέχειν ἐμαυτὸν τοῖς ξένοις.

sophists/initiators into the 'sophistic sacred truths',[108] they anticipate tortures (boiling and flaying) leading to the attainment of *arete*.[109]

Now, although Xanthias' imaginative ways of torturing never materialize, the scene *does* actually culminate in a flagellation, where master and slave in turn receive 'blow for blow (πληγὴν παρὰ πληγήν)' (643) each. A passage of Achilles Tatius (5. 23. 5–6) seems to suggest that beating was a well-known feature in Greek mysteries,[110] but the value of this kind of evidence is highly debated, and, apart from the well-known flagellation scene in the Villa of the Mysteries in Pompeii (2.12(c)), the most securely documented case of beating in an initiatory context is to be found in relation to the Spartan *agoge*, where the ephebes are flagellated ruthlessly at the sanctuary of Artemis Orthia. As in most other cases of tribal initiations, the Spartan neophytes' ordeal has the meaning of a 'resistance test',[111] the ideal of the ephebes who vie with each other for supremacy (Plut. *Mor.* 239d ἁμιλλώμενοι περὶ νίκης πρὸς ἀλλήλους) being the achievement of absolute impassivity.[112] Dionysus and Xanthias in the *Frogs* are likewise required to display utter apathy (634) by concealing every external sign of their pain (637–9). Furthermore, in the Spartan *agoge*, the ephebe who 'could endure being beaten for the longer time and the greater number of blows (ὅστις αὐτῶν ἐπὶ πλέον τε καὶ μᾶλλον καρτερήσειε τυπτόμενος)' would be 'held in especial repute (ἐν τοῖς μάλιστα ἐπίδοξός ἐστι)' (Plut. *Mor.* 239d) and appointed βωμονίκης, 'winner of the prize at the altar'.[113] Similarly, in the *Frogs*'

---

[108] *Euthd.* 277e νῦν οὖν νόμισον τὰ πρῶτα τῶν ἱερῶν ἀκούειν τῶν σοφιστικῶν (coming right after Socrates' comparison of Cleinias' bamboozlement by the sophists to the Corybantic rite of *thronosis*, 277d).

[109] *Euthd.* 285c ἀπολλύτω με, καὶ εἰ μὲν βούλεται, ἑψέτω, εἰ δ', ὅτι βούλεται, τοῦτο ποιείτω· μόνον χρηστὸν ἀποφηνάτω ... καὶ ἐὰν βούλωνται δέρειν ἔτι μᾶλλον ἢ νῦν δέρουσιν, εἴ μοι ἡ δορὰ μὴ εἰς ἀσκὸν τελευτήσει, ὥσπερ ἡ τοῦ Μαρσύου, ἀλλ' εἰς ἀρετήν.

[110] See Merkelbach (1962: 143). In *Frogs* 501 Dionysus exclaims that Xanthias/Heracles will prove to be οὐκ Μελίτης μαστιγίας, *mastigias* being, as Dover (1993: ad loc.) writes 'a term for an incorrigible slave who is often flogged.' The scholiast (ad loc.) records a tradition whereby Heracles' initiation into the Lesser Mysteries took place in that deme: ἐν γὰρ Μελίτῃ δήμῳ τῆς Ἀττικῆς ἐμυήθη Ἡρακλῆς τὰ μικρὰ μυστήρια. It is very likely that Dionysus' unprompted aside was meant to be particularly evocative for the spectators from Melite by mobilizing associations with cult practices established in that deme. If this were the case, one might push this speculation even further and surmise that Heracles' cult, such as practised in his famous Melitan sanctuary (Woodford 1971: 218), was either re-enacting (in the form of ephebic initiations?) or even merely preserving a tradition whereby the hero would have undergone a ritual *diamastigosis* as part of the ordeals of his mystic initiation. For a completely different interpretation of the line see Dover (1993: ad loc.).

[111] Cf. Plut. *Mor.* 239d μέχρι θανάτου πολλάκις διακαρτεροῦσιν ἱλαροὶ καὶ γαῦροι; an inscription (*IG* v. 1. 290) from the very sanctuary of Artemis Orthia characterizes the *diamastigosis* as καρτερίας ἀγῶνα Ὀρθείᾳ. There is 'no exact evidence for the dating of the inscription'; Woodward (1907–8: 102).

[112] See e.g. Luc. 37. 38; Cic. *Tusc.* 2. 14. 34. Cf. Eliade (1959: 86).

[113] *IG* v. 1. 554 (from Laconia) Τιβέριος ... βωμονίκης, συνέφηβος Ποπλίου ...; cf. Hyg. *Fab.* 261 *qui vocabantur Bomonicae*.

contest, he will be proclaimed as winner, who resists the most. As for the promised reward, this will be no less than full acknowledgement and recognition of his status, that is, divinity (637–9).

2.7. Ritual Nudity

Before enduring the ordeal of their flagellation, Dionysus and Xanthias have to strip their garments off (641 ἀποδύεσθε δή). If viewed as an isolated moment in the flow of the performance, nakedness[114] is obviously the first prerequisite to whipping. Nevertheless, if placed within the narrative sequence of the play in its entirety, nudity can seem invested with a more important function, mobilizing, as it does, a set of secondary associations.

Starting off his journey clad in effeminate attire, Dionysus reaches the threshold of his destination nude. It is in nudity that he presents himself to Pluto and Persephone,[115] who will confer his divine status back on him, and, in all probability at least (cf. Stone 1981: 421), it is in the Dionysiac part of his dramatic gear (i.e. his saffron robe and buskins, without the Heraclean insignia of lion-skin and club), that he assumes his civic role as a judge in the agon.[116] As in a variety of initiatory contexts nakedness mediates between liminal alterity and the reintegration of the self when the ritual transition is accomplished, this particular dimension of Dionysus' stage-presence in the *Frogs* should be considered as one more element which would induce a Greek fifth-century spectator to perceive the god in the role of a ritual passenger who undergoes initiation.[117]

[114] Now, as Alan Sommerstein points out to me, Dionysus and Xanthias are not asked to undress completely (complete nakedness would have been indicated by *ek-dyesthai* in Greek) (see Sommerstein 1996: ad loc.). However, even semi-nakedness on stage, and especially in the case of a god, is a 'sign' strong enough to mobilize in the audience a string of culturally determined associations.

[115] At least as can be gauged from the fact that both he and Xanthias are sent 'inside' right after their flagellation (669), a command of the Doorkeeper to which they immediately respond. A parallel case can be sought in the Akkadian version of Ishtar's Descent into the Underworld where, after having been progressively stripped of all her garments and jewels at each gate of the 'Land of no Return', Ishtar is finally derobed of her breechcloth at the seventh gate, and appears in front of the 'Mistress of the Nether World' completely naked; see Pritchard (1955: 107–8).

[116] An analogous change of garments in order to assume an important public function can be seen in *Knights*. After Demos has been subjected to the initiatory (cf. West 1983a: 144, 160–1) procedure of boiling as leading to rejuvenation, he appears 'magnificent in his old apparel' (1331), the *skeue* (1324) he had been wearing when, in the good old times, he had been 'dining together with Aristeides and Miltiades' (1325).

[117] In a fresco from Capua (fig. 30 in Merkelbach 1984: 288) which depicts Mithraic initiation the neophyte kneels in front of his Mystagogue naked, blindfolded, and with arms behind his back. However, this evidence cannot shed any light on mystic initiation in 5th-cent. Greece.

Nakedness is one of those signs of liminality which encapsulate and dissolve two antithetical processes simultaneously. As Turner (1967: 99) has expressed it, it is 'at once the mark of a newborn infant and a corpse prepared for burial.' One can easily understand then that nudity becomes a '"costume" in the context of the initiation of youths' (Bonfante 1989: 551), and that it is especially appropriate for the beginning and the end of the initiand's marginal seclusion.[118] The former case is comically exploited in the *Clouds*, where Strepsiades, before entering the initiatory space of Socrates' house, is asked to lay aside his cloak (497), with the explanation that it is customary to enter the Phrontisterion 'nude' (498 ἀλλὰ γυμνοὺς εἰσιέναι νομίζεται).[119] The latter possibility seems to have been fairly widespread in the Greek world in connection with rites of puberty, both male and female (Lloyd-Jones 1983: 94). Epigraphic evidence from Dreros and Malla in Crete, for example, suggests that, when the initiands were about to get out of their 'herd' (*agela*) and pronounce their ephebic oath, they had to lay aside the garments of their boyhood and to assume 'the warriors' costumes which each had received as a gift after his period of seclusion' (Willetts 1962: 175).[120] It is at such a moment, at the end of initiation, that the future Cretan citizens are described as 'without garments', πανάζωστοι or ἄζωστοι.[121]

[118] However, nakedness *during* liminality is attested in the case of the Spartan *gymnopaidiai* (taking their name from the nudity of the participants), activities that Plato (*Leg.* 633c) regards as 'tests of endurance': ἔτι δὲ κἂν ταῖς γυμνοπαιδίαις δειναὶ καρτερήσεις παρ' ἡμῖν γίγνονται τῇ τοῦ πνίγους ῥώμῃ διαμαχομένων; see Pettersson (1992: 45–8); cf. Eliade (1958: 32).

[119] For stripping as an indicator of initiatory boundary-crossing see Buxton (1987: 69). The scholiast on *Clouds* 497b (Holwerda) presents nudity as a general practice in mystic initiation (without, however, citing any sources to support his claim): ὅπερ ἐποίουν ἐπὶ τῶν μυουμένων τὰ μυστήρια, ἀποδῦσαι αὐτὸν βούλεται τὴν ἐσθῆτα. Byl (1980: 20 n. 69) refers to Plotinus 1. 6. 7, where shedding of garments and ritual nudity (καὶ ἱματίων ἀποθέσεις τῶν πρὶν καὶ τὸ γυμνοῖς ἀνιέναι) are associated with the ascent towards the most sacred sanctuaries. Unfortunately, however, this is a very late source and the initiatory context to which it refers is completely unclear.

[120] Cf. Willetts (1955: 120). Leitao (1995) has argued that the boy's prior dress was feminine: at the so-called 'Ekdysia' festival, i.e. 'Festival of Disrobing' in Phaestus (see Lambrinoudakis 1972), the ritual change of dress 'was gender-coded, meaning that the boy cast off feminine clothes and put on masculine clothes in their place' (Leitao 1995: 132). Ritual nudity before civic 're-integration' may also be suggested by the term ἐκδραμεῖν (*IC* i. XVI. 5. 21 ἐπεὶ κ' ἐγδρ⟨ά⟩μωντι), meaning 'strip and enter the stadium (*dromos*)'; as Leitao (1995: 134) has put it, 'the boy divested in order to take part for the first time in the public *dromoi*, one of the most salient characteristics of Cretan citizenship.' In Cretan Lyttos too, we hear of the 'Festival of the Garment' (*Periblemaia*) (*IC* i. XIX. 1. 17–22), suggesting that 'the order of the final stage of initiation was: undressing, being nude and donning the new adult garment' (Bremmer 1994: 45).

[121] *IC* i. IX. (Dreros) 1 A. 10–12 τάδε ὤμοσαν | ἀγελάοι παν- | ἄζωστοι . . .; *IC* i. IX. (Dreros) 1 D. 140–1 ἀζώ- | στοις. Commenting on 1 A, lines 11 ff., Guarducci (*IC* i, p. 87) collates Hesychius' gloss ἄζωστος· ἄνοπλος, ἄστολος; furthermore, the meaning of the words is

Finally, an important parallel can be sought in the ritual calendar of Athens, in the pivotal prenuptial rites of the *artkteia*[122] performed under the aegis of Artemis at Brauron. There, after a period of initiatory seclusion spent in the goddess's sanctuary and characterized by the wearing of a special dress, the *krokotos*, the *arktoi*, selected girls from Attica, cast off their saffron robe[123] and perform some ritual acts in total nudity.[124] As Sourvinou-Inwood has demonstrated in a series of detailed publications,[125] the ritual nudity of the bears signified 'the moment of the passage out of the arkteia, and the beginning of the transition into the new state' (Sourvinou-Inwood 1988: 133),[126] that of 'properly acculturated gynaikes' (ibid.: 137). It seems to be the case, then, that within the frame of Greek cultural experience nakedness can often be a step to the initiand's symbolic resurrection.[127] And, just as the bears of Brauron shed their liminary garb when the time of their reincorporation[128] into the space of the *polis* comes, Dionysus in the *Frogs* is forced to cast away the ambiguous clothing which highlighted his status as a liminal *persona* in the play's imagery and structure.[129] In other words,

corroborated by the parallel phrases: τὰν ἀγέ- | λαν τοὺς τόκα ἐ- | γδυομένους (i. xi (Dreros) 1 C. 98–100) and τὰν ἀγέ- | λαν τὰν τόκα ἐσδυομέναν (*IC* i. xix. (Malla) 17–18).

[122] Some ancient sources qualify the *arkteia* as a *mysterion*; see Seaford (1994a: 308 n. 117).

[123] See Ar. *Lys.* 645 καταχέουσα τὸν κροκωτόν (with Sourvinou-Inwood (1971) restoring the reading *katacheousa* of cod. R.); cf. Sourvinou-Inwood (1988: 136ff.).

[124] Attested in a series of krateriskoi from Brauron published by Kahil (1965 and 1977).

[125] See, most importantly, Sourvinou-Inwood (1988: 127–35); see also Lloyd-Jones (1983: 91–5).   [126] Cf. Sourvinou-Inwood (1988: 123 and 1990b: 6).

[127] Among literary remouldings of nakedness/reclothing as symbolizing loss/resumption of identity leading towards a ritual passenger's reintegration, some good examples can be sought in Homer's *Odyssey*: bereft of ships and men, stripped of all distinctive markers of the self, and socially as good as dead, Odysseus sets foot upon the island of Scheria naked (*Od.* 6. 136 γυμνός . . . ἐών; cf. 6. 222), before receiving clothes from Nausicaa and her attendants (6. 214). Nudity, however, precedes reintegration, as it is precisely upon this very island that Odysseus is first reintegrated into a society of men, after the years of his travelling among non-human, either monstrous or divine, beings. And it is now the first time when the naked, nameless hero can safely recreate for himself his own identity: taking up the role of the bard, he re-establishes and reasserts his *kleos* through a *nostos* of his memory and the immortalizing power of song; see Segal (1967).

[128] In a passage clearly influenced by mystic imagery, Plotinus refers to the ascent of the *psyche* towards the *agathon* as requiring a shedding of the garments worn during its descent (καὶ ἀποδυομένοις ἃ καταβαίνοντες ἠμφιέσμεθα) (1. 6. 7). For a literary reflection of shedding of clothes before an act of reincorporation see Hom. *Od.* 22. 1, where, just before unleashing slaughter on the suitors, i.e. just before the act which paves for him the way for his final reincorporation in his own royal *oikos*, Odysseus casts off his rags: αὐτὰρ ὁ γυμνώθη ῥακέων πολύμητις Ὀδυσσεύς.

[129] For Dionysus' sexual ambiguity manifested through his garb as a liminal characteristic see above, 2.2. For the initiands' wearing of special clothes in an initiation ritual see e.g. (initiation into Trophonius' cave): Paus. 9. 39. 8; schol. *Clouds* 508a and 508b (Holwerda); (mysteries of Andania): Sokolowski (1969: no. 65, 23–5 ὅσα δὲ δεῖ διασκευάζεσθαι εἰς θεῶν διάθεσιν, ἐχόντω τὸν εἱματισμὸν καθ' ὅ ἂν οἱ ἱεροὶ διατάξωντι; (mysteries of Isis): Apul. *Met.* 11. 23, 11. 24 (full description). For the role of dress in Dionysiac mysteries see Appendix.

Dionysus' ritual nudity in the *Frogs* could well have signified for fifth-century Athenian spectators the starting-point of his gradual reintegration.

Dionysus' Rite of Passage and Mystic Initiation

What I would now like to consider is the possibility that some of the above-mentioned constituents of the journey's liminality would have been particularly evocative for those members of the audience who were initiated into the Eleusinian and/or Dionysiac mysteries.[130] For there is reason to believe that the *tetelesmenoi* would have been able to envisage Dionysus as undergoing the experience of an initiand either in a Bacchic *thiasos* or in the Mysteries of Eleusis.[131]

2.8. *Descent/Ascent*

To start with, it is the very sequence of descent/ascent upon which the structure of the play is built that should be seen as operative in the context both of a Dionysiac and an Eleusinian initiation rite.

(a) *Dionysiac rituals*

Having assembled a wealth of evidence, Boyancé (1960–1) has proved the cardinal importance of caves in Dionysus' cult: symbol of a chthonic entrance, the cave (ἄντρον) or pit (μάγαρον) or vault (ψαλίς)[132] 'may have been seen and experienced as a kind of netherworld',[133] where the Dionysiac *thiasoi* would have been enacting

---

[130] For the Dionysiac mysteries in the classical period see Burkert (1985: 290ff.); S. G. Cole (1980); Seaford (1981, 1996: 39–44); Tsantsanoglou and Parássoglou (1987); Segal (1990); Parker (1995); Dickie (1995; new leaf-shaped gold lamellae from graves in Pella). If Xanthias' aside at *Frogs* 159 ἐγὼ γοῦν ὄνος ἄγω μυστήρια had actually a clear referential meaning in the context of Dionysiac mysteries, the μεμνημένοι could have been alert to the Dionysiac dimension of the play as early as its opening scene; see Tierney (1935: esp. 399–401) citing, most importantly, Orph. fr. 31 Kern: ὄνος βουκόλος. It would also be helpful to bear in mind that in the classical period slaves as well could be initiated (R. Osborne 1985: 174) and, therefore, *Frogs* 159 might perhaps suggest the idea of Xanthias as a celebrant in the Mysteries; on *Frogs* 159 see further Olivieri (1924: 300); Tierney (1922: 85).

[131] The reflection of various Eleusinian ritual aspects in some dramatic moments of the *Frogs* had been already noted by Thomson (1935) in his classic article on the Mysteries and the *Oresteia*.

[132] *Magaron*: see Pippidi (1964: 156 n. 2); *psalis*: Pippidi (1964: *passim*). The cultic cave of Dionysus at Eleutherae, on the boundaries between Attica and Plataea (Paus. 1. 38. 9) was apparently the setting for Euripides' Dionysiac tragedy *Antiope*. For Dionysiac scenes set in caves in black-figure iconography see refs. in Peirce (1993: 241 n. 90).

[133] Burkert (1987a: 101); cf. Bérard (1974: 108). Late hints about Bacchic mystic *katabaseis* may be detected in Liv. 39. 13. 13; cf. Bloch (1966: 396).

their mystic initiation rites: having experienced the terrors of death through his/her submergence in the cave, the initiand would emerge to light again in the newly assumed *persona* of a *bakchos*[134] or a *bakche*. The prototype of such descents/ascents[135] may have been Dionysus himself.[136] In the very old cultic hymn of the women of Elis (fr. 871 *PMG*), for example, Dionysus is invoked to 'plunge' (v. 5 δύων) into his temple, that is, as Bérard (1976: 71) has understood it, to undertake a kind of *katabasis* into the bacchic cave, while from Plutarch we learn about a ritual 'summoning up' (*anaklesis*) of Dionysus from the deep waters (*abyssos*) of the Argive lake Alcyonis.[137] But, more importantly still, myth relates how he descended once in quest for and ascended back together with his mother Semele,[138] a 'chthonic passage' that Plutarch (*Mor.* 565e–f) explicitly connects with 'a great chasm extending all the way down' and having 'the appearance of a Bacchic grotto' (τοῖς βακχικοῖς ἄντροις ὁμοίως). Boyancé (1965–6) has drawn attention to Semele's importance in the Dionysiac cult, especially to the role of the *mater*, standing for her incarnation in Dionysiac sacred pantomimes.[139] Apart from the nocturnal *dromena* performed annually in honour of Dionysus at the bottomless lake of Alcyonis at Lerna (Paus. 2. 37. 5–6), mystic rites which Pausanias did not think appropriate to divulge to the uninitiated,[140] the most important mystic *dromenon* centring around Semele about which we have some scraps of information is the feast named Herois in Delphi which, in Plutarch's view (*Mor.* 293c–d), enacted the ἀναγωγή (the 'bringing up') of the divine mother:

---

[134] Cf. Eur. fr. 472N², 15; Pl. *Phaed.* 69c. See further Cumont (1933: 258).

[135] An Attic rf. krater of the beginning of the 4th cent. BC may be illustrating the cultic sequence of a 'Dionysiac' initiatory ascent (Bérard 1974: pl. 10, no. 34). (Figs. 2.3*a* and *b*).

[136] In an impressive iconographic scene on a 4th-cent. Apulian krater (*RVAp.* Suppl. ii. 508, 18/41a1), Dionysus is depicted in the Underworld, in the midst of his *thiasos*, clasping the hand of Hades (in the presence of Persephone). According to Moret (1993), it represents Dionysus' departure from the Underworld (i.e. his ascent); however, see now the more convincing interpretation of Johnston and McNiven (1996).

[137] Plut. *Mor.* 364f ἀνακαλοῦνται δ' αὐτὸν ὑπὸ σαλπίγγων ἐξ' ὕδατος, ἐμβάλλοντες εἰς τὴν ἄβυσσον ἄρνα τῷ Πυλαόχῳ. See Farnell (1909: 183–5); Nilsson (1957: 41).

[138] Diod. 4. 25. 4; Paus. 2. 31. 2 (Dionysus brought Semele back through the temple of Artemis at Troezen, full of altars of underworld deities), 2. 37. 5; Apollod. 3. 5. 3; Plut. *Mor.* 565f–6a; and, more elaborately on Dionysus' quest in Hades, Clem. Alex. *Protr.* 2. 34 (Klotz). On Semele's cults see now Larson (1995: 93–6) and D. Lyons (1997: 120–2; cf. 132). A superb iconographic illustration of Semele's *anodos* is a 6th-cent. cup in Naples (*ABV* 203, 1 = *LIMC*, s.v. Dionysos, 55), depicting two colossal heads (Dionysus and Semele; inscribed) emerging from the ground in the midst of grape-clusters and other vegetation.

[139] However, the bulk of his evidence is of late periods.

[140] Paus. 2 37. 6 τὰ δὲ ἐς αὐτὴν Διονύσῳ δρώμενα ἐν νυκτὶ κατὰ ἔτος ἕκαστον οὐχ ὅσιον ἐς ἅπαντας ἦν μοι γράψαι. On *dromena* as denoting mystic rites especially in Plutarch and Pausanias see Richardson (1974: 304, ad 476).

2.3(a). *Anodos* of a Dionysiac mystes . . .
rf. Attic krater: British Museum, 1917. 7–21. I

The greater part of the Herois has a secret import (τὰ πλεῖστα μυστικὸν ἔχει λόγον) which the Thyiads know; but from the portions of the rites (δρωμένων)[141] that are performed in public one might conjecture that it represents the evocation of Semele (Σεμέλης . . . ἀναγωγήν).

Should this rite ever prove connected with female initiations, as has been occasionally suggested (Jeanmaire 1939: 411; Delcourt 1965: 114–15), it would corroborate beyond doubt the proposition that the sequence of descent/ascent was a solidly established Dionysiac initiatory pattern.[142]

---

[141] On *dromena* see previous note.

[142] It seems that the Theban *thiasos* of *Kataibatai* sent to Magnesia in Asia Minor (*IMagn.* 215a) had similar rites to perform; see Reinach (1890: 359); Farnell (1909: 193).

2.3(*b*). . . . in the presence of Dionysus
rf. Attic krater: British Museum, 1917. 7–21. I

(b) *Eleusis*

In the Demetrian sphere, correspondingly, both the Homeric *Hymn to Demeter*, which is our most important source for the Eleusinian myth, and the mystic ritual itself, in so far as we can safely reconstruct its stages, display clear initiatory characteristics, in accordance with van Gennep's scheme of 'separation', 'limen', and 'reintegration'. Both for Persephone and for the human brides of Persephone's age, the myth reflects initiation into marriage.[143] But, most pertinent is the fact that Persephone's death as a *kore* and her subsequent rebirth into a new state of maturity is signified in the myth's imagery through the initiatory symbol of a *kathodos* into and an *anodos* from the Underworld. And yet, as far as the ritual sequence of Eleusis is concerned, our sources do not allow us to

---

[143] See e.g. Jeanmaire (1939: 69–79, 98–305); Lincoln (1979); Foley (1993: 95–7).

gauge precisely to what extent the main cultic units of the Core myth (i.e. rape/descent, quest, and *anodos*) were mimetically performed. Clement of Alexandria speaks of a 'mystic drama' re-enacting 'the wanderings and the abduction and the mourning' of Demeter and Core.[144] This is, admittedly, a very late source, but the Homeric *Hymn* itself, which hails Demeter as having 'revealed the conduct of her rites (δρησμοσύνη θ' ἱερῶν) and taught the Mysteries' (476) to the people of Eleusis, uses the word *dresmosyne*, which suggests 'actions in a ritual context' (Foley 1993: 62). Moreover, all the sources which discuss the notorious profanation of the Mysteries in 415 BC refer to a representation, a mimetic re-enactment of the rites (see sources in Ch. 3, n. 50), a kind of spectacle. On the other hand, excavations in the area of the Sanctuary suggest that 'any theory which assumes a full-scale dramatic representation inside the Telesterion is almost certainly wrong' (Richardson 1974: 25). The *Katabasion* (subterranean chamber) mentioned in the writings of the Christian bishop Asterius (Mylonas 1961: 311) has not been brought to light up to now and, according to Mylonas (1961: 314), there is no chance of its being found in the future, since 'the territory of the Telesterion has been completely cleared and everywhere the rock was reached.' Nevertheless, although it does seem safer to conclude that no collective *katabasis* of the mystai could have been performed within the Eleusinian Initiation Hall itself,[145] I don't believe there is good reason to reject the milder suggestion for a representation of the story *outside* the Telesterion, 'around the very landmarks supposed to have been consecrated by the actual experience and presence of Demeter' (Mylonas 1961: 263). For even if Richardson (1974: 25) is right in protesting that 'one can hardly believe that vast crowds, perhaps thousands of initiates, roamed about the Sanctuary, searching for Core',[146] Clement's 'mystic drama' need not have been staged

---

[144] Clem. Alex. *Protr.* 2. 12. (p. 30 Butterworth) Δηὼ δὲ καὶ Κόρη δρᾶμα ἤδη ἐγενέσθην μυστικόν, καὶ τὴν πλάνην καὶ τὴν ἁρπαγὴν καὶ τὸ πένθος αὐταῖν Ἐλευσὶς δᾳδουχεῖ. See, however, Riedweg (1987: 121 n. 26) on this passage as being a continuation of an elaborate theatrical metaphor of Clement's preceding paragraph.

[145] Burkert (1985: 288) is dogmatic on this point: 'There was no true entrance to the nether world, no chasm, no possibility of acting out a journey into the underworld.' Cf. id. (1983: 280). Cf. Richardson (1974: 25), stressing that the Telesterion doesn't seem to have been equipped with elaborate machinery for large-scale representations, 'nor for any form of simulated "underworld-journey".' However, as Richard Seaford points out to me, to exclude even the possibility of a *simulative* representation of the story in the Eleusinian Initiation Hall is a dangerously far-fetched argument.

[146] See, however, Dowden (1980: 426): 'Such a mass mime would be a hopeless mess in the Telesterion, *but outside it would make very good sense*' (my italics). Moreover, one may say that passages such as Plut. *Mor.* 81d ὥσπερ γὰρ οἱ τελούμενοι κατ' ἀρχὰς μὲν ἐν θορύβῳ καὶ βοῇ σύνιασι πρὸς ἀλλήλους ὠθούμενοι or Plut. fr. 178 Sandbach ὄχλον . . . πατούμενον ὑφ' ἑαυτοῦ καὶ συνελαυνόμενον refer to this initial disorderly jostling of the mystai with each other.

by the whole body of initiates collectively.[147] It could still have been performed on a purely representative, symbolic, level by the officials of the Sanctuary, most importantly Demeter's and Persephone's High Priestess.[148] That is to say, the initiands would only *empathically* participate in the *dromena*, by way of identifying with the protagonists' emotions, as they would pass from the sorrow of the Mother's loss through the turbulations of the search to the supreme joy of Persephone's recovery (cf. Dowden 1980: 426). And actually, there is in Eleusis a natural grotto, the so-called Plutonion, with a small temple of Pluto built in one of its cavities.[149] As a natural chasm of the earth, it would very probably have stood for the place wherefrom Hades sprang to light (cf. Hom. *h. Dem.* 16 χάνε δὲ χθών . . .) and wherein he disappeared again with the abducted Core (Richardson 1974: 18–19, 220; cf. 150). Excavations in this cavern have revealed a well-like pit with an artificial opening and a stairway. This place would have been a perfect location for the High Priestess of the Sanctuary to mime Persephone's sudden *kathodos* and disappearance into the darkness of the Netherworld.[150] Her *anodos*, correspondingly, undoubtedly a high point in the ceremony, would have been staged inside the Telesterion, either as an appearance in

[147] Although, again, some collective performance could have been possible, even if restricted only to a limited section of initiands. For example the torchlit search for Persephone (reflected in Ar. *Thesm.* 655 ff.), which was part of the *pannychis* into which the procession from Athens to Eleusis culminated, seems to have been open exclusively to women (cf. Foley 1993: 38).

[148] Ἱέρεια Δήμητρος καὶ Κόρης was her formal title (see Clinton 1974: 68 ff.). She certainly had an important role to play in the secret *telete*; cf. a mid-5th-cent. inscription (Clinton 1974: 68) where the priestess Lysistrate identifies herself as a minister (πρόπολος) of the unspeakable rite (ἀρρήτο τελετῆς). Regretfully, however, there is no explicit information on the priestess's duty to perform a mimetic role during the celebration of the Great Mysteries. There is only one very late (2nd-cent. AD) literary allusion to the priestess's mimetically enacted abduction in a passage from Tertullian (cited in Mylonas 1961: 310): 'why is the priestess of Demeter carried off, unless Demeter herself had suffered that same sort of thing?' An even vaguer allusion (although in a negative form) can be detected in a papyrus from Antinoopolis (text in Nilsson 1960: lines 5–7): τὴν Κόρην εἶδον ἡρπασμένην οὐδὲ τὴν Δημήτερα λελυπημένην (see Riedweg 1987: 64 n. 172).

[149] See description in Mylonas (1961: 99–100, 146–9 and figs. 50–2) and Daux (1958: 800–2).

[150] Mylonas (1961: 148), on the contrary, thinks that its most probable function was to stage 'the passage from the lower world': 'a priestess impersonating Persephone could ascend the stairway and emerge through the elliptical opening into the view of spectators on the Sacred Way . . .'. But I find it highly implausible that the ascent of Core which, if enacted would certainly have formed a part of the 'secret' of Eleusis, would have taken place outside the Telesterion. For (i) it would have thus been open to the view of all the mystai rather than only the *epoptai* (for the grades see Dowden 1980), and (ii) it would have sundered the continuity between the final acts, some of which we know for sure were performed within the Telesterion, such as, for example, the revelation of the great light (μέγα φῶς) from the open gates of the Anactoron (cf. Plut. *Mor.* 81e), the sacred building at the centre of the Initiation Hall. For a different reconstruction of the Eleusinian 'sacred drama' see Clinton (1988 and 1992: 84–90).

flesh and blood or as a vision or as a statue or, at any rate, in a form that we shall probably never be able to recapture.[151] But the fact that the *telete did* eventually culminate in an *anodos*/appearance of Core can be gauged from a variety of different sources, such as the sounding of a gong by the hierophant 'when Core is being called upon' (τῆς Κόρης ἐπικαλουμένης), an act suggesting a ritual summoning from the Underworld; a papyrus fragment, where 'having seen' Core is highlighted as the 'true' initiation; the very language of the Homeric *Hymn to Demeter*, where the mourning goddess's strongest wish is to 'see' her daughter with her own eyes; and, above all, vase-paintings and reliefs portraying the ritual (as opposed to mythical) bringing back of Persephone with torches.[152]

(c) *Thesmophoria*

Nevertheless, there actually exists an elaborately dramatized Demetrian scenario comprising both a descent and an ascent, re-enacted annually within the precinct of the Athenian Thesmophorion itself and, arguably, in many other places where either *megara* or Thesmophoria existed, since the Thesmophoria festival was the most widespread form of Demeter's cult (Burkert 1985: 242). A scholion on Lucian (Rabe 1906: 275–6 (in *DMeretr. 2*.

---

[151] Vision: Pl. *Phdr.* 250b–c κάλλος δὲ τότ' ἦν ἰδεῖν λαμπρόν, ὅτε σὺν εὐδαίμονι χορῷ μακαρίαν ὄψιν τε καὶ θέαν . . . εἰδόν τε καὶ ἐτελοῦντο τῶν τελετῶν ἣν θέμις λέγειν μακαριωτάτην . . . ὁλόκληρα δὲ καὶ ἁπλᾶ καὶ ἀτρεμῆ καὶ εὐδαίμονα φάσματα μυούμενοί τε καὶ ἐποπτεύοντες ἐν αὐγῇ καθαρᾷ . . .; Plut. fr. 178 Sandbach σεμνότητας ἀκουσμάτων ἱερῶν καὶ φασμάτων ἁγίων ἔχοντες; Procl. *In Remp.* ii, p. 185, 3–4 (Kroll) φάσματά τε δεικνύντων γαλήνης μεστά. Zeitlin (1989: 160–1) suggests a literary reflection of the blissful Eleusinian *phasmata* in the Dionysiac/Eleusinian scenario of Euripides' *Ion*, where the recognition of mother and son abounds in the imagery of blessed phantoms (1354 ὦ μακαρία μοι φασμάτων ἥδ' ἡμέρα; 1395 τί δῆτα φάσμα τῶν ἀνελπίστων ὁρῶ; cf. 1444). An appearance of Core (or Demeter) as a vision is suggested by a marble votive relief from the Telesterion of Eleusis (*LIMC*, s.v. Demeter, 161), dedicated to Demeter by a certain Eucrates. On the rectangular dedicatory plaque there is the head of a female deity (Core or Demeter) surrounded by shining rays painted in red (see *LIMC*, ad loc. and Kerényi 1967: 97). It may also be interesting to note here that at the 'Oracle of the Dead' near Ephyra in Epirus traces of a piece of iron machinery for showing ghostly apparitions (probably wheeling them down from an upper floor) have been discovered; see Daux (1965: 776) and Dakaris (1973: 147). Statue: cf. *Phdr.* 254b εἶδον τὴν ὄψιν . . . ἀστράπτουσαν . . .; cf. Themistius 20. 235a–b, where he seems to be conceiving of Eleusinian *epopteia* as a revelation of a statue, which the priest ἐπεδείκνυε τῷ μυουμένῳ μαρμαρύσσον τε ἤδη καὶ αὐγῇ καταλαμπόμενον θεσπεσίᾳ (see Riedweg 1987: n. 163); cf. Boyancé (1962: esp. 471–3), who defends Kern's old suggestion about the moment of the Eleusinian *epopteia* as comprising 'un dévoilement de statues qui apparaissent dans l'éblouissante clarté de la lumière' (Boyancé 1962: 464).

[152] Gong: Apollodorus, *FGrHist* 244 F110 b (cf. below, n. 179); see Richardson (1974: 25) and Burkert (1983: 286 n. 57); for the ritual scheme of the *appel cogné* (the 'call by knocking') where such summoning belongs see Bérard (1974: 75–87). Papyri: *Pap. della R. Univ. Milano* (1937), no. 20 pp. 176–7 "μυστήρια [πολλῶ ἀ]ληθέστερα μεμύημαι . . . τὴν Κόρην εἶδον" ('I have experienced far truer mysteries . . . I have seen Kore') (Burkert 1983: 286 n. 58; his translation). Hom. *h. Dem.* 333, 339, 350. Iconography: see below, 2.14, nn. 239–40.

1)), although notoriously obscure (Brumfield 1981: 73 ff.), provides the most detailed description of the ritual core of the festival: women called Bailers (ἀντλήτριαι) descend (καταβαίνουσιν) into underground rooms (εἰς τὰ ἄδυτα) and bring up (ἀναφέρουσι) the decomposed remains of the piglets which had been previously thrown down into trenches (εἰς τὰ μέγαρα).[153] No full explanation of the rites has survived from antiquity. Yet, what lies beyond doubt is that the thematic core around which its symbolism revolved was Persephone's abduction and return.[154] And, although suggestions about the purely initiatory nature of the Thesmophoria[155] are untenable (see Versnel 1993), we *do* hear of initiation rites (*teletai*) in connection with this festival (Burkert 1985: 242 with n. 10); important characteristics of ritual liminality, such as role reversals, *can* be isolated in its cultic cycle; and, most interestingly, some of its ritual aspects may even attract mystic terminology (Burkert 1985: 242 with n. 9), a linguistic interweaving which very adequately expresses the conflation of the marital and mystic aspects of the rites.[156] Nevertheless, independently of the complex and largely impenetrable ritual logic underlying this particular Demetrian festal cycle,[157] the very strong connection of the subterranean *megara* with the cult of Demeter and Core[158] in a variety of places all over the Greek world constitutes a safe indication that both a *kathodos* and *anodos* were actually mimetically performed.[159]

After having surveyed the primary schema of descent/ascent and

---

[153] Rabe (1906: 276, 3–6); see also Broneer (1942: 258 and 264).

[154] See primarily schol. Luc. *DMeretr.* 2. 1; Burkert (1985: 243 with nn. 21–3); Zeitlin (1982); Foley (1993: 71–3, 80).

[155] The proposition that the Thesmophoria constituted the mythic pattern for female initiation rites was first argued by Jeanmaire (1939: 268 ff., esp. 296–307), and revived by Prytz Johansen (1975); Skov (1975); Lincoln (1979).

[156] For the analogy between the categories of an initiand and a bride, the use of mystic terminology in wedding ritual, and the celebration of marriage ritual in the mysteries see Seaford (1994a: 308, with n. 117); cf. Burkert (1983: 271 n. 22). The analogy is informative for the Thesmophoria, where the participant matrons are ritually reduced to the status and the role of *nymphai*, i.e. virgins on the brink of their marital transition, at the threshold between virginal and marital status (see Versnel 1993: esp. 256, 275).

[157] See most importantly Zeitlin (1982) and Versnel (1993: 228–88).

[158] Nilsson (1906: 362); see e.g. Paus. 1. 39. 5, 3. 25. 9, 9. 8. 1; L. Robert (1934: 811 nn. 6, 7, 8: inscriptions from Peiraeus, Mantinea, Eleusis). Cf. White (1967: 346 with n. 97), and see also Clinton's very interesting piece (1988), identifying *megara* over seven metres deep attached to the Telesterion of Eleusis (figs. 5–8).

[159] Cf. Festugière (1972: 58–9) for Sicily. The mimetic representation of the whole sequence (ἡ ἀνάβασις τῆς θεοῦ . . . ἡ δύσις τῆς θεοῦ) is probably reflected in a Roman calendar of Dardanus (Sokolowski 1969: no. 128). A ritual *anodos* of Core might be inferred by Paus. 1. 43. 2 (Megara) and of Demeter by Photius (s.v. Stenia). Clinton (1988) argues that at the Eleusinian Thesmophoria the Bailers descended into the *megara* to deposit the piglets during the Mysteries (perhaps on the 21 of the month Boedromion), i.e. some 20 days before the Thesmophoria.

its function within the initiatory structure of the play, let us now consider Dionysus' theatrical itinerary through the regions of the Underworld.

2.9. *Dionysus' ponos*

Shortly after his first appearance on the stage, Dionysus complains that walking is for him a source of labour: 'I walk and toil' (αὐτὸς βαδίζω καὶ πονῶ) (23). Some of the possible semantic associations of *ponos* have been explored in the previous chapter (1.6(b)). However, if the notion of 'toiling' were set against the background of a rite of passage, its connotative breadth would appear to be greater still. For the accomplishment of arduous tasks is a prominent characteristic of ritual liminality[160] and, in the narrower context of mystic cults especially, *ponoi* or *mochthoi* or *kopoi* or *agones* are almost 'technical' terms for the ordeals the initiand is required to undergo.[161] To take only some examples, the mystical imagery pervading the *Oresteia* (Thomson 1935; Tierney 1937) opens with the Watchman's prayer for a release from toils, an *apallage ponon* (*Ag.* 1; cf. *Eum.* 83). In the *Bacchae*, *ponos, mochthos, kopos, agon* qualify Pentheus' initiatory ordeals (Seaford 1981) which culminate in his death,[162] while in an often cited passage from Firmicius Maternus (*Err. Prof. Rel.* 22. 1)

---

[160] A good example may be sought in the initiatory sequence of Heracles' exploits, explicitly characterized as *ponoi* (cf. 1.7 with nn. 94–5) and leading to his ultimate salvation. As he himself reviews his life in the closing scene of Sophocles' *Philoctetes*, his *ponoi* paved the way for his *apotheosis*: καὶ πρῶτα μέν σοι τὰς ἐμὰς λέξω τύχας, | ὅσους πονήσας καὶ διεξελθὼν πόνους | ἀθάνατον ἀρετὴν ἔσχον (1418–20). It is upon his own archetypal example that Philoctetes' exit from his liminal condition should be modelled: καὶ σοί, σάφ' ἴσθι, τοῦτ' ὀφείλεται παθεῖν, | ἐκ τῶν πόνων τῶνδ' εὐκλεᾶ θέσθαι βίον (1421–2) (cf. above, n. 92).

[161] It is true that when Dionysus refers to his own toiling in *Frogs* 23, he has not yet entered the 'limen' of his initiation. However, a literary text cannot be expected to reflect ritual phases with extreme accuracy (cf. 2.1, 2.13); patterns and themes are likely to be remoulded in different order, and yet, still be recognizable by an audience for which they constitute a familiar experience.

[162] Note the striking recurrence of these terms in the scene of Pentheus' ordeal in the palace stables (626 μάτην πονῶν . . .; 627 διαμεθεὶς δὲ τόνδε μόχθον; 634–5 κόπου δ' ὕπο | διαμεθείς . . .; 964 τοιγάρ σ' ἀγῶνες ἀναμένουσιν . . .) as well as in the Stranger's conception of the nature of his death as an *agon* (974–5 τὸν νεανίαν ἄγω | τόνδ' εἰς ἀγῶνα μέγαν . . .); cf. Thomson (1935: 584. See also the reflections of mystic language and imagery in e.g. Pl. *Phdr.* 247b ἔνθα δὴ πόνος τε καὶ ἀγὼν ἔσχατος ψυχῇ πρόκειται; Plut. *Mor.* 36e φριττόντων δὲ τὸν θάνατον καὶ τὸν πόνον . . . ἔκπληξις ἴσχει καὶ ταραχὴ καὶ θάμβος. A very late text comprises *hodoiporiai* (walking), among the ordeals the initiand is required to undergo: see schol. of Nonnus Abbas on Gregorius Nazianzenus, *Against Iulianus* (Migne, *PG*, vol. 36, col. 989) Αἱ δὲ κολάσεις εἰσί, τὸ διὰ πυρὸς παρελθεῖν, τὸ διὰ κρύους, διὰ πείνης καὶ δίψης, διὰ ὁδοιπορίας πολλῆς, καὶ ἁπλῶς διὰ πασῶν τῶν τοιούτων. Furthermore, among other late sources, a passage in Maximus Tyrius (*Diss.* 39. 3) constructs the (Platonic) image of life as a long road (ὁδόν τινα . . . μακράν), whose end is a *telete* (39. 3. 102–3) and upon which many souls walk and toil: σὺν πολλῷ πόνῳ καὶ ἱδρῶτι ἀνύουσιν καματηραὶ καὶ ἐπίπονοι ψυχαί (39. 3. 111–13). See also Riedweg (1987: 65 n. 177).

ponos is the inescapable prelude to mystic *soteria* (salvation): 'take courage, mystai, for the god has been saved: so we too will be saved from our toils.'[163] In *Frogs* 185 Hades is conceived of as a place where *ponoi* are to be relieved (τίς εἰς ἀναπαύλας ἐκ κακῶν καὶ πραγμάτων;). And, although for the wider section of the audience this may simply be a reference to the forgetfulness of sorrows which traditionally characterizes the dead,[164] the *memyemenoi* would have been able to look forward to the play's action as a sequence moving towards an initiatory 'release from troubles'.[165] When the unfolding of the plot confronts Dionysus with a series of ordeals, correspondingly, the initiates, again, would have felt inclined to look backwards to the god's first toilsome task as a foreshadowing of his role as a mystes who would have to undergo *ponoi* before being able to achieve his ultimate regeneration.

2.10. The Symbol of the Journey

After a long string of jokes focusing on the diversity of roads one might take to descend to Hades (117–35), Dionysus announces his decision to reduplicate the journey of Heracles himself (135–6). Now, the notion of a journey to the other world seems to be a fixed element in afterlife mythology.[166] A good example of its wide diffusion is an impressive funerary stele from Upper Egypt, which preserves the travelling motif in a scheme closely reminiscent of the dramatic enactment of Dionysus' journey in the *Frogs*: the monument depicts a man together with his horse, saddled, as if ready

---

[163] θαρρεῖτε μύσται τοῦ θεοῦ σεσωσμένου. | ἔσται γὰρ ἡμῖν ἐκ πόνων σωτηρία. Cf. Pind. fr. 131a Maehler (on the pious dead) ὄλβιοι δ' ἅπαντες αἴσᾳ λυσιπόνων τελετᾶν. See, most importantly, Orph. fr. 232, 4–5 Kern (of Dionysus) οὕς κ' ἐθέλῃσθα, λύσεις ἔκ τε πόνων χαλεπῶν καὶ ἀπείρονος οἴστρου, and Pl. *Rep.* 365a (of private *teletai*) αἳ τῶν ἐκεῖ κακῶν ἀπολύουσιν ἡμᾶς. See further Tsantsanoglou and Parássoglou (1987).

[164] Dover (1993: ad loc.) compares 'our expression "eternal rest"'.

[165] Cf. the cry 'I have escaped bad, I have found better' (ἔφυγον κακόν, εὗρον ἄμεινον) (Dem. 18. 259) at rituals of mystic initiation in 4th-cent. BC Athens (for the possible blending of cultic features, most notably of Sabazius and Dionysus, in Demosthenes' passage see C. G. Brown 1991: 43–5 esp. with n. 19). Moreover, the formula is also applicable to a variety of initiatory contexts, most importantly, wedding ritual (see Detienne 1977: 116ff., esp. 117 n. 83; Seaford 1994a: 308). Cf. Orph. fr. 229 Kern; Alciphron 4. 17. 8 νὴ τὰ μυστήρια, νὴ τὴν τούτων τῶν κακῶν ἀπαλλαγήν; for more references to the 'release from troubles' mystic motif see Headlam and Thomson (1938; on *Ag.* 1). Zeitlin (1989: 188 n. 69) detects literary reflections in Eur. *Suppl.* 615–16 (Eleusinian context) and Eur. *Ion* 1604–5 (cf. above, n. 151). Cf. Seaford (1994b: 281 on Soph. *El.* 1489–90 κακῶν | μόνον γένοιτο τῶν πάλαι λυτήριον, 'a phrase suggestive of the mystic transition'). See also, most importantly, Pl. *Phaed.* 81a, where the immortal soul arrives at a place where it can be happy, 'freed from error and foolishness and fear and cruel loves and of the rest of the ills which beset mankind (καὶ τῶν ἄλλων κακῶν τῶν ἀνθρωπείων ἀπηλλαγμένη), and, as it is said about the initiated (ὥσπερ δὲ λέγεται κατὰ τῶν μεμυημένων), lives truly for the rest of the time with the gods'.

[166] In the Greek tradition, it goes at least as far back as the Homeric *Nekyia*.

for the journey into the afterlife.[167] Most importantly, however, it seems that the road symbol could be especially evocative for those members of the audience who were initiated into mystic cults. Within the mystic frame of Bacchic *teletai*, the Hipponion gold tablet first springs to mind, warning the deceased initiate that he or she is bound to come to a 'long road' (15 καὶ δὴ καὶ συχνὸν ὁδὸν ἔρχεαι; cf. *Frogs* 402 πολλὴν ὁδόν), a 'sacred' path which is also 'trodden by other illustrious initiates and *bakchoi*' (ἅν τε καὶ ἄλλοι | μύσται καὶ βάκχοι ἱερὰν στείχουσι κλεινοί) (15–16).[168] But within the framework of the Eleusinian ritual too, Dionysus' journey evokes reminiscences of the so called 'Sacred Way', that is, the road which leads neophytes and initiates alike in procession from Athens to Eleusis. Symbolizing, as it does, Demeter's wanderings in search of Core (Foley 1993: 43), this pilgrimage could be conceived of as a cultic analogue of Dionysus' trip in quest of a fertile poet in the *Frogs*. Finally, there is Plutarch's famous fragment (178 Sandbach) which, in comparing the soul's *pathos* at the hour of death to the sufferings of the initiate in mystic *teletai*, talks about 'wanderings astray in the beginning, tiresome walkings in circles, some frightening paths in darkness that lead nowhere'.[169] In the perspective of an Eleusinian *mystes*, then, watching Dionysus' itinerary to Hades on the comic stage might well be a vicarious re-enactment of a memorable experience of his own initiation.[170]

[167] Catalogue no. 35 in Abdalla (1992: 109), who gives as parallels two more funerary stelae, one of which (Roman, 4th cent. AD) shows frontally a man holding an unsaddled horse by the halter (Farid 1973: 25, pl. 17), while the other (dating to 2nd or 1st cent. BC) depicts a young man with a cloak, as if on a journey, holding by the muzzle an unbridled horse. However, Abdalla (1992: 109) himself thinks 'it is unlikely that it [sc. the horse] is included as the means of embarking on the journey to the after life'.

[168] For the specifically Dionysiac flavour of the term *bakchos* see S. G. Cole (1980).

[169] πλάναι τὰ πρῶτα καὶ περιδρομαὶ κοπώδεις καὶ διὰ σκότους τινὲς ὕποπτοι πορεῖαι καὶ ἀτέλεστοι. This image of a way to Hades with σχίσεις τε καὶ τριόδους πολλάς goes back to Pl. *Phaed.* 108a, where Socrates speculates on the passage of the soul to the other world ἀπὸ τῶν θυσιῶν τε καὶ νομίμων τῶν ἐνθάδε τεκμαιρόμενος, i.e. inferring 'from the rites and ceremonies practised here on earth'; Seaford (1986a: 13 with n. 52). In the Platonic myth of Er as well (where mystic imagery is pervasive), when Er's soul left his body, it 'journeyed with a great company' (πορεύεσθαι μετὰ πολλῶν), which reached τόπον τινὰ δαιμόνιον (*Rep.* 614b–c); there, the ever-arriving souls 'appeared to have come as it were from a long journey' (ὥσπερ ἐκ πολλῆς πορείας φαίνεσθαι ἥκειν) (*Rep.* 614e).

[170] There are also scattered literary allusions to a mystic road leading initiates to the Underworld. See e.g. Pind. *Ol.* 2 (an eschatological ode with distinctive mystical colouring; see Lloyd-Jones 1985), where the fulfilment of the road of Zeus (ἔτειλαν Διὸς ὁδόν) up to the tower of Cronus (70) on the Island of the Blessed (71 ἔνθα μακάρων νᾶσον) seems to have a certain mystic ring; see Farnell (1932: 19) who, nevertheless, does not mention Diogenes Laertius 6. 39, where the Islands of the Blessed feature as the well-known afterlife dwelling-place of Eleusinian mystai (μεμνημένοι ἐν ταῖς μακάρων νήσοις ἔσονται). For the road symbol in Parmenides and its possible mystic connotations see Feyerabend (1984). In an Hellenistic poem of unknown authorship (text in Lloyd-Jones 1963; lines 21–2) death is expressed with the image of a 'mystic path' (μυστικὸν οἶμον) leading up to Rhadamanthys (see, however,

2.11. Guidance to the Underworld

Dionysus does not undertake his *katabasis* totally unaided. His half-brother Heracles provides him not only with miscellaneous information on the nether regions, but also with instructions specifically relating to the way he should follow. This section argues that initiates in Bacchic mysteries and in Eleusis were familiar both with the notion of physical guidance as well as with instructions offered to the initiand for his/her journey to the Underworld, familiarity arising either through the ritual itself or through the mythical traditions accompanying the mystic *telete*.

Some Orphic versions of the Eleusinian myth claim that Demeter, in her *katabasis* to the nether regions in search for Core, was guided by Eubulus, the offspring of her own union with Dysaules.[171] In the corpus of Dionysiac legends, correspondingly, Pausanias and Clement of Alexandria preserve a tradition whereby Dionysus, in his descent into Hades in quest of his mother Semele, was at a loss about the way (Clem. Alex. *Protr.* 2. 30 (p. 72 Butterworth) ἠγνόει τὴν ὁδόν) and was guided by a certain Prosymnus (Clement) or Polymnus (Paus. 2. 37. 5 κάθοδον δεῖξαί οἱ Πόλυμνον). Pausanias' account, in particular, is especially instructive, as the site of Dionysus' *kathodos* is the Argive Lerna, a region with strong Demetrian and Dionysiac mythic/ritual/cultic associations.[172] Even if the annual mystic *dromena* mentioned by Pausanias as performed at the lake at night (see above, 2.8(a)) did not include a full-scale mimetic re-enactment of Dionysus' *katabasis*, the mythical cluster of the mysteries of Lerna *does* preserve the element of physical guidance to the Underworld.

Most importantly, however, the element of instruction offered to the deceased initiate is prominent in both the 'A' and 'B' groups of the Bacchic gold leaves. In lines 5–6 of plate A4 (Zuntz) the initiate is hailed and instructed to 'walk on the right-hand side' (δεξιὰν

Lloyd-Jones 1963: 93–4). In Apuleius' *Metamorphoses*, the initiand into the mysteries of Isis asserts that he has 'journeyed through all the elements and come back' (*per omnia vectus elementa remeavi*) (*Met.* 11. 23). Finally, I am inclined to detect an allusion to the mystic way which leads the initiand through *pathos* to salvation in Electra's joyful cry after the fictitious-ness of Orestes' death has been revealed: ἥτις μιᾷ σε τῇδ' ὁδῷ θανόντα τε | καὶ ζῶντ' ἐσεῖδον (Soph. *El.* 1314–15; cf. above, 2.3).

[171] Orph. *h.* 41. 5–8: 'you came to Hades in search of noble Persephone, having taken the chaste son of Dysaules as your guide'; see Richardson (1974: 84). For a discussion of some sources preserving Demeter's other-worldly search see Harrison and Obbink (1986).

[172] See e.g. Paus. 2. 37. 1 (statues of Demeter Prosymne and Dionysus within the sacred grove); Paus. 2. 36. 7 (legend locating Pluto's and Persephone's descent at the lake); Paus. 2. 36. 7 (*telete* enacted in honour of the Lernaean Demeter, Λερναίᾳ . . . Δήμητρι); Plut. *Mor.* 364f (see above, n. 137). However, it would seem that the Eleusinian influences on the Lerna cults are quite late (Nilsson 1906: 289).

ὁδοιπόρει), to the 'sacred meadows and groves of Persephone', while in the group B tablets the initiate is given not only specific information about things he/she will encounter (e.g. B2, 1–2: 'you will find in the house of Hades on your right hand side a fountain, and a white cypress standing next to it'), but also warnings and instructions about how he/she should react on particular occasions (e.g. B2, 3: 'do not come close to this spring'; B2, 5a: 'they [i.e. the guardians] will ask you why you have come'; B2, 6ff.: 'you must say. . .').[173]

2.12. Terror and Ordeals

(a) Terrifying visions

Overcome with fear, as he approaches the meadow of the mystai, the god advises his companion to keep quiet (321–2) before the things performed and heard, terror and silence being recorded as typical reactions of initiands in Eleusis who, 'when the holy rites are being performed and disclosed . . . are immediately attentive in awe and silence'.[174] However, it cannot be emphasized too strongly that a ritual sequence encapsulated in a work of art is not expected to constitute an accurate reflection of the actual ceremony itself. For example, whereas for the real initiands in Eleusis light dissipates terror before the moment of the great revelation, Dionysus is still required to face a variety of threats and tortures, even *after* his encounter with the Mystai and their blissful life. Thus, the first initiatory ordeal Dionysus is required to undergo is to face the terrifying apparition of the shape-changing Empusa (285ff.; see above, 2.6(a)), a psychological experience which tallies well with Plutarch's memorable account of Eleusinian psychology: 'immediately before the end [come] all the terrible things, panic and shivering and sweat, and amazement'.[175] There is a wealth of evidence, albeit late, testifying to the mystic initiand's psychological torment through various kinds of amazements (καταπλήξεις).[176] These may

---

[173] For the texts see Zuntz (1971: 300ff. and 359ff.); for the Hipponion gold tablet of the B group see (first publication) Foti and Pugliese Carratelli (1974); West (1975); Merkelbach (1975); Pugliese Carratelli (1976); Luppe (1978); Guarducci (1985).

[174] δρωμένων δὲ καὶ δεικνυμένων τῶν ἱερῶν προσέχουσιν ἤδη μετὰ φόβου καὶ σιωπῆς (Plut. *Mor.* 81e). Metaneira, a surrogate initiand in the *Hymn to Demeter* (see below, n. 187) falls into silence, panic-stricken by Demeter's epiphany (h. *Dem.* 281–2; cf. her fear at 190), while Demeter herself, an archetypal initiand in the Homeric *Hymn*, sits silent (198) in a procedure which forms the *aition* for the rite of *thronosis* (see 2.13; see further in 6.3). For silence as a typical reaction of initiands, as a high point at mystic rituals, and as a requirement imposed on every mystes see Richardson (1974: 306–7).

[175] Fr. 178 Sandbach εἶτα πρὸ τοῦ τέλους αὐτοῦ τὰ δεινὰ πάντα, φρίκη καὶ τρόμος καὶ ἱδρὼς καὶ θάμβος (tr. Burkert 1987a: 91).

[176] See e.g. Procl. *Theol. Plat.* 3. 18 (p. 64 Budé) ἔκπληξις τῶν μυουμένων; Procl. *In Remp.*

have included not only upsetting visions, but also sounds or tumult, like the sudden *psophos* (noise) that Xanthias pretends to hear in *Frogs* 285.[177] Now, alarming clatter is usually underplayed in scholarly reconstructions of Greek mystic initiations, but, as Bérard (1974: 75–87) has argued in his detailed study of ritually performed divine 'ascents' (*anodoi*), the 'calling-up through knocking', the 'appel cogné', as he characteristically terms it, plays a role of primary importance in ceremonial invocations of chthonic deities from their subterranean abodes. The acoustic code may have been prominent in a wide range of Dionysiac *teletai* as well, where bull-roarers may have been used in order to produce unnerving effects upon the neophytes.[178] Moreover, in Eleusis, according to the testimony of Apollodorus, the ascending vision of Persephone at the culmination of the Eleusinian *telete* (2.8(b)) was accompanied (or perhaps even brought about) by the sound of a gong,[179] the so called *echeion*; its rumbling noise had its replica in the theatrical *echeion* or *bronteion*, a piece of stage-machinery used in classical Greek drama in order to produce nerve-shattering effects (see schol. Ar. *Clouds* 292b. a–c (Holwerda)).[180] Among theatrical remouldings of this initiatory

ii., p. 108, 21–2 (Kroll); Ael. Arist. 22. 2 (Keil): *ekplexis* of the *dromena*; Plut. *Ages*. 24. 7; Strabo 10. 3. 7 (on Corybantic initiation). Furthermore, as Riedweg (1987: 60ff.) argues, a reflection of the fear of initiation may be detected in several Platonic passages, as e.g. *Phdr.* 251a, etc.; see Riedweg (1987: 42–3).

[177] Cf. *Frogs* 492–3 σὺ δ' οὐκ ἔδεισας τὸν ψόφον τῶν ῥημάτων | καὶ τὰς ἀπειλάς;
[178] See Bérard (1974: 83) on Aesch. *Edoni* (a Dionysiac tragedy), fr. 57 Radt ὁ δὲ χαλκοδέτοις κοτύλαις ὀτοβεῖ (6); . . . ταυρόφθογγοι δ' ὑπομυκῶνταί | ποθεν ἐξ ἀφανοῦς φοβεροὶ μῖμοι, | τυπάνου δ' εἰκών, ὥσθ' ὑπογαίου | βροντῆς, φέρεται βαρυταρβής (8–11). Cf. Pind. fr. 70b Maehler on a certain Βρομίου [τελε]τάν with ῥόμβοι τυπάνων (9); a bull-roarer, representing one of the tokens with which baby Dionysus was enticed by the Titans in the Orphic myths, features in a fragmentary papyrus of the 3rd cent. BC from Gurôb 'giving instructions, partly in note form, for a religious rite' (West 1983a: 170; text and tr. 171). On the remoulding of mystic terrifying sounds in satyric drama see Seaford (1984: 42) and on the rumble of the thunderbolt as an element of mystic initiation see now Seaford (1996: 196–7).
[179] Apollodorus, *FGrHist* 244 F110b φησὶ δ' Ἀπολλόδωρος Ἀθήνησι τὸν ἱεροφάντην τῆς Κόρης ἐπικαλουμένης ἐπικρούειν τὸ καλούμενον ἠχεῖον (cf. above, n. 152); see also Burkert (1983: 286 with n. 57).
[180] In other initiatory frames, a loud banging (ψόφῳ προσπεσόντι) precedes the striking of Timarchus' head after his (initiatory) *katabasis* into the cave of Trophonius (Plut. *Mor.* 590b). It is also interesting to mention at this point that in the so-called *Confession of St Cyprian* (a very late text composed under the reign of the Emperor Julian, when paganism was still a living reality, and in which the author's description of mystic rites 'is founded on the knowledge and the ideas of the fourth century AD'; Nilsson 1947:168), we hear of initiation 'in sounds of converse and in the recounting of noises (ἠχοῦς ὁμιλιῶν [-ίαν corr. Preller] καὶ ψόφων διήγησιν)' (text in Nilsson 1947: 168). If we can trust the author, late pagan mystic tradition used *psophoi* in initiation ceremonies. Note also, again, the confused clatter (though not explicitly linked with fear) testified for the Eleusinian initiation, as e.g. in Plut. *Mor.* 81d (quoted above, n. 146); *Mor.* 943c θορύβῳ καὶ πτοήσει; cf. Pl. *Phdr.* 248b1–2 θόρυβος οὖν καὶ ἅμιλλα καὶ ἱδρὼς ἔσχατος γίγνεται.

ordeal, one could single out the comic apparition of the Νεφέλαι in the *Clouds*, pre-empted by a 'bellowing, divinely awesome thundering' (βροντῆς μυκησαμένης θεοσέπτου) (292). In tragic drama, correspondingly, there is the alarming, infernal sound, the *ktypos* of Zeus, which calls Oedipus to his apotheosis at the end of the Sophoclean *Oedipus at Colonus*,[181] in a scene heavily indebted to mystic imagery.

As for φάσματα (spectres, apparitions) and δείματα (terrors), we learn—even if from late sources, such as Origen and Proclus—that these had a conspicuous role to play in Bacchic *teletai*.[182] At Eleusis,[183] correspondingly, on the strength of such passages as Idomeneus, *FGrHist* 338 F2 and Lucian 19. 22, C. G. Brown (1991: 42–3) argued that in the course of the Great Mysteries 'at a relatively early point in the proceedings the initiands were terrified by the appearance of a spectre like that which terrorizes Dionysus and Xanthias in the *Frogs*' (cf. above, 2.6(a)). But most importantly still, with respect to literary reflections of the same form of *pathos*, I would now like to compare the ordeal of terrifying visions in the *Frogs* to the experience undergone by the Dionysiac initiand Pentheus in Euripides' *Bacchae*.

Playing tricks with Pentheus' mind, Dionysus/the Stranger created a phantom (or a light)[184] in the palace's courtyard, thus tempting the man to enter in the vain pursuit of an hallucination (*Bacch.* 630–1). The scholiast on Aristophanes' *Wasps* 1363 comments that 'those who have already been initiated alarm those who are about to be initiated', and, if this remark refers to a specific moment in the initiatory experience,[185] it may have something to do

---

[181] See Soph. *OC* 1606 κτύπησε μὲν Ζεὺς χθόνιος; cf. 1456 ἔκτυπεν αἰθήρ; 1462–3 μέγας ἐρείπεται | κτύπος ἄφατος (followed by extreme fear, as in mystic initiations); see Kerényi (1967: 84–6).

[182] See primarily, Celsus *ap.* Origen (*Cels.* 4. 10) and Procl. *In Remp.* ii, p. 181, 5–8 (Kroll). Note also Procl. *In Remp.* ii, p. 181, 7 (Kroll), where the many *phasmata* of which Dionysus ἡγεῖται are said to be δράκουσιν ὁμοίως ἐμπίπτοντα. The initiand's terror in the course of Bacchic initiation is memorably expressed on the face of the startled girl in the Great Frieze of the 'Villa of the Mysteries' in Pompeii; see Seaford (1978: 66–8).

[183] For happy (*eudaimona*) *phasmata* in Eleusinian initiation see the sources cited above, in n. 151; see further, Graf (1974: 134 n. 34).

[184] The reading of the manuscripts is φῶς, whereas Dodds (1960), Kopff (1982), and Diggle (1994) adopt Jacob's emendation φάσμ'; Seaford (1981: 256) opts for the first, comparing the 'marvellous light' of Eleusis; see also now Seaford (1996: ad 630–1); however, the controversy does not affect my point substantially since, whether phantom or light, the text is explicit with respect to the fact that Pentheus perceives an apparition, a human-shaped vision.

[185] Schol. *Wasps* 1363b (Koster) τοὺς γὰρ μέλλοντας μυεῖσθαι οἱ προλαβόντες (v.l. οἱ μεμυη-μένοι) δεδίττονται. Now MacDowell (1971: 309) and Richardson (1974: 215) are most probably right in detecting 'a general reference to αἰσχρολογία as a preliminary to the Mysteries' in *Wasps* 1362–3, but, as the scholion refers exclusively to fear or rather to the action of *causing* fear, I am inclined to relate it, as A. M. Bowie (1993a: 236 n. 45) does, to the terrifying experiences an initiand is required to undergo.

with the relation of the mystagogue to the initiand under his care.[186] I would, therefore, like to suggest that, if in the *Bacchae* it is Dionysus who leads Pentheus, the neophyte, to his ordeal, Xanthias, as a comic mystagogue in the Empusa scene[187] fulfils a similar role as a creator of disturbing illusions in the *Frogs*: the slave's witty play with his master's cowardice could be deciphered as the comic analogue of the Euripidean god's contemptuous amusement at the initiand's excitement and agitation (esp. *Bacch.* 616–17, 620–1, 630–1), while his full power over his master's emotions would correspond to the tragic god's complete control over Pentheus' emotional turmoil. Moreover, particular attention deserves to be drawn to Xanthias' attempt to calm the fear he had previously inspired in the initiand Dionysus: 'be of good courage (θάρρει); all has turned out well for us' (302). For Xanthias' initiative, reflecting, as it does, an intrinsic element in a variety of initiatory sequences, that is, the exhortation to courage addressed to the mystai after their ordeal (cf. 2.9), could be coupled with a similar gesture of Dionysus/the Stranger in the *Bacchae*, that is, his promptness to reassure the panic-stricken (*Bacch.* 604) Chorus of Asiatic women after the palace's collapse which had been caused by his illusion-making power.[188] Besides, the analogies between the pairs of initiator–neophyte in *Frogs* and *Bacchae*, exemplified in the roles of Xanthias and Dionysus, the Stranger/god and Pentheus respectively, may be found to extend even beyond the narrow boundaries of the Empusa scene.

Astonished at his companion's dispassionate and mocking tone after another dangerous encounter with the Underworld Doorkeeper, the terrified Dionysus of the comic stage asks: 'did you

---

[186] For the responsibilities of the mystagogue see e.g. Riedweg (1987: 59).

[187] It is actually very difficult to decide whether Xanthias plays the role of a fellow-initiand (cf. above, n. 130) or that of a *mystagogos*; some moments in the play's sequence would argue for the former (e.g. the whipping scene), while others would privilege the latter (e.g. the Empusa scene). However, given the fact that Xanthias is after all only a secondary figure and, more significantly still, that our text is not a sacred document, consistency and verisimilitude in every detail are not to be expected; the poet adapts his roles in whatever way it fits the narrative and the protagonist at any given moment. Besides, in texts remoulding initiation ritual it is possible that the role and experiences of the initiand are shared between more than one character. In the Homeric *Hymn to Demeter*, for example, it is not only Core and Demeter who experience the initiatory phases of separation, limen, and reintegration, but also Metaneira (Foley 1993: 52; cf. Richardson 1974: 208–9), who reproduces the quintessential mystic reaction of silence, awe, and fear (281–3; cf. Richardson 1974: 208–9, 306–8), and the baby Demophon, 'perhaps a symbolic first initiate' (Foley 1993: 48), a surrogate *pais aph' hestias*. In Euripides' *Ion* too, initiatory experiences are shared between Ion and Creusa (Zeitlin 1989).

[188] *Bacch.* 606–7 †ἀλλ' ἐξανίστατε† | σῶμα καὶ θαρσεῖτε σαρκὸς ἐξαμείψασαι τρόμον. See Firm. Mat. *Err. Prof. Rel.* 22. 1 (quoted above, n. 163). For possible reflections of the exhortation to courage formula in Plato see Joly (1955). For an interpretation of Euripides' passage in this light see Seaford (1981: 258), who does not, however, mention the comic reflection in the *Frogs*. See also Eur. *Her.* 624–7 (with Seaford 1994a: 379 n. 48).

really not dread the sound of his language and his menaces?' (492–3). But within the range of expectations created by an initiatory ritual frame, Xanthias' defiant reply 'By Zeus, I didn't even give it a thought' (οὐ μὰ Δί' οὐδ' ἐφρόντισα) (493), emphasizing, as it does, his total apathy and lack of share in the initiand's terror, associates him with the Dionysus of Tragedy, the calm spectator of Pentheus' turmoil in the *Bacchae* (621–2; cf. 636). To put it in another way, within the initiatory frame of the *Frogs*, the comic Xanthias' boasting οὐδ' ἐφρόντισα fulfils the same ritual function as the tragic god's appearance on the stage 'not having given Pentheus a thought' (Πενθέως οὐ φροντίσας) (*Bacch.* 637).

(b) *Dismemberment*

Now, what probably constituted the most memorable experience of an Eleusinian/Dionysiac mystes is the *pathos* he/she was required to undergo, as a fragment of Aristotle[189] would suggest. An elaborate scene of prospective *pathos* in the *Frogs* is deployed in lines 464ff. where, as has already been mentioned in 2.6(b), the god is confronted with the grim menace of *sparagmos*: the enraged Doorkeeper threatens him that a viper with one-hundred heads will rend his inward parts to pieces (διασπαράξει) (474), a Tartesian eel will lay hold of his lungs, while Tithrasian Gorgons will tear apart (διασπάσονται) (477) his kidneys and intestine, dripping with blood. However, Bacchic initiands in the comedy's first audience could not have missed the specifically Dionysiac connotations of *diasparassein* and *diaspan*, for dismemberment is the typical death of Dionysus' opponents or Dionysiac initiands in myth,[190] as well as a prominent feature of commemorative maenadic mystic ritual.[191] But, more importantly still, *sparagmos* is the specific form of *pathos* the initiand Dionysus was subjected to in the Orphic tale of his death/rebirth,[192]

[189] Περὶ Φιλοσοφίας, fr. 15 Ross τοὺς τελουμένους οὐ μαθεῖν τι δεῖν ἀλλὰ παθεῖν καὶ διατεθῆναι. I hope to discuss this fragment elsewhere.

[190] Dionysiac opponents: e.g. Lycurgus, Actaeon, or infants torn apart by frenzied maenads (with frequent depictions of the act in vase-painting as well); see West (1983a: 147–8 with n. 26); Seaford (1994a: 291–2, with sources indicating the regular employment of διασπαράσσειν and διασπᾶν). Dionysiac initiands: Pentheus (see Seaford 1994a: 283–93). I discuss *sparagmos* further from a Dionysiac initiatory perspective in 4.8.

[191] See primarily Phot. s.v. νεβρίζειν . . . διασπᾶν νεβρούς· κατὰ μίμησιν τοῦ περὶ τὸν Διόνυσον πάθους; cf. Plut. *Mor.* 291a, 299e, 417c (ἡμέρας ἀποφράδας καὶ σκυθρωπάς, ἐν αἷς ὠμοφαγίαι καὶ διασπασμοί). See also Seaford (1994a: 283 n. 15).

[192] West (1983a: 174–5) argues that Athens of the late 5th cent. BC would have provided 'a suitable milieu' for the composition of the Eudemian theogony which preserves this form of the myth. Besides, some further evidence (Burkert 1983: 225 n. 43) may be adduced in corroboration of this version's early date. For some sources referring to the *sparagmos* (using actually the terms διασπᾶν or (δια)σπαράττειν), see e.g. Orph. frs. 35, 210 (*passim*), 211 and 214 Kern; Origen, *Cels.* 4. 17. 1, etc. (see further, 4.8). It would seem that the Orphic myth of Dionysus/Zagreus was not restricted to Orphic mystic circles; a testimony to its wider

probably a sacred text of mystic rites accompanying a ritual re-enactment of the divine child's initiation.[193]

In the Orphic passion the dismembered Dionysus is reborn[194] and, in so far as we are willing to pay heed to the connotations of the words οὔκουν ἀναστήσει and ἀνέστην ('won't you rise up?'; 'I've risen up')[195] uttered by Xanthias and Dionysus further on in the text (lines 480 and 490 respectively), we can legitimately speculate that a fifth-century audience of *memyemenoi* could have read the scene as the reflection of a sequence of Dionysiac *sparagmos* and resurrection.[196]

The scholiast at *Frogs* 479, that is, Dionysus' cry 'invoke the god' (κάλει θεόν), offers a crucial bit of information which helps us to visualize the scene against the background of the Dionysiac festival of the Lenaea. It reads as follows:

> In the Lenaean festival of Dionysus the torchbearer, holding a torch, says: 'Invoke the god' and the listeners reply: 'O Iacchus, son of Semele, bestower of wealth'.[197]

Now, the dearth and the confusion of the sources on the Lenaean rites is a generally accepted fact. However, there may be some ground for allowing the speculation that *inter alia* the festival re-enacted the god's dismemberment and resurrection in a sequence perhaps parallel to that which underlay the rituals of the Dionysiac groups of the so-called Hosioi and the Thyiads of Delphi,[198] very probably commemorating Dionysus' dismemberment and rising from the dead.[199] The most precious of our sources here is a gloss on

diffusion is the Leningrad Eleusinian pelike (*ARV*² 1476, 1: *LIMC*, s.v. Demeter, 404: *LIMC*, s.v. Dionysos, 528; *c.*340–330 BC), whose one side depicts Eleusinian deities (including Dionysus and Heracles), while side B portrays an infant Dionysus on Demeter's lap. If the scene on side B can be identified (cf. Simon 1966) as the birth of Dionysus/Zagreus, it is important that it belongs to the same iconographic complex with the purely Eleusinian picture on the vase's other side. However, the interpretation of the pelike's iconography is controversial (for bibliography see *LIMC*, s.v. Demeter, 404).

[193] West (1983*a*: 140–75), preceded by Harrison (1927: 13–22) and Thomson (1946: esp. 110–13), argued that the myth reflects a ritual of initiation, 'presumably' into 'a Bacchic society' (West 1983*a*: 150), the god thus taking the role of an archetypal initiand who has to die so that he can be reborn (see *contra* Detienne 1979*b*: 80). In a papyrus fragment from Gurôb that Tierney (1922; text 77–8) interprets as a description of Orphic/Dionysiac initiatory ritual, we can perhaps read (line 4): τὸν θεὸν ἔτεμον (ibid.: 83), a reading which would make dismemberment of Dionysus/Zagreus one of the central acts of a mystes' initiation.

[194] See e.g. Orph. fr. 36 Kern (διασπασθεὶς ὑπὸ τῶν Τιτάνων . . . ἀνεβίω) and Plut. *Mor.* 996c.

[195] Of course within the comic scene with the prosaic sense of 'getting up'.

[196] For this suggestion cf. Elderkin (1955: 19).

[197] Ἐν τοῖς Ληναϊκοῖς ἀγῶσι τοῦ Διονύσου ὁ δᾳδοῦχος κατέχων λαμπάδα λέγει "καλεῖτε θεόν" καὶ οἱ ὑπακούοντες βοῶσι "Σεμελήι' Ἴακχε πλουτοδότα" (test. 9 in Pickard-Cambridge 1988: 27).

[198] Where the remains of Dionysus were interred; for sources see West (1983*a*: 151 n. 31).

[199] (Hosioi) Plut. *Mor.* 365a καὶ θύουσιν οἱ Ὅσιοι θυσίαν ἀπόρρητον ἐν τῷ ἱερῷ τοῦ Ἀπόλλωνος (with Burkert 1983: 125). (Thyiads) Plut. *Mor.* 365a ὅταν αἱ Θυιάδες ἐγείρωσι τὸν Λικνίτην (with Nilsson 1957: 39–40, and Seaford 1981: 266–7). For discussions of the very slender (and

the word ληναΐζοντας in Clement's *Protrepticus* 1. 2. This scholion testifies to the existence at the Lenaea of a 'rustic song sung on the vinepress which contained Dionysus' *sparagmos*',[200] and, therefore, allows us to glimpse the first part of the sequence. As to the second part of the ceremony, a well-known vase in the Vlasto collection (*ARV²* 1249, 13) depicts two women flanking the adult Dionysus' mask placed in a winnowing fan (λίκνον). Seaford (1981: 267 n. 135) observes that this mask gives the strong impression of 'a dis-membered head' and, therefore, infers that the rite depicted may well have been analogous to the Delphic ἔγερσις, the resurrection, of Dionysus Liknites (1981: 266–7). It is unfortunate, however, that, due to the paucity of solid evidence, Seaford's further suggestion that the ritual may have been part of the Lenaea festival cannot be unequivocally accepted: (i) although the presence of the mask links the vase with the so-called corpus of 'Lenäenvasen', these have not been conclusively attributed to a particular Athenian festival to date,[201] and (ii) the vase in question is a chous, a shape very strongly, although not exclusively, connected with the Anthesteria.[202] One should be, therefore, open to the possibility that Dionysus' resur-rection—if actually enacted at some festal moment of the ritual calendar—was ceremonially performed on the day of the Choes,[203] for which Philostratus (*Vit. Apoll.* 4. 21) attests the existence of Dionysiac masquerades carried out 'in the midst of Orpheus' epic poetry and incantations' (μεταξὺ τῆς Ὀρφέως ἐποποιΐας τε καὶ θεολογίας).[204] Nevertheless, should the argument weigh conclusively in favour of the Lenaea,[205] the implications would be of primary importance, as *Frogs* 464 ff. would prove a highly self-referential

mostly late) evidence about the Lenaean festival as containing mystic elements see Nilsson (1906: 276–9); Pickard-Cambridge (1988: 35).

[200] Schol. Clem. Alex. *Protr.* 1. 2 (Pickard-Cambridge 1988: 28, test. 19 (Lenaea)) ἀγροικικὴ ᾠδὴ ἐπὶ τῷ ληνῷ ᾀδομένη, ἣ καὶ αὐτὴ περιεῖχε τὸν Διονύσου σπαραγμόν.

[201] For the debate see Frickenhaus (1912); Nilsson (1916); Wrede (1928); Coche de la Ferté (1951); Pickard-Cambridge (1988: 30–4); Durand and Frontisi-Ducroux (1982); Frontisi-Ducroux (1986, 1991); Hamilton (1992: 134 ff.).

[202] Burkert (1983: 237) connects with the Anthesteria another chous (fig. 2 in Boyancé 1960–1: 109), where a maenad pours a libation on a huge Dionysiac mask set up in a cave. In Burkert's (1983: 237) reading, this scene would give visual expression to the ritual symbolic act of restoring (bringing up from a subterranean *antron*?) 'that which had previously been dismembered and destroyed in an unspeakable sacrifice.'

[203] On the other hand, however, it cannot be emphasized too strongly that no independent (literary or other) evidence exists which would securely associate the imagery of the choes with the festive events taking place on the Choes day itself.

[204] As Burkert (1983: 226) understands this passage, it seems to be connected with the Orphic Dionysus' myth, performed on the day of the Choes. However, it is, of course, open to serious doubt whether this late evidence conveys anything at all from the enactments of the Choes in classical times. Cf. Introd., Sect. 1.

[205] Cf. also a couple of inscriptions mentioned in Seaford (1994a: 262 n. 122).

scene, remoulding in a distinctively parodic/comic way its own ritual background. In other words, its Lenaean overtones would have been even more evocative in a comedy performed at the Lenaean festival itself: to the eyes of the classical Athenian *theatai* what seems to us obscure and latent in this scene would have presented an easily detectable, familiar series of ritual allusions.

(c) *Flagellation and ritual degradation*

If Dionysus is merely threatened with *sparagmos* in lines 473–8, he is actually beaten at the threshold of Pluto's and Persephone's palace. There is some scanty information concerning beating in Dionysiac mystic rites,[206] but, regretfully, the only virtually uncontroversial piece of evidence on flagellation in a Bacchic initiatory context is of a quite late date, namely, the famous flagellation scene in the Villa dei Misteri in Pompeii. However, if the whipping scene is unparalleled in a Dionysiac/Eleusinian context *qua* flagellation,[207] it is firmly paralleled as an indication of the initiand's total humiliation and degradation (see above, 2.4(d)), that is, as a manifestation of the 'world upside-down'.

In the *Hymn to Demeter*, for example, it is Demeter herself who, as a prototype initiand in her own mystic rites, suffers a spectacular reversal of her divine role and status: a deity, radiant and beautiful, untouched by age (cf. above 1.6(b)), she assumes the guise and social position of an elderly, graceless woman (101–2), badly in need of human pity (137) and protection. Powerful and awesome though she is among Olympus' divinities, she begs to enter into servitude to a human house (138–40),[208] and finally places herself under the orders (226) of a mortal woman, accepting, as she does, the humble role of a nurse to a human child. Besides, as if she were a part of

---

[206] Beating features a couple of times in representations of Pentheus' death; see e.g. Philippart (1930), nos. 133 (rf. cup, 4th cent. BC, beating with a thyrsus), 144 (Roman sarcophagus, beating with a javelin), 145 with fig. 10 (Roman sarcophagus, 2nd cent. AD, beating with a club).

[207] Even if Plautus' *Aulularia* 408 ff. (*fustibus male contuderunt* (409): Congrio complains of the beatings he and his disciples got at a colloquium of Bacchanals) can be considered as a hint to an ordeal of Bacchic initiation, the passage is still late and the allusion quite uncertain. Simon (1961: 135) mentions the beating of women at the sanctuary of Dionysus in Alea (Paus. 8. 23. 1), but despite the fact that Pausanias offers as a parallel to the rite the flogging of Spartan ephebes at the altar of Artemis Orthia (καθὰ καὶ οἱ Σπαρτιατῶν ἔφηβοι παρὰ τῇ Ὀρθίᾳ) (cf. 2.6(c)), no independent evidence exists to place it securely within an initiatory context. Finally, there is, of course, Daphnis' beating in Longus 2. 14 (with Merkelbach 1962: 207), but once again, we are on shaky ground, as the case for Daphnis as a religious *boukolos*, a Dionysiac initiand *par excellence*, is, to say the least, by no means an uncontested issue; for an interesting discussion see Geyer (1977: 179–83 and 188 ff.). For evidence of Roman sarcophagi see Merkelbach (1988: 114).

[208] Cf. 140–4, where Demeter enumerates the variety of domestic tasks which she would happily perform.

humankind herself, she is advised to accept ungrudgingly the lot given to men by gods (147–8), a piece of traditional morality deeply entrenched in archaic and classical Greek thought. Finally, her experience of ravaging grief at Persephone's loss draws her decisively into the realm of mortals, for whom death and the sorrow of death are universal, inescapable conditions of existence (cf. Foley 1993: 88). In the Bacchic sphere, correspondingly, Pentheus, the prototype initiand in the *Bacchae*, suffers an analogous ritual degradation. Much dreaded king (see e.g. *Bacch*. 668–71, 775–6), head of the royal house of Thebes, he will be led in feminine attire through the streets of his own city, exposed to the mockery of his own subjects. As Dionysus/the Stranger plans it, 'After those threats with which he was so fierce, I want him made the laughing-stock of Thebes (χρῄζω δέ νιν γέλωτα Θηβαίοις ὀφλεῖν), paraded through the streets, a woman' (*Bacch*. 854–6). His humiliation stems not only from gender reversal but also from his transformation into the figure which best epitomizes the negation or perversion of order in both *oikos* and civilized *polis* alike, a maenad (Seaford 1993). Besides, it seems that ritual degradation was a regular feature of *myesis* in the Eleusinian mysteries as well. According to some of our sources (e.g. Hesychius, s.v. *gephyris*), masked figures[209] sitting at the bridge of the river Cephisus, a physical boundary between Athens and Eleusis, levelled abuse and obscenities at those among the mystai in procession who happened to be citizens prominent in the *polis'* social life. And, most importantly, this particular manifestation of initiatory humiliation is reflected in the *Frogs* as well (416–30), when the Chorus of Initiates, after having prayed to Demeter to allow them to 'play' and to 'jest' in a manner worthy of her festival (393–4 τῆς σῆς ἑορτῆς ἀξίως | παίσαντα καὶ σκώψαντα . . .), start firing abuse against individuals well known in the *polis*.[210]

2.13. *The Experience of Bliss*

Looking at the bright side of initiation now, Plutarch's fragment 178 (Sandbach) offers a glimpse of the delights the initiates encounter after having survived the terror and the darkness:

And then some wonderful light comes to meet you, pure regions and meadows are there to greet you, with sounds and dances and solemn,

---

[209] It is unclear whether these were male or female, one or many.

[210] See A. M. Bowie (1993*a*: 239–40); Richardson (1974: 214); Graf (1974: 45–50). *Contra*, Dover (1993) who, noting a 'striking formal resemblance' (247) to fr. 99 K–A from Eupolis' *Demes* (lines 1–20), denies Eleusinian connotations and suggests (248) that 'purely theatrical precedent is an adequate explanation.'

sacred words and holy views; and there the initiate, perfect by now, set free and loose from all bondage, walks about, crowned with a wreath, celebrating the festival together with the other sacred and pure people, and he looks down on the uninitiated, unpurified crowd in this world in mud and fog beneath his feet. (tr. Burkert 1987a: 91–2)

But, as we have already seen in 2.12(a), a play's plot cannot be expected to reflect a cultic sequence in its ritually performed order. So, Dionysus meets the blissful, dazzling light of the mystic torches which illuminate the dramatized nocturnal *telete* (313–14, 340–1, 344, 350; cf. 155) *before* having to face the Underworld Doorkeeper or being flagellated at the threshold of Persephone's dwellings. Similarly, it is *before* he is subjected to ordeals that he feels attracted by the Chorus's playful mood and dance, as he admits in lines 414a–15: 'I, for my part, feel like following her, and I'd love to join in and play and dance' (ἐγὼ δ' ἀεί πως φιλακόλου | θός εἰμι καὶ μετ' αὐτῆς | παίζων χορεύειν βούλομαι).

Now, burning of torches in imitation of Demeter's torchlit search for Core (*h. Dem.* 47–8) is one of the most conspicuous and impressive features of the Eleusinian initiation ritual, both at the Iacchus procession and the *pannychis* as well as at the very closure of the rites (2.14). In this respect, Dionysus' passage through a torchlit ritual at the meadow of the mystai in the *Frogs* is very likely to evoke the happy memories of every initiate into the Mysteries of Eleusis.[211] Moreover, a wealth of sources indicates that *paidia* and dance distil a vital experience of initiands in a variety of mystic *teletai* of Graeco-Roman antiquity.[212] Lucian, for example, in his treatise *On the Dance* claims that in the times of old there was no initiatory ceremony performed without dancing:

I forbear to say that not a single ancient mystery-cult can be found that is without dancing (τελετὴν οὐδεμίαν ἀρχαίαν ἔστιν εὑρεῖν ἄνευ ὀρχήσεως), since they were established, of course, by Orpheus and Musaeus, the best dancers of that time, who included it in their prescriptions as something exceptionally beautiful to be initiated with rhythm and dancing (σὺν ῥυθμῷ καὶ ὀρχήσει μυεῖσθαι). To prove that this is so, although it behoves me to observe silence about the rites on account of the uninitiate, nevertheless

---

[211] The 'fire' of Eleusis is such a quintessential part of the rite that it becomes virtually synonymous with the initiatory *telete* itself; see e.g. Himerius 29. 1 ἤγαγε δὲ ἄρα ὁ τοῦ πυρὸς τοῦ κατ' Ἐλευσῖνα πόθος καὶ Ἀνάχαρσιν τὸν Σκύθην ἐπὶ μυστήρια; id. 60. 4; Galen 13, p. 271f. Kühn μὰ τὸ ἐν Ἐλευσῖνι πῦρ; *Pap. della R. Univ. Milano* (1937), 20, pp. 176–7. Cf. Richardson (1974: 233) on Hippolytus' phrase ὑπὸ πολλῷ πυρί (*Ref. Haer.* 5. 8. 40 αὐτὸς ὁ ἱεροφάντης . . . νυκτὸς ἐν Ἐλευσῖνι ὑπὸ πολλῷ πυρὶ τελῶν τὰ μεγάλα καὶ ἄρρητα μυστήρια), as referring to 'the sudden blaze of torches' inside the Telesterion.

[212] See Boyancé (1937: 88–91), stressing the importance of *paidia* and dance in initiation ceremonies; to the passages he discusses add Dio Chrys. *Or.* 12. 33 and Pl. *Euth.* 277d–e. See further Riedweg (1987: 58 n. 144 with detailed list of sources) and Burkert (1983: 288: n. 65).

there is one thing that everybody has heard; namely, that those who let out the mysteries in conversation are commonly said to 'dance them out' (ἐξορχεῖσθαι). (Luc. 45. 15)

Similarly, in the *Frogs*, the prime enjoyment of Eleusinian *mystai* in the Underworld derives from dancing, an activity which also links them with Iacchus, the 'lover of dances' (φιλοχορευτά) (403, 408, 413), whom they invoke to take part in their *choroi* (326 ἐλθέ . . . χορεύσων; cf. 334–6, 395–7). Besides, the privilege to join in the mystic dances becomes for the initiates of this play a marker of identity which separates them promptly from those who are not *memyemenoi*: participation in the blessed *choroi* is expressly forbidden (354 κἀξίστασθαι τοῖς ἡμετέροισι χοροῖσιν) to anyone who 'has neither seen nor danced the rites of the noble Muses' (356 γενναίων ὄργια Μουσῶν μήτ' εἶδεν μήτ' ἐχόρευσεν; cf. 5.2). Nevertheless, a fifth-century Greek audience would have been able to perceive an 'Eleusinian' play's concentration on dancing as a natural reflection of the actual mystic rites of Demeter and Core. For these are organized to a very large extent around *choreia*, as dancing takes place both during the Iacchus procession (Richardson 1974: 214) and on its arrival at Eleusis, during the *pannychis* around the well Callichoron.[213] Moreover, in the legendary cluster of Eleusis too, the archetypal hierophant of myth, Eumolpus, is portrayed on some vases dancing (Burkert 1983: 288 n. 66), while, similarly to their fictive counterparts in the Aristophanic *Frogs*, initiates hope that in their afterlife 'they will go on playing and dancing (παίζοντες καὶ χορεύοντες) in Hades in places full of brightness' (Plut. *Mor.* 1105b). Within the Bacchic circle, correspondingly, initiates would have been able to perceive Dionysus' attraction by the Chorus's *paidia* as a reflection of his own initiatory bewitchment by the 'limb-bending toys' (παίγνια καμπεσίγυια) that the Titans offered to him in myth (Orph. fr. 34 Kern).[214] And, as far as dancing is concerned, it would appear that *choreia* is one of the most conspicuous manifestations of Dionysiac identity, as a vast number of Dionysiac / maenadic vases and a variety of texts attest. Of particular interest here are some late Bacchic funerary epigrams, which imagine the deceased initiate either as joining in the dance or even as leading it, at the invitation

---

[213] This is probably one of the oldest elements of the ritual; cf. Paus. 1. 38. 6 (the women first honoured Demeter with song and dances around this well). Dancing around the Callichoron is certainly alluded to in *Frogs* 450–1 τὸν ἡμέτερον τρόπον | τὸν καλλιχορώτατον (cf. 371).

[214] For the myth of Dionysus and the Titans as reflecting initiation see above, n. 193. An inscription from Eleusis attributes to Dionysus himself the characterization παραπαίζων; see Kourouniotes (1923: 171–4), who explains *parapaizon* as *sympaizon*, and offers an excellent defence of the appropriateness of the title for Dionysus.

of Dionysus himself.²¹⁵ But, more importantly, due to their early date, a couple of Platonic passages become invaluable testimonies to the centrality of dancing in initiatory Dionysiac ritual practice. In the first place, there is the much quoted passage from Plato's *Laws* (815c–d), which brands as 'not suitable for citizens' (οὐκ ἔστι πολιτικόν)

all the dancing that is of a Bacchic kind (ὅση μὲν βακχεία τ᾽ ἐστὶν καὶ τῶν ταύταις ἑπομένων) and cultivated by those who indulge in drunken imitations of Pans, Sileni and Satyrs (as they call them), when performing certain rites of expiation and initiation.

And secondly, there is a passage from the *Euthydemus* (277d–e) where Socrates refers to the Corybantic initiation ceremony, the so-called *thronosis*, as being performed precisely through *choreia* and *paidia*:

because it is there *par excellence* that one would encounter dancing and playing (χορεία . . . καὶ παιδιά) (as you know) if you happen to have been initiated.

And, although Hellenistic or later reliefs portraying Dionysus himself enthroned as a mystes with Corybantes dancing all around him in arms²¹⁶ are unequalled as tangible reflections of the merging of Bacchic/Corybantic *teletai*, the parodos of Euripides' *Bacchae* too (120–34) may readily confirm the 'syncretism' between Dionysiac and Corybantic elements in the late fifth century BC (see Dodds 1960: ad loc.).

Finally, the special significance of Dionysus' initiatory attraction by the Chorus's *paidia* and dancing can only come into relief if placed within the wider context of fifth-century Dionysiac drama. For it would seem that in the tragic dramatizations of Bacchic initiation dancing is not the joyful, frolicking activity of the Aristophanic mystai, but, more frequently, an ominous participation in Dionysus' frenzied *teletai*. In Euripides' *Bacchae*, for example, the quintessence of the Dionysiac experience, such as perceived not only by Dionysus/the Stranger and his faithful Chorus

---

²¹⁵ See e.g. *CIL* iii. 686 (a late Latin epigram in verse from Philippi in Macedonia; see Vollgraff 1948 for a full discussion), referring to Bacchic mystic other-worldly dances which the deceased child is invited to join as a satyr (17–19), after having been restored to life in Elysium (12). Cf. a funerary epigram from Tusculum (Merkelbach 1971), concluding with the deceased girl's words: . . . Διόνυσος ὁ Βάκχιος ἐν θιάσοισιν | ἡγήτειραν ἐμὲ σπείρης ἐνέβησσε χορεύειν (lines 6–7).

²¹⁶ See e.g. the scene depicted on the frieze (stone a. λ. 13) of the Hellenistic altar of Dionysus in Cos (see Stambolides 1987: 110, 161, with pl. 32γ); Dionysus and the Couretes on a sacrificial frieze from the *orchestra* at the theatre of Perge in Pamphylia (late 2nd cent. BC; see *AJA* 92 (1988), 116–17); Roman reliefs and coins from Asia Minor (Stambolides 1987: 151 with refs.); an ivory pyxis at Bologna (*LIMC*, s.v. Dionysos, 267).

of Asiatic women, but also by Pentheus, Cadmus, and Teiresias, is dancing the mystic rites of this god.[217]

Moreover, tragic Dionysiac dancing can be the gruesome punishment inflicted on the sceptics and the god's opponents, as a means of dragging them forcefully into his sacred *teletai*. Thus, Thebes, which is still 'uninitiated' into the 'Dionysiac revelries' (*Bacch.* 40 ἀτέλεστον οὖσαν τῶν ἐμῶν βακχευμάτων) will soon be seized by a collective dancing mania (*Bacch.* 114 αὐτίκα γᾶ πᾶσα χορεύσει), just as everybody else among barbaric tribes is already engaged in the choral dancing of the orgies of the god (*Bacch.* 482 πᾶς ἀναχορεύει βαρβάρων τάδ᾽ ὄργια; cf. 21–2). Furthermore, both Dionysiac and Eleusinian mystic dancing can also be in Tragedy a cosmic dance, a celebration encompassing all the elements of nature. In Euripides' *Ion*, for example, Iacchus, the god 'much sung of' (1074–5 τὸν πολύυ- | μνον θεόν), is envisaged (1074–85) as a witness of the dance of entire nature in honour of 'the gold-crowned Core and her awesome mother' (1085–6) at Eleusis. Now, of course, the Mystai in the *Frogs* evoke the impressive picture of Dionysus as the 'light-bringing star of the nocturnal rite' (νυκτέρου τελετῆς φωσφόρος ἀστήρ) (343), qualification which, in the literary horizon of fifth-century theatregoers, would have recalled the cosmic image of *Antigone* 1146–7, where Dionysus was invoked as 'leader of the dance of the fire-breathing stars' (ἰὼ πῦρ πνεόντων | χοράγ᾽ ἄστρων), 'in accordance with some mystic *logos*', as the scholiast comments.[218] Nevertheless, the similarity between the comic and the tragic text does not go any further. For in contrast to the *wild pannychis* of the raving Sophoclean Thyiads on the mountain,[219] the open space which negates the civilized enclosure of the city,[220] dancing as an initiatory experience in the *Frogs* is part of a communal, disciplined, nocturnal rite, the *civic* Eleusinian *pannychis*. Besides, not only is Dionysus/Iacchus invited to lead the dancing of an ordered procession which, staged by the city for the city in the theatre's orchestra, reduplicates a quintessential expression of Athenian cultic and political identity, but also, more importantly, the Coryphaeus of the comic Chorus understands mystic identity as inextricably interwoven with Athenian civic consciousness (5.2).

---

[217] See e.g. *Bacch.* 20–1, 63, 114, 132–4, 184, 190, 195, 205, 207, 220, 323–4, 482, 511.

[218] Schol. Elmsley ad loc. κατὰ γάρ τινα μυστικὸν λόγον, τῶν ἀστέρων ἐστὶ χορηγός.

[219] See Soph. *Ant.* 1149–52 προφάνηθ᾽, | ὦναξ, σαῖς ἅμα περιπόλοις | Θυίασιν, αἴ σε μαινόμεναι πάννυχοι | χορεύουσι τὸν ταμίαν Ἴακχον. On this ode see Henrichs (1990: 264–9). On dancing in the circle of Dionysus see now Lonsdale (1993: esp. ch. 3).

[220] See now Buxton (1994: 81–96).

2.14. From Simulative Death to Initiatory Rebirth

If in the *Frogs* Dionysus hopes to find fertility and revitalization, the spark of Life sepulchred in the realm of the Dead, one has to bear in mind that life rising out of death is the feeling lying at the core of every initiation sequence, since the function of a ritual passage is to place the neophyte in the midst of the 'mystery of death and resurrection',[221] 'death' being understood as the initiand's renunciation of his previous identity and 'resurrection' as his attainment of a new status, whether on the social or on the religious level. The initiand feels as if he/she has acquired a new personality; in the expression of the rhetor Sopatrus, 'I came out of the mystery hall feeling like a stranger to myself' (ἐπ' ἐμαυτῷ ξενιζόμενος) (Walz, *Rhet. Graec.* viii. 114–15). This sequence of simulative death/ rebirth lies at the heart of Graeco-Roman mystic symbolism as well. In the fragment I have drawn upon many a time up to now, Plutarch compares the *pathos* of the soul at the threshold of death to the experience of those who are 'undergoing initiation into great mysteries', an analogy explaining why 'the verbs *teleutan* (die) and *teleisthai* (be initiated), and the actions they denote, have a similarity'.[222] Firmicius Maternus (*Err. Prof. Rel.* 18.1) considers the initiand who enters the 'innermost parts' (*interioribus partibus*) of the sanctuary of Attis as 'a man who is about to die' (*homo moriturus*), while Proclus (*Theol. Plat.* 4. 9, p. 30. 17–19 Budé) finds it 'most amazing' (θαυμαστότατον) that 'in the most mystic of *teletai*' (ἐν τῇ μυστικωτάτῃ τῶν τελετῶν) the performers of sacramental rites (θεουργοί) expect the initiands 'to bury the body, leaving out only the head' (θάπτειν τὸ σῶμα . . . πλὴν τῆς κεφαλῆς). The entire symbolism comes into relief in Apuleius' *Metamorphoses* where, as the Great Priest explains to Lucius, the act of initiation (*traditio*) is performed 'in the manner of voluntary death and salvation obtained by favour' (*ad instar voluntariae mortis et precariae salutis celebrari*), since Isis' providence grants that the initiands are 'in a manner reborn . . . and set once more upon the course of renewed life' (*quodam modo renatos ad novae reponere rursus salutis curricula*) (*Met.* 11. 21). The rite accomplished, the initiand himself describes his experience as an arrival at the boundaries of death, and regards his initiation as a celebration of birth.[223] In a wider ritual frame, the

---

[221] Eliade (1959: 85). Cf. ibid.: 90: 'Les symboles de la mort initiatique et de la renaissance sont complémentaires', etc.

[222] Plut. fr. 178 Sandbach: . . . πλὴν ὅταν ἐν τῷ τελευτᾶν ἤδη γένηται· τότε δὲ πάσχει πάθος οἷον οἱ τελεταῖς μεγάλαις κατοργιαζόμενοι. διὸ καὶ τὸ ῥῆμα τῷ ῥήματι καὶ τὸ ἔργον τῷ ἔργῳ τοῦ τελευτᾶν καὶ τελεῖσθαι προσέοικε.

[223] Death: 'accessi confinium mortis et, calcato Proserpinae limine, per omnia vectus elementa remeavi' (11. 23); birth: 'Exhinc festissimum celebravi natalem sacrorum' (11. 24).

best illustration of a death/rebirth symbolism expressed through the ritual sequence of descent/ascent can be sought in the rituals of Trophonius at Lebadeia.[224] There, the descender is dragged down feet first through a vertical and oblong opening of the earth (Paus. 9. 39. 10–11), in an action which resembles the carrying out (*ekphora*) of the dead in funeral processions. Moreover, as Pausanias (9. 39. 9–10) writes, the chasm of the earth used for the *katabasis* is not natural but 'artificially constructed after the most accurate masonry' so as to resemble the shape of a bread-oven (*kribanos*), the oven being, as Page du Bois (1988: 110–29) has shown, 'a suggestive metaphor for the woman's body' (129). In this way, after having experienced in the shrine a state of emotional paralysis and non-existence,[225] the consultant of the oracle comes back to earth from the same narrow passage, as if reborn from a female womb.[226]

But most importantly still, this psychological experience of death/rebirth is especially prominent in the Eleusinian and Dionysiac mysteries. In Eleusis the ritual sequence has encoded an entire series of symbolic acts[227] intended to impart to the initiand the feeling that 'life and nourishment result from terror' (Burkert 1983: 291): having died symbolically,[228] every neophyte may hope that 'if an equilibrium exists at all at the center of being, . . . the path into death will lead to life' (ibid.: 264).[229] In the Dionysiac circle, correspondingly, the most tangible expression of this sequence can be sought in the hopes of the initiates for a new life to come after their death, hopes which sometimes convey explicitly a note of actual rebirth, as we can read in the first line of the recently discovered gold leaves from Pelinna (end of fourth century BC)

---

[224] See, most importantly, Paus. 9. 39. 1– 40. 2; Philostr. *Vit. Apoll.* 8. 19; Plut. *Mor.* 589f–92e. See Hani (1975); Clark (1968); Weinberg (1986: 142–5). The scholiast on Ar. *Clouds* 508c (Holwerda) refers to those who descend into Trophonius' cave as 'the initiands' (οἱ μυούμενοι), thus qualifying the whole rite as an initiation.

[225] Timarchus, the descender in Plut. *Mor.* 589f–92e loses consciousness (592e) within the cave; every descender has to drink the water of forgetfulness before descending, and when he re-emerges from the opening he is still 'paralysed with terror and unconscious both of himself and of his surroundings' (Paus. 9. 39. 13; see further below, 2.15).

[226] Cf. Weinberg (1986: 144), who notes that the oracular 'oven-shaped chamber clearly resembles an egg or a womb'. Cf. Hani (1975: 108).

[227] See Burkert's (1983: esp. 256–97) illuminating discussion.

[228] The piglet that the mystes had to sacrifice (note the allusion in *Frogs* 337–8) corresponded to his own ritual death (Burkert 1983: 258–9).

[229] Instrumental here is the Hierophant's announcement at the climax of the Mysteries of the birth of a divine child: "ἱερὸν ἔτεκε Πότνια Κοῦρον, Βριμὼ Βριμόν" (Hippol. *Ref. Haer.* 5. 8. 40). The symbolic value of initiation as giving birth to a new life is also evident in the practice of using the garments of Eleusinian initiates as swaddling clothes for newborn babies (schol. Ar. *Plut.* 845).

νῦν ἔθανες καὶ νῦν ἐγένου, τρισόλβιε, ἄματι τῷδε

now you have died and now you have been born, thrice blessed, on this selfsame day,[230]

or on a gold plate from Thurii (A4 Zuntz, lines 3–4), where 'Persephone or some undefined voices in the Netherworld' (Zuntz 1971: 343) greet the initiate:

χαῖρε παθὼν τὸ πάθημα τὸ δ' οὔπω πρόσθε ἐπεπόνθεις·
θεὸς ἐγένου ἐξ ἀνθρώπου

hail you who endured the suffering you've never suffered before; you were a man, you've now become a god.[231]

However, the initiatory sequence of 'death'/'rebirth', which is so deeply entrenched in rites of passage, has also important literary remouldings, that is, fictive dramatizations which, by the end of the fifth century BC would have been part and parcel of the literary 'encyclopaedia' of Greek theatre-audiences. In the Sophoclean *Electra*, for example (cf. 2.3), while the brother–sister recognition is being effected on the stage, Orestes, the much lamented 'nothingness' (1129 *ouden onta*; cf. 1165–6), the 'dust and idle shade' (1159) within his urn, is suddenly revealed as having been 'saved' and 'reborn' (Seaford 1994b: 276–8). As Electra joyfully bursts out in her celebratory lyrics:

> Ah! birth
> —birth of a person to me most beloved—
> (ἰὼ γοναί,
> γοναὶ σωμάτων ἐμοὶ φιλτάτων)
> you came but this moment . . .
>
> (1232–4; tr. Kells 1973).[232]

Similarly, as Froma Zeitlin (1989) has convincingly shown in her

---

[230] First published by Tsantsanoglou and Parássoglou (1987); see also Luppe (1989); Merkelbach (1989); Gigante (1990).

[231] Seaford (1981: 262) rightly understands the πάθημα as indicating the 'ritual death' of the initiand who is now elevated, 'reborn' into the status of a 'god' or, perhaps, sharing in the nature of Dionysus himself (Seaford 1981: 254 with n. 28), if this is the meaning of the riddling ἔριφος ἐς γάλα ἔπετες (A4 Zuntz, line 4), as immersion into milk implies not only regeneration (Graf 1993: 249) but also *apotheosis* (see *Pap. Berlin* 5025 (= *PGM*, no. 1) ἀποθέωσον εἰς γάλα βοὸς μελαίνης (line 5), with Betz (1992: 3, with n. 3)), and Eriphos or Eriphios is a widespread cult title of Dionysus (Farnell 1909: 303, no. 85c). Cf. also gold tablet A1 Zuntz (lines 7–8), implying a sequence of *katabasis*/fictive death and rebirth: δεσποίνας δ' ὑπὸ κόλπον ἔδυν χθονίας βασιλείας . . . "ὄλβιε καὶ μακαριστέ, θεὸς δ' ἔσῃ ἀντὶ βροτοῖο" (cf. above, 2.2, n. 36). Extremely important is also the phrase: βίος θάνατος βίος inscribed on three 5th-cent. bone tablets related to the mystic cult of Dionysus at Olbia of Pontus (cf. 1.4), and almost certainly implying 'a doctrine of new life after death' (West 1982a: 18).

[232] Cf. *El.* 1228–9 ὁρᾶτ' Ὀρέστην τόνδε, μηχαναῖσι μὲν | θανόντα, νῦν δὲ μηχαναῖς σεσωμένον, and 1314–15. See now Seaford (1994b: 276–8).

brilliant analysis of Euripides' *Ion*, on the ritual/initiatory level of the tragic action Ion plays the role of Dionysus Liknetes. After his recognition by Creusa who, up to that point had thought of her child as dwelling 'under the ground, together with Persephone' (1441–2 κατὰ γᾶς ἐνέρων | χθονίων μέτα Περσεφόνας; cf. 953), Ion perceives himself as 'a living apparition, who died and did not die' (1444 ὁ κατθανών τε κοὐ θανὼν φαντάζομαι), a very appropriate description of initiatory fictitious death and symbolic rebirth.[233]

What I hope to have shown in this section, then, is that the 'movement' of the *Frogs* from death and intellectual sterility to hope and renewed life is not only deeply entrenched into the mystic symbolism of the Eleusinian/Bacchic circles and related rites of passage, but also connected to a recognizable and elaborate nexus of literary imagery. In a play of a markedly initiatory structure, it significantly enhances the spectator's understanding of Dionysus as a ritual 'subject' undergoing a mystic ritual passage.

Besides, if Dionysus enacts the role of a mystes both on a Dionysiac and an Eleusinian initiation sequence,[234] Aeschylus plays the ritual role of a Semele[235] or of Core,[236] whose disappearance causes dearth and nature's desiccation and whose retrieval is followed by the blossoming of flowers and crops: 'the whole wide earth burgeoned with leaves and flowers' (Hom. *h. Dem.* 472–3).[237] Finally, Aeschylus' way up to Athens, lit with the light of the Initiates' torches (λαμπάδες), situates his theatrical ascent quite

---

[233] Zeitlin (1989) does not explicitly refer to the initiatory sequence of death/resurrection with respect to these lines, but notes the Eleusinian connotations (161) and draws the parallel with the birth of a mystic child at Eleusis (159). In a reversal of this mystic symbolism the Chorus, prior to the recognition of Ion as Creusa's son, prays that 'he dies at the moment when he celebrates his birth' (*Ion* 720; with Zeitlin 1989: n. 52).

[234] On a Demetrian axis his role conforms to that of the mourning Demeter, deprived of her daughter and embarking on a quest which in one version of the myth even brings her down to the Underworld itself (refs. in Richardson 1974: 259).

[235] Fertility of nature is closely bound up with the legend of Semele: being an Earth goddess (see *RE*, s.v. Semele; Dodds 1960 on *Bacch.* 6–12 (pp. 63–4) and Jeanmaire 1970: 343), her return coincides with the coming of the joys of the spring (Pindar, fr. 75, 16–19 Maehler).

[236] Κόρη was actually one of the so-called *merismoi*, i.e. the roles assigned to the Dionysiac actors of the sacred association of the Iobacchoi in Athens (see *Lex Iobacchorum*: Sokolowski (1969): no. 51, 121 f.).

[237] Of course, it has to be said that, in the panhellenic version of the myth reflected in the Homeric *Hymn to Demeter*, Persephone's rape and return brings about barrenness or renewed vegetation through the mediation of Demeter's grief and anger: it is *the mother's* angry withdrawal at her temple at Eleusis which threatens mankind with extinction from famine (see 305–13, 331–3, 351–6, 450–6; Richardson 1974: 258), and it is *her* appeasement, correspondingly, when Persephone is given back to her, which leads her to restore fertility on earth (471–3). However, in the annual repetition of the pattern of descent/ascent, it is Persephone's *own* return which will coincide with the burgeoning of flowers in spring: 'When the earth blooms in spring with all kinds of sweet flowers, then from the misty dark you will rise again, a great marvel to gods and mortal men' (401–3).

2.4. *Anodos* of Persephone, with Hecate as torch-bearer

rf. bell-krater: The Metropolitan Museum of Art, Fletcher Fund, 1928. (28. 57. 23) (*ARV²* 1012, 1)

2.5. Return of Persephone

rf. column-krater: Bologna, Museo Civico Archeologico, 236 (*ARV²* 532, 44)

firmly within the ritual sequence of the play. In the first place, we have the testimony of Lactantius that the entire Eleusinian ceremony culminates in 'thanksgiving and tossing of torches',[238] and Aeschylus' *Oresteia*, a trilogy pervaded with mystic imagery, ends with a torchlit procession to the heart of the city. But more significantly still, in the representations of Core's *anodos*/return in art she is frequently shown as ascending,[239] or merely escorted on her way back, with torches (Figs. 2.4 and 2.5).[240] The closest ritual parallel to Aeschylus' return—which was presumably enacted on an horizontal axis on the stage—would be the dramatized ceremony of the 'bringing back' of Core, the very much discussed Κόρης Καταγωγή, taking place in Sicily at harvest time (Diod. 5. 4. 6).[241] Epigraphical evidence from Arcadia (*IG* v. 2. 265 from Mantinea), famous for the primitiveness of its preserved *teletai*, testifies to the ritual's ultimate Greek origin: an 'Assembly of the *Koragoi*' (Σύνοδος τῶν Κοραγῶν) celebrates in honour of the Core the *Koragia* during which the image of the deity, having been taken into a private house on the previous evening, is ceremonially brought back to the *Koragion*.[242]

2.15. Reintegration

What we have seen in 2.8–14 is Dionysus' initiatory experience from the point of view of the initiates in Eleusinian and Bacchic *teletai*. Let us now return to the 'wider' audience's perspective in order to consider the final stage of a rite of passage, the phase of reintegration (cf. 2.1).

Emerging out of his marginal seclusion, the novice may have acquired a deeper understanding of himself, but by no means has he or she accomplished a real 'ontological mutation'.[243] What liminality

---

[238] Lact. *Div. Inst.* 18. 7 'facibus accensis per noctem Proserpina inquiritur et ea inventa ritus omnis gratulatione ac taedarum iactatione finitur'.

[239] Ascending Persephone with torches: see Bérard (1974: pl. 9, no. 31: lekane of Berlin); Bérard (1974: pl. 9, no. 32): lekythos from Athens, presenting the ritual *anodos* of Core lighted by a woman with two torches, on which see further Kourouniotes (1933–5). On the purely mythical plane see the famous New York krater (Bérard 1974: pl. 15, no. 50) (Fig. 2.4), with Hecate as a torch-bearer.

[240] Core brought back with torches in an horizontal scheme: Bérard (1974: pl. 9, no. 33: stamnos from Florence); on the mythical level see Bérard (1974: pl. 17, no. 59: krater of Bologna) (Fig. 2.5) and (1974: pl. 17, no. 60: krater from the Acropolis of Athens).

[241] Her annual advent signalled the return of fertility, wealth, and affluence upon the earth; for Diodorus' *katagoge* as signifying not the *Kathodos* of Core but on the contrary her *return*, her *ascent* back to earth (becoming thus a synonym for *anagoge*), see e.g. Kourouniotes (1933–5); Le Bonniec (1958: 337–8).

[242] See Stiglitz (1967: 74). Furthermore, for traces of a ritual arrival (Katagógia) of a nature goddess (Demeter? Persephone? Ariadne?) in spring in Protogeometric Cnossos see Burkert (1988).   [243] From Eliade's definition of initiation (1969: 112).

has offered to him or her was only the *potential* for becoming 'other': in the reaggregation period, using the skills and powers absorbed, the initiand has still to learn, usually from scratch, his or her new role in society.[244] As far as Greek ritual practice is concerned, a temporarily limited regression to a state of infantile dependence can be witnessed in the reintegration phase of initiation in Trophonius' cave at Lebadeia: as Pausanias (9. 39. 13) reports, when the initiate ascends, he is 'paralysed with terror and unconscious both of himself and of his surroundings' (κάτοχόν τε ἔτι τῷ δείματι καὶ ἀγνῶτα ὁμοίως αὐτοῦ τε καὶ τῶν πέλας); it is in such a state that the priests entrust him to his relatives, and it is only after some time that 'he will recover all his faculties, and the power to laugh will return to him'.

Nevertheless, the most impressive literary remoulding of initiatory learning at the time of an initiate's reincorporation into his social milieu can be found in Aristophanic Comedy itself. After having completed his reverse transition to ephebic status in the *Wasps* (A. M. Bowie 1993a: ch. 4), Philocleon is subjected by his father to a thorough re-education in the ways of one's integration into adult social life through the institution of the banquet: 'learn to be convivial and companiable' (1208–9 κατακλινεὶς προσμάνθανε | ξυμποτικὸς εἶναι καὶ ξυνουσιαστικός). Similarly, Dionysus, the ritual passenger of the Aristophanic *Frogs*, realizes gradually during the time of his reaggregation the ways in which his individual *persona* can and must be realigned with the collective perspective of the community of Athens.

This civic reincorporation which accomplishes Dionysus' initiation is effected in the comic literary agon, which will be discussed in detail in Chapters 5–9. But, for the moment, let us round off the present chapter by attempting a brief contextualization of our findings in the space of fifth-century Athenian drama. Because nothing can bring more sharply into focus the special nature of comic liminality than a comparison of its characteristic features with the ways in which the same ritual schema is remoulded on the tragic stage. Finally, narrowing the focus on the dramatization of Dionysus in the *Frogs*, this chapter will also attempt a brief *synkrisis* of *Dionysiac* comic versus tragic liminality.

---

[244] See e.g. Eliade (1969: 114); Loeb (1929: 262); and van Gennep (1960: 81) on the process of reintegration, as sometimes involving several months during which the neophytes 'must relearn all the gestures of ordinary life'. Cf. Thurnwald (1939), and for more refs. see West (1983a: 169 n. 97).

2.16. Tragedy, Comedy, and Ritual Liminality

(i) Tragedy, many a time, dramatizes missed or nearly failed ritual passages. For example, by insisting on remaining an exclusive devotee of Artemis, and thus resisting marriage, Hippolytus fails to accomplish his transition to fully grown manhood in the Euripidean tragedy which bears his name. Similarly, viewed from a different perspective, initiation of the male into adulthood can be primarily defined as his transition from the *oikos* and the sphere of influence of women, to the *polis*, where he joins the community of warriors and takes up the entire range of his civic duties. Nevertheless, in Sophocles' *Philoctetes*, a play which has served us well throughout this chapter as a rich repertory of initiatory reflections, the eponymous hero chooses to resolve his liminality with a move backwards, a regression to the safety of the starting-point, whether this be Neoptolemus' *home* (see e.g. 488) or, preferably, his paternal Oeta and his own family *oikos*; the agonizing plea 'take me home' can be heard again and again throughout the play (e.g. 468–506, 1367–8, 1398–9). Besides, what is even more unsettling is that Philoctetes' *pathos* acts as the catalyst which threatens to annihilate even Neoptolemus' own passage to adulthood. Because before the appearance of Heracles, which un-expectedly provides the play with a second ending and ensures for both of its protagonists the accomplishment of their transition towards the community of the Greek warriors, Neoptolemus' *personal* decision amounts to the resolution of his ritual passage with an irrevocable retreat to his own homeland. 'If you will, then,' he says to Philoctetes, 'let us go' (1402 εἰ δοκεῖ, στείχωμεν). It transpires, then, that in the tragic genre, ritual passages are often dramatized in a way which highlights their failure—or sometimes their near failure—to be fully and successfully accomplished.

In Comedy, on the other hand, there are no fatally missed rites of passage. The comic plot culminates either in a positive reintegration of the ritual passenger into society (e.g. *Frogs, Wasps, Knights*), or in the resolution of ambiguous liminality (cf. below, iv) and the unequivocal restoration of reversed order and polarities. To mention only one example, after the confusion of sexes and roles in the liminal space and time of the Thesmophoria festival, Euripides' Kinsman, the old man disguised as a woman, leaves the comic stage *andrikos* (Ar. *Thesm.* 1204), that is, 'in a manly way' (A. M. Bowie 1993*a*: 227).

(ii) In Tragedy, aspects of liminality which are by definition temporary and transient, tend to crystallize and become a fixture in the ritual passenger's condition. Sophocles' *Philoctetes* offers, again, the richest cluster of examples.

As we have seen in 2.2, ritual transitions are often effected through the initiands' compulsory expulsion from society and isolation or seclusion in an area situated outside the boundaries of the community to which they belong. Nevertheless, if ritual liminaries play only symbolically the role of social outcasts, expulsion from the community of the Greek warriors attacking Troy and isolation on the desert island of Lemnos (*Phil.* 257; cf. 5)[245] become for Philoctetes a fixed and immutable condition. Whereas for the Spartan *kryptos*, for example, his period of seclusion lasts only for one year (schol. Pl. *Leg.* 633b), Philoctetes leads his whole life in isolation (172 μόνος αἰεί), with spotted or shaggy beasts as his companions (183–5).[246] More importantly still, whereas ephebic hunting is an almost ubiquitous initiatory exploit, preparing the adolescent for his transition to manhood,[247] Philoctetes seems to have *actually become* what Neoptolemus or any ephebic hunter is only symbolically and for a limited period of time supposed to be: he literally lives the life of a hunter (e.g. 165, 287–9, 710–11). Frugal existence too, apparently an important aspect of Greek ephebic marginality,[248] becomes in the case of Philoctetes a permanent companion of his life, as he has actually very spare means of sustenance, and he himself employs the word *limos* (hunger, famine) to describe his condition (186, 311–13). Furthermore, although, as we have already seen in 2.6, the initiands have to face for a limited period of time trials of endurance ('prova di resistenza'), Philoctetes' style of life requires him to be perpetually *eukardios*, tolerant at heart, imposing upon him a *permanent* ordeal of steadfastness. The play's Chorus, correspondingly, amazed at his patient perseverance (e.g. 187–8, 686–90) and overwhelmed with pity, wonder: 'how can this wretched man, how can he possibly hold out?' (πῶς ποτε πῶς δύσμορος | ἀντέχει;) (175–6).[249] Finally, whereas the initiand's 'struc-

[245] More specifically, the cave, which is the focus of Philoctetes' seclusion, brings to mind the worldwide attested initiatory hut, where initiands are secluded in the period of their marginality (cf. above, n. 39).

[246] His solitude is often emphasized throughout the play; see e.g. 171–2, 183–5, 227–8, 470–1.

[247] As Sophocles' play itself implies from the start, Neoptolemus' initiatory hunting of Philoctetes and his bow, once successfully brought to an end, will reintegrate him into society in an elevated status.

[248] At least as can be gauged from the 'spare diet' (Plut. *Lyc.* 17. 4 ὀλιγοσιτία) of the Spartan *kryptoi* (see schol. Pl. *Leg.* 633b), and cf. Plut. *Lyc.* 17. 4 γλίσχρον γὰρ αὐτοῖς ἐστι δεῖπνον. For *limos* as a widespread initiatory ordeal see Brelich (1969: 73 n. 64; non-Greek references).

[249] *Antechein* belongs to the semantic field of *karteria*, as can be seen, for example, in a passage from Lucian which refers to the practice of ephebic *diamastigosis* (cf. 2.6(c)) at Sparta: '. . . if they should not bear up (ἀντέχοιεν) under the stripes' (37. 38. 25).

tural invisibility' and social death (2.3) are supposed to be restricted to the time and space of his/her liminality, Philoctetes suffers a permanent loss of name/*kleos* in the eyes of the social group to which he once belonged (cf. 2.3). The conclusion which emerges, then, is that in Tragedy features of liminality which are meant in real life to be confined to the initiand's space and time of transition tend to be remoulded in such a way as to *transgress* temporal limits and to brand permanently the ritual subject's mode of existence.

Similar observations can be made with respect to Sophocles' *Trachiniae* (Seaford 1986*b*), where Deianeira's fear, anxiety, and loneliness, the negative feelings inherently interwoven with bridal liminality,[250] are never fully overcome with the completion of her marital transition. Instead of being constricted to her ritualized crossing from her father's hearth to the *oikos* of her husband, that is, to the time when she was suspended 'betwixt and between' her old and new existence, Deianeira's liminal experience has 'engulfed her whole life' (Seaford 1986*b*: 58). 'Nurturing fear after fear' (28), the wife of Heracles is incessantly a prey to anxiety (e.g. 36–7, 106–8, 175–7) as well as perpetually tormented on a desolate bed (109–10). In other words, Sophocles' *Trachiniae* is a good illustration of Tragedy's tendency to hold the ritual passenger, so to speak, 'arrested' in the negative pole of liminality by suppressing the prospect or even the possibility of a happy consummation of the ritual transition.

To take one final example of tragic liminality crystallized abnormally in an almost irreversible condition (Seaford 1985; 1994*a*: 375–8), we may turn to Sophocles' *Electra*, where the orphaned daughter of Agamemnon, determined never to give up her lamentation,[251] seems to be fixed into a lifeless life. For, whereas mourning liminality, primarily characterized by what Aristotle called a 'likeness of experience with' or 'sympathy for' (*homopatheia*) the condition of the dead,[252] is temporarily restricted and aims at the reincorporation of the mourners into the life of the community to which they belong, the model for Electra's grief is Niobe's *incessant* weeping in her rocky tomb (150–2). Sophocles' *Electra*, then, provides one more illustration of tragic liminality degenerating into a permanent condition by transforming, as it does, temporary death-like sorrow into a *perpetual* sharing in the

---

[250] Consider how these feelings are powerfully evoked in connection with Deianeira's bridal transition, e.g. *Trach.* 7–8 (dread of marriage: νυμφείων ὄκνον | ἄλγιστον ἔσχον; cf. implicitly 145–9); 529–30 (liminal solitude).

[251] See e.g. Soph. *El.* 103–4, 231–2; cf. 122–3, 1075–7.

[252] Arist. fr. 101 Rose (= Συμπόσιον, fr. 2 Ross), *apud* Athen. 675a ὁμοπαθείᾳ τοῦ κεκμηκότος κολοβοῦμεν ἡμᾶς αὐτοὺς τῇ τε κουρᾷ τῶν τριχῶν . . .; see Seaford (1994*a*: 86).

doom of the defunct. As the women of the Chorus point out to Electra, 'you have chosen a lifetime (αἰών) shared (with your dead father) and full of weeping'.[253]

(iii) Nevertheless, transgression of temporal limits in the tragic treatment of liminality goes hand in hand with Tragedy's tendency to dwell on the *negative* imagery which can be associated with a rite of passage. For example, if initiation is, as we have seen in 2.14, a passage from symbolic death to simulative rebirth, the tragic genre tends to dramatize only the first part of the sequence. Thus, in a scene which fuses and remoulds Eleusinian and other initiatory ritual elements, Sophocles' Antigone laments her descent into her underground cave, both a tomb and simultaneously a bridal chamber (*Ant.* 891 ὦ τύμβος, ὦ νυμφεῖον), as the virgin daughter of Oedipus, doomed to death, will become the bride of Hades (*Ant.* 816 ἀλλ' Ἀχέροντι νυμφεύσω).[254] Antigone is herself conscious of the fact that, entering her bridal/funereal liminality (cf. above, 2.3, n. 45), she is unclassifiable:

Neither among the living nor the dead
do I have a home in common—neither with the living nor the dead.[255]

Both alive and buried like a corpse,[256] Antigone becomes a perfect illustration of liminary structural invisibility (see 2.3), that is, the initiand's ambiguous hovering 'betwixt and between' the categories of social structure. But far more interesting for our discussion is the fact that the *imagery* attached to Antigone's failed ritual passage is closely analogous to the imagery which dramatizes Dionysus' transition in the *Frogs*: in both the tragic and the comic play the ritual passengers enact a *katabasis*[257] into the Underworld, a realm which is connoted in the tragedy by the powerful symbol of the 'vaulted tomb' (885–6 κατηρεφεῖ | τύμβῳ), the 'deep-dug dwelling' (891–2 κατασκαφῆς | οἴκησις).[258] Yet, unlike Dionysus who, after the enactment of his initiatory descent, is granted by the comic plot the privilege of an ascent back to the upper world, the tragic heroine is never to emerge into the light again. That is to say, rather than

---

[253] Seaford's (1985: 316) translation of *El.* 1085–6 ὡς καὶ σὺ πάγκλαυτον αἰ | ῶνα κοινόν εἵλου; for a defence of κοινόν of the MSS. see Seaford (1985: n. 12).

[254] See above, n. 45 and Rose (1925).

[255] *Ant.* 850–2 ἰὼ δύστανος, βροτοῖς | οὔτε νεκρὸς νεκροῖσιν | μέτοικος, οὐ ζῶσιν, οὐ θανοῦσιν.

[256] See *Ant.* 774 κρύψω πετρώδει ζῶσαν ἐν κατώρυχι; 810–13, 821–2 ἀλλ' αὐτόνομος ζῶσα μόνη δὴ | θνητῶν Ἀίδην καταβήσῃ; 888 ἐν τοιαύτῃ ζῶσα τυμβεύειν στέγῃ; 920 ζῶσ' ἐς θανόντων ἔρχομαι κατασκαφάς.

[257] The common metaphor of 'going down' to Hades (cf. *Ant.* 821–2, 896 κάτειμι) can be taken literally in Antigone's case, as she is actually descending into an underground chamber, a cave/grave under the earth (cf. 920).

[258] Cf. *Ant.* 804–5, 848–9. For caves as entrances to the Underworld see Dietrich (1973).

providing for the redemption of the ritual passenger, the tragic plot ensures that there is no initiatory 'rebirth'. To put it in another way, when moulded by the tragic frame, ritual symbolism is fixed at the *negative* end of its potential spectrum. Besides, the fate of Sophocles' Antigone is one among the many examples on the tragic stage where the largely symbolic character of ritual marginality degenerates into grim and irrevocable reality. For just as Pentheus' Dionysiac initiation in the *Bacchae* culminates in a real rather than symbolic death, that is, a sacrificial killing, which leads to no rebirth, so the Sophoclean tragic plot transmutes the bride's symbolic immolation of virginity into irreversible doom.[259] It would, therefore, seem that Tragedy shares with myth the transposition of ritual features from a simulative to a real dimension,[260] while Comedy stands closer to its ritual background, where the symbolic element is paramount. But, of course, we should beware of assuming that any dividing lines between the genres are clear-cut. In Aeschylus' *Oresteia*, for example, gloom and death give place to joy and communal celebration: the incorporation of the benevolent power of the Furies, now converted to Semnae, renews and revitalizes the order of the *polis*, which displays its magnificent splendour in the blazing torchlight of the Great Panathenaean procession. And in a number of Euripidean tragedies which Helene Foley (1992) has perceptively termed '*anodos* dramas' (*Alcestis*, *Helen*), the underlying scenario of Core's descent into and ascent from the Underworld does not crystallize in the gloom and darkness of the world below, but culminates instead in a renewal of fertility and life on both a personal and a communal level.

(iv) Inherently interwoven with the tragic imagery's excessive dwelling on the *negative only* pole of initiatory symbolism, is Tragedy's tendency not to resolve the ambiguities of ritual liminality. Perhaps the best example at this point can be sought in Euripides' *Electra*. Being 'perpetually fixed at the moment of transition', 'perpetually on the brink'[261] between virginal and marital status, since she is both a married woman, a *gyne*, and yet still a

---

[259] See Seaford (1990a: 77, 1994a: 381). Yet, in the case of the Euripidean Pentheus, a faint echo of ritual anticipation of rebirth can be heard in Agave's concern (*Bacch.* 1300) about his lacerated body: 'Has it all been fitted together decently in its joints?' (tr. Seaford 1996; cf. ibid. ad 969).

[260] For example, what is in ritual a mock death is preserved in myth as a real death (think e.g. of the sacrificial death of Iphigeneia in myth in connection to the prenuptial preparation of girls for the symbolic death of their virginity in ritual; see Lloyd-Jones 1983); ritualized female abstinence from marital sex (e.g. Thesmophoria, Skira, Lemnian rituals) is reflected in the myths as female killing of the husband (Lemnian women; Danaids; see Burkert 1970).

[261] I draw here on Mary Beard's (1980) exemplary analysis of the ambiguous status of the Vestal Virgins at Rome (quote from p. 21).

parthenos, sexually intact, the daughter of Agamemnon is structurally unclassifiable. By consequence, dwelling, as she does, at the interstices of social structure, she shuns the company of women,[262] but feels also equally excluded from the community of the Argive maidens, who prepare themselves to celebrate a prenuptial festival at the temple of Hera Akraia.[263] It is only through a forward look to the extra-dramatic future, briefly outlined by the *dei ex machina* at the play's closing scene, that the audience learns of Electra's eventual consummation of a marital transition, as the wife given by her brother to Pylades (1249; 1284–5). Comedy, by way of contrast, is the genre where the structural ambiguity of ritual liminality tends to be unequivocally resolved (cf. 2.17). Dionysus, for example, the ritual passenger in the initiation frame of the *Frogs*, does not remain fixed in the marginal position he occupied at the beginning of the play (2.2). The comic plot gradually restores the negative attributes which demarcated his liminal existence (anonymity, loss of insignia, ordeals, etc.), so that by the end of his transition, in the phase of reaggregation, he reassumes in full his Dionysiac *persona* in the literary agon (see Chs. 5–9). To put the discussion of this section in a broader context, it appears that comic liminality tends primarily to exploit and magnify the features which narrowly defined ritual liminality (cf. Lada 1996) shares with festive occasions or civic rites of reversal, for instance, rank reversals (masters/slaves), exchanges of costume, etc. In a word, in the comic dramatization of liminary time and space, playfulness is paramount.

(v) Tragedy has been characterized as the 'misadventure of the human body' (Zeitlin 1990*a*: 72). Failed ritual passages almost always materialize on the tragic stage in the theatrical display of extreme corporeal anguish, such as the tearing apart of Pentheus' flesh or the death pangs ravaging Hippolytus' shattered frame. And, while many a comic character experiences some kind of bodily torment, the difference from tragic dramatizations lies in the depth of the experience and the way in which the tragically fragmented body is exposed to the viewer's vision. For, rather than leaving the spectator's soul intact, tragic bodily pain engages the audience in a profound psychological experience, and is viewed by Aristotle as one among the elements of *mythos* which can generate *pathos*.[264] In other words, the shaken body of the actor on the tragic stage gives rise to the spectator's psychological infection, a torment sometimes so deep

---

[262] Eur. *El.* 310–11 ἀνέορτος ἱερῶν καὶ χορῶν τητωμένη | ἀναίνομαι γυναῖκας οὖσα παρθένος; see Zeitlin (1970).

[263] Eur. *El.* 173–4 πᾶσαι δὲ παρ' Ἥ | ραν μέλλουσιν παρθενικαὶ στείχειν.

[264] Arist. *Poet.* 1452b11–13 πάθος δέ ἐστι πρᾶξις φθαρτικὴ ἢ ὀδυνηρά, οἷον οἵ τε ἐν τῷ φανερῷ θάνατοι καὶ αἱ περιωδυνίαι καὶ τρώσεις καὶ ὅσα τοιαῦτα.

as to betray signs of physical reality. A very eloquent example of this case can be sought in the experience of Neoptolemus, overwhelmed by a 'terrible pity' (965 οἶκτος δεινός) at the spectacle of Philoctetes, the exiled hero agonizing in the grip of violent bodily disease. In fact, the empathy of Neoptolemus is so intense as to transmute itself into a feeling of almost physical pain: in order to give voice to his affliction, the boy can only appropriate the language of physical suffering (806 algo, i.e. 'I am in pain'),[265] and, as Martha Nussbaum (1992: 122) has expressed it, he 'even calls out with the interjection papai (895) that the poor man had used in the throes of his torment'. Now, of course, Neoptolemus is only an 'internalized' theates, a spectator within the very structure of the tragic plot itself. For him the pathos of Philoctetes is bound to be engaging, as it is conveyed through a tangible, immediate reality of body and of flesh, un-mediated by the 'aesthetic distance'[266] that the frame of a theatrical production can create. And yet, it is not merely the play's 'inter-nalized' theatai who may be gripped by the protagonist's corporeal pathos. The tragic broken body can also generate such an all-embracing current of emotion that the private grief of kin and philoi in the ambience of the play itself may be transposed to the public realm of the theatrical community, or further out to the domain of the polis, where it may even graft itself upon the polis' collective memory. So, for example, in Euripides' Hippolytus, the Chorus of Troezenian women refer to the undoing of the young man's body (διαλυμανθείς) as a 'household grief', a πόνος οἴκων (1344), before declaring it in their exodial song as a 'common woe for all the citizens alike' (κοινὸν τόδ' ἄχος πᾶσι πολίταις),[267] a pathos that will breed a 'waterfall of tears' (πολλῶν δακρύων ἔσται πίτυλος) (1462–4), and which, according to Artemis' instructions, will be annually com-memorated in the prenuptial rites of Troezenian maidens (1423–30).[268]

To sum up, then, the bodily pain entailed by failed ritual passages dramatized on the tragic stage is not merely a physical ordeal for the sufferer, but also, most importantly, a psychological experience for the viewer. The affective reaction that it generates can bind the audience together by jolting them out of the safety of their 'spectat-ing isolation' and instigating instead their vicarious sharing in the

---

[265] Cf. Philoctetes' identical description of Neoptolemus' condition in line 1011 δῆλος δὲ καὶ νῦν ἐστιν ἀλγεινῶς φέρων.

[266] For the concept see e.g. Bullough (1912).

[267] Cf. Hipp. 1157–9, where the Messenger characterizes the misadventure of Hippolytus' body as 'a tale worthy of concern' not only to Theseus himself but also to the citizens of Athens and of Troezen: μερίμνης ἄξιον φέρω λόγον | σοὶ καὶ πολίταις οἵ τ' Ἀθηναίων πόλιν | ναίουσι καὶ γῆς τέρμονας Τροζηνίας.   [268] See Segal (1988b: esp. 62–6).

passion of the bodily discourse enacted on the stage. To push this a step further, the broken body of the actor in tragic ritual passages involves the *theates* in a way which corresponds to real-life patterns of ritual initiation, where the novice is subjected not only to physical *pathos* but to the overwhelming psychological ordeal of *sympatheia* as well.[269] Nevertheless, if the fragmented tragic body gives rise to an 'empathic joining',[270] an identity of shared feelings between performer and spectator, the primary reaction of the comic viewer at the 'misadventure' of the comic body is not empathy but alienation, not infectious grief but disengaged, self-conscious laughter. To put it in another way, if the psychology of tragic audience-response is based on the anti-Brechtian principle 'I weep when they weep, I laugh when they laugh', the viewer who is faced with, let us say, Dionysus' physical suffering and crying at his flagellation in the *Frogs* will not be moved to tears, but, instead, to laughter; here prevails the Brechtian credo 'I laugh when they weep, I weep when they laugh' (Brecht 1964: 71).

Besides, a most important difference lies in the way each of the genres chooses to highlight somatic pain on the stage. I mean that, although tragic bodily suffering reaches the spectator as physical agony, sometimes so intense as to be modelled upon the pangs of childbirth ravaging the vulnerable female *soma* (see Loraux 1981*a*), the 'misadventure' of the *comic* body is focused in such a way as to throw sharply into relief the loss of its autonomy, the affront against the comic hero's masculine integrity. And this becomes particularly evident when the comic body is put to torture, as is the case in Dionysus' flagellation in the *Frogs*, or in the binding of Euripides' Kinsman, the ritual and theatrical performer in the liminal reversed order of the *Thesmophoriazusae* (A. M. Bowie 1993*a*: ch. 9). Because it has to be remembered that a supreme marker of the freedom inextricably interwoven with civic identity in the democracy of Athens is the inviolability of the citizen's physical *persona*, the 'literally untouchable' (Winkler 1990*a*: 179) status of his body. Even 'to put your hand on a citizen's body is to insult him profoundly, implying that he is a social inferior' (Winkler 1990*a*: 179). In other words, the maltreatment of the body as part of comic remouldings of ritual liminality is focused from the point of view of the debasement and humiliation it entails for the male hero. In fact, the 'invasion' of the comic body can even cause it to adopt externally the guise of the

---

[269] See Procl. *In Remp.* ii, p. 108, 17–21 (Kroll) αἱ τελεταί . . . συμπαθείας εἰσὶν αἴτιαι ταῖς ψυχαῖς περὶ τὰ δρώμενα τρόπον ἄγνωστον ἡμῖν καὶ θεῖον. Cf. also the sharp grief which seizes Demeter's heart in the Homeric *Hymn* (e.g. *h. Dem.* 40, 50, 77, 90, 98, 201, 304).

[270] Staub (1987: 107); see further Lada (1993: 100–3).

other sex. The masculine prerogatives of Euripides' Kinsman in the *Thesmophoriazusae*, for example, are transformed so as to bestow upon him a feminine appearance (see *Thesm.* 211–68). And, although we should beware of assuming that tragic liminality is totally unaware of analogous 'invasions' of the male body, pride of place among which holds Pentheus' adornment with maenadic dress in *Bacchae* 912–70, such bodily manipulations belong to scenes where Tragedy resorts to comic means for throwing its deadly gruesomeness into relief.[271] Moreover, as can be seen again in *Frogs*, the liminary degradation of the comic body can even reach the point of its bare exposure to the eyes of the spectators at its most 'physical' moments, such as the act of defecation (*Frogs* 479–90). At such comic scenes the rules of grotesque realism prevail or, to put it in Bakchtinian language, the aesthetics of the 'lower material bodily stratum'.

(vi) Finally, Comedy has left its mark upon the moulding of initiatory ordeals in another respect as well. We may think, for example, of the solemnity of Neoptolemus' 'prova di resistenza', the firmness with which he bears the sight of Philoctetes' ills. In the *Frogs*, on the other hand, apart from the ordeal of flagellation, which poses on the initiand Dionysus a demand for patient perseverance, there is a miniature agon which, from a Greek classical perspective, could well have been received as a comic travesty of an initiand's endurance test. I mean that Dionysus is required to withstand not only the toil of rowing but also the intolerable noise of the croaking Stygian frogs.[272]

DION. brekekekex koax koax
   You will certainly not beat me in that.
CHO. Neither will *you* conquer us no matter what happens.
DION. Nor will *you* ever defeat me;
   for I will be shouting
   even all day through, if necessary,
   till I outdo you in 'koax'
   brekekekex koax koax.
   I knew I would make you sooner or later stop your 'koax'.   (*Frogs* 260–8)

Dover (1993: 222) understands Dionysus' lyric exchange with his amphibian companions as a 'shouting match', 'a competition to see who can last longer' (ibid.: 223). Nevertheless, what Dover does not take into account is the possibility that under Dionysus' sudden

---

[271] For the controversy as to the seriousness or comic tone of the scene see e.g. Seidensticker (1978: 316–19, 1982: 123–9).

[272] See his annoyance at 226–7: 'go to hell, you and your "koax"! You are nothing more than "koax"', or at 241–2a.

determination to silence his opponents lies the tenacity of any initiand undergoing a resistance test. To put it in another way, Dionysus' persistence resembles an initiand's ambition to outlast his fellow-neophytes in the forbearance of a painful experience (cf. above, 2.6(c)).

Having surveyed independently some specific points of divergence between tragic and comic liminality, let us now broaden our scope of inquiry towards the wider, the social institutions which host such scenic remouldings of ritual patterns. For Aristophanes' *Frogs*, displaying, as it does, a ritual initiation sequence grafted upon a comic dramatic plot, provides an excellent example of the complex ways in which distinct levels of representation could converge and frames interpenetrate. To put this more specifically: the liminality of the *Frogs* is metatheatrically enfolded within a wider space of carnivalesque inversions and potential subversiveness, that is, the comic frame, which is itself part of the ritual space of the Lenaean festival—like all festive occasions a time of ritual licence. To ask what is *distinctively* comic in the way those three superimposed layers of liminal transgression interact is to raise an extremely complicated question which falls outside the scope of this book. However, what should be certainly remarked at this point is that the initiation sequence of the *Frogs* unfolds along the lines of the most characteristically comic rhythm, namely, that of release, renewal, and revitalization. Either a quest or the scenic enactment of a *katabasis* intended to bring something good out of the Underworld, sometimes combined with the vertical return of a deceased helper, are standardized comic patterns,[273] while one of the generic stereotypes of satyric drama is the *anodos* of an earthgod/dess from the subterranean depths,[274] a return ensuring the

---

[273] Quest: see e.g. Trygaeus in the *Peace*, a questing hero *par excellence* or Peisthetaerus and Euelpides in *Birds*; cf. Aristophanes' Ποίησις, which stages the quest for a woman, most probably to be identified with Poiesis herself (Lloyd-Jones 1981). *Katabasis*: see e.g. Aristophanes' Γηρυτάδης (esp. fr. 156 K–A, deputation of poets sent down to Hades by the Assembly of Athens): if fr. 63 *CGFP* (= fr. 591 K–A), referring to the *anodos* of a female daimon (line 85 τὴν δαίμον' ἣν ἀνήγαγον) (Cassio 1981: 17 with n. 1), belongs to the same play (for the uncertainty see *CGFP*, p. 27), this comedy would seem to have combined the *katabasis* with an ascent, perhaps of the Ἀρχαία Ποίησις; cf. Pherecrates' Μεταλλῆς (Baldry 1953: 55) and Κραπάταλοι, probably (see fr. 100 K–A) also containing the return of Aeschylus (see Kassel and Austin, *PCG*, vol. vii, p. 143). *Anodos*: see e.g. Eupolis' Δῆμοι (cf. Plepelits 1970: 17, 24, etc., who understands the play's plot as including a *katabasis* as well; however, see *contra* Storey 1994: 117), staging the *anodos* of Solon, Miltiades, Aristeides, and Pericles; Cratinus' Χείρωνες (return of Solon), and Πλοῦτοι (return of the ancestral spirits of plenitude in Athens; see Goossens 1935a: 406; Baldry 1953: 52).

[274] See e.g. Sophocles' Ἰχνευταί: Cyllene enters the stage 'vertically' (Taplin 1977: 448 n. 2; cf. C. Robert 1912 and Guarducci 1929: 33–4); Sophocles' Πανδώρα ἢ Σφυροκόποι (Buschor 1937; see Guarducci 1929 and Simon 1982: 145 ff. for a 'theatrical' interpretation of *ARV²* 612, 1 and *ARV²* 1562, 4, illustrating Pandora's *anodos* (Fig. 2.6)); Sophocles' Ἴναχος: accord-

2.6. Pandora rising from the ground
rf. Attic volute-krater: Oxford Ashmolean Museum, G 275 (ARV² 1562, 4)

invigoration of nature's vital forces.[275] More significantly still, the thematic core of 'life arising out of death' in its symbolical dimensions is a widely established comic stance.[276] In this respect then, it is ultimately the flow and interplay of comic patterns which consummates the unsettling picture of the journey's liminality and translates it into the fictitious image of restored order, as this is anticipated at the play's closing scenes. To put it in another way, conditioned by the structure of the comic genre, the liminality of the *Frogs* is bound to be steered towards its resolution.

ing to Seaford's (1980: 29) reconstruction of the plot, 'Zeus-Plouton and his messenger Hermes . . . appear in Argos from the world below.'

[275] See e.g. Sophocles' Ἴναχος, where τοῦ Διὸς εἰσελθόντος πάντα μεστὰ ἀγαθῶν ἐγένοντο (schol. Ar. *Plut.* 806), 'the ἀγαθά in question' being 'the blessing of fertility' (Seaford 1980: 25), 'agricultural πλοῦτος' bestowed upon the 'thirsty Argos' (ibid.: 26).

[276] Consider the typical 'nostalgia' of Old Comedy, which places the *agathon* in subterranean depths; see e.g. Ar. *Frogs* 1462 ἐνθένδ' ἀνίει τἀγαθά; Pherecrates' Μεταλλῆς, esp. fr. 113 K–A; Phrynichus' Κωμασταί, fr. 16 K–A ἡμῖν δ' ἀνίει δεῦρο σύ τ' ἀγαθὰ | τοῖς τήνδ' ἔχουσι τὴν πόλιν ἵλεως; Aristophanes' Ταγηνισταί, esp. fr. 504, 14 K–A αἰτούμεθ' αὐτοὺς (sc. the dead) δεῦρ' ἀνιέναι τἀγαθά, with Photius' note (α 1993) ἀνίει τὰ ἀγαθά· τοῖς τεθνεῶσιν ἔθος εἶχον λέγειν ἐπευχόμενοι. In a wider cultural perspective cf. e.g. Pl. *Crat.* 403a ὅτι ἐκ τῆς γῆς κάτωθεν ἀνίεται ὁ πλοῦτος . . .

2.17. *Comic and Tragic Liminality in a Dionysiac Play*

Finally, as a very last step, it is now important to consider very briefly how Comedy, as a genre, shapes *Dionysus'* religious personality and ultimately creates an impression altogether different from that conveyed through the tragic stage. I shall confine my *synkrisis* to the *Frogs* and *Bacchae*, that is, the two most important extant dramatizations of Dionysus in the theatre of the Athenian *polis*. For, if they are viewed as highly sophisticated 'fin de siècle' products incorporating a wide range of traditional material, both *Frogs* and *Bacchae* can provide ample ground for comparisons as well as for the drawing of general conclusions.

In his extensive monograph devoted to Euripides' play, Charles Segal (1982) demonstrated persuasively how this drama unfolds by constructing and displaying gradually to the spectators' eyes the Dionysiac paradox. As I hope this chapter has made clear, the *Frogs* proceeds in the opposite direction. The puzzling knot of Dionysiac contradictions is stated both visually and verbally at the beginning of the play, which brings Dionysus on the stage as a strikingly indeterminate and highly ambiguous creature. Unlike Tragedy, however, Comedy effects the *dissolution* of this paradox, for the play's narrative discourse consistently steers Dionysus' *dramatis persona* towards the space of 'Culture' and the values of the 'City' (see Chs. 3–8). Besides, given that Dionysus was felt to be a liminal, an interstitial figure, lying perpetually on the margins[277] between socially definable categories, it is important to realize that Greek cultural experience could easily have visualized him as the obvious candidate for initiation, the perfect subject in a ritual transition. In fact, with respect to the thematic structure and imagery of the *Bacchae*, Richard Seaford, in an extremely influential paper (1981), showed that these are to a great extent conditioned by the ritual patterns of Dionysiac initiation. In the Aristophanic play, correspondingly, I have already argued in this chapter that the comic channelling of the *dramatis persona* of this god is similarly effected through the sequence of an initiation. Nevertheless, we should beware of overlooking that both Tragedy and Comedy have their distinctive ways of recasting and remoulding a Dionysiac rite of passage.

Concentrating, as it does, on a perverted relation between human and divine, Tragedy portrays the *dark* side of Dionysiac initiation. The city of Athens places before itself the image of an 'other' city in

---

[277] The case is most powerfully elaborated by Hoffmann (1989), but I cannot agree with all of the conclusions formulated in his paper.

a liminal suspension between the profane and the sacred. Yet, the anarchy and the disorder of this time apart, at the threshold of sacralization, are *not* to be resolved. Forced, as it is, upon unwilling ritual subjects, Dionysiac initiation fails both as a personal (i.e. for Pentheus) and as a collective rite of passage. The civic dramatic festival of Athens stages the last phase of Dionysus' *telete* as a distorted 'proto-festival' (Foley 1980) which, rather than bringing the initiand/actor into the space of the *polis*, isolates him in a space of wilderness, standing for the opposition or negation of the city's norms and values. To put it in another way: as portrayed in the tragic genre, Dionysiac initiation culminates in a cruel interplay of illusion and reality. Instead of elevating the initiand to renewed ritual and theatrical self-consciousness, Dionysus' sacred *orgia* cause individuality to be submerged and lost. Tragedy, then, dwells on the notion of the ritual passenger as a placeless being, a danger for himself, a threat and a contagion for the wider community into which he cannot be integrated anew. Enduring a real rather than a simulative death (cf. above, 2.3), the initiand of tragedy suffers both a metaphorical dismemberment of personality as well as the visual fragmentation of his theatrical *persona*.

In Comedy, on the other hand, liminality and structural indeterminacy are happily overcome and the initiand is successfully restored within a social milieu. Dionysiac initiation is steered towards the space of the City and it is a thoroughly civic ritual pattern, the Mysteries of Eleusis, which acts as the embracing frame. If I were to apply to the structure of the *Frogs* the functionalist model of Greimas (1966: 172–91), it would seem that the 'sender' or 'dispatcher' who motivates Dionysus, the ritual subject, for the journey of his initiation is the extra-dramatic city of Athens, that is, the current complex of its cultural condition. Nevertheless, 'receiver' or 'destinataire' would be, *again*, the *polis*, as in the comedy's agon the initiand's *dramatis persona* is finally reincorporated into a dramatic other-worldly 'Athens', whose ever-glowing spirit is nostalgically preserved in the mind and the soul of the poet who participated in its glory.[278] More importantly still, as the comic narrative induces Dionysus to realize that poetic fertility does not consist in verbal ingenuities, but rather in an artist's capability to help and willingness to 'save' his city, the god solves his dilemma by finally choosing Aeschylus, the dramatist whose civically oriented visions are expected to revitalize the Athenian *polis* of the real world as well.

---

[278] For a very interesting application of Propp's model in Greek Comedy see Sifakis 1992.

3

The God of Wine and the *Frogs*

The opening picture of the *Frogs* presents Dionysus in the guise of a traveller, entering the space of the Lenaean theatre in Athens. Nevertheless, the point of his departure is never stated openly for the sake of the spectators, as it is, for example, in the *Bacchae* (13–20). The god is just here, in the sight of the audience; he suddenly appears, an 'itinerant epiphany' (Detienne 1989: 5), a divinity coming from outside, arriving 'from Elsewhere' (Detienne 1989: 8). This aspect of Dionysus as a traveller and *xenos* is an essential dimension of his mythical *persona*, since this god, a missionary of his own rites, appears always in the guise of a stranger, playing the role of a divine visitor in whatever land his *thiasos* attains.[1] More significantly still, it is the Attic branch of the Dionysiac tradition which presents the god as a divinity brought 'more than once . . . into the city from outside' (Henrichs 1990: 259). Thus, in the cultic cycle of the Dionysiac festivals in Athens, the god's original advent is annually re-enacted: as part of the preliminary rites inaugurating the City Dionysia festival, the cult-statue of Dionysus Eleuthereus is taken to a temple near the Academy on the road to Eleutherae only to be escorted back, in procession, to the theatre precinct, within the centre of the *polis*.[2] It is the thesis of this chapter that the various legends clustering around Dionysus' visits and ultimate reception into Athens not only inform the thematic structure of the *Frogs* but, more importantly, provide one of the very prominent mythical models upon which the comic god's reaggregation into the dramatic *polis* of the play is built. But, in order to set the scene, let us first survey the ground of the Athenian mythical tradition.

---

[1] For this aspect of Dionysus see Burnett (1970: esp. 27); Detienne (1989: 10–14); for lengthier discussions see Massenzio (1969); Seaford (1994*a*: chs. 7 and 8).

[2] Pickard-Cambridge (1988: 59–60); S. G. Cole (1993*b*: esp. 27). For a different reconstruction of the evidence See Sourvinou-Inwood (1994), who suggests that 'the "leading in" from the *eschara* refers to the bringing of the statue to the theatre, not from the temple at the Academy, but from the *eschara* in the Agora' (283).

Dionysus' visits seem to have been considered as consecutive steps leading to his ultimate admission as a god into the pantheon of the *polis*. Pausanias, for example, reports how the Oracle of Delphi, in an attempt to boost Pegasus' enterprise for the introduction of the god, 'reminded' (ἀναμνῆσαν) the Athenians of his previous sojourn in the house of Icarius (Paus. 1. 2. 5). However, Dionysus' itinerary through Attica was the epiphany of the wine-god, and wine was not harmless from the start: mythical tradition has it that initially it represented 'a madness to be tempered, a savage power to be tamed' (Detienne 1989: 7).

Leaving the house of Icarius, Dionysus bestowed upon him a vine branch together with the secret of viticulture and wine-making. Nevertheless, the shepherds to whom the god's boons were first presented, 'having tasted the beverage and quaffed it copiously without water for the pleasure of it, imagined that they were bewitched and killed him' (Apollod. 3. 14. 7). It was only at his last epiphany to Athens that the god revealed to men the way of liberating his gift from its savagery. According to Philochorus, the king of Athens, Amphictyon, was the first to learn 'from Dionysus how to dilute wine with water' (*FGrHist* 328 F5b, 19–20), precious knowledge indeed, since it resulted in mankind's restoration to its vertical position (ibid.: 21–3) as well as in the institution of the banquet (Philochorus *FGrHist* 328 F5a). More significantly, it is precisely with a *symposion* that the Athenian king Amphictyon entertained Dionysus in the company of other gods (ἄλλους τε θεοὺς ἑστιῶν καὶ Διόνυσον), according to Pausanias' description of a clay-depiction of the scene in Athens (Paus. 1. 2. 5). Amphictyon being the last host of Dionysus in Attica, his offer of a *Theoxenia* (cf. nn. 9–10 below) symbolizes the wine-god's final integration into both the *polis'* divinities and the *polis'* community itself. It was, therefore, as a god of sympotic good cheer (εὐφροσύνη) that the mythical Dionysus entered the civic space. His itinerary to Athens represents the process of wine's domestication and hence the gradual ascent of mankind towards civilization.

Although in the play's opening scene Dionysus is never designated verbatim as a stranger, the *xenia* motif is vital not only in the comedy's plot structure but in its ritual background as well.

As set forth for the first time in the prologue, 'ritualised friendship' (Herman 1987: 10 ff.) stands for a potential link between the pseudo-Heracles/Dionysus and his prototype: ready to embark on his adventure, the god is interested to know Heracles' 'guest-friends', should the need arise for him to use them (109–12).[3] A

---

[3] For the obligations implicated in the bonds of a *xenia* see Herman (1987: 22–9).

xenos is always defined in relation to a stable and fixed familial hearth or wider community; hence, identifying himself and his slave as two *xenoi* (433), that is, newcomers in the Hades regions, Dionysus visualizes the Underworld as a community which might or might not be willing to accept them. This note of community is struck again towards the play's end, when Pluto is prepared to bid farewell to the ascending god and Aeschylus with the gesture of a *xenismos* (1480 ἵνα ξενίζω σφὼ πρὶν ἀποπλεῖν). I shall return to this point in a while; for the moment I should only emphasize that ritualized friendship is prominently apparent in Eleusinian beliefs as well, as communicated both through Heracles' Underworld description (147) and through the hymn of the Initiates themselves (456–9). However, *xenia* acquires its full significance when combined with the wine motif, an important strand which, as we shall see in this chapter, runs throughout the entire play. And I would like here to refer to Kirby's (1976: 58) eloquent expression that theatrical information comes 'in sudden bursts or "bits" scattered irregularly through the performance like stars in the night sky'. Similarly, I suggest that the disparate allusions to wine and rituals centring around wine which are embedded in this comedy's plot structure are presented to the audience in such a way as to yield, when 'reassembled', the impression of a sequence remoulding and reflecting Dionysus' mythical advent in Athens.

3.1. *Wine,* xenia, *and* symposion *in the* Frogs

In line 22 the stage-actor introduces himself as 'Dionysus, son of the Wine-Jar' (Διόνυσος, υἱὸς Σταμνίου). Now, Dionysus' self-presentation in the *Frogs* would have seemed particularly appropriate and amusing to the play's original spectators. A variety of texts exploit the god's identity with wine,[4] while the closest parallel to *Frogs* is Euripides' *Cyclops* 525, where the allusion is offered again through a receptacle of wine, the askos: 'how does he, a god, derive pleasure from dwelling in a wineskin?' Besides, in a Greek audience's perspective, Dionysus is the god *par excellence* who could have been envisaged in connection with a wine-jar: not only was his face either painted or sculpted on a multitude of drinking-cups and storage vessels, but he was often represented as a plastic vase him-

---

[4] This exploitation may be either playful (as e.g. in Eur. *Cycl.* 156, 454, 519–29; Men. *Dysc.* 946), or integrated in a literary or philosophical discourse about religion: see, most importantly, Teiresias' speech in Eur. *Bacch.* 274–85, esp. 284–5: 'He, being god, is poured out in offering to the gods' (Dodds 1960 ad loc.), and Prodicus' much discussed equation of Demeter and Dionysus with bread and wine in fr. B5 D–K (from Sext. Emp. *Adv. Math.* 9. 18), on which see Henrichs (1975b).

self (Trumpf-Lyritzaki 1969: esp. 132–5 with plates) (see Figs. 3.1
and 3.2). Moreover, in the everyday experience of a classical Greek
audience the problematic vase-shape that archaeologists have
labelled by convention 'stamnos' (Philippaki 1967: xviiff.) shared
the twofold character of the alcoholic beverage itself: its relation to
wine was known to be ambivalent, as it could be used either as a
storage vessel containing wine pure, unmixed (as e.g. in Pl. Com. fr.
205 K–A; Philippaki 1967: xix; cf. Durand and Frontisi-Ducroux
1982: 94), or as a kind of mixing-bowl, a krater (Kanowski 1984:
142; Philippaki 1967: xviii). In the 'encyclopaedic' knowledge of
fifth-century spectators, then, the jar Dionysus chooses to appropriate in his line of descent at the beginning of the *Frogs* connotes his
own intoxicating liquid in all its fundamental ambiguity, 'a mixed
blessing' and 'reminder of the god's dual nature' (Henrichs 1979: 4;
1975*a*).

While Dionysus is journeying through the spatial limen of his
initiation, the Stygian frogs, referring to sanctuaries and rites of his
cult, sing:

λιμναῖα κρηνῶν τέκνα,
ξύναυλον ὕμνων βοὰν
φθεγξώμεθ' εὔγηρυν ἐμὰν ἀοιδάν,
κοὰξ κοάξ,
ἣν ἀμφὶ Νυσήϊον
Διὸς Διόνυσον ἐν
    Λίμναισιν ἰαχήσαμεν,
ἡνίχ' ὁ κραιπαλόκωμος
τοῖς ἱεροῖσι Χύτροις χω-
    ρεῖ κατ' ἐμὸν τέμενος λαῶν ὄχλος.

Children of the marshy fountains
let us strike up the hymn in concert with the flute
my lovely sounding song,
koax koax,
which we sung for the Nysean
son of Zeus, Dionysus,
at the Marshes,
when the revelling drunken crowd
rumbles towards my precinct
on the sacred festival of Pots.   (211–19b)

The ritual moment evoked at this point belongs to the oldest
Dionysiac festival in Attica, the festival of the new wine called
Anthesteria, which is widespread in the entire Ionian region and
extends over a period of three days: the 'Opening of Jars'
(Pithoigia), the 'Wine-Pitchers' (Choes), and the 'Pots' (Chytroi).[5]

─────────────
[5] However, see Hamilton (1992: 49) (cf. next note).

3.1. The god of wine *on* wine jugs   3.2. The god of wine *as* a wine jug

bf. amphora: Tarquinia, Museo Nazionale,   plastic oenochoe: Museum of Fine Arts,
RC. 1804 (*ABV* 275, 5)   Boston, 97, 377

More precisely, however, *Frogs* 216–19b very probably refers to the
evening of the Choes, on the 12th of the month Anthesterion.[6] It is
this allusion, I suggest, which constitutes the next semantic unit in
the comedy's wine thread, representing, as it does, an important
stage in the wine's domestication, dramatized annually in the ritual
calendar of Athens. For the wine drunk on the day of the Choes is
not a savage liquid any more. In the context of the κραιπαλόκωμος,
the 'rumbling in drunken revelry' of the Anthesteria feast, the
sanctuary in the Marshes dominating the scene mobilizes an entire

[6] The consensus of opinion seems to be in favour of the evening of the second day of the
Anthesteria festival (note, most significantly, the analogy of the Aristophanic picture with
Phanodemus, *FGrHist* 325 F11); see Deubner (1932: 99–100); Immerwahr (1946: 254–5);
Burkert (1983: 231–2). The argument here runs as follows: 'One must recall that, according
to the old religious chronology, sundown signaled the end of a day and that evening and night
were reckoned as the eve of the following day. Thus, the Pithoigia and the Choes meet on the
evening of the eleventh, the Choes and the Chytroi on the evening of the twelfth. Already in
antiquity, this hazy distinction occasionally caused confusion' (Burkert 1983: 215). *Contra*,
see Jacoby, *FGrHist* IIIb (suppl.), ii. 160 on 325 F12. Hamilton (1992), on the other hand,
breaks new ground by arguing that 'the theory of calendrical confusion is weak' (47), and concludes that 'although certainty is impossible, one should allow the possibility that Choes and
Chytroi occurred on the same day' (49). However, whether the Choes and the Chytroi were
actually conflated or not does not make any difference for my argument at this point.

set of associations with the evening of the previous day: at the Pithoigia, after sunset, when the temple of Dionysus 'in the Marshes' (ἐν Λίμναις) opens, the Athenians 'bring their casks from their houses in order to have them blessed by the god' (Jacoby, *FGrHist* IIIb (suppl.), i. 185). The ritual centres on the mixing of the wine with water, as Phanodemus (*FGrHist* 325 F12) reports, while the Athenians 'pour a libation of the wine before drinking and pray that the use of the "medicine" be harmless and safe for them' (Plut. *Mor.* 655e). In this respect, then, *Frogs* 211–19b remoulds theatrically the ritual moment which follows the wine's ceremonial transformation from a poison to a mild drink.[7]

As Burkert (1983: 217) has emphasized, wine-drinking during the Choes 'is not left to the whim of the individual; . . . tasting the new wine is a collective celebration within the sanctuary'.[8] In fact, the feast becomes virtually synonymous with a collective rite of passage for a whole age-class of the Athenian city's population, as a boy's first celebration of the Choes at the age of 3 signalled for him the end of infancy. Receiving the first pitcher in his life the young Athenian was 'admitted to the religious community' (van Hoorn 1951: 17), and even in a period as late as the second century AD the Choes day still remained a conspicuous occasion in one's life, i.e. the first after birth and last before passing to adolescence, as the famous *Lex Iobacchorum* attests: 'for marriage, birth, Choes, adolescence' (γάμων, γεννήσεως, Χοῶν, ἐφηβείας) (Sokolowski 1969: no. 51, 130). As Burkert (1983: 221) has expressed it, 'Sharing in the wine signified the first step toward sharing in the life of the society, in adult life'; 'ritual wine-drinking at the Choes', therefore, 'reinforced the civic identity of the Athenian male' (Henrichs 1982: 141). In a fifth-century Athenian audience's perspective, then, Dionysus' fictitious passage through the Choes, as evoked by the singing frogs, could be regarded as an experience of transition, bringing the initiand a step closer to his final integration into the community of Athens.

Both the *xenia* and the wine/*symposion* motif meet at *Frogs* 503 ff., where Persephone's maid invites the pseudo-Heracles to feast (4.10). In other words, the scene presents Persephone in the position of a host and Dionysus/Heracles in the position of a guest, a *xenos* to be entertained with a meal, a *deipnon* of hospitality. Nevertheless, the high status of this guest (in Persephone's eyes he is a hero, in the

---

[7] I am not convinced by the arguments leading to N. Robertson's (1993: 226) conclusion that 'the *choes* contained neat wine. The ritual mixing of wine and water must belong to the third day.'

[8] The bulk of the evidence consists of choes, some with inscriptions, found on infants' graves.

spectators' eyes a god) enriches the *xenia* offered to him with an additional dimension: Persephone's invitation can be interpreted as an instance of a *Theoxenia*, that widespread ritual by which a city, an individual, or a god offers hospitality to a god(s) or hero(es).[9] Within the Greek religious experience, for example, the ritual which bears the closest affinity to the Aristophanic scene is the Delphic *Theoxenia*, where Apollo plays the role of host to gods and heroes.[10] More importantly still, a variety of sources indicates the strong connection of *Theoxenia* with a table (*trapeza*) and a meal, while in the ritual language which describes such occasions the formal designation of this cultic practice is the expression κλίνην στρῶσαι καὶ τράπεζαν κοσμῆσαι, to spread clothes over a bed and to prepare a table.[11] When seen in such a light, then, the *trapeza* and the listing of the foods which constitute the focus of the scene in *Frogs* (see 518 and 505 ff. respectively) create a semantically 'loaded' picture, carrying a complex range of ritual connotations. Besides, as both Dionysus and Heracles were formally honoured with *Theoxenia* (in Dionysus' case called *Theodaisia*) in a variety of places, the *xenia* dimension of the scene would have been readily detectable by the play's original spectators, whether the scene was deciphered along an Heraclean or a Dionysiac axis.[12]

However, the prospective *deipnon* does not merely consist in food. Persephone has mixed a 'sweetest' wine (511), while the feast will also be enriched with the elements of music and of dance, as both a flute-player (513 αὐλητρίς) and dancers (514 κὠρχηστρίδες) have been asked to perform for the distraction of the guest. In other words, Persephone's invitation is so enunciated as to construct to the eyes of a Greek classical spectator the merry setting of a banquet. Because although 'in the strict etymological sense' the word *symposion* 'designates the time after the meal when communal drinking takes place' (Schmitt-Pantel 1990: 15), the two phases are very often

---

[9] For rituals of *Theoxenia* see Deneken (1881); Nilsson (1906: 160ff., 418ff., 446f.); Gernet (1968: 32–3).

[10] Schol. Pind. *Nem.* 7. 68 (p. 217 Abel) γίνεται ἐν Δελφοῖς ἥρωσι ξένια, ἐν οἷς δοκεῖ ὁ θεὸς ἐπὶ ξένια καλεῖν τοὺς ἥρωας. For discussions of this Delphic ritual type see Vollgraff (1925: 121); Amandry (1939: 209–11, 1944–5: 413–15); Bruit (1984: 360).

[11] Connection with a table/meal: schol. Pind. *Ol.* 3 (p. 149, 18–19 Abel) Θεοξένια . . . οἱονεὶ ξενίαν καὶ τράπεζαν τῶν θεῶν; Pind. *Ol.* 3. 71–2. Cf. Athen. 137e (ἄριστον at the *Theoxenia* for the Dioscuri in Athens); see further Bruit (1989: 19) and Deneken in *LGRM*, s.v. Heros, 2507–8. Ritual language: see Ziehen, in *RE*, s.v. parasitoi, 1379 (with refs. to inscriptions), and (more detailed still), Rhomaios (1914: 230 n. 2). For the centrality of *trapeza* in cultic occasions see Dow and Gill (1965: esp. 109).

[12] Dionysus: see Deneken (1881: 47); Nilsson (1906: 279–80); more extensively on the ways of his implication into the *xenia*-code see Massenzio (1969). For Heracles see Burnett (1970: 25 with n. 8), and cf. the proverb Ἡρακλῆς ξενίζεται (Ar. *Lys.* 928 with schol.), which suggests a close link between a meal, voracity, and Heraclean *xenismos*.

fused and projected onto the same plane (cf. O. Murray 1983*a*: 50),[13] as is the case with our scene. Besides, both art and literature can prove the various segments which build up Persephone's scene to be intrinsic elements in a *symposion*'s distractions.[14] Even Dionysus' festive solitude in *Frogs* 503ff. is a familiar picture in the cultural horizon of Greek spectators. As Schmitt and Schnapp (1982: 69) observe, towards the end of the sixth century the banquet with many symposiasts yields its place to the representation of one single person—in most cases a hero or a god—in the role of a banqueter: 'The banqueter alone, in the middle of other actors who are not fellow-drinkers any more, is represented "in majesty".' And, although it is not the god himself but Xanthias/Heracles, his slave, to whom Persephone's invitation is actually addressed, the Dionysiac dimension of the scene should not be overlooked, as Persephone's symposium represents the only moment in the play's plot when the god expresses the desire to *identify* with the fate of Heracles, his prototype, rather than wishing to estrange himself from it (see in detail 4.10).

It is a common idea among social anthropologists[15] that what and how one eats or drinks 'constitute a mode of communication' (Gusfield 1987: 76), a code, which both expresses and establishes a wide variety of social relations, such as one's participation in/ exclusion from smaller or larger groups, social castes, ethnicities, religious circles, and so forth (cf. Farb and Armelagos 1980: 6). As Mary Douglas (1987*b*: 8) has put it with respect to drinks, 'drinks . . . act as markers of personal identity and of boundaries of inclusion and exclusion'.[16] Some examples can be taken from Dionysiac iconography, where types of food as well as the pictorial interplay of mixed versus unmixed wine help to signify to the viewer the space (human or divine) where Dionysus belongs. So, a painter's favourite way of signifying Dionysus' divinity is the pictorial associ-

---

[13] For such images in art see Dentzer (1982: 335) on Attic banquet reliefs from 420 to 300 BC, while for the earlier period see Schmitt and Schnapp (1982: 59). In literature cf. e.g. Ar. *Wasps* 1216ff.; Men. *Dysc.* 940ff., etc.

[14] See, most importantly, Xen. *Symp.* 2. 1–2, which bears a close correspondence to the feast in *Frogs*. For flute-girls and dancers in the banquet see e.g. (literature) Ar. *Acharn.* 1093; *Wasps* 1219; Pl. Com. fr. 71, 12–13 K–A; Men. *Dysc.* 950ff. and (art) Dentzer (1982: 111–13, 125); cf. Schmitt and Schnapp (1982: 71). The Milesian στρώματα (see schol. *Frogs* 542; cf. Theocr. *Id.* 15. 125) correspond to the various draperies and cushions which in vase-paintings cover convivial couches and seats adding thus to the symposiasts' comfort; see Schmitt and Schnapp (1982: 59–60). For erotic scenes within the banquet-setting see Dentzer (1982: 111–13, 123, 124, 126, and *passim* for Dionysiac banquets especially), and cf. Eur. *Cycl.* 495ff. For the imaginary fist-fight (545–8) see, in general terms, Pellizer (1983; cf. 1990: 181 with n. 14) and, more closely to *Frogs*, Athen. 607c–e and 592f.

[15] For a brief survey of various perspectives see Goody (1982: 10–39).

[16] Cf. Vernant's (1979*a*) analysis of the Prometheus myth (esp. 42–3).

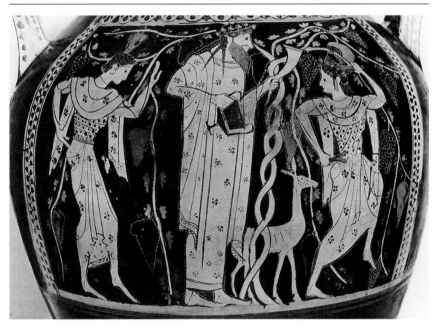

3.3. Dionysus with rhyton and kantharos

rf. Attic amphora: Munich, Staatliche Antikensammlungen, Glyptothek 2300 (*ARV*² 11, 1)

ation of the god with his distinctive drinking vessels, the kantharos or the rhyton (Fig. 3.3), which, as typical Dionysiac insignia, are supposed to contain pure, intoxicating wine. Conversely, if the painter's aim is to translate the banquet of the god into human terms, he can associate pictorially Dionysus (or even his mythical followers, the satyrs) with types of mugs which are most frequently connected with scenes of human festive drinking, such as the skyphos (Fig. 3.4) or, more importantly, the krater, the 'space' *par excellence* where wine is mixed (cf. *krasis, kerannymi*) with water. In a similar way, I suggest, Dionysus' seduction by the human mode of food and drink consumption in the *Frogs* serves as a dramatic sign of his integration into the community of human beings. To put it in another way, *Frogs* 503 ff. elaborates on the well-known motif of Dionysus as a fellow-celebrant, best exemplified in Plato's conception of this god as one among the immortal *syneortastai* that the Olympians bestowed upon mankind as companions in festivity (Pl. *Leg.* 653d), as well as in Euripides' ode in *Bacchae* 375 ff. (see below, 4.10). Furthermore, this note of Dionysus as a fellow-dancer[17] has

---

[17] Cf. Pl. *Leg.* 665a θεοὺς δὲ ἔφαμεν ἐλεοῦντας ἡμᾶς συγχορευτάς τε καὶ χορηγοὺς ἡμῖν δεδωκέ-ναι . . . καὶ δὴ καὶ τρίτον . . . Διόνυσον.

3.4. Dionysos holding a skyphos
rf. amphora: Paris, Louvre, G 201 (*ARV*² 201, 63)

already been struck at an earlier moment in the plot when the god,
as an onlooker of the Eleusinian procession, articulated his wish to
'play and dance' with a female member of the Chorus (414b–15 καὶ
μετ᾽ αὐτῆς | παίζων χορεύειν βούλομαι).

Nevertheless, Persephone's *symposion* must not be viewed as an
isolated event within this comedy's dramatic framework. Although
I would not wish to argue that the chain of 'wine moments' provides
a compelling, unmistakable, and all-embracing unifying link to the
same extent that the thread of ritual initiation does (cf. Ch. 2), I *do*
believe that sympotic pictures are more widely interspersed in the
structure of this play, and that it rests with the culturally conditioned receptiveness of the receiver to reconstruct and organize
them into a meaningful sequence. Taking, then, into account first
and foremost classical Greek sociocultural parameters, this chapter
argues for the possibility of such a reconstruction and attempts to
show the ways in which a 'sympotic' reading of the *Frogs* would
enrich the play with new dimensions.

(i) At their first entrance on the stage Dionysus and Xanthias are
accompanied by a donkey, an animal closely associated with the
context of a Dionysiac *komos* at least from the sixth century
onwards, as the extremely popular representations of the story of
Hephaestus' Return[18] attest. In the most frequently produced

---

[18] See Paus. 1. 20. 3 and Libanius, Διηγήματα ζ´ Περὶ Ἡφαίστου (Foerster, viii. 38–9). With
an artistic life of at least 200 years (T. B. L. Webster 1959: 62–3), with some 180 extant

3.5. Return of Hephaestus (early sixth cent. BC)
bf. Corinthian column-krater: British Museum, 1867. 8–5. 860 (B42)

3.6. Return of Hephaestus (late fifth cent. BC)
rf. kalyx-krater: Paris, Louvre, G404 (*ARV*² 1046, 6)

scheme, Hephaestus, inebriated with his brother's wine, is seated on a mule in a komastic posture, with drinking-cup or horn in hand, while Dionysus himself is walking, either behind or in front of him (Figs. 3.5 and 3.6). The opening picture of the *Frogs* is similar in some respects (Handley 1985: 365), for Dionysus steps onto the stage walking, while his slave rides the ὄνος, as is verbally empha-

representations in art coming from workshops from all over the Greek world (Brommer 1978: 10), and with its basic iconographic elements virtually unchanged (Schöne 1987: 44), this corpus of images was one of the most beloved Dionysiac themes. For an exhaustive analysis of iconographic types see Brommer (1978) and for the 5th-cent. Attic production in particular see Halm-Tisserant (1986).

sized in line 23. I would, therefore, like to suggest that the presence
of the donkey would activate the cultural or 'long-term' memory
(De Marinis 1985: 15) of a Greek audience in order to evoke a
picture semiotically 'loaded' with komastic associations. Furthermore, even outside the context of this specific legend, the donkey/
mule is a familiar presence in the space of a Dionysiac banquet: on
all sorts of drinking-cups and storage vessels, that is to say, in an
image which belongs to the everyday experience of Greek symposiasts, Dionysus is either drinking or holding the kantharos, whether
seated in front of the animal (*LIMC*, s.v. Dionysos, 384–5) or
walking at its side (ibid.: 386–91), or even feasting while reclining
on his mobile couch (ibid.: 392–403) (Fig. 3.7).[19] Even without
Dionysus' presence, the donkey seems to be a part of the sympotic
frame; a rhyton from Agrigento (fig. 36 in Lissarrague 1987*b*), for
example, is manipulated in a donkey shape: its cargo (cf. Xanthias'
φορτίον) constitutes the actual drinking-cup, decorated with the
image of a drinking party, while a banqueter is drinking in the space
under the donkey's legs.

(ii) In a fifth-century audience's perspective, the familiar image—
for us illustrated by numerous Choes jugs—of the drunken throngs
rumbling along the streets and alleys of Athens towards the
Dionysiac temple in the Marshes in *Frogs* 211 ff. is closely associated
with—and, therefore, can call forth—the private and civic banquets
that have taken place earlier on that same day of the Choes.
Aristophanes' *Acharnians* 1085 ff. offers an elaborate description of
such feasts: tables full of dishes, draperies and cushions, female
dancers and erotic fantasies (1147–9) conjure up an enjoyment
whose nature very much resembles the picture of Persephone's
banquet in the *Frogs*.

(iii) *Frogs* 211–19b may also be considered as a function of a more
elaborate sympotic image. For Dionysus' rowing on the Styx in
Charon's boat, accompanied, as it is, by the frogs' song of drunken
revellers evokes in its own right the motif of a symposium on the
basis of a metaphor well-known both in literature and art, whereby
sympotic space is compared to a ship floating in the sea:[20] 'the
symposiasts are depicted as, or believe themselves to be, sailors'
(W. J. Slater 1976: 163), while the splash of wine can be compared
to the sweep of oars.[21] More significantly still, the image claims a

[19] See also a mule featuring among a rich tapestry of sympotic elements in *LIMC*, s.v.
Dionysos, 372. Besides, a Dionysiac *symposion* is conceivable on the back of other animals as
well, especially the bull (ibid.: 435–6).

[20] See W. J. Slater (1976) for an exhaustive treatment of the sources, to which add
Archilochus, fr. 4 West (with E. L. Bowie 1986: 16 ff.), and Eur. *Cycl.* 503–9.

[21] As e.g. in Eur. *Alc.* 798 μεθορμιεῖ σε πίτυλος ἐμπεσὼν σκύφου, πίτυλος being taken from

3.7. Feasting on the back of a donkey
rf. column-krater: Museo Civico Archeologico, Bologna, 194 (*ARV*² 575, 21)

strong connection with Dionysus himself, as Dionysius Chalcus
(5th cent. BC) can suggest. For fr. 5 G–P: 'and there are some who
bring wine to the oarage of Dionysus, sailors of the banquet and
rowers of the wine-cups' (καί τινες οἶνον ἄγοντες ἐν εἰρεσίᾳ Διονύσου,
| συμποσίου ναῦται καὶ κυλίκων ἐρέται), not only establishes the act of
rowing as an intrinsic element in the structure of the metaphor²² but
also denotes the symposium in terms of a Dionysiac εἰρεσία, that is,
rowing.²³ The evidence from literature may be corroborated by
images as well (Fig. 3.8), portraying Dionysus as a 'mariner and
banqueter' reclining in his ship, simultaneously a sea-vessel and a
banqueting couch (Daraki 1982: 5). In *Frogs* 211 ff., then, both
visual and acoustic signs as well as the performer's bodily discourse
combine and interact for channelling the expectation of the
audience towards the banquet of Persephone.

antiquity to be a sound-word (Hesychius, πιτύλοις· τοῖς ψόφοις τῶν ὑδάτων), mostly indicating
the plash of oars in the water, the oar-beat; see examples in Barrett (1964: 418). Barrett (ibid.:
ad Eur. *Hipp.* 1464), in an extensive note on the word, argues for *pitylos* as 'a regularly
repeated rhythmical movement' rather than sound, but even this interpretation does not
exclude the working of the nautical metaphor.

²² Cf. also Dionysius Chalcus (fr. 3 G–P) extending the metaphor of rowing and rowers to
an 'intellectual' banquet: εἰρεσίᾳ γλώσσης ἀποπέμψομεν ἐς μέγαν αἶνον | τοῦδ᾽ ἐπὶ συμποσίου·
δεξιότης τε λόγου | Φαίακος Μουσῶν ἐρέτας ἐπὶ σέλματα πέμπει (3–5).

²³ Cf. Davies (1978: 80), who considers as the 'clearest illustration of such fantasy in vase-
painting' a Campanian bell-krater depicting a silen in the act of rowing the *symposion*-ship.

3.8. Dionysus' marine banquet
bf. Attic kylix by Exekias: Munich, Staatliche
Antikensammlungen, Glyptothek 2044 (*ABV* 146, 21)

(iv) The first adventure of Dionysus as he steps out of Charon's boat culminates in his yearning for a drink in a symposium. Terrified by Empusa and seeking refuge in his own priest, the god envisages himself in the happy situation of being a fellow-drinker: 'O priest, please, keep a watchful eye on me, so that I may join you for a drink at the wine party' (ἱερεῦ, διαφύλαξόν μ', ἵν' ὦ σοι συμπότης) (297). But, as Segal very aptly stressed, drinking together with the priest, Dionysus' representative in the theatrical performances of Athens, is a powerful allusion to the comic festival's communal setting (Segal 1961: 222) and, therefore, one more link in the chain of images revolving around wine which orientates gradually the god towards the very heart of the Athenian *polis*.

Finally, the thematic thread centring around wine which unites apparently disparate 'moments' of the play's imagery and structure very aptly complements the primary symbolic frame of this comedy, the mystic initiation pattern discussed at great length in Chapter 2. Because, although certainty is impossible, there are strong indications that wine was used as a means of Bacchic initiation. In the first place, wine features in the Pelinna gold leaves (lines 6 and 5 on leaves *a* and *b* respectively: οἶνον ἔχεις εὐδαίμονα τιμήν (You have wine as your fortunate honour)), belonging to the complex of Dionysiac mystic ritual (2.14; cf. 4.10, n. 140),[24] while the Euripidean *Cyclops* dramatizes the mock-initiation of Polyphemus into the Bacchic *thiasos* of satyrs through the medium of Dionysus' intoxicating drink, offered cunningly to him by Odysseus (esp. *Cycl.* 411–24).[25] In Aeschylus' satyric *Lycurgus*, Dionysus' antagonist, an archetypal mystic initiand comparable to the Euripidean Pentheus in the *Bacchae* (cf. 2.12), may have been converted to wine-drinking,[26] and a fragment of a dramatic text (most probably belonging to the period of Old Comedy; Bierl 1990) preserved in *P. Köln* VI 242a mentions a Dionysiac initiate (μύστης) in close connection with the newly invented wine.[27] As for archaeological evidence, Graf (1993: 249 with n. 26) mentions a Roman relief and a sarcophagus depicting Bacchic initiation in a sequence which 'it seems, was concluded by ritual wine drinking, marking the integration of the new member.'[28] In this respect, then, being involved in a chain of wine images in the process of his initiation, Dionysus may be thought to re-enact an experience recognizable by a number of Bacchic initiates among the Aristophanic *theatai*.

3.2. *The Poetic Agon as an Intellectual Banquet in the* Frogs

If Persephone's symposium has been gradually anticipated, it is worth investigating whether it could also have created an expectancy for its reduplication in the play's second part. Such an expectation would have been firmly situated within the framework of Greek Comedy's generic norms. For the culmination of a comic

---

[24] It is interesting to note here that a satyr labelled Oinops is depicted in the great Dionysiac Underworld scene of a 4th-cent. Apulian krater now in Toledo (cf. Ch. 2, n. 136). His drinking horn may represent the festive life which awaits the Orphic/Dionysiac initiate in the afterlife, and thus offer an iconographic parallel to the textual promise of the Pelinna tablets (Johnston and McNiven 1996: 34).

[25] On the *Cyclops* as being 'based on the process of initiation into the mysteries of Dionysos' see Seaford (1984: 57–9).

[26] See Aesch. fr. 124 Radt κἀκ τῶνδ' ἔπινε βρῦτον . . . (i.e. according to Athen. 447b, wine made from barley: κρίθινον οἶνον).

[27] Lines 14–15 . . .] εἰς θνητοὺς ἀνέφηνα ποτὸν Διονύσου | . . .] σος ὁ μύστης οὔποτε λήγων ἐπὶ Βάκχῳ (text in Bierl 1990: 354).

[28] Initiation through wine seems to have been operative in the context of other mystic cults as well; for example, Burkert (1970: 9 with n. 3) notes that wine-vessels excavated in the precinct of the sanctuary of the Cabeiri at Lemnos may point to the conclusion that 'wine-drinking played an important role' in the Cabeiric mysteries, at a site which 'offers a neat example of continuity of cult from pre-Greek to Greek population.'

play in a feast elaborately set up after the protagonist has established
his/her imaginary world[29] or even the prospect of an off-stage
banquet mingling imaginatively with the festival's official celebrations (as it happens, for example, at the closing scenes of *Peace* and
Birds), is part and parcel of Comedy's carnivalesque dimension.
And, actually, two explicit references to Dionysus and wine can be
isolated after the play's parabasis.

Before the start of the agon Xanthias offers to his fellow-slave and
the *theatai* a brief portrait of his master as somebody who 'knows
only how to drink and to have sex' (πίνειν οἶδε καὶ βινεῖν μόνον) (740),
a characterization which captures the essence of the meaning of this
god for a wide section of the Lenaean audience (cf. Eur. *Bacch.*
773–4). Nevertheless, there is an important respect in which this
brief description of Dionysus foreshadows the image offered to the
spectators in the immediately ensuing scene. For in the course of the
contest Aeschylus suddenly addresses his judge with the surprising
remark: 'Dionysus, the wine you drink does not have a fine bouquet'
(Διόνυσε, πίνεις οἶνον οὐκ ἀνθοσμίαν) (1150). No satisfactory explanation of this unexpected outburst has been proposed to date. Dover
(1993: ad loc.) wavers between 'You stink' and 'You have a hang-
over', neither of which gets us very far, because they both fail to
shed light on the way in which Aeschylus' rebuke could be smoothly
integrated with its immediate semantic and/or visual frame.[30] I
would, therefore, like to suggest a twofold possibility for placing the
dramatist's comment in an intelligible context.

To start with, it seems that in Old Comedy allusions to concrete
objects and actions had an easily detectable or tangible plane of
reference for the spectator's vision,[31] or, to put it in another way, it
seems that minimization of abstraction was one of the implicit rules
governing the staging of a comic spectacle. In this respect, then,
Aristophanes' first audience would have considered Aeschylus'
taunt as utterly inexplicable or, to say the least, as out of place, if the
god had not been holding his special drinking vessel, the kantharos,
in his hand. Nevertheless, even beyond the visual level of the comic
staging, there is a far more subtle and intrinsic way in which
Dionysus' drinking of 'not flower-scented wine' can fit in its con-

[29] As, for example, in *Acharn.* 1085 ff.; *Wasps* 1208 ff.; *Peace* 1191 ff.; *Lys.* 1182 ff.; *Eccles.*
1112 ff. (where the *theatai* and judges are also invited at 1141–3).

[30] Sommerstein's note (1996: ad loc.): 'The semantic link between "you drink evil-smelling
wine" and the message Aeschylus evidently means to convey, viz. "that remark was in very
poor taste", is presumably "your breath stinks": both the words one speaks, and the smell of
the wine one has drunk, are carried on one's breath,' is much more helpful, without, however,
answering all the questions one might wish to ask.

[31] Cf. Macleod's (1974) argument about the visible point of reference of the demonstrative
pronouns ὁδί and οὑτοσί in Ar. *Acharn.* 418 and 427.

textual frame. Its semantic integration in the literary agon operates on a purely metaphorical level, metaphor joining together two prima-facie incompatible activities: the tangible, material process of food and drink consumption and the intellectual, abstract, mental process which enables the viewer's or the listener's assimilation and enjoyment of literary *logoi*. The interpenetration of these levels is firmly rooted in both Greek and Roman culture, the archetype of *logos*/drink interrelation going as far back as the Homeric poems. In *Odyssey* 4 a banquet takes place in Menelaus' palace; before the wine is poured out to the guests, Helen mixes with it a magic drug (*pharmakon*) given to her in Egypt (219–32), and immediately proposes to take up the role of the bard by saying 'fitting' (*eikota*) things (Goldhill 1991: 62) for the distraction of her feasting audience:

ἦ τοι νῦν δαίνυσθε καθήμενοι ἐν μεγάροισι
καὶ μύθοις τέρπεσθε· ἐοικότα γὰρ καταλέξω.

Sit here now in the palace and take your dinner and listen
to me and be entertained. What I will tell you is plausible.   (238–9)

This magic drug, however, being 'grief removing, anger reducing, and inducing forgetfulness of every sorrow' (νηπενθές τ᾽ ἄχολόν τε, κακῶν ἐπίληθον ἁπάντων) (221), has the characteristic qualities of *logos* and of bardic song, whose listener 'forgets his anxious cares and doesn't give a thought to his own griefs' (Hes. *Theog.* 102–3).[32] As Plutarch (*Mor.* 614c) understood it, Helen's 'good drug' was the tale itself, her *mythos*:

This, I take it, was the 'assuaging' and pain-allaying drug, a story with a timeliness appropriate to the experiences and circumstances of the moment.

To put it in another way, in the Odyssean narrative the wine acquired the qualities of *logos*, or rather it became *logos*.[33] Nevertheless, it is not only epic poetry which can conceive of wine and *logos* as potentially interwoven. In fact, the Homeric epics themselves seem to have been viewed as banquets, as a quotation from Athenaeus (347e) suggests, where Aeschylus is said to have declared his tragedies as 'large cuts (τεμάχη) taken from Homer's mighty

---

[32] Cf. Hes. *Theog.* 53–5; Bacchyl. *Ep.* 5. 3ff. In Pl. *Phdr.* 267d *logos* can calm anger (ὠργισμένοις ἐπᾴδων κηλεῖν); cf. Gorg. *Helen* (fr. B11 D–K) 8 (λύπην ἀφελεῖν) and see, in general, Gorg. *Helen* 8–9, and esp. 14.

[33] Goldhill (1988b: 30 n. 86) notes that the connection between *pharmakon* and *mythos* made in antiquity was facilitated by 'the common use of *pharmakon* for spoken spells', but I think this perspective overlooks the true analogy between sympotic food/drink and *logos* deeply ingrained in Graeco-Roman culture. For a Roman parallel see Horace's *Odes* 1. 20, where the Sabinian wine Horace offers to Maecenas is ultimately the poem itself; see Putnam (1969).

dinners (τῶν Ὁμήρου μεγάλων δείπνων)'. More importantly still, it is obvious that in fifth-century Athens, the metaphor is well established: a dramatist can conceive of himself as a cook who feasts his audience on a modest or a sumptuous meal, as the need arises.

The comic poet Metagenes, for example, announces his intention to vary his speech in each episode, 'so that I may delight the audience with a feast of side-dishes new and many' (ὡς ἂν | καιναῖσι παροψίσι καὶ πολλαῖς εὐωχήσω τὸ θέατρον) (fr. 15 K–A). The spectators, correspondingly, on leaving the theatre, can be described as having been 'fed'. Thus, in Aristophanes' *Knights* 538–9 the Chorus refers to Crates as a comic poet who would offer to his audience 'a cheap little repast' (ὃς ἀπὸ σμικρᾶς δαπάνης ὑμᾶς ἀριστίζων ἀπέπεμπεν) and would 'knead the funniest devices' (μάττων ἀστειοτάτας ἐπινοίας), while elsewhere in Aristophanes (fr. 347, 1 K–A) the art of Comedy (the τρυγῳδοποιομουσική) is 'really a substantial meal' (ἢ μέγα τι βρῶμ').[34] Besides, the art of Tragedy as well can be presented through the comic lens in culinary terms both on the reception and the composition level. So, the comic poet Teleclides refers to the tragic Mnesilochus as 'the one who roasts a new drama (φρύγει τι δρᾶμα καινόν) for Euripides, with Socrates providing the firewood' (fr. 41 K–A), while two Aristophanic characters discuss how the language of the tragic poet Sthenelus can best be 'eaten':

> (A) καὶ πῶς ἐγὼ Σθενέλου φάγοιμ' ἂν ῥήματα;
> (B) εἰς ὄξος ἐμβαπτόμενος ἢ ξηροὺς ἅλας
>
> (A) And how am I supposed to eat Sthenelus' words?
> (B) Dipping them in vinegar or dry salt.
>
> (Ar. fr. 158 K–A)

The conception of a theatrical performance as a δαίς or as a feast of dishes, then, must have been a fairly standard image in the literary 'encyclopaedia' of fifth-century playgoers.[35]

However, if a performance can be viewed as a banquet, as a feast of dishes, a real banquet too can be conceived in abstract terms in such a way as to become a feast of words. In the range of a metaphor abundantly attested, the banquet is the soul's occasion to devote itself to its own pleasures and, therefore, feast on words (λόγοις εὐωχουμένη).[36] As Plutarch (*Mor.* 672 e) expressed it,

---

[34] Cf. also Cratinus, fr. 182 K–A. For more examples see Taillardat (1965: 439–41).

[35] In the 4th cent. Plato extends the culinary metaphor to encompass rhetorical *logos* in general: rhetoric is for the soul what cookery is for the body (*Gorg.* 465d).

[36] Plut. *Mor.* 673a; cf. Luc. 17. 2, where Philon characterizes Lycinus' anticipated tale as an ἡδίστην . . . ἑστίασιν, and Pl. *Tim.* 27b τὴν τῶν λόγων ἑστίασιν.

at parties men of wit and taste hurry at once after dinner to ideas as if to dessert, finding their entertainment in conversation that has little or nothing to do with the concerns of the body; and so they make it clear that there is a private store of delights set aside for the soul, and that these are its only true pleasures . . .

In the literary staging of a banquet, then, metaphor plays so prominent a role that 'Words become dishes, and discussions of the banquet are in their turn transformed by the imagery of the language into banquets themselves' (Lukinovich 1990: 268).[37] Athenaeus, for example, casts himself in the role of a cook, 'preparing, ordering and serving various ingredients' (Relihan 1992: 234), and prefaces his *Deipnosophists* with an elaborate analogy of literary *logos* and luxurious banquets:

καί ἐστιν ἡ τοῦ λόγου οἰκονομία μίμημα τῆς τοῦ δείπνου πολυτελείας, καὶ ἡ τῆς βίβλου διασκευὴ τῆς ἐν τῷ δείπνῳ παρασκευῆς. τοιοῦτον ὁ θαυμαστὸς οὗτος τοῦ λόγου οἰκονόμος Ἀθήναιος ἥδιστον λογόδειπνον εἰσηγεῖται[38]

In short, the plan of the discourse reflects the rich bounty of a feast, and the arrangement of the book the courses of the dinner. Such is the delightful feast of reason which this wonderful steward, Athenaeus, introduces . . . (Athen. 1b)

Levels of edible reality and abstract *logos*, therefore, intermingle in a variety of ways, so that attributes of food or wine are transferred to speeches[39] with the same ease that the primary dimension of a conversation is translated by its own right into a *deipnon*. In Athenaeus 358c, for example, a healthy conversation about fishes has the value of a healthy *deipnon*. Constructing playfully a pleasant paradox, Plutarch often treats wise *logos* as more indispensable than wine itself in an intellectual sympotic setting, so Mnesiphelus addresses the drinking company of the 'Seven Wise Men' as follows:

However, when such men as you, whom Periander has invited here, come together, I think there is nothing for the wine-cup or ladle to accomplish,

---

[37] Cf. Gowers (1993: 41): 'As an ordered form created out of selected, transformed ingredients and offered to others, the meal has a great deal in common with literary composition. The Greeks and Romans could describe the whole process of creating, presenting, and consuming a literary text in alimentary terms. Writers often characterized themselves as cooks or caterers serving feasts of words.' For a survey of classical literary *symposia* see Relihan (1992).

[38] Cf. Athen. 2b λόγοις ἑστία; 398b ζητήσεις γὰρ σιτούμεθα; 122e τῶν γὰρ τοιούτων φωνῶν ἐγὼ δυμῶ; 122f δυμᾷς γὰρ λόγων (refs. from Lukinovich 1990: nn. 25 ff.) For a philosophical 'feast of words' see e.g. Pl. *Rep.* 571d ἑστιάσας λόγων καλῶν καὶ σκέψεων; *Rep.* 352b εὐωχοῦ τοῦ λόγου; *Phdr.* 227b ἦ δῆλον ὅτι τῶν λόγων ὑμᾶς Λυσίας ἑστία;

[39] See e.g. Athen. 121e, where Cynulcus needs fountains of sweetness (γλυκέων . . . νάμασι) to wash away 'salty speeches' (ἁλμυροὺς λόγους). Cf. Plut. *Mor.* 614d, 711d and (Anon.) *Vit. Aes.* (G), chs. 51–2 (p. 52 Perry).

but the Muses set discourse in the midst before all, a non-intoxicating bowl
as it were (ἀλλ' αἱ Μοῦσαι καθάπερ κρατῆρα νηφάλιον ἐν μέσῳ προθέμεναι τὸν
λόγον), containing a maximum of pleasure in jest and seriousness combined; and with this they awaken and foster and dispense friendliness,
allowing the 'ladle', for the most part, to lie untouched 'atop of the bowl'—
a thing which Hesiod would prohibit in a company of men better able to
drink than to converse.   (Plut. *Mor.* 156d–e)

Returning now to the *Frogs*, my proposition is that lines 1149–50
would make perfect sense if viewed against the sociocultural background I have just deployed, that is, if they are deciphered as
belonging to the well-attested cluster of allegorical sympotical discourse. Connoting the smell of decay and of corpses, Dionysus'
clumsy intervention: 'Then, surely, he would have inherited the
skill of grave-robbing from his father' (οὕτω γ' ἂν εἴη πρὸς πατρὸς
τυμβωρύχος) determines in Aeschylus' mind the quality and flavour
of his drink,[40] which can certainly not be an οἶνος ἀνθοσμίας, a per-
fumed wine, a liquid with a nice fragrance.[41] In the remainder of this
chapter, then, I will explore the possibility that 'stage iconization'
and 'textual symbolization' (Pavis 1982: 32) in the agon of the *Frogs*
'cross-fertilized' each other[42] in such a way as to create for the
audience the possibility to assimilate the literary debate as an intellectual banquet. Now, needless to say, this line of inquiry is by no
means proposed as the best or only way of having access to the
play's agon. As I have already stated in the Introduction to this
book, I am deeply conscious of the fact that, at any single point of
the text, my approach illuminates and activates only *some* of the
many possible channels of communication that the reception of this
play could follow in its original context. In this respect, thinking of
the agon as a banquet is by no means exclusive of other plausible
constructions, some of which will be discussed at length in Chapters
5–9. But for the moment, I intend to concentrate on *one* particular
range of connotations, and exploit in full the fact that a Greek
audience's receptiveness was shaped to a considerable extent by
expectations such as those reflected in Astydamas' play Ἡρακλῆς
Σατυρικός:

---

[40] However, if Dionysus in the agon is placed in the midst of such an intellectual aura where
logoi can stand for food and drink, at the beginning of the play he was obliged to follow a
reverse procedure, i.e. translate *logos*/intellectual discussion into food through the means of
ainigmoi (61 δι' αἰνιγμῶν ἐρῶ) in order to reach the level of Heracles, his interlocutor.
[41] From Greek lyric poetry onwards literature can be tasted and smelt, and stylistic features
are compared to edible substances or alimentary processes; see Bramble (1974: 45–59).
[42] For the notion of 'cross-fertilization' of theatrical signs belonging to different modes of
semiosis see Veltruský (1976: 571).

ἀλλ' ὥσπερ δείπνου γλαφυροῦ ποικίλην εὐωχίαν
τὸν ποιητὴν δεῖ παρέχειν τοῖς θεαταῖς τὸν σοφόν,
ἵν' ἀπίῃ τις τοῦτο φαγὼν καὶ πιών, ὅπερ λαβὼν
χαίρει ⟨τις⟩ . . .

Like the varied bounty of a dainty dinner,
such must be the fare provided by the clever poet for the spectators,
so that each departs after having eaten and drunk
that in which he delights . . .

(Astydamas II, *TGrF* i (60) F4)

A number of cultural parameters can be adduced to support my proposition.

(i) In the first place, a gathering of intellectuals in Hades was traditionally conceived of in terms of a convivial entertainment, a banquet of 'wise men'.[43] In the Pseudo-Platonic *Axiochus*, for example, 'discourses . . . of philosophers and assemblies of poets and cyclic dances and musical sounds' are intermingled with 'agreeable symposia and self-furnished feasts' (συμπόσιά τε εὐμελῆ καὶ εἰλαπίναι αὐτοχορήγητοι) (371c–d), while in Lucian's *Vera Historia*—more likely to parody stock (either 'literary' or popular) beliefs—Homer, Arion, Anacreon, and Stesichorus are feasting in the company of their heroes, reciting literary works and singing songs (Luc. 14. 15–16). Even outside the confines of the other-worldly realm, it seems that to Greek eyes a sympotic scene would have appeared as the most appropriate milieu for the hosting of a literary discussion. For, although neither the highly refined atmosphere of Agathon's Platonic banquet nor Athenaeus' and Plutarch's selection among the learned discussions held around 'table and goblet' (ἅμα τραπέζης καὶ κύλικος φιλολογηθέντων) (*Mor.* 612e) are adequate for giving an insight into the drinking experience of the ordinary Athenian male, sympotic ethics seem to have established that 'the man of sense who comes to dinner does not betake himself there just to fill himself up as though he were a sort of pot, but to take some part, be it serious or humorous, and to listen and to talk regarding this or that topic as the occasion suggests it to the company, if their association together is to be pleasant' (Plut. *Mor.* 147f; cf. 673a–b). Hence, from early times onwards, Greek tradition has associated with the *potos* riddles (αἰνίγματα) and dark sayings (γρίφους)[44] and all kinds of philosophical inquiries (*zeteseis*)[45] which could often be pursued in the most

---

[43] In more general terms, for the *symposion* of the dead see 4.10.

[44] On riddles in the course of the Dionysiac *symposion* which forms part of the ritual of the Boeotian Agrionia see Plut. *Mor.* 717a τοῦ δείπνου τέλος ἔχοντος, αἰνίγματα καὶ γρίφους ἀλλήλαις προβάλλουσιν. I owe this reference to R. Seaford.

[45] Note, most conspicuously, the tradition about the *symposion* of the 'Seven Wise Men',

sophisticated and serious way. So Athenaeus (2b), for example, praises Larensis as a banquet host who 'never put his questions without previous study, or in a haphazard way, but with the utmost critical, even Socratic, acumen, so that all admired the keen observation shown by his questions'.

(ii) Both literary and pictorial evidence suggests that singing and recital of poetry—including improvised verse[46]—was one of the *symposion*'s most important moments.[47] As Rösler (1990: 230), reflecting the prevailing scholarly opinion, has expressed it, out 'of all possible social contexts and institutions', the *symposion* was 'the central place for the creation and performance of poetry'.[48] In this respect, then, Aeschylus' and Euripides' singing and parodying of each other's choral odes could well be understood as forming part of the 'cultural complex' inherently intertwined with a Greek sympotic framework. Furthermore, among the salient traits of conviviality are the *asteia*, the jokes, that Dionysus expects from both contestants (905–6; see below) as well as the *eikones* ('likenesses') that he forbids them to indulge in (906 μήτ' εἰκόνας),[49] for they can easily give rise to convivial *eris* as, for example, *Wasps* 1308 ff. suggests.

As for the notion of *mimesis* implicated in the dramatists' parodic re-enactment of each other's work, sympotic space could actually provide a congenial atmosphere for the staging of representational discourse. Unfortunately, not much evidence exists before the Roman period. However, scraps of information point to the conclusion that sympotic space could include mimetic spectacle as well. The earliest ascertainable example dates from the summer of 421 BC, which is the dramatic date of Xenophon's *Symposion*. The banquet given at Callias' house is praised as a perfect dinner (τελέως ἡμᾶς ἑστιᾷς), as it provides not merely a lavish *deipnon* but also 'delightful sights and sounds' (θεάματα καὶ ἀκροάματα ἥδιστα) (*Symp.* 2. 2) for the distraction of the guests. Pride of place among these is held by a pantomime performance of the story of Dionysus and Ariadne, a

going at least as far back as the 5th cent. BC (O. Murray 1983*b*: 270); cf. also Plut. *Mor.* 612e–15c (on philosophy at drinking parties).

[46] On singing ἐξ αὐτοσχεδίης in the banquet see Hom. *h. Herm.* 54–6. For later periods cf. e.g. Athen. 125c–d and 656d (on Simonides improvising epigrams in the course of *symposia*); both Aeschylus' and Euripides' recitals, *qua* parodies, contain much improvisation.

[47] See Herington (1985: 195–8), listing the relevant vase-paintings; for explicit literary evidence, cf. Ar. *Clouds* 1354 ff.; *Wasps* 1222 ff.; Δαιταλῆς, fr. 235 K–A; Pl. Com. fr. 71, 11 K–A (a *skolion* is sung).

[48] Cf. Von der Mühll (1983: 20–1); O. Murray (1983*a*: 49); E. L. Bowie (1986: esp. 21; 1990).

[49] *Eikasmos*, i.e. the game of comparing one another to something funny, was one of the commonest amusements in drinking parties; see e.g. Xen. *Symp.* 6. 8–10; Pl. *Symp.* 215a–b, etc.

vivid mimetic re-enactment of Dionysus' love (*Symp.* 9. 2–7). But, by far the most important evidence is the series of mimetic enactments during private drinking parties connected with the notorious profanation of the Eleusinian Mysteries at 415 BC. All our sources unanimously present the mysteries as 'acted out', dramatically performed,[50] and it is highly significant that the *symposion* was the chosen forum for such activities.[51] Plutarch's *Life of Alcibiades* 19. 1 is a telling passage, attributing to all the gathered symposiasts a part to play in the performance:

. . . καὶ μυστηρίων παρ' οἶνον ἀπομιμήσεις τοῦ Ἀλκιβιάδου καὶ τῶν φίλων κατηγοροῦντας. ἔλεγον δὲ Θεόδωρον μέν τινα δρᾶν τὰ τοῦ κήρυκος, Πουλυτίωνα δὲ τὰ τοῦ δᾳδούχου, τὰ δὲ τοῦ ἱεροφάντου τὸν Ἀλκιβιάδην, τοὺς δ' ἄλλους ἑταίρους παρεῖναι καὶ θεᾶσθαι, μύστας προσαγορευομένους.

. . . accused Alcibiades and his friends of making a parody of the mysteries of Eleusis in a drunken revel. They said that one Theodorus played the part of the Herald, Poulytion that of the Torch-bearer, and Alcibiades that of the High Priest, and that the rest of his companions were there in the role of initiates, and were dubbed mystai. (cf. *Alc.* 22. 4)

It would appear, then, that the vogue of Menander's New Comedy as performative material for *symposia* of the Imperial times[52] had a clear precedent in the society of the classical Athenian *polis*.

(iii) As Pellizer (1990: 183) has very aptly noted, taking part in a symposium means coming to terms with a 'confrontation with the group'. Being a *sympotes* entails 'a risking of the image, of the self-representation that each of the symposiasts has constructed as part of his participation in social life' (Pellizer 1990: 183).[53] And actually, the primary feeling communicated through the agon is that each poet's personality is put at every moment 'to the test' (Pellizer 1990: 183). Just as in a real-life convivium the participants are asked to contribute to the common *euphrosyne* by displaying their technical/artistic skills or intellectual abilities,[54] Aeschylus and Euripides

[50] e.g. Lys. 6. 51 (μιμούμενος τὰ ἱερά); Isocr. 16. 6 (συνδειπνοῦντες τὰ μυστήρια ποιήσειαν); Andoc. 1. 11 (τὰ μυστήρια ποιοῦντα), 12 (γίγνοιτο μυστήρια), 16 (μυστήρια ποιεῖν); Thuc. 6. 28. 1 καὶ τὰ μυστήρια ἅμα ὡς ποιεῖται ἐν οἰκίαις ἐφ' ὕβρει; Plut. *Mor.* 621c Ἀλκιβιάδης δὲ καὶ Θεόδωρος τελεστήριον ἐποίησαν τὸ Πουλυτίωνος συμπόσιον ἀπομιμούμενοι δᾳδουχίας καὶ ἱεροφαντίας.

[51] On the oligarchic *hetaireiai*, the groups responsible for such politically loaded 'performances', as originating in relations formed at drinking parties see O. Murray (1983*b* and 1990*c*: esp. 150).

[52] See e.g. Plut. *Mor.* 712b, where Diogenianus argues that the performance of New Comedy 'has become so completely a part of the *symposium* that we could chart our course more easily without wine than without Menander.' Cf. *Mor.* 673b, etc. For a concise overview of the mimetic element in Graeco-Roman banquets see Jones (1991).

[53] Cf. E. L. Bowie (1986: 34).

[54] e.g. in the manifold sympotic games (Lissarrague 1987*b*: 66–82), in singing, playing the lyre or the aulos, etc. Nevertheless, everybody is required to contribute in accordance with their own skills (Plut. *Mor.* 622a).

are required to recite, sing, improvise, parody or criticize one another: jeered or applauded, praised and humiliated in turn, the dramatic poets of the *Frogs*' contest reflect the banqueters' self-image, always 'fragile and exposed' (Pellizer 1990: 183), susceptible to either 'improvement' and acceptance, or to σκῶμμα (jest) and τωθασμός (scoffing). The most powerful expression of the close affinity between the nature of sympotic and theatrical exposure of the 'self' to the incisive gaze of the 'other' can be sought in Socrates' anecdotal remark quoted in Plutarch. Asked (*Mor.* 10c) whether he was not upset at his derision in Aristophanes' *Clouds*, the philosopher replied (*Mor.* 10d): '"No indeed" . . . "when they break a jest upon me in the theatre I feel as if I were at a big party of good friends"' (ὡς γὰρ ἐν συμποσίῳ μεγάλῳ τῷ θεάτρῳ σκώπτομαι).

(iv) A gathering of a restricted and selected group, a Greek *symposion* was nevertheless a blend of 'private' and 'public' (see especially Schmitt-Pantel 1990: 24–5). Its space was, therefore, felt to be appropriate for the enunciation of political advice, while from the days of Alcaeus onwards the drinking club, as a dynamic form of social grouping, has the potentiality or at least the tendency to shape and steer political events (n. 51). If placed within such a background, the question of the *polis*' salvation that the drinkers of the *Frogs* are faced with (1420–3) can be considered as an aptly set sympotic puzzle (πρόβλημα). The contestants' answers, correspondingly, extend the boundaries of the *symposion*'s horizons beyond the private sphere: in a judicious mixture of seriousness and riddling language[55] both Euripides and Aeschylus succeed in implicating the purely political dimension of the city's life in the theatrical/sympotical discourse, and are expected to exert a beneficial influence on it.

3.3. *Sympotic Imagery in the Agon of the* Frogs

What I hope to have established so far is that the cultural predisposition of this play's original spectators was such as to enable them to understand the constellation of the verbal and the visual signs interspersed in the structure of the agon as building up the 'frame' of a banquet. Moving now a step further, I would also like to focus very briefly on some specific 'moments' of literary imagery which could be viewed in a sympotic light and, therefore, support my general reading of the agon as an intellectual banquet.

---

[55] See 1427 ff.; for riddles in the *symposion* see Athen. 448b–59b and cf. Anon. *Vit. Aes.* (G) chs. 47–8 (p. 51 Perry).

(i) Like so many other social occasions, a drinking party is inaugurated with prayers (εὐχαί),[56] precisely the activity which marks the start of the contest in *Frogs* 871 ff. The hymnic invocation to the Muses in particular (875 ff.), is highly appropriate for a *potos* of assembled intellectuals, as an aetiological passage from Plutarch suggests:

The meaning of the ritual [i.e. the Agrionia] is that when drinking we ought to engage in conversation that has something speculative, some instruction in it, and that when conversation like this accompanies indulgence in wine, the wild and manic element is hidden away, benevolently restrained by the Muses. (*Mor.* 717a)

Correspondingly, the ending of the agon too may be considered as having sympotic overtones, as the rich symbolic range of the torches which accompany Dionysus' and Aeschylus' *pompe* to Athens (1524–7) fuses the Eleusinian and komastic dimensions of the play's exodos.[57]

(ii) One of the most memorable scenes in the agon is the weighing of the verses of the two contestants (1365–9, 1378 ff.) on a scale of balance (1378 ἴθι δή, παρίστασθον παρὰ τὼ πλάστιγγ'). Now, in the literary horizon of Greek fifth-century spectators, this image, situated, as it is, in the space of the nether world, could easily have been received as an ingenious parody of the well-known (and much imitated in antiquity) Homeric *psychostasia* in *Iliad* 22. 209–13, where Zeus himself put the fates of Achilles and Hector in the balance.[58] Yet, beyond the literary associations, there are also other ways, suggested by the text itself, in which the weighing act could be deciphered. As Angus Bowie points out to me, when the idea is first mooted in line 797: 'there will even be a weighing of poetry on the scales' (καὶ γὰρ ταλάντῳ μουσικὴ σταθμήσεται), the Underworld Slave who converses with Xanthias exclaims: 'What do you mean? will they weigh Tragedy on the scales, as if it were a sacrificial lamb?' (τί δέ; μειαγωγήσουσι τὴν τραγῳδίαν;) (798), the verb *meiagogein*, alluding clearly to the sacrifice of the *meion* at the Apaturia (cf. Dover 1993: ad loc.) (cf. 5.2). Moreover, when Aeschylus mentions the scales (1365 ἐπὶ τὸν σταθμόν . . .), Dionysus immediately associates with it the mundane image of weighing cheese (1369 τυροπωλῆσαι

---

[56] Cf. Xenophanes, 13–16 B1, D–K (cf. ibid.: 7 λιβανωτός, as in *Frogs* 871); Pl. *Symp.* 176a; Pl. Com. fr. 71, 9 K–A (λιβανωτόν before the banquet), etc.

[57] For torches in Eleusinian initiation see Hom. *h. Dem.* 48 (with Richardson 1974: 165–7); *Frogs* 340 ff., 446/7, and see above, 2.8(b) and 2.14. For torches in a sympotical context cf. Ar. *Wasps* 1330–1; *Eccles.* 1150.

[58] Aeschylus himself wrote a tragedy entitled *Psychostasia*, where 'Zeus weighs the fates of Achilles and Memnon while their mothers stood pleading beside each scale-pan (like A. and E. in 1378ff)' (Stanford 1963: ad loc.).

τέχνην). However, there is no reason to suppose that any of these possible—and to a greater or lesser extent fairly obvious—constructions need be exclusive of the others. In fact, the cultural frame itself of the Athenian *polis* could have oriented the imagination of classical Greek viewers towards one added possible way of deciphering *Frogs* 1365ff. I mean that the act of weighing *poiesis* on a scale of balance could also have carried a set of secondary, sympotic connotations, as exercises and displays of the drinkers' aptitude in equilibrium were among the most widespread sympotic games (Deonna 1959: 12–17; Lissarrague 1987*b*: 74–5).

Drinking-cups or amphorae which must achieve a balance on the arms, the toes, the foot, the back, or any other part of the symposiast's body are abundantly attested in an important corpus of banquet imagery (Deonna 1959: figs. 4–10; Lissarrague 1987*b*: figs. 59–66). More significantly still, it is the famous sympotic game of the *kottabos* which largely depends upon the notions of equilibrium and its breach:[59] the wine-drops the drinker aims at a πλάστιγξ (this time meaning a small disk), poised on the top of a slim rod (the ῥάβδος κοτταβική), must make it tumble and eventually strike upon a plate or cup fixed at an inferior point along the pole. Boehm[60] argued strongly that an actual scale of balance would never have been used as a *kottabos* in a symposium. Yet, it is precisely the uncertainty and the confusion of the ancient authors on this matter[61] which generates the impression of a close analogy between the two. In this respect then, I suggest that within the repertoire of images available to Greek spectators, Dionysus' weighing-scale, as a stage-prop, would have been apt for calling forth a quite familiar sympotic picture. That is to say, its introduction in the literary banqueting hall would have reversed the expectation of some *theatai* that they were going to see the *kottabos* brought in for the distraction of the drinkers, as was probably the case in Pl. Com. fr. 71 K–A (lines 4 and 11). Besides, both literature and art have freely associated this kind of game with specifically Dionysiac banquet scenes. Thus, in Dionysius Chalcus (fr. 2 G–P = 3D; Borthwick 1964), the *kottabos* becomes the punch-ball (κώρυκον) of the dining-room (metaphorically designed as the 'gymnasium of Bromios', lines 2–3),[62] while a stamnos in the Louvre (Fig. 3.9) and a kalyx-krater in the British

---

[59] For the *kottabos* see Lafaye in *DA*, s.v. kottabos; Deonna (1959: 18–23); Lissarrague (1987*b*: 75–82).

[60] C. Boehm, *De Cottabo* (diss. 1893: 13–19; *non vidi*) (argument briefly stated in Lafaye in *DA*, s.v. kottabos: 867 n. 2).

[61] Sources quoted by Lafaye (*DA*: 867 n. 2).

[62] Cf. Borthwick (1964: 49 n. 4) on the wine-drops in the kottabic game referred to as Βακχίου τοξεύμασιν or Βρομίου ψακάδεσσιν.

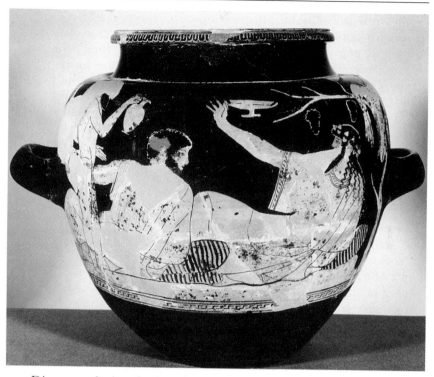

3.9. Dionysus playing the *kottabos*
rf. stamnos: Paris, Louvre, G114 (*ARV²* 257, 14)

Museum (Fig. 4.7) depict Dionysus himself in the act of *kottabizein.*[63]

(iii) Finally, considering the purely linguistic level of the agon, some specific verbal constellations in the dialogue construct a cluster of sympotic language and metaphors.

(*a*) At 843–4, as Aeschylus has almost lost control over his temper, Dionysus instructs him in a grandiloquent tone to 'shut up':

παῦ', Αἰσχύλε,
καὶ μὴ πρὸς ὀργὴν σπλάγχνα θερμήνῃς κότῳ.

Stop it, Aeschylus,
and do not angrily inflame your guts with rage.

Whether this is an Aeschylean verse (Charlesworth 1926; Goossens 1935*b*) or not is not germane to my argument. But, had the dramatist been actually portrayed as a banqueter arriving at the brink of

[63] See also Lafaye, *DA*, s.v. kottabos: 868 n. 9.

hybris while draining off his drinking-cup, the spectator could have reasonably expected Dionysus' command to be: 'stop it, Aeschylus, and do not angrily inflame your guts with *drinking*' (παῦ', Αἰσχύλε, | καὶ μὴ πρὸς ὀργὴν σπλάγχνα θερμήνῃς πότῳ) on the basis of that solidly established metaphor which attributes to wine the heating quality of fire (πῦρ) or flame (φλόξ).[64] In other words, κότῳ ('with rage') derives its strength precisely by being an unexpected reversal of the anticipated ending of the line in πότῳ ('with drinking').[65]

(*b*) As has already been mentioned above, the *symposion* can often be envisaged as a ship steered by a helmsman (κυβερνήτης),[66] while the drinker can be visualized as a sailor, sometimes in the midst of wavy seas (W. J. Slater 1976). In this respect, the Chorus's portrayal of the enraged Aeschylus as a mariner battling in the middle of a storm (999–1003) could be deciphered as bearing some affinity with drinking metaphors of the kind reflected in a fragment of Choerilus of Samos, where *hybris*, insolence, results in 'the shipwreck of the fellow-drinkers' (ἀνδρῶν δαιτυμόνων ναυάγιον).[67]

(*c*) The marine sympotic image is created once again in the Euripidean literary pastiche that Aeschylus recites. Out of lines 1317–21,

> ἵν' ὁ φίλαυλος ἔπαλλε δελ-
> φὶς πρώραις κυανεμβόλοις
> μαντεῖα καὶ σταδίους,
> οἰνάνθας γάνος ἀμπέλου,
> βότρυος ἕλικα παυσίπονον,

> where the flute-loving dolphin leaped
> at the dark-blue prows,
> oracles and race-courses,
> delight of the bloom of the grape-vine,
> curling of the grape-cluster assuaging pain,

lines 1317–18 come from Euripides' *Electra* 435–7, whereas 1320–1 are, according to the scholiast, inspired by Euripides' *Hypsipyle*, fr. 765 N²: 'the bloom of the grape breeds the sacred grape-cluster' (οἰνάνθα τρέφει τὸν ἱερὸν βότρυν). But I suggest that the ship with

---

[64] See e.g. Pl. *Tim.* 60a; *Leg.* 666a–c, 671b; Eur. *Alc.* 758–9; Timaeus, *FGrHist* 566 F149, 8–9; Plut. *Mor.* 156d. For a version most supportive of my proposition see Eur. *Cycl.* 423–4 ἐγὼ δ' ἐπεγχέων | ἄλλην ἐπ' ἄλλῃ σπλάγχν' ἐθέρμαινον ποτῷ.

[65] This would be especially apt for Aeschylus, who reputedly composed his tragedies while 'heated up' with drink; see e.g. *TrGF* iii T 117e τὸν Αἰσχύλον ὁ Καλλισθένης (*FGrHist* 124 F 46) ἔφη που λέγων τὰς τραγῳδίας ἐν οἴνῳ γράφειν ἐξορμῶντα καὶ ἀναθερμαίνοντα τὴν ψυχήν; T 117f (Plut. *Mor.* 622e) καὶ τὸν Αἰσχύλον φασὶ τὰς τραγῳδίας πίνοντα ποιεῖν καὶ διαθερμαινόμενον.

[66] See e.g. Plut. *Mor.* 712b διακυβερνῆσαι τὸν πότον.

[67] Fr. 9, 2 (Bernabé). A *symposion* getting out of control is said to 'suffer shipwreck' (ναυαγεῖν) (Plut. *Mor.* 622b).

dolphins floating around, the grape-clusters, and the vine, all joined together, as if drawn from the same picture, are very likely to be reminiscent of the Dionysiac 'symposium at sea'. For not only are vine branches and grapes *sine qua non* elements in representations of Dionysiac marine *symposia* (as the Tarquinia amphora or the kylix of Exekias can attest; see 2.4(b)), but also the dolphin, proverbially *philomousos* ('lover of the muse') and, more precisely, *philaulos* ('lover of the flute'; cf. e.g. Pindar, fr. 140b, 15f. Maehler), is a sympotic animal *par excellence*. Being a memorable presence on the famous Exekias cup, as well as featuring quite frequently in the variety of pictures decorating the inner cavity of drinking vessels (Lissarrague 1987*b*: 109–18), that is, the space which, when filled with *oinos*, resembles the Homeric 'wine dark sea', the *oinops pontos*, the dolphin seems to be a vital element in the working of the marine sympotic metaphor.[68]

3.4. *Dionysus as* Symposiarchos

Once the sympotic aspects of the literary agon have been surveyed, it is important to appreciate the role of Dionysus in this particular context. Because Dionysus' presence would have seemed highly appropriate in a convivial gathering of intellectuals *par excellence* where, blended with the Muses no less than with the Nymphs,[69] he becomes 'really gracious and a giver of joy' to the souls of the *sympotai* (Plut. *Mor.* 613d ταῖς ψυχαῖς μειλίχιον ὄντως καὶ χαριδότην). Conversely, when the drinkers 'throw themselves into the singing of any kind of song, the telling of foolish stories, and talk of shop and market-place', 'gone . . . is the aim and end of the good fellowship of the party, and Dionysus is outraged (καθύβρισται ὁ Διόνυσος)' (Plut. *Mor.* 615a).

[68] Sommerstein (1996: ad 1319) emphasizes the Apollonian connotations of the picture, based on 'The association between dolphins, oracles and race-tracks' which 'may go back to *h. Hom. Ap.* 493–4 . . .'; Borthwick (1994) argues (and Sommerstein accepts) that the puzzling words *manteia kai stadious* (oracles and race-courses) may come from Euripides' *Hypsipyle*, and, coupled with the vine, they may have been 'the three recognition motifs of *Hypsipyle*—the prophecy of Amphiaraus . . . the victory at racing . . . followed by the herald's identification, and the token of the vine . . .' (33). If this is so, then, given that the *Hypsipyle* is a play with a strong Dionysiac element (Zeitlin 1993) and that the Dionysiac connotations of οἰνάνθας γάνος ἀμπέλου | βότρυος ἕλικα παυσίπονον are unmistakable, I do not think that Apollo could have been uppermost in the audience's minds here. Besides, oracles are not exclusive properties of Apollo, as Dionysus is himself associated with Delphi and mantic power (cf. 6.2), and his close connection to Apollo in this respect is well reflected in Aesch. fr. 341 Radt ὁ κισσεὺς Ἀπόλλων, ὁ βακχειόμαντις.

[69] Plut. *Mor.* 613d ἀφήσομεν αὐτοὺς (i.e. the philosophers at the *symposion*) . . . φιλοσοφεῖν, οὐχ ἧττον ταῖς Μούσαις τὸν Διόνυσον ἢ ταῖς Νύμφαις κεραννύντας. For Dionysus' link with the Muses see 6.2.

Furthermore, Dionysus could have been easily envisaged not only as an arbitrator in debates over *potos* (as e.g. in Pl. *Symp.* 175e), but as an *archon* of the banquet, a *symposiarchos* as well (Pellizer 1990: 178 n. 7). For Plato refers to the symposiarchs as 'leaders of Dionysus' (*Leg.* 671e) and, according to Philochorus (*FGrHist* 328 F5a, 15–17; cf. F5b, 27–30), it was Dionysus himself who instituted the *symposion*'s fundamental law, its *thesmion*. Besides, as Dionysus' realm, encompassing both Tragedy and Comedy, stands for the quintessence of both the serious and the ludic, this god becomes by nature the ideal 'banquet-*archon*', who must be 'congenial to seriousness and no stranger to play', that is, he 'must have both qualities properly blended' (εὖ πως συγκεκραμένον πρὸς ἀμφότερα) (Plut. *Mor.* 620d). In full accordance with the fundamental duty of an *archon* to mingle 'seriousness with playfulness' (τῇ σπουδῇ τὴν παιδιάν) (Plut. *Mor.* 621d), Dionysus' various interventions in the course of the agon are such as to ensure that the discussion fluctuates between the levels of gravity and joke.

In Plato's work, the role of the symposiarch is placed in the same rank as that of the commander of any institution (Pl. *Leg.* 640a–c). Lack of obedience to him is envisaged as a moral slip incurring even greater shame than one's *apeitharchia* to the chieftains of the army (Pl. *Leg.* 671d–e). The primary obligation of the drinkers is, therefore, their submissive disposition (Plut. *Mor.* 620b–c) and hence, Dionysus has recourse to the notion of *peitho* when either Euripides or Aeschylus appear to be reluctant to follow his suggestion (see 1134 and 1229 ἐὰν πείθῃ γ' ἐμοί). Besides, his warning in lines 1132–3: 'if you disobey me, you will find yourself in debt of three more iambic trimeters' (εἰ δὲ μή, | πρὸς τρισὶν ἰαμβείοισι προσοφείλων φανεῖ) resembles the orders (προστάγματα) and corresponding penalties (ζημίαι) sometimes imposed on the *sympotai*, activities traditionally surveyed by the drinking party's 'king' (e.g. Plut. *Mor.* 621e–f). And just as a symposiarch's principal commission is to secure the banqueters' respect towards sympotic laws, especially the rule that each of them is speaking, being silent, drinking, and singing in his turn (Pl. *Leg.* 671c),[70] Dionysus attempts throughout the entire agon to impose an order in the speech and silence of both contestants (e.g. 926, 1020, 1125, 1132–4, 1283, 1364). Besides, as a competent symposiarch is required to ensure the banquet's 'decorum and harmony' (εὐσχημοσύνην καὶ ὁμόνοιαν) (Plut. *Mor.* 621a) by bringing 'the natural dispositions (τὰς φύσεις) of the guests from

[70] For the same ideal, realized *par excellence* at the sympotic gathering of educated men cf. Pl. *Prot.* 347d: 'each speaking and listening decently in his turn (ἐν μέρει), even though they may drink a great deal of wine.'

diversity into smooth and harmonious accord (εἰς ὁμαλότητα καὶ συμφωνίαν ἐκ διαφορᾶς)' (Plut. *Mor.* 620f),[71] Dionysus accomplishes a mediatory role, now counselling patience and lack of anger (*orge*) or bad temper (e.g. 843–4, 851–9), now preventing the sympotic jest (σκῶμμα) from disintegrating into abuse (*hybris*) and railing (*loidoria*) (see esp. 857–8).[72]

More importantly, as a symposiast in Plutarch asserts, a well-endowed and successful 'banquet-*archon*' should not only be familiar with the natures of all drinkers (*Mor.* 620e) but also favourably predisposed towards all (*Mor.* 620d and 621a) and recognized equally by all (*Mor.* 621a). More significantly still, it is Dionysus who 'softens and relaxes their characters with wine, as in a fire, and so provides some means for beginning a union and friendship with one another' (*Mor.* 156d). With respect to the Aristophanic drinkers of the *Frogs*, Dionysus unites in his *dramatis persona* as an *archon* all three presuppositions: for one could hardly think of anybody more familiar with or favourable towards or recognized by dramatic poets than the patron god of theatre himself. And this is actually the attitude which he maintains until the end of the agon, when he deliberately refrains from his initial plan to judge, precisely because he wishes to avoid becoming disagreeable to either of them: 'These men are my friends, and I will not decide their contest, because I don't want to be at feud with either of them (οὐ γὰρ δι' ἔχθρας οὐδετέρῳ γενήσομαι): the one I think is clever, yet in the other I delight' (1411–13).

Finally, taking part in a convivium is one of those activities which shape the symposiast's personality not only by forging links of friendship with his fellow-drinkers[73] but, more significantly, by imparting to him the feeling of sharing the community's values (O. Murray 1990*b*: 5) and of participating in the citizen group.[74]

Frogs 503 ff. casts Dionysus in the role of a prospective lonely banqueter in a *deipnon*/feast which is never actually materialized on the stage. Yet, the flow of the comic plot climaxes in the picture of Dionysus banqueting together with a group,[75] becoming thus a

---

[71] Cf. Pl. *Leg.* 640c–d: 'For he has both to preserve the friendliness which already exists among the company and to see that the present gathering promotes it still further.'

[72] For the *skomma* as the 'soul' of the *symposion* see Lucian 23. 8. For the requirement of its decent use see e.g. Plut. *Mor.* 631cff.

[73] Cf. Plut. *Mor.* 621c, where the party's aim (τὸ συμποτικὸν τέλος) is 'through pleasure to produce among those who are present the heightening of friendship or to bring it into existence.' Cf. *Mor.* 660a–b and Pl. *Leg.* 671e, on the ideal συμπόται who part μᾶλλον φίλοι ἢ πρότερον.

[74] See e.g. Schmitt-Pantel (1990: 24); E. L. Bowie (1986: 34).

[75] The symposiarch *does* (and must) have a share himself in the sympotic pleasures or, as Plutarch has expressed it, he must be 'the quintessence of a convivial man' (συμποτῶν

'participant' (κοινωνός) in the *logoi*[76] of the most respected represen-
tatives of the intellectual sector of the city's populace. Furthermore,
there is a qualitative difference between Persephone's entertainment
which lured Dionysus during his liminal transition and the literary
symposion over which he is presiding in his reintegration period in
the play's second part. The former recalls occasions like those which
Socrates in Plato branded as *symposia* 'of common market-folk'
(τῶν φαύλων καὶ ἀγοραίων ἀνθρώπων) who,

> owing to their inability to carry on a familiar conversation over their wine
> by means of their own voices and discussions—such is their lack of educa-
> tion—put a premium on flute-girls by hiring the extraneous voice of the
> flute at a high price, and carry on their intercourse by means of its utter-
> ance. (Pl. *Prot.* 347 c–d)

The latter, on the other hand, is obviously a *symposion* of *kaloi
kagathoi* and educated (πεπαιδευμένοι) drinkers, where

> you will see neither flute-girls nor dancing-girls nor harp-girls, but only
> the company contenting themselves with their own conversation, and none
> of these fooleries and frolics . . . (Pl. *Prot.* 347d)

In this respect, then, as the 'banquet imagery' of the *Frogs* culminates in Dionysus' implication in a refined sympotic gathering, the
god is gradually associated with the most civilized among the range
of activities which fall into his own realm.[77] To put it in another way,
his final integration in the city is effected through his participation
in a vital educational experience/institution of the city.[78]

This image of reintegration becomes much more explicit with
Pluto's final invitation, pronounced at 1479–80: 'if you would, then,
go in, Dionysus . . . so that I may entertain both of you as guests (ἵνα
ξενίζω σφώ) before you depart'. As studies on Athenian decrees
and institutions have revealed,[79] *xenia* and *xenismos* are terms used
exclusively for designating the civic hospitality and banquet at the
Prytaneion,[80] offered on special occasions to *xenoi*/visitors or to
Athenian ambassadors on their return from a mission executed

συμποτικώτατον) (*Mor.* 620c). For the banquet-*archon* who is completely sober (παντάπασι
νήφων) is characterized as 'disagreeable and more fit for tending children than for presiding
over a drinking party' (*Mor.* 620c).

[76] Cf. Plut. *Mor.* 660b ὁ γὰρ σύνδειπνος . . . λόγων κοινωνὸς ἥκει . . .
[77] For the *symposion* as a distinctively Dionysiac space see 4.10–11.
[78] For the general educational value συμποσίου ὀρθῶς παιδαγωγηθέντος see Pl. *Leg.* 641a–d.
For the educational aspect of singing, playing the lyre, and reciting at the *symposion* see
Bremmer (1990: 137–8).
[79] See primarily, Miller (1978); Henry (1983); M. J. Osborne (1981); cf. Schmitt-Pantel
(1980: 63 and 1985: 153 n. 49).
[80] This shade of meaning is entirely lost on Moorton (1989: 323) (see below, n. 87).

abroad.[81] True, no work of art —certainly not a comic fiction— is a legal document and, therefore, comic language should not be treated as evidence for the use of terms in the *polis*' official discourse.[82] Nevertheless, both the notion of the Underworld as a *polis* and its role as a public 'host' have been explicitly reiterated in an earlier passage in the text, when the Underworld Doorkeeper drew attention to the custom that whoever is the best in every *techne* receives 'public maintenance in the Prytaneion (σίτησιν . . . ἐν πρυτανείῳ) and a throne next to that of Pluto' (764–5).[83] In other words, the civic/legal institutions and the principles of real-life Athens are transferred to the dramatic *polis* of the Underworld,[84] whose representative/king exercises his right of inviting the *xenoi* to the civic hearth. Before re-entering the space of the 'real' *polis* and after the completion of his other-worldly task, Dionysus becomes the civic guest of the dramatic Athens.[85] Just as, for the ambassadors, reception at the Prytaneion signifies the renewal of their civic identity,[86] Pluto's gesture signifies for the god his reaggregation into the civic realm and could have been appreciated as such in the perspective of fifth-century Athenian *theatai*.[87] Similarly, in the Aristophanic *Knights*, the *dramatis persona* of the Athenian Demos acknowledges Agoracritus' final reincorporation into the *polis* in his new and elevated status as a 'leading citizen', a *prostates* of the people, by addressing to him a formal invitation to enjoy the privilege of *sitesis* in the Prytaneion: 'and as a reward for your services, I invite you to dine at the Prytaneion' (καὶ σ' ἀντὶ τούτων ἐς τὸ πρυτανεῖον καλῶ) (*Knights* 1404; see A. M. Bowie 1993*a*: 55–6).

Finally, as Philippe Gauthier (1973: 5) has put it, those who practise hospitality 'doivent se reconnaître, en quelque manière,

[81] The formula for such an invitation is: καλέσαι δὲ αὐτοὺς ἐπὶ ξένια εἰς τὸ πρυτανεῖον εἰς αὔριον; see Miller (1978: 4, with sources in appendix A, 132 ff.) and Henry (1983: 262 ff.). However, it is not always clear whether Athenian ambassadors are invited to *deipnon* or to *xenia*.

[82] Note, however, that on several occasions, Aristophanes abides by the distinction: *deipnon* for citizens, *xenia* for foreigners; see e.g. Miller (1978: test. nos. 32, 39, 41).

[83] Σίτησις ἐν πρυτανείῳ is actually the term used for the grant of permanent maintenance offered to outstanding citizens; see Miller (1978: 7 ff.) and Henry (1983: 275 ff.).

[84] It would be interesting to note all the instances of Hades/Athens overlap in the play; see e.g. Pluto's reference to Athens as 'our city' (πόλιν τὴν ἡμετέραν) (1501). Cf. also Woodbury (1986: 257 n. 39).

[85] Dionysus' *xenismos* by Pluto at the civic hearth may also be intrinsically 'Dionysiac', if Sourvinou-Inwood (1994) is right in suggesting that central to the City Dionysia festival was a fully fledged ritual of *xenismos* of Dionysus (at the earliest stage of the festival taking place at the Prytaneion itself, but later at the Altar of the Twelve Gods, whose *eschara* 'duplicated symbolically the *hestia* of the Prytaneion' (287)), occurring before the festival's *pompe*.

[86] See Schmitt-Pantel (1980: 63) and Gernet (1968: 396).

[87] In this respect, I cannot agree with Moorton (1989: 322–3), who understands Pluto's *xenismos* as a 'full-scale rite of separation' of Dionysus and Aeschylus from Hades.

comme des semblables'.[88] Being prepared to entertain Dionysus as a
civic guest, Pluto acknowledges him as his equal, corroborating thus
the initiand's restoration to divine status and consolidating his
position in the pantheon of a Greek religious community. In other
words, the role of king Amphictyon in myth is taken up in comedy
by Pluto, and the divine banqueter is re-established in dignity in the
space of both the comic and the 'real-life' Athens.

3.5. Symposion, *Comedy, and Ritual*

I would now like to end this chapter by paying brief attention to the
ways in which the range of meanings of this comedy in its entirety
may be enriched if one envisages its closing scenes as a *symposion.*
    The comedy begins with a visual evocation of the story of
'Hephaestus' Return', which, as our iconographic corpus can attest,
is invariably situated in a festive context of mummery and drunkenness. The association of this legend with Dionysus' revels is so deep
that the artist may feel free to label the entire scene as 'Komos',[89]
while the drunk Hephaestus features as the prototype of the riding
komast (Bron *et al.* 1989: 165). More significantly still, performed
'in different places and at different times' (T. B. L. Webster 1959:
64), most probably by padded dancers (Seeberg 1971: 45, nos.
227a–c), the story of Hephaestus belonged to the 'archetypal' ones
which 'set the rhythm for satyr play and comedy' (T. B. L. Webster
1959: 64), and which can be included among the most ancient pre-
dramatic manifestations (Ghiron-Bistagne 1976: 221). Thus, while
the opening picture of the *Frogs* intertwines comedy's quest for its
healthy ludic spirit with the reminiscence of its Dionysiac pre-
dramatic past,[90] an obvious model of carnivalesque festivity (cf.
Seeberg 1965: 107), the agon draws on the most sophisticated and
refined articulation of Dionysiac entertainments: in both its beginning and its end the Aristophanic Comedy displays itself as a merry
art-form which stages self-reflexively its own Dionysiac essence and
subject-matter,[91] while simultaneously transfusing the improvisa-
tory and coarse festivity interlocked with its origins into the frame

---

[88] More generally, from an anthropological perspective see Pitt-Rivers (1977: 107 ff.).
[89] As in an oenochoe in New York: *ARV²* 1249, 12; see Bron *et al.*, (1989: 163).
[90] That the story was understood by classical artists as one of the prototypes for Comedy
may be attested by an Attic krater in the Louvre (*c.*450 BC), where the personified Comedy
(name inscribed) is integrated into Hephaestus' *cortège* (Fig. 3.10).
[91] The self-reflexivity of the *Frogs'* agon would have seemed much greater to the play's
original spectators if Sourvinou-Inwood (1994: 289; cf. above, n. 85) is right in proposing that
some proto-form of tragedy was initially 'performed as part of the ritual of Dionysos' entertainment at the Prytaneion'.

3.10. Return of Hephaestus: Dionysus with personification of Comedy
rf. krater: Paris, Louvre, G421

of a metaphor. For the sympotical articulation of the agon is the civilized alternative that Comedy proposes to the city as a model for the transmutation of the fundamentally material aesthetics of the genre into the life of the spirit. To put it in another way, the *Frogs* incorporates through its sympotical conclusion a miniature example of Dionysiac festivity, contrived as a literary art-form sustained through a proper mixture of *spoude* and *paidia*, and placing itself at the service of the city rather than seeking to escape the constraints and boundaries imposed by the city.

Furthermore, seen in a slightly modified perspective, the komastic picture implicated in the comedy's first scene mobilizes a range of fertility associations, for in the 'encyclopaedic knowledge' of Greek spectators the Hephaestus of this corpus of Dionysiac legends is the 'divine magician' called upon to 'free the deity of the fruitful earth'.[92] The elaborate sympotic setting of the closing scenes, conversely, resumes the underlying theme of fertility (*gonimotes*) by staging the return of intellectual fertility personified by Aeschylus, the poet-

[92] See Seeberg (1965: 106); cf. T. B. L. Webster (1958: 43) and, in a much wider perspective, see Delcourt (1982: esp. 107–8). Fertility and 'new life arising out of death' are the main thematic units of the legend.

saviour expected to effect the *polis'* spiritual, instead of natural, revitalization.

Finally, one of the salient traits of conviviality is the spirit of 'playful release', that is, the individual's deliverance from inhibitions imposed by day-to-day social life, a relaxation which primarily takes the form of laughter (Halliwell 1991: 290 ff.) and, as has already been mentioned above, *skomma*.[93] Although jesting is bound to pervade an Aristophanic comic text, the sympotic *skomma* of the play's closing scenes could more profitably be appreciated in its comparison with a specific textual moment of scurrility, the *aischrologia* of the parodos, where ribaldry, taking the ritual form of the Demetrian *gephyrismoi* (*Frogs* 416 ff.) (cf. 2.12), is part of the festive procession to Eleusis:[94] while the Demetrian frame of the comedy exhibits playfulness and raillery in its most natural and primitive enunciation, as an overt obscenity (esp. 416–30)[95] linked with the regenerative powers of nature,[96] within the festive sphere of a Dionysiac intellectual banquet jesting appears in its refined, elegant, and witty form, as an *asteion*,[97] that is, 'humour esteemed as personally and socially admirable' (Halliwell 1991: 290). In other words, within the festal realm of Dionysus, encapsulated in this play as a sympotic gathering, the transgressive modes of mockery conditioning the atmosphere of a Demetrian feast yield their place to a sophisticated discourse of *paidia* which, confined to the boundaries of civic decorum, aims at the restoration rather than subversion of values and norms.

---

[93] See how Aeschylus and Euripides throw jibes at each other, esp. at 836–42.

[94] Eleusinian and sympotic *skomma* are brought together at *Wasps* 1361–3 (on which see the most pertinent note of Rusten 1977).

[95] For obscenity in Demetrian rites see e.g. Olender (1990).

[96] For *aischrologia* and fertility see Richardson (1974: 217).

[97] See Dionysus' request at 905–6 οὕτω δ' ὅπως ἐρεῖτον, | ἀστεῖα (cf. 901a). Cf. the sympotic context of the *Wasps* where *asteion*, as a socially acceptable form of convivial laughter/joke (1258), is later on subverted by the old man's *agroikon skomma* (1320).

4

Initiation through Acting

4.1. *Aristophanic Metatheatre and Dionysiac Dramatic Acting*

A primary dimension of Dionysus' *dramatis persona* in the *Frogs* is his theatricality. From the beginning of the play he steps onto the stage dressed up as Heracles, that is, like a true actor, who sets out to incarnate somebody 'other' than himself; when the comic plot gets under way, correspondingly, he fluctuates again between his own identity (most emphatically proclaimed in 631–2) and those of Heracles and Xanthias. Now, as we have already mentioned in 2.4, role-playing is a well-known feature of ritual liminality. The purpose of the present chapter is precisely to explore the initiatory significance of Dionysus' acting, that is, the ways in which his theatrical performance on the stage forges, shapes, and directs his *dramatis persona* and, together with the wine motif and his initiation into the Eleusinian and Dionysiac mystic cult (Chs. 2–3), becomes a fundamental channel for his ultimate 'reintegration' into the community of the Athenian *polis* (Chs. 5–9).

The role assigned to Dionysus in the dramatic fiction of the *Frogs* sets him quite apart from the rest of the divine stage-appearances in Aristophanes' work. Not only does it require the god to be present on the stage as a protagonist almost throughout the entire performance but, more significantly still, it displays a remarkable theatrical complexity. I mean that, rather than having one single dimension, Dionysus' role-playing oscillates between two distinct theatrical levels. On the first level, the 'god' Dionysus is playing 'Dionysus': 'when I, being Dionysus, son of Stamnias' (ὅτ' ἐγὼ μὲν ὢν Διόνυσος, υἱὸς Σταμνίου) (22).[1] However, on what we may call a 'second' level of impersonation, that is to say, a level where 'the actor, already playing a part, takes on a *second*, a *different* character' (Sharpe 1959: 36; my italics), Dionysus assumes the secondary roles of Heracles, visibly symbolized by the lion-skin and club, and (even if only

---

[1] From Aristophanes' point of view, it is 'Dionysus, the god', who is placed in the middle of the action, in the same way that Euripides in the *Bacchae* makes 'the god . . . himself a masked actor', forcing thus 'Dionysus, the patron of tragedy, to become the subject of tragedy' (Segal 1982: 233).

briefly) Xanthias, the slave. In this respect, then, Dionysus becomes an 'internalized' actor, for 'what he does and how he is regarded within the play is analogous to what an actor does and how he is regarded in respect of the play' (D. C. Muecke 1982: 77). In other words, within the boundaries of Dionysus' original role, two further impersonations are enfolded, thus placing the god at the centre of that metatheatrical phenomenon which has been denominated as 'role-playing within the role' (Hornby 1986: 67 ff.) and which, when voluntary, as here, has been considered 'the most metadramatic type' (Hornby 1986: 74). Besides, the first level of Dionysus' impersonation is always visible through the Dionysiac elements in his *skeue*, the *krokotos* and the *kothornoi* and, in all probability, through the mask that he is wearing. It is true that we lack the amount of evidence which would enable us to gauge how 'Dionysiac' his Dionysiac *persona* was,[2] but what is much more relevant to our discussion is the fact that he does not seem to be wearing the mask which corresponds to his secondary impersonation, that is, the mask of Heracles, most probably a 'special mask' reserved exclusively for the ferocious hero himself (cf. T. B. L. Webster 1970: 61). For one may reasonably assume that, had Dionysus appropriated his prototype's theatrical *persona* too, in addition to his lion-skin and club, that mask would have somehow attracted Heracles' comment. The disparity between stable mask and modified costume, then, a standard situation in comic disguise scenes, contributes here to the transparency of 'the role-playing within the role' and, therefore, to the heightening of its effect.

However, what should primarily be emphasized at this point is the remarkable degree of self-awareness with which Dionysus himself characterizes his theatrical relationship to Heracles as one of 'imitation':

> ἀλλ' ὧνπερ ἕνεκα τήνδε τὴν σκευὴν ἔχων
> ἦλθον κατὰ σὴν μίμησιν, . . .

> But this is why I've come here dressed in this garb,
> in imitation of you . . . (108–9)

---

[2] The extant evidence would not suggest a close correspondence between Dionysus' comic mask and the Dionysiac images of cult, as Stone (1981: 315) seems to imply. Only one representation of Dionysus on stage from the period of Old Comedy exists, on a fragment of an oenochoe from the Athenian Agora (*MOMC*[3], AV14), very probably illustrating Eupolis' *Taxiarchi* (see Ch. 2, n. 96): here, as T. B. L. Webster (1970: 61) remarks, Dionysus 'has nothing to distinguish him from the other fat phallic men of Old Comedy' (cf. T. B. L. Webster 1960: 262); in fact, Dearden (1976: 138) ascribes to this comic Dionysus mask-type Z from Webster's list in *MOMC*[3]. Both the wide variety of Phlyax vases, which depict Dionysus as an actor (e.g. *PhV*[2] nos. 20, 61, etc.), as well as representations of other gods (e.g. Zeus, Hermes) wearing 'normal comic masks' in illustrations of comic scenes can corroborate this conclusion; see T. B. L. Webster (1951: 593); Dearden (1976: 125).

In an important survey of the semantic field covered by the word *mimesis*[3] Halliwell (1986: 113–14) has taken *Frogs* 109 to be a 'straightforward instance' of the 'impersonation' sense, an interpretation which implicitly attributes to Dionysus an unmistakably metadramatic stance. Very much like a detached, that is, a non-theatrical observer, he is able to conceive his personal engagement in the fiction of the drama as an act of acting.[4] Nevertheless, *mimesis* in *Frogs* 109 is much more flexible a term than Halliwell would allow. With the sense of impersonation are mingled first the sense of appearance imitation, that is, the meaning of 'visual copying or resemblance' (cf. Halliwell 1986: 111), an aspect thrust sharply into relief in the stage confrontation of Dionysus with Heracles (esp. *Frogs* 38 ff.), where the focus narrows to the god's unfortunate attempt to reproduce his prototype's external outlook; and secondly, the notion of 'behavioural imitation',[5] which will subsequently be exploited in Dionysus' enactment of the role. This chapter, then, deploys the argument that Dionysus' role-playing in the *Frogs* could have been deciphered by the comedy's first audience as an exploration of the meaning of theatrical *mimesis*. The god's 'Heraclean' performance not only invites the spectator to perceive and appreciate him in the position and the function of an actor but, more importantly still, raises and explores the key dramatic question of how 'appearance' and 'behaviour' imitation interrelate and work within the boundaries of a theatrical impersonation.

It cannot be emphasized too strongly that both self-conscious assumption of a 'role within the role' and the envisaging of the 'internalized' performer as an actor are by no means restricted to the case of Dionysus in the *Frogs*. For the device of a 'secondary impersonation' is a well-established feature of Aristophanes' technique, frequently exploited for the richness of its dramatic possibilities. Thus, Dicaeopolis' gradual acquisition of Telephus' rags and props and the self-conscious enactment of his role in *Acharnians* 383 ff.; the Kinsman's preparation for his feminine performance in *Thesmophoriazusae* 211 ff., together with the striking interplay of representation levels inherent in the subsequent impersonations of

---

[3] The meaning of this word, as of the whole '*mimeisthai*-group' (Sörbom 1966: 23) in its pre-Platonic period especially, is still a matter of dispute; for the main discussions see Koller (1954); Else (1958); Sörbom (1966); Halliwell (1986: 109–37). For new perceptive insights see Nagy (1990: esp. 42–5).

[4] Note especially Dionysus' metatheatrical awareness of his Heraclean disguise as σκευή (108), i.e. a costume, a theatrical outfit for the enactment of his role (the word seems to have been a *terminus technicus* for the actor's garb; cf. Lys. 21. 4; Pollux 4. 115). For the 'awareness of costume as costume' as pertaining to the realm of the metatheatrical see F. Muecke (1982a: 23); cf. Taplin (1993: 68), who draws attention to *Frogs* 108 ff. as a nice illustration of 'the metatheatricality of σκευή/σκεύη in *Frogs*.' [5] See Halliwell (1986: 113 with n. 9).

dramatic characters (Helen, Andromeda, Perseus, Echo) within the same play (846 ff., 1008 ff.); and, finally, Praxagora's training of her cast for their male roles in the Assembly of the *Ecclesiazusae* (57–284), point clearly to the conclusion that the theatrical *mimesis* of an actor, displayed in all its manifold complexity, constitutes a constant focus of Aristophanes' attention.[6] In other words, inextricably bound up with some of Aristophanes' disguise/role-playing scenes is a skilfully and self-reflexively manipulated 'artistic' strand. And yet, although the *persona* and *mimesis* of the actor lie at the core of the above scenes, the spectator's attention is primarily directed to other aspects of the process of 'artistic' imitation[7] and, therefore, the relation of the stage-performer to his prototype is not the bedrock upon which the structure and dynamics of the narrative are built. As we shall see in Sections 4.4–10, conversely, Dionysus' role-playing in the *Frogs* is shaped in such a way that its focus narrows to the 'face-to-face' confrontation of the actor with some prominently 'Heraclean' aspects of his model's deeds. For, although after the end of the prologue Heracles is not physically on stage any more, the spectator is forcefully given the impression that he has never disappeared, he is still intensely 'there' (cf. also 7.1). This effect of uninterrupted presence is primarily due to the fact that Dionysus' journey is closely modelled upon the corresponding Heraclean labour of descent to Hades,[8] something which makes it perfectly natural that he has to meet persons more or less connected with Heracles' other-worldly past. As a result of this connection, each of the three 'encounter scenes' (460–502, 503–48, 549–604) which will be closely examined in this chapter (4.5–11), bears a distinctively 'Heraclean' flavour to the extent of bringing a particular aspect of the Heraclean nature to the fore. In other words, as the 'encounter scenes' unfold, the aim of Dionysus' *mimesis* acquires in the eyes of the audience an existence of its own. More significantly still, this existence is not delimited by any single text, despite the fact that a varied literary tradition (epic, tragic, and comic) lurks behind the re-enactment of Heracles' labour.[9] Dionysus' model rather bursts

---

[6] My own conception of these scenes is heavily indebted to F. Muecke (1977, 1982*a*, 1982*b*); Zeitlin (1981); Foley (1988).

[7] In Dicaeopolis' role-playing in the *Acharnians*, for example, the relationship primarily explored and highlighted is that of the performing stage-figure with his public, while, if viewed metatheatrically, the stage-impersonations in the *Thesmophoriazusae* tragic parodies amount to a general reflection of the poet on those conditions and conventions whose occurrence and acceptance enables a theatrical performance to unfold and work. I discuss the structure and artistic flavour of these scenes at length in Lada-Richards (1997*b*).

[8] For a detailed inspection of analogies see Lloyd-Jones (1967: esp. 218–21).

[9] For the epic *katabaseis* of Heracles see Lloyd-Jones (1967); for the paratragic flavour of *Frogs* 464 ff. see below, n. 55. For the comic tradition see Hunter (1983: 89–90).

forth with all the impact of his forceful personality *per se*, as this is shaped by the multi-levelled mythical tradition which revolves around him.[10] Consequently, in the *Frogs*, as we shall see in 4.4–11, the major concern of the scenes which frame Dionysus' secondary impersonation is precisely the actor's 'approach to' and 'deviation from' the values associated with his prototype's mythical and cultic presence. Thus, the only way one can envisage the theatrical relationship between Dionysus and Heracles is as a measurement of their 'personalities'. Furthermore, this 'actor–model' link is offered to the spectators' eyes in its irreducible, primary form. I mean that, without any intervening textual role—not even the guidelines of a mere scenario, as is the case with the Kinsman's feminine impersonation in the *Thesmophoriazusae*—the actor's 'self' passes to the sphere of the 'other' through direct appropriation of the 'other''s attributes and with the aim of re-enacting as closely as possible a pre-established mythical pattern (the pattern of a *katabasis* to Hades). In this respect, Dionysus' function in the plot resembles that of a performer in a pre-dramatic chorus, who dresses up as goat, bird, or mythical figure in order to *re*create the story in which his model was involved.[11] In the *Frogs*, then, not only is impersonation the clear focus of Dionysus' metatheatrical role-playing, but it is also displayed in its original immediacy and force: through the elementary way he assumes his role, the theatre god is linked to the very first requirement that calls forth drama into being, the transfusion of the 'self' into the 'other', which is visibly expressed in the actor's adoption of disguise.

Now, if placed within the wider context of Greek fifth-century predispositions and assumptions, dramatic focusing on Dionysus as an impersonator becomes especially evocative. For in an ancient Greek audience's perspective a deep affinity exists between 'Dionysiac psychology' and acting: both the actor's 'stepping out' of himself as well as the spectator's sympathetic fusion with the acting stage-figure (cf. Lada 1993) become possible through the Dionysiac experience of *ekstasis*. As Erwin Rohde (1925: 285) has brilliantly observed:

. . . the art of the actor consists in entering into a strange personality, and in speaking and acting out of a character not his own. At bottom it retains a profound and ultimate connexion with its most primitive source—that

---

[10] However, this proposition should only be conceived within the theoretical frame of my Introduction.

[11] See Nagy (1990: 43) on 'the fundamental meaning inherent in *mimêsis*' being 'that of reenacting the events of myth in ritual.' Consider e.g. Herodotus' 'tragic choruses' in Sicyon (5. 67. 5), re-enacting the *pathea* (sufferings) of the hero Adrastus (Nagy 1990).

strange power of transfusing the self into another being which the really inspired participator in the Dionysiac revels achieved in his *ekstasis*.

And if the hallmark of an actor's personality is his expressive versatility, his ability to assume and bring to life a thousand different *personae*, it is precisely this flexibility which sanctifies him as a 'Dionysiac' performer, since inconstancy and fickleness of shape is the principle which lies at the core of the Dionysiac nature (see e.g. Henrichs 1982). Functioning, therefore, as a divine proto-type for the Greek actor's stage-metamorphoses, Dionysiac trans-formability provides the assurance for the reintegration of the 'other' into the 'self', as Claude Calame (1986: 99) has put it. 'Dionysus', then, offers a case very unlike other trickster comic heroes, for, when on stage and performing, it is the shapelessness of his own nature which underlies the theatrical metamorphoses he may have to undergo. In other words, when acting, the fluidity of his mythical and cultic personality is quite naturally expressed through disguise and change of role, the only means that a pro-fessional performer has at his disposal in order to achieve a trans-formation. Nevertheless, in Greek society, a stage-Dionysus cast in the role of an actor is bound to be a culturally 'loaded' signifier; con-sequently, its integration, manipulation, or highlighting within a work of art may on occasions prove to be significant, the range of connotations likely to be attached to it being determined by the dramatic piece's overall milieu. *Frogs*, I believe, *does* form, in this respect, an exceptionally privileged context: concerned with play-wrights and the art of playwriting itself, it also focuses on Dionysus' mythical and cultic personality. More importantly still, its highly 'self-reflexive' nature places the god both of dramatic poetry *per se* and of dramatic performances as theatrical events precisely in the cardinal position which effects the transition from the former sphere to the latter, that is, in the status of an impersonator.

4.2. *The Ritual Value of Dionysus' Disguise*

As early as the comedy's opening lines, Dionysus interprets Heracles' astonishment at the oddity of his dress as terror, caused by the fiercer attributes in his theatrical outfit (*skeue*): 'Didn't you notice?' Dionysus asks Xanthias (40). 'Notice what?', the slave replies in astonishment. 'How terribly frightened he was of me!' (ὡς σφόδρα μ' ἔδεισε) (41). The god seems to have taken it for granted that wearing the likeness of Heracles confers upon him an air as fearsome as that of the real hero. So, when the Underworld Doorkeeper (4.5) asks him to identify himself, Dionysus, confident that his ferocious appearance lays bare a ferociousness of soul as well, replies: 'I am Heracles, the mighty one!' (Ἡρακλῆς ὁ καρτερός) (464). That is to say, in Dionysus' perspective, Heraclean appearance and Heraclean prowess are interdependent, or rather, a given *schema* (i.e. form, shape) is causally associated with the corresponding *lema* (i.e. purpose of mind, spirit): he has transformed himself in the guise of Heracles (*aition*); he is, therefore, *bound* to be suffused with Heraclean bravery and strength (result). In the mind of Dionysus, the actor, then,[12] external assimilation to the 'other' through disguise entails internal transmutation as well, participation in the *nature* of the 'other'.

Now, to us, it may seem a perfectly natural inference that, should we don a lion-skin, we would assume that, somehow or other, we look fearsome. And I say 'natural', in the sense that we are not *culturally* predisposed to attach any string of connotations to our straightforward assumption. However, things are not so simple in pre-industrial societies, where symbolic modes of thought are paramount. Thus, if focused through Greek perceptual filters, Dionysus' assumption acquires deeper implications, for syllogisms such as 'like produces like', or 'an effect resembles its cause' (Frazer 1949: 11)[13] are usual modes of reasoning in traditional cultures. Moreover,

---

[12] Silk (1990: 171) doubts the possibility that the Aristophanic people 'can . . . actually be said to have minds and thoughts', since they are not 'realist' creatures but purely 'imagist' beings. Nevertheless, the issue at stake is much broader and spans the dichotomy between 'realistic' and 'non-realistic' writings: the motivation or rather the possibility of a discussion about motivation of dramatic/narrative figures is probably the most debated aspect of the whole 'characterisation-problem' (Hochman 1985: 22–5). Hence, I find it necessary to clarify, even if only briefly, my position: I agree with Goldhill (1986*b*, 1990*b*) that it is legitimate to discuss dramatic characters' possible motivations, either explicit or even implicit, as long as we acknowledge that these creatures are just figures, not off-stage human beings '*really* and *absolutely* endowed with motivations, which, if only we could discover them, would give us "the truth" of a character' (1990*b*: 112). In other words, what is certainly futile and absurd is only the search for a 'sure and fixed answer to what a character is "really feeling", "really thinking", "really wanting"' (1990*b*: 113); it is the notion of a 'real' motivation which is bound to elude us 'at any particular moment in a text' (1990*b*: 113). It is only with such provisos in mind that I touch the point of Dionysus' 'underlying intent' in his Heraclean dressing up and, consequently, I have tried to remain as close as possible to the hints afforded by the text itself. Besides, I should like to believe that the notion of Dionysus' motives could even be dispensed with without seriously affecting the following discussion: because what I now call 'Dionysus' point of view' might equally well be ascribed to 'the logic of the narrative itself' (Hochman 1985: 22).

[13] Frazer's conception of 'sympathetic magic' has come in for a great deal of criticism in modern anthropological studies. Even at the level of terminology, 'imitative symbolism' (Tambiah 1973: 204) or 'symbolic instrumentation' (Munn 1973: 592) are the new terms broached by modern anthropological research to counteract Frazer's simplistic and deprecatory conception of magic as a pre-logical way of thought and as an illustration of a failed causal reasoning. For a theoretical overview of criticisms of Frazer's approach to magic see e.g. Jarvie and Agassi (1970); Lukes (1970) and, for a practical application of a symbolist approach see, most importantly, Tambiah's studies (esp. 1968; cf. 1973).

'analogical action' (Tambiah 1973: 204)—as would be the general term for this mode of reasoning, based on a conscious and consistent use of similes, 'suggestive metaphors', and metonymic reconstructions (Tambiah 1968: esp. 195)—proves a salient feature in many areas of human experience and thought, and is particularly operative in the ritual ceremonies of primitive societies.

   Research and fieldwork carried out by anthropologists such as Lévi-Strauss, Evans-Pritchard, Leach, Turner, Douglas, to name but a few distinguished contributors, have interestingly elucidated the subtlety and the diversity of logical and analogical relations involved in the structuring of primitive world-order, and have brought to light a series of symbolic patterns which govern the activities of pre-industrial peoples in all the areas of their life, especially in the ritual sphere. More significantly still, the analogic transference of qualities from one person or object to another can be seen most clearly at work in connection with the ceremonial action of disguise, the ritual actor's dressing up. For in the context of a ritual performance dressing up invests the individual actor with an added quality, an added faculty, which is expected to refashion him or her into a new construct. That is to say, the ritual actor becomes 'something more', with respect to a given set of qualities, than what he normally, in everyday life, is. What takes place in such cases is a complex symbolical process: the assumption of a ritual garb does not annihilate or replace or restructure the wearer's secular *persona*, as Lévy-Bruhl and other early anthropologists would have us believe,[14] but rather *assimilates* it, by an analogy sometimes clearly discernible even by mere observers of a given culture, to the existential mode of what the ritual mask or costume[15]

---

[14] In its crudest form the anthropological conception of ritual disguise is fixed by Lévy-Bruhl (1931: 128): 'lorsque, dans les cérémonies et les dances rituelles, les acteurs ont mis leurs masques . . . ils sont devenus, ipso facto, les êtres dont les masques, de notre point de vue, sont les symboles et les représentations'. In other words, according to the writings of early anthropologists, the appropriate terms to be used in such contexts are not the categories of 'resembling' or of 'representing' (Lévy-Bruhl 1931: 124, 128, etc.) but those of 'becoming' and of 'being' (Lévy-Bruhl 1931: 124; cf. J. Campbell 1960: 21, etc.). As Eliade (1964b: 179) has generalized, magico-religious transformations are governed by a '"law" well known to the history of religions: one becomes what one displays.' However, if ritual disguise is focused through a symbolist anthropological perspective, the Lévy-Bruhlian case proves untenable (for a brief critical survey of Lévy-Bruhl's work see Horton 1973: esp. 252–3; Morris 1987: 182–6, and cf. Lloyd 1990: 16ff.). For claiming that the donning of a ritual garment is perceived by the community involved as a change of *existential* status in the *literal* sense of the word (Lévy-Bruhl 1931: 125, 128) is ultimately equivalent to underplaying the richly documented capability of 'primitive mentality' to formulate metaphorical equations as well as to distinguish 'real' from 'ideal' relationships within a given culture (cf. Sperber 1975: 94).

[15] See Lévy-Bruhl (1931: 127–8): 'on ne saurait dire plus nettement que la peau et le masque ont la même vertu'; see also Eliade (1964a: col. 522; and 1964b: 167, on shamans); cf. Deonna (1964: col. 527).

represents.[16] In the case of impersonation of divinities and spirits, for example, the tribal community is perfectly aware[17] that the costumed/masked ritual 'actor' is not the god in *propria persona*, but has been elevated in a highly *symbolical* and *analogic* way into the status of the god: through the appropriation of the god's distinctive emblems and paraphernalia he/she is now a manifestation[18] of divinity, and has such power over the congregated onlookers as the god himself is deemed to have with respect to human beings.[19] As Lévi-Strauss (1961: 18) has put it, 'The mask is both the man and something other than the man: it is the mediator *par excellence* between society, on the one hand, and Nature, usually merged with the Supernatural, on the other.'

Similar is the case of disguise into animals, a form of ritual change of identity which has closer bearing on Dionysus' dressing up in *Frogs*. The wearer of, let us say, an animal's hide is not believed to be *literally transformed* into the tribe's totemic creature, so that he might be treated and regarded as having claws, beak, or mane (cf. Sperber 1975: 94),[20] and so on. However, he is certainly believed to have *symbolically* partaken of and communicated in the special functions and the sacred powers of the tribe's totem, so as to be able to perform successfully, and for the benefit of the entire community, the ritual 'drama' within which the presence of the totem's qualities is viewed as indispensable; in other words, the ritually disguised actor is taking the place of the totem. To reformulate this thesis in more general terms, there is an implicit acceptance on both parts (i.e. performers and community alike) that the masked person acts temporarily *as if he were* somebody else,[21] a being whose presence and mediation are deemed to be essential for the welfare and continuation of the tribe.

In conclusion, then, although the ritual mask or costume cannot

---

[16] Cf. Myerhoff's (1978: 230–1) interpretation of disguise as deities during an Indian ritual in Mexico: '[they] do not merely impersonate the deities by assuming their names and garb. Ritually and *symbolically* (my italics), they become supernatural, disguising the mortal coil, abrogating human functions and forms'.

[17] Albeit, 'no doubt with varying degrees of awareness'; see Evans-Pritchard (1956: 140).

[18] But *not* an incarnation, as e.g. in Eliade's (1964b: 167–8) perspective.

[19] Cf. Evans-Pritchard's (1956: 123–43) illumination of some famous Nuer equations (e.g. the sacrificial cucumber *is* an ox, twins *are* birds, etc.) as *relative* triadic statements, condensing and implying a comparison with a third term, which is not explicitly stated (in the above examples, god or Spirit). For other studies on symbolical analogy see e.g. Gordon (1980: esp. 38) and Crocker (1985: esp. 13).

[20] Except that this could happen in a symbolic way in the course of the ceremony; see e.g. Porph. *De antr. Nymph.* 15 (on Mithraic initiations): ὅταν μὲν οὖν τοῖς τὰ λεοντικὰ μυουμένοις εἰς τὰς χεῖρας ἀνθ' ὕδατος μέλι νίψασθαι ἐγχέωσι . . . οἰκεῖα νίπτρα προσάγουσι.

[21] This *acceptance* of the ritual actor's 'otherness' is essential to the performance of the rite. See e.g. Werbner (1984: 272); Gell (1975: 193 and 243 ff.), and, most importantly, Crocker (1983: 158).

transform *substantially and literally*, they are assumed precisely because of their function to infuse the wearer with the powers of the beings they represent (gods, ancestral spirits, sacred animals, etc.). And such 'magico-religious' transformations can even be effected through the wearing of mere symbols and of signs: 'one assumes the power of magical flight by wearing an eagle feather, or even a highly stylized drawing of such a feather; and so on'.[22] Now, this altered feeling and status of the ceremonial performer is well documented in various ethnological contexts and ritual circumstances.[23] Even in ancient Greece, where secure evidence on ritual masking is relatively smaller, there *are* analogous phenomena which may be open to a similar interpretation; most pertinently, the process of 'deep metamorphosis' through appearance transformation is at work *par excellence* within the field of the Dionysiac 'myth and ritual' complex, as can be inferred from such activities as maenadism, initiation rites into the Dionysiac *thiasoi*, and specific ritual services performed under the 'eye' of the god (see Appendix). I believe that this conclusion greatly assists our attempt to estimate the ways in which a classical Greek audience would have been likely to appreciate Dionysus' perception of Heracles' insignia in the *Frogs*. For, if the analogical relation 'dressing up like X': 'appropriating the qualities of X' did actually belong to the mythico-ritual experience and general cultural knowledge of Greek spectators, Dionysus' 'point of view', as he stepped onto the stage to play the role of Heracles, could well have been 'received' as illustrating the distinctive psychology of Dionysiac ritual transformation.

4.3. *Stage-Acting and Theatrical Disguise*

Dionysus' 'psychology' and 'point of view', then, make perfect sense on a purely *ritual* level. As a theatrical performer, on the other hand, Dionysus proves utterly incompetent (cf. 2.4); fluctuating 'in' and 'out' of his chosen 'character', he is manifestly unable to sustain the integrity of his theatrical *persona*. In other words, the god of drama's ritual 'approach' to stage-acting is clearly inadequate and false: although in his own, limited perspective, ritual apparel and theatrical disguise are similar or even interchangeable, in the perspective of the ancient world of Theatre the function and the power of the ritual mask can never be regarded as identical to that of a theatrical *persona*. For, if the ceremonial mask or costume invests

---

[22] Eliade (1964*b*: 180); for further examples see Frazer (1949: 31).
[23] See e.g. Hill (1972: 89–90); Ashley (1979: 107–9), and for a fascinating description of a Balinese ritual actor see Emigh (1979: esp. 32–5).

the ritual subject with a strange power and enriches his/her secular identity with new dimensions, the dramatic mask cannot convey to the wearer any kind of magical power (Calame 1986: 93–4). In the theatrical domain, the donning of a mask or costume can only cause the borderlines of the actor's personality to blur and his own 'self' to be imaginatively projected towards the sphere of any 'alterity' his mask or costume represents. Rather than readily endowing the wearer with a new identity, the 'otherness' symbolically appropriated through a mask or costume on the stage confers upon him nothing more than the mere *potentiality* of *acquiring* one (Calame 1986: 94). To put it slightly differently, when acting takes place on the civic space of the *polis*, the actor's mask is not to be regarded as a talismanic object but rather as a powerful and creative instrument in the performer's hands. That is to say, it is the actor, rather than the mask *per se*, which is the 'living force', the cause of the *metamorphosis*, as it rests entirely with the performer's own skill to integrate harmoniously his mask and costume in the play's action by exploiting to the full the entire range of their intrinsic properties. It is the actor who, as the focal point on which the multiplicity of codes traversing the performance meet (cf. Elam 1980: 52; Burns 1972: 144), must learn to co-ordinate the sum of his expressive means (i.e. body-gestures, voice, etc.) to the specific mode of being of the dramatic figure suggested by his mask.[24] In other words, the actor must train himself in such a way as to be able to attain an ideal stage of congruity or, as David Wiles (1991: 223) has put it, that 'single psychosomatic level of coherence' where dramatic role, expression of the mask, and suggestions of the costume as well as the delivery of the performer 'coalesce'.[25]

To take our example from the *Frogs*. The costumed stage-actor

[24] For the performer's need to adapt his voice, gestures, movements, and emotion to the 'character' and the emotions of the role see e.g. Arist. *Rhet.* 1403b26–30; Dem. 18. 287 (on orators: μηδὲ τῇ φωνῇ δακρύειν ὑποκρινόμενον τὴν ἐκείνων τύχην, ἀλλὰ τῇ ψυχῇ συναλγεῖν); DH *Dem.* 53; Bekker, *Anecd. Graec.* ii, p. 744; iii. p. 1165, 744. 1; Anon. *Proleg. Rhet.* (in Walz, *Rhet. Graec.* vi, p. 35, 16–19) Ἡ δὲ ὑπόκρισίς ἐστιν, ἵνα καὶ τῷ σχήματι, καὶ τῷ βλέμματι, καὶ τῇ φωνῇ, ὡς ἂν τραγῳδὸς ἄριστος καλῶς τοῖς λεγομένοις συσχηματίζηται. Cf. Cic. *De Orat.* 2. 189–90, 2. 193, 3. 216–19; Quint. 6. 2. 26–8, 2. 35, 11. 3. 61, etc.

[25] See primarily, Luc. 8. 11, 28. 31 (quoted below in the text and in n. 27 respectively); Quint. 11. 3. 73–4; Fronto, *De Eloq.* 2. 16 (m² in *margine*), p. 143 Van den Hout. See T. B. L. Webster (1965). Of course, it cannot be emphasized too strongly that the bulk of first-hand evidence on ancient acting dates from relatively later periods, thus making any hasty inferences about classical Athenian acting-style particularly hazardous; as it can be easily understood, a variety of changes are likely to have occurred even in the period of one dramatist's lifetime (cf. e.g. Arist. *Poet.* 1461b33–6). Nevertheless, when one makes due allowances for the expected changes in gestures, general movements, tone and modality of voice, the diachronic inspection of the evidence brings to the fore two elements consistently unalterable, namely, the actor's tendency towards immersion in his role and the spectator's high responsiveness to every kind of emotion (cf. Lada 1993).

who aspires to sustain his role as Heracles throughout the theatrical performance would be unwise to content himself with mere achievement of a physical resemblance with his prototype through appropriate adjustments of his garb. In order to play 'Heracles' successfully, he should first of all remember that it would be equally important to 'make up' and 'dress' his 'soul', to 'tune' his 'inner strings' to the key of the Heraclean 'personality' (cf. Magarshack 1961: 68). Only when he would achieve that complete fusion between his own life and the life of his character, whereby he would be able to 'feel the presence of bits of himself in his part and bits of his part in himself' (Magarshack 1961: 75), would he be truly and persuasively incarnating Heracles on stage. Because, by ancient acting-standards, a good impersonation is not solely dependent on external imitation, but is mainly a matter of creating one's role in inner and harmonious correspondence to the 'character' who lies behind it.[26]

To take one further example from Aristophanic metatheatre, we could consider *Ecclesiazusae*, and especially Praxagora's training of the female members of her 'cast' for the masculine impersonation they are about to perform on the *political* stage of the city, the Assembly of the Pnyx. Like an experienced stage-director, she tries to impart to her actors precisely this double requisite for imitation that we have singled out with respect to *Frogs*. I mean the fact that a good impersonation does not merely depend on outer assimilation, not even solely on eloquent delivery (*kalos legein*), but primarily on creating one's role in inner and harmonious correspondence to the model which inspires it, in the case of her actors, 'in a *manly* way': 'Come on, then, make sure that you speak well and as befits a man' (ἄγε νυν ὅπως ἀνδριστὶ καὶ καλῶς ἐρεῖς) (149). Acting which contradicts the 'spirit' of the part or which substitutes the performer's own point of view for the frame of mind of the *dramatis persona* is of no avail, even when the verbal and recitative levels of performance are impeccable. So Praxagora takes one of her actresses to task because, although playing at being a man, she has sworn by female deities, and this is bound to have a shattering effect, despite the fact that in all other matters she has spoken to perfection:

WOM. . . . . it doesn't seem so to me, by the two Goddesses!
PRAX. By the two Goddesses? Poor creature, have you lost your wits?
WOM. Why? what's amiss? Surely, I didn't ask for a drink!

---

[26] For sources implying artistic effort for character adaptability see e.g. Plut. *Mor.* 711c (ὑπόκρισις πρέπουσα τῷ ἤθει τῶν ὑποκειμένων προσώπων); Plut. *Dem.* 7. 2; Luc. 45. 67; *Vit. Soph.* 6 (*TrGF* iv, p. 32 = Istrus, *FGrHist* 334 F36); Macr. *Sat.* 2. 7. 12–15. I propose to discuss the concept of 'character acting' on the classical Athenian stage in forthcoming work.

PRAX. By Zeus, certainly not, but you invoked the two Goddesses, although you were supposed to be a man! All else you said was perfectly right. (*Eccles.* 155–9)

Incongruity, then, either between external outlook and *ethos* of the role or between delivery and 'character reality' could be perceived as a hindrance to the successful outcome of a performance. So one of Lucian's characters expresses his anxiety lest he prove himself similar to those actors who

Time and again when they have assumed the role of Agamemnon or Creon or even Heracles himself, costumed in cloth of gold, with fierce eyes and mouths wide agape, they speak in a voice that is small, thin, womanish, and far too poor for Hecuba or Polyxena.[27] (Luc. 8. 11)

In a similar way, Dionysus is primarily required to adjust his inner disposition, reflected in the style of his delivery, to the Heraclean 'appearance' (*schema*) (*Frogs* 463) he has donned. However, it would seem that such a notion of artistic effort is not meaningful for him at all. Instead of trying to adjust himself to the role (see Benedetti 1981: 14), he has finally adjusted the role to himself[28] and, although he intends to play 'Heracles', he only plays and reproduces the image of his own soft and cowardly self, a distinctively 'Dionysiac' *dramatis persona* moulded by a long theatrical tradition of which Cratinus' *Dionysalexandrus* is for us the clearest example. And yet, hopeless actor though he is, the very structure of the play itself is such as to initiate him in the specific needs of the dramatic space. For, as the 'encounter scenes' (4.5–11) unfold, the spectator comes step by step to the point of realizing that the only way in which the god would have been able to live his part would have been his attempt to see the world through the eyes of his model (cf. Rapoport 1955: 68). Such a modified perspective would have entailed for him first the rejection of his stubborn overconfidence in the magical superimposition of his model's personality upon his own and, most importantly, the scrupulous decipherment of the artistic hints that his Heraclean disguise conveys, that is, courage, bravery, ferocity in the enactment of the role. In the manner of a 'Stanislavskian' actor,[29] then, Dionysus would have had to analyse the various levels of his part (Brockett 1980: 300ff.), so that he

---

[27] Cf. Luc. 28. 31 καὶ τὸ πρᾶγμα ὅμοιον ἐδόκει μοι καθάπερ ἂν εἴ τις ὑποκριτὴς τραγῳδίας μαλθακὸς αὐτὸς ὢν καὶ γυναικεῖος [v. l. γυναικίας] Ἀχιλλέα ἢ Θησέα ἢ καὶ τὸν Ἡρακλέα ὑποκρίνοιτο αὐτὸν μήτε βαδίζων μήτε βοῶν ἡρωϊκόν, ἀλλὰ θρυπτόμενος ὑπὸ τηλικούτῳ προσωπείῳ.

[28] See S. Moore (1966: 77).

[29] Cf. Lada-Richards (1997b).

might have started to react in the way his model would have done, if placed in analogous circumstances (Rapoport 1955: 49).

Given, therefore, the dissimilar function of ritual and theatrical *skeue*, I would like to suggest that, in so far as the act of imitation is concerned, the play dramatizes a *clash* between a ritual and a theatrical standpoint: the spectator's gradual realization of the purely *theatrical* requirements for the enactment of a stage-impersonation is juxtaposed to the quite spectacular display of Dionysus' misplaced *ritual* attitude to his dramatic garb. Nevertheless, it is precisely this clash which enables the play's dominant point of view to be powerfully highlighted. For the uniqueness of being an actor in the theatre is emphasized primarily because of its projection upon the complementary, yet different, background that being an actor in the ritual constitutes. 'Complementary' because in both contexts the aspiration of the actor is to *identify* with the being whose tangible, external elements he has appropriated; and 'different' because the way in which such identification is effected is distinctive for each case, singularity being due to the dissimilar functions that ritual and theatrical disguises perform.

To round off the first part of this chapter, then, we may conclude that, setting out from a non-theatrical perspective, Dionysus is thrust, by the very *praxis* of the comedy itself and through the means of his own *pathos*, into a theatrical display of what it means to be an actor in front of the *polis*' theatre-audience. By interweaving in the same stage-character the two antithetical viewpoints, the ritual and the theatrical,[30] the play stimulates the spectator to hold in sight simultaneously the two angles from which the phenomenon of 'playing the other' is conceivable, both of which are markedly 'Dionysiac' and ultimately based on the experience of *ekstasis*. Yet, the challenging requirements of *stage*-acting that the comedy's scenario throws sharply into relief confront the actor with the obligation to abide by the ways that the *polis* has developed in order to approach, to capture, and appropriate the figure of the 'other'. Privileging, as it does, the *theatrical* over the ritual type of Dionysiac performance, Aristophanes' comedy transfuses the Dionysiac mode of ritual transformation into the distinctive moulds of Dionysiac civic drama. In what follows, therefore, we shall try to appreciate step by step the precise ways in which theatrical role-playing is able to effect Dionysus' gradual integration into civic space.

---

[30] Exemplified respectively in Dionysus' frame of mind and the actions in which he happens to become involved.

Role-Playing and Dionysiac/Heraclean Polarities

4.4. *Introduction*

As has been argued in the opening pages of this chapter, the only way in which Dionysus can be 'seen' while playing his role is in his relation to Heracles, a point of reference which lies outside his own artistic self: both the Dionysiac 'self' and the Heraclean 'other' are simultaneously and manifestly visible. Now, theoretical studies of dramatic conventions have made us aware that an important function fulfilled by a 'secondary' role-playing is the examination of the 'internalized' actor's identity:[31] how closely or how remotely does he or she relate to the specific features of the figure he/she impersonates? Similarly, with respect to our play, I should like to believe that probing the relation of Dionysus to Heracles, while the former carries out the *mimesis* of the latter, is an important step towards evaluating the direction into which stage-acting steers the *dramatis persona* of the god. Dionysus' 'approach to' or 'deviation from' the model of his imitation is intimated to the spectators through his successive reassumption and discarding of Heracles' *skeue*. The remainder of this chapter, therefore, argues that, in the eyes of fifth-century spectators sharing the same sociocultural assumptions, this comically displayed fluctuation between artistic 'self' and 'otherness' can function as a remarkably dynamic 'sign', indicating the measure of the god's appropriateness (or, for that matter, inappropriateness) for identifying with the codes of behaviour that his stage-prototype represents.

Dionysus sets aside his Heraclean *persona* after his encounter with the Underworld Doorkeeper (494–7) and after the menaces levelled at him by two Innkeepers, enraged at his model's deeds (579 ff.). Despite the fact that they do not follow each other in the flow of the performance, *Frogs* 464 ff. and 549 ff. call for a preliminary joint examination at this point, as they both result in the actor's separation from the object of his imitation. Their shared thematic background consists in their mutual evocation of a model of behaviour whose primary dimensions are: (i) use of violence and appropriation of things through corporeal force,[32] entailing defiance of rules and law,[33]

---

[31] For a theoretical discussion and the application of this principle to Shakespeare's plays see Hornby (1986: ch. 4).

[32] Consider his manual overpowering of Cerberus in 467–8, and cf. his behaviour at the inn (549 ff.), culminating in menaces with a sword (564).

[33] The Doorkeeper's account makes it clear that the dog was driven away without permission (468–9); as for the Innkeepers, they describe Heracles as a πανοῦργος (549), who broke in and grabbed food, while denying any payment for it (esp. 561–2). Cf. below, 4.9.

(ii) action in accordance with the ethic of immediate satisfaction of one's 'natural' instincts,[34] and (iii) perversion of the human norm through madness (564) and failure of articulated speech (562).

(i) Reliance on bodily strength as a means of coping with one's environment had always been regarded in Greek culture as representing a primitive stage in mankind's evolution, a period when human life was 'beastlike and subservient to brute force' (Critias, B 25, 1–2 D–K), and violence (βία) was 'enthroned with Zeus'.[35] It is the realm of wild beasts which is governed by the law of violence (cf. e.g. Lys. 2. 19; Hes. *Op.* 274 ff.), while man, inferior from the start in strength (see e.g. Isocr. 3. 6; cf. Pl. *Prot.* 322b), has either developed or received as gifts unique methods of survival, variously specified as *nomos*, *dike*, *techne*, or *peitho*, according to each writer's viewpoint and/or philosophical stance. In Lysias' perspective, the ancestors of fifth-century Athenian citizens deemed that

> it was the way of wild beasts to be held subject to one another by force (βία κρατεῖσθαι) but the duty of men to delimit justice by law, to convince by argument (λόγῳ . . . πεῖσαι), and to serve these two in act by submitting to the sovereignty of law and the instruction of reason (λόγου). (2. 19)

Correspondingly, the neglect of social rules is a constant spectre for the *polis*, paving the way for society's disintegration and relapse to a level of bestiality. In Demosthenes' words,

> if . . . every man were given licence to do as he liked, not only does the constitution vanish, but our life would not differ from that of the beasts of the field. (Dem. 25. 20; cf. Pl. *Leg.* 874e; Diod. 13. 26. 3, etc.)

(ii) Living 'only by one's senses' is for Aristotle a sign of the 'beastlike' (*EN* 1149a9–10 οἱ μὲν . . . μόνον τῇ αἰσθήσει ζῶντες θηριώδεις), and it is primarily the piggish swallowing of food which has always been considered as deeply rooted in the ways of 'nature',[36] as incompatible with philosophy and *mousike* (Pl. *Tim.* 73a). In the political discourse of democratic Athens, for example, insatiability is one of the characteristics of the potentially subversive anti-citizen, like Aeschines' opponent Timarchus, who 'wolfed down' and 'drank up' the whole of his patrimony to gratify his lusts.[37] But also, ever since the time of Homer, compliance with the

---

[34] As can be gauged from the Innkeepers' recollections (549 ff.).

[35] Moschion, *TrGF* i (97) F 6, 15 ff.; cf. Polyb. 6. 5. 7–9.

[36] For the needs of the *gaster* (in Homer and Hesiod) as interwoven with an asocial existence see Svenbro (1976: 50–9). In comedy, the glutton seems to be frequently compared to insatiable animals or monsters; see Taillardat (1965: 94–6). In a wider cultural perspective cf. Athen. 363a, where 'ἀπλήστως eating' is coupled with θηριωδῶς, and Xen. *Inst. Cyr.* 5. 2. 17.

[37] Aeschin. 1. 96 ἐνταῦθα ἤδη ἐτράπετο ἐπὶ τὸ καταφαγεῖν τὴν πατρῴαν οὐσίαν. καὶ οὐ μόνον κατέφαγεν, ἀλλ' εἰ οἷόν τ' ἐστὶν εἰπεῖν, καὶ κατέπιεν.

'law of the belly' had been regarded as reflecting a state of bestial savagery (Vernant 1979a: 92–8). The semi-feral Euripidean Cyclops, for example, may happily proclaim as the highest credo in his life 'sacrificing to no one of the gods', except to

> the greatest god of all,
> this belly of mine! To eat, to drink
> from day to day, to have no worries—
> that's the real Zeus for your clever man! (335–8)

The impression of 'naturalness' in our scene is enhanced by the coarse description of the parts of the Heraclean body (571, 572–3, 575–6), a picture which acquires much more depth if compared to the language and visual images of the *Cyclops* in those passages where Euripides describes Polyphemus' gluttony and eating manners.[38] More importantly still, the Heracles of our scene does not merely devour human food. His 'dishes' range from the most 'tame' and civilized (551 ἄρτους; cf. 553 κρέα . . . ἀνάβραστ')[39] to the most 'natural' and savage, objects inedible to men, such as the food-baskets (560). Thus, the hero's mixed diet creates an image which confounds the boundaries of bestial and human, nature and culture,[40] while his gulping down the wooden baskets would certainly appear to Greek eyes as the peak of brutishness: wood (ὕλη) was mankind's means of sustenance when man could still be satisfied 'eating and drinking the same things as bulls and horses',[41] a mode of living which was considered as 'strong' and 'beastlike'.[42] And it is especially the play's Eleusinian background which is appropriate for highlighting Heracles' relapse into bestiality as a striking deviation from the norm of civilized human beings. For ancient tradition is unanimous in praising Demeter's gift of grain as the nourishment which freed mankind 'from beastlike existence' (τοῦ . . . θηριωδῶς ζῆν) (Isocr. 4. 28), and effected the transition from a savage (*agria*) diet to a 'tame' mode of nourishment (*hemeros trophe*).[43]

[38] See e.g. 214–15, 243–5, 289, 302–3, 310, 326, 356–7, 362, 409–10, 505–6, insisting on Polyphemus' φάρυγξ, γνάθος, νηδύς, γαστήρ. Konstan's (1990: 215) judgement of the Euripidean monster would equally apply to the Heracles of *Frogs* 549 ff. as well: 'He simply consumes, and in the imagery of the play, he is all jaws, gullet, and belly.'

[39] Boiling being conceived as having followed roasting in the culinary evolution of mankind; see Seaford (1984: 152, on Eur. *Cycl.* 244–6).

[40] Besides the fact that such a fusion is distinctively Heraclean, an analogous synthesis of the two polarities into a single 'stage-act' is illustrated in the Euripidean Polyphemus' prospective sacrifice (*Cycl.* 241 ff.), both disgustingly savage and highly 'sophisticated'; see Seaford (1984: 152).

[41] Hippocr. *VM*. 3 (i. 576 Littré); see ibid. οἷον τὰ ἐκ τῆς γῆς φυόμενα, καρπούς τε καὶ ὕλην καὶ χόρτον.   [42] Hippocr. *VM*. 3 (i. 576 Littré) ἀπὸ ἰσχυρῆς τε καὶ θηριώδεος διαίτης.

[43] See e.g. Moschion, *TrGF* i (97) F 6 τόθ' ηὑρέθη μὲν καρπὸς ἡμέρου τροφῆς | Δήμητρος ἁγνῆς (23–4) . . . καὶ τὸν ἠγριωμένον | εἰς ἥμερον δίαιταν ἤγαγον βίον (28–9); Rabe (1906: 276, 22–4 in Luc. *DMeretr.* 2.1); Paus. 7. 18. 2, 8. 4. 1; Diod. 13. 26. 3, etc.

(iii) As for the attributes of articulate voice and reason, these have always been considered as distinguishing man from the sphere of the beasts.[44] Either disruptions of articulated language, therefore, or irrational fits of rage (*mania*) relegate man to a space outside social life, where both lack of sagacity (*synesis*) and inarticulate growling impede a human-like communication.[45]

Having in mind such cultural considerations, then, we may now conclude that the discarding of Heracles' *skeue* estranges Dionysus, the actor, from a bestial and uncivilized mode of being. However, *Frogs* 464–502 and 549–604 cannot be fully appreciated unless they are approached from a specifically 'Dionysiac' and 'Heraclean' angle, and this is precisely the task that I shall turn to next.

THE DOORKEEPER'S SCENE: *FROGS* 460–502

4.5. *Heracles, Dionysus, and Anomalous Hunting*

Let us start with the Underworld Doorkeeper's[46] retrospective vision of Heracles.

> ὦ βδελυρὲ κἀναίσχυντε καὶ τολμηρὲ σὺ
> καὶ μιαρὲ καὶ παμμίαρε καὶ μιαρώτατε,
> ὃς τὸν κύν' ἡμῶν ἐξελάσας τὸν Κέρβερον
> ἀπῇξας ἄγχων κἀποδρὰς ᾤχου λαβών,
> ὃν ἐγὼ 'φύλαττον.

> You loathsome, shameless and daring creature,
> and defiled, and foulest and most abominable,
> who drove away our dog Cerberus, the one that was under
>   my guard,
> and darted off throttling him, and in your flight went away
> having taken him with you!   (465–9)

Within two lines overburdened with verbal forms which vaguely connote either harsh treatment of the beast (467–8) or treacherous behaviour (468), it is only the participle ἄγχων, 'throttling' (468), which actually defines the specific mode of the hero's capture of

---

[44] *Logos*: see, most importantly, Socrates' etymology of ἄνθρωπος in Pl. *Crat.* 399c; cf. Pl. *Prot.* 322a; Isocr. 3. 6ff.; Arist. *Pol.* 1253a9–10; Diod. 1. 8. 3. *Reason*: see e.g. the collective characterization of all creatures except man in the Protagorean myth as ἄλογα (Pl. *Prot.* 321b–c); cf. Polyb. 6. 6. 4, and Pl. *Menex.* 237d.

[45] See e.g. Eur. *Troad.* 671–2; *Suppl.* 203–4; note also Diod. 1. 8. 3 and Aristotle's attribution of mere *phone* even to the beasts, as a sign τοῦ λυπηροῦ καὶ ἡδέος (*Pol.* 1253a11–12).

[46] For the problematic identification of the Doorkeeper with the exceptionally pious judge of the Underworld Aeacus see Dover (1993: 50–5) (sceptical) and Sommerstein (1996: ad 464, deeming it 'highly likely that this character was meant to be identified as Aeacus'). My reading of the scene is not affected either way.

Cerberus, implying, as it does, a corporeal fight and a mastery over the animal effected through bare hands. Studies in the rich corpus of hunting imagery revolving around Heracles have shown that the iconographic pattern 'animal grabbed by the hero' forms a fundamental principle in the depictions of Heraclean wrestlings with wild beasts (Schnapp 1987: 123). In the 'Cerynitan hind' labour, for example, it is precisely his manual grasp which differentiates Heracles from an ordinary deer-hunter. As Alain Schnapp (1987: 123 with figs. 1–4) has put it, 'Heracles can be identified because he seizes the beast. This seizure of Heracles is fundamental in red figure imagery.'[47] As presented through the Doorkeeper's recollections, then, the seizure of Cerberus belongs to the category of the cruder Heraclean exploits, where the savage monsters he combats are vanquished not through inventiveness of mind but through sheer strength of hand (cf. e.g. Soph. *Trach.* 1089ff., esp. 1097–8).[48]

However, in order to inquire into the significance of this Heraclean fighting scheme, we should first place it within the broader context of Graeco-Roman culture, where the use of bare hands in man's fight against beasts had always been considered as a feature of primitiveness. Thus, in Democritus' account of human social evolution, we read that in the first stages of mankind people 'were coming to each other's aid against the wild beasts and were engaging in battle with them unarmed, with their hands bare' (fr. B5 3, 41–2 D–K), while in Lucretius' perspective 'the ancient weapons were hands, nails, and teeth' (*De Rer. Nat.* 5. 1283). Civilized communities have gradually developed the skills of weaponry, or, as Protagoras would put it, the 'art of warfare' (*polemike techne*), a part of the supreme 'art of governing cities' (*politike techne*) (Pl. *Prot.* 322b). Hunting, then, becomes a civilizing activity in so far as it affirms the human condition through severing its bonds with the ferocity of animals. As Durand and Schnapp (1989: 59) write, 'The hunting of animals is for men the guarantor, on the anthropological level, of human identity. For the Greeks hunting is not only a simple matter of subsistence but a means of affirming themselves as men among other living beings.' Heraclean hunting, on the other hand, emphatically negates the use of man-made weapons. In a scheme which constantly recurs on vase-paintings, Heracles' bow, quiver, and arrows are shown as either 'hanging in the field or held by a patient Iolaos' (Boardman

[47] Cf. Henderson (1994: 99): 'He disdains the shield. This fighter of fighters knows only grappling, the scrap of the subhuman beast in his supernatural make-up.'

[48] e.g. in Heracles' great monologue in Sophocles' *Trachiniae* 1046ff., the snatching of the Ἅιδου τρίκρανον σκύλακα (1097–8) is presented as a purely manual task. For other cases of strangling in the labours see e.g. Diod. 4. 10. 1 (snakes), 4. 11. 3, 4. 11. 4 (Nemean lion).

1975: 11), while in other iconographic patterns, the hero's sword is 'crumpled and abandoned or inflicting only a surface wound' (Boardman 1975). 'How could one say more explicitly that the hero does not have the merest need of weapons?', Alain Schnapp (1987: 123) very aptly asks. By circumventing and annihilating the superiority that the 'technique of warfare' (πολεμικὴ τέχνη), a skill developed within an organized community, can give to man, Heracles reverts to the primitive means of overpowering savagery, by sliding backwards towards savagery himself,[49] that is, by subjugating the violence of nature through exhibiting a higher degree of 'natural' violence himself. A close look at, let us say, Sophocles' *Trachiniae* can illustrate this point very well. In the great monologue (1046–1111), where the vanquished hero laments the loss of his past splendour, the semantic category of *bia* defines not only the condition and behaviour of his savage bestial opponents, but also his personal, characteristic mode of combat, that is, the brutishness of his supreme bodily strength.[50]

Nevertheless, if Heraclean hunting, transgressing and subverting practices and norms, ends up being an exploit 'of a very idiosyncratic nature' (Schnapp 1987: 121), anomalous hunting lies also at the core of the Dionysiac realm. The persecution/hunt of the god's mythical opponents is the territory *par excellence* where the polarities of bestial, human, and divine mingle through a complex network of gruesome inversions. In Euripides' *Bacchae*, for example, Pentheus' death is strongly designated as a death in the hunt, as the king is consistently envisaged as a *ther*, a 'beast of prey' (e.g. 1107–8, 1171, 1174, 1188, 1190–1, 1196, 1214–15, 1278), while Agave cherishes the image of herself and her followers as huntresses, skilled in the art of 'seizing' (1173 ἔμαρψα), 'hunting' (1204 ἠγρεύσαμεν; 1237 ἀγρεύειν), 'catching' (1209 εἵλομεν), 'chasing' (1215 θηράσασ') wild beasts.[51] In fact, Euripides had been anticipated by Aeschylus, who saw in Pentheus' doom the fate of a hare (*Eum.* 26). But, more significantly still, it is the technique of such a hunt which

---

[49] Cf. Bond (1981: 108) on Eur. *Her.* 157–8 (ὁ δ' ἔσχε δόξαν οὐδὲν ὧν εὐψυχίας | θηρῶν ἐν αἰχμῇ, τἄλλα δ' οὐδὲν ἄλκιμος): 'No doubt, Heracles' fights with beasts seemed primitive and savage to sophisticated critics in the late fifth century . . .'. I am very much inclined to believe that this is true—although no specific piece of evidence exists for its substantiation. Note, however, Eur. *Suppl.* 314ff., where Theseus' animal-wrestling exploits are judged as coarser and inferior to real hoplitic deeds. Cf. Iambl. *Protrept.* (pp. 94. 29–95. 2 Pistelli), where subduing (χειροῦσθαι) the βλαβερώτατα τῶν θηρίων is said to be the task of the θηριώδεις men (whatever the connotations of this adjective may be); see A. T. Cole (1961: 153).

[50] The Centaurs, for example, a species 'exceedingly violent' (ὑπέροχον βίαν) (*Trach.* 1096; cf. *Trach.* 1059, where they are collectively branded as the θήρειος βία), have been forcefully overpowered (1094 βίᾳ κατειργάσασθε) by Heracles' valiant *membra corporis* (*Trach.* 1089–90 ὦ χέρες, χέρες, | ὦ νῶτα καὶ στέρν', ὦ φίλοι βραχίονες).

[51] Cf. the way she addresses her followers at *Bacch.* 731 as δρομάδες ἐμαὶ κύνες.

makes it 'exceptional',[52] a striking deviation. Thus, in Euripides' *Bacchae*, Agave harps proudly on the theme that the prey has been snatched with bare hands (1206–7), 'without a noose' (1173), 'without Thessalian thonged javelins or nets' (1205–6), while exultation in the hunt's departure from the norm culminates in outright rejection of that norm: in the 'bare-handed' hunt (Eur. *Bacch.* 1209; cf. 1206–7) that Dionysus inspires (1189–91), the 'armourers' engines' are a 'useless possession' to obtain (1207–8).

To conclude. We are now in a better position to appreciate what Dionysus' artistic failure to live up to the standards of Heracles, his prototype, would have meant for the original spectators of this scene. Dionysus' wish to abandon his Heraclean identity in *Frogs* 494–7 effects his *alienation* from a distinctively Heraclean pattern of brute strength, a model verging on bestiality and operating in the wilderness of nature, outside the boundaries of civilized space. Besides, given that the transgression of the hunting code from below is one of the most salient images in which Greek myth enregisters Dionysiac savagery, Dionysus' deviation from Heraclean primitiveness in the hunt could also have been plausibly deciphered as a departure of the actor from a mode of wildness inherent in the mythical conglomerate surrounding his own religious personality as well.

4.6. *From Hunters to Hunted*

We can now proceed with our reading of the Doorkeeper's speech.

> ἀλλὰ νῦν ἔχει μέσος·
> τοία Στυγός σε μελανοκάρδιος πέτρα
> Ἀχερόντιός τε σκόπελος αἱματοσταγὴς
> φρουροῦσι, Κωκυτοῦ τε περίδρομοι κύνες,
> ἔχιδνά θ᾽ ἑκατογκέφαλος, ἣ τὰ σπλάγχνα σου
> διασπαράξει, πλευμόνων τ᾽ ἀνθάψεται
> Ταρτησσία μύραινα, τὼ νεφρὼ δέ σου
> αὐτοῖσιν ἐντέροισιν ἡματωμένω
> διασπάσονται Γοργόνες Τειθράσιαι,
> ἐφ᾽ ἃς ἐγὼ δρομαῖον ὁρμήσω πόδα.

> But now you are firmly gripped.
> For such is the black-hearted rock of Styx
> and the blood-dripping Acherontian peak
> which guard you, and the roaming hounds of Cocytus,
> and the hundred-headed Viper, who will rend your inward
>   parts in pieces,

---

[52] Cf. the adverb περισσῶς in Eur. *Bacch.* 1197, indicating the 'special way' in which the women caught the ἄγραν . . . λεοντοφυῆ (1196).

while a Tartessian murry will lay hold of your lungs, and
     Teithrasian Gorgons,
whom I'll fetch here by setting a swiftly running foot in motion,
will tear apart your kidneys together with your guts, all in blood.

(469–78)

As we can immediately see, verse 469 introduces an abrupt change
in the Doorkeeper's speech. Heracles' success was a matter of the
past, while 'at present' (ἀλλὰ νῦν) the outlaw is trapped in a difficult
position: ἔχει μέσος.[53] As the scholiast on *Acharnians* 571 notes, this
favourite expression of the poet is a metaphor denoting the waist-
lock hold of wrestlers. But it is precisely the athletic movements
practised in the palaestra which provide the obvious model upon
which painters and sculptors fashion Heracles' locks in the representations of his bestial fights or hunting exploits (Boardman 1975:
11).[54] The 'connotative breadth' of verse 469, then, is very apt
for introducing the imagery of the monologue's ensuing part, as it
foreshadows its hunting connotations. *Frogs* 469–78[55] resumes the
hunting theme which had been only subtly enunciated in the preceding lines, and elaborates upon it through the means of a reversal:
the brave 'hunter' will now shift to the position of the 'hunted', a
danger always inherent in the confrontation between man and beast.

The monstrous creatures which will persecute the victim are
all well-known bogies of Underworld geography. Simultaneously,
however, they are closely related to each other in a complex pattern
of imagery, whose clearest illustration is the hunting theme
permeating the Aeschylean version of the myths of the Atreidae, as
metaphors borrowed from the realm of hunting play a significant
role throughout the *Oresteia*.[56]

First in the Doorkeeper's speech are mentioned the 'roaming
hounds of Cocytus' (472), glossed by the scholiast as the Erinyes,[57]
whose hunting function is abundantly illustrated, most prominently

---

[53] Cf. Ar. *Acharn.* 571; *Knights* 387; *Clouds* 1047; *Eccles.* 260. On the expression see
Poliakoff (1982: 45), and cf. the whole of his discussion of the μέσον wrestling term (ibid.:
40–9).

[54] For an analogous Heraclean bestial wrestling cf. Soph. *Trach.* 517–22 (with Poliakoff
1982: 75).

[55] The Doorkeeper's speech is unmistakably paratragic, but lack of solid evidence necessi-
tates the acceptance of Rau's (1967: 116) conclusion that, so far as we can safely establish, the
Aristophanic verses 'keinem bestimmten Vorbild folgen'. It is on this assumption that
the following discussion of the passage rests: Aristophanes has freely mixed and parodied
style and motifs from Tragedy without having been confined to one specific model. Cf.
Dover's (1993: 253–4) appreciation of lines 470–8 as 'not a parody of any particular tragic
scene . . . but an accumulation of bombastic and not always entirely coherent tragic motifs and
phrases.'

[56] See, most importantly, Vidal-Naquet (1988a).

[57] See schol. *Frogs* 472 λέγει δὲ τὰς Ἐρινύας, and further, Wüst, *RE*, s.v. Erinys, col. 127.

4.1. Orestes and Furies in hunting boots
rf. Paestan bell-krater by Python: British Museum, 1917. 12–10. 1

in the rich tradition which revolves around the figure of Orestes and his crime of matricide.[58] Aeschylus' literary picture[59] is richly supplemented by iconographic monuments for, as Prag (1985: 48) observes, the 'hunting notion' has been taken up by most vase-painters. (Fig. 4.1). In the fourth century, especially, the Erinyes are occasionally endowed with hounds, something which makes their hunting function even more explicit (Prag 1985: 118 n. 48). But hunting boots are almost indispensable accessories of painted Furies in other mythological contexts as well.[60] The Heraclean tradition more specifically offers some excellent examples: three

[58] See e.g. Prag (1985: E4, pl. 30a; F1a, pl. 33, etc.).
[59] See esp. *Choeph.* 1054ff.; *Eum.* 147–8, 231, 246–7, 325–6.
[60] See Wüst, *RE*, s.v. Erinys. For the ubiquitousness of the hunting Erinys motif in art, see *LIMC* iii, s.v. Erinys, 81–109, e.g. 85 (with Amphiaraus), 99 (with Hippolytus), 102 (with Meleagrus), etc.

vase-paintings inspired by underworld imagery portray the hero in the act of leading Cerberus away from Hades (cf. *Frogs* 467–8),[61] while a Fury in short chiton and hunting boots stands next to him in a menacing posture. Much more importantly, however, the Erinyes introduce to our scene a markedly Dionysiac flavour, for in a Greek cultural perspective Furies and Bacchae are closely inter-related. Sharing with the Bacchae aggressive movement and the frenzy of kin-killing (Seaford 1993: 140, 1994*a*: 348), tragic Furies very frequently attract the 'bacchic metaphor';[62] and, as Seaford (1994*a*: 348) emphasizes, the Fury who inspires the fratricide in Aeschylus' *Seven Against Thebes* is described as 'Melanaigis' (699), that is, 'of the black goatskin', a title otherwise occurring solely in the aetiological myth of the Apaturia festival in connection with Dionysus 'Melanaigis' (see above, 2.4(c)). Iconography as well bears splendid testimony to the fusion of Oresteian and Maenadic circles. As had been observed already in the previous century, both the dress/paraphernalia and the postures/movements of Erinyes and Bacchae many a time bear such striking similarities that they become bewilderingly hard to distinguish.[63] One of the most impressive iconographic overlaps of Oresteian and Bacchic material can be seen on an early fourth-century Apulian cup in Naples,[64] where the laurel-tree and heap of stones on which the central figure of the picture kneels qualify the setting as the altar of Apollo in Delphi and, consequently, identify the suppliant as Orestes, put to flight by the Furies.[65] Yet, this same figure is inscribed by the painter as *ΠΕΝΘΕΥΣ* and the nearby women ready to attack him wear the long *peploi* and *pardalides* so characteristic of Dionysiac followers in literature and art.[66]

---

[61] Listed by Wüst, *RE*, s.v. Erinys, col. 145, nos. 1, 3, 4 (now, *LIMC* iii, s.v. Erinyes, 9–11).

[62] See e.g. Eur. *Or.* 411 αὐταί σε βακχεύουσι συγγενῆ φόνον; Cf. Eur. *Or.* 835–6 βεβάκχευται μανίαις, | Εὐμενίσι θήραμα; Aesch. *Eum.* 499–500, where the Erinyes perceive themselves as maenads (βροτοσκόπων | μαινάδων). See also Guépin (1968: 21–3).

[63] See Knapp (1879: 149); Baumeister (1884: s.v. Erinyen, 495); Goldman (1910); Whallon (1964); and esp. Moret (1975: 114). Maenads sometimes wear the short chiton and high hunting boots so characteristic of the 'Erinys' pictorial type, while often the Furies chasing Orestes are depicted either in the long *peploi* that Bacchants almost always wear in art or as clad in animal-skins, again a typical garment of the Bacchants. Moreover, both Furies and Bacchae handle snakes, wands, and torches. On an Apulian rf. krater (*LIMC* vii, s.v. Orestes, 16), one of the Erinyes persecuting Orestes approaches with her head flung back, a posture typical of the *ekstasis* of Dionysus' followers in art; see Goldman (1910: 152, no. xxxv).

[64] *LIMC* vii, s.v. Pentheus, 7 (=Moret, 1975: no. 51, taf. 59).

[65] See Zancani Montuoro and Zanotti-Bianco (1954: 293 n. 1); Moret (1975: 114).

[66] On an Attic rf. pelike in Perugia Orestes clings to the Omphalos of Delphi, while one of the menacing female figures who surround him wears long maenadic *peploi* and dances like a maenad. See Trendall and Webster (1971: III. 1. 9). On a drinking-cup depicting Pentheus' death, conversely, the woman who storms against the Theban king is not a maenad but belongs 'to the circle of the Erinyes' (Dilthey 1874: 81).

The second monster, the 'hundred-headed viper' (473; cf. Hes. *Theog.* 295–303), is strongly linked with Erinys, as snakes hissing out of the Furies' heads or hands are an almost standard element in the iconography of the Oresteian pursuit.[67] However, since our passage mentions one single snake only, *echidna*, the most germane type of the 'Fury snake' iconography is probably the 'Erinys as snake', a pattern well documented in both literature (e.g. Eur. *IT* 286–7) and art.[68] The association of *echidna* with *myraina* (moray) (475) is reflected in the memorable depiction of the Aeschylean Clytaemnestra as a 'murry or a viper' (Aesch. *Choeph.* 994 μύραινά γ' εἴτ' ἔχιδν' ἔφυ), while the Gorgons (477), about to be fetched to tear apart the pseudo-Heracles' kidneys and intestine (475 ff.), are readily compared to the Furies in Aeschylean drama, by both Orestes and the priestess of Apollo:

> In front of this man slept a startling company
> of women lying all upon the chairs. Or not
> women, I think I call them rather Gorgons.
>
> (Aesch. *Eum.* 46–8; cf. *Choeph.* 1048)

Iconography as well confirms the existence of a strong link between the Fury and the Gorgon (Prag 1985: 48), who, even outside the corpus of Oresteian myths, is many a time depicted with 'snakes somewhere about her . . .' (Harrison 1922: 224 and 235) and, very frequently, as wearing the typical high huntress boots.[69]

The motif is closed with the involvement of the Doorkeeper himself in the hunting pattern, as, in his description of his planned movements, he seems to appropriate the running virtue of a hunting-dog: 'I will launch a swiftly running foot to fetch them (i.e. the Gorgons) here' (ἐφ' ἃς ἐγὼ δρομαῖον ὁρμήσω πόδα) (478). For the adjective *dromaios* and its cognates are inherent in the conception and vocabulary of the hunt, applicable, as they are, both to the hunter or the hounds as well as to the quarry (describing its flight in front of pursuing dogs) and the quarry's tracks.[70] In Euripides'

---

[67] e.g. Prag (1985: nos./ figs. E6, E7b–c, E8a, F1a (pls. 31–3)); Garvie (1986: 345) on Aesch. *Choeph.* 1049–50. In both Aeschylus and Euripides the Erinyes haunt Orestes' imagination πεπλεκτανημέναι | πυκνοῖς δράκουσιν (*Choeph.* 1049–50; cf. Eur. *Or.* 256).

[68] Harrison (1922: 232–7); Prag (1985: 44 and nos./figs. E1, pl. 28b; cf. pl. 28a); cf. Kossatz-Deissmann (1978: 103 with n. 582).

[69] See e.g. *LIMC* iv, s.v. Gorgo, Gorgones, 107–21a (Gorgons with snakes), 288, 289, 293 (Gorgons with hunting boots). The Gorgon's dramatic mask too may have been equipped with snakes; see e.g. *RVAp.* i. 77, 83 (*LIMC* iv, s.v. Gorgo, Gorgones, 342), probably depicting a scene from satyr drama.

[70] See e.g. Xen. *Cyneg.* 3. 5, 3. 6, 3. 7, 5. 17, 5. 21, 6. 16 (of hounds), 6. 17, 6. 19 (of the hunter), 9. 10 (of fawns). *Dromaios* applied to the quarry (e.g. Xen. *Cyneg.* 5. 9); to the quarry's tracks (Xen. *Cyneg.* 3. 8).

Bacchae, for example, the Bacchic huntresses, whom Dionysus has just spurred against Pentheus, the intruder in their rites, are said to possess 'speed of feet with intense running' (ποδῶν τρέχουσαι συντόνοις δραμήμασι) (1091; Seaford's tr.).[71] Moreover, the humour of the Aristophanic line seems to rest on its distortion of hunting language and imagery: the 'running to catch or fetch', usually expressing the relation of the hound to the quarry,[72] has been comically transposed a step backwards, that is, to the relation of the hunter to his hounds.[73]

Nevertheless, whereas hounds are normally expected to bring back their prey intact, the hunters/hounds of our scene will rather carry out a perverted hunt: taking on the role of scavengers, they will engage themselves in *diasparassein* (rending in pieces) (474) and *diaspan* (tearing apart) (477) their prey. As to the focus of the threats, this narrows to the victim's viscera (473–7). The viper, the murry, and the Gorgons are envisaged as being 'at work' upon the human prey's inner parts, while kidneys and intestine are referred to as 'full of blood' (ἡματωμένω) (476) and the setting of the scene, the 'Acherontian crag' is described as 'blood-dripping' (αἱματοσταγής) (471). Now, all these elements are strongly associated with one of the most central rituals of ancient societies, the ritual of sacrifice, which defines the human condition by demarcating its proper space as the sphere 'in between' the realms of beasts and gods. For sacrificial ritual is deployed around the victim's *splagchna* and their extraction (Durand 1979: esp. 139–50), while the flowing blood has to be sprinkled on the altar stone, the object which 'alone', as Burkert has expressed it, 'must again and again, drip blood' (1983: 5). Yet, the concentration of 'sacrificial' elements in our scene evokes a sacrificial picture only in so far as it highlights its distortion. For the eating of the victim raw curtails the sacrificial procedures of roasting and boiling, the only source of meat procurement that Greek culture sanctifies as socially acceptable (cf. 4.10). As early as the dawn of Greek literature, the desire to eat raw is associated with moments of extreme savagery, where 'wild' instincts have been stirred up by pain, anxiety, or grief.[74] In addition, the very act suggested by the verbs *diasparassein* and *diaspan*, that is,

---

[71] But see Seaford (1996: ad loc.), as lines 1091–2 are missing in the papyrus. 'Running' seems to be one of the characteristic activities of maenads; see e.g. *Bacch.* 135–6 θιάσων δρομαί- | ων, of running bands of maenads during the hunt for the goat's blood (see below, 4.7); *Bacch.* 985–6 ὀρειδρόμων . . . | Καδμείων (of Agave's running bands).

[72] Cf. e.g. Eur. *Bacch.* 871–2 θωΰσσων δὲ κυναγέτας | συντείνῃ δράμημα κυνῶν; Hom. *Il.* 11. 292–3 ὡς δ' ὅτε πού τις θηρητὴρ κύνας ἀργιόδοντας | σεύῃ ἐπ' ἀγροτέρῳ συΐ καπρίῳ ἠὲ λέοντι.

[73] Radermacher (1921: 213) regards the line 'nach Wortwahl und Stilisierung der Rede sicher tragisches Zitat'. Dover (1993: ad 478) collates Eur. fr. 495, 3f. N².

[74] See e.g. Hom. *Il.* 22. 346–7, 24. 212–14.

the indiscriminate tearing apart or cutting of the victim's limbs at random (as opposed to following the natural articulations of its body) reflects a radical deviation from the norm, intrinsically inter-woven with primitiveness and savagery. Thus, we hear in the *Odyssey* that the Cyclops Polyphemus 'cut up' Odysseus' comrades

> limb by limb (διὰ μελεϊστὶ ταμών) and got supper ready,
> and like a lion reared in the hills, without leaving anything,
> ate them, entrails, flesh and the marrowy bones alike.
>
> (*Od.* 9. 291–3)

Besides, the game's dismemberment at random and in absolute disorder transgresses irrevocably the civic and political dimension of the sacrifice, that is, the egalitarian division and subsequent dis-tribution of the sacrificial meat which, within the democratic values of a Greek community, symbolizes, reaffirms, and reproduces its political equality.[75] For, as Nicole Loraux (1981*b*) has put it, restat-ing a principal thesis of the 'French school',[76] '. . . du corps défait de la bête, naît, lors de chaque sacrifice, l'espace civique de la *polis*' (616), so that 'dans le repas communautaire surgit la figure isonomique de la cité' (620). In this respect, Dionysus' threatened dismemberment in *Frogs* 474 and 477 reshapes dramatically a fundamentally non-civic model of confusion of those levels of existence (animal, human, and divine) whose distinctiveness and incompatibility is ritually ensured through civic sacrificial practice.[77]

Finally, the image of perversion reflected in *Frogs* 464 ff. resides largely in the *intersection* of hunt and sacrifice, as the prospect of chasing and killing/dismembering suggests. The merging of these practices twists them both to their complete distortion, as, for a variety of reasons, Greek cultural perspective considers hunt and sacrifice irreconcilable; their 'combination is also a contradiction, for the unrestrained pursuit and violence of the hunt stands at the opposite pole to the calm, ordered leading of an acquiescent victim to a controlled killing in the sacrifice' (Seaford 1994*a*: 289).[78] In other

---

[75] For a fine discussion of ancient Greek urban space conceived metaphorically in sacrificial terms see Svenbro (1982).

[76] Cf. Detienne (1979*a*: 23–4); Durand (1979: 154).

[77] This is fundamental in the structuralist approach to the Promethean myth of the origin of sacrifice. See primarily Vernant (1979*a*); Detienne (1981). For a very informative general overview of sacrifice in Greek society see now A. M. Bowie (1995).

[78] For an interesting appreciation of the clash from an anthropological perspective see Solinas (1985: esp. 106–9). Nevertheless, the incompatibility of hunt and sacrifice in every single sociocultural complex is neither universally attested (see e.g. Marinatos 1986: 42–9; 1988: 18 ff.) nor unequivocally accepted in the relevant discussions. See, most importantly, Burkert's thesis on the sacrifice as originating in the hunt (1983: 12 ff.) and his arguments con-cerning the 'similarity of hunting and sacrificial customs' (15). Cf. Burkert (1987*b*: 166–7).

words, hunt translates the sacrifice to the space of 'nature', outside the confines of the *polis*. The lack of clear-cut dividing lines dispenses with altar and fire through which the victim passes gradually into the realm of 'culture' as well as with the ceremonial procedures which culminate in the securing of the animal's assent,[79] a primary prerequisite for putting death 'comme entre parenthèses', that is, for the 'legitimization' of the violent act.[80] Understandably, then, the fusion of both acts in a unique 'performance' is almost always relegated to the realm of the barbaric or non-civic space. Thus, it is on the mythical island of the Sun that Odysseus' men hunt down and kill the bulls of Helios (Hom. *Od.* 12. 339–65),[81] while a merged ritual hunt and sacrifice (ἐθήρευον . . . ἔσφαττον) of bulls occurs on the exotic Atlantis (Pl. *Critias* 119d–e), the island which, in Plato's myth, epitomizes barbaric *hybris* pitted against the civilized world within the pillars of Heracles (*Tim.* 24e).[82] In Tragedy, more specifically, the fusion of the hunting and the sacrificial codes is many a time paramount among the ritual perversions which precipitate the royal household to its ruin. A good example can be sought in the *Oresteia* where, as Vidal-Naquet (1988*a*: 142) has put it, 'Agamemnon and Orestes . . . play the role first of hunters and then of hunted, first of the sacrificers and subsequently of the sacrificed (or those threatened with this fate).' Erinyes, the huntresses, expect to feast upon Orestes in a 'corrupted' sacrificial rite (Zeitlin 1965: esp. 485–6), since the 'animal' is hunted, rather than slain on the altar, and is destined to feed its persecutors alive: 'and you shall feed me while being still alive, not after being killed at the altar' (καὶ ζῶν με δαίσεις οὐδὲ πρὸς βωμῷ σφαγείς) (*Eum.* 305). In a similarly distorted way, rather than providing the ritually procured substance of a proper sacrificial meal, the victim's *splagchna* in the *Frogs* are due to be extracted and consumed *during the hunt*.

To conclude. A contextualized reading of *Frogs* 460–502 suggests that Dionysus, the actor, is brought face to face with a comically moulded version of distorted rites. In this respect, his discarding of Heracles' insignia in *Frogs* 494–7 signifies his deviation from an aberrant fusion of those vital social codes that civilized communities

---

[79] See Detienne (1979*a*: 18–19); Vernant (1981: 7).

[80] See Durand (1985: 60). My discussion is much more indebted to the 'French school' model of the sacrificial ritual, attributing community cohesion to *commensality*, the sharing in the sacrificial meat, than to Burkert's theory (see esp. 1983: 35 ff.), whereby community perpetuation is ensured through *ritualized killing*, understood as the emotional climax of the entire 'act'.

[81] See esp. *Od.* 12. 343–4; fundamental here is Vidal-Naquet (1981).

[82] Cf. also the fusion of hunt and sacrifice in the sacrificial customs of the barbarians in the land of Tauris, where Iphigeneia is a priestess of Artemis (e.g. Eur. *IT* 280, 1163).

are anxious to preserve distinct and independent from each other, the hunting and the sacrificial. The perverted sacrifice of *Frogs* 469 ff. is even rounded off with a perverted libation, for line 479 ἐγκέχοδα· κάλει θεόν ('I have defecated: invoke the god') parodies sacrificial language. As the scholiast comments,

ἢ πρὸς τὸ ἐν ταῖς θυσίαις ἐπιλεγόμενον. ἐπειδὰν γὰρ σπονδοποιήσωνται, ἐπιλέγουσιν, ἐκκέχυται, κάλει θεόν.

Or in accordance with what is said in the aftermath of sacrifices. For, when they have poured the libations, they say in addition: 'it has been poured out: invoke the god'.[83]

4.7. *Hunt and Sacrifice in* Frogs *460–502 and Dionysiac Distortion*

We saw in the previous section that from a Greek perspective *Frogs* 460–502 can be read in hunting/sacrificial terms. I am now concerned with the primary territory where hunt and sacrifice are merged in a scheme which represents a 'radical alterity' for civic sacrificial norm, that is, the sphere of Dionysus' orgiastic rites.[84] Euripides' *Bacchae* provides the best illustration of such a fusion at the level of myth.[85] We have already seen (4.5) that Dionysiac hunting imagery plays an important role in the play's thematic structure (see further Segal 1982: 31 ff.). However, Pentheus' death is not merely a death in hunt, but also a perverted sacrificial death.[86] Ever since the play's early scenes, we are reminded that the Dionysiac women are performers of secret sacrificial rites (224 μαινάδας θυοσκόους) and, when Dionysus/the Stranger excites Pentheus' curiosity with the fascination of secret *orgia*, the king immediately imagines them as centring round sacrifice (*Bacch.* 473). When we hear the Messenger's report about the deeds of the Dionysiac *thiasoi* of women on the mountains, we understand that the shepherds have very narrowly escaped a frenzied hunt, which would have grimly ended in *sparagmos* (*Bacch.* 734–5). The hunting/sacrificial imagery culminates in the description of Pentheus' tragic fate. Cadmus ironically refers to him as a *thyma*, a sacrificial victim, which has been offered to the gods (*Bacch.* 1246). His flesh is full of blood (ᾑματωμένη) but, instead of having been ritually

---

[83] Since the preceding verses have evoked the image of the victim's death, the vocabulary of *choe*, i.e. libation, concealed in ἐγκέχοδα (modelled on ἐγ-χέω) is most appropriate, as *choai* designate, very strictly, *chthonic* offerings (Casabona 1966: 279–97).

[84] Daraki (1980*a*: 151–2); cf. Vernant (1981: 13 and 34–5); Detienne (1979*b*: 62; but see Seaford (1994*a*: 293)); Obbink (1993: 69–70).

[85] The difference between myth and cult is in this case of crucial importance.

[86] See Seidensticker's pioneering piece (1979), and now Seaford (1994*a*: 281–93), with manifold new insights.

deposited on the altar, it has become the 'handball' in the blood-dripping hands (1163 χέρ' αἵματι στάζουσαν) of the female sacrificers/huntresses:

> Every hand was smeared with blood
> as they played ball with scraps of Pentheus' body.   (*Bacch.* 1135–6)

The archetypal mythical example for the merging is, of course, Dionysus himself, whom the play's parodos celebrates as the one who 'hunts the blood of the slain goat, joy of the living flesh that is devoured'.[87] However, what is particularly significant in relation to the perverted sacrifice scene in *Frogs* is the fact that Pentheus, the tragic victim of the frenzied hunt, is not ceremonially sliced up with a sacrificial knife, but savagely rendered to pieces: 'his ribs were clawed clean of flesh' (γυμνοῦντο δὲ | πλευραὶ σπαραγμοῖς) (1134–5), in a 'sacrificial' rite that his mother Agave had gruesomely initiated as 'priestess of the slaughter' (ἱερέα φόνου) (1114). Similarly, in our Aristophanic scene, the 'inverted sacrifice' of the Dionysiac hunt is forcefully evoked through the comic use of *diasparassein* and *diaspan*, as these (together with their cognates) are the verbs most regularly employed in a variety of sources in order to denote the Dionysiac frenzied dismemberment of animals or plants or even human beings.[88]

At the level of Dionysiac cult it seems that hunting was combined with sacrifice at the annual Boeotian festival of the Agrionia where, as Plutarch attests (*Mor.* 299f), the descendants of the 'daughters of Minyas' (the mythical Minyades) had to endure a chase (δίωξις) by Dionysus' priest, armed with a sword, and to flee (φυγή).[89] Plutarch's further information that 'any one of them whom the priest catches he may kill, as in my time did the priest Zoilus' (ἔξεστι δὲ τὴν καταληφθεῖσαν ἀνελεῖν, καὶ ἀνεῖλεν ἐφ' ἡμῶν Ζωΐλος ὁ ἱερεύς) (ibid.) suggests the sacrificial culmination of the hunt. For, when enacted by ritual actors who *do not* fail 'to recognize the theatrical, playacting nature of the ritual', and hence do not pursue it '*ad absurdum*', persecution normally ends with animal sacrifice (Burkert 1983: 175). A very similar pattern of fused hunt and sacrifice is

---

[87] *Bacch.* 138–9 ἀγρεύων | αἷμα τραγοκτόνον, ὠμοφάγον χάριν. Cf. the much discussed 'feasts of raw flesh' (ὠμοφάγους δαῖτας) in Euripides' *Cretans* (472, 12 N²), forming part of a mystic initiation ritual, whereby the initiand becomes a *bakchos* (15).

[88] See most importantly Eur. *Bacch.* 739 ἄλλαι δὲ δαμάλας διεφόρουν σπαράγμασιν; 1220 διασπαρακτόν (i.e. Pentheus' body); 1127 ἀπεσπάραξεν ὦμον; schol. Ar. *Frogs* 360; Eratosth. *Catast.* 24 (= fr. 113 Kern); Plut. *Mor.* 299e; Ael. *VH* 3. 42. 25; Plut. *Mor.* 291a. Simultaneously, however, one must not lose sight of the fact that such vocabulary is also very much at home in the imagery of the Underworld; see e.g. Luc. 77. 24. 1, 38. 14 (on the tortures in the κολαστήριον) with Dieterich's (1893: 46–54) discussion.

[89] Plut. *Mor.* 299f καὶ γίγνεται παρ' ἐνιαυτὸν ἐν τοῖς Ἀγριωνίοις φυγὴ καὶ δίωξις αὐτῶν ὑπὸ τοῦ ἱερέως τοῦ Διονύσου ξίφος ἔχοντος.

ingrained in the Argive myth of the Proetides, whom the priest Melampus persecuted in a large-scale ephebic hunt which culminated in the death of Iphinoe, the eldest among Proetus' daughters (Apollod. 2. 2. 2). And, although there is no firm evidence that hunt and sacrifice were re-enacted ritually in Dionysus' Argive cult, a gloss in Hesychius (s.v. *Ἀγράνια*) testifies to the fact that the myth of the Proetides was connected with the Argive festival of Agrania in honour of Proetus' daughter, presumably the one who met her doom during the hunt (see Burkert 1983: 173). If this was actually the case, one could safely assume that the ritual would have ended in animal sacrifice. As Burkert (1983: 173) writes, 'The hunt is repeated and fulfilled in the animal-sacrifice, which marks and surmounts the crises of society.' Finally, a late piece of evidence suggests that some form of ritual chase by Bacchic women may have been one among the many ordeals imposed on a Dionysiac mystes in the course of Bacchic initiation rites: in the second century BC a '*thiasos* of Asians' dedicated a funerary epigram to its deceased member Favis, a mystes who is said to have 'fled the sacred Bacchic women on his way to Hades' (*τὰς ἱερὰς προφυγὼν εὐιάδας εἰς Ἀίδην*).[90]

We may now conclude by returning to our text. In bringing Dionysus face-to-face with the prospect of a death in the hunt, *Frogs* 460–502 displays to the god a comic version of performances which demarcate *his own* mythical and cultic realm.

4.8. *Dionysiac and Heraclean Spanning of the Poles of Hunt and Sacrifice*

In the previous section we have seen that Dionysus and Heracles are intrinsically linked to both hunt and sacrifice; it is now time to appreciate that they are also able to span the poles of both.

The mythical Heracles features not merely in the role of the 'hunter of wild beasts' that *Frogs* 464 ff. evokes. He may also shift to the position of a 'hunted beast', a reversal most clearly reflected in the Euripidean *Heracles*, where the hero 'hunts down his sons' (*κυναγετεῖ τέκνων διωγμόν*) (896)[91] only after having being chased himself by the 'Keres of Tartarus', summoned by Lyssa to accompany her (*ὁμαρτεῖν*) as hounds accompany the hunter (*ὡς κυναγέτῃ κύνας*) (860). As far as sacrifice is concerned, the same Euripidean tragedy depicts Heracles' killing of two of his offspring as a perverted sacrificial act,[92] where hunt and slaughter of a human victim

---

[90] See S. G. Cole (1993*a*: 294); Greek text in Voutyras (1984: 45).
[91] See Bond (1981: 302).
[92] In a different corpus of Heraclean legends, consider also the notorious Heraclean per-

are closely interwoven.[93] More importantly still, this perverted
sacrifice is inherently Dionysiac, in so far as it re-enacts the distinctively Dionysiac pattern of intrafamiliar killing resulting in
the household's destruction (Seaford 1994*a*: esp. 7c), a scheme
which, as Seaford (1994*a*: 354) has compellingly argued, 'acted as a
dynamic paradigm, influencing the shape of dramas on non-
Dionysiac myths.' Besides, the Dionysiac tinge is also evident in the
recurrent Bacchic metaphors conveying Heracles' killing frenzy,[94]
while the Euripidean hero himself, returning to his senses, worries
lest he has destroyed his *oikos* in a Bacchic fit.[95]

Yet, looking at the other end of the spectrum, it is Heracles' own
death which can be understood as a corrupted sacrifice, his body
being cremated in a 'sacrificial' pyre on the usual sacrificial setting of
Mt. Oeta's highest crag (Soph. *Trach.* 1191–2).[96] And, if Heracles'
immolation like a sacrificial beast upon the pyre transgresses the
norm of sacrifice 'from above', paving the way for his deification,
Sophocles' *Trachiniae* also reflects Heracles' distortion of the
sacrificial rite 'from below': while offering to the gods a splendid
hecatomb on the altar of Cape Caenaeum (*Trach.* 760–2), the
poisoned tunic 'clings to his sides' (προσπτύσσεται | πλευραῖσιν)
(767–8), 'close-glued, as if by a craftsman's hand' (ἀρτίκολλος, ὥστε
τέκτονος) (768),[97] and he is seized by 'a convulsive pain which bit into
his bones' (ἦλθε δ' ὀστέων | ὀδαγμὸς ἀντίσπαστος) (769–70).[98] The
difference between man and beast that sacrifice reproduces and
affirms is blurred; Heracles turns out to be a 'novel sacrificer'
(θυτῆρα . . . καινόν) (*Trach.* 612–13) for, strangely and paradoxically,
he is the sacrificer who eventually becomes his own sacrificial victim.
Instead of burning and eating the beast, he is being himself
devoured by the poison of the beast.[99]

version of the civic sacrifice of the ox, most importantly reflected in the story of Theiodamas
(4.9), on which see primarily Durand (1986: 149ff.). Cf. also the tradition (which, according
to Philostratus, goes back to Pindar) of Heracles' feasting at the house of Coronus, where he
dispenses with the 'Promethean' division of the victim and devours indiscriminately the
whole animal (σιτεῖται βοῦν ὅλον, ὡς μηδὲ τὰ ὀστᾶ περιττὰ ἡγεῖσθαι (Philostr. *Imag.* 2. 24. 2)).

[93] See Eur. *Her.* 974 and 984–5, suggesting that the slaughter took place at the house's very
altar; cf. *Her.* 994–5 δεύτερον δὲ παῖδ' ἑλὼν | χωρεῖ τρίτον θῦμ' ὡς ἐπισφάξων δυοῖν, where
Heracles' killings are described in sacrificial terminology, and see Seaford (1994*a*: 380 with
n. 52).
[94] See esp. Eur. *Her.* 896–7, 1086 (ἀν' αὖ βακχεύσει Καδμείων πόλιν), 1119 (Ἀΐδου βάκχος),
1122. See Seaford (1993: 130, 1994*a*: 353–4).
[95] Eur. *Her.* 1142 ἦ γὰρ συνήραξ' οἶκον †ἦ βάκχευσ' ἐμόν†;
[96] For the sacrificial connotations of the scene see Easterling (1982: ad 1192); Segal (1975:
47–9).
[97] Tr. Jebb (1892).
[98] Tr. Easterling (1982: ad loc.).
[99] In another cluster of Heraclean legends the hero faces the threat of ritual slaughter on the
altar of Busiris in Egypt; see Piccaluga (1968: 149–55; literary sources); Durand and

Returning now to our scene in *Frogs*, I suggest that the tragic Heracles' *sparagmos* in the folds of his poisoned robe is evoked by the language of the comic text itself, for line 474 πλευμόνων τ' ἀνθάψεται strikingly echoes *Trach.* 777–8 διώδυνος | σπαραγμὸς αὐτοῦ πλευμόνων ἀνθήψατο ('a spasm attacked his lungs, piercing him through and through').

Dionysus, correspondingly, can be both the 'Bacchic hunter',[100] whom Agave praises as a 'fellow-huntsman' (ξυγκύναγον) and 'comrade in the chase' (ξυνεργάτην ἄγρας) (*Bacch.* 1146) and, occasionally, the object of the hunt as well. The vivid picture of *Bacch.* 719–21, where the shepherds on the mountains are ready to 'hunt down' (θηρασώμεθα) the frenzied Agave and her *thiasos*, has its antecedent already in the legends of Lycurgus, as reflected in the *Iliad*, where the Tracian king

> once drove the fosterers of rapturous Dionysos
> headlong down the sacred Nyseian hill, and all of them
> shed and scattered their wands on the ground, stricken with an
> ox-goad
> by murderous Lykourgos, while Dionysos in terror
> dived into the salt surf, and Thetis took him to her bosom,
> frightened, with the strong shivers upon him at the man's blustering.
>
> (*Il.* 6. 132–7)[101]

There are a number of other Dionysiac legends too, where the Dionysiac women are chased and flee or, alternatively, are killed in the deadly pursuit.[102] In the cultic sphere we have already seen the Agrionia ritual of the Boeotian Orchomenos (4.7), centring around the ritualized acts of 'flight (φυγή)' and 'pursuit (δίωξις)' of the descendants of the Minyades. Elsewhere in Plutarch (*Mor.* 717a) we hear that the same festival, as celebrated in Chaeroneia,[103] comprises a search for the fleeing Dionysus himself:

Lissarrague (1983; iconography). On the other hand, Heracles could also be envisaged as offering a sacrifice in the Promethean/civic mode as well (Durand 1986).

[100] See *Bacch.* 1189–92 (Agave's boast) ὁ Βάκχιος κυναγέτας | σοφὸς σοφῶς ἀνέπηλ' ἐπὶ θῆρα | τόνδε μαινάδας, to which the Chorus responds: ὁ γὰρ ἄναξ ἀγρεύς (1192). For Dionysus in hunting boots in art see e.g. *LIMC* s.v. Dionysos, 801.

[101] Cf. Apollod. 3. 5. 1. The Homeric Dionysus' terror before the chase of his persecutor contains the germs of the Aristophanic image of the god's reaction before the imminent chase of the Doorkeeper; cf. Segal (1961: 208). For some late (and uncertain) reflections of Lycurgus' hunting of Dionysus and his nymphs in art, see *LIMC* vi, s.v. Lykourgos (I), 5 (2nd cent. BC) and 10 (Rome, imperial period).

[102] See e.g. Diod. 5. 50. 4–5 (on the Thracian king Boutes); Apollod. 2. 2. 2 (see Seaford 1988: 134); Paus. 2. 20. 4 and 2. 22. 1 (on the persecuted maenads' tomb).

[103] For Agriania/Agrionia as 'one of the most widespread of all Greek festival names' see Burkert (1983: 173 with n. 23).

παρ' ἡμῖν ἐν τοῖς Ἀγριωνίοις τὸν Διόνυσον αἱ γυναῖκες ὡς ἀποδεδρακότα ζητοῦσιν, εἶτα παύονται καὶ λέγουσιν ὅτι πρὸς τὰς Μούσας καταπέφευγεν καὶ κέκρυπται παρ' ἐκείναις.

In the Agrionia, as it is celebrated here, the women search for Dionysus as though he had run away, then desist and say that he has taken refuge with the Muses and is hidden among them. (cf. 6.2)

As Dodds (1960: xxvii) has put it, 'If we accept Plutarch's evidence, it is hard to avoid the conclusion that the pursuit of the Argive maenads by the priest Melampus, and that of the god's "nurses" by Lycurgus and Boutes, reflect a similar ritual.'[104]

On the sacrificial level too, Dionysus could be envisaged as the receiver of a raw-meat sacrifice or as rending apart in *propria persona* animals or even human beings,[105] as his epithets Ὠμάδιος/ Ὠμηστής (the Eater of raw flesh) and Ἀνθρωπορραίστης[106] (the Man-destroyer) may suggest. Most importantly, it is Dionysus who inspires intrafamiliar violence resulting in the *oikos'* sacrificial self-destruction, a pattern which has left its mark on non-Dionysiac tragic plots as well (Seaford 1994a). In the myths of Lycurgus, for example, Dionysiac frenzy inspired the Thracian king to sacrifice his son Dryas, while the Proetides and the Minyades, maddened by Dionysus, kill and devour their own children.[107] Sacrificial slaughter looms even over Dionysus' own devotees,[108] while in the Orphic branch of Dionysiac legends it is the god himself who, as a proto-typical initiand, suffers 'sacrificial' dismemberment at the hands of the impious Titans.[109] His mythical *sparagmos* is commemorated in a variety of ritual enactments, sometimes even connected with

---

[104] Cf. Seaford (1994a: 274 n. 176) on Pentheus' wish to chase the Theban maenads from the mountains with arms (see Eur. *Bacch.* 778ff.): 'This probably reflects the ritual practice of a male pursuit of the maenads from the mountain.'

[105] Although in Attic iconography the motif of Dionysus μαινόμενος is relatively rare; Maffre (1982: 203–7; examples in 205 n. 46).

[106] For the sources see Henrichs (1981: 222 with nn. 5 and 6) and Graf (1985: 74–80). Phaenias' report (*apud* Plut. *Them.* 13. 2–5) on the human sacrifice to 'Dionysus the Raw Eater' at Athens should, of course, be relegated to the realm of fiction (Henrichs 1981: 208–24), but the mere use of this epithet in a historical treatise (as well as in early Lesbian poetry: Alcaeus, fr. 127, 9 Page Ζόννυσσον ὠμήσταν) destined to be read in wider circles, is an important indication of the qualities which Greek audiences could associate with this god.

[107] Lycurgus: Apollod. 3. 5. 1; Proetides: Apollod. 2. 2. 2, 3. 5. 2. Minyades: Plut. *Mor.* 299e. See in greater detail Seaford (1994a: 291–2; cf. 256).

[108] See e.g. Pentheus' threat in Eur. *Bacch.* 796–7 θύσω, φόνον γε θῆλυν, ὥσπερ ἄξιαι, | πολὺν ταράξας ἐν Κιθαιρῶνος πτυχαῖς.

[109] Cf. 2.12(b). The sources mostly employ the verbs *diasparassein* and *diaspan* and their cognates. See e.g. Diod. 5. 75. 4 διασπώμενον ὑπὸ τῶν Τιτάνων; Origen, *Cels.* 4. 17 Διονύσου ... σπαρασσομένου ὑπ' αὐτῶν; Orph. frs. 210, 211, 214 Kern, etc. On the myth as going back to the 5th cent. see Burkert (1983: 225 n. 43).

mystic initiation,[110] during which the maenads, in imitation of the god's archetypal *pathos*, tear apart animals or plants which symbolize, that is, stand as a *mimema* of, Dionysus himself (cf. Parker 1989). Having surveyed the wide range of structural analogies in the ways in which Dionysus and Heracles are implicated in the cultural and social codes of hunt and sacrifice which sustain the thematic pattern of *Frogs* 464 ff., we can now conclude that when Dionysus deviates from Heraclean 'naturalness' by casting aside the Heraclean elements of his theatrical disguise, he also deviates from an analogous level of savagery, chaos, and confusion lurking in his own proper realm, where the acculturation process symbolically re-enacted and embedded in the *polis'* official ritual[111] becomes reduced to a 'natural' predatory instinct, and where humanity sinks to crudity, eating raw flesh, and bestiality.

THE INNKEEPERS' SCENE: *FROGS* 549–604

Our discussion of *Frogs* 460–502 paves the way for our reading of the rest of the 'encounter scenes', *Frogs* 503–48 and 549–604. While Dionysus' implicit 'meeting' with his prototype in *Frogs* 503–48 (4.10), indicated by his wish to reassume his model's garb (522 ff.), draws him close to the joyful and civilized side of his own mythical and cultic personality, his dissociation from the Heraclean element of his *skeue* and role, suggested by his determined disposal of Heracles' insignia at 579 ff., distances his *dramatis persona* from acts subversive of the *polis'* socio-religious identity.

4.9. Heracles and Dionysus, symposion and xenia

While still equipped with Heracles' insignia, Dionysus is taken by surprise by two Innkeepers, in all probability 'partners in the same inn'.[112] Mistaking him for Heracles, the women are prepared to take

---

[110] Clem. Alex. *Protr.* 12. 119 (p. 92P) maenads αἱ δυσάγνον κρεανομίαν μυούμεναι with schol. ad loc. (p. 318 Stählin) ὠμὰ γὰρ ἤσθιον κρέα οἱ μυούμενοι τῷ Διονύσῳ, δεῖγμα τοῦτο τελούμενοι τοῦ σπαραγμοῦ, ὃν ὑπέστη Διόνυσος ὑπὸ τῶν Μαινάδων. Harpocration, s.v. Νεβρίζων· Δημοσθένης ἐν τῷ Ὑπὲρ Κτησιφῶντος (18. 259). οἱ μὲν ὡς τοῦ τελοῦντος νεβρίδα ἐννημένου ἢ καὶ τοὺς τελουμένους διαζωννύντος νεβρίσιν, ⟨οἱ δὲ⟩ ἐπὶ τοῦ νεβροὺς διασπᾶν κατά τινα ἄρρητον λόγον. ἔστι δὲ ὁ νεβρισμὸς καὶ παρὰ Ἀριγνώτῃ ἐν τῷ Περὶ Τελετῶν. See further Seaford (1994a: 283, n. 15).

[111] This is symbolically re-enacted in the successive use of barley-grains on the altar (standing for alimentation in a raw/natural state); the roasting of the viscera (act mediating between nature and culture); the boiling of the meat (climax of the 'cultural' transformation of the aliments).

[112] Dover (1993: 263); cf. Sommerstein (1996: ad 549–78). For the problematic identification of the speakers in this scene see Hooker (1979: 245); Ussher (1985: 102). As far as the distribution of lines between the two women is concerned, I agree with Dover (1993: 264)

harsh revenge (568 ff.) for the hero's forceful intrusion into their property, an incident which evidently had taken place sometime in the past, during his perilous descent to Hades. Horrified at their threats, Dionysus/Heracles begs Xanthias to release him from the burden of his heroic/Heraclean identity, and allow him to reassume the guise and role of a slave (579–88). So it happens, and the scene culminates in a third exchange of identities between master and slave (589–604), Dionysiac and Heraclean roles. Now, the inn, the *pandokeion*, is by definition a place where *xenoi*/foreigners are offered bed and food on payment. However, it is obvious that in our scene even the notion of paid-for hospitality is subverted to the point of negation: Heracles' stay at the *pandokeion* was marked by a total absence of *xenia*, since not only was he uninvited, but he had not even secured the consent or the permission of the lawful owners. According to the women's recollections, he merely broke in as a *panourgos* (549), a wicked, deceitful fellow, ready for everything bad. However, this scene should be examined in direct juxtaposition to its immediately preceding one (*Frogs* 503–48), where Persephone's maid invites Heracles to feast in a sumptuously prepared banquet (3.1): as we shall see in this section, not only does the setting of *Frogs* 549 ff. stand at the diametrically opposite extreme of a *symposion*, but it also transforms and qualifies the civilized picture of eating and drinking that the prospect of Persephone's banquet has already vividly evoked. In the following pages, then, we will read *Frogs* 549 ff. in terms of a distinctively 'anti-sympotic' picture and, while doing so, we will be able to appreciate in much greater depth the gradual moulding of Dionysus' *dramatis persona* through his markedly theatrical act of discarding Heracles' *skeue* in lines 579 ff.

As we learn from the Innkeepers, Heracles had gulped down sixteen pieces of bread, as well as meat, onions, smoked fish, fresh cheese together with their baskets. What immediately strikes the listener or reader is that Heracles' roguish grabbing of the substances he needs in order to set up his dinner curtails a primary and indispensable dimension of the banquet, that is, the proper, not to say almost ceremonial, serving and offering of dishes.[113] Furthermore, the wolfish raid on food that our scene so vividly

that 'the greatest comic effect is achieved if both women rage at Dionysos in rapid alternation, so that he is battered from both sides and has no chance (after 555 f.) to utter a word.'

[113] Athenaeus (12d), for example, relegates the violent grabbing of nourishment to the primitive stages of mankind's evolution, and clearly contrasts it to decent sympotical behaviour.

portrays[114] subverts the banquet's fundamental principle that food and drink are not to be regarded as material elements in its milieu, but rather as constituents of a broader range of delights.[115] Taking part in a *symposion* means primarily to learn how to be integrated in one's society (cf. 3.4); in Plutarch's words, the guest who neglects the social aspect of a *symposion* 'makes the social occasion incomplete and unrewarding to himself; he departs after having partaken only with his stomach, not his mind' (ἄπεισι τῇ γαστρὶ σύνδειπνος οὐ τῇ ψυχῇ γεγονώς) (*Mor.* 660b). The implicit protagonist of our scene, conversely, does not display any signs of sociability. Not only does he 'give hard looks' to the bystanders (562 ἔβλεψεν εἴς με δριμύ), but he also annihilates conversation, even to the point of negating human speech: as the Innkeeper puts it, 'and he most certainly growled' (κἀμυκᾶτό γε) (562). Finally, Heracles' drawn sword (564), connotative of violent outbursts and aggressiveness, becomes the hallmark of distorted conviviality,[116] since *hybris* and abuse, violence and strife—or even tales about strife (cf. e.g. Xenophanes, B1, 21–3 D–K)—are all varieties of the perversion of sympotical discourse.

Now, the model of this Aristophanic scene is certainly 'Heraclean', as the hero's proverbial gluttony (Athen. 411a–12b) is the most famous Heraclean comic theme (Ar. *Wasps* 60; *Peace* 741), going at least as far back as Epicharmus[117] and continuing even into Hellenistic times, when Heracles was glorified as a Ptolemaic ancestor. In fact, one of the most memorable descriptions of his all too 'natural' voracity is given in the fourth book of Apollonius' *Argonautica* (4. 1442–9), where we hear how the hero, dying with thirst, created a spring in a rock, thrust himself like a grazing beast (φορβάδι ἶσος) upon the earth and drunk 'until his deep belly . . . was filled up' (ὄφρα βαθεῖαν | νηδύν . . . ἐκορέσθη) (1448–9).[118] Furthermore, the Aristophanic Heracles' defiance of civilized eating manners (e.g. by wolfing down food or devouring the food-baskets), finds its most abstract expression and highest symbolic form in his slaughter of the ploughing ox (see below), the prerequisite for the

---

[114] Consider especially the words used to describe his eating manners: 551 κατέφαγ'; 560 κατήσθιεν; 573 κατέφαγες; 576 κατέσπασας.

[115] See Dentzer (1982: 449). Note esp. Pl. *Symp.* 214a–b and cf. Athenaeus' rule (178f–9b) that the symposiast's aesthetic sense must prevail over his desire to eat gluttonously.

[116] The 'sword motif' is also a fixed detail in legendary *Katabaseis* (Hom. *Od.* 10. 535, 11. 48; Ver. *Aen.* 6. 260 and 290ff.), including the tradition of the Heraclean Descent (see Apollod. 2. 5. 12). According to Norden (1903: 206) (on Ver. *Aen.* 6. 260), *Frogs* 564 is the comic handling of this motif.

[117] See esp. fr. 21 Kaibel, from *Busiris*: πρᾶτον μὲν αἰκ ἔσθοντ' ἴδοις νιν, ἀποθάνοις· | βρέμει μὲν ὁ φάρυγξ ἔνδοθ', ἀραβεῖ δ' ἁ γνάθος, | ψοφεῖ δ' ὁ γομφίος, τέτριγε δ' ὁ κυνόδων.

[118] See Hunter (1993: 30): 'Aigle's speech in which she describes Heracles' "visit" is in fact reminiscent of the rude welcome which Dionysus, dressed as Heracles, receives in the Underworld in Aristophanes' *Frogs*.'

production of the civilized gifts of Demeter.[119] However, most distinctively Heraclean is also the *particular* perversion of the social codes of banquet and *xenia* which forms the background to our scene, as it reflects essential functions of the hero in the mythical traditions which revolve around him. Thus, any Greek fifth-century spectator would have been fully aware that Heracles is not always an invited, let alone a beneficial, guest, while an atmosphere of merriment and peace is not the sole convivial space he is able to create. We can examine at this point very briefly two well-known Heraclean episodes of myth, namely his encounter with Theiodamas and his feasting in the house of Syleus; both bear a clear resemblance to our scene in *Frogs* and bring strongly to the fore the mythical *persona* of the hero as a subverter of both hospitality[120] and banquet.

Apollodorus (2. 7. 7) tells us that while 'going through the country of the Dryopes and being in lack of food' Heracles 'met Theiodamas driving a pair of bullocks; so he unloosed and slaughtered (σφάξας) one of the bullocks and feasted (εὐωχήσατο)'. As Jean-Louis Durand (1986: 153) has rightly stressed, in all the versions of the Theiodamas episode[121] Heracles is envisaged as 'a kind of wanderer', while Theiodamas' territory (either Lindos or the country of the Dryopes) is one among his countless stopping-points. Theiodamas as a cattle-driver (βοηλάτης) labouring on the soil, his ploughing ox, and piece of land create an enclosed space, a limited and well-defined terrain into which Heracles intrudes. A 'prey' to his hunger,[122] he appropriates by force—or rather steals in Origen's expression[123]—the ploughing ox, and proceeds to create his own private space in order to accommodate his voracious instincts. Of all the versions, only Philostratus (*Imag.* 2. 24. 1) employs the colourless word σιτεῖται, 'feeds on', 'eats'. In other authors verbs with strong feasting and sympotic connotations occur (εὐωχεῖσθαι: to be sumptuously

---

[119] In the perspective of an agricultural society there is no doubt that killing the ploughing ox relegates the perpetrator to the realm of primitive savagery and causes eating to sink down to the degree of mere instinct (Durand 1986: 155–6). Cf. schol. Arat. *Phaen.* 132 ἀσεβὲς γὰρ ἦν τὸν ἀρότην βοῦν φαγεῖν.

[120] For Heracles and *xenia* see Bruit (1989: 17–19) and Flückiger-Guggenheim (1984: 70–8).

[121] The most important are: Apollod. 2. 5. 11, 2. 7. 7; Philostr. *Imag.* 2. 24; Conon, *FGrHist* 26F 1, XI; schol. Ap. Rh. *Argon.* 1. 1212–19a, pp. 110–11 (Wendel); Lact. *Div. Inst.* 1. 21. 31–7. The extant sources are quite late but, as Merkelbach and West (1965: 304–5) have argued, the encounter of Heracles with Theiodamas can be traced back to Hesiod, as it may have been narrated in his lost *Wedding of Keyx*.

[122] See Lactantius' *famemque pateretur* (*Div. Inst.* 1. 21. 33).

[123] Origen, *Cels.* 7. 54. 4–5 . . . ὁ τοῦ γεωργοῦ βίᾳ καὶ λῃστρικῶς τὸν βοῦν λαβών, a perspective which agrees with the comic Heracles' refusal to offer recompense to the Innkeepers for the damage he has caused (561–2).

entertained; θοινᾶσθαι or καταθοινᾶσθαι: to be feasted),[124] stressing Heracles' role as a lonely banqueter on an occasion where every notion of *xenia* is conspicuously absent.

A similar Heraclean feasting is set up in the house of Syleus, an uncouth landowner who 'was seizing any strangers who passed by and forcing them to hoe his vineyards' (Diod. 4. 31. 7; cf. Apollod. 2. 6. 3). In the story, as remoulded in the Euripidean satyr-play *Syleus*, Heracles has been sold to Syleus as a 'slave' (Tzetz. *Proleg. in Arist. ap.*, N², p. 575). Yet, his behaviour blatantly belies his inferior status:[125] after having 'broken his master's wine cellar open' and 'sacrificed the most impeccable of bulls' and 'opened the best of jars', he set up a private feast (εὐωχεῖτο),[126] in which he was 'eating, and drinking, and singing' (ἤσθιε καὶ ἔπινεν ἄδων),[127] or, in another version of the plot, he 'reclined, drinking gallons of wine neat' (ἀθρόον εὖ μάλα κατακλιθεὶς ἠκρατίζετο).[128] Heracles' omnivorousness was also highlighted in Ion of Chios' *Omphale*, for in a banquet represented or narrated somewhere in this satyr-drama[129] he is said to have 'devoured (κατέπινε)' 'both the firewood and the charcoal' (καὶ τὰ κᾶλα καὶ τοὺς ἄνθρακας) (*TrGF* i (19) F 29), while an annihilation of sympotic civilized setting analogous to the Aristophanic scene can be sought once more in Euripides' *Syleus*: rather than reclining on luxurious furniture and cushions, Heracles had probably been shown as dining on the doors, which served him as a table.[130] Similar Heraclean 'perversions' are abundantly reflected in iconography as well. For example, a Phlyax vase (*PhV²*, no. 41, p. 37, pl. 1c) depicts the actor/Heracles plunging his hand into a bowl full of food placed on the floor, a surface serving him as a banquet table (Hurschmann 1985: 77–8).

Furthermore, whereas a *symposion* is ideally intended to consti-

---

[124] *Εὐωχεῖτο-εὐωχήσατο* in Apollodorus (2. 5. 11 and 2. 7. 7 respectively); εὐωχεῖτο in schol. Ap. Rh. *Argon.* 1. 1212, on line 21; θοινᾶται in Conon (see above, n. 121); καταθοινησάμενος in Origen, *Cels.* 7. 54. 5. Lactantius is even more explicit with the pompous phrase *epulas apparat* (*Div. Inst.* 1. 21. 35).

[125] Philo Judaeus (*ap.* N² 576); ἐπεὶ δὲ καὶ πριαμένου Συλέως εἰς ἀγρὸν ἐπέμφθη, διέδειξεν ἔργοις τὸ τῆς φύσεως ἀδούλωτον.

[126] As in Philo Judaeus (*ap.* N² 576).

[127] Tzetz. *Proleg. in Arist.* (*ap.* N² 575).

[128] Phil. Jud. *loc. cit.* (*ap.* N² 576); κατακλίνεσθαι is included by Athenaeus in a list of verbs which are commonly used for describing the reclining posture of symposiasts (Athen. 23c). More significantly still, this episode is linked with an inversion in the roles of proprietor and visitor, since it is the uninvited 'guest' who asks his 'host' to join him in drinking (fr. 691 N²: κλίθητι καὶ πίωμεν).

[129] On the existence of this *symposion* (although its exact position in the play's action cannot be securely specified) and on Heracles' protagonistic role in it see Chourmouziades (1974: 139).

[130] See Tzetz. *Proleg. in Arist.* (*ap.* N² 575); τὰς θύρας τε ὡς τράπεζαν θεὶς ἤσθιε.

tute an opportunity for common *euphrosyne*, invigorating the spirits
of all participants alike, in the banquet that the presence of Heracles
both creates and perverts commensality and sharing in the pleasures
are impossible. It is only Heracles who feasts.[131] Bystanders cannot
participate, since the actions of the glutton and asocial hero oblige
them to retreat. For example, with the Innkeepers' jumping 'on the
mezzanine level' (ἐπὶ τὴν κατήλιφ' . . . ἀνεπηδήσαμεν) in *Frogs* 566 one
may compare Theiodamas' withdrawal onto a hill (Apollod. 2. 5.
11). Rather than partaking of Heracles' delight, the unlucky farmer
alienates himself from the banqueting intruder and curses him (all
versions). Conon's version (*FGrHist* 26F 1, XI, lines 7–8) intensi-
fies this gap to the extreme, by stressing the fact that Heracles
enjoyed his 'feast' especially because he felt observed by someone
not participating in his festal mood: 'Laughing at the curses,
Heracles said he had never enjoyed a feast (θοίνης) better than the
one accompanied by curses.' Besides, Heracles' festive isolation
seems to be so strongly intertwined with his mythical *persona* that a
dramatist may feel free to exploit this motif even in those cases
where Heracles himself initiates the offer of communication. In
Euripides' *Alcestis*, for example, where the feasting (815 κωμάζοντ')
hero/*xenos* gives the impression of being a 'trickster, thief and
robber fellow' (765–6), it is not only 'the household ills' (807) but
also the guest's extravagant behaviour (747–60) which alienate
Admetus' Servant and induce him to deny the banqueter's proposal
for a sip: 'Well, then, will you not put aside this overwhelming grief
of yours and join me with a drink . . .?'[132] The same motif of
Heracles' feasting loneliness is to be found in iconography as well.
An Apulian bell-krater (*LIMC* iv, s.v. Herakles, 1523, *c*.370–360
BC) depicting Heracles running away, while carrying on his
shoulders a *symposion* side-table laden with food, is a very eloquent
example: the hero seems to have disturbed a banquet's peaceful
conviviality in order to seclude himself in private feasting space.

Finally, it is not difficult to trace a correspondence between
Heracles' menacing anti-sympotical behaviour in the *Frogs*—his
provocations range from angry looks (562)[133] to threats of an attack
(564)—and Heraclean episodes in myth, as many of the hero's hosts
have suffered bloodstained subversions of their banquets from their
guest. So, for example, at a banquet given after the completion of

---

[131] For an interesting example of Heracles' festive solitude (curtailing *trapeza* and distribution of the meat) in sacrificial iconography see Durand (1986), figs. 81–5.

[132] Eur. *Alc.* 794–5, to which the Servant replies: ἐπιστάμεσθα ταῦτα· νῦν δὲ πράσσομεν | οὐχ
οἷα κώμου καὶ γέλωτος ἄξια (803–4).

[133] Cf. Tzetz. *Proleg. in Arist.* (ap. N² 575) on Heracles in Euripides' *Syleus*: καὶ τῷ
προεστῶτι δὲ τοῦ ἀγροῦ δριμὺ ἐνορῶν φέρειν ἐκέλευεν ὡραῖά τε καὶ πλακοῦντας.

his labours, Heracles, worsted in the food portions by Eurystheus' sons, 'deemed he had been insulted, and killed three of the lads' (Anticleides, *Nosti* = *FGrHist* 140 F 3). Similarly, at a *symposion* given in his honour by the family of Eurytus, king of Oechalia, the hero's rashness and irascibility caused the convivial exultation to result in a murderous fist-fight (*LIMC*, s.v. Eurytos I). The disruption of this banquet is well illustrated on a kylix in the Metropolitan Museum of Art, depicting both the fight and the couches 'on which the sons of Eurytus were probably reclining when Heracles began his attack' (Richter 1916: 128), while its disastrous ending may have been the subject of an Attic red-figure cup by the Brygos painter, dating from the beginning of the fifth century BC (*LIMC*, s.v. Eurytos I, 5).

However, if the comic Heracles, whose antisocial behaviour is vividly evoked in *Frogs* 549 ff., brings vividly to mind some 'primitive' and 'natural' aspects of his mythical and cultic counterpart, every spectator/participant in Greek fifth-century society would have been well aware that both *symposion* and *xenia* are cultural complexes which could also be disrupted through the presence of Dionysus.

When acting as a strange force arriving unexpectedly at places unwilling to accept him, the mythical Dionysus unleashes pitilessly upon his 'hosts' the violence of his orgiastic rites. In the murderous turmoil that such Dionysiac visits generate the rigidly defined categories of civic space fuse and the framework of well-ordered communities collapses. The myths of Lycurgus and of Pentheus, of the Proetides and the Minyades, for example, may well be read along the lines of 'missed hospitality' (Massenzio 1969: 72). Similarly, in the sphere of the banquet, Dionysus' role is not reducible either to the creation or to the perpetuation of sympotic *euphrosyne*. Wine (with which this god is frequently identified (3.1)), when offered unmixed, becomes the main obstacle to peaceful conviviality, either by preventing a banquet from taking place[134] or by leading its joyful atmosphere to disastrous endings.[135] Besides, both Heracles and Dionysus are simultaneously involved in a complex nexus of imagery revolving around the codes of banquet and hospitality, in the familiar episode of Heracles' *xenismos* on Mt. Pholoe by the Centaur Pholus. On that mountain, myth relates, Dionysus 'in times of old' (τὸ παλαιόν) had entrusted a jar of wine to a certain Centaur, to be opened only at the arrival of Heracles

---

[134] Cf. e.g. the encounter of Icarius and the shepherds in Apollod. 3. 14. 7.

[135] The primary *exemplum* is the fight of the Centaurs and the Lapiths at Peirithus' wedding-feast, due to overdrinking; for a rich discussion see Valenza-Mele (1986).

(Diod. 4. 12. 3). Time goes by and Heracles is actually 'entertained by the centaur Pholus' (ἐπιξενοῦται Κενταύρῳ Φόλῳ) (Apollod. 2. 5. 4) in a space which had been sheltering Dionysus' gift for four entire generations (Diod. 4. 12. 3). Pholus remembers the divine orders and offers Heracles a 'banquet of hospitality'[136] organized around this old pithos of wine which, half-sunk into the earth and rooted in its very place,[137] functions as 'the central good of the foreign "city", where the guest must be led, received and entertained' (Noel 1983: 146). In this respect, it is Dionysus/wine whom mythical imagery has cast in the position of the banquet's real 'host'. Simultaneously, however, this very same role is also invested with disruptive functions. For the violence of the Centaurs, who swarmed with stones and branches into the banquet, is not presented in the myth as unprovoked. In Diodorus' account, it was precisely the scent of pure Dionysiac liquid which, reaching the private dwellings of the hybrid creatures by its ancestry and strength, drove them out of their senses (Diod. 4. 12. 4) and prompted them to turn the feast into a deadly battleground (Diod. 4. 12. 5–6).

To conclude. Given the analogies in the functions of Dionysus and Heracles with respect to the codes of *symposion* and *xenia* implicated in our scene, when Dionysus, the 'actor', is estranged from the destructive side of his model's personality, he is also kept at a distance from a potential danger of subversiveness inherent in his own realm as well.

PERSEPHONE'S BANQUET: *FROGS* 503–48

4.10. *Dionysus Draws Close to his Own Realm*

As has already been mentioned in Chapter 3, *Frogs* 503–48 is the only instance in Dionysus' role-playing where he, the 'actor', wishes to take on the role and fate of his 'model'. As Persephone's maid invites Dionysus/Heracles to a sumptuous feast, Dionysus, the performer who had just discarded his prototype's troublesome insignia (494–502), is now keen to reassume them, so as to 'become' Heracles once again.

DION. Eh, you! Hang on a second! Surely, you don't take it seriously
   that I have jokingly dressed you up as Heracles?
   Come, Xanthias, won't you stop talking nonsense,
   and pick up and carry the bed-clothes again?

---

[136] See Verbanck-Piérard (1982: 146–7); cf. Noel (1983: 141).
[137] The jar is described in Diodorus as τὸν κατακεχωσμένον οἴνου πίθον (4. 12. 3).

XANTH. What's this? You don't have perhaps in mind to take back from
  me
  what you yourself have given me?
DION.   There's no 'perhaps' about it; I am
                             doing it already.
  Put down that lion-skin!
XANTH.   I call for witnesses to this insult
  and I refer the matter to the gods.
DION.   'Gods indeed!'
  Isn't it foolish and vain on your part to expect that *you*,
  a slave and a mortal, could become Alcmene's son?
XANTH. All right then, I consent. Take them. And maybe, god being
  willing,
  you will need my services again!

                                      (*Frogs* 522–33)

Now, if we look at *Frogs* 503–48 through Greek perceptual filters,
we can easily appreciate that in the wider, 'encyclopaedic' knowledge of male classical spectators the 'artistic' meeting conjured
between Dionysus and Heracles has an important cultural analogue,
namely the frequently reproduced iconographic pattern of 'Heracles
banqueting together with Dionysus' in a peaceful and relaxed sympotic setting, a theme with an unbroken life from the late sixth into
the fourth century BC.[138] More specifically, the comically conveyed
feeling of 'approach' between the two half-brothers in a joyful
sympotic frame is memorably impressed on a mid fifth-century red-
figure cup, where they recline close to each other, the hero gently
touching Dionysus' arm (*LIMC* iv, s.v. Herakles, 1506) (Fig. 4.2).[139]
However, viewed from a Greek perspective, the implicit 'meeting'
of Dionysus, the actor, with Heracles, his prototype, can take on
further connotations, for also shared by Dionysus and Heracles
alike is the afterlife *symposion*, the banquet of immortality.[140]

[138] See *LIMC* iv, s.v. Herakles, p. 820; see esp. 1503, 1504, 1508.

[139] Moreover, many a time in imagery, Dionysus and Heracles are linked through the
Dionysiac drinking-vessel, the kantharos. Perfect examples of such iconographic contacts are
LIMC iv, s.v. Herakles, 1503 and *LIMC* s.v. Dionysos, 839 (Fig. 4.3).

[140] The belief in some kind of afterlife banquet, where the virtuous may be rewarded after
their death, is extensively documented in sources ranging from 6th-cent. epic to Lucian and
Philostratus; see e.g. [Anon.] *Alcmaeonis* (fr. 2 *PEG*), . . . νέκυς δὲ χαμαιστρώτου ἔπι τείνας |
εὐρείης στιβάδος, παρέθηκ' αὐτοῖσι θάλειαν | δαῖτα ποτήριά τε, στεφάνους δ' ἐπὶ κρασὶν ἔθηκεν; [Pl.]
Axiochus 371d (on the paradise of the just as consisting of συμπόσιά τε εὐμελῆ καὶ εἰλαπίναι
αὐτοχορήγητοι); Ar. *Tagenistae* (fr. 504, 6a–8 K–A), †τοῦ γὰρ ἄν ποτε | οὕτω †στεφανωμένοι |
προύκειμεθ', οὐδ' ἂν †κατακεκρινομένοι†, | εἰ μὴ καταβάντας εὐθέως πίνειν ἔδει; Pherecrates (fr.
113 K–A (<u>Μεταλλῆς</u>)); *AP* 7. 27; Plut. *Mor.* 225d. Cf. also 3.1, n. 24. It seems that the motif
played a prominent part in Pythagorean eschatology (see e.g. Aristophon, fr. 12 K–A; Hdt. 4.
95. 3; Pl. *Rep.* 363c–d συμπόσιον τῶν ὁσίων κατασκευάσαντες ἐστεφανωμένους ποιοῦσιν τὸν ἅπαντα
χρόνον ἤδη διάγειν μεθύοντας, ἡγησάμενοι κάλλιστον ἀρετῆς μισθὸν μέθην αἰώνιον); see Graf (1974:
98 ff.). For the motif in funerary monuments (esp. *stelai* and reliefs) of classical Greece see

4.2. Dionysus and Heracles as fellow-banqueters

rf. cup: British Museum, E 66 (*ARV²* 808. 2)

4.3. Dionysus, Heracles, and kantharos

rf. Attik psykter by Cleophrades: Compiègne, Musée Antoine Vivenel, 1068 (*ARV²* 188. 66)

4.4. *Symposion* of Heracles' *apotheosis*
bf. hydria: British Museum, F 301 (*ABV* 282, 2)

Heracles' everlasting bliss among the gods is frequently conveyed through the image of a banquet.[141] A typical iconographic pattern of such a heavenly feast of Heracles is crystallized on an early sixth-century BC hydria in London (*ABV* 282, 2), where the hero, about to be crowned by Athena with a wreath, reclines on his couch, with food and a kantharos placed at his side, and with his lion-skin and weapons scattered in the field unused (Fig. 4.4).[142] As Metzger (1951: 229) concludes, in the course of the fifth century BC the popularity of this particular pictorial way of conveying Heracles' deification was such as to outnumber all other related iconographic motifs. Moreover, what is particularly relevant to the way ancient

Dentzer (1982: 529–40; note in particular R199 (grave relief from the Cerameicus in Athens) featuring what is probably Charon's boat, behind which two couples recline at a banquet); Thönges-Stringaris (1965). Finally, wine (as part of a banquet?) seems to be the fate of the blessed Dionysiac mystai in the Underworld, in so far as we can gauge from the Pelinna gold leaves (2.14): οἶνον ἔχεις εὐδαίμονα τιμήν (line 6 on the leaf with the longer text; cf. 3.1). Cf. also S. G. Cole (1984a: 45), noting that 'Dionysiac imagery associated with wine and wine-drinking was often used as decoration on tomb monuments.' For an unjustified complete denial of the 'symposion as a central part of the iconography of death' see O. Murray (1988: 241).

[141] See e.g. Hom. *Od.* 11. 602–3; Theocr. *Id.* 17. 22; Ap. Rh. *Argon.* 1. 1319.
[142] See Verbanck-Piérard (1987: fig. 6). Another common type is that of Athena pouring wine into Heracles' kantharos or other wine-vessel (see e.g. *LIMC*, s.v. Athena, 181–4 and 187).

audiences would have been able to decipher our scene in *Frogs*, is
the subsequent evolution of the scheme, witnessed from the end of
the fifth century BC, when Heracles' privileged relation with the
sphere of Dionysus, a realm with a pronounced eschatological
dimension, led to the eventual *substitution* of the Olympian by the
Dionysiac element in the hero's *apotheosis*: the deified Heracles is
now shown as banqueting in a distinctively *Dionysiac* context,
created either by vine clusters, leaves, and grapes all around and
above his couch[143] or by the presence of satyrs providing him with
food and drink in his posture of repose.[144] And, obviously, of even
greater importance are those images where Dionysus himself
features as a fellow-banqueter in Heracles' other-worldly bliss.[145]
Some truly wonderful pictorial documents provide good insight
into the cultural repertory of the play's Greek spectators.[146] The
two sides of a sixth-century 'bilingual' amphora in Munich, for
example, combine the Dionysiac and Heraclean banquet under the
eye of Athena: the black-figure side of the vase shows Heracles'
afterlife banquet (Athena, followed by Hermes, stands at the foot of
his couch in a welcoming gesture), while the red-figure side represents Dionysus himself as a solitary banqueter on a sympotic couch.
A late fifth-century BC phiale, probably of Attic provenance, displays another striking combination of the Dionysiac and Heraclean
motifs in an eschatological context. While its upper frieze depicts
Heracles' *apotheosis* in a chariot soaring up to heaven, its inner frieze
'consists of groups of figures reclining at a banquet' (Richter 1941:
369): the deified Heracles banquets leaning on his club, and
Dionysus, holding the *thyrsos*, embraces Ariadne.[147] Finally, the
widespread distribution of this motif is well illustrated in a
magnificent volute-krater in Brussels (Hurschmann 1985: A7, pl. 8):
the centrally depicted deification of Heracles, signified by the
standard motif of Athena's ascending chariot, blends harmoniously
with the portrayal of Dionysus' *thiasos* around the vase's neck as
well as with the markedly Dionysiac banquet with maenads and a
satyr which adorns its lower zone. As Hurschmann (1985: 73–4)
writes, the banquet of Dionysus depicted just below the horses
which bring Heracles to immortality, marks the 'Endpunkt des

---

[143] See e.g. *LIMC* iv, s.v. Herakles, 1487, 1491, 1492, etc.

[144] See e.g. Metzger (1951: 224–5), nos. 56–8 (4th cent. BC).

[145] Cf. Schauenburg (1963: 117), who sees 'eine besondere Form der Apotheose des Herakles' in his connection with Dionysus.

[146] On Heracles' apotheosis in art see Mingazzini (1925); Metzger (1951: 210–24); Schauenburg (1963); Verbanck-Piérard (1987).

[147] The rest of the figures may be deities but also perhaps 'mystai, taking part with Herakles in the Dionysiac banquet in a future life' (Richter, 1941: 372 n. 16, though she herself regards this last idea as unconvincing).

Weges, nämlich die zu erhoffende Tisch- und Herd-gemeinschaft der Gerechten mit den Göttern und Helden in dionysischer Glückseligkeit'.

To conclude then. Persephone's offer of a banquet to Xanthias/ Heracles in *Frogs* 503–7 and Dionysus' desire to join in by reassuming the insignia of his model (522 ff.) effects dramatically a 'meeting' of Dionysus and Heracles which, if approached from a Greek cultural perspective, has important analogues on two distinctive registers: it can remind a fifth-century spectator both of the earthly, merry drinking-party of the two half-brothers as well as of their association on the eschatological level of Dionysiac bliss. Furthermore, within the broader range of culturally determined associations that *Frogs* 503–48 is likely to generate, Greek theatre-goers could have easily deciphered Dionysus' desire to banquet as a wish for his association, or, better say, *re*unification, with a quintessential aspect of his own civic cult.

Iconography is remarkably rich in representations of Dionysus in sympotic settings which bear striking similarities to the picture that the verbal level of our scene constructs (cf. 3.1).[148] Written sources, correspondingly, treat the banquet as a realm inextricably interwoven with this god,[149] for he is frequently supposed to preside over its festive atmosphere.[150] In a memorable choral ode, for example, Euripides' *Bacchae* celebrates Dionysus as 'supreme among the blessed at the beautifully crowned festivities' (παρὰ κάλλι | στεφάνοις εὐφροσύναις δαί | μονα πρῶτον μακάρων) (376–8). The Chorus specify his cultic province (378 ὃς τάδ' ἔχει) as comprising dance (379), the merriment which accompanies the music of the flute (380), and, most importantly, the precious gift of wine, which 'sets an end to cares' when flowing either 'at the feast of gods' or at the 'ivy-crowned banquets', where the krater 'embraces' men with the all-pervasive sweetness of sleep (*Bacch.* 381–5). In other words, within the range of a Greek audience's experience, wine, the music of the flute, and dance were likely to demarcate and evoke an essentially Dionysiac area. However, it cannot be emphasized too strongly that perceptual assimilation of these elements is inextricably interwoven with the simultaneous awareness of their double function. For it is

[148] There are many representations of Dionysus as a solitary banqueter; see e.g. *LIMC*, s.v. Dionysos, 362–81; for the erotic dimension of the scene cf. Dentzer (1982: 124) and Xen. *Symp.* 9. 2–7.

[149] Ion of Chios, for example, calls Dionysus εὐθύμων συμποσίων πρύτανι (fr. 1, 14 G–P). Plato (*Leg.* 671a) regards the participants in a *symposion* as the 'chorus of Dionysus', while the comic poet Eubulus (fr. 93 K–A: fr. 94 Hunter) seems to have brought the god himself on stage as a symposiarch who is setting up 'the proper number of rounds to be drunk'; see Hunter (1983: 186).

[150] Although this presidency is interchangeable with that of Apollo.

not merely the wine which may be both a 'source of pleasure (χάρμα)' and a 'load of grief (ἄχθος)' (Hesiod, fr. 239, 1 M–W; cf. Theogn. 875), both a 'raving' liquid' (μαινόμενος . . . οἶνος), when drunk neat, and a 'gentle and tolerable potion' (ἀγαθὸν πῶμα καὶ μέτριον),[151] when it flows, mixed with water, in the space of a banquet. The flute (cf. *Frogs* 513 καὶ γὰρ αὐλητρίς τε σοι . . .) as well is both an accompaniment to the orgiastic Bacchic dances on the mountains, functioning as one of the main stimuli which translate the participants to a state of trance,[152] and an intrinsic element of the Dionysiac civic cult, lying at the centre of the dithyrambic and theatrical performances which are enacted in honour of this god.[153] Finally, dance (cf. *Frogs* 514) is not only the essential activity of mythical and cultic maenads on the wildness of open mountainsides[154] but also indispensable in Dionysus' civic realm, from the pre-dramatic dances of the 'fat men' and satyrs depicted on Corinthian 'Komos Vases' to the strictly patterned performance of the choruses in fifth-century Dionysiac drama. Nevertheless, the 'denotational' significance of a theatrical sign is primarily determined by its narrow, immediate frame. In this respect, the inclusion of all of the above mentioned elements in the context of a *symposion*, a realm conceived of as belonging—in its ideal form, at least—to the utterly enclosed, the civilized and civic space, amounts to the dissolution of their inherent Dionysiac ambiguity. To put it in another way, when situated in a convivial atmosphere, not only mixed wine but also flute and dance are dissociated from their subversive or un-civic function. The performer's wish to have a share in them, consequently, could well have been decoded as a move towards the harmless, joyful, and beneficial, the civically oriented dimension of his own attributes.

Finally, in a Greek perspective the festive image evoked in *Frogs*

[151] See Plato's metaphor in *Leg.* 773d.

[152] See e.g. Aesch. fr. 57, 5 Radt μανίας ἐπαγωγόν; Arist. *Pol.* 1341a22, 1342b1–6; cf. Pl. *Symp.* 215c; see Dodds (1951: 97 n. 95) and for a brief general discussion of *aulos* and trance see Bremmer (1984: 278–9).

[153] Flute-players wearing the *phorbeia* are a constant feature in pictorial representations of pre-dramatic choruses; see e.g. Trendall and Webster (1971: nos. 1.8; 1.9; 1.11; 1.14; 1.17; 1.19; 1.20). More significantly, it is precisely the presence of an *auletes* playing his/her double pipe (Beazley 1955: 310) which constitutes the more or less decisive criterion for the inclusion of a painted scene into the realm of theatre. Cf. Pickard-Cambridge (1988: 179). Every dramatic chorus too had its own *aulos*-player; for pictorial evidence for Comedy see Taplin (1993: 70–8).

[154] Consider e.g. Euripides' *Bacchae*, where the establishment of Dionysus' orgies is first of all connected to the initiation of the *polis* in his dances (21–2). Moreover, although the state of mind of an historical female follower of the god may remain forever impenetrable (for a balanced position see Bremmer 1984), the fact is incontestable that she applied herself in mountain-dancing; cf. e.g. Pausanias (10. 4. 3) on the maenads of his time.

503 ff. could be understood as very closely linked with sacrificial overtones. As we hear from Persephone's maid, a bull has just been broiled (506 βοῦν ἀπηνθράκιζ' ὅλον), while a cook (*mageiros*) is ready to retrieve the meat portions (τὰ τεμάχη) from the fire (517–18). Now, given that (i) meat consumption was of strictly sacrificial provenance in ancient Greece;[155] (ii) the ox had always been considered in both myth and cult as the 'sacrificial' animal *par excellence*;[156] and (iii) the functions of the sacrificer were frequently submerged within the role of the *mageiros*, who was responsible for carrying out the performance of the 'act',[157] the entertainment proposed in *Frogs* 503 ff. is, in reality, an invitation to a sacrificial banquet.[158] In the remainder of this section, then, we will compare the sacrificial setting of this scene with *Frogs* 469–78, where we have already seen that sacrificial order is perverted (4.6). We will thus be better equipped to understand that the direct juxtaposition of two diametrically opposed articulations of the city's mythical and ritual conglomerate entails important implications for the shaping of Dionysus' *dramatis persona*, as in the general 'encyclopaedic' knowledge of classical Athenian *theatai* this god was strongly linked with both.

For a modern audience, whose knowledge of Dionysiac matters is almost exclusively shaped by Euripides' *Bacchae*, it is remarkably easy to forget that the dismemberment of victims was not the only way in which this god was implicated in sacrificial norms. For 'participants' in classical Greek culture, on the other hand, Dionysiac *sparagmos* was strictly relegated and confined to the range of myth:[159] the cult calendars of the Attic demes provide ample evidence confirming beyond doubt the ritual slaughter of *domestic* animals on the *altar* at the prescribed festal days of this god.[160] As Obbink (1993: 77) writes, 'The portrait of sacrifice they present is one not of sacramentalism but of sociability and domestication.' A similar picture of Dionysiac ambivalence emerges from a variety of

[155] See e.g. Detienne (1979a: 10); cf. Peirce (1993: 240) on iconographical evidence.

[156] Consider e.g. the Hesiodic first sacrifice in *Theog.* 535 ff. and innumerable cases reflected in both literature and art. Besides, the sacrifice of the ox lies at the heart of the specifically Athenian feast of the 'Bouphonia', on which see primarily Durand (1986).

[157] See e.g. Athen. 659d . . . καὶ θυτικῆς ἦσαν ἔμπειροι οἱ παλαίτεροι μάγειροι; see further Detienne (1979a: 20–2) and more extensively Berthiaume (1982: 17–37). This double role is abundantly reflected in the comic fiction too (see Berthiaume 1982: 34 with refs. in n. 134).

[158] For iconographic parallels see below.

[159] Except that it may have been performed in a symbolic form in Orphic initiation rites, intended to re-enact Dionysus' *sparagmos* by the Titans (cf. 2.12(b)).

[160] Henrichs (1990: 262–4) on calendars from Thoricus and Erchia, late 5th and early 4th cent. BC respectively; see also Henrichs (1978: 151 n. 97 and 1982: n. 68). To Henrichs's pictorial evidence add Athen. 659f, where Olympias advertises to Alexander a μάγειρος who knows ὃν τρόπον θύεται . . . τὰ βακχικά.

Dionysiac cultic contexts, ranging from sacrificial rituals performed in the wilderness of nature to sacrifices at the heart of the Athenian city. According to Diodorus (4. 3. 3), at the trieteric rituals performed 'in many of the Greek cities' in honour of Dionysus, 'the matrons, forming in groups, offer sacrifices to the god and celebrate his mysteries', while at the Anthesteria festival of Athens, the wife of the Archon Basileus, the Basilinna, performs 'secret sacred sacrifices' on behalf of the entire city.[161] This duality inherent in Dionysiac sacrificial rites is crystallized in iconography as well. A pelike of the early fifth century BC (*LIMC*, s.v. Dionysos, 472) (Fig. 4.5), for example, shows Dionysus brandishing the two parts of a dismembered kid above an altar, which features prominently at the front of the picture's lower zone. Vase-painters could even represent Dionysus himself as the receiver or as the instructor of a sacrifice in the civic mode. Thus, on a janiform kantharos from Spina (*ARV²* 266, 85), dating from the first half of the fifth century BC, Dionysus, reclining at a banquet, is about to receive the offer of a he-goat immolated with sacrificial knife on the vase's other side (M. Robertson 1986: 84–5). Similarly, in the iconographic complex of a richly illustrated pelike (*ARV²* 558, 130) Dionysus seems to demand a sacrifice from Icarius, showing or giving him the knife he must use,[162] while an Apulian volute-krater of about 400 BC (*LIMC*, s.v. Dionysos, 863) offers a more interesting iconographic parallel to the Dionysiac sympotic scene of *Frogs*: surrounded by maenads and a silen who plays the *kottabos*, Dionysus reclines at a banquet, depicted on the vase's upper zone; emphasizing the theatrical dimension of the feast (cf. below, 4.11), a long-haired female mask is suspended in the field; in the vase's lower zone an ivy-crowned bacchant with a sacrificial knife in hand is ready to immolate a kid held above the altar, adjacent to a small statue of Dionysus equipped with *thyrsos* and kantharos. One single image, then, presents Dionysus, both in his iconic and his aniconic form, as the receiver of a sacrifice in the *civic* mode, duly performed on the altar by the female members of his entourage.[163]

Now, obviously, this ambiguity can hardly be surprising in the sphere of Dionysus, 'the deity who above all others belongs both to the heart of the savage universe and to the centre of the town'

---

[161] Diod. 4. 3. 3; [Dem] 59. 73; see Seaford (1994a: 263).

[162] According to M. Robertson's (1986: esp. 82–3) tentative reconstruction of the image.

[163] The iconographic link of Dionysus with 'civic' sacrifice dates at least as far back as the 6th cent. BC. As fragments of a volute-krater in the Acropolis Museum of Athens (no. 654) show, an enthroned Dionysus presides over a sacrificial event, where men in loincloths cut up meat and satyrs put them in the fire to boil. See Karouzou (1955: pl. IX) and Peirce (1993: 240).

4.5. Dionysus holding dismembered animal above an altar

rf. pelike: British Museum, E 362 (*ARV*² 585, 34)

(Seaford 1994*a*: 237).[164] And I believe that classical spectators would have been able to appreciate the reflection of this same inherently Dionysiac duality in the 'sacrificial' dimension of *Frogs* 469–78. To conclude, then, the dramatized clash between Dionysus' aversion to the gruesome picture of a 'bacchic'-like dismemberment (479 ff.) and his strong attraction to the prospect of a sacrificial banquet (522 ff.) qualifies for his initiatory dissociation from the wild and his alignment with the tame and civilized side of his own mythical and cultic personality.

[164] However, it has to be made clear at this point that the fusion of dismemberment with normal sacrificial practice—even in the frame of one single ritual act—is not a uniquely Dionysiac phenomenon. As we learn from Pausanias' account of the rites of the Arcadian goddess Despoina, 'the Arcadians celebrate mysteries, and sacrifice to the Mistress many victims in generous fashion. Every man of them *sacrifices* (θύει) what he possesses. But he does not cut the throats of the victims (οὐ τὰς φάρυγγας ἀποτέμνει), as is done in other sacrifices; each man chops off a limb of the sacrifice, just that which happens to come to hand (κῶλον δὲ ὅ τι ἂν τύχῃ, τοῦτο ἕκαστος ἀπέκοψε τοῦ θύματος)' (Paus. 8. 37. 8). Cf. a practice of sacrificial dismemberment in Delphi (*P. Oxy.* 1800, fr. 2 ii 32–63) quoted by Nagy (1979: 284–5). See Seaford (1994*a* : 296 with n. 74) and Burkert (1985: 280).

4.11. *Dionysus,* symposion, *and Dionysiac 'Alterity'*

The previous section has established that Dionysus' wish to participate in a banquet draws him close to a quintessential civilized space of his own realm. The question I would now like to explore is how intrinsically 'Dionysiac' is Dionysus' desire to become 'other' in the specific context of a banquet.

In literature and iconography alike, wine, the *sine qua non* element of the *symposion,* creates for the drinker happy evasions from reality, generating, as it does, illusions of wealth, luxury, and power;[165] faces of the Dionysiac satyrs, grimacing from the bottom or the sides of one's drinking-cups, confront the male symposiast with an aspect of bestiality, while head-shaped vessels[166] (sometimes even janiform),[167] or the so-called 'eye-cups' (Ferrari 1986; Kunish 1990), vases with staring eyes creating the impression of a frontal face, invite the banqueter to 'lose' his own *persona* in the sight of the 'other' (cf. Boardman 1976: 288), and become absorbed in the representation of alterity itself. But on a larger scale too, specific occasions of the Athenian festival calendar highlight the theatricality of the sympotic realm. On the day of the Choes, for example, the second day of the Dionysiac festival of the Anthesteria (3.1), banquets/revels (cf. 3.1) and indulgence in 'theatrical alterity' of various forms converge: not only do the revellers dress up as satyrs (Seaford 1984: 7), but, most impressively, the mood of 'performance' and 'otherness' is vividly captured by the so-called 'choes-jugs', the special wine-vessels used at the great public banquets of the Anthesteria (cf. 3.1). And it is especially a series of children's 'choes-jugs' (dating from the fifth and the fourth century BC) which best testify to this komastic mood of 'playing the other', for they portray young revellers at the moment they indulge in their own future 'otherness', by impersonating adult roles[168] or even by playing at being actors. In this latter category, a chous in St Petersburg[169] is most impressive, as the everyday 'self', the artistic identity aspired to, and the *dramatis persona* about to be assumed merge in the figures of four children, who play at being actors, who are about to imitate gods.[170] Furthermore, in the extant evidence on

---

[165] See e.g. Bacchyl. fr. 20B, 10–16 Maehler; Pindar, fr. 124b, 6–8 Maehler; Ar. *Knights* 92 ff.

[166] See *ARV*² appendix i, pp. 1529–52.

[167] Woman/negro, satyr/woman, satyr/Dionysus being the most frequent combinations; see Lissarrague (1987b: 57).

[168] e.g. playing at being teachers; see van Hoorn (1951: 39) and nos. 108, 244, 402, 629 (with figs.).

[169] Chous from Phanagoria (Taman), now in St Petersburg (ΦΑ 1869.47: *MOMC*³, AV8).

[170] Of similar complexity is the interaction of artistic levels on a chous from Athens (end of

the Anthesteria, several sources mention theatrical contests, the so-called 'Chytrine contests' (*agones chytrinoi*).[171] Their precise character and nature is elusive, but the very fact that some kind of theatrical performances were included in the feasting and sympotic context of that particular Dionysiac festival where banquets/revels occupied such a prominent position (cf. 3.1),[172] corroborates the impression that can be gleaned from other sources,[173] namely that a *symposion* distils the Dionysiac experience of becoming 'other'. In this respect, then, that is, in so far as the sphere of a banquet can be perceived as a space of alterity, the Aristophanic Dionysus' wish (522ff.) to 'step out' of himself in order to join Persephone's sympotic feast is not merely 'Dionysiac' (4.10) but also inherently 'theatrical' as well. Moreover, if read on a purely theatrical register, the three 'encounter scenes' (460–502, 503–48, 549–604) discussed in this chapter form an interesting dramatic triptych.

With its strongly paratragic diction and the tragically tinged perversion of the hunting/sacrificial codes (4.6–8) the Doorkeeper's scene evokes the tragic genre; with its heavy exploitation of Heraclean comic themes, conversely, the Innkeepers' scene is firmly rooted in the tradition of the comic genre. As for *Frogs* 503–48 (Persephone's prospective banquet), situated in between, it mobilizes a string of associations with the general mimetic frame which hosts both kinds of performance, that is, Theatre itself. Here the best support for my proposition can be sought in iconography. For in vase-paintings the *symposion* becomes the space *par excellence* which brings together Dionysus, poets, actors, other contributors to

5th cent. BC) and now in the Louvre (CA 2938), where a boy is dressed up as a comic actor impersonating an old man (he wears a bearded mask); see T. B. L. Webster (1953: pl. 126. 2); cf. a chous with a boy playing at being an actor dressed up as king: van Hoorn (1927: pl. III, fig. 7). On the basis of a chous now at the National Museum of Athens (Athens 17752: *PhV²*, p. 21 no. 5), Karouzou (1946: 132; fig. 10, a–c) argued that it might have been customary for children on the day of the Choes to stage a parodic re-enactment of the myth of Orestes, i.e. the myth which constitutes the *aition* for the wine-drinking ceremonies of the choes (schol. Ar. *Acharn.* 960–1). For more choes with theatre scenes, see *PhV²*, pp. 20–2.

[171] For a collection of testimonia on the Chytroi as a spectacle see Hamilton (1992: 38–42); cf. Pickard-Cambridge (1988: 15–16). For a possible reflection of the *agones chytrinoi* on a late 5th-cent. chous from Anavyssos (*PhV²*, p. 20, no. 1) see Hamilton (1978).

[172] It is possible to argue that the *agones chytrinoi* were taking place on the evening of the Choes (i.e. the day of the revels/banquets), but were called 'Chytrine' because, as we have already seen in 3.1, after sunset the day of the Choes moved into the Chytroi. Besides, the iconography of the choes-jugs perhaps suggests that the real *agones chytrinoi* were anticipated by mock performances/contests 'staged', so to speak, by revelling young boys (cf. above, n. 170) *playing at* being victorious actors/'others' (cf. the frequent crowning motif on the jugs).

[173] Cf. e.g. Ch. 3 on mimetic/pantomime performances at banquets. Moreover, Green (1989: 222) notes that on banquet vessels decorated in the so-called Gnathia technique 'most of the subject-matter is either drawn (directly or indirectly) from the theatre or concerns satyrs and maenads, likewise connected with Dionysos.' See also Frontisi-Ducroux and Lissarrague (1990) on the 'alterity' and the Anacreontic *komos* (cf. 1.3).

a theatrical performance as well as the 'alterity' represented by their masks, in one single social setting, one specific cultural context.

Thus, in the Athenian frame, the sympotic motif in iconography and sculpture has clear dramatic connotations. Votive monuments, such as the so-called 'Peiraeus' and 'Cagliari' reliefs, are prominent examples. The former (end of fifth century BC) depicts three actors (mask in hand) approaching the couch of a banqueter; although the inscription which identifies the reclining figure as Dionysus is certainly a later addition, I cannot see, as N. W. Slater (1985) does, any presumptive reason for ruling out the possibility that the symposiast is the god himself. In this case, Dionysus, actors, as well as their masks, the prime emblems of theatrical alterity, are joined together in a celebratory sympotic context: according to the majority of interpreters (see the table compiled by Dentzer 1982: 506), the relief represents an offering brought by three victorious actors to Dionysus (Dentzer 1982: 508). On the semi-preserved 'Cagliari' relief (fifth century BC) the theatrical dimension is conveyed through masks, either held or hanging from the architrave. The inscription Ἡραέες Διονύσωι ἀνέθηκ[αν] makes it quite plausible that the banqueting figure is Dionysus himself (Guarducci 1962: 276).[174] Moreover, sculpture concurs with vase-painting at this point, in so far as it treats the *symposion* as a privileged frame for the celebration of a scenic victory. The most famous iconographic monument here is the so-called 'Pronomos vase', an Attic volute-krater of the end of the fifth century BC (*LIMC*, s.v. Dionysos, 835), now in Naples. On its front side, which depicts Dionysus' Sanctuary, the theatre god, surrounded by the cast of a satyr-play who hold their masks in hand, reclines together with Ariadne in an elaborately adorned sympotic couch. Another important iconographic crystallization of the banquet as a space of Dionysiac 'otherness' is an Attic red-figure volute-krater (end of fifth century BC) from Samothrace, which bears two complementary sets of pictures: on the side which Green (1982: 238) considers to be the reverse of the vase, Dionysus, drunk and supported by a satyr, advances towards a couch near which a woman (probably a maenad) stands, holding a mask in her right hand. The vase's other side (Green 1982: 239) is decorated with the image of a banquet, where Dionysus and Ariadne recline on a couch, under columns which, most probably, stand for the architrave of a temple. From this architrave, above the heads of the reclining figures, hang a male and

---

[174] The masks suggest that Ἡραέες was a theatrical association, and it is very probable that the relief was offered to the theatre god as a token of gratitude after a victorious theatrical performance (Guarducci 1962: 276).

a female mask.[175] According to T. B. L. Webster (1972: 455), the scene, which 'may well have been painted for a symposion to celebrate a victory with tragedy', seems to be taking place in the sanctuary of Dionysus, in a setting clearly theatrical.

However, outside mainland Greece as well, it is also interesting to note that an entire series of South Italian vases depict the motif of the 'symposion under masks' in a plain or elaborate manner (*PhV²*, pp. 89 ff.). In the most usually employed scheme, a youth or youths (probably victorious actors) recline on a couch feasting, while a mask or masks (presumably the *dramatis personae* they had worn in the successful play) are shown hanging somewhere in the field above their heads. Two beautiful examples of this iconographic type are now in the Vatican. The first (Vatican AD 1 (inv. 17370)),[176] a fourth-century Paestan red-figure bell-krater, depicts three young revellers reclining on a banquet couch with three different comic masks hanging above their heads from a festoon of ivy (Fig. 4.6) (see p. 214). The theatrical dimension of the scene is enhanced by an actor dressed as *papposilenos*, asleep on the floor in front of them. On the second (Vatican T7 (inv. 17946)),[177] a fourth-century Apulian bell-krater, a maenad holding a *tympanon* is ready to crown a young banqueter reclining on a couch, under a long-haired female mask hanging in the field. Now, on a number of vases the symposiast who banquets under masks can be unequivocally identified as Dionysus, principally because of his characteristic attributes, the *thyrsos* and/or the *kantharos*.[178] However, Handley (1973: 107) has pertinently observed that in such scenes there is a very fine line separating Dionysus from his human votaries, and this is undoubtedly true with respect to the Vatican kraters as well as a fourth-century red-figure kalyx-krater now in Louisville (Kentucky) (Green 1994: 99, fig. 4.7) where, following a model well known in Dionysiac banquets, the revellers seem to have been elevated to the divine sphere (Green 1994: 98).[179]

It seems, then, that in both Greek and South Italian art the *symposion* as a space of alterity is the most privileged space for the 'framing' of a theatrical scene. But, if a banquet can be thought of as the space *par excellence* where 'Dionysiac' and theatrical, actors

[175] For pictures of the vase, see McCrede (1968: pl. 59c); Green (1982: figs. 2–3), and *LIMC*, s.v. Dionysos, 834.

[176] Hurschmann (1985: pl. 20) and Green (1994: fig. 4. 6).

[177] Hurschmann (1985: pl. 10.2).

[178] See e.g. a South Italian kalyx-krater in London (British Museum, F 275; see *JHS* 55 (1935), 230) (Fig. 4.7); a Paestan kalyx-krater of mid-4th cent. BC (*LIMC*, s.v. Dionysos, 844); an Apulian bell-krater of 4th cent. BC (*PhV²*, pl. xiv(a)), etc.

[179] More secure is the identification of the 'theatrical' symposiast as Dionysus on an Apulian kalyx-krater (*PhV²*, pl. xiv (b)), where the reclining banqueter holds a kantharos.

4.6. *Symposion* under masks
Paestan bell-krater: Vatican, Museo Gregoriano Etrusco, AD1 (inv. 17370)

and their divine patron 'meet', *Frogs* 503–48 can be considered to reflect this cultural interrelation. Dionysus desires to adopt a different *persona* in order to participate in a quintessentially Dionysiac realm, where the dividing lines between the reveller's confused 'alterity' and the performer's ordered experiments with specified forms of 'otherness' collapse and blur. *Symposion* and theatre, two provinces distinctively 'Dionysiac', meet and merge in the dramatic evocation of Persephone's sumptuous feast, and the Aristophanic plot's manipulation of Dionysus' reaction to the offer (522 ff.) links him unmistakably with both. As a general conclusion, therefore, it appears that Dionysus' theatrical role-playing is an important avenue for his initiatory reintegration into the com-

4.7. Dionysiac *Symposion* under masks

rf. kalyx-krater: British Museum, F 275.

munity of the Athenian *polis*. His *mimesis* of Heracles is fashioned in such a way as to direct his *dramatis persona* into the civic space of Athens.

5

Dionysus, the Poets, and the *Polis*

In the preceding chapters we have seen that the experience of the Eleusinian Mysteries, the 'wine/symposion' motif, and, most importantly, Dionysus' 'Heraclean' role-playing have been designed in such a way as to orientate the *dramatis persona* of the god towards the space of the *polis*. Furthermore, as has been argued in Chapter 2, the literary agon should be considered as corresponding to Dionysus' reaggregation into Athens. But, as the end of any initiation sequence is to forge the initiand's personality into a new identity, we still have to consider the ways in which the comically remoulded pattern of mystic initiation grafted on our play's plot enriches and enlarges the dramatic character attributed to Dionysus as an initiand in the comedy's first part. To put this differently, if Dionysus' liminal transition has bestowed on him the potentiality of becoming 'other', how is this 'otherness' constructed and displayed in the comedy's agon? What are the new dimensions he is now able to incorporate while arbitrating the literary contest? Chapters 5–9 aim to investigate the specific ways in which the agon effects the final remoulding of Dionysus' *dramatis persona*. What I hope to suggest is that the last part of the play's structure both illustrates and complements Dionysus' reintegration into Athens. One issue requires some preliminary clarification here, namely the much discussed and highly controversial notion of 'character development'.

Michael Silk (1990: 156) has strongly argued that fictional 'characters can be seen to do what we call "develop"' only within the boundaries of the 'realist' tradition. However, Aristophanes' stage-figures, although realistic 'in *some* degree', 'partake also of a different mode of representation' that Silk (1990: 159) proposes to call '*imagist*'. Thus, being characterized by discontinuity at every level, by inconsistent and unexpected behaviour, 'If and when they change, they change abruptly and, perhaps, entirely' (ibid.: 162). In this respect, then, Silk argues that the notion of character evolution, as it is conceivable in terms of the nineteenth-century novel, for example, is non-existent in Aristophanes' dramatic world. Now, to some extent, Silk is obviously right. Aristophanic characters, such as, let us say, Trygaeus or Peisthetaerus, are not creatures of a Dostoyevskian depth and, therefore, any attempt to analyse them through notions of character 'advancement', 'evolution', and related terms is clearly misplaced. However, it cannot be emphasized too strongly that, whether deep or shallow, consistent or discontinuous, these characters are inextricably interwoven with an action, the play's plot—and here I subscribe to Barthes's position, adopted and defended by Goldhill (1990*b*: 112), namely, that 'the character and the discourse are each other's accomplices'. Consequently, in so far as we are willing to admit that the action of any play starts off at a point A and ends at a point B, which under no circumstances can be identical with A, the characters who have, so to speak, co-operated in this action have certainly undergone a change, in the sense that at the play's end they must be seen in a different relation both to the other characters as well as to the issues of the plot. In this respect, it *is* reasonable, I think, to speak of an 'advancement'. Furthermore, the *Frogs* may be treated in a special way, as it is the play's discourse itself which contains the notion of development: reflecting the sequence of an initiation, it implicates the initiand/actor in the change that a *myesis* entails. In other words, being a function of this play's action, Dionysus' character inevitably 'evolves'.

5.1. *Dionysus' Choice: A 'Carnivalesque' Reversal?*

Inflamed by a passion for Euripides, as he sets out on his journey, Dionysus none the less returns to Athens after having chosen Aeschylus, a change of mind lending support to those who inveigh against the unified conception of the play's plot.[1] I do not intend to become entangled in the subtleties of the debate, as the whole of this book develops the position that the play is conceived and worked out in a sophisticated and organic structure. However, I *do* want to place the discussion in the light of a broader appreciation of the nature of the comic discourse. For Dionysus' choice of Aeschylus is the play's debt to the spirit of carnival, in which Old Comedy, as a genre, has a share *par excellence*.[2] As part of a comic narrative then, the initial 'crowning' of Euripides as the select poet and prospective saviour of the city creates *ipso facto* the anticipation of his subsequent 'dethronement' and 'uncrowning', in keeping with the chief rule of 'carnivalesque' reversals, that is, as Bakchtin (1968: 11) has put it, 'the peculiar logic of the "inside out" (à l'envers), of the

---

[1] e.g. Fraenkel (1962: 163–88); Hooker (1980); Harriott (1986: 115), etc.
[2] See primarily Carrière (1979: esp. 43); Rösler (1986); Goldhill (1991: esp. 176–88), and now von Möllendorff (1995); *contra*, Henderson (1990: esp. 274–5, 285–6).

"turnabout", of a continual shifting "from top to bottom" . . .', the 'upside down' in both the literal sense and the 'metaphorical meaning of the image' (ibid.: 370). And yet, the selection of Aeschylus does not obey an extraneous logic inconsistent with the play's own demands. On the contrary, Aristophanes' artistry lies in the dexterity with which he brings about this reversal in intrinsic and internal correspondence with the play's pivotal concerns. Besides, it is precisely this different decision which illustrates best the advancement that Dionysus' theatrical *persona* underwent during the fictitious initiation sequence that the *Frogs* remoulds. I will elaborate on these issues in Chapters 5–9. For the moment, I will briefly focus on the unifying effect of Dionysus' dramatic role, and will attempt a first contextualization of his judgement in the play's thematic structure and imagery.

In lines 96–7 Dionysus complains to Heracles that 'searching though one may, one would not be able to find a fertile poet (γόνιμον . . . ποιητήν) any longer, one who would utter a noble expression'. Heracles asks him to clarify the essence of this fertility (98 πῶς γόνιμον;), that is, the poetic quality he seems to be considering of primary importance, whereupon Dionysus replies:

> 'Fertile' of such a kind that he will utter
> something daring like this—
> 'air, the bed-chamber of Zeus' or 'the foot of Time'
> or 'a mind unwilling to pronounce an oath over sacrificial offerings,
> while the tongue has broken her oath independently of the mind'.
>
> (98–102)

Dionysus, then, identifies 'fertility' with airy, insubstantial features, such as verbal ingenuities, 'adventurous' (99) speech, and bold expressions, which either have no real plane of reference (100) or are morally ambiguous (101–2). At the beginning of his journey, therefore, Dionysus' poetic appreciation is displayed and exhausted at a purely artistic level. He can only envisage an author in his 'individual autonomy' (Longo 1990: 12) or, to borrow a phrase from Oddone Longo (ibid.: 12), as 'the artificer of a literary exercise utterly self-enclosed and fulfilling itself within the limits of the text.' Moreover, Dionysus' quest for such poetic 'fertility' is ascribed entirely to personal emotions, that is, the 'longing' (*pothos*) which overcame him as he was reading the *Andromeda* aboard (52–4), and the 'yearning' (*himeros*) which 'wears [him] out' (59) comparably to his half-brother's craving for soup (61–5).[3] In other

---

[3] Only in lines 66–7 does it become apparent that the object of his *pothos* is the deceased Euripides.

words, his initial criterion is essentially individual, while the reason for his *katabasis* seems to be no more than an hedonist's pursuance of his own pleasure. As he confesses, so great is his admiration of Euripides that he is 'going mad' (*mainomai*) about his verse (103).

Towards the end of the play, in lines 1467–8, Dionysus is forced by Pluto to decide (1467 κρίνοις ἄν) and announces his judgement as the choice of the will of his *psyche*:

αὕτη σφῶν κρίσις γενήσεται·
αἱρήσομαι γὰρ ὅνπερ ἡ ψυχὴ θέλει.

This will be my decision between you:
I mean, I will choose him whom my soul desires.

In Dover's (1993: 19) interpretation of the lines (and the agon as a whole), this declaration

is in effect one more admission of inability to decide; the ego of Dionysos puts the responsibility on to his 'soul', committing himself to following its guidance, not just heightening the suspense which he has created in us, but himself sharing it.

And he continues (ibid.: 20):

Dionysos follows what we would call 'the promptings of his heart'; an arbitrary, intuitive judgement, divorced from rational assessment of the poets' answers to the questions he has just put to them. Some sixty lines from the end of the play, it displays a striking identity of concept, despite the reversal of direction, with what he said fifty lines from the start: 'a desire struck [his] heart' (53 f.) and sent him off to the underworld. Now that he has heard Euripides and Aeschylus together, his ψυχή prefers Aeschylus.

What I hope to show in this part of the book (Chs. 5–9) is the simplicity as well as the inadequacy of such a reading. Dionysus may well be following 'the promptings of his heart', but such 'promptings', I will argue, do not amount to an 'arbitrary, intuitive judgement'. For, by the time he pronounces his decision, Dionysus' soul has fused and merged with the 'soul' of the *polis*, and *this* is the primary condition which sets his predilection in contrast to the earlier stages of the play. To put it in another way, by the time the agon draws to its end, Dionysus' initial egocentric attitude has been thoroughly abandoned. In a late restatement of the reason for his *katabasis* he ponders:

φέρε, πύθεσθέ μου ταδί.
ἐγὼ κατῆλθον ἐπὶ ποιητήν. τοῦ χάριν;
ἵν' ἡ πόλις σωθεῖσα τοὺς χοροὺς ἄγῃ

Come, then, learn from me this much:
I came down here to find a poet. For what reason?
so that the *polis* may be saved and may (continue to)
lead its choruses.

$$(1417-19)^4$$

A poet is now viewed as inextricably bound up with his socio-political milieu, that is, as having such a formative power over his environment as to be able to save his city through his art. The *polis* will be saved through the medium of *poiesis* and, in its turn, will both display and ensure its health and its cohesion in the 'leading' of its choruses: τοὺς χοροὺς ἄγῃ. Besides, it cannot be emphasized too strongly that the word 'choruses' (χορούς) has twofold implications, designating both the professional chorus of citizens/actors performing in a theatre's *orchestra* in the course of a dramatic festival and the performers of a cultic dance-song in honour of a god (cf. Segal 1961: 224–5).[5]

In Dionysus' modified perspective, therefore, poetry is deemed worthy of undertaking the preservation of a *polis*' community in its politico-religious identity.[6] And it is precisely this newly acquired Dionysiac perspective which lies at the furthest possible extreme from individualistic vision, as in the Greek experience participation in the ordered performance of choral dance-songs 'is both a principal means of education[7] and the medium through which mortals can relate to the gods and affirm and share with each other the values of their society' (Bacon 1995: 14).[8] In other words, the Aristophanic Dionysus' concern with the *polis*' sustained 'leading of its choruses' is the best expression of his community-oriented interest in the preservation of a social mechanism which safeguards the transmission of communal values and the body politic's collective memory.[9]

---

[4] This is essentially the line taken by Bierl (1991) who, in his very brief discussion of the play, interprets Dionysus' adventure as a quest for his own 'political' self; see esp. (1991: 42): 'Vor seiner Identitätsfindung handelte er dabei freilich aus rein individuellen ästhetischen Motiven. Nun, nachdem er sich der politischen Dimension seines Festes bewußt geworden ist, definiert er den Zweck seines Planes neu . . . (*ran.* 1419)'.

[5] In the experience of the classical Athenian *theatai* choral performances are not only part of dramatic productions but also constitute civic spectacles in their own right, both during the Great Dionysia itself (tribal competitions of dithyrambic choruses) and at other moments of the *polis*' festival calendar, as e.g. at the Great Panathenaea. In this respect, then, Dionysus' wish for the Athenian *polis* to 'lead its choruses' should be understood as having the widest possible plane of reference.

[6] Cf. Segal (1961: 224) and Bacon (1995: 19).

[7] See Plato's memorable formulation in *Leg.* 654b Οὐκοῦν ὁ μὲν ἀπαίδευτος ἀχόρευτος ἡμῖν ἔσται, τὸν δὲ πεπαιδευμένον ἱκανῶς κεχορευκότα θετέον;

[8] See primarily Pl. *Leg.* 654a (quoted below, n. 43).

[9] See, most importantly, Calame's monumental work (1977).

As can be seen in lines 1420–1, the criterion for Dionysus' selection is reformulated accordingly, as the divine arbiter declares:

ὁπότερος οὖν ἂν τῇ πόλει παραινέσειν
μέλλῃ τι χρηστόν,[10] τοῦτον ἄξειν μοι δοκῶ.

I think, then, I shall take back with me whichever of you
will give a good piece of advice to the City.

The notion of 'fertility' is not explicitly articulated any more, and yet it has clearly undergone a re-evaluation, since artistic productivity is now understood as the poet's aptitude for rendering a service, proving himself useful to his *polis*. In fact, this *polis*-orientated criterion is reiterated twice after Dionysus' selection, both by the Chorus (1487) and by Pluto himself, as he bids farewell to the ascending poet:

Go on, then, Aeschylus, rejoice[11] and may you fare well!
Save our City (σῷζε πόλιν τὴν ἡμετέραν)
with your noble thoughts, and educate
the foolish . . .   (1500–3)

The decisive factor, then, which determines the selection of the city's saviour is the conception and the notion of the *polis*, as this develops gradually throughout the play's course and culminates in Aeschylus' self-portrayal in the agon. In other words, the dimension projected in lines 1419–21 is not 'Aristophanes's rather perfunctory way of converting D.'s original literary and personal motive into a political one', as Stanford (1963: ad 1419) thought, but represents a carefully worked out progress. Because (as we shall see in detail in Chapters 7–8), the development of the contest makes it increasingly obvious that it is the figure of Aeschylus, as the comedy shapes it, who stands for the impulse inspiring the civic cohesiveness of Athens, while Euripides is interested in the inner, private, *oikos* world, showing the art of 'managing the affairs of a household in a more efficient way than before' (976–7). In contrast to Euripides' 'house-centred' images and the domestic orientation of his poetry's impact (see esp. 980–98), Aeschylus' poetry can be defined as '*polis*-centred', uniting his fellow-citizens in the desire to 'be always victorious against the enemies' (νικᾶν ἀεὶ τοὺς ἀντιπάλους) (1027). More importantly still, it is the comically shaped portrait of Aeschylus, rather than the *dramatis persona* of Euripides, which is consistent with aspects of the Athenian *polis*' collective ideology and democratic practice.

[10] On *chrestos* see 8.2(a).
[11] For the meaning of 'rejoice' in *chaire* see now Sourvinou-Inwood (1995: 210).

Thus, in the nearly defeated Athens of 405 BC, Aeschylus' emotional glorification of 'his' men, citizens of a bygone and better era, resembles the *polis'* nostalgic idealization of its ancestral *aretai*, an attitude which permeates fifth- and fourth-century Athenian texts, as, for example, Aeschines' indictment against Ctesiphon suggests:

If any one should ask you whether our city seems to you more glorious in our own time or in the time of our fathers, you would all agree, in the time of our fathers. And were there better men then than now? Then, eminent men; but now, far inferior.   (Aeschin. 3. 178)

More specifically still, considering the Aeschylean exaltation of the *Marathonomachai* to an almost superhuman status (see 8.5), it is difficult not to discern in it the notions and the tropes traditionally employed in the construction of that peculiarly Athenian 'genre', where the conceptual frontiers between reality and fantasy collapse and blur, that is, the civic funeral oration.[12] Aeschylus' sentimental 'heroization' of his men (e.g. 1013–17; cf. 8.5) is a poetic analogue of the Athenian city's heroization of its war dead (Loraux 1986: 39–42; Thomas 1989: 216)[13] through a public funeral service, in accordance with the *polis'* 'ancestral law' (Thuc. 2. 34. 1), and a specially commissioned *epitaphios logos*, adorning their sacrifice and highlighting their achievement. Furthermore, Aeschylus' privileging of the community and the collective values over the individual and the values of the *oikos* is entirely consistent with the *polis'* supreme ideal of subordinating private interest to the demands of the common good, a lofty principle reaching its noblest expression in texts such as Pericles' *Epitaphios*:

For in my judgment a state confers a greater benefit upon its private citizens when as a whole commonwealth it is successful (ξύμπασαν ὀρθουμένην), than when it prospers as regards the individual but fails as a community (καθ' ἕκαστον τῶν πολιτῶν εὐπραγοῦσαν, ἀθρόαν δὲ σφαλλομένην). For even though a man flourishes in his own private affairs, yet if his country goes to ruin he perishes with her all the same; but if he is in evil fortune and his country in good fortune, he is far more likely to come through safely.   (Thuc. 2. 60. 2–3)

or fourth-century oratory:

But it is not the diction of an orator, Aeschines, or the vigour of his voice that has any value: it is supporting the policy of the people, and having the

---

[12] See Loraux (1986: esp. ch. 6); cf. Thomas (1989: 196–237).

[13] On the notion of the 'heroization' of the dead with respect to funerary practice and iconography see Shapiro's (1991: 630) very apt remarks: 'By "heroization" I do not mean that the dead are turned into objects of cult or chthonic demi-gods . . . but rather that they are likened to the heroes whose arete was celebrated in the Homeric poems.'

same friends and the same enemies as your country (ἀλλὰ τὸ ταὐτὰ προαιρεῖσθαι τοῖς πολλοῖς καὶ τὸ τοὺς αὐτοὺς μισεῖν καὶ φιλεῖν οὕσπερ ἂν ἡ πατρίς). With such a disposition, a man's speeches will always be patriotic. . . . My purposes are my countrymen's purposes; I have no peculiar or personal end to serve (ταὐτὰ γὰρ συμφέρονθ᾽ εἱλόμην τουτοισί, καὶ οὐδὲν ἐξαίρετον οὐδ᾽ ἴδιον πεποίημαι). (Dem. 18. 280–1)

In sum, Aeschylus' civically oriented men tend rather to conform to the famous character-portrait of the Athenians, as sketched in the Corinthians' speech to the Spartan Assembly just before the out-break of the Peloponnesian war:

Moreover, they use their bodies in the service of their country (ὑπὲρ τῆς πόλεως) as though they were the bodies of quite other men (ἀλλοτριωτάτοις), but their minds as though they were wholly their own, so as to accomplish anything on her behalf. (Thuc. 1. 70. 6)

Lastly, while Euripides promotes a centrifugal, disconcerting religious individualism,[14] Aeschylus poses as a truly Eleusinian poet (see Ch. 6), representing and perpetuating the religious traditions of the *polis*. In antithesis to his antagonist's private gods (890–1), Aeschylus' mind has been 'nourished' (886) by the solemn figure of Demeter, and he therefore asks to be worthy of her mystic rites (887 εἶναί με τῶν σῶν ἄξιον μυστηρίων).

To conclude then, the contest has gradually revealed to the eyes of Dionysus, the judge, the communal setting of the dramatic festival of Athens, that is, the complex nexus of interrelation operating between the author, his work, dramatized on the stage, and the audience/citizen body to which the poetic enunciation is addressed. Encapsulated in the divine arbiter's final preference for Aeschylus is, I believe, this gradual revelation, achieved by Dionysus himself, but also shared by the theatrical spectators. Correspondingly, it is *now and only now* that Dionysus truly becomes the patron of the civic festivals of Athens (cf. Ch. 9), and this is, in my view, the most significant respect in which the agon illustrates the divine initiand's final integration into Athens.

5.2. *Foreshadowing and Anticipation*

Placed within the wider perspective of the play in its entirety, Dionysus' realization of dramatic poetry's communal function even proves to have been carefully foreshadowed in the comedy's earlier parts.

One of the most memorable choral moments in the *Frogs* is the

---

[14] See esp. his total rejection of the traditional gods in 889–94.

opening of the prorrhesis, uttered by the Chorus of the Eleusinian Initiates:

εὐφημεῖν χρὴ κἀξίστασθαι τοῖς ἡμετέροισι χοροῖσιν,
ὅστις ἄπειρος τοιῶνδε λόγων ἢ γνώμην μὴ καθαρεύει,
ἢ γενναίων ὄργια Μουσῶν μήτ᾽ εἶδεν μήτ᾽ ἐχόρευσεν,
μηδὲ Κρατίνου τοῦ ταυροφάγου γλώττης Βακχεῖ᾽ ἐτελέσθη

Let us all abstain from inauspicious words and let these stand aside
    from our choral dances—
whoever is ignorant of such utterances as this or does not have purity
    of thought,
or has neither seen nor danced the secret rites of the noble Muses
nor been initiated in the Bacchic mysteries of the tongue of Cratinus,
    the bull-devouring poet.

(354–7)

It is clear that the word *choroisin*, choral dances, is exploited by the Leader of the Eleusinian Initiates for its inherent ambiguity, which sets the tone for the intermingling of civic and cultic images throughout this passage (354–71).[15] The Aristophanic audience witnesses a civic/Dionysiac chorus performing in the civic/cultic space of the Lenaea festival in the *dramatis persona* of a cultic/ Eleusinian chorus. This double voice of the play's Chorus can be heard most clearly in lines 385a–93, where the ritual performers ask the divine foundress of their rites for civic protection and civic victory, but it also resounds throughout the parodos, where the cultic identity of the dancers enables them to function as a link between the gods invoked (Soteira, Demeter, Iacchus) and the civic community to which they belong;[16] it reverberates once again in the play's parabasis, where the Chorus is both a 'sacred band of dancers' (τὸν ἱερὸν χορόν) (686), belonging to the cult of Demeter, and a truly comic chorus undertaking the task—sanctified by Old Comedy's conventions—of offering good advice (χρηστά . . . | ξυμπαραινεῖν) and teaching (διδάσκειν) to the *polis* (686–7).

However, such an interweaving of choral identity and ritual role anticipates in many ways the grounds on which the selection of the city's saviour will be made: unusual combinations, such as the 'secret rites' (*orgia*) of the Muses (356),[17] initiation into the 'Bacchic

---

[15] Dover (1993: 239) acknowledges that 'Many ingredients in this blend are ambivalent, open to interpretation as referring either to the procession of initiates which is being enacted or to the comic chorus which is enacting it', but offers virtually no interpretation of the ambiguity *per se*.

[16] Cf. Calame (1995: 147) on the similar function of tragic choruses performing 'the role of intermediary between the *polis* and the gods invoked.'

[17] For the mystic connotations of *orgia* see e.g. Richardson (1974: ad Hom. *h. Dem.* 273); Burkert (1987a: 9, with nn. 43–4); cf. the clearly cultic use of the word by the Chorus in *Frogs* 385a–b.

mysteries of the tongue' (γλώττης Βακχεῖ')[18] of Cratinus, the 'bull-eating' poet (357),[19] as well as the 'Dionysiac ancestral rites' (ἐν ταῖς πατρίοις τελεταῖς ταῖς τοῦ Διονύσου) (368), with reference to the dramatic festivals of Athens,[20] reveal that the whole pageant of theatrical performances is conceived as inherently intertwined with mystic imagery. Moreover, it would seem that the *polis*' dramatic spectacle, mystically dressed up, is closely connected in its turn with the political, or rather civic, language of the prorrhesis: the uninitiated in the 'mysteries' of poetry (356) together with the politicians who avenge themselves on dramatists participating in the stage-*teletai* (367–8) are classed in the same rank as those who are uninitiated into the real Mysteries of Eleusis (355 ὅστις ἄπειρος τοιῶνδε λόγων) or those who endanger or betray or offend the *polis* with their actions (359–66). In other words, the Eleusinian Chorus's proclamation is not merely the theatrical remoulding of a traditional ritual utterance, the religious request for good-omened silence (*euphemia*); more importantly still, its wide-ranging proscriptions amount to the charting of an ideal citizen body, as exclusion from choral performances is a sign of not belonging to the community which 'stages' them.[21]

The primary impression, then, communicated through the Chorus's position, coincides with the quintessence of Dionysus' initiatory learning accomplished in the course of the agon, namely, that dramatic poetry is an inherent part of civic consciousness, and thus inextricably interwoven with the *polis*' religious and political discourse. And the Chorus return to poetry's communal nature towards the play's end, when they highlight the public importance of their own stage-activity, that is, singing and dancing to the accompaniment of instruments. In a privileged moment of theatrical self-referentiality,[22] they draw attention to the primacy of *mousike* as a lesson to be gained from Aeschylus' victory: 'it is therefore a mark of elegance (χαρίεν οὖν) not to sit together with Socrates and chat, having cast away *mousiken* . . .' (1491–3).[23] Now, it is, I

---

[18] For the specifically Dionysiac flavour of Bacchic terminology in the 5th cent. BC see S. G. Cole (1980); cf. Schlesier (1993: 93–4 with notes).

[19] *Taurophagos* is one of the cultic epithets of Dionysus; cf. Soph. fr. 668 Radt Διονύσου τοῦ ταυροφάγου. For the significance of Eleusinian-Dionysiac attributes in the presentation of Cratinus cf. Bierl (1991: 38 with n. 47).

[20] For the entire word-family of *telein/telete*, etc. as an integral part of mystic terminology throughout Greek antiquity see e.g. Burkert (1987a: 9–11 with notes).

[21] See Bacon's (1995: 19) fine remarks.

[22] On choral self-referentiality see primarily Henrichs (1995) and P. J. Wilson and Taplin (1993).

[23] Cf. *Clouds* 972 τὰς Μούσας ἀφανίζων (on experimenting with musical innovations). In a markedly self-referential choral ode from Euripides' *Heracles* see the tragic chorus's

think, misleadingly restrictive to translate *mousike* here, as Dover (1993: 21) does, merely as 'poetry'. Uttered by the Chorus, a civic community's most treasured medium for the transmission of its hallowed 'song culture' (Herington 1985: esp. 3–5), *mousike* should be invested with a richer range of semantic possibilities, and understood as that special co-ordination of words, melody, and dance which lie in the province of the skilled poet.[24] Besides, this almost programmatic weight placed on *mousike* forms a powerful and suggestive link with the major political worries expressed in the course of the agon. For, as Wilson and Taplin (1993: 169) have strongly emphasized, a 'deep-seated relation . . . was felt to exist between the modes of music and the fundamental conventions governing social and political life in ancient Greece.' In Plato's view, concurring with that of the famous fifth-century musical theorist and friend of Pericles, Damon,

'People should beware of change to new forms of music, for they are risking change in the whole (ὡς ἐν ὅλῳ κινδυνεύοντα) [i.e. constitution and fabric of the state]. Styles of music are nowhere altered without change in the greatest laws of the city (ἄνευ πολιτικῶν νόμων τῶν μεγίστων): so Damon says, and I concur . . . It seems then', I said, 'that it is here, in music, that the guardians must build their guard-house.'

(Pl. *Rep.* 424c–d; tr. Barker 1984: 140).

The agon of the *Frogs* is a brilliant illustration of such interdependence between the registers of *mousike* and politics, for Euripides' disorderly fusions of gender roles, social hierarchies, and classes (see 7.2–4), strongly condemned in the agon as subversive of the socio-political order, seem to go hand in hand with his musical innovations, subversive of the musical order. Against community's demand for the respect of borderlines between different types of music (Pl. *Leg.* 700a–e), Euripides is accused of having created an offensive musical mélange:

But he picks up his songs from any odd source—prostitutes' songs,
Meletus' drinking-songs, Carian pipe-tunes,
dirges, dances . . .

(1301–3)

---

abhorrence of a life deprived of *mousike*: μὴ ζῴην μετ' ἀμουσίας, | αἰεὶ δ' ἐν στεφάνοισιν εἴην (676–7).

[24] A further level of self-referentiality can be detected in the Chorus's 'χαρίεν', for Plato (*Leg.* 654a) makes an etymological pun on *choros* and *chara*: χορούς τε ὠνομακέναι παρὰ τὸ τῆς χαρᾶς ἔμφυτον ὄνομα. Moreover, the Chorus's concern with aesthetic pleasure (Dover 1993: 20–1) may take us back to Dionysus' reaction at the spectacle of Aeschylean drama: ἐγὼ δ' ἔχαιρον τῇ σιωπῇ (916); cf. also 1028–9 (involving the Chorus too) ἐχάρην γοῦν, ἡνίκ' †ἤκουσα περὶ† Δαρείου τεθνεῶτος, | ὁ χορὸς δ' εὐθὺς τὼ χεῖρ' ὡδὶ συγκρούσας εἶπεν "ἰαυοῖ".

This same interpenetration of the musical and political levels informs other pivotal moments of this comedy's discourse, such as the parabasis, where the Chorus uttered their famous plea for the restoration to full political rights of those citizens who had been 'reared in wrestling-schools and choruses and *mousike*' (729)— *mousike* standing here for the refined, upper-class intellectual education in which instrumental music always played a substantial part.

To sum up. Key 'moments' of the play manifestly converge, and their convergence helps us to make sense of Dionysus' choice. Moreover, in the play's second part it is precisely the judgement of Dionysus, in his new and elevated status, which resumes and reunites some of the cardinal thematic units interspersed up to that moment at various points of the comic *logos*.

Thus, the individualistic dimension of the Euripidean world that Dionysus rejects has already been touched upon in the prorrhesis, when the Chorus Leader castigated the most important exemplifications of private gain (360) and ambition (359–65). The Euripidean 'monkeys of politicians', whose rhetoric 'beguiles the *demos*' (1085–6), have already made their appearance in the name of those demagogues who are derided by the Mystai in a passage which most probably reflects the sceptic practice of the Eleusinian *gephyrismoi* (416–30; see above 2.12(c)). Concern about the disintegration of ethics and deterioration of *paideia*, faults which are blamed on Euripides in the agon (see 8.2(a)), has already been a major issue in the parabasis (esp. 718–33). Moreover, there is Aeschylus' voice of protest against the insufficient physical training of the 'Euripidean' men. As the elder dramatist complains,

> no one has now the strength to run with a torch any more,
> because of lack of exercise.   (1087–8)

His distress is instantly shared by Dionysus, who comically elaborates on it:

> By Zeus, certainly not, so that I laughed myself dry
> at the Panathenaea, when some slow fellow, pallid, fat,
> was running on, head down, puffing and panting, far behind the rest.
> Then the people of the Cerameicus at the gates
> slapped him at the belly, ribs, flanks, buttocks,
> while he, being slapped with the flat of their hands,
> breaking wind a little and blowing his torch to keep it alight,
> tried to get away from them.[25]
>
> (1089–98)

[25] My translation here is based on Stanford (1963: ad loc.).

Dionysus' comic alliance with Aeschylus has already been foreshadowed in the play's prologue, where the god had forcefully (νὴ
τοὺς θεούς) remarked that to the catalogue of sinners tortured in
Hades should be added 'whoever learnt Cinesias' pyrrhic dance'
(152–3). Dionysus' lament for the corruption of *pyrrhiche*, an Attic
form of armed dance,[26] anticipates his comically enunciated reaction
at the miserable sight of the Panathenaic torch-race (1089 ff.), for
both events were closely linked within the ambience of this same
festival as two impressive ways of communicating to citizens and
visitors alike the power and splendour of the 'city of Athena'.
Furthermore, sharing, as they did, the same liminal space 'in
between' the 'sacred'[27] and the 'secular', both the *lampadephoria* and
the *pyrrhiche* were not simply spectacular displays of physical
endurance, discipline, and skill but, most importantly, constituted
an integral part of the city's 'rhetoric' of self-assertion and self-
definition as a healthy and dynamic politico-religious unit. The
pyrrhic dance, especially, was taken to be a splendid preparation for
battle (see e.g. Athen. 629c)—alongside the substantial evidence for
its 'warlike' (πολεμικήν) (Pl. *Leg.* 815a) nature[28] an anecdotal tale has
it that the tragic poet Phrynichus was elected general by the
Athenians because of his breathtaking performance in some
tragedy's chorus of pyrrhic dancers (Ael. *VH* 3. 8. 7–8 ἐπεὶ τοῖς
πυρριχισταῖς ἔν τινι τραγῳδίᾳ ἐπιτήδεια μέλη καὶ πολεμικὰ ἐξεπόνησεν).[29]
In the perspective of the classical Athenian audience, then, the
pyrrhic dance reflects some of the essential civic values whose
deterioration is deplored in the contest of the *Frogs*: miming the
warrior's defensive and offensive movements (see esp. Pl. *Leg.*
815a), it inculcates upon men a warlike spirit (see e.g. Athen. 631a),

---

[26] See Scarpi (1979); for its representations in Attic iconography see Poursat (1968:
566–83). Our sources cannot provide secure information as to what exactly Cinesias' *pyrrhiche*
was. Nevertheless, as Cinesias appears to have been notorious for the qualitative deflation of
some other *technai* too (see e.g. Plut. *Mor.* 348b ἀργαλέος ἔοικε ποιητὴς γεγονέναι διθυράμβων;
schol. *Frogs* 153 μελοποιὸς κάκιστος), the particular kind of *pyrrhiche* that his name came to be
associated with must have been a strikingly innovative performance, in all probability viewed
as a perversion of the dance's military and manly nature. For a full note on Cinesias and his
pyrrhiche see Sommerstein (1996) on line 153.
[27] The Athenian pyrrhic dance is performed in honour of Athena, who is supposed to have
been the first to teach it (*Leg.* 796c), and commemorates her battles against the Giants. The
Panathenaic torch-race correspondingly, performed, like all *lampadephoriai*, under the aegis
of the Archon Basileus ([Arist.] *Ath. Pol.* 57. 1), was a ritual transfer of fire from the Academy
to the Acropolis for the sacrifice to Athena; for other festivals featuring a torch-race among
their ritual activities see Dover (1993: ad 131).
[28] On the *pyrrhiche* as part of military training see Wheeler (1982); Borthwick (1970b: 320
with n. 2); Ridley (1979: 545–7).
[29] See further ibid., lines 9–13 ὥστε παραχρῆμα αὐτὸν εἵλοντο στρατηγεῖν, πιστεύσαντες ὅτι
τῶν πολεμικῶν ἔργων ἡγήσεται καλῶς καὶ ἐς δέον, ὅπου μὴ ἀπάδοντα τοῖς ἐνόπλοις ἀνδράσιν
εἰργάσατο τὰ ἐν τῷ δράματι μέλη τε καὶ ποιήματα (the incident can be dated *c.*460 BC).

and hence it ultimately performs a social function closely parallel to
that of Aeschylus' drama, warlike and 'full of Ares' (1021). Besides,
the Chorus's instigation to themselves to proceed in a virile, courageous manner (372 χώρει νυν πᾶς ἀνδρείως) and in martial tone (377
ἀλλ' ἔμβα . . .)[30] not only foreshadows the importance of manly, fighting spirit in the agon, but also, in a self-reflexive way, calls attention
to the fact that 'The chorus was organized in a strict hierarchy on
the analogy of a hoplite battle line' (Csapo and Slater 1995: 353) and
that a clear homology existed between choral movements on the
orchestra and military manœuvres executed by the hoplites in the
phalanx.[31] For, as Socrates is reported to have said, 'those who
honour the gods most beautifully in choruses are best in war'
(Athen. 628f). Both in the prologue as well as in the agon, then,
Dionysus proves himself concerned, even if in a distinctively comic
way, with the decline of traditions largely instrumental in preserving the *polis* in its religious and political identity. The powerful
interplay of the registers of political and ritual performance which is
all-pervasive in the *Frogs* culminates in the comedy's closing scene.
For there is a strong sense in which Aeschylus' victorious return to
Athens for the benefit of the entire *polis* fuses mystic (see Ch. 2)
with civic/ceremonial imagery, as it resembles, *inter alia*, the
triumphant athlete's processional re-entry to his city[32]—with the
expectation that his talismanic powers will be imparted to his
fellow-citizens and the entire community within which he has been
reared (Kurke 1993).

Finally, if among the reasons for Dionysus' rejection of Euripides
is the lack of an acceptable religious centre both in his personal con-
victions as well as in the stage-world that he creates, such an absence
has already been castigated, albeit implicitly, at the beginning of
the play. On the 'winning' side of the Underworld are only the

---

[30] See Haldane (1964: 208) and Sommerstein (1996: ad 372–82). In modern Greek,
embaterion has the sole meaning of song or rhythm for a military march. For anapaests and
military marching see West (1982b: 53–4).

[31] See Csapo and Slater (1995: 353 ff. (with sources)); Winkler (1990b: esp. 55–6). Not
taking account of this cultural perspective Haldane (1964: 208) surmises that 'The humour of
the ode lies in the incongruity between the portrayal of the *mystae* marching to the fields of
the blessed and its mock-military style.'

[32] The contest is repeatedly designated as an agon (785, 873, 882/3), which is, of course, the
'technical term' for this part of a play; simultaneously, however, the broader semantic field of
ἀγών includes the agonistic background of an athletic contest, and such nuances are activated
through the athletic metaphors and imagery occasionally employed to describe the play's
poetic duel; see e.g. 878 (στρεβλοῖσι παλαίσμασιν ἀντιλογοῦντες), 993b ff., etc. One might also
wish to compare the Chorus's *makarismos* of Aeschylus and the example he provides (1482 ff.
μακάριός γ' ἀνήρ . . .) to the traditional *makarismos* of the athletic victor, both after his
victorious *ponos* and during his triumphant return; cf. e.g. Soph. *El.* 692–3 τούτων ἐνεγκὼν
πάντα τἀπινίκια | ὠλβίζετ' . . . (on Orestes' alleged victory at Delphi), and see W. J. Slater
(1984: 248).

memyemenoi (158), rewarded for the piety which they displayed in their earthly life (454–9; cf. 154–8). While the privileged may be entitled to the precious assistance of Demeter (385a–6) and the land in its entirety may rely on the unfailing protection of its patron deity (377–82),[33] the impious who involve themselves in sacrilegious actions (366) should be banned from the *polis'* religious rites (370). Let us consider, in particular, line 366: 'who shits on the food-offerings made to Hecate (κατατιλᾷ τῶν Ἑκαταίων),[34] while singing in accompaniment to dithyrambic choruses'. For, although the exact frame of reference of the Initiates' accusation is unknown,[35] the offence in question constitutes an 'actionable' (Burkert 1985: 274) form of *asebeia*, and as such it can be linked with Aeschylus' repre-hension of Euripides on the grounds that his heroines give birth in temples (1080; see 7.3). Moreover, if the scholiast is right in attribut-ing the sacrilegious deed to Cinesias,[36] notorious for his disdain and ridicule of gods,[37] the prorrhesis can be seen to anticipate the agon in thrusting outside the realms of the community the artist who is *asebes*.

To end this section, I would like to draw attention to one remain-ing factor which could, I think, facilitate an Aristophanic audience's early prediction of Dionysus' decision.

Even before the start of the agon, when Pluto's slave announces that Tragedy will be weighed in the balance (797), Xanthias, in astonishment, exclaims: 'How's that? Are they going to treat Tragedy like a sacrificial lamb?' (τί δέ; μειαγωγήσουσι τὴν τραγῳδίαν;) (798), the μεῖον being, as the scholiast explains, the *hiereion*, the sacrificial offering that a father would offer on the third day of the Apaturia festival, when his son would be first presented to the phratry.[38] Nevertheless, if Tragedy is envisaged as a sacrificial lamb to be led to the altar (Svenbro 1984: 220–1; cf. 3.3), the dramatist cast in the role of a sacrificial victim is Aeschylus.

In line 804 we hear that 'at any rate, he [i.e. Aeschylus] stooped down and looked angrily like a bull' (ἔβλεψε γοῦν ταυρηδὸν ἐγκύψας κάτω), the animal's lowering of its head being not only part of the

---

[33] For Σώτειρα (378) as Athena see Haldane (1964); Sommerstein (1996: ad loc.).

[34] For the possible interpretations of *Hekataia* see Sommerstein (1996: ad loc.).

[35] See the very balanced note of Sommerstein (1996: ad loc.).

[36] The allegation may refer to a fictitious action staged in his dramas (see schol. ad 366 εἰσήνεγκεν ἐν δράματι τὴν Ἑκάτην καὶ κατετίλησεν αὐτῆς) or even to a real-life incident, as Cinesias seems to have been notoriously seized by fits of diarrhoea (see Sommerstein 1996: ad 153 and 366).

[37] See Athen. 551e; cf. ibid. 551f–2b.

[38] See schol. ad loc. μειαγωγὸς δὲ ἐλέγετο ὁ προάγων τὸ ἱερεῖον (ὅτι μεῖον τὸ ἱερεῖον ἔλεγον, τὸ παριστάμενον ὑπὲρ τῶν εἰς τοὺς φράτορας εἰσφερομένων . . .). On the Apaturia festival and initiation see S. G. Cole (1984*b*).

preliminaries of ritualized killing (Burkert 1983: 4)[39] but, more importantly still, a prominent feature in dramatic remouldings of perverted sacrificial ritual; in Euripides' *Electra*, for example, the Messenger remembers how Aegisthus bends over the altar (τοῦ δὲ νεύοντος κάτω) at the moment of his 'sacrificial' killing by Orestes (Eur. *El.* 839–41). In 828 the Chorus refers to Euripides' tongue as 'distributing' Aeschylus' words (ῥήματα δαιομένη), the middle *daiomai* being inextricably linked with the distribution of sacrificial meat (*krea*) at a banquet (*dais*),[40] while Aeschylus' resemblance to a sacrificial bull resurfaces in 924, where *boeia*, 'oxhide,' is the adjective which qualifies his words. Finally, in 1262 Euripides threatens that he will 'cut short' (ξυντεμῶ) his antagonist's *mele*, meaning, of course, his lyric parts, his choral songs: 'I'm going to cut down all his lyrics to a single measure' (tr. Sommerstein 1996). *Mele*, however, can also mean limbs, parts of the body, and hence belongs to the semantic field of sacrificial imagery, especially in the expression κατὰ μέλη, that is, limb by limb, equivalent to μελεϊστί. Euripides, then, is prepared to attack Aeschylus 'like a bad sacrificial agent' (Svenbro 1984: 221), as he proposes to cut down the limbs themselves, instead of allowing the knife to 'follow the natural articulations of the body' (ibid.). Now, admittedly, these subtle indications, scattered, as they are, about the text, can easily be lost on the spectator in the flow of the theatrical event. Nevertheless, if we are hoping to achieve not *one* authentic or historical reconstruction of *the* meaning of the play, but, on the contrary, to recreate the entire spectrum of *possible*, that is to say, justifiable within a given culture, reconstructions (cf. Introd., Sect. 2), this nexus of sacrificial imagery in the agon of the *Frogs* cannot be brushed aside. And, as sacrifice is inherently intertwined with the notion of initiatory death (2.3), 'thinking *with*' members of a classical Athenian audience we can only contemplate that *he who dies* has paved the way to his rebirth (2.14). To put this in another way, the casting of Aeschylus as a sacrificial victim in the agon of the *Frogs* functions in its own right as an indication that it is *he*, instead of his opponent, who will ultimately be reborn.

5.3. *Dionysus' 'Dionysiac' Arbitration*

Immediately before the start of the contest, the Aristophanic audience witnesses a conversation between Xanthias and one of Pluto's slaves during which it transpires that a great dispute has

---

[39] Svenbro (1984: 220) notes the use of *hypokyptein* in sacrificial inscriptions.

[40] See Svenbro (1984: 221), who notes that the scholiasts (ad *Frogs* 826) explain δαιομένη with verbs which belong to the sacrificial vocabulary *par excellence*: διαμερίζουσα, διαιροῦσα, κατατέμνουσα.

broken out in Hades between Euripides and Aeschylus over the prestigious throne of tragic *techne*. The support offered to Euripides by throngs of villainous deceased (771–81) has turned the individual conflict into a 'most impressive civil strife' (760 στάσις πολλὴ πάνυ), which Pluto is now prepared to settle by a contest, a trial of artistic quality between the two contenders (785–6). Due to the shortage of suitably qualified arbiters (806), judgement is entrusted to Dionysus (810–11), 'well versed in the tragic art' (811), who happens to be visiting the area of unrest, while at the play's end it is precisely this mediation of the god, the casual *xenos* (cf. Ch. 3) in the Underworld community, which makes possible the restoration of *homonoia* in its heavily disturbed ranks. Moreover, it is precisely the verdict of Dionysus which, by deeming Aeschylus as worthy of resurrection, offers to the *real* City of the Athenian viewers' *real* world the possibility of collective education (1502–3) and the hope of salvation (1501 σῷζε πόλιν τὴν ἡμετέραν). But, as we have already seen in Chapter 3, deeply ingrained in the mythological clusters and cults of various places in the Greek world is the pattern of Dionysus coming into a city as a *xenos* from outside, his advent putting an end to internal civil strife (Seaford 1994a: 251–7).[41] In the remainder of this chapter, then, I would like to challenge Dover's (1993: 41) view that Dionysus' role as an arbiter in the contest 'has no specifically Dionysiac associations'. For many an aspect of Dionysus' arbitrative role in the agon of the *Frogs* could have invited fifth-century audiences to link his stage-performance with attributes and functions of his 'real' counterpart of myth and cult.

In Chapter 3 we discussed at length the possibility that the agon could be viewed metaphorically as an intellectual banquet, and that Dionysus, correspondingly, could be envisaged in his mythical role as a *symposiarchos*, an *archon* of the drinking party. But more significantly still, Dionysus' mediatory presence is made inherently 'Dionysiac' by the thematic orchestration of the literary contest itself. As we shall see in detail in 8.2, the debate in the agon clusters around some firmly seated social polarities, most prominently the oppositions between *polis/oikos*, and male/female. However, the work of scholars like Richard Seaford (esp. 1994a) has shed ample light not only on Dionysus' deep involvement in the *creation* of such polarities but also on the ways in which Dionysiac cult helps the civic/ritual community to span and to *transcend* them.

On the mythical level, by inspiring the destruction of the royal household for the benefit of the entire *polis*, Dionysus works

---

[41] See e.g. Diod. 3. 64. 7 καὶ τὸ σύνολον συλλύοντα τὰ νείκη τῶν ἐθνῶν καὶ πόλεων ἀντὶ τῶν στάσεων καὶ τῶν πολέμων ὁμόνοιαν καὶ πολλὴν εἰρήνην κατασκευάζειν.

towards the bridging of the *oikos*/city antinomy, while on the ritual register, such reconciliation often results in the foundation of a civic cult. The same Dionysus, correspondingly, who causes male loss of control over female kin by driving women away from the *oikos* to the open, dangerous, and savage space of the mountainside, is also the god who helps to transcend the polarity between the genders by assigning to the female an important role in the perpetuation of the body politic's collective well-being: as we have already seen in the Introduction to this book, we hear of maenadic (i.e. female) Dionysiac rituals conducted 'on behalf of' or 'in the sight of' the entire *polis* (Introd., Sect. 1), while at the heart of the classical Athenian calendar itself, at the Anthesteria festival, a sacred band of women called Γεραιραί together with the wife of the Archon Basileus, the Basilinna, performed Dionysiac sacrifices and other secret (ἄρρητα) acts 'for the sake of the *polis*' (ὑπὲρ τῆς πόλεως) ([Dem.] 59.73). Besides, the poets whose dispute the Aristophanic Dionysus is called upon to arbitrate, are tragic poets, and it is the tragic genre *par excellence* which 'takes its themes from within the *household*, and focuses consequently on gender conflict, thereby transcending the division between the male, rational, public sphere and the partially female, emotional sphere of the household' (Seaford 1994*a*: 343). But, more importantly still, I would like to end with Dionysus' essential understanding of Drama as first and foremost a choral performance with transformative powers over its socio-political environment (1418–19). For this privileging of the role of the Chorus not only illustrates very eloquently the indispensability of a body of civic dancers for the staging of Drama,[42] but also nicely befits the god who, jointly with Apollo and the Muses, 'lead[s] our choral dances, bringing us together with songs and dancing'.[43] Finally, in accordance with the self-reflexive nature of this comedy in its entirety, Dionysus' 'choral' awareness links him, the arbiter[44] in a contest of tragic *techne*, with the roots of Drama, that is, with the remote origins of his own, unique, and civic form of cult.

---

[42] *Choron aitein/lambanein* and related expressions (see P. J. Wilson and Taplin 1993: 178 n. 10) are central in the performative vocabulary of classical Athens. Cf. Dionysus' own expression in *Frogs* 94 (on bad poets) ἃ φροῦδα θᾶττον, ἢν μόνον χορὸν λάβῃ.

[43] Pl. *Leg.* 654a ἡμῖν δὲ οὓς εἴπομεν τοὺς θεοὺς συγχορευτὰς δεδόσθαι [sc. Muses, Apollo, Dionysus], τούτους εἶναι καὶ τοὺς δεδωκότας τὴν ἔνρυθμόν τε καὶ ἐναρμόνιον αἴσθησιν μεθ' ἡδονῆς, ᾗ δὴ κινεῖν τε ἡμᾶς καὶ χορηγεῖν ἡμῶν τούτους, ᾠδαῖς τε καὶ ὀρχήσεσιν ἀλλήλοις συνείροντας. For Dionysus invoked to 'take the lead' (Βάκχιος ἄρχοι) in choral dances see most importantly Soph. *Ant.* 152–4; closer to the cultic identity of the *Frogs*' Chorus cf. fr. adesp. 109d [1027d] *PMG*, where Dionysus is invoked as Ἴακχε θρίαμβε, σὺ τῶνδε χοραγέ.

[44] For Dionysus as judge cf. his cult title 'Aisymnetes' in Patrai.

6

Aeschylus: A 'Dionysiac' Poet?

I have suggested in the previous chapter that in the agon of the
Frogs Dionysus' judgement and perspective have been gradually
aligned with the perspective of the City. I would now like to argue
that in the distorting mirror of the comedy's contest it is not
Euripides' *techne* but rather Aeschylus' artistic personality which
displays the most conspicuous affinities with the psychology
familiar to the judge.[1] In the perspective of fifth-century Athenian
theatai familiar with literary matters,[2] Aeschylus' presentation in
the agon of the *Frogs* qualifies Dionysus' final verdict as a distinctively 'Dionysiac' move.

6.1. *Aeschylus,* ekplexis, *and* apate[3]

Euripidean drama demands an audience alert and critical throughout the theatrical performance (cf. Walsh 1984: 89), capable of exercising its mental faculties of 'thinking' (νοεῖν) and 'understanding'
(ξυνιέναι) (957). Among other things, Euripides is proud of having
taught (954 ἐδίδαξα) his fellow citizens

> applications of subtle rules and squarings-off of verses,
> to think, to see, to understand, to twist the hip,[4] to scheme,
> to suspect bad intentions, to consider everything on all possible sides.[5]

> (956–8)

---

[1] It cannot be emphasized too strongly that any quest for *direct* reflections of the historical
Euripides' or Aeschylus' personalities in the agon of the *Frogs* can be seriously misleading.
We shall see in this chapter, for example, that Aeschylus' poetry displays more strikingly
'Dionysiac' features, while, if we were to take into account the real dramatists' theatrical productions, we would find, with Henrichs (1995: 57), that 'Euripides takes advantage of every
conceivable dimension of the god and deserves to rank as the most Dionysiac of the three
tragedians.'

[2] The extent to which the agon reflects 5th-cent. literary criticism is still a matter of dispute. Involvement in the debate would not contribute much to my argument. The only
assumption that I take for granted is the existence of a lively interest in literary discussion in
5th-cent. Athenian society (cf. Lucas 1968: xviii).

[3] A version of this section forms part of Lada (1993).

[4] I follow here Sommerstein's text: στρέφειν ἕδραν; see Sommerstein (1996: ad loc.).

[5] On the whole passage see Dover (1993: 311–12).

Rather than allowing the spectator to abandon his everyday self, forget his actual surroundings and the pageant of the things he comprehends, in order to participate for a while in a different mode of existence, Euripidean art projects onto the stage the known and the familiar,

> introducing household matters, things we use, we are acquainted with,
>
> (οἰκεῖα πράγματ' εἰσάγων, οἷς χρώμεθ', οἷς ξύνεσμεν)
> in which I would have been shown up (sc. had I tried to deceive them).
> Because, as they shared in the same knowledge, they could have questioned my art.[6]
>
> (959–61)

The Euripidean fiction, correspondingly, when in its turn projected back onto the level of the real life, becomes thoroughly entangled in its pedantic and pragmatic rhythm.[7] In this respect, then, the drama of Euripides is an event conspicuously and strikingly 'un-Dionysiac', because Dionysus is the god *par excellence* who requires that his votary stands out of himself, 'temporarily relinquishes the safe limits of personal identity in order to extend himself sympathetically to other dimensions of experience' (Segal 1985: 156). Exploring not the conscious and the critical but the unconscious and the hidden, Dionysus is 'the god who by very simple means, or by other means not so simple, enables you for a short time *to stop being yourself*, and thereby sets you free' (Dodds 1951: 76).

The senior dramatist's performance, on the other hand, evolves in an entirely 'Dionysiac' way, as it creates a communicative channel which results in 'snatching people out of their senses'. Euripides accuses him in 961–2,

> ἀλλ' οὐκ ἐκομπολάκουν
> ἀπὸ τοῦ φρονεῖν ἀποσπάσας, οὐδ' ἐξέπληττον αὐτούς.
>
> I didn't talk big,
> thrusting them out of their wits, nor did I astound them.

Now, the notion of *ekplexis*, in particular, deserves considerable attention, for, whether it refers to Aeschylus' astounding theatrical devices[8] or to the flights of his pompous *logos* (see e.g.

---

[6] See Dover (1993: 312).
[7] See primarily 975 ff., discussed from another angle below (8.2(c)).
[8] See Aeschylus' *Bios* (*TrGF* iii. 31 ff.) ταῖς τε {γὰρ} ὄψεσι καὶ τοῖς μύθοις πρὸς ἔκπληξιν τερατώδη μᾶλλον ἢ πρὸς ἀπάτην κέχρηται (7); ibid. (9) τοσοῦτον ἐκπλῆξαι τὸν δῆμον (i.e. by the spectacle of the Erinyes); ibid. (14) κατέπληξε. Note, however, Taplin's (1977: 44–7) doubts about the real value of such testimonia. More generally, for *ekplexis* as produced from τὰ ἐν τῇ ὄψει περιπαθέστερα see schol. Soph. *Aj.* 815 and 346.

939–40),[9] it designates the complete bewilderment of the experiencer, which blunts his readiness for critical evaluation or even leads him to irrational response.[10] To narrow the focus on the effect of verbal discourse and performance, *ekplexis* or *kataplexis* conveys the power to 'unhinge' men's minds, thrusting them under the domination of affect.[11] In the Platonic *Ion*, for example, *ekplettesthai* at the singing of the rhapsode (535b) is clarified as the listeners' emotional engagement, their imaginative projection into the fictive epic world (535e), while a text as late as Polybius' *Histories* conceives of *ekplexis*, the goal (τέλος) of tragedy, as an experience inherently intertwined with the captivation of the soul (ψυχαγωγία).[12] Plato's application of the notion of *ekplexis* to signify the soul's response to *logos* is particularly significant, for the bewilderment of those overwhelmed by amazing *logoi* is such an all-pervasive feeling that it may even be compared to an experience of religious possession and conveyed through metaphors drawn from the areas of orgiastic trance. Thus, the *ekplexis* of Socrates by Phaedrus' words is elucidated as a state of *bakcheia* (*Phdr.* 234d), while Alcibiades in the *Symposion* attributes to the *logoi* of Socrates himself the power to make the listeners *ekpeplegmenoi* and possessed (*Symp.* 215d): Socrates is compared to the mythical Marsyas, for even 'without instruments, by mere words' (ψιλοῖς λόγοις) (*Symp.* 215c) he is able to emulate the flute's insuperable possessing power (*Symp.* 215b–d). Alcibiades, correspondingly, conveys his own experience of *ekplexis* with the image of the wild *ekstasis* of the Corybantic rites:

> for when I listen to him, my heart is leaping much more than that of those possessed by Corybantic frenzy, and tears stream forth from my eyes at the sound of his speech.   (*Symp.* 215e)

The parallelism just quoted is all the more important for its direct bearing on the realm *par excellence* where *ekplexis* is operative, that is, the sphere of mystic *teletai*, where the neophytes have to undergo the emotional ordeal of overwhelming terror:

---

[9] *Ekplexis* could actually be caused by stunning style. The most well-known example would be the tradition about Gorgias (test. A4 (3) D–K), who was said to have 'astounded' (ἐξέπληξε) the Athenians with his style (but cf. also e.g. Pl. *Symp.* 198b). For the possibility of a Gorgianic influence on this passage see Segal (1962: 131 with n. 20), whereas Verdenius (1981: 120 n. 25) is negative. For *ekplexis* as a recurrent term in later prose as well as literary criticism (e.g. Plut. *Mor.* 16c, 17a) see F. Pfister in *RAC*, s.v. *Ekstase*, cols. 964–5 (with refs.).

[10] In Gorg. *Hel.* 16 (fr. B11 D–K), for example, *ekplexis* is the deep turmoil of the soul inextricably interwoven with confused judgement (wrong evaluation of circumstances) and resulting in non-rational behaviour.

[11] Cf. e.g. Pericles' speeches by which λέγων κατέπλησσεν [the Athenians] ἐπὶ τὸ φοβεῖσθαι (Thuc. 2. 65. 9).

[12] Polyb. 2. 56. 11. Cf. Longin. 15. 2, where *ekplexis* as the *telos* of poetry in general is inextricably interwoven with the excitement of feelings, τὸ συγκεκινημένον.

just as in the most secret initiation rites (ἐν ταῖς ἁγιωτάταις τελεταῖς), before the sight of the mysteries the initiands are overcome by terror (ἔκπληξις τῶν μυουμένων). . .[13] (Procl. *Theol. Plat.* 3. 18, p. 64 Budé)

One of the earliest passages where *ekplexis* is interwoven with Eleusinian mystic imagery is Plato's *Phaedrus* 250a–b, where Socrates maintains that those souls who have kept a sufficient memory of the true being,

when they see here any likeness of that other world, they are stricken with amazement (ἐκπλήττονται) and can no longer control themselves (οὐκέτ' ἐν αὑτῶν γίγνονται).

But, if *ekplexis* or *kataplexis* is one of the essential emotional ordeals that an initiand into Bacchic/Eleusinian mysteries is required to undergo, the Aristophanic Aeschylus' spectacle becomes in this respect a mystical event. Dionysus, therefore, who responds to it, proves ultimately receptive to a stage-performance which distils a primary experience of his own rites.

We shall return to the mystic associations of Aeschylus' drama in 6.2 and especially 6.3. For the moment, let us concentrate on the captivating power of Aeschylean theatre, which informs another Euripidean accusation against the senior dramatist's technique, namely the *apate* that he practises at the expense of the spectator:

> τοῦτον δὲ πρῶτ' ἐλέγξω,
> ὡς ἦν ἀλαζὼν καὶ φέναξ οἵοις τε τοὺς θεατὰς
> ἐξηπάτα.

> But first of all it is him I shall expose,
> by showing what a rogue and an impostor he was
> and by what tricks he used to deceive his audience. (908–10)

Euripides elaborates on the cheating as follows:

First of all, he'd sit someone on stage, having covered them up—an Achilles or a Niobe—and he wouldn't show their face: it was a pretence at tragedy, because they wouldn't say a thing . . . The Chorus would grind out four strings of songs, one after another—but the characters would stay silent . . . He did this out of devilment so that the spectator would sit guessing when Niobe would say something. Meanwhile, the drama would drag on. (911–20; tr. A. M. Bowie 1993a: 247)

Now, it is, of course, impossible to reconstruct with any certainty a fifth-century audience's understanding of the nature of this

---

[13] Cf. Procl. *In Remp.* ii, p. 108, 21–2 (Kroll) ὡς τοὺς μὲν τῶν τελουμένων καταπλήττεσθαι δειμάτων θείων πλήρεις γιγνομένους; Ael. Arist. 22. 2 (Keil); Procl. *In Remp.* ii, p. 181, 5–8 (Kroll) (on Dionysus who ἡγεῖται πολλῶν φασμάτων whose function is καταπλήττειν τὰς ψυχάς), etc. See also Strabo 10. 3. 7. For *ekplexis* as extreme terror see e.g. Arist. *Rhet.* 1385b32–3.

'cheating', especially because, in terms of literary maturity and intellectual ability, any such audience must have been a remarkably non-homogeneous body. But, even so, the obvious issue at stake seems to centre on the handling of dramatic technique. Aeschylus' characteristic way of opening his tragic narrative is voiceless, yet impressive, self-imposing, awesome, generating a rich complex of expectations. However, as the primary criterion in Euripides' evaluation of literary art is the uninterrupted flow of dramatic *logos*,[14] what follows on the Aeschylean stage is something of a let-down, since the protagonist, instead of breaking into speech, continues to remain silent (913, 915) till the dramatic time reaches nearly half its way through the action (920). In other words, in Euripides' perspective, Aeschylus' drama is unabashed 'cheating' because, in his perception of the theatre event, nothing happens on the Aeschylean stage, 'happening' being equivalent for him to chatting, generating everyday intelligible and down-to-earth discourse. Besides, what is even more important at this point is that Euripides' line of reasoning cannot be lost on Aristophanes' audience, for ever since the comedy's prologue, it has been constantly exposed to talking (*lalein*) as the quintessential feature of Euripides' art. Thus, amazed at Dionysus' need to bring Euripides back to life, Heracles asks:

> Well, are there not more than thousands of other
> young blokes here composing tragedies,
> who are miles more talkative (πλεῖν ἢ σταδίῳ λαλίστερα) than
> Euripides? (89–91)

while after Aeschylus' victory, the Chorus draws a moralizing conclusion:

> It is an elegant thing, then,
> not to sit by Socrates and talk
> (χαρίεν οὖν μὴ Σωκράτει
> παρακαθήμενον λαλεῖν),
> discarding *mousike*
> and foresaking the most important
> elements of tragic art.
> To spend time idly on theorizing
> and nonsensical quibbling
> (τὸ δ' ἐπὶ σεμνοῖσιν λόγοισιν
> καὶ σκαριφησμοῖσι λήρων
> διατριβὴν ἀργὸν ποιεῖσθαι)
> is the sign of an insane man.[15] (1491–9)

[14] See esp. 946–7, 948–9. Besides, what he considers as his greatest achievement is the fact that he has taught his fellow-citizens to talk (954 λαλεῖν ἐδίδαξα).

[15] Translation based on Dover (1993: 21).

To resume, then, my argument so far, the junior dramatist charges his predecessor in the tragic art with fooling his spectators[16] by creating plays deficient in artistic structure.[17] He is a 'cheat' because he robs his audience of the right to be treated with a fully fledged performance, a drama replete with *logos* from the beginning to the end of its stage-action. The spectacle which he presents instead is a πρόσχημα τῆς τραγῳδίας, a mere 'pretence' at tragedy (913), devoid of essence.

Nevertheless, beyond this obvious meaning, accessible to the majority of the Aristophanic audience, the humour of lines 907–20 is also to be sought in the interaction of more than one comic level. For this passage can actually be said to constitute a masterpiece of Aristophanes' 'complex layering of parody',[18] since all its key words are fraught with connotations which can be activated *par excellence* within the frame of a literary context. Thus, ἀλαζών and φέναξ seem to be closely interwoven with enthralment and bewitchment produced by various kinds of discourse, ranging from the misleading power of sophistic *logos*[19] to the realm of magic[20] or to the confusion of the listener through a style convoluted and ambiguous to the extent that it becomes reminiscent of an oracular response. As Aristotle comments in the *Rhetoric*,

when there is much going around in a circle, it cheats (φενακίζει) the listeners and they feel the way many do about oracles: whenever the latter speak amphibolies most people nod in assent (συμπαρανεύουσιν) . . .

(1407a35–8; tr. Kennedy 1991)

[16] Something like Aristophanes' own use of *exapatan* in connection with his *techne* in *Clouds* 546 (cf. also the use of *exapatan* in the simple sense of 'cheating' in *Frogs* 1404).

[17] Cf. Pheidippides' condemnation of Aeschylus in the *Clouds*, as ἀξύστατον (1367), i.e. probably, 'incoherent'; see Dover (1968: 254), who compares Arist. *Poet.* 1453b3ff. (δεῖ γὰρ . . . οὕτω συνεστάναι τὸν μῦθον . . .) and relates the criticism to the Aristophanic Aeschylus' 'cheating' in the *Frogs*.

[18] I borrow the phrase from Goldhill (1991: 214).

[19] See Burkert (1962: esp. 50–1), from whom many of the following references are taken. Both *alazon* and *phenax* are often associated with the notion of *goeteia* (*goes/alazon*: Pl. *Hp. Mi.* 371a; *goes/phenax*: Dem. 19. 102 γοητευθέντα καὶ φενακισθέντα; Deinarchus 1. 92 ταῖς τοῦ μιαροῦ καὶ γόητος τούτου δεήσεσιν . . . τοὺς φενακισμοὺς τοὺς τούτου), *goes* being a usual prerogative of the rhetor/sophist, who plays on the listener's emotions: see e.g. Dem. 18. 276, 19. 109; Aeschin. 3. 137; Pl. *Symp.* 203d (Eros as a δεινὸς γόης καὶ φαρμακεὺς καὶ σοφιστής); *Euthd.* 288b; *Soph.* 234e–5a; *Plt.* 291c τὸν πάντων τῶν σοφιστῶν μέγιστον γόητα. For *apatan* and *goeteia* cf. Pl. *Rep.* 413c ἔοικε γάρ, ἦ δ' ὅς, γοητεύειν πάντα ὅσα ἀπατᾷ; Dem. 18. 276, 19. 109 γόης . . . οἳ' ἐξηπάτηκεν. See also Pollux, who treats ἀπάτη, φενακισμός, γοητεία (9. 132–3) and their derivatives (9. 133–5) as synonymous. Consider also Ar. *Acharn.* 370–4, where the *alazon* orator is conceived of as capable of leading the populace astray through the deceptive power of his speech: τούς τε γὰρ τρόπους | τοὺς τῶν ἀγροίκων οἶδα χαίροντας σφόδρα, | ἐάν τις αὐτοὺς εὐλογῇ καὶ τὴν πόλιν | ἀνὴρ ἀλαζὼν καὶ δίκαια κἄδικα· | κἀνταῦθα λανθάνουσ' ἀπεμπολώμενοι.

[20] See Hippocr. *Morb. Sacr.* 1 (vi. 354 Littré) μάγοι τε καὶ καθάρται καὶ ἀγύρται καὶ ἀλαζόνες; Dem. 25. 80 μαγγανεύει καὶ φενακίζει (of Aristogeiton, the son of a φαρμακίς).

As for *apate*, it is quite possible that in fifth-century literary debate it had acquired the nuance of 'illusionism'. This would most probably have centred on the illusionist power of drama, such as vividly expressed in Gorgias' famous dictum that

> Tragedy offers through its myths and sufferings 'illusion' . . . whereby he who deceives is more just than he who does not deceive, and he who is deceived is wiser than he who is not deceived.[21]　(B 23 D–K)

A similar oscillation between the word's literal sense of 'cheating' and its literary connotations of 'illusory production' is at work in Aristophanes' *Thesmophoriazusae* 890–4. In her response as an 'internalized' spectator of the paratragic performance of the *Helen*, Critylla accuses Euripides' Kinsman/actor of trying to intrigue his fellow-performer, Euripides himself, with a lie:

KINSM.　　　　　　　βιάζομαι
γάμοισι Πρωτέως παιδὶ συμμεῖξαι λέχος.
CRIT. τί, ὦ κακόδαιμον, ἐξαπατᾷς αὖ τὸν ξένον;

KINSM. I'm being forced to join Proteus' son in a bed of marriage.
KRIT. You wretch, why are you trying to deceive the gentleman, again?

(890–2)

However, as the Kinsman's 'lie' consists precisely in the construction of fictive bonds between dramatic characters within his plot, Critylla offers unconsciously to the 'informed' spectator a metatheatrical insight into the aim of the enfolded tragic play—and by extension into the goal of Greek tragic art *per se*: the illusory construction of reality through stage-action, and the spectator's submersion into it.[22] Thus, if we bear in mind the whole spectrum of potential connotations of the term *apate*, we may hear both in the *Thesmophoriazusae* as well as in the *Frogs* echoes of fifth-century

---

[21] (παρασχοῦσα) τοῖς μύθοις καὶ τοῖς πάθεσιν ἀπάτην, . . . ἣν ὅ τ' ἀπατήσας δικαιότερος τοῦ μὴ ἀπατήσαντος καὶ ὁ ἀπατηθεὶς σοφώτερος τοῦ μὴ ἀπατηθέντος. Pohlenz (1965: 452–72) and Segal (1962: 130–1) are ready to accept that Aristophanes is playing with Gorgianic notions in this passage, whereas Walsh (1984: 154 with n. 12) is sceptical and others negative. Entirely reluctant to recognize the nuance of 'illusionism' in the 5th-cent. use of the term *apate* is Cataudella (1931: 383); cf. Rosenmeyer (1955: 234 with n. 33).

[22] For a detailed discussion of Critylla's reaction from a metatheatrical perspective see Lada-Richards (1997*b*). For an analogous use of *apatasthai* cf. Soph. *Phil.* 928–9 οἴά μ' εἰργάσω, | οἳ' ἠπάτηκας and 949 νῦν δ' ἠπάτημαι δύσμορος, where Philoctetes' *epatekas* and *epatemai* convey the engaging nature of Neoptolemus' performance, the impact that the 'internalized' actor's acting had on him. See in detail Lada-Richards (1998). For another occurrence of *apate* in the meaning of dramatic illusion in Old Comedy see *P. Köln* VI 242 A, line 20 νῦν δ' εἰς ἀπάτας κεκύλισμαι, where 'the comic poet, or the speaker representing comedy, notes in the first person that he has been rolled or has rolled himself into illusion' (Bierl 1990: 385). In a lengthy note on Gorgias and theatrical illusion Bierl (367 n. 46) touches on *Frogs* 911 f., but arrives at a different interpretation of Euripides' accusation.

Athenian literary discourse, even if this is phrased in the comic idiom. In other words, it is possible that the informed *theatai*, that is, those literate enough to appreciate the subtle quality of intellectual humour upon which the whole passage rests, would have been able to perceive Aristophanes' 'tour de force': it is *Euripides*, rather than Aeschylus, who seems so unable to comply with the requirements of a game in which the deceiver is ultimately more just than the non-deceiver that he even distorts the meaning of its keyword, *apate*.[23] Dionysus' reply, on the other hand

ἐγὼ δ' ἔχαιρον τῇ σιωπῇ, καί με τοῦτ' ἔτερπεν
οὐχ ἧττον ἢ νῦν οἱ λαλοῦντες.

But, I, for my part, enjoyed those silences, and this device
gave me no less pleasure than those who now chatter   (916–17)

is pronounced on a completely different level. Testifying to the *chara* and *terpsis* of a *theates* at the dramatic spectacle that Aeschylus created, he acknowledges obliquely the power of Aeschylean theatre to bewitch and cast a spell: the silence of the protagonistic figure together with the *hormathoi* of *mele* that the chorus sang (911–15) created a sublime and transcendental atmosphere inducing the spectator to surrender. In other words, Dionysus' reaction re-attributes by implication the notion of 'illusion' to Aeschylus' *apate*[24] and qualifies the Aeschylean performance as an essentially 'Dionysiac' event. Because, if 'letting oneself go' is Dionysiac, it is the illusionism of the Aeschylean stage which translates the spectator into another sphere, enwrapping him within a web of magic. And what could possibly convey more strongly the Dionysiac flavour of Aeschylus' *poiesis* than the confession of Dionysus himself that he has frequently succumbed to it?[25]

To conclude, then, the scholarly debate centring on whether Euripides' accusation ἐξηπάτα refers or not to the illusionistic power of drama is rather a simplification of the issue. For this passage does not merely depend upon the caricature of Aeschylus' and Euripides'

---

[23] In this case, ἠλίθιος, pronounced by Euripides as a term of abuse against the god (917–18), would ultimately be understood as turned against the dramatist himself, since it is *he* who does not know how to play the scenic game δικαίως.

[24] A similar double edge might be detected in 921 ὢ παμπόνηρος, οἵ' ἄρ' ἐφενακιζόμην ὑπ' αὐτοῦ.

[25] Of course, one may easily retort that Dionysus actually *regrets* his susceptibility to the Aeschylean performance (918, 921). Nevertheless, the 'instability' of comic voices is a quite essential characteristic of the genre (Goldhill 1991: 196 and his ch. 3 *passim*) and, once a point has been uttered, it calls for our attention, even if it is subverted in the immediately ensuing verse. For a full exposition of the argument that Dionysus' fictitious emotional response to an emotionally laden performance corresponds with real patterns of response embedded in Greek culture and with the social parameters which shaped a Greek theatrical event see Lada (1993).

dramatic *techne* or even on the travesty and trivialization of Greek fifth-century discourse on art.[26] Primarily, and most importantly, it rests upon a failure of communication between Dionysus and Euripides, and thus significantly highlights both the artistic distance separating the former from the latter as well as the characteristic 'closeness' of the divine judge to Aeschylus.

6.2. *Aeschylus as a* Bakcheios anax

Euripides' dramatic 'realism' goes hand in hand with a poetic intellectualism, since the achievement he most vividly takes pride in is the reasoning and thinking powers (*logismos* and *skepsis*) he has brought into his art.

> But such were the things
> that I instructed them to think about,
> by introducing reasoning into my art (λογισμὸν ἐνθεὶς τῇ τέχνῃ)
> and speculation (καὶ σκέψιν) so that they would
>   already consider (νοεῖν)
> everything . . .   (971–5)

Just as Plato opposes the skilfulness of the professional to the divine inspiration of the gifted poet (e.g. *Phdr.* 245a; *Ion* 533d–4e; *Apol.* 22b–c), Aristophanes throws into sharp relief the contrast between Euripides' clever mannerisms and Aeschylus' spontaneous productivity. 'Overflowing with feeling, overstocked with the substance of the spirit' (Walsh 1984: 88), Aeschylus creates 'with a gigantic blowing' (γηγενεῖ φυσήματι) (825),[27] infusing even in the characters he moulds a share of his breath.[28] If Euripides' creative organ and the god to whom he prays is the Tongue (892),[29] Aeschylus' poetry is the 'mighty labour' of his lungs (829 πλευμόνων πολὺν πόνον). Besides, as I will argue in this section, it is primarily as a possessed *poietes* that Aeschylus appears in the *Frogs*.

    Discussing the *poiesis* of his lyric parts, the Chorus designates him as 'the Bacchic lord' (τὸν Βακχεῖον ἄνακτα) (1259),[30] a title which may

---

[26] *Alazon* is obviously a common comic term of abuse; see Hubbard (1991: 2–8 and n. 2). Cf. Arist. *EN* 1127a 20–2 δοκεῖ δὴ ὁ μὲν ἀλαζὼν προσποιητικὸς τῶν ἐνδόξων εἶναι καὶ μὴ ὑπαρχόντων καὶ μειζόνων ἢ ὑπάρχει. At the same time, however, as Richard Hunter has pointed out to me, *alazon* and *phenax* may have been intended as parodic degradations of more sublime terms for appreciating an artist's personality or work, as e.g. ἀπατῶν in the Gorgianic sense of the skilled artist, etc.

[27] See Dover (1993: ad loc.). Cf. the vehemence of his creativeness, implied in 903ff. For breathing linked with poetic inspiration cf. e.g. Hom. *Od.* 22. 347–8; Hes. *Theog.* 31–2.

[28] See 1016–17 ἀλλὰ πνέοντας δόρυ καὶ λόγχας . . .; cf. Walsh (1984: 87).

[29] Cf. 815 and 826–8, where he seems to be almost identified with his tongue.

[30] It may be the case that 1257–60 belong to the original production of 405 BC, substituted in 404 with 1252–6, so that the text, as we now have it, is the result of a conflation; see Dover (1993: 343) and Sommerstein (1996: ad 1251–60).

mean the 'master of the Dionysiac art of tragedy' (Sommerstein 1996: ad loc.) but also, given the play's initiatory frame, the poet who is possessed and inspired by Bacchus.[31] And, actually, tradition has it that Aeschylus received his first calling to poetry directly from Dionysus. According to Pausanias (1. 21. 2),

Aeschylus himself said that when a youth he slept while watching grapes in a field, and that Dionysus appeared and bade him write tragedy. When day came, in obedience to the vision, he made an attempt and hereafter found composing quite easy.[32]

To return to our text in *Frogs*, this 'Dionysiac' way of evaluating poetic virtue has been adequately anticipated by the Bacchic figure of Cratinus, whom the Initiates' prorrhesis had extolled as a poetic prototype. One category of people whom the Chorus Leader bans from the blessed dances of the Mystai (354) includes whosoever has not 'been initiated into the Bacchic rites of the tongue of Cratinus, the bull-eating poet' (μηδὲ Κρατίνου τοῦ ταυροφάγου γλώττης Βακχεῖ' ἐτελέσθη) (357). Like the mythical Dionysiac devotee, who participates in the god's essence by devouring his bestial incarnations,[33] Cratinus, the 'bull-eating' poet, is implicitly supposed to derive verbal eloquence from an analogous communion (357 γλώττης Βακχεῖ' ἐτελέσθη), translated metaphorically into the space of the *polis*. Moving on to the contest, the Chorus conjures up the picture of Aeschylus who, 'caught in a terrible frenzy (μανίας ὑπὸ δεινῆς), will whirl his eyes this way and that' (816–17).[34] But, within the underlying network of classical Athenian culture, the image of a dramatist caught in the grips of madness can be closely associated with the inspired poet of Democritean and Platonic writings,[35] an

---

[31] Cf. Eur. *Hec.* 676–7 μῶν τὸ βακχεῖον κάρα | τῆς θεσπιῳδοῦ δεῦρο Κασσάνδρας φέρεις; More significantly still, it is Dionysus himself who is invoked as a *Bakcheios anax* (Orph. *h.* 30.2).

[32] For the well-known iconographic scheme of 'Dionysus visiting a poet' see Handley (1973: esp. pl. 2).

[33] For Dionysus' bestial incarnations as kid, bull, goat, etc. see Seaford (1994a: 288 n. 31). Although I do not share Henrichs's (1982: 159–60) abhorrence of the application of Smith/Durkheim's sacramental theory to the Dionysiac realm, I feel that a symbolist anthropological interpretation (cf. 4.2) would provide a much better insight into the Bacchic practice of *sparagmos*: in the perspective of the ritual 'actors', the animals which are torn apart *are* the bestial doubles of the god himself, in the same way that in the Nuer sacrificial practice the cucumber *is* (i.e. is viewed, treated and accepted as) an ox (see above, Ch. 4, n. 19).

[34] For the cyclic movement of the eyes as a sign of divine κατοχή or altered state of mind see the examples discussed by Ciani (1974) *passim* (esp. 73–4, 81, 89); for διάστροφος as a sign of Dionysiac delusion see Eur. *Bacch.* 1122–3, 1166–7 (about Agave).

[35] Democritus: fr. B 18 and B 21 D–K, and cf. B 17 D–K (the Latin tradition of the Democritean theory); for Democritus and the 'inspired poet' see Delatte (1934: 28 ff.). Plato: e.g. *Phdr.* 245a; *Ion* 533e. Nevertheless, despite the fact that Plato calls it a παλαιὸς μῦθος (*Leg.* 719c), the conception of poetic *furor* may be 'no older than the fifth century BC' (P. Murray 1981: 87); *contra*, Vicaire (1963: 75).

artist who creates poetry precisely when 'he becomes possessed and out of his senses and his mind does no longer dwell in him' (ἔνθεός τε γένηται καὶ ἔκφρων καὶ ὁ νοῦς μηκέτι ἐν αὐτῷ ἐνῇ) (*Ion* 534b).[36] Furthermore, in Plato's conception, 'when the poet sits on the tripod of the Muses, he comes out of his senses (οὐκ ἔμφρων ἐστίν)' and 'resembles a fountain, which gives free course to the upward rush of water' (οἷον δὲ κρήνη τις τὸ ἐπιὸν ῥεῖν ἑτοίμως ἑᾷ) (Pl. *Leg.* 719c). Likewise, in the *Frogs*, Aeschylus is about to 'release' his 'fountain', when encouraged to do so by his judge (1005 θαρρῶν τὸν κρουνὸν ἀφίει),[37] thus satisfying in this respect Dionysus' yearning for a *gonimos* (fertile) tragedian. Finally, in the perspective of the play's original spectators, his lack of clarity (927, 1122), his words which, 'unknown (ἄγνωτα) to the spectators' (926), are not easy to decipher (929), could perhaps be 'reassembled' into the stage-signifier of a remote and obscure *poeta vates*.[38]

Aeschylus, as a poet, then, stands much closer to Dionysus than Euripides could ever claim to be. For example, the analogy that Plato traces between poets in trance and the Dionysiac bacchants is revealing. In Socrates' words,

so the lyric poets compose those fine songs when they are not in their senses (οὐκ ἔμφρονες ὄντες), but when they embark on the music and the rhythm, they become frenzy-stricken (βακχεύουσι), and it is under possession (κατεχόμενοι) —as the bacchants draw honey and milk from the rivers when they are possessed, but not when they are in their senses—that the soul of the lyric poets is doing the same thing, according to their own report.[39] (Pl. *Ion* 534a)

Dodds (1951: 82) suggests that 'The notion of the "frenzied" poet composing in a state of ecstasy' might be 'a by-product of the

[36] For an opposite conception which, nevertheless, testifies to the diffusion of the poetic *furor*-theory see Arist. *Poet.* 1455a32–3 διὸ εὐφυοῦς ἡ ποιητική ἐστιν ἢ μανικοῦ, *manikos* being the 'divinely possessed'; Lucas (1968: 178) is willing to accept Aristophanes' depiction of Aeschylus in *Frogs* 816 as an example of such a *manikos*.

[37] As Alan Sommerstein points out to me, Cratinus in his prime had also been characterized in the language of rushing water (*Knights* 526ff.) and had picked it up himself the following year in his *Pytine* (fr. 198 K–A).

[38] This conception is abundantly developed in Latin literature, although Pindar is the obvious example of a self-confessed poet/prophet in the Greek world; see e.g. fr. 150 Maehler; *Paean* VI = fr. 52f, 6 Maehler; *Parth.* I = fr. 94a, 5–6 Maehler. As Dodds (1951: 100 n. 118) remarks, traces of this very old Indo-European conception may be found in Hes. *Theog.* 31–2. Cf. Pl. *Apol.* 22b–c; *Ion* 534b, 534c–d and, most importantly, Plato's memorable image in *Leg.* 719c ποιητής, ὁπόταν ἐν τῷ τρίποδι τῆς Μούσης καθίζηται, τότε οὐκ ἔμφρων ἐστίν. For the closeness of poetry, religious initiation, and prophecy see Vicaire (1963: 79f.). As for the notorious obscurity of oracular language cf. the Aristophanic parody in *Birds* 959ff.

[39] Cf. Pl. *Ion* 533e, where the comparison is made between the poets and the κορυβαντιῶντες, who οὐκ ἔμφρονες ὄντες ὀρχοῦνται; cf. also Pl. *Phdr.* 245a, where the *mania* of the Muses is working upon the poet's soul ἐγείρουσα καὶ ἐκβακχεύουσα κατά τε ᾠδὰς καὶ κατὰ τὴν ἄλλην ποίησιν.

Dionysiac movement' but, be that as it may, Dionysus is linked unequivocally with poetic inspiration through his gift of wine which, from a very early date,[40] had been considered an important stimulus to the creation of the artist's art.[41] In fact, a long anecdotal tradition perpetuates the image of Aeschylus as creating poetry while 'out of his senses' (οὐκ εἰδώς γε) (*TrGF* iii T 117a) under the influence of drink.[42] As for Aeschylus' riddling language, it should primarily be stressed that Dionysus was also credited with prophetic faculties (Eur. *Bacch.* 298 μάντις δ' ὁ δαίμων ὅδε)[43] for, in Teiresias' words, 'the state of frenzy and madness is endowed with great mantic power' (τὸ γὰρ βακχεύσιμον | καὶ τὸ μανιῶδες μαντικὴν πολλὴν ἔχει) (Eur. *Bacch.* 298–9).[44] Besides, for those among the audience who were initiated into Bacchic *teletai*, Aeschylus' obscure, unintelligible sayings[45] could also have mobilized another set of connotations, by recalling the riddling utterances often used in mystic initiation ritual so as both to confuse and stimulate the initiand's mind (Seaford 1981: 254–5): 'Hence the mysteries too are expressed in the form of allegory, in order to arouse *ekplexis* and shudder' (Διὸ καὶ τὰ μυστήρια ἐν ἀλληγορίαις λέγεται πρὸς ἔκπληξιν καὶ φρίκην) (Demetrius, *On Style* 101).[46] And, although Demetrius' treatise dates from the Hellenistic or early Roman period, good early illustrations of mystic riddling ambiguities are encoded in the language of dithyramb and satyr drama (Seaford 1976, 1977–8), let alone in the intriguing puzzles of some of the Bacchic gold leaves as, for example, 'bull, you rushed into the milk; suddenly you rushed

[40] Cf. Archilochus, fr. 120 West. For the inherently Dionysiac and even mystic/initiatory quality of Archilochus' fragment see Mendelsohn (1992).

[41] See Dodds (1951: 101 n. 124); Lucas (1968: 178) on Arist. *Poet.* 1455a32–4; Bramble (1974: 48–9).

[42] For Aeschylus' drunkenness as a source of poetic inspiration see Pohlenz (1965: 452) and *TrGF* iii T 117a–g (cf. Ch. 3, n. 65).

[43] See Dodds (1960: ad 298–301), and cf. Aesch. fr. 341 Radt; Dionysus' role at Delphi: Plut. *Mor.* 388e τὸν Διόνυσον, ᾧ τῶν Δελφῶν οὐδὲν ἧττον ἢ τῷ Ἀπόλλωνι μέτεστιν; see Amandry (1950: 196–200).

[44] Although primarily inspired by Apollo, some prophetic figures in Greek tragedy attract Bacchic metaphors as well; see e.g. Eur. *Troad.* 408 (of the raving Cassandra) εἰ μή σ' Ἀπόλλων ἐξεβάκχευσεν φρένας.

[45] I cannot agree with A. M. Bowie's (1993a: 249) perspective at this point, who writes that 'If he [i.e. Aeschylus] is incomprehensible, then he breaks the Eleusinian prohibition on the *barbaros* (and one wonders how he will save the city through his tragedies).' As will become clear in this chapter, Aeschylus' incomprehensibility makes better sense *within* an Eleusinian context rather than against it.

[46] Cf. Plut. *Mor.* 388f–9a, where it is said that the 'more enlightened' (οἱ σοφώτεροι) refer cryptically (αἰνίττονται) to Dionysus' *pathe* and transformations as a διασπασμόν τινα καὶ διαμελισμόν. On the various levels of allegorizing in the realm of mystic cults see also Burkert (1987a: 78ff.), who remarks that 'beginning with the Hellenistic age, allegory has commonly been called "mystic"' (79), and that 'In consequence, all allegorization in a religious context could be termed "mystic"' (80).

into the milk; ram, you fell into the milk'.[47] More importantly still,
Euripides' *Bacchae* offers an excellent example, contemporary with
Frogs, of the mystic practice of offering tantalizing hints, while
simultaneously concealing deeper truths.[48] In riddling language
which obfuscates any clear information, the Stranger/Dionysus,
who plays the role of Pentheus' initiator (cf. 2.12(a)), masterfully
excites the initiand's curiosity about the form, the doings, and the
whereabouts of the god.[49] As Pentheus complains to him, 'once
again, you have diverted the matter dexterously, saying nothing'
(τοῦτ' αὖ παρωχέτευσας εὖ κοὐδὲν λέγων) (*Bacch.* 479).

Finally, Aeschylus comes closer to Dionysus through the contiguity of his *poiesis* with the Muses. Unlike Euripides, who is
charged with having cast away *mousiken* (1493), he seems to conceive his poetic task as culling the 'sacred meadow of the Muses',
albeit not the same one as Phrynichus (1299–1300). The sinister
consequences of Euripides' neglect for the outcome of the agon
have already been foreshadowed in Dionysus' wish (872) 'to judge
the contest in a manner most befitting a cultivated critic'
(μουσικώτατα) (873)[50] as well as in his suggestion to the Chorus to
sing a *melos* to the Muses (874; cf. 875 ff.). Earlier in the play the
Chorus summoned the Muse to the dance (674 ff.), while in the
prorrhesis the Chorus Leader banned everyone who 'has neither
seen nor danced the secret rites of the noble Muses' (356) (cf. 5.2).
In the parabasis too, those citizens were extolled who had been
brought up 'in poetic-musical education' (ἐν . . . μουσικῇ) (729) (cf.

[47] Lines 3–5 of the Pelinna gold leaves (Tsantsanoglou and Parássoglou 1987); see also the
gold leaves from Thurii (A1 (Zuntz 1971), 8–9 "ὄλβιε καὶ μακαριστέ, θεὸς δ' ἔσῃ ἀντὶ βροτοῖο."
ἔριφος ἐς γάλ' ἔπετον; cf. A4 (Zuntz 1971), 3–4) and the riddling short inscriptions 'life death
life', 'peace war', 'truth lie' on the 5th-cent. Orphic/Dionysiac bone tablets from Olbia (cf.
1.4), with which Seaford (1994*b*: 283) compares the riddling style and content of Heracleitus'
philosophical writings. In Seaford's view (1994*a*: 227), 'Herakleitos' riddling, antithetical
style undoubtedly derives from the language used in the mysteries, and he presents his *logos*
in the manner of the Orphic *hieroi logoi* and the *legomena* of the Eleusinian mysteries.' Cf.
Seaford's (1994*b*: 282–4) insightful interpretation of Ajax's riddling monologue in the
Sophoclean play (*Aj.* 646 ff.) in the context of mystic allusive language and concepts. Finally,
the famous Eleusinian 'password' too, the *synthema*, is expressed in riddling language. See
Richardson (1974: 22–3).

[48] However, as was the case with Aeschylus' *apate* of his *theatai*, in the perspective of those
members of a 5th-cent. audience who would have had special acquaintance with literary
matters, Euripides' rebuke of Aeschylus' unintelligibility could have been registered as
praise. For a propensity to riddling expression could also be seen as a perfect illustration of
poetic temperament and talent, as can be gauged from e.g. Pl. *Alc.* 2, 147b ἀλλ' αἰνίττεται, ὦ
βέλτιστε, καὶ οὗτος καὶ οἱ ἄλλοι δὲ ποιηταὶ σχεδόν τι πάντες. ἔστιν τε γὰρ φύσει ποιητικὴ ἡ σύμπασα
αἰνιγματώδης καὶ οὐ τοῦ προστυχόντος ἀνδρὸς γνωρίσαι or Pl. *Rep.* 332b–c ἠνίξατο ἄρα, ἦν δ' ἐγώ,
ὡς ἔοικεν, ὁ Σιμωνίδης ποιητικῶς. See further Dover (1993: 13).

[49] See esp. *Bacch.* 470, 472, 474–5, 478–9.

[50] See Dover (1993: ad loc.). Alternative translations would be 'with exceptional poetic
skill', or even 'most harmoniously'.

8.2(a)).[51] But more importantly still, Euripides' fault could also be deciphered as an offence to the person of Dionysus himself as many a time, in both literature and cultic practice, Dionysus is closely linked with the Muses. To mention only some examples, Aeschylus designated Dionysus as a μουσόμαντις, a 'poet prophet' (*Edoni*, fr. 60 Radt); Euripides (*Bacch.* 410) included Pieria, the 'seat of the Muses', among the places which would welcome the orgies of the god; in Sophocles' account of the fate of Dionysus' enemy Lycurgus, the king of the Edonians was punished precisely because he 'provoked the flute-loving Muses' (*Ant.* 965), while in Plato Dionysus, Apollo, and the Muses are the 'fellow-celebrants' (συνεορταστάς), whom the gods in pity bestowed on mankind (*Leg.* 653d).[52] Moreover, in a quite revealing metaphor, the *sophia* allegedly imparted by Dionysus to his missionary in Euripides' *Bacchae* is characterized as an instruction in the Muses' art (*Bacch.* 825). In cult practice, correspondingly, Plutarch (*Mor.* 717a) describes the ritual of the Boeotian Agrionia, where Dionysus is believed to take refuge with the Muses, while in Diodorus (4. 4. 3) the Muses are not only the followers (αὐτῷ συναποδημεῖν) but also the entertainers (ψυχαγωγεῖν τὸν θεόν) of Dionysus as well.[53]

6.3. *Aeschylus, the 'Eleusinian' Poet*

In 5.1 we have noted Aeschylus' prayer to Demeter 'who has nourished my mind' and in 6.1 we have seen in greater detail some 'mystic' aspects of Aeschylus' *poiesis*, such as the notion of *ekplexis*, which links his drama to the psychology of initiation rituals. Verbs and epithets as well applied to Aeschylus throughout the contest have a broader connotative—and possibly cultic—range. The adjectives *semnos* (i.e. revered, august, holy, worthy of respect) and *polytimetos* (i.e. highly honoured),[54] for example, can bring into play a host of Eleusinian associations, as a fifth-century Greek audience would certainly have been familiar with *semnos* both in regular connection with the rites of Demeter[55] and as a special cultic title of

---

[51] For a useful note on *mousike* see Nussbaum (1986: 476 n. 54).

[52] In early lyric poetry too (e.g. Solon, fr. 24 G–P), Dionysus can be mentioned in association with the Muses. Several epigrams in the *Greek Anthology* as well reveal such associations; see *AP* vii. 104, 82, 412.

[53] Among literary reflections of Dionysiac cult see lines 3–4 of an Hellenistic poem (Lloyd-Jones 1963), where the Muses are envisaged as παρ᾽ Ὀλύμπου | Βάκχῳ τὰς τριετεῖς ἀρχόμεναι θυμέλας.

[54] 1004 ὦ . . . πυργώσας ῥήματα σεμνά (cf. the participle *semnynomenos*, 1020); 851 ὦ πολυτίμητ᾽ Αἰσχύλε.

[55] See Richardson (1974: ad 478) with many examples from Tragedy. *Semnos*, however, can also be ascribed to Dionysus, as e.g. in Eur. *Rhes.* 973, where he is σεμνὸς τοῖσιν εἰδόσιν θεός.

Demeter and Persephone *par excellence*,[56] while three times in the *Frogs* the epithet *polytimetos* is significantly applied both to Dionysus/Iacchus as well as to Persephone (323, 398/337).[57] However, the cluster of connections between Aeschylus and Eleusis that an initiate would have been able to perceive is even more wide-ranging than would at first appear. What I hope to show in this section is that a proper understanding of Aeschylus' privileged role as an 'Eleusinian' poet deeply integrated into the play's ritual context has important implications for our attempt to 'think with' classical Greek spectators about Dionysus' final choice which decides the poetic agon of the *Frogs* (see Ch. 5).

In the first place, Aeschylus' contiguity with Eleusis can be gauged from the moulding of his dramatic figures, sitting on the stage veiled and in silence, while incomprehensible songs are sung around them (see above, 6.1).[58] As Angus Bowie (1993*a*: 247–8) has ingeniously suggested, the primary frame of reference here is that of Eleusinian myth. In the Homeric *Hymn to Demeter* we hear that, while a guest in the house of Celeus and grieving over the loss of Core, the goddess sat on a stool, veiled, motionless, and silent.

> Seated there, the goddess drew the veil before her face.
> For a long time she sat voiceless with grief on the stool
> and responded to no one with word or gesture.
> Unsmiling, tasting neither food nor drink,
> she sat wasting with desire for her deep-girt daughter.
>
> (Hom. *h. Dem.* 197–201; tr. H. Foley)

The ritual analogue of Demeter's mythical action is the pre-initiatory purification ritual that Hesychius calls 'enthronement', *thronosis*[59] (cf. 2.13 on *thronosis* in Bacchic/Corybantic mystic

---

[56] See Richardson (1974: ad 1 and 486). Of course, this is not to overlook the mundane associations of the epithet and its derivatives, which can be caricatural terms for grand airs, pride, imaginary self-importance, and pretentious gravity (Loraux 1986: 319–21). Such would be, for example, the primary, denotational significance of (*apo-)semnynesthai* in *Frogs* 703, 833, 1020.

[57] Dover (1993: ad 851) observes that 'elsewhere in comedy this epithet is given only to deities (e.g. 323/4, 337, 398)', but, instead of drawing any conclusions about its Eleusinian colouring, he merely infers 'so that here it sounds an extravagant compliment to Aeschylus.' Bierl (1991: 38 n. 47) rightly stresses the significance of the connection.

[58] For an attempt to specify the Aeschylean play Aristophanes was likely to have in mind here see Taplin (1972: 58–76).

[59] Hesychius, s.v. θρόνωσις· καταρχὴ περὶ τοὺς μυουμένους. However, it has to be made clear at this point that Bowie's reading of the analogy of Aeschylus' performance with the Eleusinian ritual differs substantially from mine. For I perceive the similarity as capable of indicating to the audience the *closeness* of Aeschylus' *dramatis persona* to Demeter's mystic rites, while in A. M. Bowie's view (1993*a*: 249) 'If he [i.e. Aeschylus] puts on stage figures in an Eleusinian mode, then we are made to wonder whether this is not another example of his "revealing the Mysteries"'.

teletai). This is best known to us through Roman replicas of what may have been 'an early Hellenistic original',[60] that is, the so-called Lovatelli urn, a sarcophagus from Torre Nova and some near-contemporary Campana clay-reliefs.[61] The scene which all these monuments portray is the Eleusinian initiation of Heracles. However, the depiction of this initiation has much broader implications. The hero was considered to be a *protomystes* in the Eleusinian *telete* (see further, 7.1 with n. 9) and, therefore, we may naturally assume that the iconographic scheme of his *myesis* provided and established the pattern for the initiatory experience of human novices as well.[62] Like every initiand, then, Heracles is portrayed as sitting on a stool veiled, while a priestess stands near him with either a winnowing fan (urn) or a torch (sarcophagus). Moreover, Burkert (1983: 275) suggests that all initiates who had not yet reached the grade of the *epoptes* may have had to veil themselves while the more secret enactments of the *telete* were taking place inside the Initiation Hall.[63]

Secondly, I would like to draw attention to a brief antode where the Chorus intervenes to admonish Aeschylus to check his temper:

μόνον ὅπως
μή σ' ὁ θυμὸς ἁρπάσας
ἐκτὸς οἴσει τῶν ἐλαῶν.

> Just make sure that
> your temper does not seize you
> and throw you off the course.   (993b–5)

Now, it is clear that the Chorus conceive of Aeschylus as a charioteer who, giving vent to his rage, risks careering off course.[64] However, an audience of Eleusinian initiates would have been able to understand the Chorus's figurative language as drawing on a cluster of imagery familiar and operative in *logoi* about Eleusinian initiation.[65] The images I am referring to are best encapsulated in

---

[60] Boardman (*LIMC* iv. 1, s.v. Herakles, p. 807).

[61] Lovatelli urn (marble relief-vase, middle of 1st cent. AD): see *LIMC* iv, s.v. Demeter/Ceres, 145 (with bibliography); sarcophagus (1st cent. AD): see *LIMC* iv, s.v. Demeter/Ceres, 146 (with bibliography). See also Burkert (1983: 267 n. 12).

[62] See Boardman (*LIMC* iv. 1, s.v. Herakles, p. 805): 'in art he becomes the typical hero-initiate and many scenes seem generic.'

[63] Inspired by the veiling of initiation may be Aesch. *Choeph.* 809–11 καί νιν ἐλευθερίας φῶς | λαμπρὸν ἰδεῖν φιλίοις | ὄμμασιν ⟨ἐκ⟩ δνοφερᾶς καλύπτρας, while Eleusinian *thronismos* informs *Clouds* 254–9.

[64] See scholion ad 995 ἐν τῷ τέλει τοῦ τόπου οὗ ἐτελεῖτο ὁ δρόμος, ἐλαῖαι στιχηδὸν ἵστανται, οὖσαι κατάντημα τοῦ δρόμου, καὶ οὐδεὶς ἐπέκεινα τούτων ἐχώρει. ὅστις οὖν πέρα τοῦ δέοντος ἔπραττέ τι, ἔλεγον ὡς ἐκτὸς τῶν ἐλαιῶν φέρεται.

[65] Burkert (1987a: ch. 3) has interesting remarks on the various ways in which *logoi* 'in the mysteries' ('esoteric') as well as *logoi* 'about the mysteries' ('exoteric') interrelated. As

the famous Platonic metaphor of the soul as the winged driver of a chariot to which are harnessed two horses, one good and one unruly, which drags the soul back to earth (*Phdr.* 247b ἐπὶ τὴν γῆν ῥέπων). The unsuccessful attempt of those souls who do not manage to soar up and catch a glimpse of the heavenly meadow is expressed as a failed initiation: 'they go away uninitiated into the vision of reality' (*Phdr.* 248b). The suffering, the *ponos*, that those souls undergo, correspondingly, is conceived in terms of the turmoil of a chariot race which went out of control:

αἱ δὲ δὴ ἄλλαι γλιχόμεναι μὲν ἅπασαι τοῦ ἄνω ἕπονται, ἀδυνατοῦσαι δέ, ὑποβρύχιαι συμπεριφέρονται, πατοῦσαι ἀλλήλας καὶ ἐπιβάλλουσαι, ἑτέρα πρὸ τῆς ἑτέρας πειρωμένη γενέσθαι. θόρυβος γοῦν καὶ ἅμιλλα καὶ ἱδρὼς ἔσχατος γίγνεται, οὗ δὴ κακίᾳ ἡνιόχων πολλαὶ μὲν χωλεύονται, πολλαὶ δὲ πολλὰ πτερὰ θραύονται.

The other souls follow after, all yearning for the upper region but unable to reach it, and are carried round beneath, trampling upon and colliding with one another, each striving to pass its neighbour. So there is the greatest confusion and sweat of rivalry, wherein many are lamed, and many wings are broken through the incompetence of the drivers.

(*Phdr.* 248a–b)

Richard Seaford (1994*b*: 279–80) has drawn the connection between this passage of the *Phaedrus* and scenes from Greek Tragedy, particularly the alleged death of Orestes during a Delphic chariot race, an incident narrated at length by the Paedagogus in Sophocles' *Electra* (680ff.). We have already seen in Chapter 2 that Aeschylus' and Sophocles' dramatization of Orestes' ephebic rite of passage assimilates and remoulds feelings and ritual patterns of the Eleusinian initiation rites. Pushing this line of thought a step further, Seaford argues that, for those among the *theatai* who were familiar with the imagery of Eleusinian initiation, Orestes' lamentable death under the feet of horses going out of control in the course of a chariot race could have evoked a cluster of metaphors connoting a failed initiatory transition. In fact, there is one more case in the extant corpus of Greek Tragedy where the failure of a rite of passage is conveyed through the image of a horse race culminating in turmoil and defeat, instead of victory. I have in mind here the

Plutarch (*Mor.* 378a) writes on the mystic rituals of Isis, it is necessary that one adopts 'the reasoning that comes from philosophy as guide in the mysteries' (λόγον ἐκ φιλοσοφίας μυσταγωγὸν ἀναλαβόντας) (Burkert 1987*a*: 72). In other words, for those versed in philosophical reading and speculation, a philosopher's metaphorical language inspired from mystic ritual could go hand in hand with the direct experience of the ritual itself, in much the same way that ritual *exegesis* is inseparable from the ritual it refers to (see Beard 1987).

Euripidean Hippolytus, the virgin male who stubbornly refused to accomplish his transition to a fully masculine role as a citizen, a husband, and a warrior. Like the tale of the Paedagogus in Sophocles' play, the Euripidean Messenger's *rhesis* narrates how Hippolytus' body is fatally mutilated when his steeds, seized by panic, get out of control:

> Then all was in confusion. Axles of wheels,
> and linch-pins flew up into the air,
> and he the unlucky driver, tangled in the reins,
> was dragged along in an inextricable knot . . .[66]

(1234–7; cf. Soph. *El.* 745 ff.)

There is, therefore, reason to believe that, for those among the audience of the *Frogs* who were both frequent theatregoers and initiated into Eleusis, the Aristophanic picture of Aeschylus as potentially carried *ektos ton elaon* was particularly evocative. Although obscure for us today, the image may have mobilized for them a wealth of associations following, as it does, not only a mystic pattern, but also a series of dramatically remoulded metaphors expressing failed ritual transitions. More importantly still, there is reason to believe that literate members of the Aristophanic audience would have been able to recognize in the Chorus's admonition to Aeschylus in *Frogs* 993*b*–5 the same picture that Aeschylus himself had hitherto applied to the archetypal initiand in his dramatic repertoire, that is, Orestes.

In an ode of the *Choephori* sung before the matricide, the Chorus had envisaged Orestes as a colt harnessed in a chariot. His prospective act of vengeance, correspondingly, was visualized as a victory in a chariot race, provided the team would keep its ordered pace over the course.[67] Within the underlying nexus of fifth-century perceptions and assumptions, an abundance of shared patterns of imagery links the winner of athletic contests to the neophyte successfully accomplishing initiation.[68] In this respect, those among the audience of the trilogy who were themselves *memyemenoi* would have been able to appreciate the mystic connotations of a victorious chariot race. However, much more relevant to the Aristophanic picture in the *Frogs* is the recurrence of the equestrian mystic

---

[66] See Segal (1988*a*: 280–1).

[67] ἴσθι δ᾽ ἀνδρὸς φίλου πῶλον εὖ | νιν ζυγέντ᾽ ἐν ἅρμασιν | πημάτων· ἐν δρόμῳ προστιθεὶς μέτρον, κτίσον |†σωζόμενον† ῥυθμόν, | τοῦτ᾽ ἰδεῖν δάπεδον ἀνόμενον | βημάτων ὄρεγμα (794–9). See Headlam and Thomson (1938: ad *Choeph.* 790–5).

[68] Especially the conception of both athlete and initiand as contestants, the crowning and the *makarismos* of the victor/successful initiand, etc. See primarily Headlam and Thomson (1938: ad *Choeph.* 579–82, 790–5); Garner (1992).

metaphor *after* the completion of the matricidal act, because this time, as in *Frogs*, the metaphor is firmly fixed at the *negative* end of its potential spectrum. While experiencing the onset of his madness, the Aeschylean Orestes comes to apprehend himself not as a triumphant charioteer, but as driven off his course by uncontrollable frenzy:

> I am a charioteer whose course is wrenched outside
> the track, for I am beaten, my rebellious senses
> bolt with me headlong and the fear against my heart
> is ready for the singing and dance of wrath.
>
> (Aesch. *Choeph.* 1022–5)[69]

We have seen, then, in this section that the imaginative depiction of Aeschylus in *Frogs* as running the risk of careering off course, if he does not succeed in keeping his surging rage under control, is informed by a well-known metaphor of the mysteries. Consequently, the tragic dramatist himself is cast, albeit momentarily, in a conspicuously Eleusinian role, as his potential failure to restrain himself is expressed in terms belonging to the mystic cluster of Eleusis. Finally, there is one further feature of this ode which invites an Eleusinian reading.

In lines 999–1003 equestrian imagery merges with a nautical metaphor, as the Chorus envisages the elder dramatist as a mariner who struggles in the middle of a storm.[70] Now, as Kamerbeek notes (1974: 102 ad 729, 30), 'The reciprocal use of shipping terms and terms of riding and driving is . . . as old as Greek literature'. Moreover, the blending of horse-riding and seafaring images is by no means unique in Aeschylean drama (Moreau 1979). Nevertheless, it is, I think, especially important that the tale of Orestes' tragic horse-racing in Sophocles' *Electra*, a narrative which, as we have seen above, draws on the Eleusinian mysteries, displays a similar conflation of equestrian and marine pictures twice. In his fictitious report of the alleged accident which caused some carts to crash and overturn each other,[71] it is with a marine

---

[69] Note esp. lines 1022–4 ὥσπερ ξὺν ἵπποις ἡνιοστροφῶ δρόμου | ἐξωτέρω· φέρουσι γὰρ νικώμενον | φρένες δύσαρκτοι. See Garvie (1986: ad 1021–5): '. . . here Orestes is himself the charioteer who is being driven off course by the onset of his madness.' Cf. Garvie (ad 1023–4): 'Orestes' φρένες are themselves the uncontrollable chariot-horses. . . . Orestes' victory is being turned into defeat by his madness.' See Seaford (1994a: 374): 'And so when shortly after the murders Orestes compares himself to a chariot crashing in a race, with the horses like his mind "hard to control", this is a potent image, probably drawn from the mysteries themselves, of the failure of the mystic transition.'

[70] ἀλλὰ συστείλας ἄκροισιν | χρώμενος τοῖς ἱστίοις | εἶτα μᾶλλον μᾶλλον ἄξεις | καὶ φυλάξεις, ἡνίκ' ἂν τὸ | πνεῦμα λεῖον καὶ καθεστηκὸς λάβῃς. See Dover's (1993) note ad loc.

[71] 728–9 κἀντεῦθεν ἄλλος ἄλλον ἐξ ἑνὸς κακοῦ | ἔθραυε κἀνέπιπτε.

metaphor that the Paedagogus expresses the confusion: 'the whole race-ground of Crisa was strewn with the wreck of chariots'.[72] Within just a couple of lines the same metaphor recurs, this time centring on the turmoil of rough waters ('the rough stream of chariots seething in the middle', 733),[73] while towards the play's end Aegisthus refers to the scene of the accident by using the expression 'equestrian wrecks' (ἱππικοῖσιν ἐν ναυαγίοις) (1444). However, nearest to Aeschylus' equestrian/marine picture in the *Frogs* comes the amalgamation of both metaphors in the Messenger's speech of Euripides' *Hippolytus*, where the unlucky rider, vainly trying to control his chariot, is compared to 'a sailor at the oar':

> And he pulled them as a sailor does an oar
> (ἕλκει δὲ κώπην ὥστε ναυβάτης ἀνήρ)
> letting his body hang backward on the throngs.
>
> (Eur. *Hipp.* 1221–2; tr. Barrett)

Finally, some wider parameters should be taken into account at this point.

According to the scholiast on *Frogs* 886 (*TrGF* iii T 8d), Aeschylus was Eleusinian by birth—hence, it was only natural that he should pray to Demeter; Athenaeus (*TrGF* iii T 103) informs us that the dress of the Eleusinian *dadouchoi* and hierophants self-consciously imitated the 'dignity' (εὐπρέπειαν) and the 'solemnity' (σεμνότητα) of the costumes worn by Aeschylus' actors on the stage; but of far greater interest is the tradition (mainly preserved by scholiasts on Aristotle's *EN* 1111a8)[74] that Aeschylus was once accused of *asebeia*, on the grounds that in some of his dramas he had spoken openly of aspects of the Eleusinian rites which were not to be divulged (*TrGF* iii T 93b). The dramatist escaped the death penalty, the story goes, by pleading ignorance of the fact that his poetical remouldings of the rites had touched on things which were supposed to be kept secret (*TrGF* iii T 93c). Now, obviously, it would be very difficult, and even perhaps impossible, to disentangle the historical truth (if any) from the layers of anecdotal ornamentation imposed on our sources. However, should we be willing to believe the main line of the story, we could safely, I think, conclude that, in a play where the dramatically remoulded Eleusinian frame

---

[72] Jebb's translation (1894) of πᾶν δ᾽ ἐπίμπλατο | ναυαγίων Κρισαῖον ἱππικῶν πέδον (729–30). For the image cf. [Dem.] 61. 29 (quoted by Jebb, ad 728ff.) ὡς ἐν τοῖς ἱππικοῖς ἀγῶσιν ἡδίστην θέαν παρέχεται τὰ ναυαγοῦντα.

[73] κλύδων᾽ ἔφιππον ἐν μέσῳ κυκώμενον.

[74] The scholia and other sources are assembled in *TrGF* iii T 93a–94.

is paramount, the real-life Aeschylus' indebtedness to Eleusis could have been a major factor in the Aristophanic audience's decipherment of his dramatic figure in the literary contest.[75]

[75] However, see *contra* A. M. Bowie (1993a: 246): '. . . if we are to believe the charge of revealing the Mysteries which was brought against Aeschylus . . . this [i.e. Aeschylus' prayer to Demeter in *Frogs* 886–7] would be not the pious prayer of the model poet, but an appeal which most inopportunely recalls a charge of grave seriousness in any circumstances, but especially so in a play which makes these Mysteries a central part of its design.' I find myself much more in agreement with Dover (1993: 303) at this point: '. . . even if this [i.e. the charge against Aeschylus] was well known, the humorous point, that in spite of being "nourished" by Demeter he had betrayed her, does not seem very appropriate here.'

7

Dionysus 'Returns' to Heracles

7.1. *Introduction*

I have argued so far that on the level of poetic *techne* Aeschylus is
the quintessence of a 'Dionysiac' poet. What still remains to be
seen is how the relationship between the three stage-characters
(Dionysus, Aeschylus, and Euripides) changes, if the contest is
evaluated from the point of view of an artist's *impact on society*, as
one of the issues which is given great prominence throughout the
agon is that of an artist's influence on the social milieu of which he
is a part (see esp. 1008–10). It is the thesis of this chapter, then, that,
if the contest is looked at from a purely *social* angle, it is Euripides'
art which exercises a 'Dionysiac' influence on its environment,
while Aeschylus, on the contrary, should rather be viewed as an
essentially 'Heraclean' figure.[1]

Now, although the agon contains no explicit reference to
Heracles, let alone to any clear indication of a possible connection
between Heracles and Aeschylus, the play's plot is built upon a
pattern of *mimesis* of Dionysus' Heraclean prototype (109 ἦλθον κατὰ
σὴν μίμησιν) (cf. Ch. 4), whose perilous descent into the domain of
the dead resulted in his victorious return to Earth together with the
dog Cerberus. In this respect, if the comedy is read in terms of a
Dionysiac re-enactment of Heracles' other-worldly labour,[2] the
city's saviour can be seen as the literary equivalent of the mythical
hell-hound,[3] in the same way that he can also be perceived as conforming to the role of Semele or Persephone (2.14), when the play
is read along the lines of either a Dionysiac or an Eleusinian initiation ritual. In fact, Pluto's cheerful willingness to let Aeschylus go
at the play's end brings the poet even closer to Cerberus in the

---

[1] Cf. Padilla's (1992: 375) argument that 'the play's vocabulary and imagery align
Aeschylus with Heracles, the frogs, and the initiates', while 'Euripides is identified as their
opposite', culminating in the conclusion that 'Dionysus learns to embrace the heroic value of
his model's catabasis' (ibid.: 381). However, the ways by which Padilla reaches this conclusion and his further exploitation of it differ substantially from mine.

[2] For Heracles' *katabasis* as a model of Dionysus' adventure in the underworld journey of
the *Frogs* see primarily Lloyd-Jones (1967); cf. Clark (1979: 79–94).

[3] Lloyd-Jones (1967: 220); cf. Padilla (1992: 381).

'Eleusinian' version of Heracles' labour,[4] in which the ferocious guardian of the Underworld is offered to him with Pluto's and Persephone's consent.[5] Besides, if I have been right in suggesting in 5.2 that Aeschylus' return to Athens resembles the triumphant re-entry of an athletic victor to his city, it is certainly important to bear in mind the consistent function of the divinized Heracles as the supreme exemplum for the victorious athlete's panegyrical return, a function he fulfils not only in Pindaric epinicians,[6] but also on the classical Athenian stage too, as the plot of Euripides' *Alcestis* may suggest (cf. Garner 1988: 67).

Towards the play's end, Heracles returns to Admetus' palace as a winning athlete, with his prize in hand, namely, a veiled woman, whom he has supposedly earned for his victory (1028–9 τήνδε νικητήρια | λαβών) at a public contest (1026 ἀγῶνα . . . πάνδημον); not much later in the same scene, it emerges that Heracles has actually fought a contest against Death himself (1141 ποῦ τόνδε Θανάτῳ φῂς ἀγῶνα συμβαλεῖν;),[7] and that the woman is actually Alcestis, whom the hero has rescued from her grave. Now, in so far as the deceased Aeschylus of the Aristophanic plot returns to the light of the upper-world, he is the comic analogue of Alcestis.[8] Simultaneously, how-ever, the tragic poet of the *Frogs* is in a much more independent, so to speak, position than that of his Euripidean counterpart, in so far as it is *he himself* who engages in a contest, ostensibly with his deceased antagonist and fellow poet, but, in reality with death, as the reward for the victorious poet is an *anodos* to light and life, while the fate of the loser is fixture in the domain of the Dead. As Euripides indignantly exclaims, just after Dionysus has pronounced

---

[4] Lloyd-Jones (1967: esp. 211–14, 220); Boardman (1975).

[5] See e.g. Apollod. 2. 5. 12; Diod. 4. 26. 1; Persephone's reception, in particular, is espe-cially welcoming and generous (see e.g. Diod. ibid. προσδεχθεὶς ὑπὸ τῆς Φερσεφόνης ὡς ἂν ἀδελφός; cf. Boardman, 1975: 8), a feature which, as Lloyd-Jones (1967: 220) has observed, is probably reflected in *Frogs* 503 ff., i.e. Persephone's cordial invitation to Heracles/Xanthias to a *symposion*; her gesture is perhaps reduplicated, albeit in a different form, at the play's end, provided, of course, we understand Pluto's suggestion at 1479–80 χωρεῖτε τοίνυν, ὦ Διόνυσ', εἴσω . . . ἵνα ξενίζω σφὼ πρὶν ἀποπλεῖν, as coming both from himself and from his wife (Sommerstein 1996: ad 1480 finds it tempting to read, along with Rogers, ξενίσωμεν).

[6] e.g. *Nemean* 1, where Heracles is proposed as the divine analogue of the chariot race winner Chromius, re-entering Hieron's court. See W. J. Slater (1984).

[7] Cf. 1140 μάχην συνάψας δαιμόνων τῷ κυρίῳ.

[8] Like Aeschylus' death, which causes intellectual barrenness (2.2), Alcestis' self-sacrifice turns Admetus' life into permanent deathlike existence (242–3, 861–71, 939–40, 960–1) (for the conformity of the Euripidean play's plot to the Eleusinian myth see Foley 1992). Moreover, in so far as Aeschylus is hailed by the Chorus as *makarios* (1482) and sent forth by Pluto χαίρων (1500), his status is exalted (for *chaire* and the heroization of the dead in 5th-cent. epitaphs see Sourvinou-Inwood 1995: 191–200), one might say in correspondence with the cult that Alcestis is destined to receive after her death; see *Alc.* 436, 445 ff., 1003–4 νῦν δ' ἔστι μάκαιρα δαίμων· | χαῖρ', ὦ πότνι', εὖ δὲ δοίης; see Sourvinou-Inwood (1995: 197–8).

his ultimate verdict, 'You, merciless fellow, will you really suffer me to remain dead?' (ὦ σχέτλιε, περιόψει με δὴ τεθνηκότα;) (1476). In other words, the Aristophanic Aeschylus is not the prize of a contest fought *for* him—and, unlike Cerberus, he is not even the sought-after goal of the descent, as Dionysus had initially set out for Euripides; instead, he *saves himself* by winning the agon through his moral standards, his devotion to the *polis*, and his 'Eleusinian' piety (5.1 and 6.3), the latter element bringing him even closer to Heracles, who in Euripides' homonymous play attributes his successful return from Hades to his Eleusinian initiation (Eur. *Her.* 610–13).[9] To sum up, then, although there are no explicit references to Heracles or his relation to Aeschylus in the agon of the *Frogs*, cultic and literary considerations belonging to a fifth-century Greek audience's 'horizon of expectations' could easily have linked the two, in such a way that, at the play's end, Aeschylus would have, so to speak, *become* Heracles.[10] And just as with Heracles' victory in the 'contest' of the *Alcestis*, Admetus, the mortal king, is a co-winner (1103 νικῶντι μέντοι καὶ σὺ συννικᾷς ἐμοί), the Aristophanic play ends with the hope that the 'Heraclean' saviour's victory will be imparted to the wider community of which he will, once more, become a part.

Let us now, then, focus on the social register, so as to begin to gauge the dynamics of interrelation between Dionysus, Heracles, and the deceased poets. The first part of the agon makes it gradually apparent that the main issue which underlies and unifies the motley shafts of Aeschylus against Euripides is the latter's heavy responsibility for having challenged the boundaries of the Athenian male spectator's self-definition in the following respects.

7.2. Euripides' 'Dionysiac' Bewilderment

One of the main functions of a Greek *polis'* civic discourse was to mould both individual and collective identities through a complex network of analogies with—and more significantly of oppositions

---

[9] In Diodorus (4. 25. 1) and Apollodorus (2. 5. 12), Heracles asks to be initiated in Eleusis, confident that *myesis* will facilitate the most dire of his labours. On Heracles' Eleusinian initiation in a Pindaric (?) fragment (*P. Oxy.* 2622), probably drawing on an epic Heraclean *katabasis* of around 550 BC see Lloyd-Jones (1967). Cf. 6.3, with nn. 61–2, on Heracles as the divine prototype of the mystic ritual of *thronosis*, a *telete* which underlies the description of Aeschylus' dramatic characters in *Frogs* 911–15.

[10] This is not to exclude the possibility that, in a different interpretative structuring of plot and roles, it might appear that it is Pluto, the Chorus, and the *daimones hoi kata gaias* (1529) who, in the *Frogs*, fulfil the function of the tragic Heracles, as it is they who 'send up' the rising poet and escort him (1525 προπέμπετε) from darkness to light, in the same way that Heracles 'sends up' Alcestis in the Euripidean play: πῶς τήνδ' ἔπεμψας νέρθεν ἐς φάος τόδε; (1139).

to—social groups which, with respect to a variable point of reference each time, might be defined as 'others'. Nevertheless, whereas
the community of Athens aimed at impressing upon its male citizen
his supremacy and singularity, Euripides, as if outrightly subverting
this civic process of differentiation, allegedly confronted him with a
picture of disorder and bewilderment, where sexes and classes mix
and boundaries collapse or fuse.

As expressed most clearly in lines 1058–62, the older dramatist's
poetic vision favoured discrimination in all respects and registers:

> Poor devil! *On the contrary*, it is necessary
> to construct such expressions as would befit great concepts
> and thoughts.
> And in any case, it is only to be expected that the demigods
> should use loftier language,
> especially because the clothes they wear are far more
> majestic than ours.
> I had revealed the proper way in which all these should
> be staged, but you spoilt it.

Euripides, on the other hand, takes pride in having assigned an
'equal' stage-presence and an 'equal' voice to all his *dramatis personae*.

> Then, from the very opening words, I wouldn't leave
> anyone idle on stage,
> but in my plays both the wife and the slave would have
> spoken just as much (ἔλεγεν . . . οὐδὲν ἧττον),
> and so would have done the master and the maiden as
> well as the old woman.   (948–50)

Thus, by annihilating the distinctions between men and women,
slaves and masters, inferiors and superiors in civic hierarchy (cf.
1063 and 1071–2), the Aristophanic Euripides puts at risk the male
citizen's secure knowledge of the place reserved for him within the
rigidly structured society of the fifth-century Athenian *polis*.[11]

Nevertheless, in the perspective of a Greek fifth-century spectator
the fusion and turmoil that Comedy lays at Euripides' door are typ-
ically Dionysiac prerogatives in both myth and cult. For, in the
powerful experience that Dionysus creates, man and beast, male and
female, human and divine merge, while his worship brings together
social classes, age groups, and sexes.[12] As a Delphic oracle given to

[11] The antithesis with Aeschylus is clearer in 950–1, where to Euripides' boastful claims,
Aeschylus retorts: 'you should have been put to death for such audacity!'

[12] Even the peculiar kind of disarray that Euripides' mixture of musical types and forms
(1301–3; see in detail 5.2) creates could be envisaged in 'Dionysiac' terms, at least in Plato's
perspective, who deems that those bent on 'mixing' (κεραννύντες) θρήνους τε ὕμνοις καὶ παίωνας

the Athenians of the distant past commands, Dionysus must be honoured 'by all the citizens . . . all mixed up together (ἄμμιγα πάντας)'.[13] The intrusion of the bestial element is prominent not only in Dionysiac secret initiation ritual[14] but also even in the great Dionysiac festivals of the Athenian *polis*. In the Anthesteria, for example, literary sources (mainly late) but also sixth-century vase-paintings indicate that men dressed up as satyrs, especially in order to escort Dionysus in his annual ship-cart journey, which was meant to re-enact his original advent from the high seas to Athens.[15] The same festival, we hear, annihilated boundaries of age: infants, who now have reached the third year of their lives, receive for the first time a pitcher (3.1) and thus participate in the blessing of Dionysus' wine, side by side with the older generations. This interaction is inherently Dionysiac for, as the god himself puts it in Aeschylus' satyr-play *Theori*, 'no one, whether young or old, willingly abstains from these double rows of dancers' (fr. 78c 37–8 Radt). Most impressively, in the ambience of this same Dionysiac feast, master and slave distinctions too are blurred: on the 'Day of the Jars', the Pithoigia (cf. 3.1), we are told that 'it was not allowed to ban either a slave or a hired servant from the enjoyment of the wine, but all those who had offered a sacrifice were obliged to let everybody have a share in Dionysus' gift'.[16] And, although it seems that cultic maenadism of the classical Greek period excluded males (Henrichs 1984*b*),[17] there were other important Dionysiac ritual manifestations (e.g. Lenaea, Rural Dionysia, City Dionysia, Anthesteria), where the entire civic community was welcome to participate irrespectively

διθυράμβοις, καὶ αὐλῳδίας δὴ ταῖς κιθαρῳδίαις μιμούμενοι, καὶ πάντα εἰς πάντα συνάγοντες were 'in a Bacchic frenzy', βακχεύοντες καὶ μᾶλλον τοῦ δέοντος κατεχόμενοι ὑφ' ἡδονῆς (*Leg.* 700d). Even Euripides' Muse, envisaged as playing *ostraka*, i.e. a kind of percussion instrument 'like a castanet, made either from pottery or from shell' (Barker 1984: 115 n. 65), has Dionysiac connotations, for percussion instruments, such as drums, cymbals, rattles, etc. were closely associated with Eastern, orgiastic, and mystic cults (Dionysus/Sabazius, Cybele, etc.); see West (1992: 122ff.). Moreover, the 'backgrounded' Euripidean text as well places the parody on firm Dionysiac ground, as Euripides' *Hypsipyle*, which is satirized here (Dover 1993: ad 1305; Borthwick 1994), is a distinctively 'Dionysiac' play (Zeitlin 1993: 171–82).

[13] Cited in Dem. 21. 52. See Seaford (1994*a*: 246, esp. n. 49 and 1996: ad 206–9).

[14] See Pl. *Leg.* 815c; for the initiand's assumption of bestial identities see the ritual puzzles 'kid/ram/bull/you rushed into the milk' in the Bacchic gold leaves (Ch. 2, n. 231 and Appendix).

[15] For the evidence see Seaford (1984: 8–9 and 1994*a*: 266–9). See also Seaford (1994*a*: 267 n. 146) for great 'Dionysiac' civic occasions of the Hellenistic cities, where revellers dressed up as satyrs.

[16] Schol. Hes. *Op.* 368; cf. Dionysus' cult title Ἰσοδαίτης (Plut. *Mor.* 389a), i.e. 'he who divides portions equally at the feast'. See Dodds (1960: ad 421–3).

[17] In the sphere of myth, however, the 'mixed satyr-maenad band' was a 'dominant theme' in iconography 'from the beginning of the recognisably Dionysiac scenes' (McNally 1984: 109).

of sex. Besides, a multiplicity of cult titles honour Dionysus as the god of the entire *polis*. In various Greek communities we hear of him as 'the Citizen' (Polites), 'the Saviour' (Saotes), 'the god adopted by the whole people' (Demoteles), 'the Leader' (Kathegemon, Archegetes), 'the god of righteous judgement' (Aisymnetes), and so on (Farnell 1909: 135–8). Besides, one of the most memorable and vivid illustrations of such a Dionysiac befuddlement is the picture of Dionysianism that Euripides himself reflected (or, to some extent, created) in the *Bacchae*. Thus, in lines 35–8 the entire 'female seed' of the Cadmeians are said to have mingled on the mountains without distinction with the daughters of the king,[18] while Teiresias asserts that Dionysus, far from discriminating between young and old, wishes that his worship may embrace the whole community alike.

> For the god has not determined, either for the young
> or for the older, that only he should dance,
> but wishes to receive the same honours from the whole of mankind,
> and to be magnified without having anyone excluded from his
>   worship.

> (*Bacch.* 206–9)

Finally, the Chorus, the mouthpiece of Dionysiac religion in the play, celebrate Dionysus as the democratic god who 'offers the griefless joy of wine in equal measure to both rich and humble' (*Bacch.* 421–3), and declare their unreserved acceptance of the thoughts and norms espoused by the 'simple people' (πλῆθος . . . τὸ φαυλότερον) (430 ff.).[19] It emerges, then, that the Aristophanic figure of a 'democratic' Euripides[20] in the poetic agon not only has close affinities with the *polis*' Dionysus, 'magnified by the lack of distinctions in his worship' (Seaford 1996: 170),[21] but at the same time consolidates the confusion of identities and picture of disorder already exemplified by the comic Dionysus' disguise in the prologue of the *Frogs*.

---

[18] *Bacch.* 37 ὁμοῦ δὲ Κάδμου παισὶν ἀναμεμειγμέναι. See Dodds (1960: ad loc.) and Seaford (1996: ad loc.).

[19] See Dodds (1960: ad loc.): 'The φαῦλοι are the "simple" people both in the social and in the intellectual sense.' Seaford (1996: 91) translates 'the mass, the ordinary people.'

[20] See Euripides' defence against Aeschylus' accusations, in line 952: 'I did such things in the name of democracy (δημοκρατικὸν γὰρ αὖτ' ἔδρων)' with Sommerstein's note (1996: ad loc.): 'Euripides is thus presented as having an extreme and warped understanding of the meaning of democracy, and as a subverter of the privileges of male Athenian citizens.'

[21] For the 'democratic' nature of Dionysus' cult see Seaford (1996: 48–9 and ad 37, 192, 206–9): cf. Connor (1996: 224), who argues that the democratic practices of equality and shared decision-making characterizing Athenian political life originated in the internal organization of Dionysiac *thiasoi*, while 'the transference of these religious practices into public space, and their modification into acceptable forms, was . . . Cleisthenes' accomplishment.'

7.3. *Euripides' 'Dionysiac' Subversion of the Male* oikos

The Aristophanic Euripides calls into question the security of the male spectator's self-definition as the dominant sex, an important component of masculine civic identity in a society where the generic discourse was highly polarized. With her proneness to adultery the 'Euripidean' wife challenges her husband's undisputed right to be in control of an *oikos* perpetuating itself through stable patrilineal succession. However, the clash between the two opponents, as far as their conception and shaping of the feminine gender is concerned, can be considered as symbolically epitomized in the antithesis between the deities with whom each one of them is linked, Demeter and Aphrodite respectively. As we have already seen above (5.1), Aeschylus proclaims his special link with Demeter as early as the beginning of the agon (886), while later on, in an almost 'Hippolytean' horror, he rejects the touch of Aphrodite-love.

EUR. By Zeus, surely not! Not the merest soupçon of Aphrodite
  ever rested upon you!
AESCH. Heaven forbid that it would ever do.[22]   (1045)

Simultaneously, however, Aeschylus vividly conveys the sensual dimension prominent in Euripidean drama by conjuring up the image of the junior dramatist oppressed by the weight of Aphrodite-love:[23]

But on you and your own people[24] she was sitting with full force.[25]
                                                                    (1046)

When asked to comment on the influence exerted on the *polis* by female adultery dramatized on the stage, Aeschylus focuses—

---

[22] The humour of these lines is created by the fact that what each of the two contestants understands by 'Aphrodite' is different. For Euripides (1045), Aphrodite means 'beauty or charm' (Dover 1993: ad loc.), 'sensual beauty and loveliness (like the Latin Venus)' (Stanford 1963: ad loc.), while 'In A.'s reply she represents passionate love' (Stanford: ad loc.).

[23] The dramatically created antithesis between Demeter and Aphrodite has an important analogue on the cultic/ritual register, for in the sphere of eroticism and women Aphrodite and her festival (the Adonia) stand for 'the very image of female licence' (Detienne 1977: 78), whereas Demeter Thesmophoros 'represents a particular image of marriage and legitimate union' (ibid.: 81). With the mistresses and courtesans who participate in the Adonia, i.e. women closer to the Euripidean 'whores' (1043), are contrasted the legitimate spouses of Athenian citizens, who gather at the Thesmophoria (Detienne 1977: 78), i.e. those women closer to the 'wives' of Aeschylus' dramas who, allegedly, have 'never' been portrayed 'in the throes of love' (1044). As Detienne has put it, 'the sexual liberty encouraged by the Adonia contrasts with the enforced continence of the Thesmophoria' (1977: 79).

[24] Cf. *Frogs* 1408 αὐτός, τὰ παιδί᾽, ἡ γυνή, Κηφισοφῶν.

[25] On the almost adverbial use of the adjective πολύς (πολλή . . . ᾽πικαθῆτο) see Barrett (1964: 155) on Eur. *Hipp.* 1–2. The image evokes, perhaps deliberately, Aphrodite's boasting in the opening line of Euripides' *Hippolytus*, or even better, *Hipp.* 443 Κύπρις γὰρ οὐ φορητὸν ἦν πολλὴ ῥυῇ.

surprisingly enough—on the feelings of the women: they are driven
to 'drinking hemlock', 'seized with shame (αἰσχυνθείσας)' because of
Euripides' Bellerophons (1051). The first part of Aeschylus' reasoning, the *aischyne* felt by women,[26] is comparable to the deep annoyance of the Aristophanic 'Women celebrating the Thesmophoria' at
the disgraceful deeds ascribed by Euripides to their counterparts in
dramatic fiction: 'I feel terribly aggrieved (βαρέως φέρω)' says
Cleonymus' wife to the feminine assembly (*Thesm.* 385). In other
words, the women spectators of Euripidean drama feel *aischyne*
by a bind of 'collective guilt'—exacerbated by Tragedy's tendency
to pronounce generalized statements about the female sex, as
though all women shared the same faults. The second part, however, blaming the trouble on the male agent, that is, dramatic
characters such as Bellerophon, is clearly a humorous inversion. In
the first place, it inverts the dynamics of the Euripidean plot itself
for, as can be inferred from the *Hypothesis*[27] and the surviving fragments of *Stheneboea*, Bellerophon *rejected* the amorous advances of
the Tirynthian queen, Proetus' wife;[28] if he pretended to succumb to
her passion, it was only in order to entrap the adulteress and throw
her off Pegasus, to the sea. But secondly, and most importantly, it
inverts the ways in which the concept of *aischyne* is involved in the
disruptions of the marital discourse, because *aischyne* refers primarily to the disgrace brought by the offender on the insulted part
(or even on the marital bed or house).[29] Such is, for example, the
concern of Phaedra, which leads her to suicidal thoughts: 'so that I
would never be discovered disgracing my husband' (ὡς μήποτ' ἄνδρα
τὸν ἐμὸν αἰσχύνασ' ἁλῶ) (Eur. *Hipp.* 420). Besides, within the
Mediterranean value system termed by anthropologists as the
'honor/shame syndrome' (Gilmore 1987a: 2), it is primarily the
insulted husband who is 'diminished in relation to other men' (ibid.:
4), since he has failed in his foremost masculine responsibility of
safeguarding the chastity of his kinswomen against external out-
rage.[30] In other words, in societies where male honour resides almost
entirely with the sexual purity and the behaviour of their women
(Pitt-Rivers 1977: 79), it is cuckoldry, rather than adultery, which

---

[26] Of course, Aeschylus is here toying with female psychology, comically exploiting the
feeling of 'sexual shame' (*aischyne*), i.e. the primary quality expected from the feminine
gender within the cluster of values dominant in most Mediterranean communities, both
ancient (cf. Lysias' exaggerated comment at 3. 6) and modern. See e.g. Du Boulay (1974:
112–13); J. K. Campbell (1964: 269–70, 277, 286–7); Peristiany (1965b: 182), etc.

[27] Now in Collard, Cropp, and Lee (1995: 84).

[28] See fr. 661 N² 19–21 οὐπώποτ' ἠθέλησα δέξασθαι λόγους, | οὐδ' εἰς νοσοῦντας ὑβρίσαι δόμους
ξένος, | μισῶν ἔρωτα δεινόν, ὃς φθείρει βροτούς.

[29] See Parker (1983: 95 n. 84, with refs.).

[30] See e.g. Pitt-Rivers (1977: 23–4); J. K. Campbell (1964: 271).

constitutes the 'most humiliating of all social states',[31] and it is the cuckold, rather than the adulteress herself, who, 'in the eyes of the watchful . . . community' (Gilmore 1987*b*: 96) becomes 'the object of ridicule and opprobrium'.[32] In this respect, Euripides himself is presented as cuckolded and feminized in the agon,[33] through the recurrent mention of his slave Cephisophon,[34] the man who was alleged to have seduced his wife (Dover 1993: 54 with n. 6). But, to return to lines 1049–51 in *Frogs*, I take it that the issue at stake is the wreck of lawful marriage bonds of 'noble' (γενναίας) women with 'noble' (γενναίων) men when the latter, like Bellerophon,[35] become the objects of uncontrollable female lust. The point would then be parallel to that raised in gnomic tone by Bellerophon himself in Euripides' *Stheneboea*:

> many a man exulting in his wealth and birth
> has been disgraced by a foolish woman in the house.[36]

But, let us now be more precise on the nature of the threat posed by Euripidean heroines to the *polis'* male order.

Aeschylus' disparagement of the way his antagonist was shaping the female figures of his dramas amounts to his disapproval of the Euripidean exploitation of the uncontrollable and lustful nature inherent in the feminine gender. Thus, within the distorting mirror of the comedy's discourse, Euripides is accused of having sought his inspiration in the feminine openness to Aphrodite,[37] while Aeschylus is presented as never having staged a 'woman in love' (ἐρῶσαν . . . γυναῖκα) (1044).[38]

Now, as King (1983: 110) has emphasized, 'the Greek word for woman, gyne, is also the word for "wife", and it was as a wife and mother that woman was most fully brought into male culture.' Purged of her premarital savagery,[39] tamed by the yoke of marriage,

---

[31] See Cohen (1991: 142 with n. 30).

[32] Pitt-Rivers (1977: 23); cf. Peristiany (1965*b*: 181–2).

[33] It is cuckoldry which is most closely associated with femininity; see Cohen (1991: 142 with n. 30).   [34] 944 Κηφισοφῶντα μειγνύς; 1408 (cf. above, n. 24); 1452f.

[35] Of course it is possible that διὰ τοὺς σοὺς Βελλεροφόντας (1051) refers to Euripides' play *Bellerophon*, where, as Collard, Cropp, and Lee (1995: 99) suggest, Euripides 'may have used the version in which she took her own life from shame (e.g. Hygin. *Fab.* 57. 5)—before the play began.' In this respect, 'on account of your Bellerophons' would mean 'because of plays presenting women in such shameful situations as your play *Bellerophon* did'.

[36] Fr. 661 N² 4–5 πολλοὺς δὲ πλούτῳ καὶ γένει γαυρουμένους | γυνὴ κατῄσχυν' ἐν δόμοισι νηπία; Collard, Cropp, and Lee (1995: 93) understand 'foolish' as 'promiscuous', i.e. the wife who 'destroys a house's stability'.

[37] See 1046 (quoted above). For the conception of the feminine susceptibility to daemonic infiltration see Padel (1983: esp. 11–12, on the Euripidean *Hippolytus*).

[38] See Dover (1993: ad loc.) and Sommerstein (1996: ad loc.).

[39] See e.g. Bekker, *Anecd. Graec.* i. 445. 11–12, for the definition of the function of the *arkteia*.

the chaste female/wife can be considered as an integral part of culture, as 'best representing the positive values and structures of the house' (Zeitlin 1990a: 76–7) and even as protecting and enforcing 'the male model of society' (King 1983: 110). Nevertheless, the taming of a woman can never be complete: women remain forever 'liminal'[40] and, when they happen to surrender to their unbridled sexual desires, the mediatory function of the *oikos* as one of society's 'crucial agencies for the conversion of nature into culture' (Ortner 1974: 84) is subverted and negated. In other words, presenting women as whores, Phaedras,[41] or Stheneboeas (1043), Euripides captures the female at the moment she relapses into the wild, into this state of wantonness and promiscuity that the institution of monogamous marriage is supposed to terminate.[42] In making a woman yield to the violence of her passions, Euripides exhibits and exploits the unsevered ties of femininity with nature.[43]

And yet, adultery is not the only way in which the Euripidean woman displays her 'naturalness'. Incest, another sexual deviation linking the offender with the annihilation of incest taboos reigning in the wild,[44] also has a share in Euripides' dramatic world, as line 1081 ('mating with their brothers') would suggest.[45] Moreover, Euripides does not refrain from staging the female gender as meeting love and Aphrodite in the state of raw and elemental lust. The precise target of lines 849–50 'You, who collect Cretan arias and introduce unholy marriage-ties in our art'[46] is elusive, but an obvious common ground between Cretan monodies and impious love-ties is provided by the characters of Phaedra and Pasiphae, the Cretan princess, wife of Minos, who mated with a bull.[47] As Reckford (1974: 327) has observed, Crete stands already in the

---

[40] For the concept of female liminality see Gould (1980: 58); Versnel (1993: ch. 4).

[41] Aeschylus probably refers to the lost first *Hippolytus*, in which Euripides, according to one of his biographers, τὴν ἀναισχυντίαν θριαμβεύει τῶν γυναικῶν (*Schol. in Eur.* i, p. 5. 5–6 (Schwartz)).

[42] See the traditions clustering around Cecrops who, as the mythical inventor of marriage (Athen. 555d), prevented women from mixing in beast-like promiscuity (cf. Joh. Antioch., fr. 13 *FHG* (iv. 547) . . . πρότερον θηριωδῶς μιγνυμένας) and thus led mankind ἀπὸ ἀγριότητος εἰς ἡμερότητα (schol. Ar. *Plut.* 773). For the civilizing function of marriage in general see e.g. Vernant (1980: 138–9); Detienne (1977: 116–18); Seaford (1987b: 106 with n. 8).

[43] See, however, Foley's warnings (1981b: esp. 147–8) against not properly 'contextualized' applications of the nature/culture dichotomy.

[44] See, in general, Parker (1983: 97–100); incest was actually advocated as 'natural' by nature's aggressive supporters; see Parker (1983: 100 with n. 104).

[45] Referring to the incestuous love of Macareus for Canace in the *Aeolus*; cf. also Ar. *Clouds* 1371–2.

[46] See Dover (1993: 298–9) and Sommerstein (1996: ad 849 and 850).

[47] Schol. *Frogs* 849; Cantarella (1963: 47–8); Collard, Cropp, and Lee (1995: 53–8). It seems that Pasiphae herself refers to her adultery as 'marriage'; see fr. 472e in Collard, Cropp, and Lee (1995): νυμφίου (16); λέκτρων (17); πόσιν (19).

Hippolytus (see 372, 719) for 'the pull backward into the subhuman past', while Pasiphae's *eros* for the bull (Eur. *Hipp.* 337–8), 'symbolic extension of the bestial element in man' (Segal 1986*b*: 201), reduces sexuality to the level of a 'fundamental life instinct' which, as such, has no place in the realm of an organized city (Segal 1981: 22–3). Finally, Aeschylus rebukes Euripides for presenting the female in her most natural—and hence polluting—function of child-bearing,[48] a sacrilege when taking place in a sacred precinct.[49]

But, if Euripides exploits the potentially dangerous side of women, it is Dionysus among all Greek gods who arouses and unleashes upon the ordered male world the catalytic and irrational powers inherent in the feminine gender. Working through the easily invaded, 'enterable' female nature (Padel 1983), he challenges and calls into question civic stability, as epitomized in the ideals of the male-oriented Greek *polis* (Segal 1984: 197). Thus, as Euripides' women shatter their nuptial bond by succumbing to Aphrodite-passion, Dionysus' women annihilate the function of the *oikos* as an element of culture by transferring it to the wild, that is, by dwelling on the mountains and on 'roofless rocks'.[50] To put it in another way, if Euripides' woman can be defined as 'natural', it is Dionysus *par excellence* who returns women 'to the natural state from which men and civilization plucked them' (Just 1989: 260).[51] Bringing women to a state of inner communication with nature (whether this means suckling baby animals or tearing beasts apart with bare hands), the maenadic *thiasos* strengthens the bonds of the unmarried with the wild[52] and renews in the married 'that centrifugal opposition to marriage that had supposedly been permanently overcome in their marital transition'.[53] In fact, this Dionysiac disruption of the household's civilizing functions through female unrestrained emotionality is well exemplified in one of Euripides' own *dramatis personae*, Phaedra (albeit the Phaedra of the extant, rather than the lost, *Hippolytus*), the figure of his tragic repertoire which constitutes the most prominent target of Aeschylus' moral accusations in the contest of the *Frogs*. As Renata Schlesier (1993: 108–10) has

---

[48] *Frogs* 1080, referring to the Euripidean *Auge*. Cf. Ortner (1974: 84). Auge herself seems to have defended her act as 'natural' (see Eur. fr. 266 N² with Clement's remark, probably still Euripidean).

[49] For birth in a temple as sacrilege see Parker (1983: 33 with n. 5).

[50] See the carefully worded and balanced antithetical images in *Bacch.* 32–3, 35–8, 116–19.

[51] More subtly on the maenads' implication in the nature/culture polarity see Foley (1981*b*: 142 ff.).

[52] See e.g. the comparison of the maenad to a filly in *Bacch.* 165 f. For the maenads' Dionysiac power of destruction of the *oikos* see Seaford (1993).

[53] Seaford (1988: 127), discussing *Bacch.* 1056 (ἐκλιποῦσαι ποικίλ' ὡς πῶλοι ζυγά), a 'reversal of the hymenaial image'. See now also Seaford (1994*a*: 309).

recently suggested, Phaedra's delirious wish to be led εἰς ὄρος, to the mountain (215–18), is shot through with maenadic overtones which, it can be argued, would have been easily discernible by 'participants' in a fifth-century Greek culture. In this respect, the recurrence of Phaedra's name in the agon of the *Frogs* is particularly significant: cast by her theatrical creator in the role of a 'maenadic bride destroying the household' (Seaford 1993: 127 n. 59), Phaedra's figure can aptly draw attention to the similar ways in which Euripides depicts and Dionysus affects a *polis*' female gender.

In general, while the Aristophanic Euripides' poetry has a disruptive impact upon society, causing the ruin of legal conjugal unions, 'the . . . attitude inspired by Dionysos . . . is antithetical . . . to the whole process by which girls become the wives of citizens', as Seaford (1988: 127) has expressed it. For, if Euripides' woman is prone to adultery and does not resist the lusts of nature, the image of a maenad indulging in extramarital sex is not merely a creation of Pentheus' neurotic phantasy.[54] Accusations levelled against the orgiastic rites on moral grounds (Dodds 1960: ad *Bacch.* 222–3); the New Comedy stories of girls seduced at an all-night festival (*pannychis*) (Dodds 1960: ad *Bacch.* 487–9); or stories like the conception of Ion in Delphi, where his father mated 'with Bacchus' Maenads' (Μαινάσιν. . . Βακχίου) (Eur. *Ion* 552) at a Dionysiac nocturnal celebration, prove that maenads could indeed be thought of as 'slinking off one by one to lonely places to serve the lusts of men, pretending to be sacrificing priestesses, but in reality ranking Aphrodite higher than the Bacchic god' (Eur. *Bacch.* 222–5).[55] If one confines the inquiry to the sphere of Dionysiac myth, pictures of the mixed satyr-maenad *thiasoi* offer a wealth of instances characterized by affection, not to say lust. Of course, it is impossible for us to gauge to what extent such pictures reflected popular imagination or even, perhaps, helped in its formation (cf. McNally 1984: 110). However, it is important to emphasize that, especially in the black-figure imagery of the Archaic period,

the nymphs fully consent to the silens' interests and desires. Some black-figure scenes even depict sexual intercourse between silens and nymphs . . . . The nymphs . . . occasionally. . . lift their skirts as if to entice or encourage the silens. (Hedreen 1994: 59).

And although maenadic hostility—and hence chastity—against the attacking satyrs is a common iconographic motif, 'The depictions

---

[54] The point has frequently been stressed, e.g. by March (1989: 45); Seaford (1988: 126; 1990b: 163).

[55] Cf. Aesch. fr. 382 Radt, where Dionysus is addressed as πάτερ Θέοινε, μαινάδων ζευκτήριε.

of conflict between satyr and maenad . . . are limited to specific situations and reach a climax at one period: the end of archaic and beginning of classical art' (McNally 1984: 108). In any case, maenadic sexual surrender to the unrestrained animal drives of the semi-bestial satyrs (Lissarrague 1990*a*) is ultimately a yielding to 'natural' sexuality closely analogous to the Euripidean Pasiphae's mating with the bull.

In a brief comment on the agon of the *Frogs*, Froma Zeitlin (1990*a*: 89) writes:

Broadly stated, the contest develops into one between masculine and feminine sides, with Aiskhylos espousing a manly, virile art which exhorts its citizens to military valor, and Euripides representing a feminine, slender muse who is weaker and more insubstantial, leaning toward the sensual and the pathetic.

Furthermore, it seems that Aeschylus' concern, as regards male–female relationships in the agon, comes very close to the ideology expressed in his own dramas. To quote Zeitlin (1984: 160) once more,

If Aeschylus is concerned with world-building, the cornerstone of his architecture is the control of woman, the social and cultural prerequisite for the construction of civilization.

But Aeschylus' theatrical *persona* as presented in this play, full of fear for the corruption of the male order through the deviant outbursts of femininity dramatized on the Attic stage, approaches Heracles as much as the comically shaped Euripides stands close to Dionysus. For, whether as protector of his home and marriage,[56] or as totally 'run through' and 'pierced' by the 'frightful yearning' of extramarital passion,[57] giving in to his virile sexuality, Heracles never acts against male rights, as the 'Euripidean'/'Dionysiac' woman does. Even when he commits adultery, either violating his marital bond with Deianeira (Iole)[58] or seducing the female dependants of free men[59] (Auge, Astydameia, the fifty daughters of Thespius, etc.),[60] his behaviour, rather than being a challenge and a

[56] By vanquishing Achelous and slaying Nessus, the former wooing, the latter attempting to rape his bride/wife Deianeira (see Sophocles' *Trachiniae*).

[57] See Soph. *Trach.* 476–7 ταύτης [sc. Iole's] ὁ δεινὸς ἵμερός ποθ' Ἡρακλῆ | διῆλθε.

[58] Apparently a crime he frequently committed, as Deianeira herself is aware of in Soph. *Trach.* 459–60.

[59] See the definition of adultery in Dover (1974: 209): 'It was *moicheia*, "adultery", to seduce the wife, widowed mother, unmarried daughter, sister or niece of a citizen; that much is made clear from the law cited by Demosthenes 23. 53–5.'

[60] See e.g. (Auge): Diod. 4. 33. 8; Paus. 8. 74. 4; Apollod. 2. 7. 4; (Astydameia): Diod. 4. 37. 4–5; (daughters of Thespius or Thestius): Apollod. 2. 4. 10 (50 daughters in 50 nights); Diod. 4. 29. 3 (50 daughters in one night); Paus. 9. 27. 5–7.

threat, upholds the structure and gratifies the interests of the *male* order in society. Rather than placing the female outside male control, as Dionysus does, Heracles holds firmly the female gender in the grasp of his virile sexuality. To put it in another way, in all these cases, Heracles indulges fully and without restraints in his virile *physis*. Finally, one of the many achievements of the mythical Heracles reproduced in pottery and sculpture in infinite variations throughout the Greek and Roman world is the submission of the Amazons (see *LIMC* i, s.v. Amazones, 1–167).[61] In so far as these creatures are emblematic of the recalcitrant female,[62] his victory not only is equivalent to a triumph of the patriarchal order (Merck 1978), but it also confers upon him the status of a champion of male rights (Keuls 1985: 44).[63] More importantly still, in so far as Amazons live outside and in defiance of society, undisciplined to the bonds of marriage and propagating their race through sexual promiscuity, Heracles subdues the archetype of the 'natural' woman who stands at the core of the 'Euripidean'/'Dionysiac' world. And it is interesting to note at this point that Amazons and maenads are often coupled by Greek artists as images of the most radical 'alterity' which may threaten to subvert the 'norm',[64] that is, the model of the 'tame', civilized, woman/wife of the *polis* and the male-dominated *oikos*.[65]

In conclusion, then, much like the Aristophanic Aeschylus, the mythical Heracles is concerned with the preservation of the male order in a *polis'* community. Much like Dionysus, on the other hand, the comic Euripides disrupts the civilizing functions of the household by encouraging the deviant outbursts of female sexuality and emphasizing the ties of femininity with the wilderness of nature.

7.4. *Euripides' 'Dionysiac' Subversion of the* polis' *Hoplitic Code*

In Athenian society citizenship and military status were inextricably interwoven. As Ehrenberg (1969: 80) put it,

---

[61] For Heracles and the Amazons see e.g. Boardman (1982).

[62] For the complex ways in which Amazons subverted the Greek norm with regard to the female sex see Tyrrell (1984) and Du Bois (1982).

[63] The anti-feminine significance of Heracles' combat, as illustrated in Athenian vase-painting, is underlined by the fact that Heracles' adversary is very frequently inscribed as *ANΔPOMAXE* (see e.g. *LIMC* i, s.v. Amazones, 5, 7, 9, 48, 62, 67, etc.).

[64] See e.g. Lissarrague (1990*b*: 185–6, fig. 109 (=*ARV*² 98, 2)), an alabastron depicting a maenad and an Amazon face to face. As Lissarrague writes, 'Deux aspects périphériques du féminin sont ici associés' (186).

[65] Of course, it cannot be emphasized too strongly that, as images have no fixed, inherent, meanings, their decodification depends to a large extent on the status, disposition, etc. of the viewing subject.

The Polis had derived from the people in arms; it was essentially the state of the citizens . . . There was no question of compulsory military service; it was the other way round: the capability to serve constituted the fully qualified citizen.[66]

Reflecting such an intertwinement of citizenship and military status, Aeschylus' civic world might be defined as the orbit of warriors and hoplitic values.[67]

The senior dramatist is the poet who infuses in his audience war-like spirit and the passion for successive victories. Thus, everyone who saw the *Seven against Thebes* 'was seized by a desire to become a fighter' (1022). With his *Persae*, a production which 'adorned a splendid achievement' (1027),[68] the Greek victory over the barbarians, he had wanted to teach his fellow-citizens 'to be always yearning to vanquish their enemies' (1026–7). What he mostly admires in Homer, whom he regards as his chief source of inspiration (1040),[69] is his display of army ranks (τάξεις), heroic valour (ἀρετάς), and armings of men (ὁπλίσεις ἀνδρῶν) (1036). The citizens whom he has moulded correspondingly, can be identified by their hoplitic armour, as they are 'breathing' (πνέοντας)

> spears and lances and white-crested helmets
> and casques and greaves and sevenfold-oxhide passions.[70]

Moreover, the men whom he counts as his 'disciples' (964; but see Sommerstein 1996: ad loc.), Phormisius and Megaenetus (965), have the reputation of being rough military types, that is, men of action, unpolished, unrefined and uncivil, coarse and soldierly in their outlook and manners.[71] And, generally speaking, the goal of his poetry, which dramatized the valour of 'men like Patroclus and lion-spirited Teucer' (Πατρόκλων, Τεύκρων θυμολεόντων), was 'to excite the male citizen so that he would strain to equal them in bravery,

[66] Cf. Vernant (1980: 26); however, as Alan Sommerstein rightly points out to me, this was not true at the time of the play's production (405 BC), as *everyone* had been encouraged to serve in the fleet for the naval battle of Arginusae.

[67] Of course naval values too play an important role in Aeschylus' world (as they also played a central role in the Athenian society of 405 BC; cf. Strauss 1996); see Aeschylus' concern in 1071–3 and his answer to the civic riddle in 1463–5.

[68] For the meaning of κοσμήσας in 1027 see Dover (1993: ad 1004f.).

[69] According to Athenaeus (347e), Aeschylus himself regarded his dramas as 'slices from Homer's great banquets' (cf. above, 3.2).

[70] 1016–17 πνέοντας δόρυ καὶ λόγχας καὶ λευκολόφους τρυφαλείας | καὶ πήληκας καὶ κνημῖδας καὶ θυμοὺς ἑπταβοείους.

[71] Phormisius (schol. ad loc.) δραστικὸς ἦν . . . καὶ τὴν κόμην τρέφων καὶ φοβερὸς δοκῶν εἶναι. Megaenetus (schol. ad loc.) οὐ πάντως βάρβαρος, ἀλλ' ἀναίσθητος καὶ οὐκ ἀστεῖος. αὐθάδης δὲ οὗτος καὶ τῶν στρατηγιώντων ἐστὶ καὶ ἄλλως θρασύς. See also the scholion on σαλπιγγολο-γχυπηνάδαι (966): Σάλπιγγας καὶ λόγχας καὶ ὑπήνας ἔχοντες, which Sommerstein (1996: ad loc.) translates as 'beard-lance-and-trumpet types', i.e. 'rough, "macho" men who are good at soldiering but at little else.'

whenever he would hear the sound of the battle trumpet'.[72] Submitting to the trumpet's blast means accepting the supreme hoplitic values of discipline and subordination, something that Euripides' men clearly lack. Nevertheless, hoplitic status 'involves an attitude of mind, a quality of discipline and stability which stands at the opposite extreme from the female emotionality associated with Dionysus' (Segal 1984: 204). And although Euripides' *Bacchae* never openly stages a conflict of the maenads with Pentheus' hoplites, the poet seems to take every care to juxtapose the two armies in his audience's imagination.[73] Thus, not only is Dionysus the self-proclaimed military leader of his frenzied troops,[74] but his soldiers as well display vividly to the spectators' eyes the ways in which their fighting mode subverts the tactics of a city's army. *Thyrsoi*, naturally provided, prove more effective than fabricated, iron weapons (798–9). Fighting in the mountain glens[75] replaces the phalanx's fighting on flat ground, while pursuit/hunt (734–5) or raid[76] takes the place of the noble frontal attack of the hoplites. In short, male supremacy is overthrown by feminine affinity to the divine.[77] As the Messenger in *Bacchae* 763–4 puts it, 'they were inflicting wounds and attacking from behind, women turning men to flight, not without the help of some god'.

In iconography as well, when artists portray Dionysus' dressing up in hoplitic armour,[78] they take every care to emphasize that it is only by magical and *non*-hoplitic means, such as the *thyrsos* and the kantharos,[79] that Dionysus annihilates his opponents, while his 'warlike' army, made up of satyrs, maenads, and felines,[80] provides the most spectacular contrast to the discipline and order (*taxis,*

---

[72] 1041–2 ἵν' ἐπαίροιμ' ἄνδρα πολίτην | ἀντεκτείνειν αὐτὸν τούτοις, ὁπόταν σάλπιγγος ἀκούσῃ.

[73] See *Bacch.* 50–2, 780–6, 798–9, 809, 837, 845.

[74] *Bacch.* 52 ξυνάψω μαινάσι στρατηλατῶν. Cf. Aesch. *Eum.* 25–6, where Dionysus' leadership is stated as a fact. March (1989: 35–43) draws on pictorial evidence to argue that the standard version of the Pentheus story, as dramatized before Euripides, culminated in a military conflict between Pentheus/*polis* and Dionysus' maenads.

[75] As implied in *Bacch.* 790–1, 796–7.

[76] See *Bacch.* 752–4, where the maenads are explicitly compared to hostile troops.

[77] Graf (1984: 251) refers to a story related by Polyaenus (*Strateg.* 4. 1), whereby Macedonian girls in Bacchic attire (θύρσους ἀντὶ δοράτων πάλλουσαι) terrified the enemy's army and drove it to retreat; a temple of Dionysus Pseudanor, the 'False Man', was built to celebrate the victory.

[78] See *LIMC*, s.v. Dionysos, 609–11, part of a small corpus of Dionysiac warrior images, centring on the god's participation in the Gigantomachy (cf. 1.1 and 1.4, with nn. 11 and 36).

[79] *Thyrsos* (*LIMC*, s.v. Dionysos, 609, 610) and kantharos (ibid.: 610, 611) are extended to Dionysus alongside a breastplate and a helmet (Figs. 7.1 and 7.2).

[80] In *LIMC*, s.v. Dionysos, 611 (Fig. 7.2), a small feline stands close to Dionysus, while a serpent is the emblem on his shield, serpents and felines being regularly portrayed as warriors in the painters' depictions of the battle between gods and giants; see Villard (1947: 11), and cf. 1.1.

7.1. Dionysus goes to war in hoplitic armour and thyrsos
rf. Attic pelike: Paris, Cabinet des Médailles, 391 (*ARV*² 286, 15)

7.2. Dionysus ready to don hoplitic armour; small feline at his side
rf. Attic oenochoe: Bologna, Museo Civico Archeologico, 338 (*ARV*² 595, 65)

syntaxis, eutaxia) of the *polis*' hoplites.[81] Similar patterns of antithesis are evident when the painters portray the satyrs by themselves
as fighters. As Lissarrague (1990*b*: esp. 172 ff.) has shown, satyrs
almost never feature as hoplites on vases. By way of contrast, all the
iconographic signs employed in the pictures serve to emphasize the
deviation of their fighting mode from the hoplitic pattern. On a late
sixth-century cup painted by Epictetus, for example, satyrs are
portrayed on the front and the reverse, holding the ephebic half-
shield (*pelte*) and, instead of offensive arms, a drinking-horn and
wine-jug.[82] Even when the iconographic scheme of 'satyr warrior'
seems to be modelled on patterns familiar from the arming scenes of
citizens/warriors, the analogy and closeness serve only to highlight
the deviation and inversion. A London pelike, for example (*ARV*²
501, 35), portrays a helmeted satyr in the course of putting on his
greaves, while the female figure standing next to him assimilates the
scene to the well-established motif of the wife's farewell to her
departing husband/soldier.[83] However, whereas in the images
depicting the arming of citizens the wife hands over to her warrior
husband a spear and a shield, the female companion of the satyr is
about to offer him a *thyrsos* and a leopard-skin (fig. 99 in Lissarrague
1990*b*: 175). In general, then, it cannot be emphasized too strongly
that, in order to depict 'satyrs in arms', the imagination of the artists
draws on the most marginalized, non-hoplitic forms of war.

However, if Dionysus subverts hoplitic tactics, subversion of the
hoplitic ideal constitutes the third way in which Euripides' drama
challenges the male order of the *polis*.

Taking refuge in petty bureaucratic tasks (1083–4 ἡ πόλις ἡμῶν |
ὑπογραμματέων ἀνεμεστώθη), instead of longing to become a fighter
(1022 δάϊος),[84] and shrinking selfishly from state burdens (1014
διαδρασιπολίτας),[85] the citizen moulded by Euripides' drama is in
his behaviour a complete anti-hoplite. In the eyes of fifth-century

---

[81] Krentz (1985: 58–9); Pritchett (1974: 236–8).

[82] Cf. a cup in the Louvre (CA 4356), where satyrs kneeling in ambush, like ephebes, hold
a wineskin in their left hand and a rhyton in their right; Lissarrague (1990*b*: 173, fig. 98).

[83] See e.g. fig. 193 in Arias, Hirmer, and Shefton (1962).

[84] See schol. ad 1084 ἀνεπληρώθη τῶν γραμματεύειν βουλομένων καὶ μὴ στρατεύεσθαι . . . ἄλλως.
ἐπειδὴ ἀφέντες τὰ γενναῖα πράγματα φορολόγοι γεγένηνται. Cf. Lysias' speech *Against
Nicomachus*, a 'transcriber' of Solon's laws who was accused that, although appointed for a
term of 4 months, he managed to hold office for 6 entire years: 'And what reason is there for
acquitting this man? Because he has taken a brave man's part in many battles by land and sea
against the enemy? But *while you were facing danger on naval expeditions, this man stayed at
home* and corrupted the laws of Solon' (Lys. 30. 26).

[85] It is easily conceivable that the semantic field of such a word (which Sommerstein 1996
nicely translates as 'duty-dodging citizens') would have included one's responsibility in the
battlefield as well, since the figures of the citizen and warrior in the democratic Athens merge
(Vernant 1980: 26, 28, 35, 36, 42).

spectators, the Aristophanic 'Euripidean' men could have seemed to have transferred to the political arena and civic life the principles and values dominating the anti-hoplitic, antisocial period of ephebic marginality (cf. 2.4(c)): reversing the fair, open, and honourable hoplitic fighting,[86] they pursue all the means and paths of guile, dishonesty, *apate*. As Aeschylus complains, they are 'impudent rogues' (κοβάλους) and 'knavish' (πανούργους) fellows (1015), 'monkeys of the *demos*, constantly leading the people astray' (δημοπιθήκων | ἐξαπατώντων τὸν δῆμον ἀεί) (1085–6). The political conduct of Theramenes in particular, that celebrity among his students of whom Euripides seems to be especially proud (967), is an outright negation of hoplitic ideals. For, while the hoplite has sworn not to abandon his comrade in the battle rank wherever he be stationed,[87] Theramenes is never firm to his own party.[88] As *Frogs* 969–70 seems to imply, he rather shuns his share in the collective danger and alters his position in search of the most favourable winds: 'Who, if he gets somewhere into trouble and stands close beside it, extricates himself from danger . . .' (cf. *Frogs* 536–41 with 2.4(c)). In other words, Theramenes embodies the vices of inconstancy,[89] individualism, and selfishness, which stand at the opposite extreme to the staunchness and collective spirit upon which the strength of the hoplitic phalanx rests. Furthermore, both Aeschylus and Dionysus complain about the newfangled attitudes of 'questioning one's orders' (1076 νῦν δ' ἀντιλέγει) and 'answering back' (ἀνταγορεύειν) to one's commanders (τοῖς ἄρχουσιν) (1072), which seem to have replaced the old virtues of discipline, *taxis*, and subordination of those rowing a warship.[90] Finally, hoplitic battle 'required above all . . . unyielding physical and moral strength' (Cartledge 1977: 15–16), for the acquisition of which adolescents exercised in the gymnasiums and wrestling-schools of their cities.[91] Euripides, however, instead of prompting

[86] For the ancient hoplitic *ethos* see e.g. Polyb. 13. 3. 3–5; Thuc. 2. 39. 1 (especially for Athens).

[87] Οὐδὲ λείψω τὸν παραστάτην ὅπου ἂν στ⟨οι⟩χήσω. For the text on the Acharnian stele and its variants see Daux (1971: 370ff.). For the hoplitic rule of steadfastness in battle see e.g. Tyrtaeus 10, 15 West; Hdt. 7. 104. 5; Pl. *Lach.* 190e.

[88] For the notoriously opportunist political career of Theramenes see Sommerstein's (1996) concise note ad 541.

[89] As illustrated especially by his notorious nickname *kothornos*; see e.g. Plut. *Nic.* 2. 1 and Xen. *Hell.* 2. 3. 31.

[90] On the necessity for perfect co-ordination and order, and on the largely 'communitarian' and 'egalitarian' character of rowing a trireme in classical Athens see Strauss (1996: esp. 317–18).

[91] See esp. Delorme (1960: esp. 24–6); cf. Vernant (1980: 26). Besides, the *gymnasia* never ceased to be used as places for military training before battles; see e.g. Ar. *Peace* 355–6 with schol. 356a–c (Holwerda), and Delorme (1960: 26). For wrestling as a preparation for hoplitic fighting see Borthwick (1970a: 18 with n. 11).

the young to physical exercise, 'taught them how to be silver-tongued and wordy' (λαλιὰν ἐπιτηδεῦσαι καὶ στωμυλίαν ἐδίδαξας) (1069), qualities which caused them to abandon the wrestling-schools (1070 'ξεκένωσεν τάς τε παλαίστρας) and to remain collectively untrained, to the point of being unable to carry the torch at a torch-race (1087–8; cf. 5.2). Aeschylus' distress is not dissimilar to the disapprobation expressed by the 'Just Logos' in the *Clouds*:

> That—that's the stuff that the young men are always blabbering about all day (ἀεὶ δι' ἡμέρας λαλούντων), which makes the bath-house full and the wrestling-schools empty. (*Clouds*, 1052–4; tr. Sommerstein 1982)

Moreover, the pivotal antithesis between the 'old' and 'new' *paideia* as envisaged by the 'Just Logos' in the *Clouds* is, again, between a life of exercise in the gymnasium and a life of talking in the *agora*. As the 'Just Logos' promises to Pheidippides, 'you will spend your time in the *gymnasia*, not babbling in the *agora* coarse rude jests, like people do in our days' (1002–3) (cf. Dover 1993: 22). However, lack of outdoor activity and exercise results in effeminate delicacy. The typical male citizen of the Aristophanic Euripides' world is pale, *leukos* (1092), a fair complexion always signifying effeminacy in men.[92] But it is also this same 'virtue' which brings the Euripidean citizen much closer to Dionysus, who, as we have seen in 1.3, is frequently portrayed in fifth-century art and literature as an effeminate, soft, and sensual youth. In Euripides' *Bacchae*, in particular, Pentheus taunts Dionysus for his 'white . . . complexion' (λευκήν . . . χροιάν), which he acquired 'by avoiding the rays of the sun and by keeping in the shade' (Eur. *Bacch.* 457–8).[93]

Aeschylus, conversely, and his virile world have a close affinity with Heracles. For within the repertory of mythical and cultic images available to Greek spectators, Heracles' deeds are never placed exclusively outside the boundaries of civic space. An equally important aspect of his contradictory and multifarious mythical *persona* is his dimension as a 'culture' hero, a figure raising and promoting the standards of civilized life 'from within' (Lacroix 1974). Even his purely manual labours performed in the wild have a prominent social aspect, since Heracles, in his role of beast-slayer, stands for the archetypal model of muscular strength and heroic valour against which adolescents could measure their own down-to-earth achievements (Bérard 1987a).

---

[92] See Irwin (1974: 129, 133–4) and Seaford (1996: ad 457–8).

[93] For the ἐσκιατροφηκώς as effeminate see Dodds (1960) on *Bacch.* 458 (to his refs. add Luc. 54. 28); it also connotes inability for fighting (Irwin 1974: 131 and n. 51). Cf. also his long hair, a sign of his abstinence from the palaestra, οὐ πάλης ὕπο (*Bacch.* 455; with Dodds's note ad loc.).

Thus, when integrated into the Athenian and other cities' state cults, Heracles presides over the virile values and activities that Aeschylus boasts he is fostering through his *poiesis*. In the first place, he functions as the archetype for the agonistic and initiatory exploits of ephebes. Particularly eloquent is the story of Polydamas, a victor in the Olympic game of pancratium. From Pausanias (6. 5. 5) we learn that this young man, who slew a huge and powerful lion 'without the help of any weapon', was

led to this exploit (προήχθη δὲ ἐς τὸ τόλμημα) by an ambition to rival the labours of Heracles (φιλοτιμίᾳ πρὸς τὰ Ἡρακλέους ἔργα), for Heracles as well, legend has it, vanquished the lion of Nemea.[94]

More importantly, in Athens itself, civic propaganda chose Heracles' exploits as the primary exemplum upon which to model the ephebic deeds of Theseus, the 'national' hero of the *polis* (Boardman 1982: 2–3 and *passim*). Besides, being himself a master-wrestler (Boardman 1975: 11 with n. 45), Heracles has also a very privileged bond with adolescents in exercise (Jourdain-Annequin 1986: 286). Thus, not only did Heraclean sanctuaries serve as appropriate places for the enactment of athletic games and contests,[95] but Heracles was also one of the gods enshrined in the palaestras and *gymnasia* all over the Greek land.[96]

Furthermore, as far as war, the second pole of Aeschylean drama, is concerned, Heracles is once again a stimulus to warlike deeds. In the first place, given the initiatory function of the hunt in ancient Greek society, that is to say, its value as a preparation for the confrontation of the human enemy,[97] Heracles' hunting exploits operate as the prototype for ephebic integrations into the hoplitic rank. It is therefore not surprising that the hero is one of the deities invoked as witnesses in the Acharnian stele of the ephebic oath, and that he also plays a prominent role in the Athenian ephebic festival *par excellence*, the Apaturia. As Athenaeus informs us, during this festival the ephebes-to-be sacrifice their hair and 'offer to Heracles a large cup which they have filled with wine and which they call *oinisteria*'.[98] We even hear that Heracles is often conceived as

---

[94] It is interesting to note here that in art as well Polydamas' deed was glorified precisely through the commemoration of his fight along the exact lines of the iconographic pattern of 'Heracles, strangler of the lion' (Bérard 1987a: 183).

[95] See Paus. 6. 23. 5 and Woodford (1971: 223 with refs.).

[96] See e.g. Paus. 4. 32.1; Athen. 561d; for shrines or sanctuaries of Heracles in or close to *gymnasia* in Sicyon, Arcadia, Megalopolis, Ithome, Thebes, etc. see Jourdain-Annequin (1986: 286–7). For the Attic evidence (from Cynosarges, Academy, Melite, Tetracomos, Marathon) see Woodford (1971).

[97] Xen. *Cyneg.* 12. 1–9; *Inst. Cyr.* 1. 2. 10; *Lac.* 4. 7; see in general Schnapp (1973).

[98] Athen. 494f οἱ μέλλοντες ἀποκείρεσθαι τὸν σκόλλυν ἔφηβοι, φησὶ Πάμφιλος, εἰσφέρουσι τῷ Ἡρακλεῖ μέγα ποτήριον πληρώσαντες οἴνου, ὃ καλοῦσιν οἰνιστηρίαν, καὶ σπείσαντες τοῖς συνελθοῦσι

having played a special part in historical battles of Greek cities. In the classical Athenian *polis*, most importantly, Heracles was thought to have contributed to the illustrious victory of Marathon (Woodford 1971: 217). According to Herodotus (6. 116. 1), when the Athenians, after having defeated the Persians at Marathon, rushed home to defend their city, they encamped in Heracles' precinct at Cynosarges, just as their camp at Marathon had been pitched in a precinct of the same hero (cf. Hdt. 6. 108. 1). From Pausanias (1. 15. 3) we learn that a wall-painting in the Stoa Poikile in Athens depicted Heracles together with the fighters of Marathon. On a panhellenic scale too, a wealth of evidence reveals that Heracles featured among those gods whose military epiphanies could prove to be salutary for the party under their protection. I will just cite a couple of examples from two corners of the Greek world geographically apart.

In order to boost the fighters' morale before the battle of Leuctra (371 BC), the Theban leaders thought it worth while to exploit rumours that 'the arms from the sanctuary of Heracles had disappeared, indicating that Heracles had gone forth to the battle' (Xen. *Hell.* 6. 4. 7).[99] A similar stratagem was devised by the Pythagorean Milo, at the end of the sixth century BC, in order to encourage the inhabitants of Croton in Magna Graecia: Milo, the athlete, entered into battle 'crowned with his Olympic crowns and equipped with lion-skin and club, the gear of Heracles' (Diod. 12. 9. 6).[100]

Finally, Heracles is not merely the celebrated archer, the lonely fighter who excels in his handling of the bow, a *kakiston* and non-hoplitic weapon (Eur. *Her.* 160–1), but also the χάλκασπις ἀνήρ, the 'warrior with the bronze shield', as he is referred to by the Chorus in Sophocles' *Philoctetes* (726). In fact, it is Heracles himself who in this very play urges both Neoptolemus and the exiled hero Philoctetes to their hoplitic mission in the Trojan plain. Neoptolemus' attainment of hoplitic status and Philoctetes' reintegration into the hoplitic world of the Argive camp (Vidal-Naquet 1988*b*) are clearly implied in Heracles' pronouncement of the hoplitic ideal of standing firm by one's comrade in the rank, so that the safety of both depends on their mutual steadfastness. Addressing both the boy and the man, he orders:

διδόασι πιεῖν. See Kearns (1989: 35). For the role of Heracles as a paradigm for the young reflected in Euripides' *Heracleidae* see Wilkins (1990).

[99] Cf. Diod. 15. 53. 4 and Polyaen. *Strateg.* 2. 3. 8. Diodorus (16. 44. 3) also relates that the Argive general Nicostratus, being himself superior in bodily strength, ἐμιμεῖτο τὸν Ἡρακλέα κατὰ τὰς στρατείας καὶ λεοντῆν ἐφόρει καὶ ῥόπαλον ἐν ταῖς μάχαις.

[100] For more examples of Heraclean military epiphanies see Lonis (1979: 216–17). On divine/heroic epiphanies in the battlefield see Pritchett (1979: 14–46).

> You shall not have the strength to capture Troy
> without this man, nor he without you,
> but, like twin lions hunting together,
> he shall guard you, you him.[101]   (*Phil.* 1434–7)

Moreover, besides literature, iconography can also depict Heraclean battles as hoplitic exploits. On an early vase from Corinth, for example,[102] the artist has portrayed Heracles in full hoplitic gear leading the fight against the Amazons. As John Henderson (1994: 93) has put it, 'he is shown to be a man among men, "othered", or differentiated, from his fellows only by leading their way, and otherwise as social a hoplite as any burgher should aspire to prove himself.'

To sum up, then, Euripides' un-hoplitic character draws him closer to the anti-hoplitic figure of Dionysus, while Aeschylus' war-like and hoplitic spirit displays substantial affinities with Heracles, the heroic warrior and patron of ephebic tasks.

7.5. *Conclusion*

We have seen in this chapter that within the cultural experience of fifth-century spectators, the Aristophanic Aeschylus, the chosen poet, exercises an 'Heraclean' impact on society, while Euripides' influence seems to be carrying distinctively 'Dionysiac' overtones. However, in the previous chapter we have also seen that on the level of poetic *techne* Aeschylus is a 'Dionysiac'/'Eleusinian' poet, a *Bakcheios anax*, with his mind nourished by Demeter and *dramatis personae* bearing a close resemblance to initiates in Demeter's secret *teletai*. We can therefore start to appreciate the 'advancement' in Dionysus' *dramatis persona*, as expressed through his choice in the agon.

Given the 'Heraclean' connotations of Aeschylus' *poiesis* and the 'Dionysiac' tendencies of Euripidean art, as presented in the *Frogs'* contest, Dionysus' choice is equivalent to a circular approach, a return from another road, of the 'actor' to his 'prototype'. As we have discussed at length in Sections 3–4 of the present chapter, purged of his inherent ambiguity and focused on his positive and beneficial side, Heracles is an implicit presence within the *dramatis persona* of the city's saviour. In this respect, by discarding the rather feminine, cuckolded, un-hoplitic, sophistic, and *oikos*-oriented (cf. 8.2(b)–(c)) Euripides while choosing the 'Heraclean' Aeschylus, a

---

[101] See Vidal-Naquet (1988*b*: 173–5): 'It is the oath that the ephebe swears, never to abandon his comrade in the ranks' (174).

[102] See *LIMC* i, s.v. Amazones, 1: Corinthian alabastron, end of 7th cent. BC.

virile, martial, and *polis*-oriented (cf. Ch. 5) poet, the god is ultimately reintegrating in his dramatic figure the Heraclean dimension
which was incongruously combined with his stage-presence in the
comedy's prologue. In other words, the Dionysiac 'self', as moulded
during the initiation's limen, and the Heraclean 'other', as reshaped
in the literary contest, can be finally conceived as having fused and
merged. However, there are two important issues which deserve
particular attention at this point. First, Dionysus' 'return to
Heracles' by no means entails the loss of his 'Dionysianism', for the
'fertile' poet he selects is, as an artist, a *Bakcheios anax*. Secondly,
a reading of the agon as a 'meeting' of Dionysiac and Heraclean
neither circumvents nor contradicts Dionysus' differentiation from
the Heraclean side of his personality, a process gradually effected
during the limen of his initiation. As has been argued in Chapter 4,
the 'encounter scenes' set Dionysus apart from the model of his
imitation *only* in the measure that this model was evoked before his
eyes in its 'natural' and brutish side (*Frogs* 464 ff. and 549 ff.). In the
agon of the *Frogs*, conversely, which corresponds to the 'reintegration' period of Dionysus' initiation, the Heraclean values which
confront Dionysus are devoid of any antisocial or subversive tinge.
Remoulded, as they are, in the Aristophanic portrait of the senior
poet, not only do they represent a positive exemplum, but they are
also dramatically exploited for the multivalent contrast which they
create with modes of subversiveness and of disruption, such as those
incarnated in the drama of Euripides and the era it reflects.
Dionysus, consequently, is now put in touch with the cultural
dimension of his prototype and, in this respect, is reunited with the
social side of his model's personality.

　　To conclude. In a classical Greek audience's perspective, the
agon of the *Frogs* can be said to complement the divine actor's
'character advancement' not only by effecting the reincorporation
of 'Heracles', the model, into the *persona* of Dionysus, the impersonator, but also, most importantly, by steering and transfusing the
Dionysiac and Heraclean sides into the space and the moulds of the
polis.[103]

---

[103] Meeting the civilized Heracles through the Aeschylean figure implies for Dionysus an
encounter with the civic side of his own self as well. For example, as an 'ally' of the Greeks at
Salamis in the distinctively Athenian visage of the Eleusinian Iacchus (Polyaen. *Strateg.* 3.
11. 2 σύμμαχον ἔσχον τὸν Ἴακχον; cf. Hdt. 8. 65; Plut. *Them.* 15), he was conceived of as the
god able to inspire the *polis*' greatest fights against invaders. His followers, the satyrs, correspondingly, engaged in a broad range of manly skills, e.g. dancing the *pyrrhiche* (see e.g.
Poursat 1968: 583, no. 27), or athletics (Seaford 1984: 105 n. 39 (with refs.); cf. 39–40; Sutton
1975: esp. 208 with nn. 19–21; Simon 1982: 129–31), esp. in the imagery of his own
Anthesteria festival, which included a series of athletic contests (van Hoorn 1951: 33–5).

8

Dionysus the Civic Viewer

8.1. *Dionysus' Spectating Roles*

If 'playing the other' in his liminal transition has already introduced Dionysus into civic space (4.11), in the agon the god mingles imaginatively with an audience of tragic plays. In this respect, the agon brings Dionysus into another metatheatrical position, that of an 'internalized' spectator, a role culminating in the highest function reserved for him within the play, namely, the role of a civic judge.

The metatheatrical position of Dionysus as a spectator has been adumbrated twice in the play's early part. In the comedy's opening scene Dionysus evokes the picture of himself among the thousands of the Athenian and foreign *theatai*, as a critical beholder of the happenings on the stage:

> . . . for I, as a spectator (ὡς ἐγὼ θεώμενος),
> whenever I see some of these clever tricks,
> I walk out of the theatre feeling more than a year older than I am.

(16–18)

While journeying through the regions of the Underworld, Dionysus becomes an 'internalized' viewer of the Eleusinian procession. His response to the 'enfolded' spectacle and rite of the mystic Chorus illustrates the double reaction of every theatrical spectator, constantly oscillating between emotional participation and critical, rational disposition:[1] lines 414a–15 in particular,

> ἐγὼ δ᾽ ἀεί πως φιλακόλου-
> θός εἰμι καὶ μετ᾽ αὐτῆς
> παίζων χορεύειν βούλομαι,
>
> I, for my part, feel like following her,
> and I'd love to join in and play and dance,

whereby Dionysus gives voice to his 'sympathetic' projection

---

[1] On the spectator's fluctuation between these two poles of theatrical response see (in the case of Greek Tragedy) Bain (1977: 6); Taplin (1986: 164), and for a full discussion Lada (1993).

towards what is being enacted, is a good illustration of the psychological process of the audience's 'identification' with the actors. On
the other hand, his admonitions to Xanthias to keep 'still' and
'quiet' (321–2, 339) as the Initiates enter the orchestra, so that a
better 'understanding'[2] of the spectacle can be achieved, reflects the
need for some degree of critical detachment from the events enacted
on the stage, if the dramatic images are to be clearly deciphered and
assimilated (cf. Lada 1993).

Being an actor is an individual process, involving the performer's
secret dialogue with his role. Nevertheless, being a spectator can
also be an isolated experience since, even when amid thousands of
other *theatai*, one can still be viewing things differently, appreciating or disapproving of the spectacle alone. Dionysus, the theatrical
spectator of the prologue (16–18), for example, differentiates his
own discerning and refined tastes (1–18) from the coarse sensations
experienced by the bulk of the assembled unsophisticated *theatai*
(1–2). In the agon, on the other hand, Dionysus' spectating solitude
is not an issue any more. Mediating, as he does, between the clashing worlds of Aeschylus and of Euripides, he actively identifies with
a variety of possible viewpoints. For example, wavering from
sympathy for the former to approval of the latter, Dionysus spans
two opposite ends of the Athenian spectating body, that is, the
predilections of the older and the younger generations respectively.
The mutual exclusiveness of those sympathies can be seen very
clearly in the final scenes of Aristophanes' *Clouds*, where the aged
Strepsiades, a fervent admirer of Aeschylus (1365), comes to blows
with his young son Pheidippides when the latter, a fan of Euripides,
starts singing a Euripidean monody on incestuous love (1371–2).
But, more importantly still, as we shall see in what follows,
Dionysus' metatheatrical spectating role in the agon could be
envisaged as an amalgam of possible audience-responses in other
respects as well.[3]

Now and again, the manner of his involvement in the debate of
the two antagonists proves him intellectually incompetent: remarks
which are nonsensical or off the mark, together with comments
which merely disrupt the continuity of the discourse,[4] seem to
justify Cornford's (1914: 205) appreciation of his role as that of an
'almost idiotic buffoon'. Nevertheless, there are also instances
where his interventions are manifestly shrewd and pertinent, like,

---

[2] *Frogs* 322 ὡς ἂν εἰδῶμεν σαφῶς.

[3] For Dionysus' spectating role as 'dramatizing a range of responses to the poets for the
audience' see Goldhill (1991: 217) who does not, however, elaborate this point any further.

[4] See e.g. 1149, 1195–6 (at which point Euripides cuts him short: ληρεῖς, 1197), 1278–80, etc.

for example, his comment on the political conduct of Theramenes (968–70) or on the deceitful behaviour of the self-lamenting rich (1067–8). At other times, again, he may be able to mount a clever parody of one of the contestants, as he does in lines 980–91, where he constructs a hilarious trivialization of Euripides' claim to have taught men how to administer their households in a better way than they were doing in the past. And there are also cases when he admirably lives up to his arbitrative function and succeeds in playing a reserved and sensible mediative role (e.g. 851–9). A similar fluctuation in the quality of his response is also detectable where literary matters are concerned. Most of the time, he is conspicuously incapable of subtle textual appreciation. To put it in the language of the Chorus, one would rather say he belongs to the ranks of those *theatai* whose *amathia*, lack of education, might prevent them from discerning intellectual subtleties (1109–11). For, just like Heracles in the *Frogs*' prologue or Strepsiades in the *Clouds*, he seems to be unable to conceptualize abstractions. In consequence, his response is hopelessly confined to the level of a concrete and personalized terminology (e.g. 1036–8). And yet, even in literary matters, his concrete way of thinking can sometimes lead him to remarks cleverly worded and presented. In lines 1175–6, for example, in his attempt to defend Aeschylus against the charge of tautology with the simultaneous use of *klyein* ('hear') and *akouein* ('listen to', 'hear and understand') (1174), he readily comes up with a smart and fitting comment:

> he was talking to the dead, you poor wretch,
> whom we cannot reach even through triple invocations.

Moreover, in the parodic 'psychostasia' scene (1364–1413), where Aeschylus' and Euripides' verses are competitively weighed on the scales, Dionysus seems to have so well mastered the technique of literary parody that he is able to play a clever trick on Euripides. Trying to help the younger poet to find something 'mighty and big' (1398 καρτερόν τε καὶ μέγα) to place on the scales, he constructs[5] a line which starts impressively, on a grand, majestic tone (1400 'Achilles threw . . .'),[6] but plummets abruptly into bathos, as he incongruously pastes in a Eupolidean 'piece of comic triviality' (Sommerstein 1996: ad 1400): 'two ones and a four' (fr. 372 K–A).

Finally, this same pattern of ambiguous intellectual ability recurs in the field of language as well. In this same 'weighing of verses

---

[5] On the uncertain provenance of 1400 see Sommerstein's balanced note (1996: ad loc.).

[6] See Dover (1993: ad 1400), on the expectation that 'the object of βέβληκε may be a vast rock (cf. Diomedes in *Il.* v. 302–4)' or something comparable in terms of epic grandeur.

scene' (1364–1413), for example, Dionysus' criterion seems to be a conception of the *'onoma-pragma'* relationship similar to that espoused by Cratylus in the Platonic dialogue that bears his name, that is, that words convey the real nature of things in such a way that 'whoever comes to know the words (τὰ ὀνόματα) will also know the things (τὰ πράγματα) themselves' (Pl. *Crat.* 435e; cf. 435d). It seems to be in compliance with such theories that he reckons that Aeschylus' word 'Death', a 'heaviest ill' (βαρύτατον κακόν) (1394), tilts the balance in his favour, while Euripides' 'Persuasion', albeit a word employed 'with perfect aptness' (ἔπος ἄριστ' εἰρημένον) (1395),[7] does not weigh much, for it is 'light and devoid of sense' (1396). Thus, in so far as the *onoma* is an imitation (μίμημα) of the *pragma* itself (Pl. *Crat.* 430a–b), Dionysus, as we have just seen, advises Euripides to

> search again for something heavy,
> which will drag your scale down, something mighty and big   (1397–8)

and finally proclaims victory in favour of Aeschylus, who had put into the scale 'two chariots and two corpses, whom not even one hundred Egyptians could have raised' (1405–6). Similarly, at an earlier point in the contest, Dionysus appears to be playing the part of the 'Protagorean' educated man, who ought 'to be skilled in the subject of poetry' (περὶ ἐπῶν δεινὸν εἶναι) to the extent of 'understanding the compositions of the poets' (τὰ ὑπὸ τῶν ποιητῶν λεγόμενα), so as to be able to discern 'which ones have been composed correctly and which ones have not' (ἅ τε ὀρθῶς πεποίηται καὶ ἃ μή) (Pl. *Prot.* 338e–9a). For, in the tone of an assured connoisseur, he insists on checking Euripides' prologues:

> οὐ γάρ μουστὶν ἀλλ' ἀκουστέα
> τῶν σῶν προλόγων τῆς ὀρθότητος τῶν ἐπῶν.
>
> I absolutely have to listen to
> the accuracy of the wording of your prologues.   (1180–1)

And, as we know from a variety of sources that *orthoepeia* ('correct diction') or *orthotes onomaton* ('the correctness of names') was 'something of a standard theme' in sophistic discussions of the day,[8] we can safely assume that, in the perspective of a fifth-century audience's intellectual élite, Dionysus would have been momentarily assimilated to the 'avant-garde', educated Athenian citizen, who knows well his Prodicus, Democritus, or Protagoras.[9] Never-

---

[7] Tr. Sommerstein. See also Sommerstein's note (1996: ad loc.).

[8] Kerferd (1981: 68), and see his entire discussion at 68–77; cf. Guthrie (1971: 204 ff.).

[9] For *orthoepeia* in the doctrines of the sophists see Kerferd (1981) and Guthrie (1971); for

theless, in the painstaking analysis of language that immediately precedes this scene (1119–79), Dionysus is so puzzled by Aeschylus' and Euripides' argument as to whether *hekein* ('coming back') and *katerchesthai* ('returning') are synonyms or not, that, while praising Euripides on his answer ('Well done, by Hermes!'), he simultaneously admits: 'I don't understand what you are talking about' (1169). Moreover, the parody of sophistic 'rationalization' of linguistic matters, which informs the entirety of this scene (1119–96), resembles *Clouds* 658–93, where the grammatical definition of the correct gender of names becomes the comic game's foremost target; the ignorant Dionysus of 405 BC corresponds to the boorish Strepsiades of Aristophanes' earlier play, totally bewildered by 'philosophical' distinctions between cock and hen, male and female kneading-trough and the like.

To conclude then, we can say that Dionysus' intellectual ability displays affinities both with the point of view of the ignorant, uneducated, unperceptive member of the audience as well as with the mental framework of the educated minority, preoccupied with issues of semantics, definition, and accuracy of diction. However, a thorough evaluation of the significance inherent in Dionysus' spectating position in the agon of the *Frogs* requires a close look at the symbolical dimension inextricably interwoven with the *dramatis personae* of the two contestants. As Whitman (1964: 232) has correctly emphasized, 'the symbolic role of the two poets cannot be denied': Euripides embodies

the divisive and centrifugal forces of relativism, irresponsible rhetoric, and in general the new education, while Aeschylus stands for the staunch beliefs and public solidarity of the days of Marathon.[10]

The following section, then, argues that both the thematic texture and the dramatic structure of the agon exploit and explore in full 'Euripides' and 'Aeschylus' as socially distinct polarities, conditioned by fundamentally irreconcilable cultural overtones.

8.2. *Aeschylus versus Euripides: A Social Drama*

If the two poets represent two worlds colliding with each other, the clashing images emerging out of the contest cluster around three prominent thematic units.

Aristophanes' special indebtedness to Protagoras in *Frogs* 1119–97 see Segal (1970). Note also 1158–9 (with which cf. *Clouds* 658 ff.).

[10] Cf. Dover (1993: 23) '. . . by Aristophanes' time Aeschylus had become a symbol of Athenian power, wealth, and success, Euripides a symbol of decline.'

(a) *Old and new* paideia

The old *ethos*/education of the citizen together with the panoply of the old values in the political arena are focalized in their collision with a new, perverted conception of civic responsibilities, a new model for civic education, and a depraved type of political leadership. This antithesis is vividly conveyed through Aeschylus' conception of Euripides as a corrupter of those very citizens whom he himself had moulded to be

γενναίους καὶ τετραπήχεις, καὶ μὴ διαδρασιπολίτας,
μηδ' ἀγοραίους μηδὲ κοβάλους, ὥσπερ νῦν, μηδὲ πανούργους

brave and six-foot tall and not escaping civic-duties,
neither uncultured nor knavish, as they now are, nor rogues.

(1014–15)

Under Euripides' destructive influence, then, the *chrestoi* and *gennaioi* of Aeschylus' epoch have become 'manifestly worse fellows' (μοχθηροτέρους ἀπέδειξας) (1011). However, the semantic field of these conflicting qualities and, more significantly, the range of values determining the nature of the Aeschylean *chrestoi politai* cannot be properly understood without a retrospective look at the play's parabasis, where Aristophanes' advice was precisely to 'make use of the *chrestoi* again' (χρῆσθε τοῖς χρηστοῖσιν αὖθις) (735). For it was precisely at that moment that the *chrestoi* were defined as

εὐγενεῖς καὶ σώφρονας
ἄνδρας ὄντας καὶ δικαίους καὶ καλούς τε κἀγαθοὺς
καὶ τραφέντας ἐν παλαίστραις καὶ χοροῖς καὶ μουσικῇ,

men well-born and of sound sense,[11]
righteous, good upstanding citizens[12]
and reared in wrestling-schools and dances and music.   (727–9)

In other words, the Aeschylean ideal is the brave and steadfast citizen, highly alert to his responsibilities towards the *polis*, well-

---

[11] For the predominantly moral sense of *sophrosyne* (prudence, good sense in the service of the *polis*, self-control, moderation, and the like) in Euripides and the sophists see North (1966: 68–84, 96) and cf. Lanza (1977: 71 ff.). In *Clouds* 962, 1061–2, 1071–2 *sophrosyne*, as a hallmark of the old education, is linked with physical hardiness, devotion to athletics, modesty, chastity, etc. However, for the political colouring of *sophron* see Reverdin (1945: 210), and cf. Dover (1993: ad 727): 'there was a strong tendency in Aristophanes' time for anti-democratic forces to claim the virtue for themselves and those who acquiesced in their leadership.'

[12] I use Sommerstein's translation (1996) of *kaloi kagathoi* in *Frogs* 719. See also his note (1996: ad loc.) on *kaloi kagathoi* as a phrase 'that may refer to birth, wealth and education, or to physical and moral excellence, or (as here, cf. 727–9) to a combination of both.' On the moral qualities associated with the expression see Dover (1974: 41–3); cf. also *kalos kagathos* in *Knights* 735, as a virtue applied to the spectators and designating them as 'honest citizens', 'good men and true' (with Gomme 1953: 66–7).

educated, loyal, decent, and honest.[13] The depravity blamed on Euripides, conversely, may be considered at work in two respects, which both contradict and complement each other.

On the one hand, corruption seems to have been brought on by the excesses or rather abuses of intellectualism (956–8, 1069) at the expense both of the old values (e.g. respect and obedience to the *archontes*: 1072, 1076/7) and of physical education (e.g. 1070–1, 1087–98; cf. *Clouds* 417, 987–9). Emblematic for Euripides becomes the vocabulary of *metis*. A number of 'keywords' in its semantic field,[14] such as *strephein* (957), 'twist and turn (arguments)', *technazein* (957), 'scheme', *noein/perinoein* (957/8), 'think'/'contrive cunningly' or even 'consider on all sides', *apatan* (cf. 1086), 'deceive', as well as the advanced intellectual activities of *logismos* (973) and *skepsis* (974), 'reasoning' and 'speculation', are amply used to qualify actions or reflect characteristics of Euripides' men.[15] In fact, those whom he proudly acknowledges as his 'disciples' (964 *mathetas*) belong to the circle of the sophists.[16] On the other hand, the healthy social fabric of Aeschylus' days has been threatened by that complete lack of education, *amathia*, which belongs to the semantic field of *agoraioi* men (1015), that is, according to a scholiast's information on the word *agoraios*, 'men ignorant and uneducated'.[17] One could also compare Pl. *Prot.* 347c–d, where the *pepaideumenoi* symposiasts are contrasted with the *agoraioi anthropoi*, distinguished for their *apaideusia* (Connor 1971: 154 with n. 39). But, more importantly still, this interpretation of Aeschylus' conception of the Euripidean citizens as *agoraious* and knavish (κοβάλους) (1015) is in perfect accord with the portrait of the Sausage-Seller in the *Knights*, a self-confessed 'rogue, and vulgar . . . and rash' (πονηρὸς κἀξ' ἀγορᾶς . . . καὶ θρασύς) (181). Of course, κἀξ ἀγορᾶς here has the sense of 'not of the gentry', but the dialogue

---

[13] On *Frogs* 729 see Sommerstein (1996: ad loc.). I would not happily interpret the terms *eugeneis*, etc., of the antepirrhema as strictly and solely political labels; although de Ste Croix (1972: 373) rightly stresses that the all-rounded education presupposed by the status of *kalos kagathos* could only be achieved by the men of the propertied class (and cf. Sommerstein 1996: ad 729), it is also worth remembering that 5th-cent. democratic theory, at least, regards *arete*, i.e. the sum of an individual's skills, his personal excellence, as entirely separate from his lineage; see e.g. Pericles' proud declaration in Thuc. 2. 37. 1 κατὰ δὲ τὴν ἀξίωσιν, ὡς ἕκαστος ἔν τῳ εὐδοκιμεῖ, οὐκ ἀπὸ μέρους τὸ πλέον ἐς τὰ κοινὰ ἢ ἀπ' ἀρετῆς προτιμᾶται. On the 'discrepancies between the ideology and the reality of democratic equality' see Raaflaub (1996: 158 and *passim*).

[14] See Detienne and Vernant (1974: 27, 33–4, 42, 49, 147–8, 160, etc.).

[15] In line 1451 Dionysus even identifies Euripides with the archetypal heroic inventor Palamedes: εὖ γ' ὦ Παλάμηδες, ὦ σοφωτάτη φύσις.

[16] For Cleitophon see e.g. Pl. *Rep.* 340a–b and for Theramenes as a disciple of Prodicus cf. e.g. schol. Ar. *Clouds* 361; Athen. 220b.

[17] See Bekker, *Anecd. Graec.* i. 339. 11–12 οἱ γὰρ ἀγοραῖοι ἄνθρωποι ἀμαθεῖς καὶ ἀπαίδευτοι.

which follows in the play makes it clear that the most important issue at stake is not low lineage *per se*, but rather the series of low prerogatives associated with it. The Sausage-Seller's protest that his entire intellectual armour consists of ignorance of *mousike*, 'except the alphabet, and I'm right bad at that' (188–9) is answered by the confident assertion of the Athenian Demos' Slave:

> This is your only disadvantage, that you *do* know your 'abc',
> even if 'right bad'.
> For leadership of the people goes neither to educated
> nor to good-mannered fellows any more,
> but is assigned to the ignorant and loathsome instead.[18]   (190–3)

But, if scurrility and *amathia* are the key to demagogic leadership in *Knights*,[19] the *polis* in the Aristophanic Euripides' days in the *Frogs* is 'full of ribald monkeys of the *demos*, who have made it their daily business to deceive the public' (1085–6). In sum, Aeschylus' shafts of criticism construct the picture of the Euripidean citizen as the coarse and uncultured (*agoraios*) yet wily and 'ready for everything' (*panourgos*; cf. 1015) *demos*-flatterer, the political orator who panders to the whims of his mass audience and, in so doing, leads the assembly astray by channelling its power into directions contrary to its collective interests. This type of public speaker is largely familiar from the literary constructions of Thucydides and Aristotle[20] as well as the parodic discourse of Aristophanic comedy itself.[21]

Nevertheless, it is impossible to grasp fully the dynamics of the literary contest of *Frogs* without first identifying the social undercurrents feeding into Aristophanes' constructions. In particular, the comic Aeschylus' repudiation of Euripides on the double ground of having promoted both extreme intellectualism and contemptible *amathia* reflects a paradox deeply ingrained in Athenian social life, that is, the Assembly's simultaneous distrust *both* of the excessively skilful, trained, wily speaker/sophist *as well as* of the boorish and uncouth, the under-educated member of the *polis'* community. To deal with the top end of the spectrum first, Aeschylus' picture in

---

[18] For the demagogues' lack of 'culture', as reconstructed in Old Comedy, the Socratic dialogues, and Thucydides see Connor (1971: 163–8); cf. also Eupolis' *Maricas* (fr. 208 K–A) and Eur. *Hipp.* 988–9. On the level of ability and education of the public speakers see Ober (1989: ch. 4).

[19] See e.g. *Knights* 331–4, where the Sausage-Seller is hailed as the perfect replacement for Cleon, surpassing him πανουργίᾳ τε καὶ θράσει καὶ κοβαλικεύμασιν, and is asked to show ὡς οὐδὲν λέγει τὸ σωφρόνως τραφῆναι.

[20] See primarily Thuc. 2. 65. 10–11 (on Pericles' successors); [Arist.] *Ath. Pol.* 28. 3–5; cf. Isocr. 8. 5. For the Assembly's proneness to demagogic flattery (ἥδεσθαι θωπευομένους) and its expertise in λίαν ἐξαπατᾶσθαι see Ar. *Acharn.* 634–5; *Knights* 1115–20; Dem. 9. 4, 23. 145–7; Isocr. 8. 9–10; Thuc. 3. 38. 5. For a general discussion see de Romilly (1975: 43 ff.).

[21] See e.g. *Knights* 45 ff., 215–16, 719–20, 763 ff., 790 ff., 1086 ff., 1152 ff., 1340–5, 1355 ff.

1085–6 along with his horrified reaction at Euripides' boast that he has taught his fellow-citizens 'to talk' (954 λαλεῖν ἐδίδαξα)[22] exploits the widespread popular mistrust of exceptional, above-average ability in *legein*, that is, the characteristic quality of the slick and unscrupulous sophist, who has the intellectual power to masquerade the truth and thereby corrupt justice. A typical case of such an adroit speaker is the Euripidean rich man, who, 'wrapped up in rags, weeps and claims to be destitute' (1066). Aeschylus' accusation cannot but refer to types of court procedures,[23] whereby rich litigants, to whom an expensive liturgy had been assigned, would try to persuade their judges that their personal fortunes were actually less than estimated, and hence did not make them liable to undertake the financing of the public service imposed upon them.[24] Besides, Dionysus' astute elaboration (1067–8) of the Aeschylean picture of the Euripidean man, who feigns poverty in order to eschew his civic duty to equip a warship (1065–6; see below, 8.2.(b)), lays bare the underlying social danger that the perfidious rich man may succeed in deceiving his hearers through his persuasive *logos* (1068 κἂν ταῦτα λέγων ἐξαπατήσῃ), or rather by means of a well-polished, fine-honed speech bought from a professional logographer. The 'egalitarian' attack against Euripides' above-average citizens, who are experts in 'applications of subtle rules and squarings-off of verses' (956), originates in the same strong tendency of mistrust of *logos* which makes it necessary for most speech-writers first to defend themselves against the charge of skilled, painstaking preparation of sophistic products, and secondly to put the *demos* on its guard against those who are ready to deceive the masses into voting against the interest of the community and *polis*.[25] In the Demosthenic corpus, for example, a rhetor warns his audience that

The honourable course for you, men of the jury, is, not to put the laws or your own selves in the power of those who speak (μήτε τοὺς νόμους μήθ' ὑμᾶς αὐτοὺς ἐπὶ τοῖς λέγουσι ποιεῖν), but to keep the speakers in your power, and to make a distinction between those who speak well and lucidly, and

---

[22] See Aeschylus' reply in 954–5 φημὶ κἀγώ· | ὡς πρὶν διδάξαι γ' ὤφελες μέσος διαρραγῆναι.

[23] Tears and lamentation were traditional recipes for conditioning the emotions of a jury panel; see e.g. Aeschin. 3. 209, 210 (ὅλως δὲ τί τὰ δάκρυα; τίς ἡ κραυγή; τίς ὁ τόνος τῆς φωνῆς;), Dinarchus 1. 108, 109, 110 (καὶ ὅταν Δημοσθένης ἐξαπατῆσαι βουλόμενος καὶ παρακρουόμενος ὑμᾶς οἰκτίζηται καὶ δακρύῃ). See further Lada (1993: n. 98).

[24] Cf. Sommerstein (1996: ad 1065 and 1066). For the *trierarchia* in connection with the legal procedure of *antidosis* see now Gabrielsen (1994: esp. 91–5).

[25] The extent to which this had become a *topos* can be inferred, for example, from Aeschines' scornful remark to Ctesiphon: 'For surely you will not put forth this excuse, that you have not the ability to speak' (οὐ γὰρ δή που τοῦτό γε σκήψῃ, ὡς οὐ δυνατὸς εἶ λέγειν) (Aeschin. 3. 242).

those who speak what is just; for it is concerning justice that you have sworn to cast your votes.   (Dem. 58. 61)

And as Ober (1989: 182) has put it, the 'basic scenario' for the private litigant is always the same: 'he, an average citizen without experience or skill in public speaking, was opposed by a trained and experienced speaker who threatened both the individual and the state.' Like the clever people of Euripides, who have been taught how to 'practise fine talking' (λαλιὰν ἐπιτηδεῦσαι) (1069), the orator's opponents are portrayed as slick demagogues who, considering themselves to be clever (οἰομένους δεινοὺς εἶναι) and trusting in their verbal skills (τῷ λόγῳ πιστεύοντας), look down (καταφρονοῦντας) on their honest, unsophisticated audience, and have no scruples in attempting to lead it astray (Dem. 35. 40). In other words, Euripidean sophistry is exposed to the 'egalitarian' attack on the dangers of expert oratory, that is, its great potential for undermining 'the validity of democratic institutions by destroying the ability of mass Assemblies and juries to come to the right decisions' (Ober 1989: 189), a danger which also threatens in its turn the entire fabric of the *polis*' society as well.

However, the 'attitude of the demos toward the entire subject of rhetoric, rhetorical ability, and rhetorical education' is 'highly ambivalent' (Ober 1989: 177). The 'egalitarian' attack against the overtly clever could perfectly well coexist with the 'élitist' attack against ill-educated politicians as well as with the praise lavished on élite education. In other words, the disparaging claim that one's political opponent was a dextrous orator 'could be directly associated with the seemingly incongruous claim' that he was an 'undereducated knave' (Ober 1989: 183). Demosthenes' tirade against Aeschines is perhaps one of the most well-known examples of the latter:

Virtue! you filth! what have you or your family to do with virtue? How do you distinguish between good and evil report? Where and how did you qualify as a moralist? Where did you get your right to talk about education? (ποῦ δὲ παιδείας σοὶ θέμις μνησθῆναι;) No really educated man would use such language about himself, but would rather blush to hear it from others; but people like you, who make stupid pretensions to a culture of which they are utterly destitute, succeed in disgusting everybody whenever they open their lips, but never in making the impression they desire.

(Dem. 18. 128)

In a very similar way, then, Euripides' 'new' citizens, whom Aeschylus abhors, display the characteristics both of the wily sophist and of the uncouth (*amousos*), uneducated (*apaideutos*) rhetor,[26] that is, the ignorant, boorish, and dull-witted *agoraios* citizen, entirely deprived of culture.[27] Correspondingly, Aeschylus' accusations of Euripides are informed by the social dissonance between deep distrust of oratorical skill and the Athenian *polis*' repudiation of the uncultured and unrefined politician/orator.

(b) *Public and private, civic and household duties*

While Aeschylus' poetry moulds the civic identity of the male Athenian citizen by impressing upon him the weight of his responsibility towards the *polis* and the goal of his adult life, that is, his participation in the hoplitic battle-lines, Euripides' concern is focused on the private, inner space, the indoor world. Having introduced 'household issues' (οἰκεῖα πράγματ') (959) in his art, Euripides boasts of having initiated his audience into the skill (*techne*) of 'managing a household in a more efficient way than before' (τὰς οἰκίας | οἰκεῖν ἄμεινον ἢ πρὸ τοῦ) (976–7). To put it in more general terms, by imparting to Athenian citizens the collective *ethos* of the *polis*, self-discipline and the restriction of one's claims to the most essential individual needs (1072–3), Aeschylus' poetry lies at the opposite extreme of Euripides' world, full of individualistic, centrifugal tensions (e.g. 968–70, 1071–2, 1076/7). One might profitably compare *Wasps* 1094–7, where the Chorus nostalgically articulate the contrast between the corrupt, individualistic world of the sophistic *polis* and the martial, civic-orientated community of an idealized past:

> In those days, we did not care
> about how to make a good speech or
> how to inform on people;
> all we cared for was who would be an unsurpassable rower.

Similarly in the *Frogs*, while the elder poet's citizens had been nourished in the collective *ethos* and ideals of the city, the political arena of Euripides' day resounds with deceitful rhetoric (1085–6), a notion almost inextricably interwoven with the orator's pursuit of private motives at the expense of the public good.[28] Moreover, the

---

[26] See e.g. Aeschin. 1. 166 (of Demosthenes) καὶ γὰρ πρὸς τοῖς ἄλλοις κακοῖς ἄμουσός τις οὗτος καὶ ἀπαίδευτος ἄνθρωπός ἐστι. Cf. 3. 241 (of Demosthenes and Ctesiphon) Ἄξιον δ' ἐστὶ καὶ τὴν ἀπαιδευσίαν αὐτῶν θεωρῆσαι.

[27] See e.g. Aeschin. 3. 117 ἀναβοήσας τις τῶν Ἀμφισσέων, ἄνθρωπος ἀσελγέστατος καὶ ὡς ἐμοὶ ἐφαίνετο οὐδεμιᾶς παιδείας μετεσχηκώς. See Ober (1989: 182–3).

[28] See the demagogue's flattery of the *demos* in order to satisfy personal goals in *Wasps* 665 ff.; *Knights* 809, and 1340–5 (*exapatan* the people while vying for private ends), etc.; cf. [Arist.] *Ath. Pol.* 28. 4, where deceitful pandering to the Assembly's tastes (θρασύνεσθαι καὶ χαρίζεσθαι τοῖς πολλοῖς) is motivated by the desire to satisfy immediate ambitions (πρὸς τὰ παραυτίκα βλέποντες). Cf. Thuc. 2. 65. 10; Lys. 18.16 (where the *kerdos* of the rhetors is opposed to the πόλει βέλτιστον); Dem. 18.138, etc.

Euripidean *polis* is 'filled up with under-secretaries' (1084), that is, low-ranking civil employees who, in seeking to avoid military service (cf. 7.4), were, naturally, untrained in the feeling of common purpose and the co-operation skills characterizing those citizens who marched in the hoplitic phalanx or rowed triremes.

Now, what is particularly interesting for our reading of the *Frogs* is the realization that this comically constructed clash between 'house-centred' and 'city-centred' imagery reflects a real tension deeply ingrained in fifth-century Athenian social life. I mean that the juxtaposition of the Euripidean citizen, characterized by his introverted look and his excessive interest in his own private affairs, to the civic *ethos* of the Aeschylean drama evokes the all-pervasive antagonism between the values, aspirations, and prosperity of household (*oikos*) and *polis*. Let us take an example from the economic sphere, where 'the opposition between public welfare and private interest was perhaps most clearly and frequently formulated' (Humphreys 1983: 9). For, if we focus, let us say, on the *oikos* as an economic unit, we shall easily understand that the *polis*' demand on individuals to carry the burden of expensive civic duties (*leitourgiai*) was strongly antithetical to the household's autonomy and financial prosperity. This type of *polis* versus *oikos* conflict is comically remoulded in the Aristophanic Aeschylus' accusation that, in stark contrast to his own, non-*diadrasipolitai* citizens, Euripides' poetry inspired the rich to feign poverty[29] in order to avoid the expenses of a *trierarchia*, the responsibility for the fitting out of a trireme on behalf of the *polis* (cf. above, 8.2(a)).

> Well, at any rate, it is for this reason that no rich man is
>   willing to equip a warship
> but, wrapping himself round in rags, he weeps and claims
>   he is poor.[30]   (1065–6)

Moreover, the anti-state individualism of the Euripidean man is clearer in Dionysus' imaginative addition to the picture:

> Yes, by Demeter, while having underneath his rags a vest
>   of thick wool.
> And, if his tale is successful in deceiving, next moment
>   he pops up round the fish-stalls in the market.   (1067–8)

[29] On the tension between family and state as varying 'in intensity according to class' see Maitland (1992: 27).

[30] In general, private gain as destructive of the *polis*' welfare seems to be a very genuine Aristophanic concern. See e.g. *Thesm.* 356–60, 365–7; *Eccles.* 206–8.

Consequently, then, if approached through a classical audience's perceptual filters, the parody of Euripides' and Aeschylus' social roles in the agon of the *Frogs* reflects—and can, therefore, be deciphered in terms of—the important fifth-century polarity of *oikos* versus *polis*. Because, whereas in poetic or political idealized visions, in comic utopia or in philosophical constructions, the interests of the two areas are interchangeable or even identical,[31] everyday social life always felt the privileging of one's own interests and the promotion of one's personal ambitions as potentially subversive of the very foundations of the *polis*.[32] The tension is eloquently crystallized in one of the most frequently quoted passages of Thucydides:

> But they [i.e. the post-Periclean leaders] . . . were led by private ambition and private greed to adopt policies which proved injurious both as to themselves and their allies; for these policies, so long as they were successful, merely brought honour or profit to individual citizens, but when they failed proved detrimental to the state in the conduct of the war.
>
> (Thuc. 2. 65. 7)

(c) *Male and female*

While the Aeschylean citizen is presented as having a truly male and civic role to perform for the benefit and the promotion of the entire *polis*, the Euripidean man is alleged to consume his energy in meaningless household discourse, that is, in 'examining closely' (κἀνασκοπεῖν): 'What's the situation with this? Where has this gone? Who has taken this?' (978–9). Moreover, in the immediately following lines (980–8) Dionysus carries the image a step further:[33]

---

[31] See e.g. Soph. *Ant.* 187–90; Thuc. 2. 60. 2 (Pericles' speech); cf. Thuc. 2. 40. 2 with Loraux's discussion (1986: 182ff.); Ar. *Lys.* (see Rosellini 1979: 15f.) and *Eccles.* Aristotle and Xenophon as well detect the similarities of *oikos* and *polis* as economic institutions aiming at *autarkeia* and good quality of life. On the evidence of different kinds of sources, then, *oikos* and *polis* may indeed be seen as mutually defining one another, i.e. as parts of a 'theoretical continuum' (Foley 1982b: 21) constituting a 'contradictory unity' rather than a rigid 'structural opposition' (ibid.: 4). Strauss (1990: 105) takes such reflections a step further by emphasizing that our evidence on this matter 'cuts both ways'. Although 'Democracy sharpened the public-private distinction', Athenians 'were as aware of the homologies between *oikos* and *polis* as of the differences', so that 'The relationship between *oikos* and *polis* was, by and large, complementary rather than antithetical' (105).

[32] Cf. Thuc. 2. 65. 10, 3. 82. 8, 6. 12. 2, 8. 50. 3, 8. 83. 3. See also e.g. Pl. *Gorg.* 502e; Isocr. 12. 133, etc. The clash of interests becomes extremely clear in cases of embezzlement of public funds; see e.g. Isocr. 8. 127; Aeschin. 3. 173; Ar. *Knights* 205, 258, 715f., 826–7, 1145ff., 1218ff., etc.

[33] See Dover (1993: ad loc.): 'Dionysos takes up the theme of τὰς οἰκίας οἰκεῖν ἄμεινον and trivializes it . . .'.

> Aye, by the gods, hence now every single Athenian
> barely enters his house
> and immediately starts shouting to the servants,
> and asks: 'Where's the jug?
> Who has eaten off
> this sprat's head? Alas, my last year's soup bowl
> is dead and gone!
> Where's yesterday's garlic?
> Who has nibbled at this olive?'

In the first place Aristophanes' parody implies that Euripides' poetry contributes to the dishonour of the male Athenian citizen, as it strengthens his bonds with the domestic space, a space which is culturally defined as the primary domain of the 'other', the feminine, sex.[34] One has only to remember Oedipus' repudiation of his male offspring for 'staying within the house like unmarried girls' (κατ᾽ οἶκον οἰκουροῦσιν ὥστε παρθένοι) (Soph. *OC* 343). Secondly, it signifies that Euripides has transferred to the male Athenian citizen that range of responsibilities which, according to the traditional division of household labour, belong to the sphere of the feminine,[35] that is the care for the preservation and the arrangement of the various belongings of the *oikos*.[36]

Broadly speaking, then, the pivotal social tension between male and female genders is acted out on stage through the antagonism between the rival poets in the agon of the *Frogs*. The comic Aeschylus is associated not only with the manly sphere of war but also with the characteristically male ideology of 'keeping the woman in her place'. And, as we have seen at length in 7.3, his accusations against Euripides stem primarily from the indomitable male fear of female uncontrollable sexuality, that is, of female adultery, which puts in danger man's position in society and casts doubt over the legitimacy of his offspring. The Aristophanic Euripides, conversely, together with the men that he creates and represents on stage, falls as far as possible from the socially acceptable ideal of manliness. Implicated in female household discourse, he verges upon femininity. Unable to keep firm hold of his female kin and, therefore, cuckolded, he is himself transformed symbolically into a woman as, in the Mediterranean code of sexual honour, a wife's infidelity 'can deprive her husband of his precious masculinity and

---

[34] See e.g. Xen. *Oec.* 7. 2. 29–30; cf. du Boulay (1974: 129) and Bourdieu (1965: 222–3).

[35] The *locus classicus* is Xen. *Oec.* 7. 22. For the possibility of a pan-cultural application of the male/public/outside vs. female/private/inside polarity see Rosaldo (1974: 24). Nevertheless, for the Greek evidence, see now Cohen's (1990, 1991) very nuanced discussions.

[36] Cf. e.g. Xen. *Oec.* 7. 25, 7. 36; cf. 8. 10; Ar. *Eccles.* 211–12; Pl. *Menon* 71e. For the wife as an οἴκου φύλαξ (Xen. *Oec.* 7. 42) in the Graeco-Roman world see Pearce (1974).

even go so far as to convert him symbolically into a member of her own sex' (Brandes 1980: 91). Moreover, Euripides' citizens verge on femininity both through their proneness to trickery (7.4), a quality inherently associated with women from as early as the Odyssean Penelope, and through minimal outdoor and physical exercise, lack of which results in pallor (cf. 1092 *leukos*) and effeminate delicacy in men.

8.3. *Witnessing the Festival of Athens: Dionysus as a Metadramatic* theates

The previous section has suggested that, if viewed from a 'social' angle, the *dramatis personae* of Euripides and Aeschylus reflect powerful and active fifth-century polarities. However, we may take this observation one step further still, because, in the eyes of the comedy's first audience, the clash of the competing civic images evoked by the literary contest recreates and re-enacts *in vivo* conflicts deeply ingrained and intrinsic in fifth-century Athenian plays. It is on the Athenian stage then that we shall focus our attention next.

Let us first take, for example, the clash of the new and old *ethos* in education and politics. A play such as Aristophanes' *Clouds* dramatizes the disruptive impact of progressive ideas, advanced dialectic, and moral relativism upon the ordered world of the *archaia paideia* (961), the 'old education', when justice was flourishing and '*sophrosyne* held in high esteem' (962).[37] The contrast of 'effeminacy', 'physical weakness' (τὸ δ' ἀσθενές μου καὶ τὸ θῆλυ σώματος) (fr. 199, 1 N²), and 'over-ingenious sly tricks' (κομψὰ σοφίσματα) (fr. 188, 5 N²) with the 'strong arm' (καρτεροῦ βραχίονος) (fr. 199, 3 N²), the virile and martial duties of a real man, is one of the threads contriving the multilateral antithesis between Zethus' 'vita activa' and Amphion's 'vita contemplativa' in Euripides' *Antiope*.[38] Corrupt demagogues and their deceitful rhetoric catering for the wishes of the masses clash with true nobility of character and ideal civic education. Thus, in Euripides' *Hecuba* the dignity of the nobly born Trojan queen proves unavailing and ineffective against the base tactics of Odysseus, the 'wily, lying, honey-tongued mob-courtier' (*Hec.* 131–2), a stern exponent of 'realpolitik' (Arrowsmith 1963: 37). In Euripides' *Orestes*, a play which reflects 'an omnipresent atmosphere of political decay and disarray' (Euben

---

[37] For the close analogies between the agon of the *Frogs* and the contest of the two *Logoi* in the *Clouds* see Dover (1968: 209–10) and Martin (1960: 256 ff.).

[38] See esp. frs. 185, 188, 199 N²; cf. Snell (1964: 70–98).

1986: 222), the Assembly of the Argives is swayed not by the manly and courageous citizen (918 ἀνδρεῖος . . . ἀνήρ), the one described as 'rarely loafing in the market or public places . . . intelligent, willing to come to grips with reasoned thinking, uncorrupted' (*Or.* 919–22), but by 'a ceaseless babbler' (903), a politician who, like the comic Euripides' *demopithekos*, 'trusts in his loudness and ignorant loquacity' (905), and 'derives his power from his insolence' (903). In Euripides' *Suppliants* the idealized view of Athenian democracy (403–8, 426–62) as a regime in which the people 'follow the will of a high-minded leader' (Burian 1985*b*: 140) is strongly challenged by the realistic outlook of the political outsider, the Theban Herald, who questions the *demos*' ability to 'give right guidance to a city' in the absence of straight, honest assembly-debating,[39] and portrays the democratic ruler as the man who 'puffing the city up with words, twists her this way and that for private gain; now he flatters her with a wealth of favours, in time he harms her; then, he goes off free of charge, covering up his previous blunders by laying the blame on others' (*Suppl.* 412–16).

Moving to the conflict of domestic and public obligations, it is important to remember that many a time the tragic hero's competing loyalties to *oikos* and *polis* give fuel to the tragic clash.[40] In tragic representations of the ills befalling the house of Atreus, for example, Agamemnon is torn between his obligations as head of *oikos* and head of *polis*. His dilemma (most elaborately dramatized in Euripides' *Iphigeneia in Aulis*) is solved in favour of his obligation to the common cause and his place of responsibility within society: forfeiting his domestic duty as a father and a husband, he fulfils his civic and military role as a king and leader, thus enabling the Panhellenic expedition to sail forth. Similarly, the personal ambition (*philotimia*) of Eteocles and Polyneices in Euripides' *Phoenissae* (esp. 499ff.) as well as Creon's selfish response (*Phoen.* 962–76) to the *oikos* versus *polis* dilemma (*Phoen.* 951–2) that he faces clash both with Jocasta's noble appeal for reconciliation (*diallage*) (452–68, 528–85) and with Menoeceus' self-sacrifice for the sake of the *polis* (991–1018) (Raaflaub 1990: 53–4). Along the same lines, civic ideology and the *polis*' collective *ethos* in the Euripidean *Suppliant Women* are challenged by the individualistic careers of glory-loving political upstarts, who 'promote unjust wars at the expense of the citizens, one in order to become a general, the other in order to run riot, having taken power in his hands, another

---

[39] *Suppl.* 417–18, with Collard's note (1975: ad loc.); cf. *Suppl.* 243. On the constitutional debate in Euripides' *Suppliants* see Raaflaub (1990: esp. 45–6 and 51–2).

[40] On the whole subject see primarily Seaford (1994*a*: esp. ch. 9).

motivated by his greed for profit, without considering whether the majority is harmed by receiving such treatment' (*Suppl.* 232–7).[41] Coming, finally, to the dynamics of gender discourse in fifth-century Athenian plays, a rich variety of studies has shown both the rigour as well as the pervasiveness of male/female antagonistic dialogue in classical Greek drama. The stage-image of the unruly woman, steered time and again against the male public order, puts patriarchal authority at risk. More importantly still, by confirming through her attitude and actions the conception of femininity as a synonym for evil, openness to passion, and surrender to untamed sexual instincts, the tragic or comic woman 'out of her place' reinstates and reinforces the male-constructed stereotype of the female character as a primary source of danger, subversiveness, pollution, and destruction. But it is now time to draw this section to some more general conclusions.

In the agon of the *Frogs* theatre reflects self-consciously upon its own conditions of creation and performance. Yet its artistic 'self-reflexiveness', that is, its representation of poets who speak *about* their art *within* a work of art, is not the sole or even primary constituent of its metatheatricality. The agon's 'metatheatrical' character lies rather in its structure, designed in such a way as to bring into relief both the 'tensions and the ambiguities'[42] inherent in the texts themselves as well as the complex dynamics of the inter-action operating between the sequence of 'images' projected as a spectacle on the stage and the recipient of those images, that is, the citizen-body, or, to put it in another way, the spectator/*polis*.[43] As a spectator, then, of the social and dramatic clash between Euripides and Aeschylus, Dionysus is cast metatheatrically in the role of the *Athenian city in its entirety* as a spectator (cf. also 8.4–5). Moreover, as an 'internalized' viewer of the play's poetic competition, Dionysus fulfils one further quintessentially dramatic function: in many respects his 'internalized' spectating role can be considered as the counterpart of the *dramatis persona* traditionally assigned to the tragic chorus. For, just as the tragic chorus constitutes a body of 'internalized' viewers exposed directly to the flow of the stage-action and empathizing intensively with the fate of the protagonists, Dionysus 'identifies' sometimes with Aeschylus' and sometimes with Euripides' perspective. And, like the young male dancers of

---

[41] Cf. the antithesis between the catalogue of the warmongers and Trygaeus' patriotic unselfishness in Aristophanes' *Peace* (441–53).

[42] I borrow the expression from Vernant's title (1988*a*).

[43] For the interchangeability of the categories of *theatai* /*politai* underlying the whole discussion of the agon see Lada (1993: 139 n. 84).

the chorus,[44] for whom their confrontation with the positive and negative examples embodied by the actors on the stage is a kind of general *paideia* and civic education, Dionysus completes his initiation into civic space by having to reflect upon, and ultimately to choose among, the positive and negative images pertaining to the two contestants in the agon of the *Frogs*. Finally, just as the tragic chorus is frequently engaged in vivid interaction with characters on the stage, Dionysus reacts incessantly to the competing poets—praising or condemning, encouraging or dissuading, admonishing or criticizing.

Yet, the resemblance of Dionysus' role to the function of the tragic chorus requires some qualification. Oliver Taplin (1996: 194) has very perceptively stressed the 'helplessness' of tragic choruses: 'However emotionally involved and distressed the chorus may be by what is happening, they can do nothing about it . . .'. Dionysus of the *Frogs*, conversely, has full, unconditional, and undisputed power over the outcome of the agon/spectacle which he attends and arbitrates; in this respect, one could rather say that Dionysus' role displays affinities with the *dramatis persona* of the *comic*, as opposed to the tragic, chorus, for this particular body of civic dancers 'becomes one of the *determinants* of the contents of the play' (Taplin 1996: 194; my italics). Dionysus' ultimate amalgamation of comic and tragic moods and features in the agon will preoccupy us more thoroughly in Chapter 9. For the moment, I would simply like to return to a point already raised in Chapter 5. Given that the genesis of drama is inextricably interwoven with choral ritual performances in honour of Dionysus and that, even in the fifth century BC, drama, as a fully developed art form, can be primarily conceived as the 'dancing' of a trained civic chorus (cf. 5.2), the casting of Dionysus in a role which bears close similarities to the function of the chorus is bound to be powerfully suggestive. For, even apart from anything else, it is with 'Dionysus' that the tragic choruses competing at the great dramatic festival of Athens ultimately 'unite'. After having changed their masks and, therefore, their identity, three times in the course of three successive tragic plays, they plunge in the alterity which is, undoubtedly, the greatest of all: they become satyrs, that is, semi-bestial dancers in Dionysus' retinue and in the markedly Dionysiac frame and stage of satyr-drama.[45]

---

[44] Irrespective of whether one accepts or not Winkler's hypothesis (1990*b*) about the ephebic status of the choreuts, it seems that they were regularly enlisted from the young, since the kind of dancing required of them was physically demanding. Cf. Csapo and Slater (1995: 352).

[45] I owe this insight to Pat Easterling.

8.4. *The Plays in their Festival Setting: Re-contextualization*

A great deal of modern work pioneered by Jean-Pierre Vernant and Pierre Vidal-Naquet has amply illuminated the complex links of Greek Tragedy with social institutions. The results of such a line of inquiry are too well known to require restatement, hence I will only draw attention to the issue most relevant to our discussion, namely the special nature of the Great Dionysia festival of Athens as one of the *polis'* greatest occasions 'to celebrate its power, display its wealth and proclaim its vitality both to its own citizens and to foreign visitors' (Connor 1990: 7). Simon Goldhill (1990*a*), in particular, was among the first to make us alert to the importance of the civic ceremonies taking place in the theatre before the actual staging of the plays, for it was those social performances *par excellence* which constituted the most carefully contrived and elaborate display of the *polis'* sense of authority, dignity, and power. Dramatic performances, Goldhill argues, are enriched with new dimensions if viewed against the background of the festival in its entirety, that is, in correlation with the city's official self-image, as constructed by and promoted through its lavish festive setting (cf. Connor 1990: 23). What I primarily hope to show in this section is that our understanding of the Aeschylus/Euripides polarity in the agon of the *Frogs* would be greatly enhanced by our awareness of at least some of the ways in which plays performed at the Great Dionysia interacted both with their immediate sociocultural frame and with the civic order implicated in it. For I believe that such a line of inquiry will help us to achieve both a better appreciation of the comedy's agon through fifth-century perceptual filters and a more contextualized evaluation of Dionysus' role as a spectator and a judge of the poetic confrontation.

One of the most important ceremonial aspects of the Great Dionysia festival was the parade, on the theatre's stage, of the orphaned sons of those Athenian men who, fighting for the city, had died on the field of battle. Having acted the role of substitute father on their behalf (Pl. *Menex.* 249a ἐν πατρὸς σχήματι καταστᾶσα), the *polis* now crowns the expression of her gratitude by providing each young man at the threshold of civic majority with a full hoplitic uniform. In front of the entire body politic, assembled in the theatre to take part in the great festival, a herald introduces the *polis'* young protégés with a proclamation most 'honourable' and most 'incentive to valour':

These young men, whose fathers showed themselves brave men and died in war, have been supported by the state until they have come of age; and

now clad thus in full armor by their fellow citizens, they are sent out with
the prayers of the city, to go each his way; and they are invited to seats of
honor in the theater.   (Aeschin. 3. 154)

The complex network of profound obligations which bind the
individual to the city is thus publicly affirmed and officially proclaimed. Having gratefully received their *panoplia*, the male
offspring of the *polis*' deceased valiant members undertake, in their
turn, the duty to repay their debt to their benefactors by equalling
their fathers in bravery as well as in submission to the *polis*' communal cause. As Goldhill (1990a: 113) puts it, 'It is quite clearly a
moment in which the full weight of civic ideology is felt'. The
Athenian city, then, turns a political performance into 'spectacle',
by means of its display on the *polis*' most public and prestigious
scene, the stage of the Great Dionysia festival of Athens. But, how
does this civic 'theatre' relate to the literary and purely dramatic
spectacle with which it is inherently connected, that is, the tragic,
comic, and satyric plays themselves? This is the question that will
preoccupy us next.

Let us think, for example, of Neoptolemus in Sophocles'
Philoctetes, an orphan of war entrusted to the care of Odysseus, the
military commander who represents the will of the community of
the Achaeans at Troy. What kind of example does he offer to those
real-life orphans of the city's real wars who, fully armed and
applauded by the city, have just taken seats of honour at a spectacle
staged *by* the City *for* the City? What kind of performance has this
privileged Athenian audience been invited to attend? As viewers of
Sophocles' *Philoctetes*, are the *polis*' young warriors faced with
dramatis personae longing to acquire hoplitic armour and to take the
place of their deceased fathers in the battle-rank?[46] Are they faced
with dramatic characters resolved to die so as to avoid handing over
their hoplitic weapons to the enemy or turning them against their
own companions-in-arms? None of these positive, or even better,
normative attitudes and actions are exemplified in the role of
Achilles' orphaned son, the play's ephebe. The spectacle presented
to the city's youth as well as to those orphaned young boys who have
just attained the ranks of manhood is rather full of disturbing and
unsettling images.[47]

When receiving Philoctetes' *toxon* Neoptolemus is asked to
promise he will 'keep and guard it safely' (σῷζ' αὐτὰ καὶ φύλασσε)
(766), giving it up—whether willingly or unwillingly—to no man's

---

[46] Such as, for example, is the wish of the Chorus of boys at the end of Euripides' *Suppliant Women* (1142–4 and 1149–51).

[47] I propose to discuss these issues in greater detail in separate work.

hands (769–72). He does, indeed, consent that 'It shall not pass except to your hands and to mine' (774–5), and in the male audience's perspective his agreement recalls the oath which every Athenian citizen has sworn as an ephebe not to disgrace the sacred weapons (Οὐκ αἰσχυνῶ τὰ ἱερὰ ὅπλα), confirming in this way his allegiance to hoplitic arms. Moreover, a classical Greek audience of the play would have been quick to discern a reflection of the Athenian *polis*' hoplitic oath 'not to abandon' one's 'comrade in the battle-rank', wherever one may have been stationed,[48] in Neoptolemus' pledge to 'keep firm' (*menein*) on the side of the desperately anxious Philoctetes:

PH. Only I entreat you, do not leave me (μή με καταλίπῃς) alone.
N. Do not be afraid. We shall stay (μενοῦμεν).

> PH. You will? (ἦ μενεῖς;)
> N. You may be sure of it.

PH. Your oath, I do not think it fit to put you to your oath
(οὐ μήν σ' ἔνορκόν γ' ἀξιῶ θέσθαι, τέκνον).
N. I may not go without you, Philoctetes.
PH. Give me your hand upon it.

> N. Here I give it you, to remain (ἐμβάλλω μενεῖν)

> (*Phil.* 809–13)

It is clear, then, that civic/hoplitic ideology is deeply implicated both in the relationships forged between this play's protagonists as well as in the language which expresses them.[49] However, it cannot be emphasized too strongly that such a reflection of civic ideology in the play's dramatic world is by no means straightforward and uncomplicated.

The only piece of armour that this play's ephebe acquires and reveres as sacred is the *toxon*, a distinctively anti-hoplitic weapon.[50] More significantly still, in a blatant subversion of the spirit of the civic oath, he is prepared to allow this very weapon to be used *against* the warrior community of the Argive camp of which he

---

[48] οὐδὲ λείψω τὸν παραστάτην ὅπου ἂν στ⟨οι⟩χήσω. Note also the reflection of hoplitic language in Philoctetes' designation of Neoptolemus as a *xymparastates* in lines 674–5 as well as the negative imagery of abandoning one's comrade, moulded in Philoctetes' fears in lines 910–11.

[49] For possible reflections of the oath and more specifically the hoplitic *menein* in 5th-cent. texts see Siewert (1977), who nevertheless does not include the *Philoctetes* in his discussion.

[50] For the bow as an anti-hoplitic weapon see, most importantly, Eur. *Her.* 159–64, 190–201; Soph. *Aj.* 1120–3. In an hoplitic perspective, a *toxotes* can be qualified as an effeminate warrior, a *gynnis* (cf. Plut. *Mor.* 234e ὑπὸ γύννιδος τοξότου). For the antithesis *toxotes/hoplites* in texts see Lissarrague (1990b: 13–34), whose work explores aspects of the 'hoplitic vs. non-hoplitic' polarity in Attic imagery. Moreover, in 5th-cent. Athenian cultural discourse the *toxon* is turned 'into a powerful symbol of barbarism in general' (Hall 1989: 139), ascribed to the non-Greek 'others', such as Persians (see e.g. Aesch. *Pers.* 556, where Darius is called *toxarchos*), Scythians, bowmen *par excellence* (Hartog 1988: 43–4), etc.

forms a part. For his final decision to secede from the Argive cause is based on Philoctetes' promise to protect his homeland by stringing the Heraclean bow against the Achaean invaders:

N. How shall I avoid the blame of the Greeks?
                                        PH. Give it no thought.
N. What if they come and harry my country?
                                        PH. I shall be there.
N. What help will you be able to give me?
                                        PH. With the bow of Heracles.
N. Will you?
      PH. I shall drive them from it.

                                                    (1404–7)

Moreover, although Neoptolemus does actually honour his oath of steadfastness (*emballo menein*, 813) and stands firm,[51] his tenacity does not refer either to the communal cause or to his comrade-in-arms in the hoplitic phalanx, but only to Philoctetes, the man who, through his reluctance to contribute to the common good, qualifies as an enemy of the entire camp. In this respect, rather than offering a positive example of hoplitic staunchness, Neoptolemus' version of abiding by one's oath ratifies his loyalty to a remote, pre-hoplitic past, that is, the pre-*polis* epic world of private, individual honour (see below, 8.5), most clearly illustrated in his 'Achillean' conception of *time* and *arete*. In other words, the primary hoplitic duty of enduring, 'staying firm to one's position' (*menein*), is perverted in this play to the extent of signifying an anti-civic loyalty, the fulfilment of a private, individual obligation. True, the play ends with Heracles who, as a deus ex machina, enforces on both Neoptolemus and Philoctetes the values of the phalanx and hoplitic fighting (Vidal-Naquet 1988*b*). Yet, as I will argue elsewhere,[52] even in the play's closing scene, the ephebe's own, anti-hoplitic resolution to defy the communal cause in order to restore the exiled man back to his *oikos*, remains fresh and paramount in the mind of the male, citizen/warrior Greek spectator.

After this long excursus, which has touched upon some aspects of the Athenian dramatic festival's socio-political backdrop, we may finally return to *Frogs*. For I would like to suggest that the Aristophanic 'Euripidean' man, who undermines the hoplitic *ethos* of the Aristophanic 'Aeschylean' *polis*, embodies a challenge similar to that which either anti-military plays or self-reliant military conduct, such as the recalcitrant dramatic gestures of Neoptolemus,

---

[51] See Philoctetes' generous acknowledgement of Neoptolemus' steadfastness in lines 869–71 οὐ γάρ ποτ', ὦ παῖ, τοῦτ' ἂν ἐξηύχησ' ἐγώ, . . . μεῖναι παρόντα καὶ ξυνωφελοῦντά μοι.

[52] Cf. above, n. 47.

thrust against civic ideals of collective unity and solidarity, ideals which, as we have seen above, are publicly proclaimed in grand-style ceremonies, like the 'orphans of war' parade on the very stage of the Dionysiac theatre of Athens.

Moreover, as the agon leads us to believe that an important aspect of Euripides' world is *apate* (cf. 7.4 and 8.2), we may now identify a broader frame within which to understand the comic Euripides' deflation of his dramatic predecessor's staunch, soldierly morale: the juxtaposition of Euripides' anti-hoplitic trickery and Aeschylus' military sturdiness can be compared to the disquieting juxtaposition of the spectating *polis'* hoplitic youth with *dramatis personae* whose mode of operation is determined by deceit and guile.[53] To take one final example from the plays' civic frame, one important ceremonial aspect of the Great Dionysia festival is the honorific proclamation of the names of those citizens who have rendered some great service to the *polis* (Goldhill 1990a: 104–5). This illustrious honour conferred on the city's benefactors was intended to encourage the entire audience to emulate them.[54] As Demosthenes (18. 120) understands the underlying reason for the practice, 'the whole vast audience is stimulated to do service to the city'. However, this imposing ceremonial stressing of 'the moral and social imperative of doing good for the city' (Goldhill 1990a: 105) is time and again sub-verted in the ensuing plays by those *dramatis personae* whose individualistic and ambitious actions put a *polis'* society at risk. A similar polarity between the stating of the norm and its subsequent subversion can be sought in the actions of those citizens whom the comically moulded contenders of the *Frogs* have allegedly created. We may take, for example, the juxtaposition of the Aristophanic 'Euripidean' man, who tries to eschew his duty as a trierarch, to the Aristophanic Aeschylus' citizens, his stalwart and unswerving non-*diadrasipolitas* (1014; see 8.2). Their comically exploited clash is parallel to the disquieting juxtaposition of that despicable *philo-timia*, dramatized in many a tragic play, with the festive proclama-tion of the city's benefactors in front of the assembled *theatai*.

In a pioneering piece first published in 1972, Jean-Pierre Vernant wrote with respect to classical Athenian drama that the city 'turned itself into a theater', in the sense that 'its subject . . . was itself and it acted itself out before its public'.[55] Nevertheless, as he himself was

---

[53] Such as Orestes, for example, in the plays which revolve around him, or even any comic trickster hero.

[54] Although it has to be said that, as Goldhill (1990a: 105 n. 26) himself notes, the evidence for proclamations of benefactors and presentations of crowns to Athenian citizens in the 5th cent. is 'much less secure than for the fourth century.'

[55] Quote from Vernant (1988a: 33).

quick to point out, implication of civic ideology is by no means
equivalent to passive and acquiescent reflection of socio-political
conditions.[56] For the civic image evoked through both Tragedy and
Comedy very often questions or subverts social reality, challenges
or transgresses the *polis'* self-image that the festival officially
projects.[57] Now, it cannot be emphasized too strongly that, within
the boundaries of classical Greek culture, the dramatic vision, however challenging, disturbing, and unsettling it may be, never sets
out to deconstruct to its constituents the edifice of socio-political
reality in order to refashion it in new configurations.[58] As I have
argued elsewhere (Lada 1996), the ritual embracing frame of the
Great Dionysia festival in its entirety is there to guarantee communal order and stability and, hence, contain or subdue the tensions
and transgressions generated by the inset narrative of the dramatic
texts. Yet, even if the fictive challenges do not materialize in subversive action on the social plane of real life, the audience/*polis*
which attends the festival as a spectator is captured in the midst of
an idiosyncratic civic discourse. It becomes an eyewitness in the
constant interplay of conflicting civic images engaged in active
dialogue with one another: images of idealized civic reality versus
images of fictive remoulding and questioning of this reality or, to
put it in another way, images of 'norm' versus images of 'transgression'.

Having such social parameters in mind, then, I would like to
suggest that the original spectators of the *Frogs* were culturally
equipped to understand the literary contest between Euripides and
Aeschylus as the dramatic analogue of the more general, political
and civic discourse lying at the core of the Great Dionysia festival
of the Athenian *polis*. The Aristophanic Aeschylus is cast in such a
light as to represent the 'norm', that is, poetry inextricably bound
up with a healthy civic image, an image that it both reflects and, in
many ways, creates. The comic Euripides, conversely, embodies the
catalyst, who challenges and questions the stable masculine world,
the staunch and one-dimensional reality of which his civically
oriented predecessor formed a vital part. When juxtaposed to
Aeschylus, he represents the dangerous, unsettling force which

---

[56] See further Goldhill (1990*a*); cf. Lada (1996).

[57] However, I do share Seaford's (1994*a*: 365) worry that, although 'ambiguity' and 'the
interplay of unresolved oppositions' are important elements of tragedy, 'the *privileging* (so
dear to the postmodern Academy) of ambiguity, transgression, and instability—the exclusively intellectualist view that the essence of tragedy is to question rather than to affirm—is to
abstract the tragic text from Athenian cultic and political practice.' I have myself argued that
Greek drama strikes a fine balance between affirmation and negation of order in Lada (1996).

[58] In the same way that, let us say, a Brechtian performance does.

always threatens to burst out, a social dynamite which permanently forebodes the deconstruction of the building-blocks of *polis*, society, and culture. To conclude this section, then, I return to my earlier formulation at the end of 8.3, namely, that, as an 'internalized' viewer and arbiter of the contending parts, Dionysus is fully drawn into the civic orbit, for he seems to be placed metatheatrically in the position of the entire *polis* as a *theates*.

8.5. *The Mythical and the 'Deglamorized' World*

A paramount impression to be gained from the poetic contest of the *Frogs* is that the Aristophanic lens effects the distancing of Aeschylus' men into a nebulous, remote past, while simultaneously extolling them to an almost superhuman level.

Aeschylus' own self-conscious exaltation of the social impact of his martial dramas (1021–2, 1025–7, 1039–42) brings sharply into relief his privileged link with a specific historical moment of Athenian glory, that is, the *polis*' victory against the Persian invaders. His citizens are the hoplites who fought at Marathon 'with spear and shield' (ξὺν δορὶ ξὺν ἀσπίδι), 'each man standing beside the next' (στὰς ἀνὴρ παρ' ἄνδρ') (*Wasps* 1081–3), and the sailors who, in 'ship-fenced army' (ναυφάρκτῳ στρατῷ) (*Knights* 567), triumphed at Salamis.[59] Nevertheless, infused as they are by the 'valours' (*aretai*) of 'lion-spirited Patrocluses and Teucers' (1041) and eulogized as 'brave' (*gennaioi*) and 'six feet high' (τετραπήχεις) (1014), both his *dramatis personae* and the Athenians of his day conspicuously defy their confinement to and their definition by spatio-temporal classifications.

'Full of spears and lances and white-crested helmets and casques and greaves' (1016–17), they are equipped with hoplitic armour (7.4). Yet, rather than resembling fifth-century citizen-warriors marching against the enemy in strict hoplitic *sophrosyne*,[60] Aeschylus' men, imbued with 'sevenfold-oxhide passions' (θυμοὺς ἑπταβοείους) (1017), bear closer relation to the Homeric, not to say the Indo-European hero, who fights under the impulse of *menos*, frenzy,[61] and follows the commands of his heart (*thymos*). One might compare another Aristophanic idealized picture of the warriors of Marathon, *Knights* 570: 'their courage sprang instantly to their defence' (ὁ θυμὸς εὐθὺς ἦν Ἀμυνίας). Besides, these splendid creatures

[59] For Aristophanes' patriotic and nostalgic references to the *Marathonomachai* see Thomas (1989: 225–6).
[60] See Detienne (1968: 122–3); cf. Vernant (1980: 40).
[61] See Vidal-Naquet (1986: 122); Detienne (1968: 121–2); Clarke (1995: esp. 148); for the picture of the Homeric warrior see Daraki (1980b) and now Clarke (1995).

are recreated comically in language which carries an unmistakably
Homeric ring. Not only does their collective depiction employ
distinctively Homeric epithets and nouns, such as *tryphaleia*,
heptaboeios, *thymoleon* (see 7.4),[62] but also the entire construction
of 1016–17 (*pneontas dory*, etc.) is clearly modelled on the central
Homeric formula *menos/menea pneiontes* (e.g. *Il.* 2. 536, 3. 8, 11. 508,
24. 364; *Od.* 22. 203) while, most importantly still, the *aretai* (1040)
that Aeschylus' mind (ἡμὴ φρήν) has moulded recall the epic
aristeiai, the individual encounters for personal triumph and glory to
which the great Homeric heroes commit themselves (see e.g. Kirk
1968: 110). In other words, the Aristophanic Aeschylus' poetry
draws heavily upon a mythical, heroic world. His epoch is both
closely akin to myth and idealized in its turn to such an extent as
to be itself transformed into 'myth'.[63] Besides, the Aristophanic
fashioning of Aeschylus himself displays a streak of epic lustre. Not
only does Aeschylus attract epic adjectives like ἐριβρεμέτας ('the
mighty-thunderer') (814) and λασιαύχην ('with shaggy neck-hair')
(822) and conventional epic pictures, like that of a river in spate
uprooting trees (902–4) or the threatening approach of a black
whirlwind (848 τυφὼς γὰρ ἐκβαίνειν παρασκευάζεται)[64] but, more
importantly still, from the very start of the agon, the Aristophanic
portrayal of Aeschylus' character creates the impression of an
intractable, impetuous Achillean temper, a wrath (*cholos*) and a
thymos of Achillean dimensions. The first glimpse of the elder
dramatist afforded by the Chorus to the audience at the very start of
the contest, is that of a tempestuous creature, rearing a dreadful
anger in his heart (814 ἦ που δεινὸν ἐριβρεμέτας χόλον ἔνδοθεν ἕξει)—
anger, *menis*, being the distinctive hallmark of the Homeric Achilles

---

[62] The noun τρυφάλεια does not seem to appear anywhere else except in Homer (see *LSJ*);
ἑπταβόειος is an Homeric epithet; the epic θυμολέων is reserved for the great epic heroes like
Achilles (Hes. *Theog.* 1007; *Il.* 7. 228), Heracles (*Od.* 11. 267; *Il.* 5. 639), Odysseus (*Od.* 4.
724, 814).

[63] Conceptualizing the *Marathonomachai* as belonging to the city's mythical past would not
have been a strange feeling, particularly for the Athenians of the end of the 5th cent. For, even
before the Periclean era, the cluster of symbolical associations attributed to Amazonomachies
and Centauromachies signified the transposition of the Persian Wars into the sphere of myth;
see du Bois (1982: 56 and 61 f.); Podlecki (1966: 13 ff.). Fourth-cent. epitaphs as well, passing
'without transition from the actions of epic to the battle of Marathon', make 'mythical
Athenians the mere predecessors of those of the Pentecontaetia' (Loraux 1986: 61); cf.
Thomas (1989: 233) on the democracy of the classical period as 'often not distinguished from
the legendary past in the epitaphios.'

[64] Achilles in the *Iliad*, for example, is compared to threatening natural phenomena, like
the appearance in heaven of the ominous Dog-Star (22. 29–31) Τὸν δ' ὁ γέρων Πρίαμος πρῶτος
ἴδεν ὀφθαλμοῖσι, | παμφαίνονθ' ὥς τ' ἀστέρ' ἐπεσσύμενον πεδίοιο . . . (22. 25–6); Aeneas' deadly
spear in Vergil's *Aeneid* is compared to a dark whirlwind carrying death and destruction with
it: '*volat atri turbinis instar* | *exitium dirum hasta ferens*' (*Aen.* 12. 923–4).

(*Il.* 1. 1).[65] And, as the agon takes its course, the Achillean colouring of Aeschylus' *dramatis persona* crystallizes.

In Euripides' perspective, Aeschylus possesses a mouth 'un-bridled, uncontrollable, not fitted with a gate' (838), and as Aeschylus himself admits (1006), he is, in an Achillean way, a prey to his indomitable *thymos*: 'I am burning with anger (θυμοῦμαι) at this turn of events and my inward parts are vexed (τὰ σπλάγχν' ἀγανακτεῖ)'. In fact, the Chorus even addresses him as 'glorious Achilles' (φαίδιμ' Ἀχιλλεῦ) (992), in a line which should not be simply viewed as a random quote from the dramatist's own *Myrmidons* (fr. 131 Radt), but as perfectly consistent with aspects of Aeschylus' theatrical *persona* within the Aristophanic text itself. And, just as the most recurrent advice given to the Iliadic Achilles is precisely to curb, to keep in check, or to restrain his 'great-hearted soul' (μεγαλήτορα θυμόν),[66] the comic Aeschylus is constantly admonished both by the Chorus as well as by Dionysus himself to quench his anger: 'take care lest your anger (θυμός) seizes you . . .' (993b–4); 'only make sure, o you noble-born, that you do not answer back in wrath (μὴ πρὸς ὀργὴν ἀντιλέξεις)' (998); 'Hush, Aeschylus! do not angrily inflame your guts with drinking' (παῦ', Αἰσχύλε, | καὶ μὴ πρὸς ὀργὴν σπλάγχνα θερμήνῃς κότῳ) (843–4). As moulded by Aristophanes, then, Aeschylus embodies the tension between the characteristically epic drive for self-assertion and the markedly democratic ideal of contributing to the common good,[67] in the same way that the characters he fashions conflate paradoxically two con-secutive and diametrically opposed periods in Greek city-state evo-lution: the heroic, pre-state individualism of myth and the collective spirit appropriate to a *polis* defended by hoplites.[68] This conflation[69]

---

[65] For a full and perceptive discussion of the 'Achillean basis' of Aeschylus' characteriza-tion see Tarkow (1982), who nevertheless does not linger on Aeschylus' *cholos*.

[66] e.g. *Il.* 9. 255–6 (Odysseus to Achilles, reminding him of Peleus' parting words) σὺ δὲ μεγαλήτορα θυμὸν | ἴσχειν ἐν στήθεσσι; 260 ἔα δὲ χόλον θυμαλγέα; 496 (Phoenix to Achilles) δάμασον θυμὸν μέγαν; cf. 646–7 (Achilles) ἀλλά μοι οἰδάνεται κραδίη χόλῳ, ὁππότε κείνων | μνήσομαι.

[67] Cf. Loraux's (1982b: 38) very interesting remark that in the classical Athenian funerary oration, a storehouse of democratic ideology, 'Tout se passe . . . comme si Athènes y tenait la place qu'a, dans l'épopée, occupe Achille.'

[68] However, as Raaflaub (1994: 139) writes, 'it was the hoplites [as opposed to the *nautai*] who inherited the ethics and enjoyed the prestige of heroic man-to-man combat—despite the stress on collective discipline and the increased anonymity brought about by the phalanx.'

[69] Interestingly, the sacrifice of the historical *Marathonomachai* too was commemorated by a monument 'far from ambiguous in its meaning' (Whitley 1994: 230): as Whitley has put it, in so far as 'in honoring the defenders of the new democracy, the Athenians revived practices that were once the preserve of the old pre-democratic aristocracy,' the Marathon tumulus 'stands "betwixt and between" the symbolic order of the Late Archaic aristocracy and the demands of the new democracy, demands that were eventually to lead to the evolution of a new symbolic form, the *demosion sema*.'

is obvious even in the language used to qualify the Aeschylean men: on the one hand, the plurals *Patroklon, Teukron thymoleonton* 'collectivize', as it were, the individual heroes; individuality gives way to anonymity and, in this respect, the collective treatment of the legendary characters is consonant with the rules which govern the democratic institutions of the public burial ceremony and the funerary oration in honour of the Athenian *polis*' war dead: 'at the demosion sema all distinctions, individual or familial, economic or social, that might divide Athenians even in their graves were abolished' (Loraux 1986: 23; Thomas 1989: 214–15). On the other hand, in stark contrast to the Athenian democratic practice of the *epitaphios logos*, which grants 'no one man, even the strategos, the honour of a special mention' (Loraux 1986: 52), individual names (Patroclus, Teucer) can indeed be heard behind the levelling plurals, and the goal is to spur the citizen to individual action (*Frogs* 1041–2).[70] However, before we go any further, two issues need clarification at this point. First, it cannot be emphasized too strongly that, despite the *conjunctio oppositorum* in the Aristophanic sketching of the long-deceased Aeschylean men, the balance is tilted in the direction of the *City*, as their heroism is poignantly *addressed* to the City, *framed* by the City, *created* for the City, and *inspiring* the entire City. Secondly, the very emphasis placed on the mythical, sublime character of the Aristophanic Aeschylus' dramatic art creates *ipso facto* an antithesis with the prevalent dimension of his successor's stage constructions. It is this latter issue to which I now turn.

Apart from having irredeemably undercut the Aeschylean communal spirit by fuelling the personal *philotimia* of his men (cf. 8.2(b), 5.2), the comic Euripides casts a shadow over the gleam of epic glory which pervades the Aeschylean stage by conjuring up the picture of an 'unglamorized' (Arnott 1981: 181) world. Legendary figures stripped of their heroic stature (1058–64; cf. 842), that is, *dramatis personae* reduced to the dimensions of ordinary human beings (cf. Arrowsmith 1963: 37; Arnott 1981: 181), are the characters most frequently incarnated in his dramas, while a realistic atmosphere of petty actuality and the disconcerting intrusion of the city's intellectual ferment (see e.g. 954–8, 971 ff.) constitute the all-embracing frame of his work. Consequently, the viewer of the agon is given the impression that the comic Aeschylus and his heroic standards fit

---

[70] A similar conflation of epic competitive excellence and democratic egalitarian spirit can be, I think, detected in a fragment from Euripides' *Erechtheus* (360 N²), where Praxithea wishes for sons who 'would not only fight but also distinguish themselves among men' (μετ' ἀνδράσιν πρέποι) (25–6), while simultaneously acknowledging that 'if they die in battle, [they] earn a common tomb and glory shared equally (with their fellow-fighters)' (τύμβον τε κοινὸν ἔλαχον εὔκλειάν τ' ἴσην) (32–3).

uneasily into the new social, moral, intellectual order of the Aristophanic Euripides' world, while for the latter and his citizens, conversely, the old system of values seems outdated, insufficient, not to say meaningless. Yet, what is of primary importance for our attempt to reconstruct some of the ways in which the play's agon could have been deciphered in its own sociocultural milieu, is to appreciate that those very clashes which the Aristophanic comic text encodes correspond to actual conflicts of values and competing world-views within the classical Athenian city.

In the chronotope of the fifth-century Athenian *polis* the Homeric epics which Aeschylus reveres were regarded, in Gould's (1983: 35) expression, 'as belonging to an alien past and as offering a model of man's existence that by its very distance from contemporary reality had little to say to the "new" men of the fifth century'. Similarly, all legendary heroes, devoid of their appropriate milieu and 'translated'[71] to another world, the world of the fifth-century Athenian stage, find their integration problematic. Hence, Tragedy again and again dramatizes the disconcerting encroachment of the heroic code on the ideals of the city. Take, for example, the Sophoclean Ajax who, 'rejecting anything which might mitigate his fierce concentration upon the pursuit, the maintenance, and the restoration, of his prestige' (Winnington-Ingram 1980: 19), 'carries the implications of the heroic code to the extreme possible point' (ibid.). The intrusion of the older, Homeric and aristocratic *ethos* of individual *aristeiai*, that is, the craving for personally acquired glory in the battlefield, clashes with some deeply grounded democratic concepts of the classical Athenian *polis*. For, as Vernant (1991: 220) has put it, in a fifth-century perspective,

the individual exploit, extraordinary as it may be, and even if it lead to a heroic death on the battlefield, has no value if it deviates from the collective discipline of the phalanx . . . The prize for *aristeia* goes to the one who best contributes to the common victory by keeping his place in the ranks during combat next to his companions-in-arms. To be 'the best' one must surpass the others, all the while remaining with them, making common cause with them, being like them.

In this respect, the spectator's emotional involvement with Ajax's pathetic death calls into question his civically infused belief in corporate hoplitic practice, collective action which demands not only *sophrosyne* but also allegiance to the democratic spirit of egalitarianism. Conversely, many a time, Tragedy blatantly exposes

---

[71] 'Translation' of heroic characters into realistic 5th-cent. terms is the phrase employed by Arrowsmith (1963 *passim*) to describe the tension between the past and the present, more intensely felt in Euripidean drama.

the inadequacies of the traditional assumptions about society and the individual's place within it. Take, for example, a play like Euripides' _Electra_, where terms with heavy social connotations, such as _gennaios_ and _eugeneia_, are wrenched from their original semantic field: from class/aristocratic attributes[72] they are turned into mere ethical qualifications, that is, statements about human character. Thus, Electra's husband, a man of brilliant ancestry, and yet, by aristocratic standards, devoid of _eugeneia_ because of his impoverishment (35–9), can be hailed provocatively as a _gennaios_ in the sense of 'noble in mind': 'You have spoken of a nobly spirited fellow' (γενναῖον ἄνδρ' ἔλεξας) (262).[73] The old amalgamation of 'want' with ethical _dysgeneia_ is sundered,[74] as democratic ideology begins to appropriate—or rather to usurp—an entire range of 'class code' terms which were hitherto regarded as exclusive traits of the aristocratic rank.[75] In the experience of the aristocratic sections of fifth-century Greek audiences, then, 'identification' with Orestes cannot be a painless psychological process. For, despite being well-born himself, Orestes steps provocatively out of the _ethos_ of his social status and, inveighing (367 ff.) against the whole 'traditional panoply of birth, wealth, military and physical prowess as indicators of true nobility' (Arnott 1981: 181), acclaims Electra's peasant husband as an _aristos_ (382). In other words, Orestes' evaluation of a man's associates and character as more secure criteria for the measurement of civic _arete_ (383–5) destabilizes the firmly grounded aristocratic concept of hereditary transmission of _eugeneia_ as well as the corollary belief in its exclusive power to secure both individual dignity and social superiority.[76]

What we have undertaken in this section, then, is surveying from a different angle the same phenomenon which had been analysed in 8.3, that is to say, that the agon of the _Frogs_ dramatizes some social-intellectual conflicts which are active in fifth-century Athenian drama and the society with which it interacts (cf. 8.2). Moreover, we have also seen from an additional perspective that the dramatized

---

[72] See e.g. Arist. _Rhet._ 1390b21–2 ἔστι δὲ εὐγενὲς μὲν κατὰ τὴν τοῦ γένους ἀρετήν; Soph. _OT_ 1469 ὦ γονῇ γενναῖε, etc.

[73] Cf. _El._ 253 (and in the same vein Eur. fr. 1066 N²). _Gennaios_ is freely used in a variety of ethical and moral contexts by 5th/4th.-cent. writers; see, most impressively, Eur. _Hel._ 729–31 (of a good slave); Ar. _Knights_ 787 γενναῖον καὶ φιλόδημον; see further Dover (1974: 95).

[74] See his self-presentation in 362–3 καὶ γὰρ εἰ πένης ἔφυν, | οὔτοι τό γ' ἦθος δυσγενὲς παρέξομαι.

[75] Cf. Donlan (1980: 146), and for a brief overview of 'political label' terms see Reverdin (1945).

[76] On the other hand, however, as Alan Sommerstein rightly points out to me, despite the abundance of praise that Orestes lavishes upon the Autourgos, he never deigns to actually address him, and talks instead to his wife, as though he were not there.

clash of Aeschylus and Euripides is the metadramatic analogue of the same clash of cultural and social perspectives that we find remoulded again and again in the extant tragic dramas. To recast the argument in the most general way possible, the agon of the *Frogs* could have evoked in the original spectators' eyes that pivotal social dialectic which throughout the fifth century BC continued to feed into the tragic genre. I mean the conflict between the remote legendary past, encapsulated in the dramatic myth enacted, and the new forms of juridical and political thinking belonging to the City, the fifth-century democracy of Athens (Vernant 1988*a*).[77] In other words, the tragic genre is constantly sustained by a dynamic inter-action, an 'interference', as Loraux (1973: 910) has put it, of *mythos* and of *logos*.[78] In this respect, Dionysus' role as a spectator and judge of the agon of the *Frogs* takes on an added tinge. He could be perceived as the witness of the clash of diametrically opposed tendencies, whose precarious coexistence within the boundaries of every single tragic play moulds the unique physiognomy of classical tragic discourse. For even in the most contemporary, sophisticated, or realistic Euripidean pieces, the action is firmly situated in a mythical landscape. In Euripides' *Phoenissae*, for example, the scenic game's gloomy actuality (de Romilly 1965) is constantly projected onto its remote antecedents evoked through the play's choral odes, which extend the mythical dimension vertically so as to encompass the city's glorious prehistory (Arthur 1977). In the plays centring around Trojan heroines (*Troades, Andromache, Hecuba*) the manifold reminiscences of a lost world, Troy, and the values that it stands for, fabricate a rich mythical backdrop to the first plane of fifth-century rhetoric, of that clever intermingling of 'subtle rules' and 'squarings-off of verses' (956; cf. 6.2) which Euripides himself ascribes to his *poiesis*. Or, to put it in another way, being required to evaluate the conflict of the Euripidean 'everyday' characters with the distanced heroes of the Aeschylean past, Dionysus is confronted with the same game of perspectives in which

[77] Cf. Vernant (1970: 288) and Loraux (1973: 909): '. . . la tragédie se construit sur un perpétuel échange entre mythe et cité, un incessant va-et-vient de la *polis* à l'*épos*.' According to the French school's extremely influential account of the origins of Tragedy, this is the archetypal dialectic which brought Athenian drama into being. However, if taken in isolation, this model can be seriously misleading for, instead of placing drama in its sociocultural context, as it purports to do, it actually alienates it from it, by obfuscating the vital contribution of other cultural factors whose influence has been decisive for the Athenian theatre's *genesis* and subsequent development. And I mean, of course, here, the entire complex of cultic and ritual patterns which, as Seaford (1994*a*) has superbly demonstrated in his authoritative synthesis, have moulded the form and content of Greek drama as we know it today.

[78] Cf. Loraux (1973: 908) and note Euripides' insistence on the element of *logos* introduced in his *techne* (973–5, 956–8).

the *polis*/spectator of a drama such as, say, the *Electra* is involved. I mean, of course, the constant interplay of mythical and realistic strands, the remote, faded glory of the Argive royal house and the present misery of the characters on the stage (see e.g. Goldhill 1986a: 251 f.). Furthermore, this tension between myth and actuality, past and present language, and order which is thrust into sharp relief in the contest of the *Frogs* is an important element within the very structure of the tragic hero himself. A legendary character drawn from the sphere of myth, while at the same time communicating in iambic trimeters, a rhythm which comes much closer to the everyday language of Attic speech, and steeped in the intellectual controversies of the fifth-century Athenian *polis*,[79] the tragic hero should rather be conceived as both 'Aeschylean' and 'Euripidean' at once.[80] Finally, the spectator of a tragic play is often required to assess the *ethos* or the actions of the stage-characters with respect to mythical *exempla*, models of behaviour belonging to an even more remote past. I would like to suggest that in a similar way Dionysus becomes a witness in a conflict structured in such a way as to convey the impression that Euripides' men and *dramatis personae* are constantly measured against the standards set by Aeschylus' theatrical dimensions, that is, the titanic figures of his dramas and the code of values which determine their actions.

As a conclusion to this section, then, I would like to revert to the 'past' versus 'present', and *mythos* versus *logos* polarity, as remoulded in the agon of the *Frogs*. For, speaking the language of the *Frogs*, we could say that the tragic moment, 'moment historique fragile et menacé où, dans la cité, coexistent des valeurs hétérogènes' (Loraux 1973: 911), is nourished unremittingly by the clash of an 'Aeschylean' upon a 'Euripidean' element, a formidable conflict which in the classical Athenian city is still 'painfully felt' (Vernant 1970: 288). As a judge and arbitrator, Dionysus is called upon to mediate between these two irreconcilable systems of values which, symbolically embodied in the *dramatis personae* of Aeschylus and Euripides, are engaged in a lively 'dialogue' throughout the contest. We can, therefore, round off our whole discussion of Dionysus' 'internalized' spectatorship in the agon (8.3–5), by emphasizing, once again, that in the play's second part Dionysus becomes, in all respects, a 'civic' viewer. In so far as the *dramatis personae* of Aeschylus and Euripides symbolically incarnate conflicting social

---

[79] Consider, for example, the tensions encoded in the *dramatis persona* of Teiresias in the *Bacchae*; see Dodds (1960: 91).

[80] This clash of mythical and contemporary context had been perceived as 'anachronism' by ancient scholiasts; see Easterling (1985: 9 with refs.).

forces, active in the classical Athenian frame and sustaining the intellectual ferment of the developing Athenian *polis*, Dionysus witnesses a piece of social drama, enacted and presented on the stage by the creators of theatrical performances themselves. In this respect, Dionysus, as a privileged spectator and judge, as well as the Aristophanic play's real audience are treated with a vivid picture 'in the making' of the dynamics of interdependence between 'social' and 'stage' drama.

9

Dionysus, Comedy, and Tragedy

The previous chapters have suggested that Dionysus' perspective has broadened so much during the agon of the *Frogs* as to become identical with the perspective of the entire Athenian *polis* as a *theates*. Correspondingly, however, although Dionysus is clearly the god of Drama when he first sets out on his quest for a 'fertile' poet (cf. 1.7), it is only in the frame of the literary contest that his patronage of the theatrical events acquires its full range of implications. The present chapter, therefore, argues that, in clear contrast to the play's earlier parts, Dionysus' 'viewpoint' in the agon of the *Frogs* encompasses both Tragedy and Comedy at once.

9.1. *Tragic and Comic before the Agon of the* Frogs

The general mood pervading the imagery of the *Frogs* up to its parabasis is intensively comic. Nevertheless, a close inspection of the text is likely to reveal specific moments within its plot structure, where Dionysus' role seems to have been deliberately contrived in such a way as to create the impression that his acting is cast unequivocally within the distinctive moulds of the *comic*—as opposed to those of the tragic—genre.[1] In fact, the play's thematic density is greatly enriched through the challenge it presents to the spectator to respond to its intertextuality, that is, to set the representation of Dionysus against the well-established background of the tragic stage's conception of this same god.[2] Some of the play's

---

[1] Cf. Gredley (1996), whose discussion corroborates mine, since he reaches similar conclusions regarding the distinctively comic (as opposed to tragic) nature of Dionysus in the *Frogs*, by focusing largely on issues other than those I have chosen to highlight, and most importantly: the Euripidean Dionysus' 'completeness of . . . transformation' (204), as opposed to the comic Dionysus' fluidity of disguise; Dionysus' journeying in the *Bacchae*, indicative of 'unstoppable power, and . . . accomplished with the eerie effortlessness characteristic of gods' (205), as opposed to the Aristophanic Dionysus' advent to Heracles in need of help; the Euripidean Dionysus' 'rigid fixity of purpose' (205), as opposed to the comic Dionysus' 'endless ability to change his mind' (205). On the subject of tragic and comic laughter that I discuss in 9.1(a) cf. Gredley (1996: 206–7).

[2] My reading of the agon from the point of view of literary intertextuality does not imply or entail the assumption of the prior composition and/or staging of Euripides' *Bacchae*. For the notion of 'intertextuality' is not applied here in the restricted sense of a close-circuited

distinctively comic 'moments', then, which can be more insightfully appreciated through the comparative perspective of an 'intertextual' reading, we shall examine in this chapter.

(a) *Dionysus in the prologue and Dionysus* katagelastos *(Frogs 480)*

Confronted with Dionysus' incongruous appearance in the comedy's prologue, Heracles cannot restrain an unquenchable stream of laughter:

> By Demeter, I can't force myself not to laugh.
> I *do* bite my lips, and yet, I *still* laugh.
>
> . . . .
>
> I just can't scare my laughter away . . .   (42–3, 45)

After his encounter with the Underworld Doorkeeper (4.5–6), when Dionysus/Heracles admits 'I have messed; summon the god' (479), Xanthias replies 'Won't you get up immediately, you, ridiculous fellow (ὦ καταγέλαστ'), before any stranger catches sight of you? (πρίν τινά σ' ἰδεῖν ἀλλότριον;)' (480–1). Dionysus is explicitly pointed out as a spectacle,[3] a ridiculous sight. Nevertheless, to relegate 'Dionysus' to the position of a 'spectacle' or even to expose him blatantly to outright derision and contempt lies in sharp contrast with Tragedy's privileged way of shaping the *dramatis persona* of this god. In so far as we can infer from Euripides' *Bacchae*, rather than being himself a spectacle, the tragic Dionysus is assigned a more distinguished function: 'master of representational forms' (Goldhill 1986a: 276), he mounts his own plot and stages his own spectacle (*Bacch.* 912 ff.), 'replete with set, costume and spectators' (Foley 1980: 110), so that the whole community of Thebes may 'see'.[4] Contriving thus a scenic 'game' in which not only the barriers between illusion and reality but also the distinctiveness of such theatrical categories as 'actor', 'spectator', and 'spectacle' collapse and blur,[5] Dionysus exposes his adversary to the sight of

---

interrelation between a *single* comic and a *single* tragic text but, on the contrary, should be defined as a 'dialogue' between the practices and the discursive modes traditionally adopted in the shaping and representation of a 'stage-Dionysus' by both generic forms of Athenian drama. In other words, 'foregrounded' text in my discussion is the *Frogs*, but only in the measure that this stands for Comedy in general, while as a 'backgrounded' text I take Euripides' *Bacchae*, in so far as it stands as a specimen of the entire genre. For the notions of 'foregrounded' and 'backgrounded' text see Hutcheon (1985: 34).

[3] An impression much more vividly conveyed through the underlying ironical denial of other possible spectators except 'internalized' ones, lurking somewhere on the stage. See Sommerstein's nice note (1996: ad loc.) on *allotrios*, meaning 'anyone belonging to a different group', 'anyone who is not "one of us".'

[4] *Bacch.* 61 ὡς ὁρᾷ Κάδμου πόλις. For a fascinating discussion of Dionysiac 'vision' in the *Bacchae* see Vernant (1988c : esp. 390–7).

[5] For excellent discussions see Foley (1980); Segal (1982: 215–71; and 1985).

the *theatai*[6] as an 'unhappy', painful, spectacle (1282), a disembodied πρόσωπον/dramatic mask (1277):

CADM. Whose face, then, are you holding in your arms?
AG. A lion's—or, at least, so the hunting women were telling me.
CADM. Examine (σκέψαι) it properly, then! beholding it (εἰσιδεῖν) is but
      a brief effort.
AG. Ah! What do I see? (τί λεύσσω;) What is this that I have in my hands?
CADM. Observe it closely (ἄθρησον), so as to understand more clearly.
AG. Oh wretched me, I see the greatest grief of all (ὁρῶ μέγιστον ἄλγος).[7]

(*Bacch.* 1277–82)

Furthermore, Comedy's highlighting of Dionysus' exposure to physical eyesight reverses one of the essential 'Dionysiac' truths that Tragedy efficiently communicates, namely that access to Dionysus' divinity is only 'indirect and symbolic' (Foley 1980: 112): 'This god—for you claim you saw him clearly—what was he like?' (ὁ θεός, ὁρᾶν γὰρ φῂς σαφῶς, ποῖός τις ἦν;) (477), Pentheus indignantly prods Dionysus/the Stranger. 'Of whatever form he wanted; it was not up to me to determine this' (ὁποῖος ἤθελ'· οὐκ ἐγὼ 'τασσον τόδε) (478), the Euripidean masked god replies, stressing thus the absolute inadequacy of 'human eyes' to grant the viewer an insight into the 'real' nature of Dionysus' divinity.[8] For the mass of the uninitiated, Dionysus remains elusive and invisible.

ΠΕΝΘ. καὶ ποῦ 'στιν; οὐ γὰρ φανερὸς ὄμμασίν γ' ἐμοῖς.
ΔΙΟΝ. παρ' ἐμοί· σὺ δ' ἀσεβὴς αὐτὸς ὢν οὐκ εἰσορᾷς.

PENTH. And where *is* he, eh? For I can certainly not see him
      with *my* eyes.
DION. *Where I am.* But, being impious yourself, you cannot
      behold him.[9]

(501–2)

In contrast to Comedy, where the whole audience is cast meta-theatrically into the role of Dionysus' *theatai* (see *Frogs* 480–1, quoted above), in Tragedy it is only the initiate who can have a 'face-to-face' (ὁρῶν ὁρῶντα) (470) encounter with the god. And it is only with his gradual—and fatal—approach to the Dionysiac space that Pentheus is able to experience a newly acquired possibility to 'see' (924 νῦν δ' ὁρᾷς ἃ χρή σ' ὁρᾶν).

As for ridicule of Dionysus, this seems to be an element intrinsically interwoven with the stories of those mortals who resisted the

---

[6] Both the real, theatrical, audience and the 'internalized' spectators on the stage, i.e. the maenads; for a full discussion see Goldhill (1986a: 274f.).
[7] See Vernant (1988c: 393) on the *Bacchae*: 'No other text so insistently, almost obsessively, repeats such a plethora of words signifying seeing and visibility.'
[8] Cf. Goldhill (1986a: 276); Foley (1980: 124 and 131f.).
[9] Cf. Dodds (1960: ad loc.).

propagation of his cult. In the *Lycurgeia*, for example, mockery at the god's expense is focused on his outward appearance (frs. 61, 61a, 62 Radt). In the *Bacchae* not merely Dionysus/the Stranger but anyone reckless enough to associate with him becomes for Pentheus an object of contempt. Thus, Teiresias understands Pentheus' attitude towards the god as 'scorn',[10] while Cadmus, who performs Bacchic movements with the aid of the Dionysiac *narthex* (251), is in the young king's eyes a 'very laughable' sight (250 πολὺν γέλων; cf. 322). But for the classical spectators acquainted with the myths, such laughter (*gelos*) is replete with a foreboding. Its sinister side becomes apparent when the roles are reversed, and the γελῶν, 'the one who laughs', is himself turned into an object of disdain. Thus, after having moved to the position of the strong, the Euripidean Stranger/god requires that Pentheus is ludicrously exposed to the sight of the inhabitants of Thebes (854), while his gruesome revenge is warranted precisely on the grounds that the king has scorned (1081 γέλων τιθέμενον . . .)[11] him and his rites (cf. 1293).[12] Comedy, on the other hand, does not allow such intimations. The comic genre takes for granted and exploits the innocent, the jocular, and happy side of Dionysus' association with *gelos*,[13] and hence, not only Heracles but also Xanthias, the slave, can freely play with either the appearance or the behaviour of the god.

(b) *The whipping scene*

The second scene open to an intertextual reading is the whipping scene (*Frogs* 605–73), which calls for a comparison with those scenes of the *Bacchae* which touch upon Dionysus' *pathe*, namely, *Bacch.* 434–518 (Dionysus' captivity and miraculous release; Dionysus threatened with *pathos*) and 614–41 (Dionysus' 'effortless' liberation; Dionysus' calm viewing of the initiand's ordeal; cf. 2.12(a)).

In *Frogs* 628–32 Dionysus proclaims threateningly his identity as a divine creature and the 'son of Zeus':

ΔΙΟΝ.   ἀγορεύω τινὶ
ἐμὲ μὴ βασανίζειν ἀθάνατον ὄντ'· εἰ δὲ μή,
αὐτὸς σεαυτὸν αἰτιῶ.
ΘΥ.   λέγεις δὲ τί;

---

[10] See 272 οὗτος δ' ὁ δαίμων ὁ νέος, ὃν σὺ διαγελᾷς; cf. 286 καὶ διαγελᾷς νυν.

[11] Cf. Gredley (1996: 207): 'Pentheus laughs through a failure to see what he should see: the irresistible power of Dionysos and, metatheatrically, the fact that he lives in the world of tragedy.'

[12] In Euripides' *Bacchae* it is precisely Dionysus' smile which most effectively conveys his hidden power and his ambiguity. Wearing a smiling mask for the performance (Foley 1980), Dionysus himself is, throughout the dramatic spectacle, γελῶν (439, 1021).

[13] See Eur. *Bacch.* 378–80 ὃς τάδ' ἔχει, | θιασεύειν τε χοροῖς | μετά τ' αὐλοῦ γελάσαι.

ΔΙΟΝ. ἀθάνατος εἶναί φημι, Διόνυσος Διός,
τοῦτον δὲ δοῦλον.

DION.   I proclaim to you
not to torture me, for I am immortal. Otherwise
blame your own self!
DOORKEEPER.   What do you mean?
DION. I declare that I am immortal, Dionysus, son of Zeus,
while *he* is a slave.

One can profitably compare *Bacchae* 504: 'Being sane in my mind,
I warn *you*, fools, not to bind me' (αὐδῶ με μὴ δεῖν σωφρονῶν οὐ
σώφροσιν) and *Bacchae* 516–17: 'However, be sure that, as an atone-
ment for these outrages of yours, Dionysus will punish you, the one
you claim does not exist' (ἀτάρ τοι τῶνδ᾽ ἄποιν᾽ ὑβρισμάτων | μέτεισι
Διόνυσός σ᾽, ὃν οὐκ εἶναι λέγεις).[14] What can be seen through this comparison is that in *Frogs* 628–32 Dionysus has unexpectedly switched
over to the tragic mode.[15] In other words, within the generic idiolect
of Comedy, Dionysus' proclamation can be read as a semantic
'ungrammaticality'. But the entire scene of *Frogs* 605 ff. as well is a
good illustration of what Riffaterre has designated as 'intertextual
humor', that is, humour which arises from 'the presence in the text
of codes semantically or formally incompatible' (Riffaterre 1974:
278). For in the first place the whipping scene is structured in such
a way as to invert a traditional Dionysiac pattern of effortlessness
and freedom from pain (n. 16), a pattern that is more appropriate to
epic and tragedy, than it is to comedy (i). And secondly, the whipping scene can be thought to constitute a miniature Dionysiac
retribution story (Dodds 1960: xxv f.) in reverse (ii). Let us, then,
examine these two suggestions in detail.

(i) In *Bacchae* 614 ff. Dionysus/the Stranger reveals how he saved
himself 'easily, without any toil'.[16] Tortures were inflicted on him
only in the troubled mind of his persecutor,[17] while he himself was
in reality entirely intact:

[14] The parallel is noted by Cantarella (1974: 293).

[15] This impression is further enhanced by Dionysus' threatening *autos seauton*, for, as
Seaford (1996: 32, 497–8, 614) has perceptively noted, phrase combinations with *autos* often
attach to Dionysus as initiator and liberator (cf. line 2 of the Pelinna gold leaves (see 2.14):
εἰπεῖν Φερσεφόνᾳ σ᾽ ὅτι Βάκχιος αὐτὸς ἔλυσε), and occur a couple of times in the *Bacchae*, as
in *Bacch.* 32 (νιν αὐτός), 498 (λύσει μ᾽ ὁ δαίμων αὐτός . . .), 614 (see n. 16). A Dionysiac
formula (?), then, underlining Dionysus' own mystic power is here comically twisted in order
to underscore the magnitude of the imprudent torturer's regret.

[16] *Bacch.* 614 αὐτὸς ἐξέσωσ᾽ ἐμαυτὸν ῥᾳδίως ἄνευ πόνου. For the typical effortlessness of
Dionysus (imparted also to his devotees) see e.g. *Bacch.* 194 ἀμοχθεί (reflected in *Frogs* 402;
cf. 1.7).

[17] See 616 δεσμεύειν δοκῶν; 631 ὡς σφάζων ἐμέ; cf. the Homeric *Hymn to Dionysus*, where
the instruments of *pathos* did not have any effect on the god: τὸν δ᾽ οὐκ ἴσχανε δεσμά, λύγοι δ᾽
ἀπὸ τηλόσε πῖπτον | χειρῶν ἠδὲ ποδῶν (13–14).

οὔτ᾽ ἔθιγεν οὔθ᾽ ἥψαθ᾽ ἡμῶν, ἐλπίσιν δ᾽ ἐβόσκετο

he neither touched nor grasped me, but was feeding on hopes.   (617)

In the *Frogs*, on the other hand, the god participates in his *pathos* in flesh and blood.[18] The immunity enjoyed by his tragic counterpart becomes visible pain (660 ἤλγησεν; cf. 664). The tragic and the epic god's serenity (*Bacch.* 622 ἥσυχος; 436 πρᾶος; 438 οὐκ᾽ ὠχρός) and cheerfulness or tranquil smile (*Bacch.* 439 γελῶν; cf. Dionysus μειδιάων in Hom. *h. Dion.* 7. 14, as his opponents try to bind him) give place to weeping: τί δῆτα κλαίεις; (*Frogs* 654). More importantly still, that same ease of action which has been detracted from the comic god has been strikingly passed over to his mortal flagellator:

XANTH. How, then, will you put us to the test in a fair manner?
DOORKEEPER. Easily (ῥᾳδίως): I'll give blow for blow to each of you in turn.

(*Frogs* 642–3)

One conclusion, then, already forms itself: Dionysus, the god who, throughout the Greek world, is venerated as Lysios and Lyaios, 'the Deliverer', 'the Liberator', he who, as Aelius Aristeides (2. 331 Keil) has put it, 'releases from everything',[19] is totally unable to free himself from his predicament and the impending torture.

(ii) In the *Bacchae* Dionysus' true identity is carefully concealed throughout his confrontation with the Theban king (see especially 498–502). Even when he faces the threat of *pathos* (492ff.), the Stranger/god does not attempt to seek refuge in his divine status. Explicit unveiling of the self comes *last* in the sequence of events dramatized in the play, as it is only in lines 1340–1 that Dionysus declares:

ταῦτ᾽ οὐχὶ θνητοῦ πατρὸς ἐκγεγὼς λέγω
Διόνυσος, ἀλλὰ Ζηνός.

So say I, Dionysus, born of no mortal father,
but of Zeus.

---

[18] Of course, what we should primarily have in mind when making this distinction is that while in the *Frogs* Dionysus is himself undergoing mystic initiation (see Ch. 2), in the *Bacchae* it is primarily Dionysus' opponent, Pentheus, who re-enacts on stage a Bacchic initiand's experience and *pathos*. See Seaford (1981, 1996) and cf. above, 2.12(a).

[19] See e.g. the cult of Dionysus Lysios in Corinth (Paus. 2. 2. 6), in Sicyon (Paus. 2. 7. 5–6), and Thebes (Paus. 9. 16. 6); Dionysus' mystic *teletai* are described as 'releasing' (see e.g. Phot. s.v. λύσιοι τελεταί) and, as Jaccottet (1990) and Connor (1990) have emphasized, the worship of Dionysus is in many places, including Athens itself, intrinsically interwoven with political liberation and civic freedom. On Dionysus' liberating powers on all registers (mystic, psychological, political) see Seaford's lengthy note (1996: ad 497–8). On the City Dionysia as a 'freedom festival' see Connor (1996: 222–4).

And yet, while Dionysus elusively avoids any premature uncovering of his divine nature, his *super*-human status is hinted at obliquely through all the stages of his passion. When first arrested by Pentheus' attendants, he is described as calm, eager to be put to fetters, not turning pale because of fear, and, in sum, a willing captive, whose remarkable composure expedites the burden of his guards.[20] His followers, the bacchants, correspondingly, those whom Pentheus had 'snatched and bound in the chains of the public prison' are now 'released and gone, leaping off to the mountain glens, summoning Bromios as their god' (444–6).[21] Because, as Pentheus' guard relates,

> The chains on their legs snapped apart
> by themselves. Untouched by any human hand,
> the doors swung wide, opening of their own accord.   (*Bacch.* 447–8)[22]

And the narrator ends with the formidable conclusion: 'this man has come to Thebes, our town, full of many wonders' (πολλῶν δ' ὅδ' ἀνὴρ θαυμάτων ἥκει πλέως | ἐς τάσδε Θήβας) (449–50). In fact, although he had been shut 'in Pentheus' . . . dark prisons' (611; cf. 618), Dionysus still manages to liberate himself 'easily, without any toil' (614; see above) and to escape unharmed (617) and calm (636 ἥσυχος δ' ἐκβὰς ἐγώ . . .) from the ordeals of his passion. Also, the lengthy narrative in which the Shepherd from Mt. Cithaeron describes to Pentheus the miraculous things performed by the maenads on the mountains (660–774), encodes both subtle and explicit hints that the king's conception of the Stranger's followers is wrong,[23] and culminates in an open exhortation to Pentheus to accept Dionysus in the *polis*: 'So, master, whoever this god may be, *do* receive him into Thebes, our city' (769–70).[24]

---

[20] *Bacch.* 436–40 ὁ θὴρ δ' ὅδ' ἡμῖν πρᾶος οὐδ' ὑπέσπασεν | φυγῇ πόδ', ἀλλ' ἔδωκεν οὐκ ἄκων χέρας, | οὐδ' ὠχρός, οὐδ' ἤλλαξεν οἰνωπὸν γένυν, | γελῶν δὲ καὶ δεῖν κἀπάγειν ἐφίετο | ἔμενέ τε, τοὐμὸν εὐτρεπὲς ποιούμενος.

[21] Miraculous liberation of 'Dionysiac' captives seems to be a recurrent feature of Dionysiac myths. Apollodorus (3. 5. 1), for example, refers to Lycurgus' imprisonment of maenads and satyrs belonging to Dionysus' retinue and tells of their sudden release: αὖθις δὲ αἱ Βάκχαι ἐλύθησαν ἐξαίφνης. Miraculous loosening of bonds (τῶν δεσμῶν αὐτομάτως λυθέντων) also features in the Dionysiac story of Antiope (Apollod. 3. 5. 5), the subject of Euripides' *Antiope*.

[22] Tr. Arrowsmith (in Grene and Lattimore).

[23] Subtle hints: *Bacch.* 693, 707, 760, 764. Open address to Pentheus: 686, 712–13, 769–70.

[24] In so far as it is safe to speculate on the basis of our scanty evidence, a similar pattern of events may also have occurred in Aeschylus' *Edoni*. Having entered the action in human disguise, Dionysus was subjected to Lycurgus' abuses and arrest (frs. 61–2 Radt; the persecution of Dionysus and the punishment of Lycurgus were both included in the first part of the trilogy; see West 1983*b*: 63 ff.), 'evidently in ignorance of his identity' (Dodds 1960: xxxi). Dionysus may even have been subjected to real *pathe* too, for although the *Bacchae* constitutes for us a 'unique specimen of a Dionysiac passion-play', 'The πάθη of Dionysus . . . may well be the oldest of all dramatic subjects' (Dodds 1960: xxviii).

Finally, moving to a different genre, a condensed version of a Dionysiac transition from *pathos* to epiphany is preserved in the Homeric *hymn* addressed to this god. There, Dionysus, in the guise of a young man (*h.* 7. 3–4), does not even try to prevent the pirates from maltreating him (12 ff.). Yet, his divinity gives overwhelming visual signs (13–14; quoted in n. 17), which help the helmsman of the ship to 'realize' (νοήσας) his true identity (15–24). Consequently, Dionysus' final epiphany (44 ff.) in the Homeric *hymn* is staged only *after* he has successfully overcome his *pathos*. Now, declaration of identity and *pathe* are also the essential elements of our scene in *Frogs*. We can note especially the analogy of *Bacchae* 492 ff.[25] with the Doorkeeper's and Xanthias' speculations on possible ways of torturing in *Frogs* 618 ff. (cf. 2.6(c)). Yet, it is especially important that the *order* in which they are arranged is conspicuously *reversed*: unlike the epic and the tragic versions, Dionysus' *pathos* does not lead to *theophaneia*. Instead, it is *preceded* by a pompous verbal claim to his divinity, which nevertheless remains the only proof he can adduce for its substantiation.

The whipping scene, then, is one of those particular 'moments' of the *Frogs* which have been fashioned in such a way as to impress upon the viewer that Dionysus has been distinctively cast in the characteristic mould of a comic—as opposed to a tragic—hero. Unable to sustain for long any tragic overtones in his comic role, his stage-performance is conditioned entirely by the logic of the comic genre within which he acts. Moreover, we could reasonably generalize that in Dionysus' perspective, as this is evidenced in the play's first part, 'serious' and 'comic' seem to be conceived as mutually exclusive.

Responsible for the apparelling of his performer, Dionysus, the stage-director, understands the very core of the dramatic action, an actor's dressing up, as mere child's play, *paidia* :

> οὔ τί που σπουδὴν ποεῖ,
> ὁτιή σε παίζων Ἡρακλέα 'νεσκεύασα;

> Surely, you didn't take it *seriously*,
> that, *jestingly*, I dressed you up as Heracles? (522–3),

he asks his companion on the journey and fellow-actor Xanthias. Like the theatrical spectator, Xanthias could have taken the god's 'game' seriously, treated it as a *spoude*, had he only wished to do so. Nevertheless, his master seems to be implying he had better not. The genre's 'point of view' is comic and it is *playfulness* which must

---

[25] See 492 εἴφ' ὅ τι παθεῖν δεῖ· τί με τὸ δεινὸν ἐργάσῃ; followed by an enumeration of tortures to be inflicted.

remain the spectacle's prevailing dimension. More significantly still, Dionysus' comic dressings and re-dressings, swappings and reswappings of attire and props with Xanthias share an important point with Dionysus' costuming of Pentheus in the *Bacchae*. I mean that both the tragic and the comic scenes display transparently to the theatrical spectator's eyes that archetypal, indispensable, and fundamental action which Theatre and Ritual have in common, the action of 'becoming other', adopting a different identity (cf. 4.1).[26]

However, similarities do not go any further. Xanthias, who takes the 'play' seriously, stands at the antipodes of Pentheus, who treats his newly donned robe as a 'play'.[27] The comic Dionysus, correspondingly, ludicrously entrapped in a dressing up which he regards as a *paidia* (523 ὅτιή σε παίζων . . .), invites a comparison with his counterpart of tragic drama, who baffles his adversary by playfully adorning him with the costume of his death.[28] In other words, the Aristophanic comedy exploits and brings into relief the innocent connection of Dionysus to playing, a link strongly emphasized not only in literature[29] but also in late fifth-century iconography as well. As Shapiro (1993: 180) has shown in his study of personified abstract concepts in Greek art, in the brief period from 425 to 400 BC vase-painters used the figure and name of Paidia 'more often than that of virtually any other personification.' On several among those vases, Paidia is part of a variety of Bacchic contexts, as she is depicted in the form of a maenad in the circle of Dionysus (Shapiro 1993: 183–5). A very impressive scene comes from a depiction of the Gigantomachy on a fragmentary kalyx-krater in Naples (*LIMC*, s.v. Paidia, 10), where, among Dionysus' retinue of satyrs and maenads, Paidia wields a rock in one hand and stretches out her *thyrsos* in the other. And, as Paidia is also a familiar figure in erotic pictures of the satyr-maenad bands (*LIMC*, s.v. Paidia, 8–12a), her presence consecrates the playful dimension as an intrinsic element of peaceful and martial Dionysiac activities alike. However, let us emphasize once again that such an innocently cheerful mood is fundamentally opposed to the experience that the god of Tragedy creates. Because, although in the Dionysiac ritual,

---

[26] From a markedly metatheatrical viewpoint see Goldhill (1991: 220) on these scenes as illustrating 'drama's ability to reflect its own processes, to act out its own strategies of fictional representation'. See, however, Seaford's (1994a: 273) reaction to such readings as being 'not wholly mistaken' but putting 'the cart before the horse', for 'The theatricality is primarily a feature of the Dionysiac ritual from which theatre emerged.'

[27] See esp. *Bacch.* 925–6, 930–1, 941–2.

[28] See e.g. *Bacch.* 928–9, 932–3, 935–6, 943–4.

[29] See esp. Anacreon, fr. 357, 1–4 *PMG* ὦναξ (i.e. Dionysus), ᾧ δαμάλης Ἔρως | καὶ Νύμφαι κυανώπιδες | πορφυρῆ τ᾿ Ἀφροδίτη | συμπαίζουσιν.

as reflected in the *Bacchae*, the ludic dimension is important (*Bacch.* 160–1, 866–7), *paizein* can be uplifting and rewarding for the follower of the god only in so far as he or she has consented to unlimited participation in Dionysiac exuberance and pleasure. For the sceptic and the stern[30] there lies in store the grim manifestation of the 'playful' god's revenge. To quote Charles Segal (1982: 267),

The very manner of his revenge is itself ludic: he *plays* with Pentheus, deceives him, involves him in his own realm of disguise and deception . . . the god's elusive playfulness slips past his guard into house, city and self.

9.2. The Agon

Shifting my attention now to the agon, I would like to propose that in this part of the play Dionysus' bonds with Comedy are manifestly intensified and consolidated. The god who has already ranged the entire span of the comic theatrical event (comic actor, stage-director, spectator, and *geloion* spectacle) comes finally to be identified with the role and function of Old Comedy itself:[31] in a fifth-century audience's perspective, Dionysus' vote for Aeschylus was very likely to be perceived as analogous to the typical generic predilection of Old Comedy, that is to say, comparable with the comic genre's characteristic act of privileging and extolling an idealized past over the dissolution and decay of a degraded and inglorious present. To quote Froma Zeitlin (1990*a*: 89),

In any case, the solution of the *Frogs* in bringing back the archaic spirit of Aiskhylos as a solution to the city's problems is also a formal, generic one. It is predicated on the controlling convention of Old Comedy that fulfills its festive function of social renewal by consistently choosing the idealized past over the distressing, chaotic present, even as it prefers to rejuvenate the old (father) rather than, as in New Comedy, to promote the young (son).

Moreover, the mode of his engagement and intervention in the various phases of the literary contest bears close similarities with an important way in which Old Comedy implicates itself in the discourse of Athenian dramatic festivals. For, if Old Comedy presents a challenge to the *polis*' socio-political and intellectual articulation by constantly testing and subverting the images expressed either in the real social life or through the mirror of the tragic genre, Dionysus satirizes, undermines, and undercuts both the 'theatrical'

[30] Cf. *Bacch.* 212 Πενθεὺς πρὸς οἴκους ὅδε διὰ σπουδῆς πέρα.

[31] For a diametrically opposite—and poorly substantiated—view see Heiden (1991: 99): 'He [i.e. Dionysus] says nothing about comedy, and when he judges the *agon* there is no reason to suppose that he does so as the god of comedy.'

and the 'civic' pictures that the agon brings into relief.[32] Never-theless, rather than following the play's earlier parts in reinforcing a generic segmentation, the dramatic narrative in the agon is wrought in such a way that *both* perspectives, tragic *and* comic, ultimately intersect.[33] At the focal point of this intersection lies, of course, Dionysus, the arbiter, whose privileged position in the literary contest grants him unrestrained manipulation of discursive modes and levels of representation. In what follows, then, we shall see that the masterful complexity that Aristophanes bestowed on the theatrical *persona* of Dionysus, the judge, reunifies and reintegrates symbolically in his dramatic figure both the tragic and the comic genre simultaneously.[34] More importantly still, the play's culmina-tion in a generic amalgam presided over, or even, at some points, fashioned by Dionysus himself, is one among the many ways in which the contest of the *Frogs* can be considered as effecting the final accomplishment of the divine initiand's incorporation into the community of the Athenian *polis*.

The play's opening scene creates the impression that the god is linked to both aspects of the city's theatrical experience. For although a performer on the comic stage, the comic quest he is about to undertake is motivated by his desire to resurrect a 'fertile' *tragedian*. Nevertheless, the blending of the 'comic' and the 'tragic' remains superficial. As early as the opening verses of the play, Dionysus rebukes the worn-out jokes his slave is merely hinting at, only to reproduce the jest himself, through the very act of his rejection.

ΞΑΝΘ. εἴπω τι τῶν εἰωθότων, ὦ δέσποτα,
   ἐφ᾽ οἷς ἀεὶ γελῶσιν οἱ θεώμενοι;
ΔΙΟΝ. νὴ τὸν Δί᾽ ὅτι βούλει γε, πλὴν "πιέζομαι".
   τοῦτο δὲ φύλαξαι· πάνυ γάρ ἐστ᾽ ἤδη χολή.
ΞΑΝΘ. μηδ᾽ ἕτερον ἀστεῖόν τι;
                              ΔΙΟΝ. πλήν γ᾽ "ὡς θλίβομαι"

XANTH. Master, can I say one of the usual things,
   that the spectators always laugh at?

---

[32] See e.g. his function in 968–70, 1023–4, 1036–8, 1067–8, 1149, 1195–6, 1278–80 etc.; cf. Goldhill's (1991: 212) remark on Dionysus as regularly adding 'incisively comic counter-examples to Aeschylus' grand claims (1034–37).'

[33] In this respect, I disagree with both Taplin (1996) and Gredley (1996), who see Dionysus of the *Frogs* as the embodiment of a generic dichotomy, i.e. Taplin as 'the Dionysos of comedy, that brings back the contemporary equivalent of Aischylos to the city' (198), and Gredley as 'primarily the Dionysos of tragedy' (213). I read these pieces far too late to be able to discuss them in detail in the main body of my text.

[34] Segal (1961: 229) states that in the play's last scene Dionysus appears 'as the god of *both* comedy and tragedy,' but without fully analysing this development.

DION. By Zeus, most certainly, say whatever you wish, except 'I'm hard
   pressed'.
   This one in particular you must avoid, as by now I am totally sick of it!
XANTH. Then, can I say some other smart joke?
DION. Anything, except 'how tightly squeezed I am.'

(*Frogs* 1–5; cf. 6–11)

Being enclosed within the sphere of the 'most ridiculous' (τὸ πάνυ
γέλοιον, 6), Dionysus is still unable to surpass the level of theatrical
performance he so obstinately disdains. In other words, seeking
though he is for something better, he proves incompetent to
extricate himself from the restrictions and inadequacies involved in
some popular manifestations of the genre within which he acts. As
Segal (1961: 211) has put it, the prologue of the *Frogs* implies
Dionysus' realization of 'the inadequacy of a conception of the
comic limited to mere buffoonery'.

Yet, Segal's further statement (1961: 212) that Dionysus'
'problem, on the literary level, is to be able both to amuse and
instruct, to appear in the age of the degenerate Phrynichus, Lykis,
and Ameipsias as he did in the days of the "bull-eating" Cratinus,'
cannot be substantiated by the comedy's first part. For even if
Dionysus, as he sets out for his quest, may be considered to embody
'Comedy's' will to resurrect 'Tragedy', nothing in the text testifies
to his perception of the two genres as co-operative articulations of
the city's voice. The need for a dramatic interplay of *spoude* and
paidia that he has failed to realize (522–3; quoted above) is publicly
proclaimed only through the stage-*persona* of the Chorus; for it is
only the Initiates who seem to understand the blending of *geloia* and
spoudaia both as an essential constituent of their cultic song and as
a safe path leading towards a dramatic victory (cf. Segal 1961: 229).

> καὶ πολλὰ μὲν γέλοιά μ' εἰ-
> πεῖν, πολλὰ δὲ σπουδαῖα, καὶ
> τῆς σῆς ἑορτῆς ἀξίως
> παίσαντα καὶ σκώψαντα νι-
> κήσαντα ταινιοῦσθαι.

> And grant me to say much in jest
> as well as much in earnest,
> and, having played and joked worthily of your festival,
> to win and wear the victor's wreath.   (389–93)

In the agon, on the other hand, generic boundaries tend to dissolve
and fuse. The dichotomies seem to submerge. Hard and fast dividing lines disappear. The ludic and 'playful' Comedy is now enriched
with a more sublime dimension, since it incorporates and reflects

upon the serious, the *spoudaia* themes, sanctified by tradition as the property of Tragedy. Tragedy, conversely, loses its monolithic rigidness and enters into a 'dialogue' with the comic milieu into which it is metatheatrically enfolded.

In other words, the agon of the *Frogs* recreates and re-enacts the interplay of conflicting moods and tensions which builds the real event of the Great Dionysia dramatic festival, the primary civic occasion which hosts the theatrical performance of both genres. As in the City Dionysia festival, so in the Aristophanic *Frogs*, serious and ludic tone mingle freely under the eye of the god: engaged in a 'conversation' with Tragedy without for a moment relinquishing the distinctive Comic mode, Dionysus effects a fictional convergence of both genres under his aegis. The generic self-consciousness implicitly interwoven with his arbitrative role is openly expressed in line 1439:

γέλοιον ἂν φαίνοιτο, νοῦν δ' ἔχει τίνα;

It could be an amusing sight, but, what would be the point of it?

Reproaching the comical one-sidedness of Euripides' proposed solution (1437–8) of the civic 'riddle' (1436), Dionysus reveals his realization that both moods and, therefore, genres have an equal part to play in the *polis*' communal life.[35] Besides, the Aristophanic god's conviction that the saviour of the city should be sought in the *persona* of a tragic poet by no means implies that Comedy is either unworthy or incapable of such a noble, salutary function.[36] In the metatheatrical dimension of the play, it is Tragedy *obeying* its comic judge[37] which is assigned the noble undertaking of the Athenian *polis*' salvation. And, in this respect, I cannot see why Taplin's (1996) and Gredley's (1996) perspectives should be mutually exclusive. The very fact that Dionysus, the god of Drama, brings about a 'fin de siècle' resurrection of Tragedy, as part of his comic role as a judge in a contest of tragic poetry metatheatrically 'enfolded' in a comic play, *does* amount to 'a kind of bid for comedy to stand on a civic pedestal beside that of tragedy' (Taplin 1996: 198). As the century draws to its end, it would appear that Dicaeopolis' famous claim at the Lenaea of 425 still reverberates: 'even Comedy is acquainted with justice' (τὸ γὰρ δίκαιον οἶδε καὶ τρυγῳδία) (*Acharn.* 500). Both then, and now, 'The jealous sibling is, in effect, making

---

[35] Cf. Segal (1961: 229): 'The proper combination of laughter and seriousness is symbolic of the proper unity of the *polis* . . .'.

[36] I therefore disagree with Heiden (1991), who is troubled by 'the silence about comedy in the *agon*' (105) and by the agon's exaltation of 'tragic poetry as the city's educator and a tragic poet as the city's savior, instead of comic poetry and a comic poet' (95).

[37] See 1134 and 1229 (discussed from another angle in 3.4).

its characteristically metatheatrical bid for serious attention'
(Taplin 1996: 198). Yet, all the same, and irrespective of whether
Dionysus, as a *dramatis persona* in the agon of the *Frogs*, partakes of
the tragic or the comic mode, the resurrected Aeschylus *does*
embody 'the kind of tragedy which once gave voice to a value-
system now effectively undermined by Euripides and his spiritual
descendants' (Gredley 1996: 212–13).

Epilogue

I end this book with a quick look at the play's exodos (1500–33), that is, the staging of Aeschylus' ascent, a scene displaying striking visual and verbal similarities to the exodos that he himself had once composed for his own tragic *Eumenides*. For not only does the blaze of the Mystai's torches (1524–5 φαίνετε τοίνυν ὑμεῖς τούτῳ | λαμπάδας ἱεράς) evoke the spectacular ending of the Aeschylean trilogy, with its processional escorting of the Dread Goddesses 'by the light of flaring torches' (φέγγει λαμπάδων σελασφόρων) (*Eum.* 1022; cf. 1041–2 πυριδάπτῳ | λαμπάδι), but the clear adaptation of *Eumenides* 1012–13 in *Frogs* 1530,[1] heard immediately after Pluto's instruction that the departing poet should be accompanied to the world of light by the melodies of his own songs,[2] is also instrumental in sustaining the audience's awareness of an underlying Aeschylean sub-text. Nevertheless, beyond the external markers of the final scene's inter-textuality, a much deeper analogy between the Aeschylean and Aristophanic performances emerges. For in both cases the theatri-cally enacted sequence seems to defy confinement to the dramatic space and to spill over to the world of the spectating *polis*.

Inviting the entire audience to join their voices in the ritual *ololyge* (*Eum.* 1043 = 1047 ὀλολύξατέ νυν ἐπὶ μολπαῖς),[3] 'the *Oresteia* ends with a united cry of triumphant joy from over ten thousand mouths as all Athens hails the birth of a new era' (Sommerstein 1989: ad *Eum.* 1047). As Pat Easterling (1988: 109) has put it with special reference to Aeschylus' trilogy, 'some sequences of words, music and actions could be felt to have exceptional power, some-thing that went beyond the fictive world of the drama and was able to affect the world of the audience for good or ill'. In the Aristophanic play, correspondingly, the *politai* to whom Aeschylus is expected to bring blessings (1487 ἐπ' ἀγαθῷ μὲν τοῖς πολίταις . . .) are not only the imaginary inhabitants of the dramatic Athens but,

---

[1] τῇ δὲ πόλει μεγάλων ἀγαθῶν ἀγαθὰς ἐπινοίας; cf. Aesch. *Eum.* 1012–13 εἴη δ' ἀγαθῶν | ἀγαθὴ διάνοια πολίταις; see Dover (1993: ad loc.) and Sommerstein (1996: ad loc.).

[2] *Frogs* 1525–7 χἄμα προπέμπετε | τοῖσιν τούτου τοῦτον μέλεσιν | καὶ μολπαῖσιν κελαδοῦντες.

[3] See Sommerstein (1989: ad *Eum.* 1047): 'The singer or singers probably here again turn to the audience', and cf. ad *Eum.* 1039: 'πανδαμεί is hardly appropriate if addressed only to a dozen or so Areopagites, and is therefore probably directed mainly to the audience.'

more significantly, the real-life citizens of the distressed and tormented *polis* of 405 BC.

Now, it may be quickly counter-argued that, although Aeschylus' Oresteian trilogy ends with the establishment of the Erinyes/ *Semnai* as awesome goddesses in Athens (*Eum.* 1003 ff.), Aeschylus' comic return is without a parallel in civic ritual and therefore remains utterly fictitious: no matter how deeply 'involved' the audience of the play's first performance felt, consciousness that the chosen saviour of the *polis* was in reality 'dead and gone' and that Athens was being tossed dangerously κυμάτων ἐν ἀγκάλαις ('in the cradle of the waves') (704)[4] must have been constantly and painfully present. To quote Whitman (1964: 256),

> . . . the resurrection of Aeschylus is really a paradox. Like the *Frogs* as a whole, it is far less cheerful than it seems. Though it follows externally the comic design in achieving the impossible, the lack of revelry, the gravity of the issue, and the sorrowful tone betray the underlying lament . . . the effect is funereal. . . . To resurrect the poet in this sense, and in the terms used, comes close to confessing that he is gone forever.

Yet, there is much in this play to suggest that, by the time its plot has drawn to its end, the spectator has been given the impression that Aeschylus has been granted almost divine status or, at least, that he may never have to be confined to Hades again.[5]

We have seen in 6.2 that in line 1259 the Chorus referred to him as 'the Bacchic Lord' (τὸν Βακχεῖον ἄνακτα), that is, an inspired, possessed poet, participating in Dionysus' divinity: just as the god's entranced female followers partake of his cultic title (*Bakchos—Bakchai*), Aeschylus' denomination in the *Frogs* acknowledges his share in the Dionysiac nature. Moreover, being prepared to entertain Dionysus and Aeschylus as civic guests (1480), Pluto acknowledges them both as his equals, for those who practise hospitality inevitably recognize themselves as more or less sharing a similar status (3.4). And, if I have been right in detecting Heraclean over-

---

[4] See Sommerstein (1996: 5): 'Athenians in 405 had every reason to believe that defeat would mean the end not only of their empire, but of their city, their homes, their families, and their lives. It is impossible to understand *Frogs* without appreciating that this was the shadow that hung over spectators, performers, and author alike,' and cf. Sommerstein (1996: 4 n. 23): 'At one moment in *Frogs* (736–7) it is implied that the best Athens can realistically hope for is to perish with honour ("[to be hanged] on a respectable tree")'.

[5] Cf. Aeschylus' request to Pluto in *Frogs* 1517–18 ἦν ἄρ' ἐγώ ποτε | δεῦρ' ἀφίκωμαι, 'if I ever sometime come back here', with Sommerstein's note (1996: ad loc.): 'this strongly suggests that the risen Aeschylus may be immortal: that he will ever return to Hades is no more than a possibility. The holding of a procession, by the light of the "sacred torches" of the Eleusinian initiates, in *his* honour (and not, apparently, in honour of Dionysus-Iacchus who is also present) likewise implies that Aeschylus now enjoys a status little if at all short of divine.'

tones in Aeschylus' *persona* as moulded by the agon (Ch. 7), it is
certainly significant that banqueting together with Dionysus or
other gods is a well-established scheme communicating Heracles'
attainment of everlasting immortality (4.10). But most importantly,
attention should be paid to the precise wording of Pluto's farewell
to the ascending poet:

$$\mathring{a}γε \; δὴ \; χαίρων, \; Αἰσχύλε, \; χώρει \ldots$$

go on, then, Aeschylus, rejoice, and may you have a safe journey . . .

(1500)

Pluto's implicit address 'chaire' heroizes its recipient for, as
Sourvinou-Inwood (1995: 199) has persuasively argued, 'one of the
main uses of *chaire* was to address deities and other supernatural
beings in invocations, salutations and the like.'[6] And, given the
mystic frame of the play in its entirety, Pluto's respectful greeting
assigns to Aeschylus a status parallel to that of Dionysiac initiates,
whom the Orphic/Bacchic gold leaves salute for their achievement
of immortality and sharing in the nature of their god:

$$χαῖρε \; παθὼν \; τὸ \; πάθημα \; τὸ \; δ' \; οὔπω \; πρόσθε \; ἐπεπόνθεις·$$
$$θεὸς \; ἐγένου \; ἐξ' \; ἀνθρώπου \ldots$$

hail, you who have endured the suffering you've never suffered before;
you were a man, you've now become a god . . .

(tablet A4 Zuntz (1971), 3–4; cf. 2. 14)

Besides, special status is assigned to Aeschylus through the
makarismos, the 'blessing', pronounced on his behalf by the Chorus
of the Eleusinian Initiates (1482 μακάριός γ' ἀνήρ . . .), an utterance
resembling the ritual *makarismoi* of Eleusinian/Dionysiac mystic
teletai: 'Happy and blessed one (ὄλβιε καὶ μακαριστέ), you will
become a god instead of a man (θεὸς δ' ἔσῃ ἀντὶ βροτοῖο)', reads one
of the gold leaves (A1 Zuntz (1971), line 8), making explicit the link
between ritually pronounced blessing and conferment of immortality, earthly *pathos* and the supreme, divine serenity that only
initiates may hope to achieve beyond the grave.[7]

---

[6] Cf. Sourvinou-Inwood (1995: 197) on *chaire* in 5th-cent. tragedy as 'never addressed to
anyone either about to die or dead to whom such special status [i.e. heroic/divine] is not
assigned.'

[7] See primarily (for Eleusis) Hom. *h. Dem.* 480; Isocr. 4. 28; Pind. fr. 137a Maehler; Soph.
fr. 837 Radt. In the Bacchic circle, which concentrates on earthly (as well as afterlife)
happiness, blessings can also demarcate a special existence during one's lifetime, full of the
presence of Dionysus himself; cf. e.g. Eur. *Bacch.* 72–7: 'Blessed is he who, truly happy,
knowing the mystic rites of the gods . . . joins his soul to the *thiasos* performing Bacchic
ritual on the mountains . . .' (ὢ μάκαρ, ὅστις εὐδαί | μων τελετὰς θεῶν εἰ | δώς . . . θιασεύεται
ψυ | χὰν ἐν ὄρεσσι βακχεύ | ων . . .).

If Pluto's greeting, then, and the Chorus's *makarismos* heroize Aeschylus, *Frogs* does not belie its genre, as Whitman would have us believe. Effected as they are through comically remoulded yet clearly recognizable ritual schemes, *both* Dionysus' reincorporation into Athens *and* Aeschylus' resurrection/attainment of higher status could have been felt by classical Athenian audiences as exercising a beneficial influence on the *polis* as a whole and on its cultural vitality. Rather than ending in funereal tones, the Aristophanic play fills both stage and auditorium with light and hope. The 'performative' power of words[8] and ritual structures guarantee the *efficacy* of the utopian plot's outcome.[9] As Aeschylus himself promises, ταῦτα ποιήσω, 'I will bring these into effect' (1515).[10]

[8] In J. L. Austin's (1962) sense of the term, whereby some utterances do not simply describe, state, or report an action but 'perform' it instead: 'to say something may be to do something' (91).

[9] It could prove very fruitful to think about the Chorus's exodial song (1528–33) while bearing in mind the special power of words uttered by those invested with some kind of ritual authority within the community to which they belong. Like fertility spells commanding crop growth or other forms of magic, the Chorus's final song may be thought of as instilling in its real-life Athenian audience 'the proper cognitive, emotional, and behavioral attitudes and dispositions', and thus becoming 'self-fulfilling' by imparting to the listeners/spectators 'the necessary motivations for achieving the tasks culturally set for them' (Ray 1973: 28, summing up Tambiah's and Beattie's theories on the ritual power of words).

[10] I take Aeschylus' reply to refer to the entire set of instructions he receives from Pluto, including the great undertaking enjoined on him in lines 1501–3 καὶ σῷζε πόλιν τὴν ἡμετέραν | γνώμαις ἀγαθαῖς, καὶ παίδευσον | τοὺς ἀνοήτους. On 'promising' as a way of 'doing things with words' see Searle (1969: 54–61).

APPENDIX

Ritual Disguise in the Greek World

The subject of ritual disguise in ancient Greece requires a study in its own right.[1] Hence, this brief Appendix is not intended as a comprehensive list of the material available, but merely as an indication of its scope and variety, as well as of the nature of the interpretative problems it involves.

(i) Perhaps the most widely cited case of ritual disguise on Greek land relates to the *telete* that Pausanias designates as 'Greater' in the region of the Arcadian Pheneos. There, at a peculiar stone construction called Petroma, which stands beside the sanctuary of Demeter (surnamed 'Eleusinian') (Paus. 8. 15. 1–2), the priest of Demeter Cidaria, 'putting on the mask of the goddess', beats with rods those who dwell under the earth.[2]

(ii) A wealth of archaeological findings from Lycosura relate to the cult of the Arcadian 'Great Goddess' Despoina. Although the riddle of the animal-headed votive terracotta statuettes and the animal-headed figures depicted along the selvage of the marble drapery of Despoina's cult statue has not been deciphered yet,[3] scholars agree that such representations testify to the existence of ritual masked dances in the area,[4] on whose function Kahil (1977: 95) writes: 'Porter le masque d'un animal, c'est lui emprunter une partie de sa puissance: une fois de plus nous remontons ici à des rites ancrés dans la mentalité primitive.'

(iii) Bull-headed archaic figurines from Cypriot sanctuaries have been interpreted as priests of a fertility god who, wearing his most sacred symbol, the bucranium, are overwhelmed by the god's vitality and enter into direct association with him (Karageorghis 1971: 261–2).

(iv) A male and female figure depicted on a fragment of a krateriskos from Brauron reflecting rites of the *arkteia* (cf. 2.7) wear bear-masks. Kahil (1977: 93) recognizes in them the masked priest and priestess of Artemis.[5] Wearing the likeness of the goddess's most sacred animal, they partake symbolically in her nature and, through analogy, become assimilated to

---

[1] I have not been able to consult F. Back, *De Graecorum caerimoniis, in quibus homines deorum vice fungebantur* (diss., Berlin, 1883).

[2] Paus. 8. 15. 3 τοῦτο ὁ ἱερεὺς περιθέμενος τὸ πρόσωπον ἐν τῇ μείζονι καλουμένῃ τελετῇ ῥάβδοις κατὰ λόγον δή τινα τοὺς ὑποχθονίους παίει. See Stiglitz (1967: 135 and 136 (although in a Lévy-Bruhlian interpretative line)); Croon (1955: 13); Jost (1985: 320).

[3] See, most importantly, Perdrizet (1899); Nilsson (1906: 347); Jost (1985: 332); Stiglitz (1967: 36, 38); Dietrich (1962: 139).

[4] See e.g. Nilsson (1906: 347–8); Stiglitz (1967: 37); Jost (1985: 333); Kenner (1970: 41 n. 115).

[5] Cf. Jost (1985: 409–10); Sourvinou-Inwood (1990b: 9); see *contra* Simon (1983: 87–8).

her. Similarly, according to a very late source (Polyaen. *Strateg.* 8. 59), there was a ritual custom in Pellene whereby the priestess of Athena would wear a likeness of the goddess's panoply and helmet.

Literary reflections of this cultural pattern of 'dressing up like *x*' : 'being perceived as *x*' in a ritual ceremonial frame can be found in the novels of the Second Sophistic, Anthia's likeness to Artemis in Xenophon's *Ephesian Tale* being the most striking example:

> She wore a purple tunic down to the knee, fastened with a girdle and falling loose over her arms, with a fawnskin over it, a quiver attached, and arrows for weapons; she carried javelins and was followed by dogs. Often as they saw her in the sacred enclosure the Ephesians would worship her as Artemis. And so on this occasion too [i.e. a local festival of Artemis] the crowd gave a cheer when they saw her . . . some were amazed and said it was the goddess in person (τῶν μὲν ὑπ' ἐκπλήξεως τὴν θεὸν εἶναι λεγόντων); some that it was someone else made by the goddess in her own image. But all prayed and prostrated themselves and congratulated her parents.

> (Xen. Eph. *Ephes.* 1. 2. 6–7; tr. G. Anderson 1989) (see Connor 1987: 44)

(v) The sacred rules of the Andanian Mysteries in Messenia imply that some of the 'sacred women' have to be 'dressed in the manner of the gods' and to 'wear the clothing that the sacred men specify'.[6]

Moving away from the sphere of regular cultic occasions taking place at fixed points in the Greek *poleis*' sacred calendar, an interesting corpus of evidence relates to the frequent appropriation of divine apparel in battle as a stratagem against the enemy,[7] while divine costume can prove an indispensable 'stage-prop' when theatricality is 'latent', that is, when the 'performers' know they are 'performing', but the audience must not (cf. Schechner 1990: 29): the best Greek example here is undoubtedly the exiled Peisistratus' return to Athens in the 550s. His bold political move, travestied as a ritual procession (Sinos 1993), is carried out in distinctively 'performative' terms, primarily through ritual disguise: the prospective tyrant is driven on a chariot by a tall beautiful girl dressed up in complete armour as Athena:

> They fitted her with full armor, put her on a chariot, arranged her pose so that she would appear at her most striking, and drove her into the city. They had sent heralds to run ahead of them, and these, when they arrived, spoke as they had been ordered: 'Men of Athens, receive with good will Pisistratus, whom Athena herself, having honored him above all mankind, is bringing back from exile to her own Acropolis.' So the heralds went about, saying these things, and the word immediately spread through the demes that Athena was bringing Pisistratus back. The people in the city believed that this woman was the goddess herself (πειθόμενοι τὴν γυναῖκα εἶναι αὐτὴν τὴν θεόν) and offered prayers to her, for all that she was only human, and they welcomed Pisistratus.[8]   (Hdt. 1. 60. 4–5; tr. D. Grene 1987)

---

[6] See Sokolowski (1969: no. 65, lines 23–5) ὅσα δὲ δεῖ διασκευάζεσθαι εἰς θεῶν διάθεσιν, ἐχόντω τὸν εἱματισμὸν καθ' ὃ ἂν οἱ ἱεροὶ διατάξωντι.

[7] Cf. 7.4, on Milo's and Nicostratus' disguise as Heracles in battles.

[8] Cf. Paus. 4. 17. 2–3, on two Messenian young men who, 'riding on the finest horses and

Now, the problems and questions inextricably interwoven with the success of this 'performance' are fascinating and intriguing (see primarily Connor 1987; Sinos 1993); for my purposes, however, it is enough to underline the bare fact that, within a ritual (or even a mock-ritual) frame, it is primarily the assumption of *external* attributes which ensures the creation of a link between 'performer'/imitator and model.

To enter more specifically into the Dionysiac circle, as far as maenadism of myth is concerned, the best example of ritual dressing up is Pentheus' 'robing scene' in Euripides' *Bacchae*. Having worn the 'attire of a woman, a maenad, a bacchant' (σκευὴν γυναικὸς μαινάδος βάκχης) (*Bacch.* 915) and, therefore, having been externally assimilated to his prototypes,[9] he undergoes a change of personality.[10] For not only is he suffused with the illusion of superhuman strength (*Bacch.* 945–6, 949–50)[11] but, more significantly still, his 'point of view' has switched from 'male' to 'female', from authoritative self-control to child-like surrender and dependence (Segal 1982, *passim*). Putting on the likeness of Dionysus, the initiand Pentheus enters into the proper space of this god and is, therefore, able to perceive him in his bestial incarnation (*Bacch.* 920–2).[12] This altered state of consciousness seems to vanish at the moment Pentheus tears off the ritual *mitra* (1115–16): his 'bondage to Dionysiac delusion' (Segal 1982: 206) is symbolized by a tangible accessory of his ritual dress.[13]

Now, in the sphere of cultic maenadism, the question of whether the historical bacchants' external *mimesis* of the mythical companions of Dionysus (Diod. 4. 3. 3) entailed also their 'transubstantiation', that is, their inner fusion with the god, cannot be answered 'in good conscience' (Henrichs 1982: 159; cf. 146–7). Nevertheless, it seems to me that the Henrichs/Vernant (1988c) methodological polarity is a misleading and unnecessary complication of the issue, obfuscating the essential point, which lies simply in the fact that ritual garb confers on the Dionysiac follower a new 'social'/'religious' identity and role, as it detaches her from the realm of the 'profane' and elevates her by analogy to the status of Dionysus' mythic entourage: independently of her own internal disposition, the woman of the city who enwraps herself in Dionysiac garb takes

---

dressed in white tunics and scarlet cloaks, with caps on their heads and spears in their hands', infiltrated the Lacedaemonians' feast of the Dioscuri, with the result that 'when the Lacedaemonians saw them they bowed down and prayed, thinking that the Dioscuri themselves had come to their sacrifice.'

[9] Note the *mimesis*-language in *Bacch.* 917, 927, esp. 980 (ἐπὶ τὸν ἐν γυναικομίμῳ στολᾷ).

[10] Henrichs (1982: 159); cf. Dodds (1960: 181, ad 854–5).

[11] Cf. the same effect of the Dionysiac attributes upon Teiresias and Cadmus (esp. *Bacch.* 187 ff.).

[12] See especially Seaford (1987a) who also stresses that Pentheus' loss of personality is independent of the *lyssa* promised by Dionysus in *Bacch.* 850–1; cf. Gallini (1963b: 212).

[13] See Picard (1932: 719) on the Dionysiac *mitra* functioning as a talismanic object, responsible for the communication of the 'νοῦς divin, folie ou extase' to those possessed by the god. Cf. also Dodds (1960: ad 111).

symbolically, but *ipso facto*, in the eyes of the 'spectating' community, the place of a Dionysiac raving nymph.

The dearth of classical evidence on initiations into Dionysiac *thiasoi* is a well-known fact; nevertheless, it is still possible to reassemble some scattered bits of information, so as to reconstruct a picture, even if only shadowy, of the importance of the ritual garb in the Dionysiac cultic sphere. Here are a few examples.

Mimesis of the outward appearance, the *schema*, of Nymphs, Pans, Silenoi, and Satyrs in the midst of ritual dancing is perceived by Plato (*Leg.* 815c) as the distinguishing characteristic of those who engage in various kinds of initiatory activities (περὶ καθαρμούς τε καὶ τελετάς τινας) within the Dionysiac realm and, if the *Bacchae* can be thought of as portraying a collective initiation of the Theban town into the god's βακχεύματα (see esp. *Bacch.* 40), the *polis*' assumption of the ritual garb (*Bacch.* 34) is highlighted from the start as the prerequisite for the achievement of Dionysiac exultation.[14] In the frame of the quite similar Sabazian rites too, Aeschines is denigrated by Demosthenes (18. 259) as νεβρίζων,[15] that is, conferring on the initiands the sacred vestment of the fawn-skin,[16] an action which confirms the importance of the ritual dress in effecting the transition from a candidate's secular identity to the 'sacred' personality of an initiate.[17] Furthermore, we can be almost certain that some kind of ritual disguise underlies the riddle of the Dionysiac animals (kid, ram, bull) falling 'into the milk' in the Dionysiac/Orphic gold leaves (Ch. 7, n. 14), especially as we know that entrance into the Dionysiac sphere can be achieved through the appropriation even of very simple attributes, such as the god's *kothornoi*, which consecrate a bull-calf in Tenedos as a Dionysiac sacrificial victim (Ael. *NA* 12. 34), or merely his horns, which mark the 'Laphystian women' as Dionysiac devotees.[18]

Dionysiac iconography may also prove of help. For example, representations of ritual sequences in which satyrs appear, such as the satyrs depicted together with Dionysus in his ship, during the ship-cart procession at the Lenaea or the Anthesteria festival in Athens (2.4(b)), can be taken as indications that the painters were inspired by '*men dressed as satyrs*—rather than merely imaginary satyrs, as they did when depicting female rituals they had not seen' (Seaford 1994a: 267; my italics).[19] Moving

---

[14] Note the explicit correlation between the verb ἀνωλόλυξα (24), expressing the first impact of Dionysiac psychology upon the land of Thebes, and the forceful imposition of the sacred fawn-skin: νεβρίδ' ἐξάψας χροός (24).

[15] This passage may have more to do with Dionysiac initiation ritual than is usually assumed; see S. G. Cole (1980: 236), and C. G. Brown (1991: 44–5 with notes).

[16] See Harpocration, s.v. Νεβρίζων (qtd. in Ch. 4, n. 110).

[17] Cf. the later rite of the κατάζωσις, i.e. the investment of the mystes with the sacred girdle which transforms him into a *bakchos* ἀπὸ καταζώσεως, i.e. 'du degré le plus élevé' (Boyancé 1966: 52).

[18] Schol. Lycophr. *Alexandra* 1237 Λαφυστίας ὁ Διόνυσος, ἀπὸ Λαφυστίου, ὄρους Βοιωτίας ὅθεν Λαφύστιαι λέγονται αἱ ἐν Μακεδονίᾳ βάκχαι . . . κερατοφοροῦσι κατὰ μίμησιν Διονύσου. See Schachter (1981: 177).

[19] Men dressed as satyrs may have been part of the ritual celebration of Dionysus' union with the Basilinna at the Anthesteria (Seaford 1994a: 267). For much later evidence on

A1(*a–c*) 'Becoming' a maenad
rf. cup: Oxford, Ashmolean Museum,
1924. 2 (*ARV*² 865, 1)

A2(*a–b*) 'Becoming' a satyr
rf. krater: Paris, Louvre, G 485

away from the sphere of particular and easily identifiable Dionysiac rituals, Christiane Bron (1987) has isolated a small corpus of images which she regards as illustrating 'the initiation of a new bacchant in classical Greece' (1987: 145). In a pictorial triptych on a cup from Oxford, for example, (Fig. A1), the contrast between pre and full maenadic status is conveyed through an antithesis in the initiand's dress and instruments: to the draped, seated figure of the first two pictures (Fig. A1*a–b*) is opposed the dancing woman of the last, clad in the typical maenadic dress and equipped with the Dionysiac attributes (Fig. A1*c*). Thus, as Bérard and Bron (1989: 146) have written elsewhere on that same cup, one can 'from image to image, watch the subtle transformation of existential status of the woman who gradually becomes identified with the maenads of the mystic thiasos.'[20] More explicit is the function of disguise on a krater in the Louvre (Bron 1987: fig. 14) (Fig. A2), centring on the metamorphosis of a young male initiand into a satyr: portraying him four times, that is, naked (A2*a*), then draped in an himation (A2*b*), and in the last two pictures identical in his appearance with a mythical satyr (A2*c–d*),[21] the painter draws attention to his symbolical assimilation to the existential status of his model (Bron 1987: 152).[22] Of course, it cannot be emphasized too strongly that, taking

Dionysiac processions where satyrs, maenads, Pans, and Dionysus himself were impersonated see Seaford (1994*a*: 267 n. 146).

[20] In the entire corpus of Dionysiac imagery as well it is precisely her ἱερὸν ἐνδυτόν, i.e. the *nebris* and the rest of the paraphernalia complementing it (e.g. *thyrsoi*, snakes, etc.) which constitute the hallmark of a female figure's Dionysiac identity; see Edwards (1960: 80–1, with notes, esp. 11).

[21] i.e. without any visual signs which would betray the artificiality of his ritual *skeue*, such as e.g. the shaggy loincloth of a human actor/satyr. I intend to discuss the possible ritual meanings of this iconographic sequence (and especially of the dead (?) satyr of Fig. A2*d*) in separate work.

[22] However, Bron (1987: 152) herself emphasizes that 'Bien sûr, cette interprétation suscite beaucoup de questions et n'est qu'une hypothèse de lecture . . .'.

A2(*c–d*) 'Becoming' a satyr (*continued*)

Vernant's line of interpretation,[23] the French school archaeologists tend to oversimplify the issue, for there is no criterion certifying beyond doubt the reflection of 'mental states'—in the case of maenadism, anyway, irrecoverable—in the iconographical representations. On the other hand, however, the images discussed most probably portray a Dionysiac ritual sequence divided into easily distinguished individual 'acts' where the most conspicuous sign of status differentiation is the absence or the change of garb.

[23] Especially his assumptions concerning the deep transformative effect of the initiand's/bacchant's contact with Dionysus. See esp. Vernant (1988*c*).

References

ABDALLA, A. (1992), *Graeco-Roman Funerary Stelae from Upper Egypt* (Liverpool).

ALEXIOU, M., and DRONKE, P. (1971), 'The Lament of Jephtha's Daughter: Themes, Traditions, Originality', *Studi Medievali* (3rd ser.), 12. 2: 819–63.

AMANDRY, P. (1939), 'Convention religieuse conclue entre Delphes et Skiathos', *BCH* 63: 183–219.

——(1944–5), 'Note sur la convention Delphes-Skiathos', *BCH* 68–9: 411–16.

——(1950), *La Mantique Apollinienne à Delphes: Essai sur le fonctionnement de l'Oracle* (Paris).

AMYX, D. A. (1988), *Corinthian Vase-Painting of the Archaic Period*, vol. ii (Berkeley, Los Angeles, and London).

ANDERSON, G. (1989), 'Xenophon of Ephesus: *An Ephesian Tale*', in B. P. Reardon (ed.), *Collected Ancient Greek Novels* (Berkeley, Los Angeles, and London), 125–69.

ARIAS, P. E., HIRMER, M., and SHEFTON, B. B. (1962), *A History of Greek Vase Painting* (London).

ARNOTT, W. G. (1981), 'Double the Vision: A Reading of Euripides' *Electra*', *G&R* 28: 179–92.

ARROWSMITH, W. (1963), 'A Greek Theater of Ideas', *Arion*, 2. 3: 32–56.

ARTHUR, M. B. (1977), 'The Curse of Civilization: The Choral Odes of the *Phoenissae*', *HSCP* 81: 163–85.

ASHLEY, W. (1979), 'The Teyyam Kettu of Northern Kerala', *The Drama Review*, 23. 2: 99–112.

AUSTIN, J. L. (1962), *How to Do Things with Words* (Oxford).

BABCOCK, B. A. (1978) (ed.), *The Reversible World: Symbolic Inversion in Art and Society* (Ithaca, NY, and London).

BACON, H. H. (1995), 'The Chorus in Greek Life and Drama', *Arion* (3rd ser.), 3. 1: 6–24.

BAIN, D. (1977), *Actors and Audience: A Study of Asides and Related Conventions in Greek Drama* (Oxford).

BAKCHTIN, M. (1968), *Rabelais and his World* (tr. H. Iswolsky) (Cambridge, Mass., and London).

BAL, M., and BRYSON, N. (1991), 'Semiotics and Art History', *The Art Bulletin*, 73: 174–208.

BALDRY, H. C. (1953), 'The Idler's Paradise in Attic Comedy', *G&R* 22: 49–60.

BALENSIEFEN, L. (1990), *Die Bedeutung des Spiegelbildes als ikono-*

graphisches Motiv in der antiken Kunst (Tübinger Studien zur Archäologie und Kunstgeschichte, 10; Tübingen).

BARKER, A. (1984) (ed.), *Greek Musical Writings*, vol. i: *The Musician and his Art* (Cambridge).

——(1989) (ed.), *Greek Musical Writings*, vol. ii: *Harmonic and Acoustic Theory* (Cambridge).

BARRETT, W. S. (1964), *Euripides: Hippolytos* (Oxford).

BARTHES, R. (1975*a*), *S/Z* (tr. R. Miller) (London).

——(1975*b*), 'An Introduction to the Structural Analysis of Narrative', *NLH* 6. 2: 237–72.

BAUMEISTER, A. (1884), *Denkmäler des klassischen Altertums* (Munich and Leipzig).

BEARD, M. (1980), 'The Sexual Status of Vestal Virgins', *JRS* 70: 12–27.

——(1987), 'A Complex of Times: No more Sheep on Romulus' Birthday', *PCPS* 33: 1–15.

BEAZLEY, J. D. (1955), 'Hydria-Fragments in Corinth', *Hesperia*, 24: 305–19.

BENEDETTI, R. L. (1981), *The Actor at Work* (Englewood Cliffs, NJ).

BÉRARD, C. (1974), *Anodoi: Essai sur l'imagerie des passages chthoniens* (Bibliotheca Helvetica Romana, 13; Neuchâtel).

——(1976), '*AΞIE TAYPE*', in *Mélanges d'histoire ancienne et d'archéologie offerts à P. Collart* (Cahiers d'Archéologie romande, 5; Lausanne), 61–73.

——(1983), 'Héros de tout poil: d'Héraklès imberbe à Tarzan barbu', in Lissarrague and Thelamon, 111–18.

——(1987*a*), 'Étrangler un lion à mains nues', in Bérard, Bron, and Pomari, 177–86.

——(1987*b*), 'Le Manteau de lion', *AION* (*ArchStAnt*), 9: 159–65.

——and BRON, C. (1986), 'Bacchos au cœur de la cité', in *L'Association dionysiaque dans les sociétés anciennes* (Actes de la table ronde organisée par l'École Française de Rome (Rome 24–5 May 1984)) (Collection de l'École Française de Rome, 89; Rome), 13–27.

————(1989), 'Satyric Revels', in Bérard *et al.* 131–50.

————and POMARI, A. (1987) (eds.), *Images et société en Grèce ancienne: L'Iconographie comme méthode d'analyse. Actes du Colloque International, Lausanne 8–11 février 1984* (Cahiers d'Archéologie romande, 36; Lausanne).

——*et al.* (1989), *A City of Images: Iconography and Society in Ancient Greece* (tr. D. Lyons of *La Cité des images: Religion et société en Grèce antique*; Lausanne and Paris, 1984) (Princeton).

BERTHIAUME, G. (1982), *Les Rôles du mágeiros: Étude sur la boucherie, la cuisine et le sacrifice dans la Grèce ancienne* (*Mnemosyne*, suppl. 70; Leiden).

BETZ, D. H. (1980), 'Fragments from a Catabasis Ritual in a Greek Magical Papyrus', *History of Religions*, 19. 4: 287–95.

——(1992), *The Greek Magical Papyri in Translation* (2nd edn.; Chicago and London).

BIEBER, M. (1907), *Das Dresdner Schauspielerrelief: Ein Beitrag zur Geschichte des tragischen Costüms und der griechischen Kunst* (Bonn).

BIERL, A. F. (1990), 'Dionysus, Wine, and Tragic Poetry: A Metatheatrical Reading of *P. Köln* VI 242 A = *TrGF* II F 646a', *GRBS* 31: 353–91.

——(1991), *Dionysos und die griechische Tragödie: politische und 'metatheatralische' Aspekte im Text* (*Classica Monacensia*, 1; Tübingen).

BLOCH, R. (1966), Review of F. Matz, Διονυσιακὴ τελετή. *Archäologische Untersuchungen zum Dionysoskult in hellenistischer und römischer Zeit* (Mainz, 1964), *Gnomon*, 38: 393–7.

BOARDMAN, J. (1975), 'Herakles, Peisistratos and Eleusis', *JHS* 95: 1–12.

——(1976), 'A Curious Eye Cup', *AA* 281–90.

——(1982), 'Herakles, Theseus and Amazons', in Kurtz and Sparkes, 1–28.

BOND, G. W. (1981), *Euripides: Heracles* (Oxford).

BONFANTE, L. (1989), 'Nudity as a Costume in Classical Art', *AJA* 93: 543–70.

BORTHWICK, E. K. (1964), 'The Gymnasium of Bromius—A Note on Dionysius Chalcus, Fr. 3', *JHS* 84: 49–53.

——(1968), 'Seeing Weasels: The Superstitious Background of the Empusa Scene in the *Frogs*', *CQ* 18: 200–6.

——(1970a), 'Two Scenes of Combat in Euripides', *JHS* 90: 15–21.

——(1970b), '*P.Oxy.* 2738: Athena and the Pyrrhic Dance', *Hermes*, 98: 318–31.

——(1994), 'New Interpretations of Aristophanes *Frogs* 1249–1328', *Phoenix*, 48. 1: 21–41.

BOSANQUET, R. C. (1905–6), 'The Cult of Orthia as Illustrated by the Finds', *ABSA* 12: 331–43.

BOURDIEU, P. (1965), 'The Sentiment of Honour in Kabyle Society', in Peristiany (1965a), 191–241.

BOWIE, A. M. (1993a), *Aristophanes: Myth, Ritual and Comedy* (Cambridge).

——(1993b), 'Religion and Politics in Aeschylus' *Oresteia*', *CQ* 43: 10–31.

——(1995), 'Greek Sacrifice: Forms and Functions', in Powell, 463–82.

BOWIE, E. L. (1986), 'Early Greek Elegy, *Symposium* and Public Festival', *JHS* 106: 13–35.

——(1990), '*Miles Ludens*? The Problem of Martial Exhortation in Early Greek Elegy', in Murray (1990a), 221–9.

BOYANCÉ, P. (1937), *Le Culte des Muses chez les philosophes Grecs: Études d'histoire et de psychologie religieuses* (Paris).

——(1960–1), 'L'Antre dans les Mystères de Dionysos', *Atti della Pontificia Accademia Romana di Archeologia* (3rd ser., Rendiconti), 33: 107–27.

——(1962), 'Sur les Mystères d'Eleusis', *REG* 75: 460–82.

——(1965–6), 'Dionysos et Sémélé', *Atti della Pontificia Accademia Romana di Archeologia* (3rd ser., Rendiconti), 38: 79–104.

BOYANCÉ, P. (1966), 'Dionysiaca: A propos d'une étude récente sur l'initiation dionysiaque', *REA* 68: 33–60.

BRAMBLE, J. C. (1974), *Persius and the Programmatic Satire: A Study in Form and Imagery* (Cambridge).

BRANDENBURG, H. (1966), *Studien zur Mitra* (Münster).

BRANDES, S. (1980), *Metaphors of Masculinity: Sex and Status in Andalusian Folklore* (Philadelphia).

BRECHT, B. (1964), *Brecht on Theatre: The Development of an Aesthetic* (ed. and tr. J. Willett) (London).

BRELICH, A. (1969), *Paides e Parthenoi*, i (Rome).

BREMMER, J. N. (1984), 'Greek Maenadism Reconsidered', *ZPE* 55: 267–86.

——(1990), 'Adolescents, *Symposion*, and Pederasty', in Murray (1990a), 135–48.

——(1992), 'Dionysos Travesti', in A. Moreau (ed.), *L'Initiation: Actes du Colloque international de Montpellier 11–14 Avril 1991*, i: *Les Rites d'adolescence et les mystères* (Montpellier), i. 189–98.

——(1994), *Greek Religion* (*Greece and Rome: New Surveys in the Classics*, 24; Oxford).

BROCKETT, O. G. (1980), *The Essential Theatre* (2nd edn.; New York and London).

BROMMER, F. (1967), *Die Metopen des Parthenon: Katalog und Untersuchung*, 2 vols. (Mainz).

——(1978), *Hephaistos: Der Schmiedegott in der antiken Kunst* (Mainz am Rhein).

BRON, C. (1987), 'Porteurs de thyrse ou bacchants', in Bérard, Bron, and Pomari, 145–53.

——CORFU-BRATSCHI, P., and MAOUENE, M. (1989), 'Hephaistos bacchant ou le cavalier comaste: Simulation de raisonnement qualitatif par le langage informatique LISP', *AION* (*ArchStAnt*) 11: 155–72.

BRONEER, O. (1942), 'The Thesmophorion in Athens', *Hesperia*, 11: 250–74.

BROWN, C. G. (1991), 'Empousa, Dionysus and the Mysteries: Aristophanes, *Frogs* 285 ff.', *CQ* 41: 41–50.

BROWN, C. S. (1966), 'Odysseus and Polyphemus: The Name and the Curse', *Comparative Literature*, 18. 3: 193–202.

BRUIT, L. (1984), 'Sacrifices à Delphes: Sur deux figures d'Apollon', *RHR* 201: 339–67.

——(1989), 'Les Dieux aux festins des mortels: Théoxénies et *xeniai*', in Laurens, 13–25.

BRUIT ZAIDMAN, L. (1991), 'Les Filles de Pandore: Femmes et rituels dans les cités', in G. Duby and M. Perrot (eds.), *Histoire des femmes en Occident*, i: *L'Antiquité* (ed. P. Schmitt-Pantel) (Paris), 363–403.

BRUMFIELD, A. C. (1981), *The Attic Festivals of Demeter and their Relation to the Agricultural Year* (New York).

BULLOUGH, E. (1912), '"Psychical Distance" as a Factor in Art and an

Aesthetic Principle', *British Journal of Psychology*, 5: 87–118.

BULMER, R. (1977), 'Why is the Cassowary not a Bird? A Problem of Zoological Taxonomy among the Karam of the New Guinea Highlands', in Douglas, 167–93 (1st pub. in *Man*, NS 2 (1967), 5–25).

BURIAN, P. (1985a) (ed.), *Directions in Euripidean Criticism: A Collection of Essays* (Durham, NC).

——(1985b), '*Logos* and *Pathos*: The Politics of the *Suppliant Women*', in id. (1985a), 129–55.

BURKERT, W. (1962), 'Γόης: Zum griechischen "Schamanismus"', *RhM* 105: 36–55.

——(1966a), 'Kekropidensage und Arrhephoria', *Hermes*, 94: 1–25.

——(1966b), 'Greek Tragedy and Sacrificial Ritual', *GRBS* 7: 87–121.

——(1970), 'Jason, Hypsipyle, and New Fire at Lemnos: A Study in Myth and Ritual', *CQ* 20: 1–16.

——(1983), *Homo Necans: The Anthropology of Ancient Greek Sacrificial Ritual and Myth* (1st pub. 1972; tr. P. Bing) (Berkeley, Los Angeles, and London).

——(1985), *Greek Religion: Archaic and Classical* (1st pub. 1977; tr. J. Raffan) (Oxford).

——(1987a), *Ancient Mystery Cults* (Cambridge, Mass., and London).

——(1987b), 'The Problem of Ritual Killing', in R. G. Hamerton-Kelly (ed.), *Violent Origins: Walter Burkert, René Girard, and Jonathan Z. Smith on Ritual Killing and Cultural Formation* (Stanford, Calif.), 149–76.

——(1988), '*Katagógia-Anagógia* and the Goddess of Knossos', in Hägg *et al.* 81–7.

BURNETT, A. P. (1970), 'Pentheus and Dionysus: Host and Guest', *CPh* 65: 15–29.

BURNS, E. (1972), *Theatricality: A Study of Convention in the Theatre and in Social Life* (London).

BUSCHOR, E. (1937), 'Feldmäuse', *Sitzungsberichte der Bayerischen Akademie der Wissenschaft*, 1 (Munich).

BUXTON, R. G. A. (1987), 'Wolves and Werewolves in Greek Thought', in J. Bremmer (ed.), *Interpretations of Greek Mythology* (London), 60–79.

——(1994), *Imaginary Greece: The Contexts of Mythology* (Cambridge).

BYL, S. (1980), 'Parodie d'une initiation dans les Nuées d'Aristophane', *RBPh* 58: 5–21.

——(1988), 'Encore une dizaine d'allusions éleusiniennes dans les *Nuées* d'Aristophane' *RBPh* 66: 68–77.

CAIRNS, F. (1992), 'The Power of Implication: Horace's Invitation to Maecenas (*Odes* I.20)', in T. Woodman and J. Powell (eds.), *Author and Audience in Latin Literature* (Cambridge), 84–109.

CALAME, C. (1977), *Les Chœurs de jeunes filles en Grèce archaïque*, 2 vols. (Rome).

——(1986), *Le Récit en Grèce ancienne: Énonciations et représentations de poètes* (Paris).

CALAME, C. (1995), 'From Choral Poetry to Tragic Stasimon: The Enactment of Women's Song', *Arion* (3rd ser.), 3. 1: 136–54.

CAMERON, A., and KUHRT, A. (1983) (eds.), *Images of Women in Antiquity* (London).

CAMPBELL, J. (1960), 'Introduction: The Lesson of the Mask', in id., *The Masks of God: Primitive Mythology* (London), 21–9.

CAMPBELL, J. K. (1964), *Honour, Family and Patronage: A Study of Institutions and Moral Values in a Greek Mountain Community* (Oxford).

CANTARELLA, R. (1963), *Euripide: I Cretesi* (Milan).

——(1974), 'Dioniso, fra *Baccanti* e *Rane*', in J. L. Heller and J. K. Newman (eds.), *Serta Turyniana: Studies in Greek Literature and Palaeography in honor of Alexander Turyn* (Urbana, Chicago, and London), 291–310.

CARPENTER, T. H. (1986), *Dionysian Imagery in Archaic Greek Art: Its Development in Black-Figure Vase Painting* (Oxford).

——and FARAONE, C. A. (1993) (eds.), *Masks of Dionysus* (Ithaca, NY, and London).

CARRIÈRE, J. C. (1979), *Le Carnaval et la politique: Une introduction à la comédie grecque suivie d'un choix de fragments* (Centre de Recherches d'Histoire Ancienne, 26; Paris).

CARTER, J. B. (1987), 'The Masks of Ortheia', *AJA* 91: 355–83.

CARTLEDGE, P. (1977), 'Hoplites and Heroes: Sparta's Contribution to the Technique of Ancient Warfare', *JHS* 97: 11–27.

——(1990), *Aristophanes and his Theatre of the Absurd* (Classical World Series, Bristol).

CARUSO, C. (1987), 'Travestissements dionysiaques', in Bérard, Bron, and Pomari, 103–10.

CASABONA, J. (1966), *Recherches sur le vocabulaire des sacrifices en grec des origines à la fin de l'époque classique* (Publication des Annales de la Faculté des Lettres, Aix-en-Provence).

CASKEY, L. D., and Beazley, J. D. (1954), *Attic Vase Paintings in the Museum of Fine Arts, Boston* (Part ii) (Oxford).

CASSIO, A. C. (1981), 'A "Typical" Servant in Aristophanes (*Pap. Flor.* 112, Austin 63, 90 ff.)', *ZPE* 41: 17–18.

CATAUDELLA, Q. (1931), 'Sopra alcuni concetti della poetica antica', *RFIC*, NS 9: 382–90.

CHARLESWORTH, M. P. (1926), 'Aristophanes and Aeschylus', *CR* 40: 3–6.

CHOURMOUZIADES, N. (1974), *Σατυρικά* (Athens).

CIANI, M. G. (1974), 'Lessico e funzione della follia nella tragedia greca', *BIFG* 1: 70–110.

CLARK, R. J. (1968), 'Trophonios: The Manner of his Revelation', *TAPA* 99: 63–75.

——(1979), *Catabasis: Vergil and the Wisdom-Tradition* (Amsterdam).

CLARKE, M. (1995), 'Between Lions and Men: Images of the Hero in the *Iliad*', *GRBS* 36. 2: 137–59.

CLINTON, K. (1974), *The Sacred Officials of the Eleusinian Mysteries* (*Transactions of the American Philological Society*, NS 64. 3; Philadelphia).

——(1988), 'Sacrifice at the Eleusinian Mysteries', in Hägg *et al.* 69–80.

——(1992), *Myth and Cult: The Iconography of the Eleusinian Mysteries* (Stockholm).

COCHE DE LA FERTÉ, E. (1951), 'Les Ménades et le contenu réel des représentations de scènes bachiques autour de l'idole de Dionysos', *RA* 38: 12–23.

COHEN, D. (1990), 'The Social Context of Adultery at Athens', in P. Cartledge, P. Millett, and S. Todd (eds.), *Nomos: Essays in Athenian Law, Politics and Society* (Cambridge), 147–65.

——(1991), *Law, Sexuality, and Society: The Enforcement of Morals in Classical Athens* (Cambridge).

COLE, A. T. (1961), 'The Anonymus Iamblichi and his Place in Greek Political Theory', *HSCP* 65: 127–63.

COLE, S. G. (1980), 'New Evidence for the Mysteries of Dionysos', *GRBS* 21: 223–38.

——(1984*a*), 'Life and Death: A New Epigram for Dionysos', *Epigraphica Anatolica*, 4: 37–49.

——(1984*b*), 'The Social Function of Rituals of Maturation: The Koureion and the Arkteia', *ZPE* 55: 233–44.

——(1984*c*), *Theoi Megaloi: The Cult of the Great Gods at Samothrace* (Leiden).

——(1993*a*), 'Voices from beyond the Grave: Dionysus and the Dead', in Carpenter and Faraone, 276–95.

——(1993*b*), 'Procession and Celebration at the Dionysia', in R. Scodel (ed.), *Theater and Society in the Classical World* (Ann Arbor), 25–38.

COLLARD, C. (1975) (ed.), *Euripides: Supplices*, 2 vols. (Groningen).

——CROPP, M. J., and LEE, K. H. (1995), *Euripides: Selected Fragmentary Plays*, i (Warminster).

COMMAGER, S. (1962), *The Odes of Horace: A Critical Study* (New Haven and London).

CONNOR, W. R. (1971), *The New Politicians of Fifth-Century Athens* (Princeton).

——(1987), 'Tribes, Festivals and Processions: Civic Ceremonial and Political Manipulation in Archaic Greece', *JHS* 107: 40–50.

——(1990), 'City Dionysia and Athenian Democracy', in Connor *et al.* 7–32

——(1996), 'Civil Society, Dionysiac Festival, and the Athenian Democracy', in Ober and Hedrick, 217–26.

——*et al.* (1990), *Aspects of Athenian Democracy* (*Classica et Mediaevalia. Dissertationes*, 11; Copenhagen).

CORNFORD, F. M. (1914), *The Origin of Attic Comedy* (London).

CROCKER, J. C. (1983), 'Being an Essence: Totemic Representation among the Eastern Bororo', in N. R. Crumrine and M. Halpin (eds.), *The*

Power of Symbols: Masks and Masquerade in the Americas (Vancouver), 157–96.

CROCKER, J. C. (1985), 'My Brother the Parrot', in G. Urton (ed.), *Animal Myths and Metaphors in South America* (Salt Lake City), 13–47.

CROON, J. H.(1955), 'The Mask of the Underworld Daemon—Some Remarks on the Perseus-Gorgon Story', *JHS* 75: 9–16.

CROSBY, M. (1955), 'Five Comic Scenes from Athens', *Hesperia*, 24: 76–84.

CRUMRINE, N. R. (1969), 'Capakoba, the Mayo Easter Ceremonial Impersonator: Explanations of Ritual Clowning', *Journal for the Scientific Study of Religion*, 8. 1: 1–22.

CSAPO, E., and Slater, W. J. (1995), *The Context of Ancient Drama* (Ann Arbor).

CULLER, J. (1981), 'In Pursuit of Signs', in id., *The Pursuit of Signs: Semiotics, Literature, Deconstruction* (London), 18–43.

CUMONT, F. (1933), 'La Grande Inscription bachique du Metropolitan Museum', *AJA* 37: 232–63.

DAKARIS, S. (1973), 'The Oracle of the Dead on the Acheron', in E. Melas (ed.), *Temples and Sanctuaries of Ancient Greece* (London), 139–49.

DARAKI, M. (1980a), 'Aspects du sacrifice dionysiaque', *RHR* 197: 131–57.

——(1980b), 'Le Héros a *menos* et le héros *daimoni isos*. Une polarité homérique', *ASNP* (Classe di lettere e filosofia), 10. 1: 1–24.

——(1982), '*ΟΙΝΟΨ ΠΟΝΤΟΣ*: La Mer dionysiaque', *RHR* 199: 3–22.

DAUX, G. (1958), 'Chronique des fouilles et découvertes archéologiques en Grèce en 1957', *BCH* 82: 644–830.

——(1965), 'Chronique des fouilles et découvertes archéologiques en Grèce en 1964', *BCH* 89: 683–1008.

——(1971), 'Sur quelques inscriptions (anthroponymes, concours à Pergame, serment éphébique)', *REG* 84: 350–83.

DAVIES, M. I. (1978), 'Sailing, Rowing, and Sporting in One's Cups On the Wine-Dark Sea', in *Athens Comes of Age: From Solon to Salamis* (Papers of a Symposium Sponsored by the Archaeological Institute of America, Princeton Society, and the Department of Art and Archaeology, Princeton University) (Princeton), 72–95.

DAWKINS, R. M. (1905–6), 'Laconia. Excavations at Sparta, 1906: Remains of the Archaic Greek Period', *ABSA* 12: 318–30.

DEARDEN, C. W. (1976), *The Stage of Aristophanes* (London).

DEKKER, R. M. (1989), *The Tradition of Female Transvestism in Early Modern Europe* (Basingstoke).

DELATTE, A. (1934), 'Les Conceptions de l'enthousiasme chez les philosophes présocratiques', *AC* 3: 5–79.

DELAVAUD-ROUX, M. H. (1995), 'L'Énigme des danseurs barbus au parasol et les vases "des Lénéennes"', *RA* 227–63.

DELCOURT, M. (1961), *Hermaphrodite: Myths and Rites of the Bisexual Figure in Classical Antiquity* (tr. J. Nicholson) (London).

——(1965), *Pyrrhos et Pyrrha: Recherches sur les valeurs du feu dans les légendes helléniques* (Paris).

—— (1982), *Héphaistos ou la légende du magicien* (2nd edn.; 1st pub. 1957, Liège) (Paris).

DELORME, J. (1960), *Gymnasion: Étude sur les monuments consacrés à l'éducation en Grèce (des origines à l'Empire romain)* (Paris).

DE MARINIS, M. (1985), 'Toward a Cognitive Semiotic of Theatrical Emotions' (tr. B. Thorn), *Versus*, 41: 5–20.

DENEKEN, F. (1881), *De Theoxeniis* (diss.; Berlin).

DENTZER, J.-M. (1982), *Le Motif du banquet couché dans le proche-Orient et le monde grec du VIIe au IVe siècle avant J.-C.* (École Française de Rome).

DEONNA, W. (1959), 'Un divertissement de table "à cloche-pied"', *Collection Latomus*, 40: 5–39.

—— (1964), 'Masks', in *Encyclopedia of World Art* (New York, Toronto, and London), 9: cols. 525–30.

DETIENNE, M. (1968), 'La Phalange: Problèmes et controverses', in Vernant, 119–42.

—— (1977), *The Gardens of Adonis: Spices in Greek Mythology* (tr. J. Lloyd) (Hassocks).

—— (1979a), 'Pratiques culinaires et esprit de sacrifice', in Detienne and Vernant, 7–35.

—— (1979b), *Dionysus Slain* (tr. M. Muellner and L. Muellner of *Dionysos mis à mort*; Paris, 1977) (Baltimore and London).

—— (1981), 'Between Beasts and Gods', in Gordon, 215–28.

—— (1989), *Dionysos at large* (Eng. tr. A. Goldhammer) (Cambridge, Mass., and London).

—— and VERNANT, J.-P. (1974), *Les Ruses de l'intelligence: La Mètis des Grecs* (Paris).

—— —— (1979), *La Cuisine du sacrifice en pays grec* (Paris).

DEUBNER, L. (1932), *Attische Feste* (2nd edn.; Berlin).

DICKIE, M. W. (1995), 'The Dionysiac Mysteries in Pella', *ZPE* 109: 81–6.

DICKINS, G. (1929), 'The Masks', in R. M. Dawkins (ed.), *The Sanctuary of Artemis Orthia at Sparta* (London), 163–86.

DIETERICH, A. (1893), *Nekyia: Beiträge zur Erklärung der neuentdeckten Petrusapokalypse* (Leipzig).

DIETRICH, B. C. (1962), 'Demeter, Erinys, Artemis', *Hermes*, 90: 129–48.

—— (1973), 'A Religious Function of the Megaron', *Rivista Storica dell'Antichità*, 3: 1–12.

DIGGLE, J. (1994) (ed.), *Euripidis Fabulae*, vol. iii (Oxford).

DILTHEY, K. (1874), 'Tod des Pentheus: Galenische Trinkschale', *Archaeologische Zeitung*, 31: 78–94.

DODDS, E. R. (1951), *The Greeks and the Irrational* (Berkeley and Los Angeles).

—— (1960) (ed.), *Euripides: Bacchae* (2nd edn., Oxford).

DONLAN, W. (1980), *The Aristocratic Ideal in Ancient Greece: Attitudes of Superiority from Homer to the End of the Fifth-Century B.C.* (Lawrence, Kans.).

DOUGHERTY, C., and KURKE, L. (1993) (eds.), *Cultural Poetics in Archaic Greece: Cult, Performance, Politics* (Cambridge).

DOUGLAS, M. (1966), *Purity and Danger: An Analysis of the Concepts of Pollution and Taboo* (London).

——(1975*a*), 'Animals in Lele Religious Symbolism', in ead., *Implicit Meanings: Essays in Anthropology* (1st pub. in *Africa*, 27 (1957)) (London), 27–46.

——(1975*b*), 'Self-Evidence', in ead., *Implicit Meanings: Essays in Anthropology* (London), 276–318.

——(1977) (ed.), *Rules and Meanings: The Anthropology of Everyday Knowledge. Selected Readings* (London).

——(1987*a*), (ed.), *Constructive Drinking: Perspectives on Drink from Anthropology* (Cambridge and Paris).

——(1987*b*), 'A Distinctive Anthropological Perspective', in ead. (1987*a*), 3–15.

DOVER, K. J. (1968), *Aristophanes: Clouds* (Oxford).

——(1972), *Aristophanic Comedy* (London).

——(1974), *Greek Popular Morality in the Time of Plato and Aristotle* (Oxford).

——(1993), *Aristophanes: Frogs* (Oxford).

DOW, S., and GILL, D. H. (1965), 'The Greek Cult Table', *AJA* 69: 103–14.

DOWDEN, K. (1980), 'Grades in the Eleusinian Mysteries', *RHR* 197: 409–27.

DU BOIS, P. (1982), *Centaurs and Amazons: Women and the Pre-History of the Great Chain of Being* (Ann Arbor).

——(1988), *Sowing the Body: Psychoanalysis and Ancient Representations of Women* (Chicago and London).

DU BOULAY, J. (1974), *Portrait of a Greek Mountain Village* (Oxford).

DUCAT, J. (1966), *Les Vases plastiques rhodiens archaïques en terre cuite* (Paris).

DUCHEMIN, J. (1955), *Pindare poète et prophète* (Paris).

DUPONT, F. (1977), *Le Plaisir et la loi: Du 'Banquet' de Platon au 'Satiricon'* (Paris).

DURAND, J.-L. (1979), 'Bêtes grecques: Propositions pour une topologique des corps à manger', in Detienne and Vernant, 133–57.

——(1985), 'Sacrificier, partager, repartir', *L'Uomo*, 9. 1/2: 53–62.

——(1986), *Sacrifice et labour en Grèce ancienne: Essai d'anthropologie religieuse* (Paris and Rome).

——and FRONTISI-DUCROUX, F. (1982), 'Idoles, figures, images: Autour de Dionysos', *RA* 81–108.

——and LISSARRAGUE, F. (1983), 'Héros cru ou hôte cuit: Histoire quasi cannibale d'Héraklès chez Busiris', in Lissarrague and Thelamon, 153–67.

——and SCHNAPP, A. (1989), 'Sacrificial Slaughter and Initiatory Hunt', in Bérard *et al.* 53–70.

EASTERLING, P. E. (1982), *Sophocles: Trachiniae* (Cambridge).

—— (1985), 'Anachronism in Greek Tragedy', *JHS* 105: 1–10.

—— (1988), 'Tragedy and Ritual: "Cry 'Woe, woe', but May the Good Prevail!"', *Métis*, 3: 87–109.

—— (1990), 'Constructing Character in Greek Tragedy', in Pelling, 83–99.

ECO, U. (1979), *The Role of the Reader: Explorations in the Semiotics of Texts* (Bloomington, Ind., and London).

EDMUNDS, L. (1990) (ed.), *Approaches to Greek Myth* (Baltimore and London).

EDWARDS, M. W. (1960), 'Representation of Maenads on Archaic Red-Figure Vases', *JHS* 80: 78–87.

EHRENBERG, V. (1969), *The Greek State* (2nd edn.; London).

ELAM, K. (1980), *The Semiotics of Theatre and Drama* (London and New York).

ELDERKIN, G. W. (1955), *Mystic Allusions in the Frogs of Aristophanes* (Princeton).

ELIADE, M. (1958), *Birth and Rebirth: The Religious Meanings of Initiation in Human Culture* (tr. W. R. Trask) (New York).

—— (1959), *Initiation, rites, sociétés secrètes, naissances mystiques: Essai sur quelques types d'initiation* (Paris).

—— (1964a), 'Masks', in *Encyclopedia of World Art* (New York, Toronto, and London), 9: cols. 520–5.

—— (1964b), *Shamanism: Archaic Techniques of Ecstasy* (tr. W. R. Trask) (London).

—— (1969), *The Quest: History and Meaning in Religion* (Chicago).

—— (1972), *Zalmoxis: The Vanishing God* (tr. W. R. Trask) (Chicago and London).

ELSE, G. F. (1958), '"Imitation" in the Fifth Century', *CPh* 53: 73–90.

EMIGH, J. (1979), 'Playing with the Past: Visitation and Illusion in the Mask Theatre of Bali', *The Drama Review*, 23. 2: 11–36.

EUBEN, J. P. (1986), 'Political Corruption in Euripides' *Orestes*', in id. (ed), *Greek Tragedy and Political Theory* (Berkeley, Los Angeles, and London), 222–51.

EVANS-PRITCHARD, E. E. (1956), *Nuer Religion* (Oxford).

FARB, P., and ARMELAGOS, G. (1980), *Consuming Passions: The Anthropology of Eating* (Boston).

FARID, S. (1973), 'Preliminary Report on the Excavations of the Antiquities Department at Kôm Abû Billo', *ASAE* 61: 21–6.

FARNELL, L. R. (1909), *The Cults of the Greek States*, v (Oxford).

—— (1921), *Greek Hero Cults and Ideas of Immortality* (Oxford).

—— (1932), *The Works of Pindar* (tr. with Literary and Critical Commentaries), vol. ii: *Critical Commentary* (London).

FERRARI, G. (1986), 'Eye-Cup', *RA* 5–20.

FESTUGIÈRE, A. J. (1972), 'Les Mystères de Dionysos', in id., *Études de religion grecque et hellénistique* (Paris), 13–63.

FEYERABEND, B. (1984), 'Zur Wegmetaphorik beim Goldblättchen aus

Hipponion und dem Proömium des Parmenides', *RhM* 127: 1–22.

FISH, S. E. (1970), 'Literature in the Reader: Affective Stylistics', *NLH* 2. 1: 123–61.

——(1976), 'Interpreting the *Variorum*', *Critical Inquiry*, 2. 3: 465–85.

FLÜCKIGER-GUGGENHEIM, D. (1984), *Göttliche Gäste: Die Einkehr von Göttern und Heroen in der griechischen Mythologie* (Berne, Frankfurt am Main, and New York).

FOLEY, H. P. (1980), 'The Masque of Dionysus', *TAPA* 110: 107–33.

——(1981*a*) (ed.), *Reflections of Women in Antiquity* (New York and London).

——(1981*b*), 'The Conception of Women in Athenian Drama', in ead. (1981*a*), 127–68.

——(1982*a*), 'Marriage and Sacrifice in Euripides' *Iphigeneia in Aulis*', *Arethusa*, 15: 159–80.

——(1982*b*), 'The "Female Intruder" Reconsidered: Women in Aristophanes' *Lysistrata* and *Ecclesiazusae*', *CPh* 77: 1–21.

——(1988), 'Tragedy and Politics in Aristophanes' *Acharnians*', *JHS* 108: 33–47.

——(1992), '*Anodos* Dramas: Euripides' *Alcestis* and *Helen*', in R. Hexter and D. Selden (eds.), *Innovations of Antiquity* (New York and London), 133–60.

——(1993) (ed.), *The Homeric Hymn to Demeter: Translation, Commentary, and Interpretive Essays* (Princeton).

FOTI, G., and PUGLIESE CARRATELLI, G. (1974), 'Un Sepolcro di Hipponion e un Nuovo Testo Orfico', *La Parola del Passato*, 29: 91–126.

FOUCAULT, M. (1979), 'What Is an Author?', in J. V. Harari (ed.), *Textual Strategies: Perspectives in Post-Structuralist Criticism* (Ithaca, NY, and London), 141–60.

FRAENKEL, E. (1962), *Beobachtungen zu Aristophanes* (Rome).

FRAZER, J. G. (1949), *The Golden Bough: A Study in Magic and Religion* (abridged edn.) (London).

FRICKENHAUS, A. (1912), *Lenäenvasen* (Berlin).

FRŒHNER, W. (1876), *Anatomie des vases antiques* (Paris).

FRONTISI-DUCROUX, F. (1983), 'L'Homme, le cerf et le berger: Chemins grecs de la civilité', *TR* 4: 53–76.

——(1986), 'Images du ménadisme féminin: Les Vases des "Lénéennes"', in *L'Association dionysiaque dans les sociétés anciennes* (Actes de la table ronde organisée par l'École Française de Rome (Rome, 24–5 May 1984)) (Collection de l'École Française de Rome, 89; Rome), 165–76.

——(1991), *Le Dieu-masque: Une figure du Dionysos d'Athènes* (Paris and Rome).

——and LISSARRAGUE, F. (1990), 'From Ambiguity to Ambivalence: A Dionysiac Excursion through the "Anakreontic" Vases', in Halperin *et al.* 211–56 (1st pub. in *AION* (*ArchStAnt*) 5: 1983).

GABRIELSEN, V. (1994), *Financing the Athenian Fleet: Public Taxation and Social Relations* (Baltimore and London).

GALLINI, C. (1963*a*), 'Katapontismós', *SMSR* 34: 61–90.

——(1963*b*), 'Il travestismo rituale di Penteo', *SMSR* 34: 211–28.

GARDNER, P. (1881), 'Boat-Races Among the Greeks', *JHS* 2: 90–7.

GARLAND, R. (1985), *The Greek Way of Death* (London).

GARNER, R. (1988), 'Death and Victory in Euripides' *Alcestis*', *ClAnt* 7: 58–71.

——(1992), 'Mules, Mysteries, and Song in Pindar's *Olympia 6*', *ClAnt* 11: 45–67.

GARRARD, M. D. (1989), *Artemisia Gentileschi: The Image of the Female Hero in Italian Baroque Art* (Princeton).

GARTON, C. (1957), 'Characterisation in Greek Tragedy', *JHS* 77: 247–54.

——(1972), *Personal Aspects of the Roman Theatre* (Toronto).

GARVIE, A. F. (1986), *Aeschylus: Choephori* (Oxford).

GAUTHIER, P. (1973), 'Notes sur l'étranger et l'hospitalité en Grèce et à Rome', *Ancient Society*, 4: 1–21.

GELL, A. (1975), *Metamorphosis of the Cassowaries: Umeda Society, Language and Ritual* (LSE Monographs on Social Anthropology, 51; London).

GENTILI, B., and PAIONI, G. (1977) (eds.), *Il Mito Greco: Atti del Convegno Internazionale (Urbino 7–12 maggio 1973)* (Rome).

GERNET, L. (1968), *Anthropologie de la Grèce antique* (Paris).

GEYER, A. (1977), 'Roman und Mysterienritual: Zum Problem eines Bezugs zum dionysischen Mysterienritual im Roman des Longos', *WJA*, NS 3: 179–96.

GHIRON-BISTAGNE, P. (1976), *Recherches sur les acteurs dans la Grèce antique* (Paris).

GIGANTE, M. (1990), 'Una nuova lamella Orfica e Eraclito', *ZPE* 80: 17–18.

GILL, C. (1996), *Personality in Greek Epic, Tragedy, and Philosophy: The Self in Dialogue* (Oxford).

GILMORE, D. D. (1987*a*), 'Introduction: The Shame of Dishonor', in id. (ed.), *Honor and Shame and the Unity of the Mediterranean* (A special publication of the American Anthropological Association, 22; Washington, DC), 2–21.

——(1987*b*) 'Honor, Honesty, Shame: Male Status in Contemporary Andalusia', in id. (ed.), *Honor and Shame and the Unity of the Mediterranean* (A special publication of the American Anthropological Association, 22; Washington, DC), 90–103.

GINOUVÈS, R. (1962), *Balaneutikè: Recherches sur le bain dans l'antiquité grecque* (Paris).

GLUCKMAN, M. (1966), *Custom and Conflict in Africa* (1st pub. 1956) (Oxford).

GOLDHILL, S. (1986*a*), *Reading Greek Tragedy* (Cambridge).

——(1986*b*), 'Goldhill on Molehills', *LCM* 11. 10: 163–7.

——(1988*a*), 'Doubling and Recognition in the *Bacchae*', *Métis*, 3: 137–56.

GOLDHILL, S. (1988*b*), 'Reading Differences: The *Odyssey* and Juxtaposition', *Ramus*, 17. 1: 1–31.

——(1990*a*), 'The Great Dionysia and Civic Ideology', in Winkler and Zeitlin, 97–129.

——(1990*b*), 'Character and Action, Representation and Reading: Greek Tragedy and its Critics', in Pelling, 100–27.

——(1991), *The Poet's Voice: Essays on Poetics and Greek Literature* (Cambridge).

GOLDMAN, H. (1910), 'The *Oresteia* of Aeschylus as Illustrated by Greek Vase-Painting', *HSCP* 21: 111–59.

GOMBRICH, E. H. (1977), *Art and Illusion: A Study in the Psychology of Pictorial Representation* (5th edn.; London).

GOMME, A. W. (1953), 'The Interpretation of ΚΑΛΟΙ ΚΑΓΑΘΟΙ in Thucydides 4. 40. 2', *CQ* 3: 65–8.

GOODY, J. (1982), *Cooking, Cuisine and Class: A Study in Comparative Sociology* (Cambridge).

GOOSSENS, R. (1935*a*), 'Les "Ploutoi" de Kratinos', *REA* 37: 405–34.

——(1935*b*), 'Un vers d'Eschyle parodié dans le *Cyclope* et dans les *Grenouilles*', in *Mélanges offerts à M. Octave Navarre par ses élèves et ses amis* (Toulouse), 225–30.

GORDON, R. L. (1980), 'Reality, Evocation and Boundary in the Mysteries of Mithras', *Journal of Mithraic Studies*, 3. 1: 19–99.

——(1981) (ed.), *Myth, Religion and Society: Structuralist Essays* (Cambridge and Paris).

GOULD, J. P. (1978), 'Dramatic Character and "Human Intelligibility" in Greek Tragedy', *PCPS* 24: 43–67.

——(1980), 'Law, Custom and Myth: Aspects of the Social Position of Women in Classical Athens', *JHS* 100: 38–59.

——(1983), 'Homeric Epic and the Tragic Moment', in T. Winnifrith, P. Murray, and K. W. Gransden (eds.), *Aspects of the Epic* (London), 32–45.

GOWERS, E. (1993), *The Loaded Table: Representations of Food in Roman Literature* (Oxford).

GRAF, F. (1974), *Eleusis und die orphische Dichtung Athens in vorhellenistischer Zeit* (Berlin and New York).

——(1984), 'Women, War, and Warlike Divinities', *ZPE* 55: 245–54.

——(1985), *Nordionische Kulte* (Rome).

——(1993), 'Dionysian and Orphic Eschatology: New Texts and Old Questions', in Carpenter and Faraone, 239–58

GREDLEY, B. (1996), 'Comedy and Tragedy—Inevitable Distinctions: Response to Taplin', in Silk, 203–16.

GREEN, J. R. (1982), 'Dedications of Masks', *RA* 237–48.

——(1989), 'Motif-Symbolism on Gnathia Vases', in H.-U. Cain, H. Gabelmann, and D. Salzmann (eds.), *Beiträge zur Ikonographie und Hermeneutik: Festschrift für Nikolaus Himmelmann-Wildschütz* (Mainz am Rhein), 221–6.

——(1994), *Theatre in Ancient Greek Society* (London and New York).

GREIMAS, A.-J. (1966), *Sémantique structurale: Recherche de méthode* (Paris).

GRENE, D. (1987), *Herodotus: The History* (Chicago and London).

——and LATTIMORE, R. (1959) (eds.), *The Complete Greek Tragedies*, vols. i–iv (Chicago and London).

GUARDUCCI, M. (1929), 'Pandora, o i Martellatori: Un dramma satirico di Sofocle e un nuovo monumento vascolare', *MonAL* 33: 5–38.

——(1962), 'Bryaktes: Un contributo allo studio dei "banchetti eroici"', *AJA* 66: 273–80.

——(1985), 'Nuove riflessioni sulla laminetta "orfica" di Hipponion', *RFIC* 113: 385–97.

GUÉPIN, J.-P. (1968), *The Tragic Paradox: Myth and Ritual in Greek Tragedy* (Amsterdam).

GUSFIELD, J. R. (1987), 'Passage to Play: Rituals of Drinking Time in American Society', in Douglas (1987a), 73–90.

GUTHRIE, W. K. C. (1971), *The Sophists* (Cambridge).

HÄGG, R., MARINATOS, N., and NORDQUIST, G. C. (1988) (eds.), *Early Greek Cult Practice: Proceedings of the Fifth International Symposium at the Swedish Institute at Athens* (26–9 June 1986) (Stockholm).

HALDANE, J. A. (1964), 'Who is Soteira? (Aristophanes, *Frogs* 379)', *CQ* 14: 207–9.

HALL, E. (1989), *Inventing the Barbarian: Greek Self-Definition through Tragedy* (Oxford).

HALLIDAY, W. R. (1909–10), 'A Note on Herodotos VI. 83, and the *Hybristika*', *ABSA* 16: 212–19.

——(1925), *The Pagan Background of Early Christianity* (London).

HALLIWELL, S. (1986), *Aristotle's Poetics* (London).

——(1991), 'The Uses of Laughter in Greek Culture', *CQ* 41: 279–96.

HALM-TISSERANT, M. (1986), 'La Représentation du retour d'Héphaïstos dans l'Olympe: Iconographie traditionelle et innovations formelles dans l'atelier de Polygnotos (440–430)', *AK* 29: 8–22.

HALPERIN, D. M. (1990), 'The Democratic Body: Prostitution and Citizenship in Classical Athens', in *One Hundred Years of Homosexuality* (London), 88–112.

——WINKLER, J. J., and ZEITLIN, F. I. (1990) (eds.), *Before Sexuality: The Construction of Erotic Experience in the Ancient Greek World* (Princeton).

HAMILTON, R. (1978), 'A New Interpretation of the Anavyssos Chous', *AJA* 82: 385–7.

——(1992), *Choes and Anthesteria: Athenian Iconography and Ritual* (Ann Arbor).

HANDLEY, E. W. (1973), 'The Poet Inspired?', *JHS* 93: 104–8.

——(1982), 'Aristophanes' Rivals', *PCA* 79: 23–5.

——(1985), 'Comedy', in P. E. Easterling and B. M. W. Knox (eds.), *The Cambridge History of Classical Literature*, i: *Greek Literature* (Cambridge), 355–425.

HANI, J. (1975), 'Le Mythe de Timarque chez Plutarque et la structure de l'extase', *REG* 88: 105–20.

HARRIOTT, R. M. (1986), *Aristophanes, Poet and Dramatist* (London and Sydney).

HARRISON, G., and OBBINK, D. (1986), 'Vergil, *Georgics* I 36–39 and the Barcelona *Alcestis* (*P. Barc.* inv. no. 158–161) 62–65: Demeter in the Underworld', *ZPE* 63: 75–81.

HARRISON, J. E. (1922), *Prolegomena to the Study of Greek Religion* (3rd edn.; repr. 1991, Princeton; 1st pub. 1903, Cambridge) (Cambridge).

——(1927), *Themis: A Study of the Social Origins of Greek Religion* (2nd edn., revised with a preface and supplementary notes; 1st pub. 1912) (Cambridge).

HARTOG, F. (1988), *The Mirror of Herodotus: The Representation of the Other in the Writing of History* (tr. J. Lloyd of *Le Miroir d'Hérodote: Essai sur la représentation de l'autre*; Paris, 1980) (Berkeley, Los Angeles, and London).

HEADLAM, W. G., and THOMSON, G. (1938), *The Oresteia of Aeschylus*, 2 vols. (Cambridge).

HEDREEN, G. (1994), 'Silens, Nymphs, and Maenads', *JHS* 114: 47–69.

HEIDEN, B. (1991), 'Tragedy and Comedy in the *Frogs* of Aristophanes', *Ramus*, 20. 1: 95–111.

HENDERSON, JEFFREY (1975), *The Maculate Muse: Obscene Language in Attic Comedy* (New Haven and London).

——(1990), 'The *Demos* and the Comic Competition', in Winkler and Zeitlin, 271–313.

HENDERSON, JOHN (1994), '*Timeo Danaos*: Amazons in Early Greek Art and Pottery', in S. Goldhill and R. Osborne (eds.), *Art and Text in Ancient Greek Culture* (Cambridge), 85–137.

HENRICHS, A. (1969a), 'Μέγαρον im Orakel des Apollon Kareios', *ZPE* 4: 31–7.

——(1969b), 'Lollianos, *Phoinikika*: Fragmente eines neuen griechischen Romans', *ZPE* 4: 205–15.

——(1969c), 'Die Maenaden von Milet', *ZPE* 4: 223–41.

——(1972), *Die Phoinikika des Lollianos: Fragmente eines neuen griechischen Romans* (Bonn).

——(1975a), 'Die Beiden Gaben des Dionysos', *ZPE* 16: 139–44.

——(1975b), 'Two Doxographical Notes: Democritus and Prodicus on Religion', *HSCP* 79: 93–123.

——(1978), 'Greek Maenadism from Olympias to Messalina', *HSCP* 82: 121–60.

——(1979), 'Greek and Roman Glimpses of Dionysos', in C. Houser (ed.), *Dionysos and his Circle: Ancient through Modern* (Fogg Art Museum, Harvard University; Cambridge, Mass.), 1–11.

——(1981), 'Human Sacrifice in Greek Religion: Three Case Studies', in *Le Sacrifice dans l'antiquité* (*Entretiens sur l'Antiquité Classique*, Fondation Hardt, 27; Vandœuvres and Geneva), 195–242.

——(1982), 'Changing Dionysiac Identities', in B. F. Meyer and E. P. Sanders (eds.), *Jewish and Christian Self-Definition*, iii: *Self-Definition in the Graeco-Roman World* (London), 137–60 and 213–36.

——(1984*a*), 'Loss of Self, Suffering, Violence: The Modern View of Dionysus from Nietzsche to Girard', *HSCP* 88: 205–40.

——(1984*b*), 'Male Intruders among the Maenads: The So-Called Male Celebrant', in H. D. Evjen (ed.), *MNEMAI: Classical Studies in Memory of Karl. K. Hulley* (Chico, Calif.), 69–91.

——(1990), 'Between Country and City: Cultic Dimensions of Dionysus in Athens and Attica', in M. Griffith and D. J. Mastronarde (eds.), *Cabinet of the Muses: Essays on Classical and Comparative Literature in Honor of Thomas G. Rosenmeyer* (Atlanta), 257–77.

——(1993), '"He Has a God in Him": Human and Divine in the Modern Perception of Dionysus', in Carpenter and Faraone, 13–43.

——(1995), '"Why Should I Dance?": Choral Self-Referentiality in Greek Tragedy', *Arion* (3rd ser.), 3. 1: 56–111.

HENRY, A. S. (1983), *Honours and Privileges in Athenian Decrees: The Principal Formulae of Athenian Honorary Decrees* (Hildesheim).

HERINGTON, C. J. (1985), *Poetry into Drama: Early Tragedy and the Greek Poetic Tradition* (Berkeley, Los Angeles, and London).

HERMAN, G. (1987), *Ritualised Friendship and the Greek City* (Cambridge).

HIGGINS, W. E. (1977), 'A Passage to Hades: The *Frogs* of Aristophanes', *Ramus*, 6: 60–81.

HILL, E. (1972), *The Trinidad Carnival* (Austin and London).

HOCHMAN, B. (1985), *Character in Literature* (Ithaca, NY, and London).

HOFFMANN, R. J. (1989), 'Ritual License and the Cult of Dionysus', *Athenaeum*, NS 67: 91–115.

HOLWERDA, D. (1977) (ed.), *Prolegomena de Comoedia; scholia in Acharnenses, Equites, Nubes. Pars I. fasc. III, i: Scholia Vetera in Nubes* (Groningen).

——(1982) (ed.), *Scholia in Vespas; Pacem; Aves et Lysistratam. Pars II, fasc. ii, continens scholia vetera et recentiora in Aristophanis Pacem* (Groningen).

HOOKER, J. T. (1979), 'Two Passages in the "Frogs"', *Maia*, 31: 245–6.

——(1980), 'The Composition of the *Frogs*', *Hermes*, 108: 169–82.

HORNBY, R. (1986), *Drama, Metadrama, and Perception* (London and Toronto).

HORTON, R. (1973), 'Lévy-Bruhl, Durkheim and the Scientific Revolution', in Horton and Finnegan, 249–305.

——and FINNEGAN, R. (1973) (eds.), *Modes of Thought: Essays on Thinking in Western and Non-Western Societies* (London).

HOUSEMAN, M. (1993), 'The Interactive Basis of Ritual Effectiveness in a Male Initiation Rite', in P. Boyer (ed.), *Cognitive Aspects of Religious Symbolism* (Cambridge), 207–24.

HUBBARD, T. K. (1991), *The Mask of Comedy: Aristophanes and the Intertextual Parabasis* (Ithaca, NY, and London).

HUMPHREYS, S. C. (1983), *The Family, Women and Death: Comparative Studies* (London).

HUNTER, R. L. (1983), *Eubulus: The Fragments* (Cambridge).

——(1993), *The Argonautica of Apollonius: Literary Studies* (Cambridge).

HURSCHMANN, R. (1985), *Symposienszenen auf unteritalischen Vasen* (Würzburg).

HUTCHEON, L. (1985), *A Theory of Parody: The Teachings of Twentieth-Century Art Forms* (New York and London).

IMMERWAHR, H. R. (1946), 'Choes and Chytroi', *TAPA* 77: 245–60.

IRWIN, E. (1974), *Colour Terms in Greek Poetry* (Toronto).

ISER, W. (1974), *The Implied Reader: Patterns of Communication in Prose Fiction from Bunyan to Beckett* (Baltimore and London).

IVANOV, V. V. (1984), 'The Semiotic Theory of Carnival as the Inversion of Bipolar Opposites', in U. Eco *et al.*, *Carnival!* (ed. T. A. Sebeok) (Berlin, New York, and Amsterdam), 11–35.

JACCOTTET, A. F. (1990), 'Le Lierre de la liberté', *ZPE* 80: 150–6.

JAMESON, M. (1993), 'The Asexuality of Dionysus', in Carpenter and Faraone, 44–64.

JARVIE, I. C., and Agassi, J. (1970), 'The Problem of the Rationality of Magic', in B. R. Wilson, 172–93.

JAUSS, H. R. (1970), 'Literary History as a Challenge to Literary Theory' (tr. E. Benzinger), *NLH* 2. 1: 7–37.

JEANMAIRE, H. (1939), *Couroi et Courètes: Essai sur l'éducation spartiate et sur les rites d'adolescence dans l'antiquité hellénique* (Lille).

——(1970), *Dionysos: Histoire du culte de Bacchus* (1st pub. 1951) (Paris).

JEBB, R. C. (1892), *Sophocles: The Plays and Fragments*, part v: *Trachiniae* (Cambridge).

——(1894), *Sophocles: The Plays and Fragments*, part vi: *The Electra* (Cambridge).

JENKINS, I. D. (1983), 'Is There Life after Marriage? A Study of the Abduction Motif in Vase Paintings of the Athenian Wedding Ceremony', *BICS* 30: 137–45.

JOHNSTON, S. I. (1990), *Hekate Soteira: A Study of Hekate's Roles in the Chaldean Oracles and Related Literature* (Atlanta).

——and McNIVEN, T. J. (1996), 'Dionysos and the Underworld in Toledo', *MH* 53: 25–36.

JOLY, R. (1955), 'L'Exhortation au courage (θαρρεῖν) dans les mystères', *REG* 68: 164–70.

JONES, C. P. (1991), 'Dinner Theater', in W. J. Slater (ed.), *Dining in a Classical Context* (Ann Arbor), 185–98.

JOST, M. (1985), *Sanctuaires et cultes d'Arcadie* (Paris).

JOURDAIN-ANNEQUIN, C. (1986), 'Héraclès Parastates', in *Les Grandes Figures religieuses: Fonctionnement pratique et symbolique dans l'Antiquité, Besançon 25–26 avril 1984* (Centre de Recherches d'Histoire Ancienne, 68; Paris), 283–331.

JUST, R. J. (1989), *Women in Athenian Law and Life* (London).

KAHIL, L. (1965), 'Autour de l'Artémis attique', *AK* 8. 1: 20–33.
——(1977), 'L'Artémis de Brauron: Rites et mystère', *AK* 20. 2: 86–98.
KAIBEL, G. (1899), *Comicorum Graecorum Fragmenta* (Berlin).
KAMERBEEK, J. C. (1974), *The Plays of Sophocles*, part v: *The Electra* (Leiden).
KANNICHT, R. (1969), *Euripides: Helena*, ii: *Kommentar* (Heidelberg).
KANOWSKI, M. G. (1984), *Containers of Classical Greece: A Handbook of Shapes* (London).
KARAGEORGHIS, V. (1971), 'Notes on Some Cypriote Priests Wearing Bull-Masks', *HThR* 64: 261–70.
KAROUZOU, S. (1945), 'Vases from Odos Pandrosou', *JHS* 65: 38–44.
——(1946), 'Choes', *AJA* 50: 122–39.
——(1955), 'Fragments d'un cratère à volutes provenant de la collection Hélène Stathatos', *BCH* 79: 177–204.
KASSEL, R. (1966), 'Kritische und exegetische Kleinigkeiten II', *RhM* 109: 1–12.
KEARNS, E. (1989), *The Heroes of Attica* (*BICS* suppl. 57; London).
KELLS, J. H. (1973) (ed.), *Sophocles: Electra* (Cambridge).
KENNEDY, G. A. (1991), *Aristotle, On Rhetoric: A Theory of Civic Discourse* (New York).
KENNER, H. (1970), *Das Phänomen der verkehrten Welt in der griechisch-römischen Antike* (Klagenfurt).
KERÉNYI, C. (1967), *Eleusis: Archetypal Image of Mother and Daughter* (tr. R. Manheim) (London).
KERFERD, G. B. (1981), *The Sophistic Movement* (Cambridge).
KEULS, E. C. (1985), *The Reign of the Phallus: Sexual Politics in Ancient Athens* (Berkeley, Los Angeles, and London).
KING, H. (1983), 'Bound to Bleed: Artemis and Greek Women', in Cameron and Kuhrt, 109–27.
KIRBY, M. (1976), 'Structural Analysis/Structural Theory', *The Drama Review*, 20. 4: 51–68.
KIRK, G. S. (1968), 'War and the Warrior in the Homeric Poems', in Vernant, 93–117.
——(1977), 'Methodological Reflexions on the Myths of Heracles', in Gentili and Paioni, 285–97.
KNAPP, P. (1879), 'Mänaden und Mänadentracht auf Vasenbildern', *Archaeologische Zeitung*, 36: 145–9.
KOLB, F. (1977), 'Die Bau-, Religions- und Kulturpolitik der Peisistratiden', *JDAI* 92: 99–138.
KOLLER, H. (1954), *Die Mimesis in der Antike: Nachahmung, Darstellung, Ausdruck* (Berne).
KONSTAN, D. (1986), 'Poésie, politique et rituel dans les *Grenouilles* d'Aristophane', *Métis*, 1: 291–308.
——(1990), 'An Anthropology of Euripides' *Kyklops*', in Winkler and Zeitlin, 207–27.
——(1995), *Greek Comedy and Ideology* (New York).

KOPFF, E. C. (1982), *Euripides: Bacchae* (Leipzig).

KOSSATZ-DEISSMANN, A. (1978), *Dramen des Aischylos auf westgriechischen Vasen* (Mainz am Rhein).

KOSTER, W. J. W. (1978) (ed.), *Scholia in Vespas; Pacem; Aves et Lysistratam. Pars II, fasc. i: Scholia Vetera et Recentiora in Aristophanis Vespas* (Groningen).

KOUROUNIOTES, K. (1923), '*Ἐλευσινιακά*', *AD* 8: 155–74.

——(1933–5), '*Κόρης Ἄνοδος*', *AD* 15: 1–15.

KRENTZ, P. (1985), 'The Nature of Hoplite Battle', *ClAnt* 4: 50–61.

KRISTEVA, J. (1974), *La Révolution du langage poétique. L'Avant-Garde à la fin du XIXe siècle: Lautréamont et Mallarmé* (Paris).

KRITZAS, C. B. (1973), '*Ἡρακλῆς Παγκάμης*', *AE* 106–19.

KUNISH, N. (1990), 'Die Augen der Augenschalen', *AK* 33: 20–7.

KURKE, L. (1993), 'The Economy of *Kudos*', in Dougherty and Kurke, 131–63.

KURTZ, D. C., and BOARDMAN, J. (1986), 'Booners', in *Occasional Papers on Antiquities, 2: Greek Vases in the J. Paul Getty Museum* (The J. Paul Getty Museum, Malibu, California, 3), 35–70.

——and SPARKES, B. (1982) (eds.), *The Eye of Greece: Studies in the Art of Athens* (Cambridge).

LACROIX, L. (1974), 'Héraclès, héros voyageur et civilisateur', *Bulletin de la classe des Lettres de l'Académie Royale de Belgique*, 60: 34–60.

LADA, I. (1993), 'Empathic Understanding: Emotion and Cognition in Classical Dramatic Audience Response', *PCPS* 39: 94–140.

——(1996), '"Weeping for Hecuba": Is it a "Brechtian" Act?', *Arethusa*, 29: 87–124.

LADA-RICHARDS, I. (1997a), 'Neoptolemus and the Bow: Ritual *Thea* and Theatrical Vision in Sophocles' *Philoctetes*', *JHS* 117: 179–83.

——(1997b), '"Estrangement or Reincarnation"? Performers and Performance on the Classical Athenian Stage', *Arion*, 5. 2: 66–107.

——(1998), 'Staging the *Ephebeia*: Theatrical Role-Playing and Ritual Transition in Sophocles' *Philoctetes*', *Ramus* 27. 1.

——(forthcoming), '"Foul Monster or Good Saviour"? Reflections on Ritual Monsters', *Nottingham Classical Literature Studies*, 6.

LA FONTAINE, J. S. (1986), *Initiation* (Manchester).

LAMBRINOUDAKIS, B. (1972), '*Τὰ Ἐκδύσια τῆς Φαιστοῦ*', *AE* 99–112.

LÄMMLI, F. (1962), *Vom Chaos zum Kosmos: Zur Geschichte einer Idee* (Schweizerische Beiträge zur Altertumswissenschaft, 10; Basel).

LANZA, D. (1977), 'Lo spettatore sulla scena', in D. Lanza *et al.* (eds.), *L'ideologia della città* (Naples), 57–78.

LAPALUS, E. (1934), 'Le Dionysos et l'Héraclès des "Grenouilles"', *REG* 47: 1–20.

LARSON, J. (1995), *Greek Heroine Cults* (Madison, Wis.).

LATTIMORE, R. (1965), *The Odyssey of Homer* (New York).

LAURENS, A. F. (1989) (ed.), *Entre hommes et dieux: Le Convive, le héros, le prophète* (Centre de Recherches d'Histoire Ancienne, 86; Paris).

LEACH, E. R. (1966), *Rethinking Anthropology* (1st edn. 1961) (London).

LE BONNIEC, H. (1958), *Le Culte de Cérès à Rome: Des origines à la fin de la République* (Paris).

LEITAO, D. D. (1995), 'The Perils of Leukippos: Initiatory Transvestism and Male Gender Ideology in the Ekdusia at Phaistos', *ClAnt* 14: 130–63.

LÉVY-BRUHL, L. (1931), *Le Surnaturel et la nature dans la mentalité primitive* (Paris).

LÉVI-STRAUSS, C. (1961), 'The Many Faces of Man', *World Theatre*, 10. 1: 11–20.

LINCOLN, B. (1979), 'The Rape of Persephone: A Greek Scenario of Women's Initiation', *HThR* 72: 223–35.

LINFORTH, I. M. (1946), 'The Corybantic Rites in Plato', *University of California Publications in Classical Philology*, 13. 5: 121–62.

LISSARRAGUE, F. (1987a), 'Dionysos s'en va-t-en guerre', in Bérard, Bron, and Pomari, 111–20.

——(1987b), *Un flot d'images: Une esthétique du banquet grec* (Paris).

——(1990a), 'The Sexual Life of Satyrs', in Halperin *et al.* 53–81.

——(1990b), *L'Autre Guerrier: Archers, peltastes, cavaliers dans l'imagerie attique* (Paris and Rome).

——and THELAMON, F. (1983) (eds.), *Image et céramique grecque* (*Actes du Colloque de Rouen, 25–6 Nov. 1982*) (Publications de l'Université de Rouen, 96; Rouen).

LLOYD, G. E. R. (1990), *Demystifying Mentalities* (Cambridge).

LLOYD-JONES, H. (1963), 'The Seal of Posidippus', *JHS* 83: 75–99.

——(1967), 'Heracles at Eleusis: *P. Oxy. 2622 and PSI 1391 [= Pindar fr. 346 S.-M.]*', *Maia*, NS 19: 206–29

——(1981), 'Notes on P. Turner 4 (Aristophanes, Ποίησις)', *ZPE* 42: 23–5.

——(1983), 'Artemis and Iphigeneia', *JHS* 103: 87–102.

——(1985), 'Pindar and the After-life', in *Pindare* (*Entretiens sur l'Antiquité Classique*, Fondation Hardt, 31; Vandœuvres and Geneva), 245–83.

LOEB, E. M. (1929), 'Tribal Initiations and Secret Societies', *University of California Publications in American Archaeology and Ethnology*, 25. 3: 249–88.

LONGO, O. (1990), 'The Theater of the *Polis*', in Winkler and Zeitlin, 12–19.

LONIS, R. (1979), *Guerre et religion en Grèce à l'époque classique: Recherches sur les rites, les dieux, l'idéologie de la victoire* (Centre de Recherches d'Histoire Ancienne, 33; Besançon and Paris).

LONNOY, M. G. (1985), 'Arès et Dionysos dans la tragédie grecque: Le Rapprochement des contraires', *REG* 98: 65–71.

LONSDALE, S. H. (1993), *Dance and Ritual Play in Greek Religion* (Baltimore and London).

LORAUX, N. (1973), 'L'Interférence tragique', *Critique*, 29, no. 317: 908–25.

LORAUX, N. (1981a), 'Le Lit, la guerre', *L'Homme*, 21. 1: 37–67.

LORAUX, N. (1981*b*), 'Note critique: La Cité comme cuisine et comme partage', *Annales, ESC*, 36. 4: 614–22.

——(1982*a*), 'PONOS: Sur quelques difficultés de la peine comme nom du travail', *AION (ArchStAnt)*, 4: 171–92.

——(1982*b*), 'Mourir devant Troie, tomber pour Athènes: De la gloire du héros à l'idée de la cité', in G. Gnoli and J. P. Vernant (eds.), *La Mort, les morts dans les sociétés anciennes* (Cambridge and Paris), 27–43.

——(1986), *The Invention of Athens: The Funeral Oration in the Classical City* (tr. A. Sheridan, of *L'Invention d'Athènes: Histoire de l'oraison funèbre dans la 'cité classique'*; Paris, 1981) (Cambridge, Mass., and London).

——(1990), 'Herakles: The Super-Male and the Feminine', in Halperin *et al.* 21–52 (1st pub. in *Revue française de psychanalyse*, 46; 1982).

LUCAS, D. W. (1968), *Aristotle: Poetics* (Oxford).

LUKES, S. (1970), 'Some Problems about Rationality', in B. R. Wilson, 194–213.

LUKINOVICH, A. (1990), 'The Play of Reflections between Literary Form and the Sympotic Theme in the *Deipnosophistae* of Athenaeus', in Murray (1990*a*), 263–71.

LUPPE; W. (1978), 'Abermals das Goldblättchen von Hipponion', *ZPE* 30: 23–6.

——(1989), 'Zu den neuen Goldblättchen aus Thessalien', *ZPE* 76: 13–14.

LYONS, C. R. (1987), 'Character and Theatrical Space', in *Themes in Drama*, 9: *The Theatrical Space* (Cambridge), 27–44.

LYONS, D. (1997), *Gender and Immortality: Heroines in Ancient Greek Myth and Cult* (Princeton).

MAASS, E. (1888), '*ΔΙΟΝΥΣΟΣ ΠΕΛΑΓΙΟΣ*', *Hermes*, 23: 70–80.

MAAS, M., and SNYDER, J. (1989), *Stringed Instruments of Ancient Greece* (New Haven and London).

McCREDE, J. R. (1968), 'Samothrace: Preliminary Report on the Campaigns of 1965–1967', *Hesperia*, 37: 200–34.

MacDOWELL, D. M. (1971), *Aristophanes: Wasps* (Oxford).

MACLEAN, I. W. F. (1977), *Woman Triumphant: Feminism in French Literature* (Oxford).

——(1980), *The Renaissance Notion of Woman: A Study in the Fortunes of Scholasticism and Medical Science in European Intellectual Life* (Cambridge).

MACLEOD, C. W. (1974), 'Euripides' Rags', *ZPE* 15: 221–2.

McNALLY, S. (1984), 'The Maenad in Early Greek Art', in Peradotto and Sullivan, 107–41.

MAFFRE, J. J. (1982), 'Quelques scènes mythologiques sur des fragments de coupes attiques de la fin du style sévère', *RA* 195–222.

MAGARSHACK, D. (1961), 'Introduction', in K. S. Stanislavsky, *Stanislavsky on the Art of the Stage* (2nd edn.; London).

MAITLAND, J. (1992), 'Dynasty and Family in the Athenian City State: A View from Attic Tragedy', *CQ* 42: 26–40.

MARCH, J. (1989), 'Euripides' *Bakchai*: A Reconsideration in the Light of Vase-Paintings', *BICS* 36: 33–65.

MARINATOS, N. (1986), *Minoan Sacrificial Ritual: Cult Practice and Symbolism* (Stockholm).

——(1988), 'The Imagery of Sacrifice: Minoan and Greek', in Hägg *et al.* 9–20.

MARTIN, V. (1960), 'Euripide et Ménandre face à leur public', in *Euripide* (*Entretiens sur l'Antiquité Classique*, Fondation Hardt, 6; Vandœuvres and Geneva), 245–72.

MASSENZIO, M. (1969), 'Cultura e crisi permanente: La "xenia" dionisiaca', *SMSR* 40: 27–113.

MENDELSOHN, D. (1992), '*Συγκεραυνόω*: Dithyrambic Language and Dionysiac Cult', *CJ* 87: 105–24.

MERCK, M. (1978), 'The City's Achievements: The Patriotic Amazonomachy and Ancient Athens', in S. Lipshitz (ed.), *Tearing the Veil: Essays on Femininity* (London), 95–115.

MERKELBACH, R. (1962), *Roman und Mysterium in der Antike*, (Munich and Berlin).

——(1967), 'Der Eid der Isismysten', *ZPE* 1: 55–73.

——(1971), 'Dionysisches Grabepigramm aus Tusculum', *ZPE* 7: 280.

——(1975), 'Bakchisches Goldtäfelchen aus Hipponion', *ZPE* 17: 8–9.

——(1984), *Mithras* (Hain).

——(1988), *Die Hirten des Dionysos: Die Dionysos-Mysterien der römischen Kaiserzeit und der bukolische Roman des Longus* (Stuttgart).

——(1989), 'Zwei neue orphisch-dionysische Totenpässe', *ZPE* 76: 15–16.

——and WEST, M. L. (1965), 'The Wedding of Ceyx', *RhM* 108: 300–17.

METZGER, H. (1951), *Les Représentations dans la céramique attique du IV siècle* (Paris).

MILLER, S. G. (1978), *The Prytaneion: Its Function and Architectural Form* (Berkeley, Los Angeles, and London).

MINGAZZINI, P. (1925) 'Le rappresentazioni vascolari del mito dell'apoteosi di Herakles', *Atti della Reale Accademia Nazionale dei Lincei* (Classe di scienze morali, storiche e filologiche) (6th ser.), 1: 417–90.

MITTEN, D. G., PEDLEY, J. G., and SCOTT, J. A. (1971) (eds.), *Studies Presented to George M. A. Hanfmann* (Mainz).

MOORE, M. B. (1979), 'Lydos and the Gigantomachy', *AJA* 83: 79–99.

MOORE, S. (1966), *The Stanislavski System: The Professional Training of an Actor. Digested from the Teachings of K. S. Stanislavski* (London).

MOORTON, R. F., Jr. (1989), 'Rites of Passage in Aristophanes' *Frogs*', *CJ* 84: 308–24.

MOREAU, A. (1979), 'L'Attelage et le navire: La Rencontre de deux thèmes dans l'œuvre d'Eschyle', *RPh* (3rd ser.), 53: 98–115.

MORET, J.-M. (1975), *L'Ilioupersis dans la céramique Italiote*, 2 vols. (Geneva).

——(1993), 'Les Départs des enfers dans l'imagerie apulienne', *RA* 293–51.

MORRIS, B. (1987), *Anthropological Studies of Religion: An Introductory Text* (Cambridge).

MOSSMAN, J. (1995), *Wild Justice: A Study of Euripides' Hecuba* (Oxford).

MUECKE, D. C. (1982), *Irony and the Ironic* (2nd edn.; London and New York).

MUECKE, F. (1977), 'Playing with the Play: Theatrical Self-Consciousness in Aristophanes', *Antichthon*, 11: 52–67.

——(1982a), ' "I Know You—By Your Rags": Costume and Disguise in Fifth-Century Drama', *Antichthon*, 16: 17–34.

——(1982b), 'A Portrait of the Artist as a Young Woman', *CQ* 32: 41–55.

MUNN, N. D. (1973), 'Symbolism in a Ritual Context: Aspects of Symbolic Action', in J. J. Honigmann (ed.), *Handbook of Social and Cultural Anthropology* (Chapel Hill, NC), 579–612.

MURRAY, O. (1983a) 'Symposion and Männerbund', in P. Oliva and A. Frolíková (eds.), *Concilium Eirene XVI: Proceedings of the 16th International Eirene Conference* (Prague, 31. Aug.–4. Sept. 1982) (Prague), i. 47–52.

——(1983b), 'The Greek Symposion in History', in E. Gabba (ed.), *Tria Corda: Scritti in onore di Arnaldo Momigliano* (Como), 257–72.

——(1988), 'Death and the Symposion', *AION (ArchStAnt)*, 10: 239–57.

——(1990a) (ed.), *Sympotica: A Symposium on the Symposion* (Oxford).

——(1990b), 'Sympotic History', in id. (1990a), 3–13.

——(1990c), 'The Affair of the Mysteries: Democracy and the Drinking Group', in id. (1990a),149–61.

MURRAY, P. (1981), 'Poetic Inspiration in Early Greece', *JHS* 101: 87–100.

MYERHOFF, B. G. (1978), 'Return to Wirikuta: Ritual Reversal and Symbolic Continuity on the Peyote Hunt of the Huichol Indians', in Babcock, 225–39.

——(1982), 'Rites of Passage: Process and Paradox', in Turner, 109–35.

MYLONAS, G. E. (1961), *Eleusis and the Eleusinian Mysteries* (Princeton).

NAGY, G. (1979), *The Best of the Achaeans: Concepts of the Hero in Archaic Greek Poetry* (Baltimore and London).

——(1990), *Pindar's Homer: The Lyric Possession of an Epic Past* (Baltimore and London).

NILSSON, M. P. (1906), *Griechische Feste von religiöser Bedeutung, mit Ausschluss der attischen* (Leipzig; repr. Stuttgart, 1957).

——(1916), 'Die Prozessionstypen im griechischen Kult: Mit einem Anhang über die dionysischen Prozessionen in Athen', *JDAI* 31: 309–39.

——(1947), 'Greek Mysteries in the Confession of St. Cyprian', *HThR* 40: 167–76.

——(1951), 'Dionysos im Schiff', in *Opuscula Selecta*, 1: 21–4 (Lund).

——(1957), *The Dionysiac Mysteries of the Hellenistic and Roman Age* (Lund).

——(1960), 'Royal Mysteries in Egypt', in *Opuscula Selecta*, 3: 326–8 (Lund).

Noel, D. (1983), 'Du vin pour Héraklès!', in Lissarrague and Thelamon, 141–50.

Norden, E. (1903), *Vergilius Aeneis VI* (Leipzig).

North, H. (1966), *Sophrosyne: Self-Knowledge and Self-Restraint in Greek Literature* (Ithaca, NY).

Nussbaum, M. C. (1986), *The Fragility of Goodness: Luck and Ethics in Greek Tragedy and Philosophy* (Cambridge).

——(1992), 'Tragedy and Self-Sufficiency: Plato and Aristotle on Fear and Pity', *Oxford Studies in Ancient Philosophy*, 10: 107–59.

Obbink, D. (1993), 'Dionysus Poured Out: Ancient and Modern Theories of Sacrifice and Cultural Formation', in Carpenter and Faraone, 65–86.

Ober, J. (1989), *Mass and Elite in Democratic Athens: Rhetoric, Ideology, and the Power of the People* (Princeton).

——and Hedrick, C. (1996) (eds.), *Dêmokratia: A Conversation on Democracies, Ancient and Modern* (Princeton).

O'Brien, M. J. (1985), 'Xenophanes, Aeschylus, and the Doctrine of Primeval Brutishness', *CQ* 35: 264–77.

Olender, M. (1990), 'Aspects of Baubo: Ancient Texts and Contexts', in Halperin *et al.* 83–113.

Olivieri, A. (1924), 'Rituale di misteri recentemente scoperto', *Atti della Reale Accademia di Archeologia, Lettere e belle Arti*, ns 8: 273–305.

Ortner, S. B. (1974), 'Is Female to Male as Nature is to Culture?', in Rosaldo and Lamphere, 67–87.

Osborne, M. J. (1981), 'Entertainment in the Prytaneion at Athens', *ZPE* 41: 153–70.

Osborne, R. (1985), *Demos: The Discovery of Classical Attica* (Cambridge).

Otto, W. F. (1965), *Dionysus: Myth and Cult* (Eng. tr. R. B. Palmer) (Bloomington, Ind., and London).

Padel, R. (1983), 'Women: Model for Possession by Greek Daemons', in Cameron and Kuhrt, 3–19.

Padilla, M. (1992), 'The Heraclean Dionysus: Theatrical and Social Renewal in Aristophanes' *Frogs*', *Arethusa*, 25: 359–84.

Paquette, D. (1984), *L'Instrument de musique dans la céramique de la Grèce antique: Études d'organologie* (Paris).

Parker, R. (1983), *MIASMA: Pollution and Purification in Early Greek Religion* (Oxford).

——(1989), 'Dionysus at Agrai', *LCM* 14. 10: 154–5.

——(1995), 'Early Orphism', in Powell, 483–510.

Pascal, C. (1911), *Dioniso: Saggio sulla religione e la parodia religiosa in Aristofane* (Catania).

Pavis, P. (1982), *Languages of the Stage: Essays in the Semiology of the Theatre* (Performing Arts Journal Publications; New York).

Pearce, T. E. V. (1974), 'The Role of the Wife as custos in Ancient Rome', *Eranos*, 72: 16–33.

Peirce, S. (1993), 'Death, Revelry, and *Thysia*', *ClAnt* 12: 219–66.

PELLING, C. (1990) (ed.), *Characterization and Individuality in Greek Literature* (Oxford).

PELLIZER, E. (1983), 'Della zuffa simpotica', in Vetta (1983*a*), 29–41.

——(1990), 'Outlines of a Morphology of Sympotic Entertainment', in Murray (1990*a*), 177–84.

PERADOTTO, J., and SULLIVAN, J. P. (1984) (eds.), *Women in the Ancient World: The Arethusa Papers* (Albany).

PERDRIZET, M. (1899), 'Terres-cuites de Lycosoura, et mythologie arcadienne', *BCH* 23: 635–8.

PERISTIANY, J. G. (1965*a*) (ed.), *Honour and Shame: The Values of Mediterranean Society* (London).

——(1965*b*), 'Honour and Shame in a Cypriot Highland Village', in id. (1965*a*), 171–90.

PETTERSSON, M. (1992), *Cults of Apollo at Sparta: The Hyakinthia, the Gymnopaidiai and the Karneia* (Stockholm).

PFISTER, M. (1988), *The Theory and Analysis of Drama* (tr. J. Halliday) (Cambridge).

PHILIPPAKI, B. (1967), *The Attic Stamnos* (Oxford).

PHILIPPART, H. (1930), 'Iconographie des "Bacchantes" d'Euripide', *RBPh* 9: 5–72.

PICARD, C. (1932), 'Dionysos ΜΙΤΡΗΦΟΡΟΣ', in *Mélanges G. Glotz* (Paris), ii. 707–21.

PICCALUGA, G. (1968), *Lykaon: Un tema mitico* (Rome).

PICKARD-CAMBRIDGE, A. (1988), *The Dramatic Festivals of Athens* (2nd edn. (1968), rev. J. Gould and D. M. Lewis; reissued with supplement and corrections) (Oxford).

PIPPIDI, D. M. (1964), 'Grottes dionysiaques à Callatis', *BCH* 88: 151–8.

PITT-RIVERS, J. (1977), *The Fate of Shechem or The Politics of Sex: Essays in the Anthropology of the Mediterranean* (Cambridge).

PLEPELITS, K. (1970), *Die Fragmente der Demen des Eupolis* (Vienna).

PODLECKI, A. J. (1966), *The Political Background of Aeschylean Tragedy* (Ann Arbor).

POHLENZ, M. (1965), 'Die Anfänge der griechischen Poetik', in *Kleine Schriften*, ed. H. Dörrie (Hildesheim), ii. 436–72.

POLIAKOFF, M. (1982), *Studies in the Terminology of the Greek Combat Sports* (Beiträge zur klassischen Philologie, 146; Meisenheim).

POURSAT, J. C. (1968), 'Les Représentations de danse armée dans la céramique attique', *BCH* 92: 550–615.

POWELL, A. (1995) (ed.), *The Greek World* (London and New York).

PRAG, A. J. N. W. (1985), *The Oresteia: Iconographic and Narrative Tradition* (Warminster).

PRICE, S. D. (1990), 'Anacreontic Vases Reconsidered', *GRBS* 31: 133–75.

PRITCHARD, J. B. (1955), *Ancient Near Eastern Texts Relating to the Old Testament* (2nd edn.; Princeton).

PRITCHETT, W. K. (1974), *The Greek State at War*, ii (Berkeley, Los Angeles, and London).

——(1979), *The Greek State at War*, iii: *Religion* (Berkeley, Los Angeles, and London).

PRYTZ JOHANSEN, J. (1975), 'The Thesmophoria as a Women's Festival', *Temenos*, 11: 78–87.

PUGLIESE CARRATELLI, G. (1976), 'Ancora sulla Lamina Orfica di Hipponion', *La Parola del Passato*, 31: 458–66.

PUTNAM, M. C. J. (1969), 'Horace *c*. 1. 20', *CJ* 64: 153–7.

RAAFLAUB, K. A. (1990), 'Contemporary Perceptions of Democracy in Fifth-Century Athens', in Connor *et al.* 33–70.

——(1994), 'Democracy, Power, and Imperialism in Fifth-Century Athens', in J. P. Euben, J. R. Wallach, and J. Ober (eds.), *Athenian Political Thought and the Reconstruction of American Democracy* (Ithaca, NY, and London), 103–46.

——(1996), 'Equalities and Inequalities in Athenian Democracy', in Ober and Hedrick, 139–74.

RABE, H. (1906) (ed.), *Scholia in Lucianum* (Leipzig).

RADERMACHER, L. (1921), *Aristophanes' "Frösche"* (Einleitung, Text und Kommentar) (Vienna).

RAPOPORT, I. (1955), 'The Work of the Actor', in T. Cole (ed.), *Acting: A Handbook of the Stanislavski Method* (revised edn.; New York), 33–68.

RAPP, A. (1872), 'Die Mänade im griechischen Cultus, in der Kunst und Poesie', *RhM* 27: 1–22 and 562–611.

RAU, P. (1967), *Paratragodia: Untersuchung einer komischen Form des Aristophanes* (Munich).

RAY, B. (1973), '"Performative Utterances" in African Rituals', *History of Religions*, 13. 1: 16–35.

RECKFORD, K. J. (1974), 'Phaedra and Pasiphae: The Pull Backward', *TAPA* 104: 307–28.

——(1987), *Aristophanes' Old-and-New Comedy*, i: *Six Essays in Perspective* (Chapel Hill, NC, and London).

REHM, R. (1994), *Marriage to Death: The Conflation of Wedding and Funeral Rituals in Greek Tragedy* (Princeton).

REINACH, S. (1890), 'Oracle de la Pythie de Delphes adressé à la ville de Magnésie du Méandre', *REG* 3: 349–61.

RELIHAN, J. C. (1992), 'Rethinking the History of the Literary Symposium', *ICS* 17: 213–44.

REVERDIN, O. (1945), 'Remarques sur la vie politique d'Athènes au Ve siècle', *MH* 2: 201–12.

RHOMAIOS, K. A. (1914), 'Tegeatische Reliefs', *MDAI (A)* 39: 189–235.

RICHARDSON, N. J. (1974), *The Homeric Hymn to Demeter* (Oxford).

RICHTER, G. M. A. (1916), 'A New Euphronios Cylix in the Metropolitan Museum of Art', *AJA* 20: 125–33.

——(1941), 'A Greek Silver Phiale in the Metropolitan Museum', *AJA* 45: 363–89.

RIDLEY, R. T. (1979), 'The Hoplite as Citizen: Athenian Military Institutions in their Social Context', *AC* 48: 508–48.

RIEDWEG, C. (1987), *Mysterienterminologie bei Platon, Philon und Klemens von Alexandrien* (Berlin and New York.).

RIESS, E. (1897), 'Superstitions and Popular Beliefs in Greek Comedy', *AJP* 18: 189–205.

RIFFATERRE, M. (1974), 'The Poetic Functions of Intertextual Humor', *Romanic Review*, 65. 4: 278–93.

ROBERT, C. (1912), 'Aphoristische Bemerkungen zu Sophokles' *Ἰχνευταί*, *Hermes*, 47: 536–61.

ROBERT, L. (1934), 'Sur deux inscriptions grecques', in *Annuaire de l'Institut de Philologie et d'Histoire Orientales*, ii. 2: *Mélanges Bidez* (Brussels), 793–812.

ROBERTSON, M. (1986), 'Two Pelikai by the Pan Painter', in *Occasional Papers on Antiquities, 2: Greek Vases in the J. Paul Getty Museum* (The J. Paul Getty Museum, Malibu, California, 3), 71–90.

ROBERTSON, N. (1993), 'Athens' Festival of the New Wine', *HSCP* 95: 197–250.

ROGERS, B. B. (1924), *Aristophanes* (Eng. tr.), 3 vols. (Cambridge, Mass., and London).

ROHDE, E. (1925), *Psyche: The Cult of Souls and Belief in Immortality among the Greeks* (tr. from the 8th edn. by W. B. Hillis; 1st pub. 1894, Freiburg) (London).

ROMILLY, J. de (1965), 'Les *Phéniciennes* d'Euripide ou l'actualité dans la tragédie grecque', *RPh* 39: 28–47.

——(1975), *Problèmes de la démocratie grecque* (Paris).

ROSALDO, M. Z. (1974), 'Woman, Culture, and Society: A Theoretical Overview', in Rosaldo and Lamphere, 17–42.

——and LAMPHERE, L. (1974) (eds.), *Woman, Culture, and Society* (Stanford, Calif.).

ROSE, H. J. (1925), 'The Bride of Hades', *CPh* 20: 238–42.

ROSELLINI, M. (1979), '*Lysistrata*: Une mise en scène de la féminité', in D. Auger, M. Rosellini, and S. Saïd (eds.), *Aristophane, les Femmes et la Cité* (Les Cahiers de Fontenay, 17; Fontenay-aux-Roses), 11–32.

——and SAÏD, S. (1978), 'Usages de femmes et autres *nomoi* chez les "sauvages" d'Hérodote: Essai de lecture structurale', *ASNP* (Classe di lettere e filosofia) (3rd ser.), 8. 3: 949–1005.

ROSENMEYER, T. G. (1955), 'Gorgias, Aeschylus and *Apate*', *AJP* 76: 225–60.

RÖSLER, W. (1986), 'Michail Bachtin und die Karnevalskultur im antiken Griechenland', *QUCC* 23. 2: 25–44.

——(1990), '*Mnemosyne* in the *Symposion*', in Murray (1990*a*), 230–7.

ROUX, J. (1970–2), *Euripide: Les Bacchantes*, 2 vols. (Paris).

RUSTEN, J. S. (1977), '*Wasps* 1360–1369: Philokleon's *Τωθασμός*', *HSCP* 81: 157–61.

STE CROIX (DE), G. E. M. (1972), 'The Political Outlook of Aristophanes' (appendix xxix), in id., *The Origins of the Peloponnesian War* (London), 355–76.

SCARPI, P. (1979), 'La pyrrhíchê o le armi della persuasione', *DArch* 1: 78–97.

SCHACHTER, A. (1981), *Cults of Boiotia*, 1: *Acheloos to Hera* (*BICS* suppl. 38. 1; London).

SCHAUENBURG, K. (1963), 'Herakles unter Göttern', *Gymnasium*, 70: 113–33.

SCHECHNER, R. (1985), 'Performers and Spectators Transported and Transformed', in id., *Between Theater and Anthropology* (Philadelphia), 117–50.

——(1990), 'Magnitudes of Performance', in R. Schechner and W. Appel (eds.), *By Means of Performance: Intercultural Studies of Theatre and Ritual* (Cambridge), 19–49.

SCHEFOLD, K. (1981), *Die Göttersage in der klassischen und hellenistischen Kunst* (Munich).

SCHLESIER, R. (1993), 'Mixtures of Masks: Maenads as Tragic Models', in Carpenter and Faraone, 89–114.

SCHMITT-PANTEL, P. (1980), 'Les Repas au Prytanée et à la Tholos dans l'Athènes classique. *Sitesis, Trophé, Misthos*: Réflexions sur le mode de nourriture démocratique', *AION* (*ArchStAnt*) 2: 55–68.

——(1985), 'Banquet et cité grecque: Quelques questions suscitées par les recherches récentes', *MEFRA* 97: 135–58.

——(1990), 'Sacrificial Meal and *Symposion*: Two Models of Civic Institutions in the Archaic City?', in Murray (1990*a*), 14–33.

——and SCHNAPP, A. (1982), 'Image et société en Grèce ancienne: Les Représentations de la chasse et du banquet', *RA* 57–74.

SCHNAPP, A. (1973), 'Représentation du territoire de guerre et du territoire de chasse dans l'œuvre de Xénophon', in M. I. Finley (ed.), *Problèmes de la terre en Grèce ancienne* (Civilisations et Sociétés, 33; Paris and The Hague), 307–21.

——(1987), 'Héraclès, Thésée et les chasseurs: Les Ambiguïtés du héros', in Bérard, Bron, and Pomari, 121–30.

SCHÖNE, A. (1987), *Der Thiasos: Eine ikonographische Untersuchung über das Gefolge des Dionysos in der attischen Vasen-malerei des 6. und 5. Jhs. v. Chr.* (Göteborg).

SEAFORD, R. (1976), 'On the Origins of Satyric Drama', *Maia*, 28: 209–21.

——(1977–8), 'The "Hyporchema" of Pratinas', *Maia*, 29: 81–94.

——(1978), *Pompeii* (London).

——(1980), 'Black Zeus in Sophocles' *Inachos*', *CQ*, NS 30: 23–9.

——(1981), 'Dionysiac Drama and the Dionysiac Mysteries', *CQ* 31: 252–75.

——(1984), *Euripides: Cyclops* (Oxford).

——(1985), 'The Destruction of Limits in Sophokles' *Elektra*', *CQ* 35: 315–23.

——(1986*a*), 'Immortality, Salvation, and the Elements', *HSCP* 90: 1–26.

——(1986*b*), 'Wedding Ritual and Textual Criticism in Sophocles' "Women of Trachis"', *Hermes*, 114: 50–9.

SEAFORD, R. (1987a), 'Pentheus' Vision: *Bacchae* 918–22', *CQ* 37: 76–8.
——(1987b) 'The Tragic Wedding', *JHS* 107: 106–30.
——(1988), 'The Eleventh Ode of Bacchylides: Hera, Artemis, and the Absence of Dionysos', *JHS* 108: 118–36.
——(1990a), 'The Imprisonment of Women in Greek Tragedy', *JHS* 110: 76–90.
——(1990b), 'The Structural Problems of Marriage in Euripides', in A. Powell (ed.), *Euripides, Women, and Sexuality* (London and New York), 151–76.
——(1993), 'Dionysus as Destroyer of the Household: Homer, Tragedy, and the Polis', in Carpenter and Faraone, 115–46.
——(1994a), *Reciprocity and Ritual: Homer and Tragedy in the Developing City-State* (Oxford).
——(1994b), 'Sophokles and the Mysteries', *Hermes* 122: 275–88.
——(1996), *Euripides Bacchae* (with an introd., tr. and comm.) (Warminster).
SEARLE, J. R. (1969), *Speech Acts: An Essay in the Philosophy of Language* (Cambridge).
SEEBERG, A. (1965), 'Hephaistos Rides Again', *JHS* 85: 102–9.
——(1971), *Corinthian Komos Vases* (*BICS* suppl. 27; London).
SEGAL, C. P. (1961), 'The Character and Cults of Dionysus and the Unity of the *Frogs*', *HSCP* 65: 207–42.
——(1962), 'Gorgias and the Psychology of the Logos', *HSCP* 66: 99–155.
——(1967), 'Transition and Ritual in Odysseus' Return', *La Parola del Passato*, 22: 321–42.
——(1970), 'Protagoras' *Orthoepeia* in Aristophanes' "Battle of the Prologues" (*Frogs* 1119–97)', *RhM* 113: 158–62.
——(1975), 'Mariage et sacrifice dans les *Trachiniennes* de Sophocle', *AC* 44: 30–53.
——(1977), 'Sophocles' *Trachiniae*: Myth, Poetry and Heroic Values', *YClS* 25: 99–158.
——(1981), *Tragedy and Civilization: An Interpretation of Sophocles* (Cambridge, Mass., and London).
——(1982), *Dionysiac Poetics and Euripides' Bacchae* (Princeton).
——(1984), 'The Menace of Dionysus: Sex Roles and Reversals in Euripides' *Bacchae*', in Peradotto and Sullivan, 195–212.
——(1985), 'The *Bacchae* as Metatragedy', in Burian (1985a), 156–73.
——(1986a), *Pindar's Mythmaking: The Fourth Pythian Ode* (Princeton).
——(1986b), 'The Tragedy of the Hippolytus: The Waters of Ocean and the Untouched Meadow', in id., *Interpreting Greek Tragedy: Myth, Poetry, Text* (Ithaca, NY, and London), 165–221.
——(1988a), 'Confusion and Concealment in Euripides' *Hippolytus*: Vision, Hope, and Tragic Knowledge', *Métis*, 3: 263–82.
——(1988b), 'Theatre, Ritual and Commemoration in Euripides' *Hippolytus*', *Ramus*, 17: 52–74.

——(1990), 'Dionysus and the Gold Tablets from Pelinna', *GRBS* 31: 411–19.

SEIDENSTICKER, B. (1978), 'Comic Elements in Euripides' *Bacchae*', *AJP* 99: 303–20.

——(1979), 'Sacrificial Ritual in the *Bacchae*', in G. W. Bowersock *et al.* (eds.), *Arktouros: Hellenic Studies presented to Bernard M. W. Knox on the occasion of his 65th birthday* (Berlin and New York), 181–90.

——(1982), *Palintonos Harmonia: Studien zu komischen Elementen in der griechischen Tragödie* (*Hypomnemata*, 72; Göttingen).

SHAPIRO, H. A. (1983), ' "Hérôs Theos": The Death and Apotheosis of Herakles', *CW* 77: 7–18.

——(1991), 'The Iconography of Mourning in Athenian Art', *AJA* 95: 629–56.

——(1993), *Personifications in Greek Art: The Representation of Abstract Concepts, 600–400 B.C.* (Zurich).

SHARPE, R. B. (1959), *Irony in the Drama: An Essay on Impersonation, Shock, and Catharsis* (Chapel Hill, NC).

SHAUENBURG, K. (1963), 'Herakles unter Göttern', *Gymnasium*, 70. 2: 113–33.

SIEWERT, P. (1977), 'The Ephebic Oath in Fifth-Century Athens', *JHS* 97: 102–11.

SIFAKIS, G. (1992), 'The Structure of Aristophanic Comedy', *JHS* 112: 123–42.

SILK, M. S. (1985), 'Heracles and Greek Tragedy', *G&R* 32: 1–22.

——(1990), 'The People of Aristophanes', in Pelling, 150–73.

——(1996) (ed.), *Tragedy and the Tragic: Greek Theatre and Beyond* (Oxford).

SIMON, E. (1961), 'Zum Fries der Mysterienvilla bei Pompeji', *JDAI* 76: 111–72.

——(1966), 'Neue Deutung zweier eleusinischer Denkmäler des vierten Jahrhunderts v. Chr.', *AK* 9: 72–91.

——(1982), 'Satyr-Plays on Vases in the Time of Aeschylus', in Kurtz and Sparkes, 123–48.

——(1983), *Festivals of Attica: An Archaeological Commentary* (Madison, Wis.).

SINOS, R. H. (1993), 'Divine Selection: Epiphany and Politics in Archaic Greece', in Dougherty and Kurke, 73–91.

SKOV, G. E. (1975), 'The Priestess of Demeter and Kore and her Role in the Initiation of Women at the Festival of the Haloa at Eleusis', *Temenos*, 11: 136–47.

SLATER, N. W. (1985), 'Vanished Players: Two Classical Reliefs and Theatre History', *GRBS* 26: 333–44.

SLATER, W. J. (1976), 'Symposium at Sea', *HSCP* 80: 161–70.

——(1978), 'Artemon and Anacreon: No Text without Context', *Phoenix*, 32: 185–94.

——(1984), 'Nemean One: The Victor's Return in Poetry and Politics', in

D. E. Gerber (ed.), *Greek Poetry and Philosophy: Studies in Honour of Leonard Woodbury* (Chico, Calif.), 241–64.

SMITH, K. K. (1905), 'The Use of the High-Soled Shoe or Buskin in Greek Tragedy of the Fifth and Fourth Centuries B.C.', *HSCP* 16: 123–64.

SNELL, B. (1964), *Scenes from Greek Drama* (Berkeley and Los Angeles).

SOKOLOWSKI, F. (1955), *LSAM: Lois sacrées de l'Asie Mineure* (École Française d'Athènes, travaux et mémoires, 9; Paris).

——(1962), *LSCGS: Lois sacrées des cités grecques: Supplément* (École Française d'Athènes, travaux et mémoires, 11; Paris).

——(1969), *LSCG: Lois sacrées des cités grecques* (École Française d'Athènes, travaux et mémoires, 18; Paris).

SOLINAS, P. G. (1985), 'Chasse, partage, société', *L'Uomo* 9: 99–120.

SOMMERSTEIN, A. H. (1982), *The Comedies of Aristophanes*, vol. 3: *Clouds* (ed. with tr. and notes) (Warminster).

——(1989), *Aeschylus: Eumenides* (Cambridge).

——(1994), *The Comedies of Aristophanes*, vol. 8: *Thesmophoriazusae* (ed. with tr. and notes) (Warminster).

——(1996), *The Comedies of Aristophanes*, vol. 9: *Frogs* (ed. with tr. and notes) (Warminster).

SÖRBOM, G. (1966), *Mimesis and Art: Studies in the Origin and Early Development of an Aesthetic Vocabulary* (Uppsala).

SOURVINOU-INWOOD, C. (1971), 'Aristophanes, *Lysistrata*, 641–647', *CQ* 21: 339–42.

——(1973), 'The Young Abductor of the Locrian Pinakes', *BICS* 20: 12–21.

——(1978), 'Persephone and Aphrodite at Locri: A Model for Personality Definitions in Greek Religion', *JHS* 98: 101–21.

——(1988), *Studies in Girls' Transitions. Aspects of the Arkteia and Age Representation in Attic Iconography* (Athens).

——(1990*a*), 'Myths in Images: Theseus and Medea as a Case Study', in Edmunds, 395–445.

——(1990*b*), 'Ancient Rites and Modern Constructs: On the Brauronian Bears Again', *BICS* 37: 1–14.

——(1994), 'Something to do with Athens: Tragedy and Ritual', in R. Osborne and S. Hornblower (eds.), *Ritual, Finance, Politics: Athenian Democratic Accounts Presented to David Lewis* (Oxford), 269–90.

——(1995), *'Reading' Greek Death: To the End of the Classical Period* (Oxford).

SPERBER, D. (1975), *Rethinking Symbolism* (tr. A. L. Morton) (Cambridge).

STAMBOLIDES, N. C. (1987), Ὁ βωμός τοῦ Διονύσου στὴν Κῶ. Συμβολὴ στὴ μελέτη τῆς ἑλληνιστικῆς πλαστικῆς καὶ ἀρχιτεκτονικῆς (Athens).

STANFORD, W. B. (1963), *Aristophanes: Frogs* (2nd edn. London).

STAUB, E. (1987), 'Commentary on Part I', in N. Eisenberg and J. Strayer (eds.), *Empathy and its Development* (Cambridge), 103–15.

STIGLITZ, R. (1967), *Die Grossen Göttinnen Arkadiens: Der Kultname ΜΕΓΑΛΑΙ ΘΕΑΙ und seine Grundlagen* (Vienna).

STONE, L. M. (1981), *Costume in Aristophanic Comedy* (New York).

STOREY, I. (1994), 'The Politics of Angry Eupolis', *The Ancient History Bulletin*, 8. 4: 107–20.

STRAUSS, B. S. (1990), '*Oikos/Polis*: Towards a Theory of Athenian Paternal Ideology 450–399 B.C.', in Connor *et al.* 101–27.

——(1996), 'The Athenian Trireme, School of Democracy', in Ober and Hedrick, 313–25.

STYAN, J. L. (1975), *Drama, Stage and Audience* (Cambridge).

SULEIMAN, S. R. (1980), 'Introduction: Varieties of Audience-Oriented Criticism', in Suleiman and Crosman, 3–45.

——and CROSMAN, I. (1980) (eds.), *The Reader in the Text: Essays on Audience and Interpretation* (Princeton).

SUTTON, D. F. (1975), 'Athletics in the Greek Satyr Play', *RSC* 23: 203–9.

SVENBRO, J. (1976), *La Parole et le marbre: Aux origines de la poétique grecque* (Lund).

——(1982), 'A Mégara Hyblaea: Le Corps géomètre', *Annales, ESC*, 37: 953–64.

——(1984), 'La Découpe du poème: Notes sur les origines sacrificielles de la poétique grecque', *Poétique*, 58: 215–32.

TAILLARDAT, J. (1965), *Les Images d'Aristophane: Études de langue et de style* (2nd edn. revised and corrected; 1st pub. 1962) (Paris).

TAMBIAH, S. J. (1968), 'The Magical Power of Words', *Man*, NS 3: 175–208.

——(1973), 'Form and Meaning of Magical Acts: A Point of View', in Horton and Finnegan, 199–229.

——(1977), 'Classification of Animals in Thailand' (excerpt from Tambiah, 'Animals are good to think and good to prohibit', *Ethnology*, 8. 4 (1969), 424–59), in Douglas, 127–66.

TAPLIN, O. (1972), 'Aeschylean Silences and Silences in Aeschylus', *HSCP* 76: 57–97.

——(1977), *The Stagecraft of Aeschylus: The Dramatic Use of Exits and Entrances in Greek Tragedy* (Oxford).

——(1986), 'Fifth-Century Tragedy and Comedy: A Synkrisis', *JHS* 106: 163–74.

——(1993), *Comic Angels and Other Approaches to Greek Drama through Vase-Paintings* (Oxford).

——(1996), 'Comedy and the Tragic', in Silk, 188–202.

TARKOW, T. A. (1982), 'Achilles and the Ghost of Aeschylus in Aristophanes' "Frogs"', *Traditio*, 38: 1–16.

TEDESCHI, G. (1982), 'Solone e lo spazio della comunicazione elegiaca', *QUCC* 10: 33–46.

THOMAS, R. (1989), *Oral Tradition and Written Record in Classical Athens* (Cambridge).

THOMSON, G. (1935), 'Mystical Allusions in the *Oresteia*', *JHS* 55: 20–34.

THOMSON, G. (1946), *Aeschylus and Athens: A Study in the Social Origins of Drama* (2nd edn.) (London).

THÖNGES-STRINGARIS, N. (1965), 'Das griechische Totenmahl', *MDAI (A)* 80: 1–99.

THURNWALD, R. (1939), 'Primitive Initiations- und Wiedergeburtsriten', *Eranos-Jahrbuch* (*Vorträge über die Symbolik der Wieder-geburt in der religiösen Vorstellung der Zeiten und Völker*), 321–98.

TIERNEY, M. (1922), 'A New Ritual of the Orphic Mysteries', *CQ* 16: 77–87.

——(1935), '*ΟΝΟΣ ΑΓΩΝ ΜΥΣΤΗΡΙΑ*', in *Mélanges offerts à M. Octave Navarre par ses élèves et ses amis* (Toulouse), 395–403.

——(1937), 'The Mysteries and the *Oresteia*', *JHS* 57: 11–21.

TRENDALL, A. D., and WEBSTER, T. B. L. (1971), *Illustrations of Greek Drama* (London).

TRUMPF-LYRITZAKI, M. (1969), *Griechische Figurenvasen des reichen Stils und der späten Klassik* (Bonn).

TSANTSANOGLOU, K., and PARÁSSOGLOU, G. M. (1987), 'Two Gold Lamellae from Thessaly', *Hellenika*, 38: 3–16.

TÜMPEL, K. (1889), '*Διόνυσος Ἁλιεύς*', *Philologus*, 48: 681–96.

TURATO, F. (1979), *La crisi della città e l'ideologia del selvaggio nell'Atene del V secolo a. C.* (Rome).

TURNER, V. (1967), *The Forest of Symbols: Aspects of Ndembu Ritual* (Ithaca, NY, and London).

——(1969), *The Ritual Process: Structure and Anti-Structure* (London).

——(1974), *Dramas, Fields, and Metaphors: Symbolic Action in Human Society* (Ithaca, NY, and London).

——(1978), 'Comments and Conclusions', in Babcock, 276–96.

——(1982) (ed.), *Celebration: Studies in Festivity and Ritual* (Washington, DC).

——and TURNER, E. (1982), 'Religious Celebrations', in Turner, 201–19.

TYRRELL, W. B. (1984), *Amazons: A Study in Athenian Mythmaking* (Baltimore and London).

USSHER, R. G. (1985), 'Aristophanes, *Frogs* 549–578', *LCM* 10. 7: 102.

VALENZA-MELE, N. (1986), 'Il Ruolo dei Centauri e di Herakles: Polis, Banchetto e Simposio', in *Les Grandes Figures religieuses: Fonctionnement pratique et symbolique dans l'antiquité* (Centre de Recherches d'Histoire Ancienne, 68; Besançon and Paris), 333–70.

VAN GENNEP, A. (1960), *The Rites of Passage* (tr. M. B. Vizedom and G. L. Caffee) (1st edn. 1909; Paris) (London).

VAN HOORN, G. (1927), 'L'idole de Dionysos Limnaios', *RA* 25: 104–20.

——(1951), *Choes and Anthesteria* (Leiden).

VELTRUSKÝ, J. (1976), 'Contribution to the Semiotics of Acting', in L. Matejka (ed.), *Sound, Sign and Meaning: Quinquagenary of the Prague Linguistic Circle* (Ann Arbor), 553–606.

VERBANCK-PIÉRARD, A. (1982), 'La Rencontre d'Héraklès et de Pholos: Variantes iconographiques du peintre d'Antiménès', in *Rayonnement*

Grec: Hommages à Charles Delvoye (Brussels), 143–54.

——(1987), 'Images et croyances en Grèce ancienne: Représentations de l'apothéose d'Héraklès au VIe siècle', in Bérard, Bron, and Pomari, 187–99.

——(1989), 'Le Double Culte d'Héraklès: Légende ou réalité?', in Laurens, 43–64.

VERDENIUS, W. J. (1981), 'Gorgias' Doctrine of Deception', in G. B. Kerferd (ed.), *The Sophists and their Legacy* (*Hermes Einzelschriften*, 44; Wiesbaden), 116–28.

VERNANT, J.-P. (1968) (ed.), *Problèmes de la guerre en Grèce ancienne* (Civilisations et Sociétés, 11; Paris).

——(1970), 'Greek Tragedy: Problems of Interpretation', in R. Macksey and E. Donato (eds.), *The Languages of Criticism and the Sciences of Man: The Structuralist Controversy* (Baltimore and London), 273–95.

——(1979a), 'À la table des hommes: Mythe de la fondation du sacrifice chez Hésiode', in Detienne and Vernant, 37–132.

——(1979b), 'Manger aux pays du Soleil', in Detienne and Vernant, 239–49.

——(1980), *Myth and Society in Ancient Greece* (tr. J. Lloyd) (Brighton and Atlantic Highlands, NJ).

——(1981), 'Théorie générale du sacrifice et mise à mort dans la θυσία grecque', in *Le Sacrifice dans l'antiquité* (*Entretiens sur l'Antiquité Classique*, Fondation Hardt, 27; Vandœuvres and Geneva), 1–39.

——(1988a), 'Tensions and Ambiguities in Greek Tragedy', in Vernant and Vidal-Naquet, 29–48.

——(1988b), 'Ambiguity and Reversal: On the Enigmatic Structure of *Oedipus Rex*', in Vernant and Vidal-Naquet, 113–40.

——(1988c), 'The Masked Dionysus of Euripides' *Bacchae*', in Vernant and Vidal-Naquet, 381–412.

——(1991), *Mortals and Immortals: Collected Essays*, ed. F. I. Zeitlin (Princeton).

——and FRONTISI-DUCROUX, F. (1988), 'Features of the Mask in Ancient Greece', in Vernant and Vidal-Naquet, 189–206.

——and VIDAL-NAQUET, P. (1988), *Myth and Tragedy in Ancient Greece* (tr. J. Lloyd) (orig. pub. as *Mythe et Tragédie en Grèce Ancienne*, Paris, 1972, and *Mythe et Tragédie en Grèce Ancienne Deux*, Paris, 1986) (New York).

VERSNEL, H. S. (1990a), 'What's Sauce for the Goose Is Sauce for the Gander: Myth and Ritual, Old and New', in Edmunds, 25–90.

——(1990b), *Inconsistencies in Greek and Roman Religion*, i: *TER UNUS. Isis, Dionysos and Hermes: Three Studies in Henotheism* (Leiden, New York, and Cologne).

——(1993), *Inconsistencies in Greek and Roman Religion*, ii: *Transition and Reversal in Myth and Ritual* (Leiden, New York, and Cologne).

VETTA, M. (1983a) (ed.), *Poesia e simposio nella Grecia antica: Guida storica e critica* (Rome and Bari).

VETTA, M. (1983*b*), 'Introduzione: Poesia simposiale nella Grecia arcaica e classica', in id. (1983*a*), xi–lx.

VIAN, F. (1952), *La Guerre des Géants: Le Mythe avant l'époque hellénistique* (Paris).

VICAIRE, P. (1963), 'Les Grecs et le mystère de l'inspiration poétique', *BAGB* (4th ser.), 1: 68–85.

VIDAL-NAQUET, P. (1981), 'Land and Sacrifice in the *Odyssey*: A Study of Religious and Mythical Meanings', in Gordon, 80–94.

——(1986), *The Black Hunter: Forms of Thought and Forms of Society in the Greek World* (tr. A. Szegedy-Maszack) (Baltimore and London).

——(1988*a*), 'Hunting and Sacrifice in Aeschylus' *Oresteia*', in Vernant and Vidal-Naquet, 141–59 (1st pub. in *Parola del Passato*, 1969).

——(1988*b*), 'Sophocles' *Philoctetes* and the Ephebeia', in Vernant and Vidal-Naquet, 161–79 (earlier version in *Annales, ESC*, 1971).

VILLANUEVA PUIG, M. C. (1986), 'A propos des Thyiades de Delphes', in *L'Association dionysiaque dans les sociétés anciennes* (Actes de la table ronde organisée par l'École Française de Rome (Rome 24–5 May 1984)) (Collection de l'École Française de Rome, 89; Rome), 31–51.

VILLARD, F. (1947), 'Dionysos combattant le géant', *RA* 28: 5–11.

VOLLGRAFF, W. (1925), 'Le Péan delphique à Dionysos', *BCH* 49: 104–42.

——(1948), 'Remarques sur une épitaphe latine de Philippes en Macédoine', in *Hommages à Joseph Bidez et à Franz Cumont* (*Collection Latomus*, 2; Brussels), 353–73.

VOLLKOMMER, R. (1988), *Herakles in the Art of Classical Greece* (Oxford).

VON DER MÜHLL, P. (1983), 'Il simposio greco', in Vetta (1983*a*), 3–28.

VON MÖLLENDORFF, P. (1995), *Grundlagen einer Ästhetik der Alten Komödie: Untersuchungen zu Aristophanes und Michail Bachtin* (Tübingen).

VOUTYRAS, M. (1984), 'Παρατηρήσεις σὲ τρία ἐπιγράμματα', *Hellenika*, 35: 38–50.

WALSH, G. B. (1984), *The Varieties of Enchantment: Early Greek Views of the Nature and Function of Poetry* (Chapel Hill, NC, and London).

WEBSTER, H. (1932), *Primitive Secret Societies: A Study in Early Politics and Religion* (New York).

WEBSTER, T. B. L. (1951), 'Grave Relief of an Athenian Poet', in G. E. Mylonas (ed.), *Studies Presented to D. M. Robinson* (St Louis), i. 590–3.

——(1953), 'Notes to Supplementary Plates, cxxv–cxxviii: Some Comic Monuments', *G&R* 22: 47–8.

——(1958), 'Some Thoughts on the Pre-History of Greek Drama', *BICS* 5: 43–8.

——(1959), *Greek Art and Literature, 700–530 BC: The Beginnings of Modern Civilization* (London).

——(1960), 'Greek Dramatic Monuments from the Athenian Agora and Pnyx', *Hesperia*, 29: 254–84.

——(1965), 'The Poet and the Mask', in M. J. Anderson (ed.), *Classical Drama and its Influence: Essays Presented to H. D. F. Kitto* (London), 5–13.

—— (1970), *Greek Theatre Production* (2nd edn.; London).

—— (1972), 'Scenic Notes II', in R. Hanslik, A. Lesky, and H. Schwabl (eds.), *Antidosis: Festschrift für W. Kraus* (Vienna), 454–7.

WEIDKUHN, P. (1977), 'The Quest for Legitimate Rebellion: Towards a Structuralist Theory of Rituals of Reversal', *Religion*, 7: 167–88.

WEINBERG, F. M. (1986), *The Cave: The Evolution of a Metaphoric Field from Homer to Ariosto* (New York).

WERBNER, R. P. (1984), 'World Renewal: Masking in a New Guinea Festival', *Man*, NS 19. 2: 267–90.

WEST, M. L. (1975), 'Zum neuen Goldblättchen aus Hipponion', *ZPE* 18: 229–36.

—— (1982a), 'The Orphics of Olbia', *ZPE* 45: 17–29.

—— (1982b), *Greek Metre* (Oxford).

—— (1983a), *The Orphic Poems* (Oxford).

—— (1983b), 'Tragica VI', *BICS* 30: 63–82.

—— (1992), *Ancient Greek Music* (Oxford).

WHALLON, W. (1964), 'Maenadism in the *Oresteia*', *HSCP* 68: 317–27.

WHEELER, E. L. (1982), '*Hoplomachia* and Greek Dances in Arms', *GRBS* 23: 223–33.

WHITE, D. (1967), 'The Post-Classical Cult of Malophoros at Selinus', *AJA* 71: 335–52.

WHITLEY, J. (1994), 'The Monuments That Stood Before Marathon: Tomb Cult and Hero Cult in Archaic Attica', *AJA* 98: 213–30.

WHITMAN, C. H. (1964), *Aristophanes and the Comic Hero* (Cambridge, Mass.).

WILES, D. (1991), *The Masks of Menander: Sign and Meaning in Greek and Roman Performance* (Cambridge).

WILKINS, J. (1990), 'The Young of Athens: Religion and Society in *Herakleidai* of Euripides', *CQ* 40: 329–39.

WILLETTS, R. F. (1955), *Aristocratic Society in Ancient Crete* (London).

—— (1962), *Cretan Cults and Festivals* (London).

WILSON, A. M. (1974), 'A Eupolidean Precedent for the Rowing Scene in Aristophanes' *Frogs*?', *CQ* 24: 250–2.

WILSON, B. R. (1970) (ed.), *Rationality* (Oxford).

WILSON, P. J. (1991), 'Demosthenes 21 (*Against Meidias*): Democratic Abuse', *PCPS* 37: 164–95.

—— and TAPLIN, O. (1993), 'The "Aetiology" of Tragedy in the *Oresteia*', *PCPS* 39: 169–80.

WINKLER, J. J. (1980), 'Lollianos and the Desperadoes', *JHS* 100: 155–81.

—— (1990a), 'Laying Down the Law: The Oversight of Men's Sexual Behavior in Classical Athens', in Halperin, Winkler, and Zeitlin, 171–209.

—— (1990b), 'The Ephebes' Song: *Tragoidia* and *Polis*', in Winkler and Zeitlin, 20–62 (earlier version in *Representations*, 11 (1985)).

—— and ZEITLIN, F. I. (1990) (eds.), *Nothing to Do with Dionysos? Athenian Drama in its Social Context* (Princeton).

WINNINGTON-INGRAM, R. P. (1980), *Sophocles: An Interpretation* (Cambridge).

WOODBURY, L. (1986), 'The Judgment of Dionysus: Books, Taste, and Teaching in the *Frogs*', in M. Cropp, E. Fantham, and S. E. Scully (eds.), *Greek Tragedy and its Legacy: Essays Presented to D. J. Conacher* (Calgary), 241–57.

WOODFORD, S. (1971), 'Cults of Heracles in Attica' in Mitten *et al.* 211–25.

WOODWARD, A. M. (1907–8), 'Laconia', *ABSA* 14: 74–141.

WREDE, W. (1928), 'Der Maskengott', *MDAI (A)* 53: 66–95.

ZANCANI MONTUORO, P., and ZANOTTI-BIANCO, U. (1954), *Heraion alla foce del Sele*, ii (Rome).

ZEITLIN, F. I. (1965), 'The Motif of the Corrupted Sacrifice in Aeschylus' *Oresteia*', *TAPA* 96: 463–508.

——(1970), 'The Argive Festival of Hera and Euripides' *Electra*', *TAPA* 101: 645–69.

——(1981), 'Travesties of Gender and Genre in Aristophanes' *Thesmophoriazusae*', in Foley (1981*a*), 169–217.

——(1982), 'Cultic Models of the Female: Rites of Dionysus and Demeter', *Arethusa* 15: 129–57.

——(1984), 'The Dynamics of Misogyny: Myth and Mythmaking in the *Oresteia*', in Peradotto and Sullivan, 159–94.

——(1989), 'Mysteries of Identity and Designs of the Self in Euripides' *Ion*', *PCPS* 35: 144–97.

——(1990*a*), 'Playing the Other: Theater, Theatricality, and the Feminine in Greek Drama', in Winkler and Zeitlin, 63–96 (original version in *Representations*, 11 (1985)).

——(1990*b*), 'Thebes: Theater of Self and Society in Athenian Drama', in Winkler and Zeitlin, 130–67.

——(1993), 'Staging Dionysus between Thebes and Athens', in Carpenter and Faraone, 147–82.

ZUNTZ, G. (1963), 'Once More: the So-Called "Edict of Philopator on the Dionysiac Mysteries" (BGU 1211)', *Hermes*, 91: 228–39.

——(1971), *Persephone: Three Essays on Religion and Thought in Magna Graecia* (Oxford).

General Index

Achilles 52, 304–5
actors and acting 3, 9, 29, 159–64, 168–72,
    173, 320
  ritual 9, 166–8, 172, 320
  see also Dionysus; kothornos; Molon
adultery, female 261–6
Aeschylean drama:
  and apate 237–42
  bewitching power of 241
  and ekplexis 235–7
  legendary characters in 304, 306
  mystic associations of 236–7, 245–6,
    247–54
  see also Aeschylus
Aeschylus 9, 56, 69, 106–8, 125, 138, 142,
    144, 145–6, 147, 149–50, 152; Chs. 5–9
    passim
  Achillean colouring of 304–5
  and Alcestis 256–7
  Athens, moulded by 56
  Bassarae 35
  and Cerberus 255
  Choephori 251–2
  citizens moulded by 221, 269–70, 284–5,
    289, 293, 301
  as civic guest 154, 327
  and Demeter 223, 261
  as a 'Dionysiac' poet 44, 235–47, 277–8,
    327
  Edoni 18 n. 3, 23, 34, 318 n. 24
  as Eleusinian poet 223, 247–54, 257
  epic adjectives of 304
  favouring social discrimination 258
  as an Heraclean figure 44, 255–7, 267–8,
    274–8
  and Homer 139–40, 269
  and hoplitic values 269, 273, 277, 289,
    301
  Lycurgeia 315
  Lycurgus 137
  as a mariner 150
  makarismos of 256 n. 8, 328–9
  and Marathonomachai 222, 303–4
  and Muses 246–7
  near divine status of 327–9
  Oresteia 48, 86, 107, 114, 180–3, 186,
    326–9
  Persae 269
  as returning Persephone 106

Pluto's greeting of 328–9
poeta vates 244
polis-oriented 10, 122, 221–3, 257, 289,
    302, 306
polytimetos 247
as a possessed poet 242–7
rejecting Aphrodite 261
resembling triumphant athletes 229, 256
and riddling language 245
as sacrificial victim 230–1
as Semele 106
semnos 247
Seven against Thebes 269
Theori or Isthmiastae 23, 259
and virility 274
and women 261–2, 263, 267, 292
  see also Aeschylean drama; anodos;
    Dionysus; Euripides
Agathon 14, 25, 33–6
'aggregation', see rites of passage
Agrionia 143 n. 44, 147, 188–9, 191–2, 247
Alcyonis lake 79
  see also Lerna
Alea, sanctuary 97 n. 207
amathia see education
Amphictyon 124, 156
Anacreontic komasts 25–6, 34 n. 63
  see also komos/komastic
'analogical action' 166–8
Andanian Mysteries 331
  see also mystic initiation
animal skins:
  connotations of 30–2, 52
  in initiation ritual 334–5
  see also Dionysus
anodos 56, 91, 256
  of Aeschylus in Frogs 106–7
  of Dionysiac mystai 78–80
  in initiation rites 54
  of Persephone 81–4, 91, 106–8, 114
  in satyric drama 119–20
  of Semele 79–80
  at Thesmophoria festival 84–5
  see also 'anodos dramas'; Dionysiac
    Mysteries; Eleusinian Mysteries
'anodos dramas' 114
  see also anodos
Anthesteria festival 5, 14, 96–7, 126–8, 208,
    233, 259, 335

Index of *Frogs* Passages

DATE DUE

MAY 2 3 2002			